D1189870

THE POEMS OF ALEXANDER POPE

VOLUME I

PASTORAL POETRY
AND
AN ESSAY ON CRITICISM

The Twickenham Edition of the Poems of Alexander Pope

★

GENERAL EDITOR: JOHN BUTT

★

VOLUME I

PASTORAL POETRY and AN ESSAY ON CRITICISM. E. Audra, formerly Professor of English, Lille University, and Aubrey Williams, Professor of English, The Rice Institute, Houston, Texas.

VOLUME II

THE RAPE OF THE LOCK and other poems. Geoffrey Tillotson, Professor of English, Birkbeck College, University of London.

VOLUME III i

AN ESSAY ON MAN. Maynard Mack, Professor of English and Fellow of Davenport College, Yale University.

VOLUME III ii

EPISTLES TO SEVERAL PERSONS (MORAL ESSAYS). F. W. Bateson, University Lecturer in English, Corpus Christi College, Oxford.

VOLUME IV

IMITATIONS OF HORACE and AN EPISTLE TO DR ARBUTHNOT and THE EPILOGUE TO THE SATIRES. John Butt, Regius Professor of Rhetoric and English Literature, University of Edinburgh.

VOLUME V

THE DUNCIAD. James Sutherland, Lord Northcliffe Professor of English, University College, University of London.

VOLUME VI

MINOR POEMS. Norman Ault and John Butt.

First published 1961
Editorial matter © 1961 E. Audra and Aubrey Williams
Printed in Great Britain by The Broadwater Press Ltd
Welwyn Garden City, Hertfordshire
Catalogue number (Methuen) 2/4776/10

PREFACE

THIS volume is the last to be published, though the first in order, of what was originally intended as a six-volume edition of Pope's poems excluding the translation of Homer. During the course of work certain modifications have been made in the original design. Experience showed that *An Essay on Man* and the *Moral Essays* could be dealt with more conveniently in separate volumes, and volume III was therefore divided into two parts. A more important change became possible when the difficulty of including Pope's *Homer* was overcome. Accordingly the edition will be completed in four more volumes, two of which will be given to the *Iliad* and two to the *Odyssey*.

Each volume has presented an individual editorial problem. Thus the editor of *The Dunciad* had to devise a system of easy cross-reference between the two versions of the poem; and besides struggling with an already voluminous commentary, he had to supply further illustration of Pope's dealings with contemporary writers. The editor of the *Imitations of Horace* was necessarily more concerned with Pope's political affiliations, but he was faced with a similar task of establishing the identity of a large number of obscure persons. These editors each had recourse to a biographical appendix, a device not required by the editors of the *Minor Poems*, whose chief task was to establish the canon, nor by the editor of the *Epistles to Several Persons*, who had to grapple with a difficult textual problem, nor by the editor of the *Essay on Man*, who was mainly concerned with analogues of phrase and idea. The editors of the first two volumes have given much consideration to analogues, but they have needed to pay more attention to questions of literary kinds.

The result has been much diversity of treatment. Yet this diversity does not disturb the basic harmony of purpose both in the presentation of the text and in the type of annotation required throughout. A notable character of the edition has been the displacement of Warburton's text, which had hitherto been treated as the final authority. In the preface to his edition of 1751 Warburton states that he had had the advantages of printing the corrections that Pope had made in his last illness, and that by the terms of Pope's will he had been bequeathed the property of the poet's work to be published "without future alterations". It is neither possible nor desirable to overlook Warburton altogether, but his readings are not always above suspicion. Pope did not complete the revision of his poems on which he was engaged at his death, and where a poem was unrevised Warburton did not always choose the most suitable copy-text; thus he failed to discover Pope's final corrections in several of the *Imitations of Horace*, notably the imitation of the seventh epistle of the first book. Where he had the poet's final revisions before him, he did not trouble to inquire whether the text subjected to correction was itself free from error. Thus for some of the poems which now appear in volume IV, Pope seems to have recorded his revisions in a copy of the *Works* in octavo published in 1740 or in the reprint of 1743. But the printer of 1740 committed some errors in following the text of 1736, the printer of 1743 added a few more, and neither Pope nor Warburton noticed all of them.

Warburton's treatment of the text was not limited to a mechanical and imperfect reproduction of a more or less authoritative copy before him. He seems to have felt justified in taking such liberties as transposing passages in the *Moral Essays*, presenting the *Epistle to Bathurst* and the *Epistle to Arbuthnot* as dialogues, and even altering the name of the last of these poems. What authority he had for these changes is discussed in the notes to the text in volumes III ii and IV. He also states that he has "ornamented this Edition with all the advantages which the best Artists in Paper, Printing, and Sculpture could bestow upon it". Since printing-house practice was changing at the time, the effect is that, in the use of capital letters and italic type, Warburton's text differs from any text with which Pope was acquainted.

Except for one poem in volume VI, for which Warburton is the sole authority, it is possible to choose a copy-text preferable to 1751. This may be done simply for the four-book *Dunciad* by taking the quarto of 1743, where Theobald was dethroned in favour of Cibber, and for the *Essay on Man* by taking the quarto prepared during 1743 by Warburton under Pope's direction. In each instance the modern editor has followed Warburton's lead, though he has been able to improve upon him by returning to the source of his authority. In other instances the choice has been more complicated; but full consideration has shown the advantages of choosing the first edition, or the earliest for which it may be confidently asserted that Pope was

responsible, except where more powerful reasons dictated otherwise. Where Pope has corrected that text, the typography of his
corrections has been modified so as to accord with the printing-
house practice, recognized then, and unmistakable now. It will be
admitted that this is a matter of taste, about which a general agreement can never be reached. We prefer to see Pope in a dress of his
own day rather than in the new style which Warburton chose for
him.

Divergences from the copy-text in matters of type and punctuation are not recorded in the textual notes of this edition, except
where the meaning is thereby changed. Printers' errors have also
been excluded. The textual notes record only the readings rejected
from the authorized editions and from Warburton's edition of 1751.

For some of the shorter poems in volume vi the text could not
have been established without recourse to manuscript authority,
but adequate treatment of all but a few of the surviving autograph
manuscripts has been precluded on grounds of space. To have presented the manuscript variants of the *Essay on Man* alone would
have doubled the size of that volume; and even such a costly addition as photographic facsimiles could not have been profitably supplied without a lengthy exposition of layer upon layer of changes.
None of these manuscripts was intended as copy for press, with the
exception of the Bodleian manuscript of *An Essay on Criticism*. Their
readings belong to the partially formed, prenatal history of the
poems; they were provisional only, liable to rejection, and frequently in fact rejected. Our chief regret in omitting them is that
we have not catered for the student of poetical origins.[1]

The editor of Pope is in the happy position of having received a
lead from his author in the matter of annotation. The second volume of his *Works*, published in 1735, contained Pope's own notes
both expository and textual, and more were added in later editions
of the poet's lifetime. The expository notes are of two kinds; they
explain obscure allusions, and they adduce parallel passages from
earlier writers. These still remain the editor's principal exegetic
tasks, though the language has changed sufficiently in two hundred
years to make the need of linguistic notes felt also. Pope's lead was

---

1. Some idea of their range and complexity can be obtained from J. Butt,
'Pope's Poetical Manuscripts', *Proceedings of the British Academy*, XL (1955), 1–39.

followed by his contemporaries: the Dublin publishers of *The Dun-ciad* and other poems used what knowledge they had to supply names in replacement of the blanks and initial letters of the English texts; the second Earl of Oxford, Horace Walpole, William Cole, and John Wilkes amused themselves by annotating their copies of the poems; and in 1740 William Clarke and William Bowyer began to make arrangements for publishing a collection of what Pope called his 'imitations', those passages of earlier poetry that assisted his expression of a new but related meaning. Misunderstanding the poetic relationship between old and new, Clarke and Bowyer desisted from their project for fear of displeasing Pope by discovering what they supposed to be his "plagiarisms" (Nichols, *Literary Anecdotes*, IV 429–37). Warburton explained some allusions and could have explained more. So too could Joseph Warton, who began to publish his garrulous notes in 1756 under the title of *An Essay on the Genius and Writings of Pope* (vol. II, 1782), and used them for his edition of 1797. Warton's energies, like those of his immediate predecessor, the acute and learned Gilbert Wakefield,[1] were mainly directed towards collecting Pope's imitations, and from their ample collections all succeeding editors have borrowed, though not all have recognized that these collections, while illustrating Pope's artistic skill, also direct attention to "the meaning, provenience, and prevalence of the ideas out of which the poetic whole was made" (vol. III i, p. v).

Since the eighteenth century, Bowles (1806), Carruthers (1853), Ward (1869), and Boynton (1903) have all produced editions which may occasionally be consulted with profit. The most important edition, made possible by the researches of Dilke[2] and Croker, was that of which publication was begun by Elwin in 1871 and completed by Courthope in 1889. This great edition has many defects, not the least of which is the harshly unsympathetic attitude of Elwin: the text was crudely modernized; collations were spas-

---

1. His first volume was published in 1794. Finding that Warton was already engaged in an edition he desisted, but published a further volume of *Observations* in 1796. At the same time, Malone was working on an edition, which he relinquished for the same reason. His notes are in the Bodleian Library (MS Malone 30).

2. Assembled in *The Papers of a Critic*, 1875. Croker's collections were handed over to Elwin when he began work on his edition.

modic; and little use was made of Pope's letters in the annotations. Yet in spite of this there is a wealth of illustrative and explanatory material in the notes, to which every subsequent editor must necessarily be indebted.

The present editors are conscious of inheriting the work of their predecessors, as well as the discoveries about Pope and his contemporaries that have been made since 1889. They believe that they have selected what is most valuable; and they have incorporated the discoveries which they themselves have made.

JOHN BUTT

Newcastle upon Tyne,
1959.

CONTENTS

ACKNOWLEDGEMENTS

THE editors of this volume, jointly and separately, gratefully acknowledge the generous support of their work by the following agencies and foundations:

A Morse Fellowship awarded to Aubrey Williams by Yale University for the year 1954–5. A John Simon Guggenheim Memorial Fellowship awarded to Aubrey Williams for the year 1956–7. A Fulbright Research Fellowship awarded by the United States Government to Aubrey Williams for study at Birkbeck College, University of London, 1956–7.

It is a pleasure to make grateful acknowledgement to:

Mr Arthur A. Houghton, Jr, for permission to publish from the autograph manuscripts of the *Discourse on Pastoral Poetry*, the *Pastorals*, and the manuscript exchange between Pope and William Walsh concerning the *Pastorals*.

The Yale University Library for permission to publish from the autograph manuscript of the Preface to the 1717 *Works*.

The Bodleian Library for permission to publish from the autograph manuscript of *An Essay on Criticism* and the manuscript memoranda accompanying it.

The Pierpont Morgan Library for permission to publish from the autograph manuscript of *Sapho to Phaon*.

The staffs of the Yale University Library, the London University Library, the Birkbeck College Library, the British Museum, the Pierpont Morgan Library, the Bibliothèque Nationale, the Bibliothèque Sainte-Geneviève, the Bibliothèque de l'Université de Lille, and the Bodleian Library for their many kindnesses.

For special aid and assistance the editors wish to thank Mr Joseph Trapp, of The Warburg Institute, who contributed the note to *An Essay on Criticism*, l. 706; Miss Marjorie Wynne, Librarian of the Rare Book Room, Yale University, for her endless patience and smiling efficiency; Mr Richard Robey, undergraduate assistant to Mr Williams at Yale University. For special help the editors also wish to thank Mr A. J. V. Chapple, Professor Marshall Waingrow, and Professor Stuart G. P. Small.

The editors can express only inadequately their gratitude to the following for their unfailing advice, criticism, and friendship: Professor John Butt, Professor Maynard Mack, Professor W. K. Wimsatt, Professor George Sherburn, Professor Geoffrey Tillotson, Mr James M. Osborn, Professor Cleanth Brooks, the late Norman Ault, the late Professor R. H. Griffith, and Professor Robert M. Schmitz.

NOTE ON THE ILLUSTRATIONS

Frontispiece. George Vertue's engraving of Pope can be dated 1715 by a letter from Charles Jervas to Pope, written about July 31, 1715 (*Corr.*, I 310). Jervas states that he is "just going to Vertue to give the last hand to that Enterprize which is our Concern." The *Daily Courant* of August 20, 1715, announced that "On Tuesday next will be Published, A Print of Mr. Alexander Pope, done from the Original Painting of Mr. Jervasi (*sic*), by Mr. Vertue. Printed for Bernard Lintott . . ."

A portrait of Pope attributed to Jervas and now in the Bodleian is probably the one from which Vertue made his engraving. On the frame is an inscription commemorating the gift of the picture in 1722 by Edward Lord Harley (see the *Illustrated Catalogue of a Loan Collection of Portraits of English Historical Personages Who Died between 1714 and 1837. Exhibited in the Examination Schools, Oxford, April and May, MDCCCCVI*, Oxford, 1906, p. 33). A letter to Harley of April 1, 1723, from Robert Shippen, Principal of Brasenose College and Vice-Chancellor of Oxford, states that Shippen "has received his Lordship's kind present of the three pictures of Lord Dorset, Mr. Prior, and Mr. Pope, for which he is to return his own and the University's thanks" (*Hist. MSS. Comm., Report on the Manuscripts of His Grace The Duke of Portland*, 1899, v 634). The editors are indebted to Professor W. K. Wimsatt for the information contained in this note.

Plate facing page 202. The autograph manuscript of *An Essay on Criticism* is the one Pope sent to the printer (see Percy Simpson, *Proof-Reading in the Sixteenth, Seventeenth and Eighteenth Centuries*, 1935, pp. 99–104). For further discussion of this manuscript, see the Introduction to *An Essay on Criticism*, pp. 197–202, below.

GENERAL NOTE ON THE TEXT
of this volume

THE textual basis of the poems in this volume is in every instance that of the first edition. Each text has been corrected and revised in the light of new readings introduced into later editions, but in so far as it is possible to do so, the spelling, punctuation, and typography of the first editions have been preserved. The preservation of the capitals and italics of the first printed texts has seemed particularly important, for there is little doubt that Pope used these typographical devices, particularly in the *Essay on Criticism*, to point up elements in his couplet structures. Such devices disappear from the later editions of these poems, apparently in conformity to contemporary changes in typographical fashion, but Pope certainly used them with pointed effect in his manuscripts and they have been considered a valuable part of the texts of this volume. When new readings introduced in late editions of the poems have lacked the emphasis supplied by capitals and italics, this emphasis has been supplied, sparingly and conservatively, on the analogy of the original reading or of Pope's general procedure.

A few modifications in punctuation have been introduced to avoid particular confusions. Thus Pope's use of the genitive singular to indicate the genitive plural has been altered to conform to modern practice, and when quotation marks have not been present to close a speech or quotation they have been added. Other minor revisions in punctuation have warrant from editions printed during Pope's lifetime. Changes such as these have been recorded in the textual notes, but obvious misprints have been silently corrected.

A number of readings introduced into editions of the *Works* in 1740 and 1743 have seemed of doubtful authenticity. Such variants usually involve the change of a single letter, and may be misprints. Except when such changes seem clearly warranted in some way, the authority of earlier editions has been followed and the new reading preserved in the textual notes. Warburton in his 1751 edition of the *Works* occasionally follows these doubtful readings, but his authority has not always seemed infallible. The textual history of the poems in this volume ends, for our purposes, with Warburton's edition of 1751, and except in such doubtful instances as those just cited, the new readings appearing in his edition have been admitted to the text.

Pope's manuscripts of many of the poems in this volume have come down to us. There are manuscripts for the *Preface* to the 1717 edition of the *Works*, the *Discourse on Pastoral Poetry*, the *Pastorals*, *Windsor-Forest*, the *Essay on Criticism*, and *Sapho to Phaon*. These manuscripts have been used to explain or clarify the meaning of the texts on occasion, but they have not been used to correct the texts. Some of these manuscripts were apparently ones Pope sent to the printer, but in these instances Pope seems to have corrected his text in proof stage. Because of this it has seemed inadvisable to correct the first printed texts by the use of manuscripts. Variations between the manuscripts and the first printed texts are innumerable, and the recording of manuscript variations has seemed to be outside the scope of this volume. Two manuscripts, however, have been reproduced in type in appendixes. These, a manuscript memorandum recording Pope's jottings for the revision of certain lines in the *Essay on Criticism* and a manuscript colloquy between Pope and Walsh about passages from the *Pastorals*, have seemed worth printing as illuminating samples of Pope at work.

In the editions of his *Works* from 1736 on, Pope printed, usually at the bottom of the page, Latin texts along with his translations from Ovid and Statius. These relatively straightforward translations have not seemed to involve the kinds of questions raised by Pope's *Imitations of Horace*, and so the Latin texts for them are not presented in this volume. Since these Latin texts made their appearance in his works twenty or twenty-five years after the first appearance of most of the translations, there is no assurance that they represent the particular Latin texts used by Pope at the time he made the translations.

Jonathan Richardson the younger tells us that he suggested to Pope "the making an edition of his works in the manner of *Boileau*'s . . .". Richardson alluded to the famous edition brought out by Brossette after Boileau's death. It had been prepared over a period of years through personal acquaintance and correspondence with Boileau, and Brossette aimed at a perfect edition of the text. He gave passages which Boileau had suppressed in certain editions, and explanations of the text he had received from Boileau himself.

Brossette divided his notes into "Changemens, Remarques, & Imitations", and a similar scheme was partly carried out in the 1736 edition of Pope's *Works*, at least in the *Pastorals*, where one finds "Remarks", "Imitations", and also variant readings from earlier editions. In 1751 the scheme was completed, for in the edition of that year we find "Notes", "Imitations", and "Variations" (that is, variants from MSS and previous editions). The content, though not the exact form, of this material is presented in the notes in this volume. The extensive and often irrelevant commentary of Warburton has been quoted only when it seemed to be useful.

CHRONOLOGICAL TABLE

The standard biographies are G. Sherburn's *The Early Career of Alexander Pope*, 1934, and W. J. Courthope's life in vol. v of the Elwin-Courthope edition of Pope's works, 1871–89. Sherburn's account stops at 1727.

1688 (May 21) Alexander Pope born in London of elderly parents.

c.1700 Pope's family moved to Binfield, in Windsor Forest, [?] to comply with anti-Catholic regulations.
Death of Dryden.

c.1705 Pope began to make acquaintance with the literary society of London.

1709 (May) The *Pastorals* published in the sixth part of Tonson's *Miscellanies*.

1711 (May) *An Essay on Criticism* published; praised in *The Spectator* by Addison, and damned by Dennis.

1712 (May) The *Messiah* published by Steele in *The Spectator*. Lintot's *Miscellany* published, containing the first version of *The Rape of the Lock*, and other poems by Pope. Pope was becoming acquainted with Swift, Gay, Parnell, and Arbuthnot, who together formed the Scriblerus Club.

1713 (March) *Windsor-Forest.*
(April) Addison's *Cato* first acted, with a prologue by Pope. Pope was contributing to Steele's *Guardian.*
(October) Proposals issued for a translation of the *Iliad.*

1714 (March) The enlarged version of *The Rape of the Lock.*
(August) Death of Queen Anne.

1715 (February) *The Temple of Fame.*
(June 6) The *Iliad*, Books I–IV, published; followed two days later by Tickell's translation of *Iliad* I. During this year [?], Pope wrote his character of Addison, and became acquainted with Lady Mary Wortley Montagu.

1716 (March) *Iliad*, vol. II.
Pope's revenge by poison on Curll the publisher [Sherburn, chap. VI; N. Ault, *Pope's Prose*, pp. xciv*ff.*].
(April) Pope's family sold their house at Binfield, and settled at Chiswick, where their neighbour was Lord Burlington.

1717 (January) *Three Hours after Marriage* by Pope, Gay, and Arbuthnot, first acted.
(June) *Iliad*, vol. III.
The collected volume of Pope's *Works*, containing *Verses to the Memory of an Unfortunate Lady* and *Eloisa to Abelard.*
(October) Pope's father died.

1718 (June) *Iliad*, vol. IV.
Death of Parnell. Pope and his mother moved to Twickenham late in the year.

1719 Death of Addison.

1720 (May) *Iliad*, vols. V and VI.

1721 (September) The *Epistle to Addison* prefixed to Tickell's edition of Addison's *Works.*
(December) The *Epistle to Oxford* prefixed to Pope's edition of Parnell's *Poems.*

1723 (January) Pope's edition of John Sheffield, Duke of Buckingham's *Works* published, and seized by the Government on suspicion of Jacobitish passages.
(May) Pope called before the House of Lords as a witness at Atterbury's trial.

1725   (March) Pope's edition of Shakespeare published in six volumes.
(April) *Odyssey*, vols. I–III.
Bolingbroke returned from exile, and settled near Pope at Dawley Farm, Uxbridge.

1726   (March) Theobald's *Shakespeare Restored : or, a Specimen of the Many Errors . . . Committed . . . by Mr Pope.*
(June) *Odyssey*, vols. IV–V.
Pope visited by Swift. *Gulliver's Travels* published in October.

1727   (June) Pope-Swift *Miscellanies*, vols. I and II.
Swift's second visit to Pope.

1728   (March) Pope-Swift *Miscellanies*, "last" volume.
(May) *The Dunciad*, in three books, with Theobald as hero.

1729   (April) *The Dunciad Variorum.*

1731   (December) *Epistle to Burlington* [Moral Essay IV].

1732   (October) Pope-Swift *Miscellanies*, "third" volume.
(December) Death of Gay.

1733   (January) *Epistle to Bathurst* [Moral Essay III].
(February) The first *Imitation of Horace* [Sat. II i].
(February–May) *An Essay on Man*, Epistles I–III.
(June) Death of Pope's mother.

1734   (January) *Epistle to Cobham* [Moral Essay I].
An Essay on Man, Epistle IV.
(July) *Imitation of Horace* [Sat. II ii].
(December) *Sober Advice from Horace.*

1735   (January) *Epistle to Dr Arbuthnot.*
(February) *Of the Characters of Women* [Moral Essay II].
Death of Arbuthnot.
(April) The *Works*, vol. II.
(May) Curll's edition of Pope's letters.
Bolingbroke returned to France.

1737 (April) *Imitation of Horace* [Ep. ii ii].
      (May) Pope's edition of his letters.
      Imitation of Horace [Ep. ii i].
      An Essay on Man attacked by Crousaz, Professor of Mathe-
      matics and Philosophy at Lausanne.

1738 (January–March) *Imitations of Horace* [Eps. i vi and i i].
      (May–July) *Epilogue to the Satires.*
      Warburton commenced his replies to Crousaz.
      Pope visited by Bolingbroke.

1740 (April) Pope's first meeting with Warburton.

1742 (March) *The New Dunciad* [i.e. Book iv].

1743 (October) *The Dunciad* in four books with Cibber enthroned
      in the place of Theobald.

1744 (May 30) Death of Pope.

LIST OF THE PRINCIPAL POEMS
of Pope to be found in the other volumes

The translation of Homer will appear in four supplementary volumes of this edition. The remaining poems will be found in volume VI. The three-book *Dunciad* is referred to as *Dunciad A*, the four-book as *Dunciad B*.

ABBREVIATIONS

used in the Notes to the Introductions and to the Poems

ADD. MSS = British Museum Additional MSS.

A.P. = The Art of Poetry, Written in French by the Sieur de Boileau, Made English [by Sir William Soames and John Dryden], 1683.

AV = The Authorized (King James) Version of the Bible.

BOWLES = The Works of Alexander Pope, Esq. Ed. W. L. Bowles. 10 vols., 1806.

CARRUTHERS = The Poetical Works of Alexander Pope. Ed. Robert Carruthers. 4 vols., 1853.

COLLINS = Pope's Essay on Criticism. Ed. John Churton Collins, 1925.

CORR. = The Correspondence of Alexander Pope. Ed. George Sherburn. 5 vols., 1956.

CROKER = Notes by Croker in the Elwin-Courthope edition of Pope's Works.

DB = The Rheims and Douai version of the Bible. New Testament, 1582. Old Testament, 2 vols., 1609–10.

DNB = Dictionary of National Biography.

EC = The Works of Alexander Pope. Ed. W. Elwin and W. J. Courthope. 10 vols., 1871–89.

EARLY CAREER = The Early Career of Alexander Pope. By George Sherburn, 1934.

ESSAYS = Essays of John Dryden. Ed. W. P. Ker. 2 vols., 2nd impression, 1926.

GRIFFITH = Alexander Pope: A Bibliography. By R. H. Griffith. 2 vols., 1922–7.

HOOKER = The Critical Works of John Dennis. Ed. E. N. Hooker. 2 vols., 1939–43.

OED = Oxford English Dictionary.

P = Note by Pope; usually followed by dates of the editions in which it was printed.

PROSE WORKS = The Prose Works of Alexander Pope. Ed. Norman Ault. Vol. 1, The Earlier Works, 1936.

SARGEAUNT= Pope's Essay on Criticism. Ed. John Sargeaunt, 1924.

SPENCE= Anecdotes, Observations, and Characters, of Books and Men. Collected . . . by the Rev. Joseph Spence. Ed. S. W. Singer, 1820.

SPINGARN= Critical Essays of the Seventeenth Century. Ed. J. E. Spingarn. 3 vols., 1908–9.

WAKEFIELD= The Works of Alexander Pope, Esq. Ed. Gilbert Wakefield. Vol. 1 only, 1794. Observations on Pope. By Gilbert Wakefield, 1796.

WARBURTON= The Works of Alexander Pope Esq. Ed. William Warburton. 9 vols., 1751.

WARD= The Poetical Works of Alexander Pope. Ed. A. W. Ward, 1893.

WARTON= The Works of Alexander Pope, Esq. Ed. Joseph Warton. 9 vols., 1797.

WEST= Pope: Essay on Criticism. Ed. A. S. West, 1896.

THE

PREFACE

OF

1717

NOTE ON THE TEXT

The text printed here follows the spelling, punctuation, and typography of the 1717 edition of the *Works*, when the Preface was first published, but observes the revisions introduced into subsequent editions. Very few changes were made by Pope in the editions from 1736 to 1743; most of the changes occur in Warburton's edition of 1751.

Warburton printed two long passages from the MS of the Preface which is now in the Chauncey B. Tinker collection in the Yale University Library. The MS is heavily corrected and incomplete, ending about l. 185 of the printed text. It consists of ten pages, on two double sheets and a single sheet. Page [9] is a working draft of parts of pp. 5–6, and p. [10] is a fair copy of p. 5. Warburton's presentation of the two MS passages is somewhat misleading, and neither they nor any other portion of the MS is reproduced here.

KEY TO THE CRITICAL APPARATUS

1717 = Works, quarto, Griffith 79.
1736*a*= Works, vol. 1, octavo, Griffith 413.
1736*b*= Works, vol. 1, octavo, Griffith 414.
1740 = Works, vol. 1, part 1, octavo, Griffith 510.
1743 = Works, vol. 1, part 1, octavo, Griffith 582.
1751 = Works, ed. Warburton, vol. 1, octavo, Griffith 643.

PREFACE.

I Am inclined to think that both the writers of books, and the readers of them, are generally not a little unreasonable in their expectations. The first seem to fancy that the world must approve whatever they produce, and the latter to imagine that authors are obliged to please them at any rate. 5
Methinks as on the one hand, no single man is born with a right of controuling the opinions of all the rest; so on the other, the world has no title to demand, that the whole care and time of any particular person should be sacrificed to its entertainment. Therefore I cannot but believe that writers and readers 10
are under equal obligations, for as much fame, or pleasure, as each affords the other.

Every one acknowledges, it would be a wild notion to expect perfection in any work of man: and yet one would think the contrary was taken for granted, by the judgment commonly 15
past upon Poems. A Critic supposes he has done his part, if he proves a writer to have fail'd in an expression, or err'd in any particular point: and can it then be wonder'd at, if the Poets in general seem resolv'd not to own themselves in any error?
For as long as one side will make no allowances, the other will 20
be brought to no acknowledgements.

I am afraid this extreme zeal on both sides is ill-plac'd; Poetry and Criticism being by no means the universal concern of the world, but only the affair of idle men who write in their closets, and of idle men who read there. 25

Yet sure upon the whole, a bad Author deserves better usage

20–1 side . . . acknowledgements.] side despises a well-meant endeavour, the other will not be satisfy'd with a moderate approbation. *1717–43.*
26 *No new paragraph 1717–43.*

---

14. *perfection*] Cf. *Ess. on Crit.*, 253–4.
20 var. Warburton, after quoting this variant, added: "But the Author altered it, as these words were rather a consequence from the conclusion he would draw, than the conclusion itself, which he has now inserted."

3

than a bad Critic: for a Writer's endeavour, for the most part, is to please his Readers, and he fails merely through the misfortune of an ill judgment; but such a Critic's is to put them out of humor; a design he could never go upon without both   30
that and an ill temper.

I think a good deal may be said to extenuate the fault of bad Poets. What we call a Genius, is hard to be distinguish'd by a man himself, from a strong inclination: and if his genius be ever so great, he can not at first discover it any other way, than   35
by giving way to that prevalent propensity which renders him the more liable to be mistaken. The only method he has, is to make the experiment by writing, and appealing to the judgment of others: now if he happens to write ill (which is certainly no sin in itself) he is immediately made an object of   40
ridicule. I wish we had the humanity to reflect that even the worst authors might, in their endeavour to please us, deserve something at our hands. We have no cause to quarrel with them but for their obstinacy in persisting to write; and this too may admit of alleviating circumstances. Their particular   45
friends may be either ignorant, or insincere; and the rest of the world in general is too well bred to shock them with a truth, which generally their Booksellers are the first that inform them of. This happens not till they have spent too much of their time, to apply to any profession which might better fit their   50
talents; and till such talents as they have are so far discredited,

27–31 for a . . . temper.] a man may be the former merely thro' the misfortune of an ill judgment, but he cannot be the latter without both that and an ill temper. *1717–43*.
34–5 if his genius be ever] if it be never *1717–43*.
36 giving way to] *Add. 1751*.   39 now] And *1717–43*.
42 might . . . deserve] might endeavour to please us, and in that endeavour, deserve *1717–43*.
44 persisting to write; and] persisting, and *1717–43*.
47 in general is] *Add. 1751*.

32–49. This passage is quoted, with slight alterations, in a note to *Dunciad* A, I 258 (vol. v, p. 94), to prove, à propos of Ogilby, that "Our author shows here and elsewhere, a prodigious Tenderness for a *bad writer*."

as to be but of small service to them. For (what is the hardest
case imaginable) the reputation of a man generally depends
upon the first steps he makes in the world, and people will
establish their opinion of us, from what we do at that season   55
when we have least judgment to direct us.

On the other hand, a good Poet no sooner communicates his
works with the same desire of information, but it is imagin'd
he is a vain young creature given up to the ambition of fame;
when perhaps the poor man is all the while trembling with the   60
fear of being ridiculous. If he is made to hope he may please
the world, he falls under very unlucky circumstances; for from
the moment he prints, he must expect to hear no more truth,
than if he were a Prince, or a Beauty. If he has not very good
sense (and indeed there are twenty men of wit, for one man of   65
sense) his living thus in a course of flattery may put him in no
small danger of becoming a Coxcomb: If he has, he will con-
sequently have so much diffidence, as not to reap any great
satisfaction from his praise; since if it be given to his face, it can
scarce be distinguish'd from flattery, and if in his absence, it is   70
hard to be certain of it. Were he to be commended by the
best and most knowing, he is as sure of being envy'd by the
worst and most ignorant, which are the majority; for it is with
a fine Genius as with a fine fashion, all those are displeas'd at it
who are not able to follow it: And 'tis to be fear'd that esteem   75
will seldom do any man so much good, as ill-will does him
harm. Then there is a third class of people who make the largest part of mankind, those of ordinary or indifferent capacities;
and these (to a man) will hate, or suspect him: a hundred
honest gentlemen will dread him as a wit, and a hundred inno-   80
cent women as a satyrist. In a word, whatever be his fate in
Poetry, it is ten to one but he must give up all the reasonable
aims of life for it. There are indeed some advantages accruing
from a Genius to Poetry, and they are all I can think of: the
agreeable power of self-amusement when a man is idle or   85

65–6 (and . . . sense)] *Add. 1751.*
73 which are the majority;] *Add. 1751.*

64–7. Cf. *Ess. on Crit.*, 25–7.   77 *ff.* Cf. *Ess. on Crit.*, 494–507.

alone; the privilege of being admitted into the best company; and the freedom of saying as many careless things as other people, without being so severely remark'd upon.

I believe, if any one, early in his life should contemplate the dangerous fate of authors, he would scarce be of their number   90 on any consideration. The life of a Wit is a warfare upon earth; and the present spirit of the learned world is such, that to attempt to serve it (any way) one must have the constancy of a martyr, and a resolution to suffer for its sake. I could wish people would believe what I am pretty certain they will not,   95 that I have been less concern'd about Fame than I durst declare till this occasion, when methinks I should find more credit than I could heretofore: since my writings have had their fate already, and 'tis too late to think of prepossessing the reader in their favour. I would plead it as some merit in me,   100 that the world has never been prepared for these Trifles by Prefaces, byast by recommendations, dazled with the names of great Patrons, wheedled with fine reasons and pretences, or troubled with excuses. I confess it was want of consideration that made me an author; I writ because it amused me; I cor-   105 rected because it was as pleasant to me to correct as to write; and I publish'd because I was told I might please such as it was a credit to please. To what degree I have done this, I am really ignorant; I had too much fondness for my productions to judge of them at first, and too much judgment to be pleas'd with   110 them at last. But I have reason to think they can have no reputation which will continue long, or which deserves to do so: for they have always fallen short not only of what I read of others, but even of my own Ideas of Poetry.

If any one should imagine I am not in earnest, I desire him 115 to reflect, that the Ancients (to say the least of them) had as much Genius as we; and that to take more pains, and employ more time, cannot fail to produce more complete pieces. They constantly apply'd themselves not only to that art, but to that

92 learned] *Add. 1736a–51.*
94–104 I could ... excuses.] *Add. 1736a–51.*

---

91. *a warfare upon earth*] Cf. *Ess. on Crit.*, 394*ff.*, 508*ff.*

single branch of an art, to which their talent was most power- 120
fully bent; and it was the business of their lives to correct and
finish their works for posterity. If we can pretend to have used
the same industry, let us expect the same immortality: Tho' if ⌉
we took the same care, we should still lie under a farther misfortune: they writ in languages that became universal and 125
everlasting, while ours are extremely limited both in extent,
and in duration. A mighty foundation for our pride! when the
utmost we can hope, is but to be read in one Island, and to be
thrown aside at the end of one Age.   ⌄

All that is left us is to recommend our productions by the 130
imitation of the Ancients: and it will be found true, that in
every age, the highest character for sense and learning has
been obtain'd by those who have been most indebted to them.
For to say truth, whatever is very good sense must have been
common sense in all times; and what we call Learning, is but 135
the knowledge of the sense of our predecessors. Therefore they
who say our thoughts are not our own because they resemble
the Ancients, may as well say our faces are not our own, because they are like our Fathers: And indeed it is very unreasonable, that people should expect us to be Scholars, and yet 140
be angry to find us so.

I fairly confess that I have serv'd my self all I could by reading; that I made use of the judgment of authors dead and living; that I omitted no means in my power to be inform'd of my
errors, both by my friends and enemies. But the true reason these 145

145 enemies. But] enemies; and that I expect not to be excus'd in
      any negligence on account of youth, want of leisure, or any
      other idle allegations: But *1717–43*.

128–9. Cf. *Ess. on Crit.*, 476*ff*.

130. Cf. *Spectator* 253, in which Addison gave an account of the *Essay on Criticism*: "We have little else left us, but to represent the common Sense of Mankind
in more strong, more beautiful, or more uncommon Lights. . ."

133. *indebted to them.*] Cf. *A Discourse on Pastoral Poetry*, 161. Also Walsh's
letter to Pope (*Corr.*, 1 20): "The best of the modern Poets in all Languages, are
those that have the nearest copied the Ancients."

145. *enemies*] Cf. *Ess. on Crit.*, 213–14.

145 var. Pope may have omitted this passage because, as EC say, it "was

pieces are not more correct, is owing to the consideration how
short a time they, and I, have to live: One may be ashamed to
consume half one's days in bringing sense and rhyme together;
and what Critic can be so unreasonable as not to leave a man
time enough for any more serious employment, or more agree-   150
able amusement?

The only plea I shall use for the favour of the publick, is, that
I have as great a respect for it, as most authors have for themselves; and that I have sacrificed much of my own self-love for
its sake, in preventing not only many mean things from seeing   155
the light, but many which I thought tolerable. I would not be
like those Authors, who forgive themselves some particular
lines for the sake of a whole Poem, and *vice versa* a whole Poem
for the sake of some particular lines. I believe no one qualification is so likely to make a good writer, as the power of re-   160
jecting his own thoughts; and it must be this (if any thing) that
can give me a chance to be one. For what I have publish'd, I
can only hope to be pardon'd; but for what I have burn'd, I
deserve to be prais'd. On this account the world is under some
obligation to me, and owes me the justice in return, to look   165
upon no verses as mine that are not inserted in this collection.
And perhaps nothing could make it worth my while to own
what are really so, but to avoid the imputation of so many dull
and immoral things, as partly by malice, and partly by ignorance, have been ascribed to me. I must farther acquit my self   170
of the presumption of having lent my name to recommend any

156–9 I would . . . lines.] *Add. 1736a–51.*

---

inconsistent with his request, at the conclusion of his preface, that those who
condemned his poems would remember his youth when he composed them.''

163. *burn'd*] This may allude to the epic poem called *Alcander, Prince of Rhodes*,
which Pope says (Spence, pp. 276–7) he began a little after he was twelve. "I
wrote four books toward it, of about a thousand verses each; and had the copy
by me, till I burnt it, by the advice of the Bishop of Rochester, a little before he
went abroad." Atterbury went into exile in 1723, but the poem had been destroyed by February, 1718. See Atterbury's letter to Pope, Feb. 18, 1718 (*Corr.*,
I 467).

171. Pope had not "lent his name" to a Miscellany, but Ault has presented
evidence (*Pope's Own Miscellany*, 1935, pp. xxi–xxviii) to show that he was en-

Miscellanies, or works of other men, a thing I never thought
becoming a person who has hardly credit enough to answer
for his own.

In this office of collecting my pieces, I am altogether uncer- 175
tain, whether to look upon my self as a man building a monument, or burying the dead?

If time shall make it the former, may these Poems (as long as
they last) remain as a testimony, that their Author never made
his talents subservient to the mean and unworthy ends of Party 180
or self-interest; the gratification of publick prejudices, or private passions; the flattery of the undeserving, or the insult of
the unfortunate. If I have written well, let it be consider'd that
'tis what no man can do without good sense, a quality that not
only renders one capable of being a good writer, but a good 185
man. And if I have made any acquisition in the opinion of any
one under the notion of the former, let it be continued to me
under no other title than that of the latter.

But if this publication be only a more solemn funeral of my
Remains, I desire it may be known that I die in charity, and in 190
my senses; without any murmurs against the justice of this age,
or any mad appeals to posterity. I declare I shall think the
world in the right, and quietly submit to every truth which
time shall discover to the prejudice of these writings; not so
much as wishing so irrational a thing, as that every body should 195
be deceiv'd, meerly for my credit. However, I desire it may
then be consider'd, that there are very few things in this collection which were not written under the age of five and twenty;
so that my youth may be made (as it never fails to be in Execu-
tions) a case of compassion. That I was never so concern'd 200
about my works as to vindicate them in print, believing if any
thing was good it would defend itself, and what was bad could
never be defended. That I used no artifice to raise or continue
a reputation, depreciated no dead author I was oblig'd to,
brib'd no living one with unjust praise, insulted no adversary 205

gaged at this time in editing, anonymously, a volume entitled *Poems on Several
Occasions*, published by Lintot in 1717.

198. *five and twenty*] Pope was twenty-five in 1713; by that time he had published the *Pastorals* (1709), *An Essay on Criticism* (1711), *The Rape of the Lock* (original version) and *Messiah* (1712), *Windsor-Forest* (1713).

B

with ill language, or when I could not attack a Rival's works, encourag'd reports against his Morals. To conclude, if this volume perish, let it serve as a warning to the Critics, not to take too much pains for the future to destroy such things as will die of themselves; and a *Memento mori* to some of my vain co- 210 temporaries the Poets, to teach them that when real merit is wanting, it avails nothing to have been encourag'd by the great, commended by the eminent, and favour'd by the publick in general.

Nov. 10,   215
   1716.

215–16 Nov. 10, 1716.] *Add. 1736a–51.*

Nov. 10, 1716] The date is corroborated by Atterbury's letter to Pope of December, 1716 (*Corr.*, I 378).

A DISCOURSE
ON PASTORAL POETRY

INTRODUCTION

I

A Discourse on Pastoral Poetry is in all probability the earliest surviving piece of formal prose written by Pope.[1] It was not printed with the *Pastorals* in 1709, but made its first appearance in the 1717 *Works*, where a half-title page announced that both the *Discourse* and the *Pastorals* were "Written in the Year 1704." If this date is correct, Pope was sixteen years old when he composed these pieces, a fact he called to the attention of his readers in various ways.[2]

Two letters appear to support the date Pope gave to these works, but both rest upon Pope's sole authority. In a letter of April 7, 1705, Wycherley writes to Pope that "Your Papers are safe in my Custody".[3] Less than two weeks later, on April 20, Walsh writes to Wycherley that he is returning Pope's "Papers", and goes on to say that "The Preface is very judicious and very learned; and the Verses very tender and easy."[4] In the 1751 edition of the *Works* Walsh's letter was cited in the first note to *Spring* as evidence in support of the date to which Pope had assigned the *Discourse* and the *Pastorals*.

A version of the *Discourse*, entitled *An Essay on Pastoral*, has come down to us, along with the *Pastorals*, in MS.[5] On the fly-leaf opposite the title page of the MS Pope again names 1704 as the date for the two works, but also says that the third eclogue, *Autumn*, was written after the other three.[6] At least one leaf is missing at the end of the MS version of the *Discourse*, and the last paragraphs of the MS differ significantly from the corresponding paragraphs in the printed version. A portion of the last MS paragraph has been cited

---

1. See *Prose Works*, I cxv.
2. See Pope's notes to his letters in *Corr.*, I 5, 7.
3. *Corr.*, I 7.   4. Ibid.
5. The manuscript, according to EC (I 239–40), was among the papers of Jonathan Richardson the younger, and was used by Wakefield and EC. It is now in the possession of Mr Arthur A. Houghton, Jr, who has kindly permitted the editors to make use of it.
6. For a transcription of the entire passage, see Intro. to the *Pastorals*, p. 38, below.

as evidence that the *Essay* was written after the completion of all four of the *Pastorals*, including *August*, and it has been argued from this that the *Essay* may date "as late as 1706 or even 1707."[1] Here is the MS passage:

> 'Twas from hence [*The Shepherd's Calendar*] I took my first Design of the following Eclogues. For looking upon Spĕcer as the Father of English Pastoral, I thought my self unworthy to be esteem'd even the meanest of his Sons, unless I bore some Resemblance of him. But as it happens with degenerate Ofspring, not only to recede from yᵉ Virtues, but to dwindle from the Bulk of their Ancestors; So I have copy'd *Spencer* in *Miniature*, and reduc'd his Twelve *Months* into Four Seasons.

A letter of undoubted authenticity from Jacob Tonson to Pope of April 20, 1706 (exactly one year after the letter from Walsh to Wycherley cited above), informs us that the publisher had lately seen a copy of at least one (Tonson's words, "a pastoral", may or may not refer to the *Pastorals* as a group) of Pope's *Pastorals* in "mr. Walsh's & mr Congreves hands".[2] It has been thought quite possible that Walsh saw Pope's eclogues as much as a year before they came to Tonson's attention,[3] and if this be true, then Walsh may have seen an original version of the *Discourse* at the same early date. And even if the third eclogue, *Autumn*, had not been written at that time, it is still possible to see the MS passage cited above as having been written immediately after the other three eclogues (rather than in 1706 or 1707), or even perhaps as referring to the *Pastorals* as planned, and not as completed poems.

On the whole it seems impossible either to confirm or deny the date Pope gave for the composition of the *Discourse*. The fact that the treatise was not published until 1717 has little bearing on the matter. Pope may have designed originally to publish the *Discourse* and the *Pastorals* together, but then may have been persuaded by friends to publish only the poems in Tonson's poetical miscellany, where even so small a prose treatise as the *Discourse* would have been out of place. If this is true, then the *Works* of 1717 offered the first suitable opportunity to publish the *Discourse* with the *Pastorals*, and the intervening years (with the *Guardian*'s contribution to the

---

1. *Prose Works*, 1 cxvi.   2. *Corr.*, 1 17.   3. See *Early Career*, p. 55.

subject) would have made the introductory treatise more rather than less appropriate.

II

Two dominant, and opposing, theories of pastoral poetry existed side by side in late 17th- and early 18th-century England. One of these, which has been called the "neo-classic" theory, derives its principles mainly from Rapin, while the other, which has been called the "rationalistic", stems mainly from Fontenelle.[1] Pope cites both of these writers in his *Discourse*, and it is only by a brief survey of the tenets of the two schools of thought that we may estimate Pope's own contribution to pastoral theory and the place of his treatise in a quarrelsome literary situation.

The two schools differ fundamentally in the sources from which each sought its ultimate authority. The "neo-classic" school looked mainly for support to the writings of the Ancients, principally Virgil; from their pastorals, and from the criticism of Aristotle and Horace, Rapin derived his premises and rules for pastoral poetry. The main point on which this school agreed was that a pastoral should be an "imitation" of the action of a shepherd living in the Golden Age. From this precept stemmed certain subsequent ones: a pastoral should reflect the innocence and peace of that age and the virtues and simplicity of the shepherds who lived in it; because shepherds in this ancient past were often princes or men of affairs, the characters and language should be simple and pure rather than "clownish"; the scene should be simple and decorous, as in Virgil; the matter should reflect only the simple affairs of shepherds, that is, the loves and sorrows of a simple rural life; the fable should be simple and plain, the style neat and plain.

Rapin had set forth the main principles of the "neo-classic" school in his *Dissertatio de Carmine Pastorali*,[2] a preface to his own pastorals, *Eclogae Sacrae*, in 1659. In 1688 Fontenelle published his *Discours sur la nature de l'églogue*, which offered a set of premises at

---

1. See J. E. Congleton, *Theories of Pastoral Poetry in England, 1684–1798* (1952). The discussion throughout this section is indebted to Professor Congleton's study.

2. Translated into English by Thomas Creech in his *The Idylliums of Theocritus With Rapin's Discourse of Pastorals* (1684).

variance with those of Rapin and which formed the basis for the development of the "rationalistic" school in England. Whereas Rapin had accepted the authority of the Ancients and had extracted a set of rules from the pastorals of Virgil and Theocritus, Fontenelle, in the formulation of his theory, let himself be guided by the "Natural Light" of his own Reason. Fundamentally, then, the conflict is one between the authority of the Ancients and self-sufficient Reason.[1]

Instead of the idea that Pastoral should be an image of the Golden Age, Fontenelle maintains that Pastoral is simply a representation of the tranquillity of rural life, and bases this notion on psychological foundations: the laziness of man's nature finds delight in representations of the quietness and leisure of a shepherd's life, while the passion most congenial to this laziness, love, also delights. Fontenelle also maintains that the pleasure of Pastoral arises from the use of "Illusion", or half-truths, which "consists, in exposing to the Eye only the Tranquility of a Shepherd's Life, and in dissembling or concealing its meanness, as also in showing only its Innocence, and hiding its Miseries."[2] The rules which Rapin derived from the Ancients are thus opposed by the independent conclusions of Fontenelle's mind. At the same time, opposed as the two critics are in the methods by which they arrive at their conclusions, it is possible to imagine pastorals written according to the premises of the one being very much like pastorals written according to the premises of the other.

The opposition between Rapin and Fontenelle was transferred to England, and made explicit, in Knightly Chetwood's *Preface* to Dryden's translation of Virgil's *Pastorals*, the full title of which included these words: *With a short Defence of Virgil, Against some of the Reflections of Monsieur Fontanelle*. Chetwood's essay reflects the passion characteristic of the battles long to continue between the supporters of the Ancients and those of the Moderns, for Fontenelle's *Discours* was regarded as one of the earliest attacks upon the authority of the Ancients and, indeed, inspired Sir William Temple to

---

1. See Congleton, op. cit., p. 65.

2. See p. 284 of Motteux's translation of Fontenelle's *Discours*, which appears at the end of the English translation of Le Bossu's *Treatise of the Epick Poem* (1695), under the title of *Of Pastorals*.

write his *An Essay Upon the Ancient and Modern Learning* (1690).[1] Thus
Chetwood passionately defends the premises and rules of Rapin,
and scornfully denounces Fontenelle as one who "ingenuously
owns" that he "first Compos'd his Eclogues, and then studied the
Rules."[2]

After Chetwood's essay the next important phase of the conflict
between the two schools occurs in the disputes over the relative
merits of the pastorals written by Pope and Ambrose Philips. Six
pastorals by Philips, four of which had appeared previously,[3] were
printed as the opening poems in *Poetical Miscellanies, The Sixth Part*,
while Pope's *Pastorals*, in their first appearance in print, concluded
the volume. The opposing principles on which the two poets had
fashioned their poems could not have been more dramatically suggested.

Philips had written his pastorals according to principles totally
at variance with the "neo-classic" principles of Rapin. Far from
giving an image of shepherds living in a Golden Age, he introduced
English rustics in an English landscape, substituted English folk-
lore for classical mythology, employed native archaisms instead of
language "simple and pure", eschewed the decorous scenery admired by the "neo-classic" school in favour of more "realistic"
English settings. For his efforts he received the praise of Addison,
who (in *Spectator* 523, October 30, 1712) said that Philips had given
"a new life, and a more natural beauty to this way of writing by
substituting, in the place of . . . antiquated fables, the superstitious
mythology which prevails among the shepherds of our own country."

The most important and self-conscious formulation of the "rationalistic" position in England is to be found, however, in the five
Guardian essays of April, 1713, supposedly written by Thomas
Tickell.[4] In the first two essays Tickell repeats the fundamental
ideas set forth by Fontenelle, but here the resemblance between the
two ends, and from this point on Tickell constructs his own ration-

---

1. See Spingarn, III 32–3.
2. See Dryden, *The Works of Virgil*, 2nd edn (1698), p. 23.
3. In *Oxford and Cambridge Miscellany Poems*, n.d. (presumably printed in 1708).
4. See nos. 22, 23, 28, 30, 32. See J. E. Butt, 'Notes for a Bibliography of
Thomas Tickell', *Bodleian Quarterly Record*, v (1928), p. 302.

alistic theory, making explicit the cardinal principles of the new school of pastoral poetry.[1] Using examples from Philips's pastorals to support his argument, Tickell informs his readers how one "may lawfully deviate from the Ancients".[2] He endorses the use of native rustics, native customs, native superstitions, native scenery, drawing his Rules, as he says, "from what our Countrymen *Spencer* and *Philips* have performed in this way". Unlike the "neo-classic" school, moreover, Tickell ranks Theocritus above Virgil as a writer of pastorals, and finds that, among his own countrymen, Spenser and Philips have most nearly approached the excellence of the Greek in their use of language appropriate to pastoral. If there is much to be said for the ideas voiced by Tickell, there is less to admire in his scale of values.

Tickell's essays were followed by Pope's famous *Guardian* 40, where the poet ironically adopts the views of the "rationalistic" school to expose the absurdities and inanities of Philips's verse. This essay has long been attributed to anger Pope is supposed to have felt at Tickell's failure to mention his pastorals along with those of Philips.[3] Pope probably was offended by the omission, but here, as in other quarrels in which Pope engaged, there were issues which transcended the purely personal and which reflected not only literary, but also social and political, divisions. On the side of the "rationalistic" group were such men as Addison, Steele, Tickell, Philips, Dennis, and Welsted; the "neo-classic" sympathizers were men such as Temple, Swift, Walsh, Pope, and Gay. If Pope, moreover, did compose a version of his *Discourse* as early as 1704, he had set down, long before Tickell's *Guardian* essays, his own considered statement of the "neo-classic" position. Tickell's essays may have been, therefore, as much an affront to that position as to Pope's pride.

III

Tickell had accepted the basic premises of Fontenelle's pastoral theory, but had gone far beyond them in his construction of a rationalistic theory of English pastoral. Pope also accepts Fontenelle's

---

1. See Congleton, op. cit., p. 87.   2. See *Guardian* 30.
3. Tickell does mention favourably some lines from Pope's version of *The Merchant's Tale* in *Guardian* 30.

premises, but in doing so shows that the principles Fontenelle derived from Reason are no different from the Rules which Rapin
derived from the Virgilian and Theocritean "Nature". Nature,
Reason, and the Rules, as the *Essay on Criticism* was to say, are one
and the same. Pope saw that the differences between Rapin and
Fontenelle were more apparent than real, and that they differ less
in their conclusions than in the methods by which they arrived at
these conclusions.[1] Pope's own method here, as in the *Essay on Criticism*,[2] is eclectic and synthetic, and by means of it he makes an
advance over the more narrow "neo-classic" theory of Rapin and
Chetwood, and at the same time gives that theory its most balanced
and polished expression.

In the opening paragraph of his *Discourse* Pope says plainly that
his design is to give the "substance of those numerous dissertations
the Criticks have made on" pastoral poetry, and to reconcile "some
points" about which "they seem to differ". As the notes to this edition show, the overwhelming majority of his observations have their
source in Rapin, and Pope's allegiance in the main to the principles
of "neo-classic" pastoral theory is thus plainly evident. At the same
time Pope incorporates into his essay the more fundamental principles stated by Fontenelle : thus pastoral is not only an image of the
Golden Age (as Rapin and Chetwood had maintained), but is also
a representation of the ease and tranquillity of country life (as Fontenelle had maintained). Pope also follows Fontenelle's principle
of "illusion", which consisted in "exposing to the Eye only the
Tranquility of a Shepherd's Life, and in dissembling or concealing
its meanness, as also in showing only its Innocence, and hiding its
Miseries."[3] Both Rapin and Fontenelle had shared a distaste for the
grosser language of Theocritus, and both too had thought that
some of Theocritus's and Virgil's eclogues were not truly pastoral:
this agreement is also reflected in Pope's *Discourse*.

In the concluding paragraph of the MS version of the *Discourse*
Pope, as we have seen, had termed himself a "degenerate Ofspring"
of Spenser, whom he called the "Father of English Pastoral". These
suggestions are not to be found in the printed version of 1717, for

---

1. See Congleton, op. cit., p. 81.
2. See Intro. to *Essay on Criticism*, pp. 210–12, below.
3. See *Discourse*, 65n.

by then Ambrose Philips had long been hailed as Spenser's legitimate heir, and in such a lineage Pope evidently did not care to participate. Besides, Pope in his *Guardian* 40 had also linked Philips and
Spenser together, claiming for himself a likeness with Moschus,
Bion, and Virgil.

Here again, however, Pope reveals the discrimination and balance which characterize his *Discourse* as a whole. He may criticize
Spenser for his verse form, his archaic and rustic language, the re-
petition necessarily involved in his "Calendar" of twelve months; yet he also praises Spenser for his "manners, thoughts, and characters", where "he comes near to *Theocritus* himself", for his "general
moral of innocence and simplicity", and for his "very beautiful"
Calendar, by which "he compares human Life to the several Seasons, and at once exposes to his readers a view of the great and little
worlds, in their various changes and aspects."[1]

Pope's *Discourse* can be regarded as the culminating statement of
"neo-classic" theory; historically it was almost immediately super-
seded by the victory of the "rationalistic" theory and by Romantic
tendencies. The "neo-classic" position has grave weaknesses, it
should be admitted, yet it is to Pope's *Discourse* that one must look
for the most flexible, balanced, and polished statement of that position. It is this fact which justifies Walsh's praise of the *Discourse* as
"very judicious and very learned".

---

1. Cf. Pope's letter to John Hughes of October 7, 1715 (*Corr.*, 1 316):
". . . Spenser has been ever a favourite poet to me: he is like a mistress, whose
faults we see, but love her with 'em all."

PASTORALS,

WITH A

DISCOURSE on *PASTORAL*.

Written in the Year 1704.

Rura mihi & rigui placeant in vallibus amnes,
Flumina amem, ſylvaſque, inglorius!

VIRG.

NOTE ON THE TEXT

Pope's *Pastorals* were first printed in 1709, but it was not until the
1717 edition of his *Works* that the poet published the *Discourse on
Pastoral Poetry* which introduces them here. The text offers little
difficulty: a few changes (at ll. 42, 60, 90, 135) were introduced into
the editions of 1736, but most of the revisions appear for the first
time in Warburton's edition of the *Works* in 1751. One doubtful
change found in Warburton's text, at l. 48, has been considered a
misprint, but it is preserved in the textual notes.

The text printed here observes the revisions of later editions, but
follows the spelling, punctuation, and typography of the first edition.

KEY TO THE CRITICAL APPARATUS

1717 = Works, quarto, Griffith 79.
1736a = Works, vol. I, octavo, Griffith 413.
1736b = Works, vol. I, octavo, Griffith 414.
1740 = Works, vol. I, part I, octavo, Griffith 510.
1743 = Works, vol. I, part I, octavo, Griffith 582.
1751 = Works, ed. Warburton, vol. I, octavo, Griffith 643.

A
DISCOURSE
ON
PASTORAL POETRY.

THERE are not, I believe, a greater number of any sort of verses than of those which are called Pastorals, nor a smaller, than of those which are truly so. It therefore seems necessary to give some account of this kind of Poem, and it is my design to comprize in this short paper the substance of those numerous dissertations the Criticks have made on the subject, without omitting any of their rules in my own favour. You will also find some points reconciled, about which they seem to differ, and a few remarks which I think have escaped their observation.

   The original of Poetry is ascribed to that age which succeeded the creation of the world: And as the keeping of flocks seems to have been the first employment of mankind, the most ancient sort of poetry was probably pastoral. 'Tis natural to imagine, that the leisure of those ancient shepherds admitting and inviting some diversion, none was so proper to that soli-

5

10

15

15–16 admitting and inviting] requiring *1717–43*.

Written at sixteen years of age. [P. *1751.*]

  11. Cf. Rapin, *A Treatise de Carmine Pastorali* (tr. by Thomas Creech, 1684), p. 14: "Pastorals were the invention . . . of that time which succeeded the beginning of the World."

  13. Cf. Rapin, *Treatise,* p. 7: ". . . *Pastoral* . . . was the most antient kind of Poetry, and resulting from the most *antient* way of Liveing. . ."

  14. *pastoral*] *Fontenelle's Disc. on Pastorals.* [P. *1751.*]

  See Fontenelle's *Of Pastorals* (in Le Bossu's *Treatise of the Epick Poem,* 1695), p. 277: "Of all kinds of Poetry the Pastoral is probably the most Ancient, as the keeping of Flocks was one of the first Employments which Men took up. 'Tis very likely that these primitive Shepherds, amidst the Tranquility and Leisure which they enjoy'd, bethought themselves of singing their Pleasures and their Loves." Cf. Rapin, *Treatise,* p. 7: "For since the first men were either *Sheapards* or *Ploughmen,* and *Sheapards* . . . were before the others, they were the first that either invited by their leisure, or . . . in imitation of Birds, began a tune."

tary and sedentary life as singing; and that in their songs they
took occasion to celebrate their own felicity. From hence a
Poem was invented, and afterwards improv'd to a perfect
image of that happy time; which by giving us an esteem for the   20
virtues of a former age, might recommend them to the present.
And since the life of shepherds was attended with more tranquillity than any other rural employment, the Poets chose to
introduce their Persons, from whom it receiv'd the name of
Pastoral.   25

A Pastoral is an imitation of the action of a shepherd, or one
considered under that character. The form of this imitation is
dramatic, or narrative, or mix'd of both; the fable simple, the
manners not too polite nor too rustic: The thoughts are plain,
yet admit a little quickness and passion, but that short and   30

17 and sedentary] *Add. 1751.*   26–7 or . . . character] *Add. 1751.*

19–20. *perfect image*] Rapin, *Treatise*, p. 5, speaks of a shepherd's life as being
"a perfect image of the state of Innocence, of that golden Age, that blessed
time . . ."

27. *character*] Knightly Chetwood, *Preface to the Pastorals*, p. 22: "As all sorts of
Poetry consist in imitation; Pastoral is the *imitation of a Shepherd consider'd under
that Character.*" This definition is almost word for word that given by Rapin,
Treatise, p. 19, where it is said that Pastoral "*is the imitation of the Action of a
Sheaphard, or of one taken under that Character.*"
All references to Chetwood's preface are to the 1698 (2nd edn) of Dryden's
Virgil.

28. *mix'd of both*] Heinsius in Theocr. [P. *1751.*]
Pope may have known Heinsius only through Rapin's *Treatise*, p. 29: "And
the same observation is made by *Heinsius* in his Notes on *Theocritus,* for thus he
[says] very plainly to our purpose, *the Character of* Bucolicks *is a mixture of all sorts
of Characters, Dramatick, Narrative, or mixt.*"

the fable simple] Rapin, *Treatise*, p. 31: "Thus every Eclogue or Idyllium must
have its Fable, which must be the groundwork of the whole Design . . . that it
might be agreeable to the Person[s] it treats of, it must be plain and simple."

29. *too rustic*] Cf. Rapin, *Treatise*, p. 33: "Now as too much neatness in *Pastoral*
is not to be allow'd, so rusticity . . . must not in my opinion be endur'd." Again,
p. 33: ". . . we must consult unstain'd, uncorrupted Nature; so that the manners
might not be too Clownish nor too Courtly."

The thoughts] Rapin, *Treatise*, p. 34: ". . . the Thought . . . must be suitable to
the *manners*; as those must be plain and pure that must be so too."

30. *quickness and passion*] Rapin, *Treatise*, p. 35: ". . . lest the Thought be cold
and flat, it must have some quickness of Passion . . ."

flowing: The expression humble, yet as pure as the language will afford; neat, but not florid; easy, and yet lively. In short, the fable, manners, thoughts, and expressions, are full of the greatest simplicity in nature.

The complete character of this poem consists in simplicity, 35 brevity, and delicacy; the two first of which render an eclogue natural, and the last delightful. |

If we would copy Nature, it may be useful to take this Idea along with us, that pastoral is an image of what they call the Golden age. So that we are not to describe our shepherds as 40 shepherds at this day really are, but as they may be conceiv'd then to have been; when the best of men follow'd the employment. To carry this resemblance yet farther, it would not be

38 Idea] consideration *1717–43*.
42 when the best] when a notion of quality was annex'd to that name, and the best *1717*.
43–5 farther . . . And an] farther, that *1717–43*.

31. *expression humble*] Rapin, *Treatise*, p. 35: "Let the Expression be plain and easy, but elegant and neat, and the purest which the language will afford."

34. *greatest simplicity*] Rapin, *Treatise*, p. 37: ". . . as Simplicity was the principal vertue of that [golden] Age, so it ought to be the peculiar Grace, and as it were *Character* of *Bucolicks*: in which the Fable, Manners, Thought, and Expression ought to be full of the most innocent simplicity imaginable." See l. 35*n* below.

35. *simplicity*] *Rapin de Carm. Past. p. 2.* [P. *1751*.]
Cf. Rapin, *Treatise*, p. 44: "Then there are three things in which, as in its parts, the whole *Character* of a *Pastoral* is contain'd: *Simplicity* of Thought and expression: *Shortness* of Periods full of sense and spirit: and the *Delicacy* of a most elegant ravishing unaffected neatness."

40. *Golden age*] Rapin, *Treatise*, p. 14: "Pastorals were the invention of the simplicity and innocence of that Golden age, if there was ever any such, or certainly of that time which succeeded the beginning of the World."

40*f.* Rapin, *Treatise*, p. 37, says that "*Pastoral* belongs properly to the *Golden Age*" because "Poetry fashions its subject as Men imagine it should be, and not as really it is. . ." He also states, pp. 33–4, that the manners of shepherds should "be represented according to the *Genius* of the *golden Age*, in which . . . every man follow'd that employment. . ."

42–3. *the employment*] Knightly Chetwood, *Preface*, pp. 22–3: "It is commonly known, that the Founders of three of the most renown'd Monarchies in the

amiss to give these shepherds some skill in astronomy, as far as
it may be useful to that sort of life. And an Air of piety to the   45
Gods should shine thro' the Poem, which so visibly appears in
all the works of antiquity : And it ought to preserve some relish
of the old way of writing; the connections should be loose, the
narrations and descriptions short, and the periods concise. Yet
it is not sufficient that the sentences only be brief, the whole   50
Eclogue should be so too. For we cannot suppose Poetry in
those days to have been the business of men, but their recreation at vacant hours.

But with a respect to the present age, nothing more con-

48 connections] connection *1751.*
51–2 in those days] *Add. 1751.*
52 of men,] of the ancient shepherds, *1717–43.*

World, were Shepherds: And the Subject of Husbandry has been adorn'd by
the *Writings* and *Labour* of more than twenty *Kings.*"

44. *astronomy*] The idea that shepherds, being of necessity weather-wise, should
be endowed in Pastorals with some knowledge of the stars, does not seem to
occur in other treatises on pastoral. The idea may have been suggested by Dryden, *Dedic. of the Æn.* (*Essays,* ii 207) : "By some passages in the *Pastorals,* but
more particularly in the *Georgics,* our poet is found to be an exact astronomer,
according to the knowledge of that age."

45. *Air of piety*] Chetwood, *Preface,* p. 26 : ". . . an air of Piety upon all occasions should be maintain'd in the whole Poem. . ."

48. *old way of writing*] Chetwood, *Preface,* p. 29 : ". . . as the Style ought to be
natural, clear, and elegant, it should have some particular relish of the Ancient
Fashion of Writing."

connections] Chetwood, *Preface,* p. 29 : "Nor ought the Connexions and Transi-
tions to be very strict, and regular. . . The over-scrupulous care of Connexions,
makes the Modern Compositions oftentimes tedious and flat."

49. *descriptions short*] Rapin, *Reflex. sur l'Art Poet. d'Arist. p. 2. Refl.* xxvii. [P.
1751.]

Pope refers to the following passage (*Reflections on Aristotle's Treatise of Poesie,*
1674, p. 135) : ". . . its [the eclogue's] *Narrations* are short, *Descriptions* little . . ."

51. *so too*] Chetwood, *Preface,* p. 29 : "Another Rule omitted by *P. Rapine* . . .
is, that not only the Sentences should be *short,* and *smart* . . . but that the whole
piece should be so too."

52–3. *recreation*] Chetwood, *Preface,* p. 29 : "For Poetry and Pastime was not
the Business of Mens Lives in those days, but only their seasonable Recreation
after necessary Labours."

duces to make these composures natural, than when some   55
Knowledge in rural affairs is discover'd. This may be made to
appear rather done by chance than on design, and sometimes
is best shewn by inference; lest by too much study to seem
natural, we destroy that easy simplicity from whence arises the
delight. For what is inviting in this sort of poetry proceeds not   60
so much from the Idea of that business, as of the tranquillity of a country life.

   We must therefore use some illusion to render a Pastoral delightful; and this consists in exposing the best side only of a
shepherd's life, and in concealing its miseries. Nor is it enough   65
to introduce shepherds discoursing together in a natural way;
but a regard must be had to the subject; that it contain some
particular beauty in itself, and that it be different in every

59 that ... arises] *Add. 1751.*
60 poetry proceeds] poetry (as *Fontenelle* observes) proceeds *1717.*
61–2 Idea . . . life.] Idea of a country life itself, as from that of its
       Tranquillity. *1717–43.*
63 *No new paragraph 1717–43.*
66–7 together in a natural way; but] together, but *1717–43.*

55. *composures*] Compositions. *Composure* is consistently used in this sense in
Creech's translation of Rapin.
   56. *discover'd*] *Pref. to Virg. Past. in Dryd. Virg.* [P. *1751.*]
   Cf. Chetwood, *Preface*, p. 28: ". . . the Writer should shew in his Compositions, some competent skill of the Subject matter, that which makes the Character of Persons introduc'd."
   61–2. *tranquillity*] Cf. Fontenelle, *Of Pastorals*, p. 284: ". . . 'tis only on that tranquility that whatever pleases in a Pastoral Life is grounded." Cf. also p. 281:
"Pastoral Poetry cannot be very charming if it is as low and clownish as Shepherds naturally are; or if it precisely runs upon nothing but rural Matters. For,
to hear one speak of Sheep and Goats, and of the care that ought to be taken of
those Animals, has nothing which in it self can please us; what is pleasing is the
Idea of quietness, which is inseparable from a Pastoral Life."
   65. *its miseries*] *Fontenelle's Disc. of Pastorals.* [P. *1751.*]
   Cf. p. 284: "The Illusion and at the same time the pleasingness of Pastorals
therefore consists in exposing to the Eye only the Tranquility of a Shepherd's
Life, and in dissembling or concealing its meanness, as also in showing only its
Innocence and hiding its Miseries."

Eclogue. Besides, in each of them a design'd scene or prospect
is to be presented to our view, which should likewise have its   70
variety. This Variety is obtain'd in a great degree by frequent
comparisons, drawn from the most agreeable objects of the
country; by interrogations to things inanimate; by beautiful
digressions, but those short; sometimes by insisting a little on
circumstances; and lastly by elegant turns on the words, which   75
render the numbers extremely sweet and pleasing. As for the
numbers themselves, tho' they are properly of the heroic mea-

---

69. *design'd scene*] Chetwood, *Preface*, p. 27: ". . . there should be some Ordon-
nance, some Design, or little Plot, which may deserve the Title of a Pastoral
Scene."

70-1. *its variety*] *See the forementioned Preface*. [P. *1751*.]
Pope may refer to the passage by Chetwood cited at l. 69*n* or to the following,
p. 27 of the *Preface*: "A Fourth Rule . . . is, that there be choice diversity of Subjects; that the *Eclogues*, like a Beautiful Prospect, should Charm by its [sic]
Variety."

71-2. *frequent comparisons*] Rapin, *Treatise*, p. 66: ". . . your *Comparisons* must be
frequent, and the more often you use them the better and more graceful will be
the Composure; especially if taken from such things, as the Shepherds must be
familiarly acquainted with: They are frequent in *Theocritus*, but so proper to the
Country, that none but a *Shepherd* dare use them."

73. *interrogations*] Rapin, *Treatise*, p. 62: "To these he may sometimes joyn
some short Interrogations made to *inanimate Beings*."

75. *circumstances*] Cf. Fontenelle, *Of Pastorals*, p. 292: "There are no persons
whom it becomes better to lengthen a little their Narrations with Circumstances
than Lovers."

76. *sweet and pleasing.*] Cf. Rapin, *Treatise*, p. 66: ". . . as likewise often *repetitions*, and doublings of some words: which, if they are luckily plac'd, have an
unexpressible quaintness, and make the Numbers extream sweet, and the turns
ravishing and delightful." Cf. also Pope's words to Spence, p. 312: "There is a
sweetness, that is the distinguishing character of pastoral versification. The
fourth and fifth syllables, and the last but two, are chiefly to be minded: and
one must tune each line over in one's head, to try whether they go right or
not."

77-8. *heroic measure*] Rapin, *Treatise*, p. 63, says: "Concerning the *Numbers*, in
which *Pastoral* should be written, this is my opinion; the *Heroick* Measure, but
not so strong and sounding as in *Epicks*, is to be chosen. . . *Virgil* useth no Numbers but *Heroick*, from whence it may be inferr'd, that those are the fittest." But
cf. what Pope told Spence, p. 312: "Though Virgil, in his Pastorals, has sometimes six or eight lines together that are epic: I have been so scrupulous as scarce
ever to admit above two together, even in the Messiah."

sure, they should be the smoothest, the most easy and flowing
imaginable.

It is by rules like these that we ought to judge of Pastoral.   80
And since the instructions given for any art are to be deliver'd
as that art is in perfection, they must of necessity be deriv'd
from those in whom it is acknowledg'd so to be. 'Tis therefore
from the practice of *Theocritus* and *Virgil*, (the only undisputed
authors of Pastoral) that the Criticks have drawn the foregoing   85
notions concerning it.

Theocritus excells all others in nature and simplicity. The
subjects of his *Idyllia* are purely pastoral, but he is not so exact
in his persons, having introduced Reapers and fishermen as
well as shepherds. He is apt to be too long in his descriptions,   90
of which that of the Cup in the first pastoral is a remarkabie
instance. In the manners he seems a little defective, for his
swains are sometimes abusive and immodest and perhaps too

90 too] *Add. 1736a–51.*

81*ff.* Rapin, *Treatise*, pp. 52–3: "I will gather from *Theocritus* and *Virgil*, those
Fathers of *Pastoral*, what I shall deliver on this account. For all the Rules that
are to be given of any Art, are to be given of it as excellent, and perfect, and
therefore ought to be taken from them in whom it is so."

87. Rapin, *Treatise*, p. 38, says that "*Theocritus* excells *Virgil* in this [simpli-
city]."

89. *Reapers*] ΘΕΡΙΣΤΑΙ *Idyl.* x. *and* ΑΛΙΕΙΣ *Idyl.* xxi. [P. *1751.*]

Cf. Rapin, *Treatise*, pp. 27–8: "Some are of opinion that . . . the discourse of
Fishers, Plow-men, Reapers, Hunters, and the like, belong to this kind of Poetry:
which according to the Rule that I have laid down cannot be true for, as I have
before hinted nothing but the action of a Shepherd can be the Subject of a
Pastoral." Cf. Fontenelle, p. 283: "As the Pastoral Life is the most idle of all
others, 'tis also the most fit to be the Ground-work of those Ingenious Representations of which we are speaking. So that no Ploughmen, Reapers, Vine-
dressers or Huntsmen, can by any means be so properly introduc'd in Eclogues,
as Shepherds."

91–2. *a remarkable instance*] Cf. Rapin, *Treatise*, p. 65: "[Theocritus] in his first
Idyllium makes such a long immoderate description of his *Cup*, that *Criticks* find
fault with him." Cf. also Fontenelle, *Of Pastorals*, p. 292.

93. *abusive and immodest*] Cf. Rapin, *Treatise*, p. 67, speaking of "Manners":
". . . in this part *Theocritus* is faulty, *Virgil* never. . . There is another thing in
which *Theocritus* is faulty, and that is making his Shepherds too sharp, and abusive to one another." Cf. also Fontenelle, *Of Pastorals*, pp. 278*ff.*

much inclining to rusticity; for instance, in his fourth and fifth
Idyllia. But 'tis enough that all others learn'd their excellencies   95
from him, and that his Dialect alone has a secret charm in it
which no other could ever attain.

   Virgil who copies *Theocritus*, refines upon his original: and
in all points where Judgment is principally concerned, he is
much superior to his master. Tho' some of his subjects are not   100
pastoral in themselves, but only seem to be such; they have a
wonderful variety in them which the *Greek* was a stranger to.
He exceeds him in regularity and brevity, and falls short of
him in nothing but simplicity and propriety of style; the first
of which perhaps was the fault of his age, and the last of his   105
language.

   Among the moderns, their success has been greatest who
have most endeavour'd to make these ancients their pattern.
The most considerable Genius appears in the famous *Tasso,*

99–100 Judgment . . . much] Judgment has the principal part, is
   much *1717–43.*

---

   96. *a secret charm*] Dryden, Dedic. of *Pastorals,* p. 3: "After all, I must confess
that the Boorish Dialect of *Theocritus* has a secret charm in it, which the *Roman*
Language cannot imitate."

   102. *a stranger to.*] *Rapin Refl. on Arist. part* ii. *refl.* xxvii.—*Pref. to the Ecl. in
Dryden's Virg.* [P. *1751.*]

Pope's first reference probably relates to the beginning of his paragraph and
refers to this passage in Rapin's *Reflections on Aristotle's Treatise of Poesie* (1674),
p. 135: "After all, *Theocritus* is the Original, *Virgil* is only the Copy. . . *Virgil* is
more judicious, more exact, more regular, more modest. . . *Virgil* has more of
good sense, more vigor, more nobleness, more modesty." For the second reference,
see Chetwood, *Preface,* p. 27: "*Virgil* is admirable in this point ["that the *Eclogue*
. . . should charm by its Variety"] and far surpasses *Theocritus,* as he does every
where, when Judgment and Contrivance have the principal part."

   105–6. *his language*] Cf. Rapin, *Treatise,* p. 36: ". . . 'twas much harder for the
Latines to write *Pastorals,* than for the *Greeks*; because the *Latines* had not some
Dialects peculiar to the Country, and others to the City, as the *Greeks* had; Besides the *Latine* Language . . . is not capable of the neatness which is necessary
to Bucolicks, no, that is the peculiar priviledge of the *Greeks.* . ."

   107. *Among the moderns*] Cf. the letter from Walsh to Pope of July 20, 1706
(*Corr.,* I 20): "The best of the modern Poets in all Languages, are those that have
the nearest copied the Ancients."

and our *Spenser*. *Tasso* in his *Aminta* has as far excell'd all the 110
Pastoral writers, as in his *Gierusalemme* he has outdone the Epic
Poets of his country. But as this piece seems to have been the
original of a new sort of poem, the Pastoral Comedy, in *Italy*, it
cannot so well be consider'd as a copy of the ancients. *Spenser*'s
Calender, in Mr. *Dryden*'s opinion, is the most complete work of 115
this kind which any Nation has produc'd ever since the time of
Virgil. Not but that he may be thought imperfect in some few
points. His Eclogues are somewhat too long, if we compare
them with the ancients. He is sometimes too allegorical, and
treats of matters of religion in a pastoral style as *Mantuan* had 120
done before him. He has employ'd the Lyric measure, which
is contrary to the practice of the old Poets. His Stanza is not
still the same, nor always well chosen. This last may be the
reason his expression is sometimes not concise enough: for the
Tetrastic has oblig'd him to extend his sense to the length of 125
four lines, which would have been more closely confin'd in the
Couplet.

In the manners, thoughts, and characters, he comes near to
Theocritus himself; tho' notwithstanding all the care he has

117 that] *Add. 1751.*   128 to] *Add. 1751.*

110. *Aminta has*] Cf. Fontenelle, *Of Pastoral*, p. 289: "And indeed *Tasso*'s *Amynta* is the best Thing that *Italy* has produc'd in the *Pastoral* kind." Cf. also Walsh's letter to Pope, June 24, 1706 (*Corr.*, 1 18).

113. *Pastoral Comedy*] Cf. Walsh's letters to Pope, June 24 and July 20, 1706 (*Corr.*, 1 18, 20).

117. *Virgil*] *Dedication to Virg. Ecl.* [P. *1751.*]

In his Dedic. of the *Pastorals* to Lord Clifford, Dryden, p. 3, says: ". . . the Sheapherd's Kalendar of *Spencer*, is not to be match'd in any Modern Language."

120. *Mantuan*] Baptista Mantuanus (1448–1516), the "Christian Virgil", wrote Latin eclogues which enjoyed great popularity during the Renaissance and did not disappear from English classrooms until the beginning of the 18th century. Some of his eclogues dealt allegorically with the religious life, and others attacked ecclesiastical abuses. Spenser had imitated Mantuan in his "July" and "September" eclogues.

123. *nor . . . well chosen*] In *A Disc. conc. . . . Sat.* (*Essays*, ii 28–9), Dryden had made the same criticism of Spenser's stanza in *F.Q.*

taken, he is certainly inferior in his Dialect: For the *Doric* had 130
its beauty and propriety in the time of *Theocritus*; it was used
in part of *Greece*, and frequent in the mouths of many of the
greatest persons; whereas the old *English* and country phrases
of *Spenser* were either entirely obsolete, or spoken only by
people of the lowest condition. As there is a difference between 135
simplicity and rusticity, so the expression of simple thoughts
should be plain, but not clownish. The addition he has made of
a Calendar to his Eclogues is very beautiful: since by this, besides the general moral of innocence and simplicity, which is
common to other authors of pastoral, he has one peculiar to 140
himself; he compares human Life to the several Seasons, and
at once exposes to his readers a view of the great and little
worlds, in their various changes and aspects. Yet the scrupulous division of his Pastorals into Months, has oblig'd him
either to repeat the same description, in other words, for three 145
months together; or when it was exhausted before, entirely to
omit it: whence it comes to pass that some of his Eclogues (as
the sixth, eighth, and tenth for example) have nothing but
their Titles to distinguish them. The reason is evident, because
the year has not that variety in it to furnish every month with 150
a particular description, as it may every season.

Of the following Eclogues I shall only say, that these four
comprehend all the subjects which the Critics upon *Theocritus*
and *Virgil* will allow to be fit for pastoral: That they have as

135 lowest] basest *1717*.   139 the] that *1717–43*.

---

130. *the Doric*] Dryden, Pref. to *Sylvæ* (*Essays*, 1 265–6), says of Theocritus:
"Even his Doric dialect has an incomparable sweetness in its clownishness, like
a fair shepherdess in her country russet, talking in a Yorkshire tone. . . Spenser
has endeavoured it [to imitate him] in his *Shepherd's Calendar*; but neither will it
succeed in English. . . Theocritus writ to Sicilians, who spoke that dialect. . ."

137. Cf. Rapin, *Treatise*, p. 58: ". . . for though the Thought ought to be rus-
tick, and such as is suitable to a Shepherd, yet it ought not to be Clownish. . ."

150. *has not that variety*] Perhaps Pope's criticism of Spenser's division of his
eclogues into twelve months derives from Addison's remark on Hesiod in his *An
Essay on the Georgics* (prefixed to Dryden's *Virgil*, p. 99): "His Method in describing Month after Month with its proper Seasons and Employments, is too
grave and simple; it takes off from the surprize and variety of the Poem. . ."

much variety of description, in respect of the several seasons, 155
as *Spenser*'s: That in order to add to this variety, the several
times of the day are observ'd, the rural employments in each
season or time of day, and the rural scenes or places proper to
such employments; not without some regard to the several
ages of man, and the different passions proper to each age. 160

But after all, if they have any merit, it is to be attributed to
some good old Authors, whose works as I had leisure to study,
so I hope I have not wanted care to imitate.

PASTORALS

INTRODUCTION

I: DATE OF COMPOSITION

THE *Pastorals* were the poems which, even before publication, first established Pope's reputation in a small circle of friends and patrons. They were also among the first group of poems to be published by Pope, appearing in 1709 in *Poetical Miscellanies, The Sixth Part*.[1] According to Pope, the *Pastorals* were written when he was sixteen, that is in 1704, and subsequently passed, in manuscript, through the hands of a number of poets and critics. In the first note to *Spring*, part of which was not published until 1751, the poet says that all of these gave him the "greatest encouragement, and particularly Mr. *Walsh*". In the same note Pope quotes a letter from Walsh to Wycherley in which the *Pastorals* and the *Discourse on Pastoral Poetry* are highly praised, and which concludes thus: " 'Tis no flattery at all to say, that *Virgil* had written nothing so good at his Age". Pope is the sole authority for this letter, which is dated April 20, 1705.[2]

Another letter, published by George Granville, Lord Lansdowne, in 1732,[3] is also cited by Pope in this same note to *Spring*. Writing to an unidentified person,[4] Lansdowne speaks of "a young Poet, newly inspir'd", whom Wycherley and Walsh "have taken under their Wing; his Name is *Pope*; he is not above Seventeen or Eighteen Years of Age, and promises Miracles: If he goes on as he has begun, in the Pastoral way, as *Virgil* first try'd his Strength, we may hope to see *English* Poetry vie with the *Roman*. . ." From the mention of Pope's age the letter can be dated 1705 or 1706, and it provides independent support to Pope's various statements[5] that his *Pastorals* were written when he was about sixteen.

Even more impartial testimony is offered by a letter from Jacob Tonson to Pope of April 20, 1706,[6] in which the publisher says: "I have lately seen a pastoral of yours in mr. Walsh's & mr Congreves

---

1. Also known as Dryden's, or Tonson's, Miscellany. Other poems by Pope in this volume are *January and May* and *The Episode of Sarpedon*.

2. *Corr.*, 1 7.   3. See Lansdowne's *Works*, 1 437.

4. See *Early Career*, p. 52.   5. See *Corr.*, 1 5n, 7n.   6. Ibid., 1 17.

hands, which is extreamly ffine & is generally approv'd off by the best Judges in poetry." Tonson's words "a pastoral" have led to the belief that only one of Pope's eclogues had been written at the time,[1] but the fact that Tonson saw only one does not prove that others had not been written. The date of Tonson's letter would again support the date of composition given by Pope, for it is surely not unreasonable to suppose that the poems were written little more than a year before they came to Tonson's attention.

The MS of the *Pastorals* which circulated among Pope's friends is still in existence.[2] On the fly-leaf of the MS version of the *Discourse on Pastoral Poetry*, which accompanies the MS of the poems, in a handwriting certainly of a later date than that of the MS texts, Pope wrote: "Mem: This Copy is that wch past thro ye hands of Mr Walsh, Mr Congreve, Mr Mainwaring, Dr. Garth, Mr Granville, Mr Southern, Sr H. Sheers, Sr W. Trumbull, L^d. Halifax, Ld Wharton, Marq. of Dorchest^r. D. of Bucks. &c. Only ye 3rd Eclog was written since some of these saw ye other 3. wch were written as they here stand wth ye Essay, anno 1704.—Ætat. meæ, 16./ The Alterations from this Copy were upon ye Objections of some of these, or my own."

Pope's statement that the third eclogue, *Autumn*, was written after the others (indeed, after these were seen by the people he lists), is supported by a letter from Walsh of September 9, 1706.[3] Walsh expects to be in London for the reassembly of Parliament, and tells Pope that he hopes "by that time you will have finisht your Pastorals as you would have them appear in the world, and particularly the third of *Autumn* which I have not yet seen." Some slight further confirmation of delay in the composition of *Autumn* is offered by the MS itself. Little difference can be detected between the beautiful script of *Autumn* and that of the other eclogues, but the capitals U, M, and N in the title of *Autumn* are adorned with a flourish which is absent from the other titles. Furthermore, while

---

1. See *Prose Works*, I cxvi. Tonson's words could refer to the poems as a group. The poems may also have been written on separate sheets, only one of which Tonson saw.

2. It is now the property of Mr Arthur A. Houghton, Jr, who has very kindly authorized the use of it by the editors.

3. *Corr.*, I 21–2.

each of the other poems is spread over seven pages, *Autumn* takes up
only six, with an evident crowding of lines on page six. It appears
from the arrangement of the sheets that Pope, by beginning *Winter*
on the recto instead of the verso of a page, left himself only six blank
pages between *Summer* and *Winter*, and therefore found himself
crowded when he came to transcribe *Autumn* in the space he had
allotted.

Another MS accompanies that of the *Pastorals*, and consists of
pages on which Pope copied out passages from the eclogues for
Walsh's criticism, and on which Walsh recorded his opinion.[1]
There are fourteen such passages, five from *Spring*, five from
Summer, three from *Winter*, and, coming last, one from *Autumn*.
Each passage is preceded by the number of the *Pastoral* and the
number of the line quoted, e.g., Past. 1. lin. 1, as if Pope had referred Walsh to a MS which accompanied this list of emendations. If
so, it was a MS different from the one we know, for although the
recorded passages correspond in a general way with the existing
MS, there are many minor differences, and some major ones. Thus
Pope submitted to Walsh's judgment a couplet which is not in the
existing MS but which forms the basis of a passage in the printed
text of *Spring*, ll. 69–76; the MS passage in *Spring* which was replaced by the revision becomes in turn the starting point of ll. 17*ff*,
in *Autumn*. Now if we are to believe the letter from Walsh to Pope of
September 9, 1706, at that date the *Pastorals* were not in final state
and Walsh had not yet seen *Autumn*. Walsh's advice was still being
sought, therefore, either late in 1706 or in 1707.

That the *Pastorals* were being remodelled at so late a date seems
confirmed by the only passage in the text which permits us to guess
at a historical allusion. This is the riddle which Daphnis puts to
Strephon in *Spring*, and which at one time stood thus in the MS
(where Strephon is the questioner):

> Say *Daphnis*, say, what Region canst thou find,
> In which by *Thistles*, *Lillies* are outshin'd?

Queen Anne revived the Order of the Thistle in 1703, and the

---

1. The MS, entitled "Alterations to the Pastoralls: (The Solutions of the
Queries are written by Mr. Walsh.)", is now in the possession of Mr Arthur A.
Houghton, Jr. It is reprinted, by the kind permission of Mr Houghton, in
Appendix A.

Thistle could henceforth be considered emblematic of the reigning monarch. The idea for the riddle may therefore have suggested itself to Pope as early as 1704, the date when he said he first composed his poems. If so, the riddle probably alluded to the victory of the Allies over the French, and to the "region" where the battle was fought, Blenheim in Bavaria. There, on August 13, 1704, Marlborough and Prince Eugene outgeneralled Tallard, and the Thistle triumphed over the Fleur de Lis.

Another version of the riddle, which became the final reading, was then proposed in the passages submitted to Walsh:

> Nay tell me first in what more happy Fields
> The Thistle springs to which the Lilly yields?

This was accompanied by a note: "Alluding to ye Arms of Scotland & France." Thus to the riddle was added a pun on "Fields", which suggests not only the "more happy Fields" ruled by Queen Anne (whose uncle, Charles II, as the preceding riddle in the eclogue indicates, had had to seek refuge in an oak tree[1]), but also the heraldic fields of the Royal Arms of England, on which, in 1707, the French Lily had "yielded" pride of place to Scotland, now united with England.[2] As early as April, 1706, the Commission assembled for the projected union of England and Scotland had recommended that the arms of the two countries be conjoined, and Queen Anne gave the royal assent to the proposals on March 6, 1707. Article one of the Act of Union provided that the two kingdoms be united on May 1, 1707, and that the "ensigns armorial of the said united kingdom be such as her Majesty shall appoint". The final version of the riddle would seem to date, therefore, from some time in 1707, after the change in the Royal Arms had occur-

---

1. In the MS passage submitted to Walsh, Pope notes that the word "more" referred to something "going before", i.e., to the riddle concerning Charles II and the oak tree. See Appendix A.

2. See Robert Steele, *Bibliotheca Lindesiana*, vol. VI, *A Bibliography of Royal Proclamations of the Tudor and Stuart Sovereigns* (vol. II), 1910, p. 498: "Another change in the Royal Arms of England took place in 1707 on the union of Scotland and England. Henceforward England and Scotland impaled were borne in the first and fourth quarters, the fleur-de-lis of France in the second, and the harp of Ireland in the third." Previous to this change, England and France had often shared, quarterly, the first and fourth quarters (the most important quarters) of the shield.

red. This would confirm the previous conclusion that Pope submitted MS fragments to Walsh for criticism as late as 1707.[1]

Toward the end of 1707 the work of revision must have been finished, or nearly so. On October 28 the Rev. Ralph Bridges wrote to his uncle Sir William Trumbull: "Near the Temple met 'little Pope' . . . He designs in the spring to print . . . his Pastorals. They are to be inscribed each to some Patron, one of which you are to be . . ."[2] Not long after, in February, 1708, Wycherley wrote to Pope: "I am pleas'd with the good News of your going to print some of your Poems, and proud to be known by them to the Publick for your Friend."[3]

The verses dedicating *Spring* to Trumbull, *Summer* to Garth, and *Autumn* to Wycherley, are not in the MS of the poem which has come down to us, and because of many other differences between the MS and the printed text one is compelled to think that Pope sent a different MS to Tonson. This was probably done at the date indicated on Pope's receipt for his poems: "Receiv'd ten Guinea's for ye Tale of Chaucer, and the Eclogues, amounting to ab^t one thousand and 2 hundred lines, of M^r. Tonson, / March 4th: 170$\frac{7}{8}$/ A: Pope."[4] The 820 lines of the "Tale of Chaucer" and the 386 lines of the *Pastorals* (including the dedicatory verses) total 1206 lines. Walsh, who apparently gave Pope more advice than anyone else and to whose memory *Winter* is dedicated in an allusive man-

---

1. Pope spent part of the summer of 1707 with Walsh. Cf. the following extract from a letter by Sir William Trumbull to Ralph Bridges, dated Aug. 5, 1707: ". . . our little Poet . . . is gone a dreadful long Journey into Worcestershire, to M^r. Walsh". A transcription of this extract, made by Bishop Thomas Percy, is preserved in the Bodleian Library (MS Eng. letters d. 59). Microfilm of many such transcriptions was made available to the editors by the kindness of Professor George Sherburn. See "New Anecdotes about Alexander Pope", *N & Q*, N.S., v (Aug., 1958), pp. 343–9.

2. *Hist. MSS Comm.: Report on the Manuscripts of the Marquess of Downshire*, I ii 853. On May 2, 1709, the day the *Pastorals* were published, Trumbull wrote to Bridges that he had had a visit from Pope two days before, and that he had seen "after he was gone" that "y^e. Miscell. is publish'd or publishing . . . wherein are his Pastoralls, & (wch. is worse) I am told, One of y^m. is inscrib^d to my Worship." Trumbull had forgotten, or pretended to forget, what Bridges had written to him eighteen months before. A transcription of Trumbull's words is preserved in the Bodleian Library (MS Eng. letters d. 59). See previous note.

3. *Corr.*, I 41.   4. The receipt is reproduced in *Early Career*, facing p. 85.

C

ner,[1] died less than a fortnight after the date of the receipt, on March 16, 1708. A year later Tonson was ready to publish his Miscellany, and on May 2, 1709, Pope's first poems appeared in print.

The Miscellany included, besides Pope's *Pastorals*, those of Ambrose Philips, which were printed at the beginning of the volume, while Pope's came last. If we are to believe a letter from Wycherley of May 17, 1709,[2] Pope's poems were admired at once: "In earnest all the best Judges, of good Sense, or Poetry are Admirers of Yours; and like your part of the Book so well, that the rest is lik'd the worse." But Philips had his admirers too, and in 1713 Thomas Tickell, Addison's friend and protégé, wrote five *Guardian* essays in which Philips's *Pastorals* were highly praised and Pope's were not even mentioned. Pope in his turn wrote a sixth essay in which he praised Philips with such exquisite irony as to heap ridicule on his rival.[3] With these events the *Pastorals* entered the history of Pope's quarrels, that "warfare upon earth" which was the life of a Wit in his time.

II: THE GENERAL LITERARY BACKGROUND

Pope's *Pastorals* follow the general patterns of classical pastorals: *Spring* is an amoebaean eclogue in which two shepherds contend in song, and *Autumn* is based on a similar alternate scheme, though in it the competitive element is missing; *Summer* is a love-complaint, and *Winter* an elegy in memory of a dead shepherdess. Pope himself indicated the models for each poem but his indications are brief, and a glance at the notes in this edition will enable the reader to realize further the number and variety of his imitations. What is proposed here is a brief survey of the principal models Pope used.

I

The first lines of *Spring* deliberately recall the first lines of Virgil's sixth Eclogue, but Pope's poem on the whole rather resembles Virgil's third and seventh Eclogues. In each of these last, two shepherds engage in a song-contest, treating similar themes in alternate

---

1. See below, p. 47.   2. *Corr.*, I 59.
3. For a discussion of this controversy, see Intro. to *Discourse on Pastoral Poetry*, pp. 17*ff*.

stanzas. Virgil's third Eclogue begins with an abusive dialogue in irregular stanzas (fifty-nine lines), and then enters the contest proper, which is composed of twenty-four alternate distichs. After these last the judge of the contest concludes, as does the judge in Pope's *Spring*, by awarding a prize to each contestant. Structurally, however, Pope's poem appears to resemble Virgil's seventh Eclogue even more closely. Here, after an introduction of twenty lines, the contest unfolds itself in twelve quatrains, and a narrator concludes in two lines. If no account is taken of the lines to Trumbull (ll. 7–16) which Pope added late, it is evident that *Spring* follows a similar plan: an introductory section in thirty-four lines, followed by twelve quatrains, and a conclusion in ten lines.

From Virgil's third Eclogue Pope also borrowed certain episodes, particularly that of the riddles which the shepherds put to each other, and also that of the bowl placed as a stake. Theocritus had preceded Virgil in the use of a cup as a prize, and a comparison of the ways in which the different poets treat these cups or bowls is instructive. In his first Idyll Theocritus describes at length the several scenes wrought within his cup: a woman besieged by two suitors, a fisherman handling his net, a young boy who neglects the care of a vineyard, two foxes that seek to plunder the grapes. The whole description is one of realistic detail, and takes up nearly thirty lines: a description too long for Pastoral, Rapin had said, and with this critic's judgment Pope was in general agreement.[1] The description of the cups in Virgil is reduced to brief mention of two figures, one of whom the speaker cannot even remember by name.[2] Spenser, in *August*, ll. 27*ff.*, returns to the detail and realism of Theocritus: his "mazer" is wrought with warring bears and tigers, a lamb in the jaws of a wolf, the rescue of the lamb by shepherds who kill the wolf. Pope, as one would expect from the tradition in which he consciously wrote,[3] chose the Virgilian concision and restraint: the "Four Figures" of his bowl represent the seasons (and recall the plan of his *Pastorals* as he outlines it in his *Discourse*[4]), while above them the twelve signs of the Zodiac in "beauteous Order lye".

---

1. See Intro. to *Discourse on Pastoral Poetry*, pp. 15*ff.*, for the relationship in which Pope stood to Rapin.
2. See *Ecl.* III 35–42.   3. See Intro. to *Discourse on Pastoral Poetry*, pp. 15*ff.*
4. See above, pp. 32–3.

If the transition from Theocritus to Virgil, and from Virgil to Pope, reveals in some respects a decline in realistic detail, it also happens that, in other respects, Virgil adds to Theocritus, and Pope to Virgil. Thus Theocritus (*Idyll*, v 88–9) describes a shepherdess who pelts a passing goatherd with apples and, at the same time, makes sounds to attract him. Virgil (*Ecl.* III 64–5), in a famous passage, adds to the feminine coquetry:

> Malo me Galatea petit, lasciva puella,
> et fugit ad salices, et se cupit ante videri.

Pope gives the idea a further turn, ll. 59–60:

> While a kind Glance at her Pursuer flies,
> How much at variance are her Feet and Eyes!

On the whole Pope's model for *Spring* was certainly Virgil, though it was often Virgil seen through Dryden, as is indicated by the number of rhymes and phrases borrowed from Dryden's translation of the Eclogues. Pope may have used Dryden as he did Sandys's translation of Ovid, as an introduction to the Latin text. At the same time, his borrowings from Dryden were a means of revealing to his readers the discipleship in which he stood to Virgil, and to Virgil's greatest English interpreter. With the same openness Pope also borrowed from Milton,[1] proof that he knew and admired Milton's early poems at a time when they were little known.

II

Pope opens *Summer* with a close imitation of the first line of *The Shepherd's Calendar*, and thus not only suggests that he is one of Spenser's heirs,[2] but also associates the amorous complaint of his Alexis with that of Spenser's Colin in *Januarye*. But though there are several recollections of Spenser in this pastoral, Pope also establishes a more ancient ancestry for his poem. Thus the dedication to the physician Garth immediately relates the poem to Theocritus's eleventh Idyll, which was also addressed to a physician. Theocritus's poem is also a love-complaint: the Cyclops Polyphemus grotesquely laments the indifference of Galatea to his love, and there are lines in *Summer* which recall particulars of Polyphemus's

---

1. See notes to ll. 5, 23. 2. See also ll. 39 *ff.* of *Summer*.

complaint. Pope's poem is also closely related to Virgil's second Eclogue, which in its turn was also based largely on Theocritus's eleventh Idyll. Like Virgil's poem, Pope's eclogue develops a relationship between the heat of summer and the fire which consumes a lover.

As the notes to *Summer* show, the poem continually recalls a situation, a theme, or a phrase from Virgil's eclogues, yet the love-theme itself rather recalls Spenser than either Virgil or Theocritus. In the eleventh Idyll Theocritus seems to suggest that the rejected lover has found relief in the very act of voicing his grief; in putting his grief to music the Cyclops has in some manner put it from him. Polyphemus then appears able to assume a philosophical attitude towards his rejection by Galatea: there are daily tasks to be performed, and other maidens to be wooed. In Virgil's second Eclogue, even Corydon can perceive that the love which possesses him is a self-destructive madness, and at the end of his complaint he, like the Cyclops, turns to daily tasks and thoughts of other loves. These perspectives in Theocritus and Virgil, in which the lover may appear ridiculous or mad, are wholly absent from Spenser's *Januarye* and Pope's *Summer*. In Spenser the prevailing mood is one of melancholy self-absorption, to which Pope's poem, for all its sophisticated gallantry, is more closely related than to the mood of Theocritus and Virgil. Too, in both Spenser and Pope one is made aware of how greatly Nature shares in and reflects man's feelings of grief and despair in love; in Virgil's second Eclogue, on the contrary, the madness of love appears to alienate man from the peace and harmony in Nature.

III

In his first note to *Autumn* Pope says that "This Pastoral consists of two parts, like the 8th of *Virgil*", in which two amorous shepherds lament, in turn, their faithless loves. Virgil divides his poem almost equally between the two speakers, each of whom punctuates his verses with a refrain, and Pope's poem reflects this structure. Virgil's eclogue had been inspired by Theocritus's second and third Idylls: in the second Idyll a maiden, forsaken by her lover, makes use of magic to win him back, and in the third Idyll a goatherd endeavours to win the love of a disdainful Amaryllis, with so little success that he talks of throwing himself into the sea and of letting

the wolves devour him where he lies. Virgil had brought the two
themes of Theocritus together in one amoebaean poem, and Pope
follows suit. In both Theocritus and Virgil, however, one is made
aware in a forceful way of the more grim and sinister aspects of per-
jured and faithless love, qualities which appear almost submerged
by the extravagant compliment and conceit in Pope's *Autumn*. The
love tradition in which Pope is writing is suggested by the fact that
the source of his refrain, "Go gentle Gales, and bear my Sighs
away", is the famous "Go, lovely Rose," of Waller.

Originally Hylas, the first lover of Pope's *Autumn*, had complained of the harshness of a young man named Thyrsis, a relationship
apparently designed to recall that between Corydon and Alexis in
Virgil's second Eclogue. In 1709 Pope must have decided to ignore
Walsh's censure of Theocritus and Virgil for their faults against
"Innocence".[1] In 1736, however, Pope apparently chose to take
seriously his own statement in *Guardian* 40 that "*Corydon*'s criminal
Passion for *Alexis*" is inadmissible in true pastoral because it is not
in accord with the moral climate of the Golden Age. At any rate,
in 1736 the homosexual suggestions were eliminated by the metamorphosis of Thyrsis into Delia.

IV

The first line of Pope's *Winter* echoes the first line of Theocritus's
first Idyll, in which a shepherd by the name of Thyrsis (the name
also of the main character in Pope's *Winter*) expresses the universal
mourning felt at the death of Daphnis, a legendary figure regarded
as the inventor of bucolic song. Theocritus's Idyll had also been
used by Virgil in his fifth Eclogue, and to this last Pope is also indebted. Virgil had presented two shepherds, the first to express the
universal grief caused by Daphnis's death, the second to describe
Daphnis's apotheosis. As a god Daphnis appears to represent some
principle of cosmic order, and Virgil suggests he is to rule over a
peaceful and joyous pastoral world. The sudden passage from the
sadness of his death to exultation in his immortality is imitated
closely by Pope (as, indeed, by Spenser and Milton[2] before him).

---

1. See Walsh's Preface to his *Letters and Poems, Amorous and Gallant*, 1692.
2. That Pope intended his poem to recall *Lycidas* is perhaps indicated by the

Pope also imitated the two successors to Theocritus, Bion and Moschus, or perhaps only used Oldham's adaptations of these poets. How free and remote these adaptations were can be guessed from Oldham's own words. For Bion, Oldham made use of the French translation of Le Fèvre: "Him I chiefly chose to follow, as being most agreeable to my way of translating, and where I was at a loss for want of his guidance, I was content to steer by my own Fancy".[1] However reliable the guidance offered by Oldham, he yet enables Pope to associate the ancient elegiac utterances of the Greek poets with his own lament for Daphne, the modern, and feminine, counterpart of the great or legendary figures of Adonis, Bion, and Daphnis.

One other name should be mentioned here, that of Walsh. *Winter* is the only pastoral which is not inscribed to one of Pope's personal friends or patrons. Possibly Pope would have dedicated it to Walsh if the latter had not died before its publication. In MS the poem is entitled *The Fourth Pastorall; or Daphne*; in 1709 it was dedicated "To the Memory of a Fair Young Lady", in 1717 "To the Memory of Mrs. Tempest". Only in 1736, in a note to the poem, did Pope explain that Walsh had celebrated this lady in a pastoral elegy, and that Walsh had wished him to celebrate her also. In 1751 Pope added to this note by quoting from a letter Walsh had written to him on September 9, 1706: "Your last Eclogue being upon the same Subject as that of mine on Mrs. *Tempest*'s Death, I shou'd take it very kindly in you to give it a little turn, as if it were to the Memory of the same Lady . . ."[2] The "little turn" which Pope gave to his poem in memory of this event may be found in the refrain, which is based on two lines of Walsh's elegy upon the lady's death.[3] The connection between the poems may have been obscure to others, but no doubt in Pope's mind it sufficed to memorialize the bond of friendship between himself and his "Judge and Friend".

fact that the part of Lycidas in the printed text went under the name of Meliboeus in the MS.

1. See the Advertisement preceding Book II of Pope's copy of Oldham's *Works*, 1685 (Brit. Mus. shelf mark c. 45. a. 1).

2. *Corr.*, I 22.

3. See ll. 27-8*n*.

III: THE *PASTORALS* AS POEMS

I

In his *Discourse on Pastoral Poetry* (written, supposedly, the same year as the *Pastorals*) Pope stated that pastoral should be an imitation of the action of a shepherd as he may be conceived to have been in the Golden Age, and that it should reflect the tranquillity of a country life, "exposing the best side only of a shepherd's life, and ... concealing its miseries."[1] In addition, Pope was in agreement with a group of critics who believed that the more "allegorical" eclogues of Virgil and Theocritus were not truly "pastoral"; eclogues such as Virgil's first, which pointedly exposed, rather than concealed, the "miseries" brought upon shepherds by a callous government's policy of land-seizure, and his sixth, which dealt with profound metaphysical questions, were thus not regarded as "true pastoral", but as "something else".[2]

A theory of pastoral conceived within such limits as these inevitably reduced the range and depth possible in such poetry and narrowed the pleasure it might produce. This effect can be observed in the theory of Fontenelle, who stated that the pleasure of pastoral derived from representations of rural leisure, which appealed to the innate laziness of man's nature, and further maintained that love was the passion most congenial to this laziness.[3] Walsh, in the Preface to his *Letters and Poems, Amorous and Gallant* (1692), suggests a similar limitation of subject: "There are three sorts of Poems that are proper for Love: *Pastorals*, *Elegies*, and *Lyrick Verses* ... Of all these, *Pastoral* is the lowest, and upon that account, perhaps most proper for Love". Seemingly mesmerized by such theories, critics of the period appear determined to exclude from the realm of pastoral an eclogue by Virgil which mentions soldiers,[4] or one by Spenser which deals with ecclesiastical vices. That Pope

---

1. Much of the discussion in this section relates to the background supplied in the introduction to the *Discourse on Pastoral Poetry*, pp. 15*ff*., above.

2. By the time he came to write his essay on pastoral in *Guardian* 40, Pope was ready to call Virgil's eclogues "*something better*" than pastoral.

3. See Intro. to *Discourse on Pastoral Poetry*, p. 16.

4. In one of the apparently more straightforward passages in *Guardian* 40 Pope says that Virgil's first and ninth Eclogues "must be rejected, because they describe the Ravages of Armies, and Oppressions of the Innocent."

was influenced by such devitalizing notions of pastoral is shown not
only by his statement quoted above, but also by the fact that he described his eclogues as comprehending "all the subjects which the
Critics upon *Theocritus* and *Virgil* will allow to be fit for pastoral."

Comparison of Pope's pastorals with those of Virgil is inevitable.
As we have seen,[1] Pope was hailed by his contemporaries as a youthful Virgil. In addition, as the preceding section has shown, Pope
sought to model the structures of his eclogues on those of Virgil, and
his poems are filled with Virgilian allusions. These Virgilian suggestions that permeate Pope's poems do, of course, serve important
functions, but it is well to recognize in the beginning that the two
poets are not often concerned with the same kind of issues. There
is nothing in Pope's eclogues to compare with the procedure by
which Virgil, in the course of ten eclogues, leads the reader both
into and out of a mythical world which is tremulous in its stability,
and in the process elucidates and comments upon the most profound reaches of human experience. This is not to say that Pope's
poems do not have their own important meaning; it is simply to
note that ultimately Pope's methods and purposes are not Virgil's.

Strictly presented, a pastoral Age of Gold in which the miseries
of human life are carefully concealed is all too likely to appear to be
a "never-never" land with a fatal irrelevance to human actuality.
Faced with such a world one may feel inclined to exclaim as Chetwood did against Fontenelle's pastorals: "Begin where you please,"
he cried, "the Subject is still the same . . .

> *Toujours, toujours de l'Amour.*

He seems to take *Pastorals* and *Love-Verses* for the same thing. Has
Human Nature no other Passion?"[2]

The practices of poets, however, are not always best accounted
for by the poets themselves, and there is certainly evidence that
Pope's own practice was inconsistent with his theory. Thus in
Summer one finds the following couplet, ll. 67–8:

> This harmless Grove no lurking Viper hides,
> But in my Breast the Serpent Love abides.

Theoretically, there should be no room in the Golden Age for the

---

1. See above, p. 37.
2. See Chetwood's Preface to the Pastorals in Dryden's *Virgil.*

confusions and disasters imaged by the snake, yet even among
Pope's innocent shepherds one finds the kind of "misery" that
prompts a lover, as in *Autumn*, to throw himself over a cliff. The
limitations his theory imposed were perhaps realized by Pope too
late, else he might have used to greater purpose than he did the
realities that inevitably forced their way into the world of his eclogues.

If it is necessary to recognize that Pope wrote within bounds
more limited than those of Virgil and Spenser, it is also necessary
to recognize the success Pope achieves within these bounds. The
contemplation of the kind of world the poet creates in his *Pastorals*
is not without its own legitimate pleasures, nor is that world without its ultimate relevance to human existence. Like the pastorals of
so many poets before him, Pope's poems may offer a means of
escape from a certain kind of actuality. They also offer a means of
engaging a different kind of actuality.

II

Criticism of the *Pastorals* has tended from the beginning to prize
the craftsmanship revealed in their verse and to minimize the
worth of their substance. Thus Johnson said that "To charge these
Pastorals with want of invention is to require what never was intended . . . It is surely sufficient for an author of sixteen . . . to have
obtained sufficient power of language and skill in metre to exhibit
a series of versification, which had in English poetry no precedent,
nor has since had an imitation."[1] Praise such as this, generous
though it is, tends to reduce Pope's achievement to something
approaching the level of mere technical virtuosity. One may wonder, on the other hand, if verse of such exceptional brilliance does
not reflect something more than the commonplace, or at least if
it is not a means of bringing new life into the commonplace. At
any rate, an examination of the verse itself should be a means of
gaining entry to whatever substance these poems possess.

Pope told Spence that "There is scarce any work of mine in
which the versification was more laboured than in my pastorals."[2]

---

1. *Lives of the English Poets*, ed. G. B. Hill (1905), III 224–5.
2. *Anecdotes*, p. 312.

The same concern for the formal properties of his verse is seen in his *Discourse on Pastoral Poetry*. There he states that the "expression" in pastoral should be "humble, yet as pure as the language will afford; neat, but not florid; easy, and yet lively." The "numbers . . . should be the smoothest, the most easy and flowing imaginable". The "character" of a pastoral "consists in simplicity, brevity, and delicacy." The same care is shown for the organization of the poems as a whole. Thus Pope is proud of his "improvement" upon Spenser's plan: he shortens Spenser's Calendar of twelve months to one of four seasons, thus keeping, he says, the variety but avoiding the repetition involved in Spenser's scheme. He further organizes his poems by way of the time and the scene: early morning in the vale, mid-day by the river, afternoon on a hill, night in a grove.

The best evidence of the care Pope lavished on the verse of these poems, however, is to be found in the MS corrections which the poet submitted to Walsh's judgment and in the differences which exist between the MS text and the printed text. In the passages submitted to Walsh[1] he is seen struggling with nice questions of grammar and vocabulary, repetition of words, inversions, hyperbole, alliteration, proper rhyme, and so on. On these work-sheets one sees a steady evolution of the verse from the slack and dull to the precise and lively. Thus Pope asks Walsh if the description of the lamb near the fountain in *Spring* should be kept as in MS, "And *his own Image* from the Brink surveys",[2] or altered to "And from the Brink *his dancing Shade* surveys". The latter, said his "knowing" Walsh, and the line gained in particularity and charm by the change. Again, in the MS of *Winter* the poet had written the following:

> Now in warm Folds the tender Flock *remains*,
> The Cattle slumber on the silent Plains.

"Objection to the word *remains*", writes Pope, and since the word affects the rhyme, he contemplates modifying the couplet completely, and proposes three alterations. "I think yᵉ last best", Walsh says, "but might not even yᵗ bee mended". Under such stimulation as this Pope finally produces for the printed text one of the most original and successful couplets in all the *Pastorals* (*Winter*, ll. 5–6):

---

1. See Appendix A.
2. The MS text has "Bank" for "Brink".

> Now sleeping Flocks on their soft Fleeces lye,
> The Moon, serene in Glory, mounts the Sky.

The differences between the MS text (as distinct from the record submitted to Walsh) and the printed text illustrate the evolution further. Thus l. 31 of *Winter*, "Now hung with Pearls the dropping Trees appear", appears in the MS as "Now hung with Pearls the weeping Groves appear", while the original of l. 32 in *Spring*, "Here Western Winds on breathing Roses blow", was the far less satisfactory "There Western Winds on Beds of Roses blow". Here too we sometimes see Pope bringing a blurred scene into sharp, and haunting, focus by the change of a mere word or two. For example, the MS line, "And the fleet Shades fly gliding o'er the Green", becomes in the printed version "And the fleet Shades glide o'er the dusky Green" (*Autumn*, l. 64).

The words Pope laboured to discover may still seem to a modern reader too general or too "poetic" to be really rich in their suggestions. Yet the course of his revisions suggests that Pope was aiming at one kind of precision and not another, and that he had his eyes always on the larger context his words were to serve. It is this fact that perhaps justifies showing what he rejected: in this process we are at least led to focus on the changes and to inquire into the purposes served by them. An example of the way in which Pope subdued his imagery to the larger purposes of an eclogue is to be found in *Winter*, ll. 9–10. Originally the couplet read:

> Behold the Trees, that shine with silver Frost,
> Whose Arms are wither'd, and whose Leaves are lost.

In the printed version the lines become:

> Behold the *Groves* that shine with silver Frost,
> Their Beauty wither'd, and their Verdure lost.

The subject of *Winter* is the death of Daphne, based, as we have seen, on the death of the legendary founder of bucolic poetry, Daphnis. In Virgil's poem on the same theme Daphnis appears to represent a law of love which, at the return of the Golden Age, will prevail in the world. Pope's poem does not encompass the whole of Virgil's theme, yet in the death of his Daphne the world is involved also: the death of one is mirrored in that of the other. In the reciprocal relationship which is established between the two the image of the "wither'd Arms" may have seemed altogether too particular.

The chief value of this record of revision perhaps lies in the fact that it tends to disprove the notions that Pope did not observe nature closely and that he merely dealt in verbal counters.[1] The very contrary to the first notion is shown by such revisions as that dealing with the lamb's shadow, while the choice of the more general terms to establish the sympathetic relationship between Daphne and Nature was evidently the product of careful second-thought. Pope frequently aims at particular detail, yet he does not wish the details to distract from the scene or context as a whole. As the change from "Trees" to "Groves" in the Daphne passage suggests, he does not wish us to miss the forest for the trees.

It is with this last idea in mind that we should recall Pope's statement in his *Discourse on Pastoral Poetry* that in every eclogue "a design'd scene or prospect is to be presented to our view, which should likewise have its variety". It is the landscape itself which dominates in Pope's pastorals, for it is a background into which human activity and experience are to be absorbed and harmonized. And because the "scene" in which man is placed has this importance, the reader is never directed to the kind of particulars that would absorb his attention or distract from the kind of world in which the men of these poems live. It is an ordered world, and one which answers to man's needs, always offering to him its shades for rest. But amidst the order there is also variety: the "breathing Roses" of *Spring*, the "blushing Berries" which "paint the yellow Grove" of *Autumn*; "Green Retreats" in *Summer*, "dropping Trees" in *Winter*.

Scattered throughout the *Pastorals* are smaller individual "scenes" that typify the activity in which Pope is engaged at large. In these smaller settings man is placed against the background of the rolling year, and the changes it brings in nature. Here is such a scene from *Autumn*, ll. 59–64:

> Here where the *Mountains* less'ning as they rise,
> Lose the low Vales, and steal into the Skies.
> While lab'ring Oxen, spent with Toil and Heat,
> In their loose Traces from the Field retreat;
> While curling Smokes from Village-Tops are seen,
> And the fleet Shades glide o'er the dusky Green.

---

1. See the discussion of this point by C. V. Deane, *Aspects of Eighteenth Century Nature Poetry*, 1935, p. 116.

Such perspectives as these, in which man is, so to speak, "contained", may be suggested in little more than a pair of lines, as in the
description of the bowl in *Spring*, with its puns on the words "rising"
and "Work":

> And I this Bowl, where wanton Ivy twines,
> And swelling Clusters bend the curling Vines:
> Four Figures rising from the Work appear . . .

The very conventionality of the little dramas—the singing-
matches, the love-complaints—that Pope uses in these eclogues
serves the purpose of not distracting from the settings in which they
occur. The world in which these shepherds live and which in one
way or another they celebrate in their songs is itself that which defines their existence. This is as it should be, for what the scenery of
the poems does is gather man and his concerns into the larger har-
monies of Nature. In these poems man should sing "by turns" because that is the way Nature also does things:[1]

> Now Hawthorns blossom, now the Daisies spring,
> Now Leaves the Trees, and Flow'rs adorn the Ground.

If, in some of the perspectives, man's stature appears reduced to a
place alongside his sheep, or to the "curling Smokes" amidst the
fields, it is also true that he is made at one with something larger
than himself.

The theme of time, and of the changes wrought by time, is central to the scheme of these poems. We have seen that Pope modelled
his *Pastorals* on the scheme of Spenser's Calendar, and we should
recall also his praise of Spenser for his comparison of "human Life
to the several Seasons", by which he "exposes to his readers a view
of the great and little worlds, in their various changes and aspects".
The same praise can be given to Pope himself, for in the scenes he so
frequently establishes in his poems man is seen in a perspective
which links him with the cattle that leave the field and the fleet
shades which glide over the dusky green. As Thyrsis says at the end
of *Winter*, "Time conquers All, and We must Time obey."

Slight though one may find the *Pastorals* to be in some respects,
they are yet the proper starting point for a study of Pope's later development. For throughout the eclogues one finds him working

---

1. See *Spring*, 41–4.

with the internal couplet structures that he was to use with such
devastating effect when he had left the softer subjects of the Age of
Gold for the Iron Age of satire. Balance and measured imbalance,
inversion and antithesis, can be found operating even in this world
of breathing roses and rural strains, and show how early Pope had
begun to fashion the structures that were later to support more
weighty themes. [1] Thus early too one finds his consummate capacity
to suggest the uttermost limits of time and space in the compass of a
single line. The movement and suggestions of such a line as "While
yon slow Oxen turn the furrow'd Plain" impart a sense of the turning point about which a whole world still turns, and forecast directly the poet who could later bring all Arabia breathing from a box.
With the publication of these poems, Pope showed that, despite his
youth and the limitations which it necessarily imposed upon him,
the Age of Pope had indeed begun.

1. See the discussion by Geoffrey Tillotson, *On the Poetry of Pope*, 2nd edn,
1950, pp. 124–31.

PASTORALS.

Rura mihi, & rigui placeant in vallibus amnes,
Flumina amem, ſylvaſque, Inglorius!——

Virg.

NOTE ON THE TEXT

The *Pastorals* were first published on May 2, 1709, in *Poetical Miscellanies, The Sixth Part*. A second edition of this volume of the set known as Dryden's or Tonson's *Miscellanies* appeared in 1716 with the title *The Sixth Part of Miscellany Poems*. In both editions Pope's *Pastorals* were preceded by their own half-title. In the first edition the half-title read as follows: PASTORALS./BY/Mr. *ALEXANDER POPE.*/Rura mihi, & rigui placeant in vallibus amnes,/ Flumina amem, sylvasque, Inglorius!——/Virg./LONDON,/ Printed in the Year, 1709./With the publication of the 1717 *Works* the *Pastorals* were preceded by the *Discourse on Pastoral Poetry* and a new half-title introduced the two works jointly. A third edition of *The Sixth Part of Miscellany Poems* appeared in 1727, but the revisions of the *Pastorals* made by Pope in 1717 do not appear therein and it is ignored as a text here.

After 1717 there were revisions in 1736 and 1751. One new reading was introduced in 1740 (see *Winter*, l. 16), and there is a strong possibility that this is a misprint perpetuated by *1743* and Warburton's edition of 1751. The text printed here observes the revisions of later editions, but follows the punctuation, spelling, and typography of the first edition. The editors have closed with inverted commas the quotations in *Winter*, ll. 18 and 28.

KEY TO THE CRITICAL APPARATUS

1709 = Poetical Miscellanies, The Sixth Part, octavo, Griffith 1.
1716 = The Sixth Part of Miscellany Poems, duodecimo, Griffith 61.
1717 = Works, quarto, Griffith 79.
1736*a* = Works, vol. 1, octavo, Griffith 413.
1736*b* = Works, vol. 1, octavo, Griffith 414.
1740 = Works, vol. 1, part 1, octavo, Griffith 510.
1743 = Works, vol. 1, part 1, octavo, Griffith 582.
1751 = Works, ed. Warburton, vol. 1, octavo, Griffith 643.

SPRING.

The First Pastoral,

OR

DAMON.

To Sir WILLIAM TRUMBULL.

Irst in these Fields I try the Sylvan Strains,
Nor blush to sport on *Windsor*'s blissful Plains:
Fair *Thames* flow gently from thy sacred Spring,

OR DAMON.] *Om. 1717–43.* *To Sir*] *Inscrib'd to Sir 1709–16.*

These Pastorals were written at the age of sixteen, and then past thro' the hands of Mr. *Walsh*, Mr. *Wycherley*, G. *Granville*, afterwards Lord *Lansdown*, Sir *William Trumbal*, Dr. *Garth*, Lord *Halifax*, Lord ⟨John⟩ *Somers* ⟨1651–1716, lord chancellor of England, friend and patron of Addison, Congreve, Steele⟩, Mr. ⟨Arthur⟩ *Mainwaring* ⟨1668–1712, prominent Whig writer and politician⟩, and others. All these gave our Author the greatest encouragement, and particularly Mr. *Walsh*, (whom Mr. *Dryden*, in his Postscript to Virgil, calls the best critic of his age.) ⟨Dryden, *Essays*, II 244, says that Walsh, "without flattery, is the best critic of our nation."⟩ "The Author (says he) "seems to have a particular genius for this kind of Poetry, and a judgment that much exceeds his years. He has taken very freely from the Ancients. But what he has mixed of his own with theirs is no way inferior to what he has taken from them. It is not flattery at all to say that Virgil had written nothing so good at his Age. His Preface is very judicious and learned." *Letter to Mr. Wycherley, Ap.* 1705. ⟨See *Corr.*, I 7.⟩ The Lord Lansdown about the same time, mentioning the youth of our Poet, says (in a printed Letter of the Character of Mr. Wycherley) "that if he goes on as he has begun in the Pastoral way, as Virgil first tried his strength, we may hope to see English Poetry vie with the Roman," etc. ⟨See Lansdowne's *Works*, 1732, I 437. All these gave . . . etc. *Add. 1751*⟩ Notwithstanding the early time of their production, the Author esteem'd these as the most correct in the versification, and musical in the numbers, of all his works. The reason for his labouring them into so much softness, was, doubtless, that ⟨was, that *1736a–43*⟩ this sort of poetry derives almost its whole beauty from a natural ease of thought and smoothness of verse; whereas that of most other kinds consists in the Strength and fulness of both. In a Letter of his to Mr. *Walsh* about this time ⟨Oct. 22, 1706; *Corr.*, I 22⟩, we find an enumeration of several Niceties in Versification, which perhaps have never been strictly observ'd in any *English* poem, except in these Pastorals. They were not printed till 1709. [P. *1736a–51*.]

Sir *William Trumbal*] Our Author's friendship with this gentleman commen-

59

> While on thy Banks *Sicilian* Muses sing;
> Let Vernal Airs thro' trembling Osiers play,   5

ced at very unequal years; he was under sixteen, but Sir William above sixty, and had lately resign'd his employment of Secretary of State to King William. [*P. 1751.*]

Trumbull (1639–1716) had in fact retired in 1698. He was sixty-five when Pope was sixteen. Pope used the spelling *Trumbal* from 1717 onwards.

1.   *Prima Syracosio dignata est ludere versu,*
          Nostra nec erubuit sylvas habitare Thalia.

This is the general Exordium and opening of the Pastorals, in imitation of the 6th of *Virgil*, which some have therefore not improbably thought to have been the first originally. In the beginnings of the other three Pastorals, he imitates expressly those which now stand first of the ⟨those of the *1736a–43*⟩ three chief Poets in this kind, *Spencer, Virgil, Theocritus,* ⟨*Theocritus, Virgil, Spencer; 1736a–43*⟩

          A Shepherd's Boy (he seeks no better name)—
          Beneath the shade a spreading Beech displays,—
          Thyrsis, *the Music of that murm'ring Spring,—*

are manifestly imitations of

          A Shepherd's Boy (no better do him call)—
          Tityre, tu patulæ recubans sub tegmine fagi.—
          'Αδύ τι τὸ ψιθύρισμα καὶ ἁ πίτυς, αἰπόλε, τήνα.—
                                                   [*P. 1736a–51.*]

Cf. respectively Spenser, *Januarye,* 1; Virgil, *Ecl.* 1 1; Theocritus, *Idyll* 1, 1.

According to Warton (*Works,* 1 59n), "The collection of passages imitated from the Classics, marked in the margin with the letter P. was made by the accurate and learned Mr. Bowyer the Printer, and given to Pope at his desire, as appears from MSS. Notes of Mr. Bowyer now before me." Some account of William Bowyer's efforts to collect passages from the ancients imitated by Pope can be found in the correspondence of William Clarke (1696–1771), printed in *Miscellaneous Tracts, By . . . William Bowyer* (1785), pp. 560ff.

1f. Cf. Dryden's tr. of Virgil, *Ecl.* VI 1–2:
          I First transferr'd to *Rome Sicilian* Strains:
          Nor blush'd the *Dorick* Muse to dwell on *Mantuan* Plains.

3. Cf. Spenser, *Prothalamion*: "Sweete *Themmes* runne softly, till I end my Song."

4. *Sicilian Muses*] The pastoral Muses, so called because Theocritus, the first writer of pastoral, was Sicilian.

5. Wakefield cites Milton, *Par. Reg.,* II 26, "Where winds with Reeds, and Osiers whisp'ring play", and Dryden, *Theodore and Honoria,* 79: "The Winds, within the quiv'ring Branches plaid." Cf. also *Par. Lost,* IV 264–6:
                    airs, vernal airs,
          Breathing the smell of field and grove, attune
          The trembling leaves . . .

And *Albion*'s Cliffs resound the Rural Lay.
  You, that too Wise for Pride, too Good for Pow'r,
Enjoy the Glory to be Great no more,
And carrying with you all the World can boast,
To all the World Illustriously are lost!   10
O let my Muse her slender Reed inspire,
'Till in your Native Shades You tune the Lyre:
So when the Nightingale to Rest removes,
The Thrush may chant to the forsaken Groves,
But, charm'd to Silence, listens while She sings,   15
And all th'Aerial Audience clap their Wings.

6. *Rural Lay*] Wakefield compares Roscommon, *An Essay on Translated Verse*,
18–19:
            Theocritus do's now to *Vs* belong,
            And *Albion*'s *Rocks* repeat his *Rural Song*.
EC note that the "term 'Albion's cliffs', which is usually appropriated to the
steeps that bound the seashore, is applied by Pope to the hills about Windsor."
  7 *ff.* Wakefield compares Lucan, VIII 493–5:
                                Exeat aula,
            qui volt esse pius. Virtus et summa potestas
            non coeunt.
  9. EC compare Waller, *The Maid's Tragedy Alter'd* (Note to the Epil., 13–14):
            Happy is she that from the World retires,
            And carries with her what the World Admires.
  11. *slender Reed*] Cf. Virgil, *Ecl.* VI 8: "agrestem tenui meditabor harundine
Musam."
  inspire] Breathe into.
  12. *in your Native Shades*] Sir *W. Trumbal* was born in *Windsor*-Forest, to
which he retreated after he had resign'd the post of Secretary of State to King
William III. [P. *1736a–51*.]
  Cf. *Windsor-Forest*, 258.
  13. *the Nightingale*] An excessive compliment. Trumbull did not pretend to
poetry. See *Windsor-Forest*, 235n.
  13 *f.* Pope may have had in mind the fact that the song of the thrush is often
mistaken for that of the nightingale.
  16. *clap their Wings*] Matthew Concanen, in his *Supplement to the Profound*
(1728), p. 12, commented ironically on this passage. By way of answer, Pope,
in the margin of his own copy of Concanen's work (Brit. Mus., shelf mark C.
116. b. 2. (4)), wrote "Dryden", alluding doubtless to the final couplet in Dryden's *Verses to Her Highness the Duchess* [of York]:
            Each Poet of the Air her Glory sings,
            And round him the pleas'd Audience clap their Wings.

    Soon as the Flocks shook off the nightly Dews,
Two Swains, whom Love kept wakeful, and the Muse,
Pour'd o'er the whitening Vale their fleecy Care,
Fresh as the Morn, and as the Season fair: 20
The Dawn now blushing on the Mountain's Side,
Thus *Daphnis* spoke, and *Strephon* thus reply'd.

DAPHNIS.

    Hear how the Birds, on ev'ry bloomy Spray,
With joyous Musick wake the dawning Day!
Why sit we mute, when early Linnets sing,   25

17–21   *Daphnis* and *Strephon* to the Shades retir'd,
        Both warm'd by Love, and by the Muse inspir'd;
        Fresh as the Morn, and as the Season fair,
        In flow'ry *Vales* they fed their fleecy Care;
        And while *Aurora* gilds the Mountain's Side, *1709–17.*

---

   17 ff. The Scene of this Pastoral a Vally, the Time the Morning. It stood originally thus; ⟨Pope, *1736a–51,* here quotes the *1709–17* variant.⟩
   Wakefield compares Congreve, *The Tears of Amaryllis for Amyntas,* 5–6:
        When woolly Flocks their bleating Cries renew,
        And from their fleecy Sides first shake the silver Dew.
   19. "The epithet *whit'ning* most happily describes a *progressive* effect" [Wakefield].
   20. *Fresh as the Morn*] Wakefield compares Dryden, *Palamon and Arcite,* I 182: "Fresh as the Month, and as the Morning fair."
   21. *Mountain's Side*] OED points out that down "to the 18th c." the word *mountain* was "often applied to elevations of moderate altitude." Cf. *To Mr. Gay,* 3–4 (in vol. VI, p. 225), *Summer,* 37, *Windsor-Forest,* 87, 212, *Corr.,* IV 173.
   22. Wakefield cites Virgil, *Ecl.* VII 20: "hos Corydon, illos referebat in ordine Thyrsis."
   23. *bloomy Spray*] Wakefield cites Milton, Sonnet I:
        O Nightingale, that on yon bloomy Spray
         Warbl'st at eeve. . .
   24. *dawning Day*] Wakefield cites Congreve, *Tears of Amaryllis,* 3–4:
        When grateful Birds prepare their Thanks to pay,
        And warble Hymns to hail the dawning Day.
   25. Wakefield recalls Waller, *Chloris and Hilas,* 1–2:
        Hilas, oh *Hilas,* why sit we mute,
        Now that each Bird saluteth the Spring?

When warbling *Philomel* salutes the Spring?
Why sit we sad, when *Phosphor* shines so clear,
And lavish Nature paints the Purple Year?

STREPHON.

Sing then, and *Damon* shall attend the Strain,
While yon slow Oxen turn the furrow'd Plain.   30
Here the bright Crocus and blue Vi'let glow;
Here Western Winds on breathing Roses blow.
I'll stake yon' Lamb that near the Fountain plays,
And from the Brink his dancing Shade surveys.

DAPHNIS.

And I this Bowl, where wanton Ivy twines,   35

31 Here on green Banks the blushing Vi'lets glow; *1709–43*.
33 yon'] my *1709–17*.

---

27. *Phosphor*] The morning star; the planet Venus before sunrise.

28. *lavish Nature*] Wakefield cites Dryden, *The Cock and the Fox*, 456: "How lavish Nature has adorn'd the Year." Cf. also Dryden, *Ecl.* VII 76, "And lavish Nature laughs", a passage Pope marked with a comma in the margin of his copy (Brit. Mus., C. 28 f. 6). Warton cites Spenser, *Muiopotmos*, 163.

Purple Year] "Purple here used in the Latin sense of the brightest most vivid colouring in general, not of that peculiar tint so called" [Warburton]. Cf. Dryden, *Ecl.* II 62: "With all the Glories of the Purple Spring."

31 var. Of the variant EC remark: "It probably at last occurred to the poet that as people do not blush blue or purple, the epithet 'blushing' was inapplicable to the violet." Pope probably used *blushing* with the proverbial modesty of the violet, rather than its colour, in mind. But see Ault, *New Light on Pope* (1949), p. 84.

32. *breathing*] Emitting fragrance. Cf. Milton, *Arcades*, 32: "breathing Roses of the Wood". Cf. also *Par. Lost*, II 244–5, IX 193; *Messiah*, 24; *Rape of the Lock*, I 134.

34. The first reading was, *And his own Image from the bank surveys.* [P. *1736a–51*.]

35*f*.   *Lenta quibus torno facili superaddita vitis,*
                    Diffusos edera vestit pallente corymbos.
                    Virg. ⟨*Ecl.* III 38–9⟩ [P. *1736a–51*.]

Cf. the description of the mazer in Spenser, *August*, 29–30:
                    And ouer them spred a goodly wild vine,
                    Entrailed with a wanton Yuie twine.
Cf. also the lines by Dryden quoted in l. 38*n*.

And swelling Clusters bend the curling Vines:
Four Figures rising from the Work appear,
The various Seasons of the rowling Year;
And what is That, which binds the Radiant Sky,
Where twelve fair Signs in beauteous Order lye?   40

DAMON.

Then sing by turns, by turns the Muses sing,

40 fair] bright *1709–43.*

---

36. *And clusters lurk beneath the curling vines.* [P. *1736a–51.*]

37. *rising*] The word refers to the figures carved in relief on the bowl. Wakefield recalls Dryden, *Æn.*, VIII 830: "And *Roman* Triumphs rising on the Gold."
Cf. also Pope's *Thebais*, 636 (describing a goblet): "With Sculpture grac'd, and
rough with rising Gold."

38. *The various Seasons*] The Subject of these Pastorals engraven on the bowl
is not without its propriety. The Shepherd's hesitation at the name of the *Zodiac,*
imitates that in *Virgil* ⟨*Ecl.* III 40–1⟩,

————————*Et quis fuit alter?*
Descripsit radio totum qui gentibus orbem. [P. *1736a–51.*]

The bowl described by Virgil's shepherd bears the figures of two astronomers.
One is identified as Conon. He hesitates at the name of the other, who, as he
says, marked out the Zodiac in the heavens, and who was probably Eudoxus of
Cnidus. EC compare Dryden, *Ecl.* III 55–62:

Two Bowls I have. . .
The Lids are Ivy, Grapes in clusters lurk,
Beneath the Carving of the curious Work.
Two figures on the sides emboss'd appear;
Conon, and what's his Name who made the Sphere,
And shew'd the Seasons of the sliding Year. . .

Cf. also Creech's tr. of the same passage: "And show'd the various Seasons of
the year"; and Dryden, *Georgics* I 439: "And the four Quarters of the rolling
Year."

40. *beauteous Order*] Wakefield cites Dryden, *Georgics* I 328–9:

And cross their limits cut a sloaping way,
Which the twelve Signs in beauteous order sway.

41. *Then sing by turns.*] Literally from *Virgil* ⟨*Ecl.* III 59, 56–7⟩,

Alternis dicetis, amant alterna Camœnæ:
Et nunc omnis ager, nunc omnis parturit arbos,
Nunc frondent sylvæ, nunc formosissimus annus. [P. *1736a–51.*]

Pope inverts the order of the verses in Virgil to conform to the order of the
thought in his own verse. Dryden translates (81*ff.*):

Now Hawthorns blossom, now the Daisies spring,
Now Leaves the Trees, and Flow'rs adorn the Ground;
Begin, the Vales shall ev'ry Note rebound.

STREPHON.

Inspire me *Phœbus*, in my *Delia*'s Praise,   45
With *Waller*'s Strains, or *Granville*'s moving Lays!
A Milk-white Bull shall at your Altars stand,
That threats a Fight, and spurns the rising Sand.

DAPHNIS.

O Love! for *Sylvia* let me gain the Prize,

---

44 ev'ry Note rebound.] Echo to the Sound. *1709–17*.

       Sing then; the Shade affords a proper place;
       The Trees are cloath'd with Leaves, the Fields with Grass;
       The Blossoms blow; the Birds on bushes sing. . .
       Each in his turn your tuneful numbers bring;
       By turns the tuneful Muses love to sing.
44. *rebound*] Wakefield cites Dryden, *Ecl.* x 10–11:
       The vocal Grove shall answer to the Sound,
       And Echo, from the Vales, the tuneful Voice rebound.
45. EC compare Virgil, *Ecl.* vii 21–3:
                            mihi carmen,
       quale meo Codro, concedite (proxima Phoebi
       versibus ille facit).
46. *Granville*—] *George Granville* ⟨see vol. IV, p. 363⟩, afterwards Lord *Lans-down*, known for his Poems, most of which he compos'd very young, and pro-pos'd *Waller* as his model. [P. *1736a–51*.]
    The association of Granville's name with that of Waller had peculiar propri-ety. Waller had praised, in some of the last verses he wrote, the poetry of the young Granville. It was "Granville's constant boast, and the praise most fre-quently offered him, that he was the 'poetical son' of Waller, upon whose shoulders the dying poet's mantle had fallen." See E. Handasyde, *Granville the Polite* (1933), p. 19. Pope was probably introduced to Granville about 1706. See *Early Career*, p. 52.
47. *A Milk-white Bull.*] Virg. ⟨*Ecl.* iii 86–7⟩
                         ——*Pascite taurum,*
     Qui cornu petat, & pedibus jam spargat arenam. [P. *1736a–51*.]
Wakefield compares Dryden, *Æn.*, ix 859, 862:
       A snow-white Steer, before thy Altar led. . .
       And dares the Fight, and spurns the yellow Sands.

And make my Tongue victorious as her Eyes;   50
No Lambs or Sheep for Victims I'll impart,
Thy Victim, Love, shall be the Shepherd's Heart.

STREPHON.

Me gentle *Delia* beckons from the Plain,
Then hid in Shades, eludes her eager Swain;
But feigns a Laugh, to see me search around,   55
And by that Laugh the willing Fair is found.

DAPHNIS.

The sprightly *Sylvia* trips along the Green,
She runs, but hopes she does not run unseen,
While a kind Glance at her Pursuer flies,
How much at variance are her Feet and Eyes!   60

STREPHON.

O'er Golden Sands let rich *Pactolus* flow,

---

56. *willing Fair*] Wakefield compares Horace, *Carm.* I ix 21–4, and EC note
Dryden's tr., 34–7:

> The half unwilling willing kiss,
>   The laugh that guides thee to the mark,
> When the kind Nymph wou'd coyness feign,
> And hides but to be found again.

58. *She runs, but hopes.*] Imitation of *Virgil* ⟨*Ecl.* III 64–5⟩,

> *Malo me Galatea petit, lasciva puella,*
> *Et fugit ad salices, sed se cupit ante videri.* [P. *1736a–51*.]

Wakefield cites Dryden, *Don Sebastian*, IV i 102–4:

> A brisk *Arabian* Girl came tripping by;
> Passing, she cast at him a side-long glance,
> And look'd behind in hopes to be pursu'd;

and also Creech's tr. of the lines from Virgil cited by Pope. Dryden translates
the same lines:

> My *Phyllis* Me with pelted Apples plyes,
> Then tripping to the Woods the Wanton hies:
> And wishes to be seen, before she flies.

61. It stood thus at first,

> Let rich Iberia *golden fleeces boast,*
> Her purple wool the proud Assyrian *coast,*
> Blest Thames's *shores,* &c. [P. *1736a–51*.]

And Trees weep Amber on the Banks of *Po*;
Blest *Thames*'s Shores the brightest Beauties yield,
Feed here my Lambs, I'll seek no distant Field.

DAPHNIS.

Celestial *Venus* haunts *Idalia*'s Groves,   65
Diana Cynthus, *Ceres Hybla* loves;
If *Windsor*-Shades delight the matchless Maid,
Cynthus and *Hybla* yield to *Windsor*-Shade.

The first line here evidently alludes to the Spanish Order of the Golden
Fleece. The wool of Assyria recalls Virgil, *Georgics* II 465: "alba neque Assyrio
fucatur lana veneno". Assyria was apparently confused in ancient times with
Tyre, the source of the famous purple dye both Virgil and Pope seem to have
had in mind.

Pactolus] A river in Lydia, in Asia Minor, famous for the gold dust once
carried in its waters.

62. In Ovid, *Met.*, II, Phaethon, having been hurled down from the sky, fell
on to the banks of the Po (Eridanus); his sisters, the Heliades, were transformed
into poplars weeping tears of amber (ll. 364–5):

> inde fluunt lacrimae, stillataque sole rigescunt
> de ramis electra novis. . .

63. Wakefield compares *Cooper's Hill*, 165–8:

> Though with those streams he no resemblance hold,
> Whose foam is Amber, and their Gravel Gold;
> His genuine, and less guilty wealth t'explore,
> Search not his bottom, but survey his shore.

Cf. *Windsor-Forest*, 357–8.

65. *Celestial Venus*] Aphrodite Urania, the "heavenly" Aphrodite, to distinguish her from Aphrodite Pandemos, the common, or sensual, Aphrodite.

Idalia] A town in Cyprus consecrated to Aphrodite.

66. *Cynthus*] Diana was said to have been born on Mt Cynthus, in Delos.

Hybla] A mountain in Sicily, famous for its thyme and honey. Cf. Virgil, *Ecl.*
VII 37: "thymo mihi dulcior Hyblae"; and also *Ecl.* I 54.

67*f*. Wakefield compares Virgil, *Ecl.* VII 67–8:

> saepius at si me, Lycida formose, revisas,
> fraxinus in silvis cedat tibi, pinus in hortis.

But, as EC point out, the "entire speech is a parody of the lines quoted by Wakefield, and of the lines [61–4] which immediately precede them". EC then cite
the tr. of Virgil done by "Mr. Adams", which appeared in vol. I of Tonson's
Miscellany Poems (1684):

> *Bacchus* the Vine, the Laurel *Phoebus* loves,
> Fair *Venus* cherishes the myrtle Groves,

STREPHON.

All Nature mourns, the Skies relent in Show'rs,
Hush'd are the Birds, and clos'd the drooping Flow'rs; 70
If *Delia* smile, the Flow'rs begin to spring,
The Skies to brighten, and the Birds to sing.

DAPHNIS.

All Nature laughs, the Groves are fresh and fair,
The Sun's mild Lustre warms the vital Air;
If *Sylvia* smiles, new Glories gild the Shore,   75
And vanquish'd Nature seems to charm no more.

STREPHON.

In Spring the Fields, in Autumn Hills I love,
At Morn the Plains, at Noon the shady Grove;
But *Delia* always; absent from her Sight,
Nor Plains at Morn, nor Groves at Noon delight.   80

73 are fresh and fair,] fresh Honours wear, *1709–17.*
75 smiles,] smile, *1709–16.*
79 absent from her Sight,] forc'd from *Delia*'s Sight, *1709–17.*

> *Phillis* the Hazels loves, while *Phillis* loves that Tree,
> Myrtles and Lawrels of less fame shall be.

69. *All nature mourns.*] Virg. ⟨vII 57, 59⟩

> *Aret ager, vitio moriens sitit aëris herba,* &c.
> *Phyllidis adventu nostræ nemus omne virebit*— [P. *1736a–51.*]

Cf. Congreve, *The Mourning Muse of Alexis*, 167: "All Nature Mourns; the Flouds and Rocks deplore. . ."

relent] To "assume a liquid form; to dissolve into water" (OED).

69 *ff.* These verses were thus at first;

> All nature mourns, the birds their songs deny,
> Nor wasted brooks the thirsty flow'rs supply;
> If Delia smile, the flow'rs begin to spring,
> The brooks to murmur, and the birds to sing. [P. *1736a–51.*]

To the above variation Wakefield compares the Epil. written by Addison for Granville, *The British Enchanters*, 11–12:

> The desart smiles; the woods begin to grow,
> The birds to warble, and the springs to flow.

DAPHNIS.

Sylvia's like Autumn ripe, yet mild as *May*,
More bright than Noon, yet fresh as early Day,
Ev'n Spring displeases, when she shines not here,
But blest with her, 'tis Spring throughout the Year.

STREPHON.

Say, *Daphnis*, say, in what glad Soil appears 85
A wondrous *Tree* that Sacred *Monarchs* bears?
Tell me but this, and I'll disclaim the Prize,
And give the Conquest to thy *Sylvia*'s Eyes.

DAPHNIS.

Nay tell me first, in what more happy Fields
The *Thistle* springs, to which the *Lilly* yields? 90

85 *Daphnis*,] Shepherd, *1709–43*.

81*f.* Wakefield compares Cowley, *Davideis*, III 553–4:
    Hot as ripe *Noon*, sweet as the *blooming Day*,
    Like *July* furious, but more fair than *May*.
86. *A wondrous Tree that Sacred Monarchs bears*] An allusion to the Royal Oak,
in which *Charles* the second had been hid from the pursuit after the battle of
Worcester. [P. *1736a–51*.]
    On Sept. 6, 1651, Charles II concealed himself in the boughs of an oak that
stood in Boscobel Wood, on the border of Worcestershire and Shropshire.
    90. *The Thistle springs, to which the Lilly yields*] alludes to the Device of the *Scots*
Monarchs, the *Thistle*, worn by Queen *Anne*; and to the Arms of *France*, the *Fleur
de Lys*. The two Riddles are in imitation of those in *Virg. Ecl.* 3 ⟨106–7⟩.
        Dic quibus in terris inscripti nomina Regum
        Nascantur Flores, & Phyllida solus habebis ⟨*habeto 1751*⟩.
                                            [P. *1736a–51*.]
    For discussion of this riddle, see Intro. to the *Pastorals*, p. 39, above. EC com-
pare Dryden's tr. of the Virgil, 163–6:
        Nay tell me first, in what new Region springs
        A Flow'r, that bears inscrib'd the names of Kings:
        And thou shalt gain a Present as Divine
        As *Phœbus* self, for *Phillis* shall be thine.
Cf. Chetwood, Pref. to the *Pastorals* (in Dryden's *Virgil*, p. 22): "But there are
some Prints still left of the Ancient Esteem for Husbandry and their plain

And then a nobler Prize I will resign,
For *Sylvia*, charming *Sylvia* shall be thine.

DAMON.

Cease to contend, for (*Daphnis*) I decree
The Bowl to *Strephon*, and the Lamb to thee:
Blest Swains, whose Nymphs in ev'ry Grace excell; 95
Blest Nymphs, whose Swains those Graces sing so well!
Now rise, and haste to yonder Woodbine Bow'rs,
A soft Retreat from sudden vernal Show'rs;
The Turf with rural Dainties shall be Crown'd,
While opening Blooms diffuse their Sweets around.
For see! the gath'ring Flocks to Shelter tend,   101
And from the *Pleiads* fruitful Show'rs descend.

Fashion of Life in many of our Sir-Names, and in the *Escutcheons* of the most
Ancient Families, even those of the greatest Kings, the *Roses*, the *Lillies*, the
Thistle, &c."

99. was originally,
> *The turf with country dainties shall be spread,*
> *And trees with twining branches shade your head.* [P. *1736a–51.*]

100. Cf. Pope, *The Garden*, 3 (vol. VI, p. 47).

102. *from the Pleiads*] The Pleiades were the mythical daughters of Atlas. Because of their sorrow at the burden imposed on their father they were changed
into a small bright group of stars in the constellation Taurus and rose with the
sun in April. They were associated with the vernal equinox and the westerly
rains of spring.

SUMMER.

The Second Pastoral,

OR

ALEXIS.

To Dr. GARTH.

A Shepherd's Boy (he seeks no better Name)
  Led forth his Flocks along the silver *Thame*,
  Where dancing Sun-beams on the Waters play'd,
And verdant Alders form'd a quiv'ring Shade.
Soft as he mourn'd, the Streams forgot to flow,   5

OR ALEXIS.] *Om. 1717–43.*
To Dr. GARTH.] *Add. 1717–51.*
1–4 A Faithful Swain, whom Love had taught to sing,
  Bewail'd his Fate beside a silver Spring;
  Where gentle *Thames* his winding Waters leads
  Thro' verdant Forests, and thro' flow'ry Meads. *1709–17.*
5 Soft as] There while *1709–43.*

Ver. 1, 2, 3, 4. were thus printed in the first edition; ⟨Pope, *1736a–51*, here gave the *1709–17* variant cited above.⟩
 1f. Cf. Spenser's *Januarye*, *1ff.*:
     A Shepeheards boye (no better doe him call) . . .
     Led forth his flock . . .
 2. *Thame*] "An inaccurate word, instead of Thames", says Warton, and EC note the confusion resulting from "the fact that there is a real river Thame, which is a tributary of the Thames." Cf. Milton, *At a Vacation Exercise*, 100: "Royal Towred Thame"; also *Windsor-Forest*, 339*n.*
 3. The Scene of this Pastoral by the River's side; suitable to the heat of the season; the Time, Noon. [P. *1736a–51.*]
 4. *quiv'ring Shade*] Wakefield compares Virgil, *Ecl.* v 5, "sub incertas Zephyris motantibus umbras"; Dryden, *Theodore and Honoria*, 79–80,
    The Winds, within the quiv'ring Branches plaid,
    And Dancing-Trees a mournful Musick made;
and Spenser, *Colin Clouts come home againe*, 58–9:
        the cooly shade,
  Of the greene alders . . .
 5. *the Streams forgot to flow*] A conceit frequent in pastoral poetry. Wakefield

The Flocks around a dumb Compassion show,
The *Naiads* wept in ev'ry Watry Bow'r,
And *Jove* consented in a silent Show'r.
   Accept, O *Garth*, the Muse's early Lays,
That adds this Wreath of Ivy to thy Bays;   10
Hear what from Love unpractis'd Hearts endure,
From Love, the sole Disease thou canst not cure!
   Ye shady Beeches, and ye cooling Streams,
Defence from *Phœbus'*, not from *Cupid*'s Beams;
To you I mourn; nor to the Deaf I sing,   15

14 *Phœbus'*,] *Phœbus, 1709–43.*

---

cites Virgil, *Ecl.* VIII 4: "et mutata suos requierunt flumina cursus"; and Dryden's tr.:

> To which the salvage *Linxes* listning stood.
> The Rivers stood on heaps, and stop'd the running Flood.

EC compare Garth, *Dispensary,* IV 222–3:

> The Banks of *Rhine* a pleas'd Attention show,
> And Silver *Sequana* forgets to flow.

Cf. l. 84, below.

   6. *Compassion show*] EC cite Congreve, *The Tears of Amaryllis for Amyntas,* 14: "And dumb Distress and new Compassion shew."

   7. *Watry Bow'r*] Cf. l. 51*n*, below.

   8. *And* Jove *consented*] Virg. ⟨*Ecl.* VII 60⟩

> *Jupiter & læto descendet plurimus imbri.* [P. *1736a–51.*]

   9. Dr. *Samuel Garth,* Author of the *Dispensary,* was one of the first friends of the author, whose acquaintance with him began at fourteen or fifteen. Their friendship continu'd from the year 1703, to 1718, which was that of his death. [P. *1736a–51.*]

   10. *Ivy to thy Bays*] Cf. Virgil, *Ecl.* VIII 11–13, and Dryden's tr., 17–18:

> Amidst thy Laurels let this Ivy twine,
> Thine was my earlyest Muse...

Cf. also Dryden, *To the Memory of Mr. Oldham,* 24: "Thy brows with ivy, and with laurels bound." For extended discussion of this image, see *Ess. on Crit.,* 706*n* (pp. 320–2, below).

   12. "This is a handsome compliment to the professional merit of his poetic friend; but the original occurs in a most admirable *idyllium* of *Theocritus,* xi 1. inscribed also to a *physician*" [Wakefield].

   15. *nor to the Deaf I sing*] *Non canimus surdis, respondent omnia sylvæ.* Virg. ⟨*Ecl.* x 8⟩ [P. *1736a–51.*]

   Wakefield cites Ogilby's tr., 9–10:

The Woods shall answer, and their Echo ring.
The Hills and Rocks attend my doleful Lay,
Why art thou prouder and more hard than they?
The bleating Sheep with my Complaints agree,
They parch'd with Heat, and I inflam'd by thee.   20
The sultry *Sirius* burns the thirsty Plains,
While in thy Heart Eternal Winter reigns.
    Where stray ye Muses, in what Lawn or Grove,
While your *Alexis* pines in hopeless Love?
In those fair Fields where Sacred *Isis* glides,   25

---

17 The] Ev'n *1709–17*.   23 stray] are *1709–16*.

Nor to the deaf do we our numbers sing,
Since woods in answering us with echoes ring.

16. *The woods shall answer, and their Echo ring*, is a line out of *Spenser*'s *Epithalamion*. [P. *1736a–51*.]

20. Bowles, criticizing the conceit, points out that Pope did not find it in Virgil, who says (*Ecl.* II 13) "sole sub ardenti resonant arbusta cicadis", but in Dryden's tr., 13–14:

The creaking Locusts with my Voice conspire,
They fry'd with Heat, and I with fierce Desire.

21. EC compare Virgil, *Georgics* II 353: "hiulca siti findit Canis aestifer arva." Pope repeated the image in *On the Statue of Cleopatra*, 64 (vol. VI, p. 67). From ancient times the Dog-star, especially when it rose in conjunction with the sun, was regarded as the source of the sultry heat of summer and of the maladies which prevailed at that time.

22. EC compare Spenser, *Januarye*, 25: "Such rage as winters, reigneth in my heart."

23. *Where stray ye Muses*, &c.]

Quæ nemora, aut qui vos saltus habuere, puellæ
Naiades, indigno cum Gallus amore periret?
Nam neque Parnassi vobis juga, nam neque Pindi
Ulla moram fecere, neque Aonia Aganippe.
                Virg. ⟨*Ecl.* X 9–12⟩ out of *Theoc.* ⟨*Idyll* I 65–7.⟩
                        [P. *1736a–51*.]

Wakefield compares Ogilby's tr., 11–12:

Say *Naiades* where were you, in what Grove,
Or Lawn, when *Gallus* fell by ill-match'd love.

Also *Lycidas*, 50.

25. *Isis*] Name given to the Thames about Oxford.

D

Or else where *Cam* his winding Vales divides?
As in the Crystal Spring I view my Face,
Fresh rising Blushes paint the watry Glass;
But since those Graces please thy Eyes no more,
I shun the Fountains which I sought before.   30
Once I was skill'd in ev'ry Herb that grew,
And ev'ry Plant that drinks the Morning Dew;
Ah wretched Shepherd, what avails thy Art,
To cure thy Lambs, but not to heal thy Heart!
    Let other Swains attend the Rural Care,   35

29 Eyes] Sight *1709–17*.   30 I] I'll *1709–16*.

---

26. *winding Vales divides*] Wakefield compares Addison, *The Campaign*, 323–4:
    Or where the *Seine* her flow'ry fields divides,
    Or where the *Loire* through winding vineyards glides.
EC remark that the Cam does not divide vales, but creeps through one of the flattest districts in England.

27.   *Oft in the crystal spring I cast a view,*
     And equal'd Hylas, if the glass be true;
     But since those graces meet my eyes no more,
     I shun, &c.
Virgil ⟨*Ecl.* ɪɪ 25–7⟩ again from the *Cyclops* ⟨*Idyll* xɪ⟩ of *Theocritus,*
     ——————*nuper me in littore vidi*
     Cum placidum ventis staret mare, non ego Daphnim,
     Judice te, metuam, si nunquam fallit imago. [P. *1736a–51.*]
EC compare Dryden's tr., 33–4: ". . . and if the Glass be true, / With Daphnis I may vie."

31*f.* Wakefield compares *Il Penseroso,* 172: "And every Herb that sips the dew." Cf. below, l. 69, and Pope's *Iliad,* xɪ 876–7.

34. *not to heal thy Heart*] Wakefield cites Ovid, *Met.,* ɪ 522–4:
        et herbarum subiecta potentia nobis.
   ei mihi, quod nullis amor est sanabilis herbis
   nec prosunt domino, quae prosunt omnibus, artes;
and EC cite Dryden's tr., 701–2, 706–7:
        what Herbs and Simples grow
    In Fields and Forrests, all their pow'rs I know . . .
    To cure the pains of Love, no Plant avails:
    And his own Physick, the Physician fails.

35.*ff.* "This is a pretty, but inferior, imitation of a most elegant passage in *Theocritus,* viii. 53" [Wakefield].

Feed fairer Flocks, or richer Fleeces share;
But nigh yon' Mountain let me tune my Lays,
Embrace my Love, and bind my Brows with Bays.
That Flute is mine which *Colin*'s tuneful Breath
Inspir'd when living, and bequeath'd in Death;   40
He said; *Alexis*, take this Pipe, the same
That taught the Groves my *Rosalinda*'s Name—
But now the Reeds shall hang on yonder Tree,
For ever silent, since despis'd by thee.
O were I made by some transforming Pow'r,   45
The Captive Bird that sings within thy Bow'r!
Then might my Voice thy list'ning Ears employ,
And I those Kisses he receives, enjoy.
      And yet my Numbers please the rural Throng,
Rough *Satyrs* dance, and *Pan* applauds the Song: 50

36 share;] sheer: *1751*.   37 yon'] that *1709–17*.
43 But now] Yet soon *1709–16*.

---

36. *share*] I.e., *shear*. *Share* is the spelling of the MS and all editions till 1751,
when *sheer* was adopted. See H. C. Wyld, *Studies in English Rhymes*](1923), pp. 64 *ff*.

37. *Mountain*] Cf. *Spring*, 21*n*.

39. *Colin*] The name taken by *Spenser* in his Eclogues, where his mistress is
celebrated under that of *Rosalinda*. [P. *1736a–51*.]

Note that Pope claims here to be the successor of Spenser. *Alexis* suggests
Pope's Christian name, *Alexander*.

40. *Virg. Ecl.* 2. ⟨36–8⟩
    Est mihi disparibus septem compacta cicutis
    Fistula, Damœtas dono mihi quam dedit olim
    Et dixit moriens, Te nunc habet ista secundum. [P. *1736a–51*.]

42. Wakefield cites Virgil, *Ecl.* 1 5: "formosam resonare doces Amaryllida
silvas." Cf. the tr. by John Caryll (1625–1711), uncle to Pope's friend, in vol. 1
of *Miscellany Poems* (1684), l. 6: "And every Grove learns *Amarillis* name."

43. EC cite Dryden, *Ecl.* VII 33–4:
    The praise of artful Numbers I resign:
    And hang my Pipe upon the Sacred Pine.

45–6. Wakefield cites Dryden's tr. of Theocritus, *Idyll* III 28–9:
    Some God transform me by his Heavenly Pow'r
    Ev'n to a *Bee* to buzz within your Bow'r.

49. Wakefield cites Virgil, *Ecl.* IX 33–4: "me quoque dicunt / vatem pastores."

50. *Rough Satyrs*] Pope may have remembered *Lycidas*, 34: "Rough *Satyrs*

The Nymphs forsaking ev'ry Cave and Spring,
Their early Fruit, and milk-white Turtles bring;
Each am'rous Nymph prefers her Gifts in vain,
On you their Gifts are all bestow'd again!
For you the Swains the fairest Flow'rs design,   55
And in one Garland all their Beauties join;
Accept the Wreath which You deserve alone,
In whom all Beauties are compriz'd in One.
    See what Delights in Sylvan Scenes appear!
Descending Gods have found *Elysium* here.   60
In Woods bright *Venus* with *Adonis* stray'd,
And chast *Diana* haunts the Forest Shade.
Come lovely Nymph, and bless the silent Hours,
When Swains from Sheering seek their nightly Bow'rs;

---

danc'd." The couplet, however, was modelled (as EC note) on Dryden, *Ecl.* VI
42–3:

> He [Silenus] rais'd his voice; and soon a num'rous throng
> Of tripping Satyrs crowded to the Song.

51. EC compare Spenser, *The mourning Muse of Thestylis*, 1–2:

> Come forth ye Nymphes come forth, forsake your watry bowres,
> Forsake your mossy caues . . .

52*ff*. EC compare Spenser, *Astrophel*, 43–8:

> And many a Nymph both of the wood and brooke,
> Soone as his oaten pipe began to shrill:
> Both christall wells and shadie groues forsooke,
> To heare the charmes of his enchanting skill.
> And brought him presents, flowers if it were prime,
> Or mellow fruit if it were haruest time.

54. EC cite Spenser, *Januarye*, 57–60:

> His clownish gifts and curtsies I disdaine,
> His kiddes, his cracknelles, and his early fruit.
> Ah foolish *Hobbinol*, thy gyfts bene vayne:
> *Colin* them giues to *Rosalind* againe.

60. *Descending Gods have found* Elysium *here.*]
    ——*Habitarunt Di quoque sylvas*—Virg. ⟨*Ecl.* II 60⟩
    Et formosus oves ad flumina pavit Adonis. Idem. ⟨x 18⟩ [P. *1736a–51.*]
EC compare Dryden's tr. of the first line, "The Gods to live in Woods have
left the Skies", and note that Dryden expanded the second line into a couplet:

> Along the Streams his Flock *Adonis* fed;
> And yet the Queen of Beauty blest his Bed.

When weary Reapers quit the sultry Field,   65
And crown'd with Corn, their Thanks to *Ceres* yield.
This harmless Grove no lurking Viper hides,
But in my Breast the Serpent Love abides.
Here Bees from Blossoms sip the rosie Dew,
But your *Alexis* knows no Sweets but you.   70
Oh deign to visit our forsaken Seats,
The mossie Fountains, and the Green Retreats!
Where-e'er you walk, cool Gales shall fan the Glade,
Trees, where you sit, shall crowd into a Shade,
Where-e'er you tread, the blushing Flow'rs shall rise, 75

70 Sweets] Sweet *1709–43*.
71 Some God conduct you to these blissful Seats, *1709–17*.

---

65. *sultry Field*] Wakefield compares Virgil, *Ecl.* II 10, "rapido fessis messoribus aestu", and Ogilby's tr., 11: "And for the Reapers, tir'd with sultry heats."

67. *lurking Viper*] Wakefield cites Virgil, *Ecl.* III 93: "frigidus, o pueri, fugite hinc, latet anguis in herba."

69. Cf. Dryden, *Georgics* IV 76 (of bees), "They skim the Floods, and sip the purple Flow'rs", and also *Ecl.* I 110: "No more my Sheep shall sip the Morning Dew." Cf. above, ll. 31–2*n*.

71 var. Of the variant line Wakefield remarks that Pope doubtless later thought it "of too heathenish an aspect".

72. *mossie Fountains*] Wakefield compares Virgil, *Ecl.* VII 45: "muscosi fontes". Cf. *Messiah*, 3.

Green Retreats] Cf. Fenton, *The Dream, Imitated from Propertius*, 1: "To green Retreats, that shade the Muses Stream", and *Windsor-Forest*, 1.

73–6. Introduced into Handel's oratorio *Semele* (1744), which was based on Congreve's opera of the same title. Congreve's *Semele* was first printed in his collected works of 1710, but it probably was written several years previously. John Eccles composed music for it in 1707, but it was not performed during Congreve's lifetime (John C. Hodges, *William Congreve the Man*, 1941, p. 73). Congreve's text was altered for Handel, and the lines borrowed from Pope, perhaps by Newburgh Hamilton (O. E. Deutsch, *Handel: A Documentary Biography*, 1955, pp. 581–2).

75. *Where-e'er you tread*] An ancient conceit. Wakefield cites Persius, II 38, and Jonson, *The Sad Shepherd*, I i 1–9. E. Handasyde (*Granville the Polite*, pp. 21–2) compares Granville, *To Flavia*, 8–11, which in its turn derives from Waller, *At Pens-hurst* ("Had *Sacharissa* . . ."), 11–16:

> The Plants acknowledge this, and her admire,
> No less than those of old, did *Orpheus*'s Lire:

> And all things flourish where you turn your Eyes.
> Oh! how I long with you to pass my Days,
> Invoke the Muses, and resound your Praise;
> Your Praise the Birds shall chant in ev'ry Grove,
> And Winds shall waft it to the Pow'rs above.   80
> But wou'd you sing, and rival *Orpheus'* Strain,

81 *Orpheus'*] *Orpheus 1709–16.*

> If she sit down, with tops all towards her bow'd,
> They round about her into Arbors crowd;
> Of if she walk, in even ranks they stand,
> Like some well-Marshal'd and obsequious band.

The conceit perhaps originated in the mythical events following Aphrodite's birth. Shortly after emerging from the sea the goddess was wafted ashore in Cyprus, and there, at the touch of her foot on the earth, grass sprang up and flowers burst into bloom. Cf. *Autumn*, 35–6. Charles Hopkins, *White-hall* (1698), 198–9, has:

> Grass springs where e're she goes, the flow'ry Mead
> Receives new Flowers, where she vouchsafes to tread.

77. *to pass my Days*] Wakefield cites Virgil, *Ecl.* x 43: "hic ipso tecum consumerer aevo."

79 *ff.*   *Your praise the tuneful birds to heav'n shall bear,*
            And list'ning wolves grow milder as they hear.

So the verses were originally written. But the author, young as he was, soon found the absurdity which *Spenser* himself overlooked, of introducing Wolves into England. [*P. 1736a–51. The prose comment appeared only in 1751.*]

Spenser introduces wolves into England in *Iulye*, 56. But he did not "overlook the absurdity", for in *September*, 151–3, he makes Hobbinoll say:

> Well is knowne that sith the Saxon king,
> Neuer was Woolfe seene many nor some,
> Nor in all Kent, nor in Christendome.

Wolves are said to have disappeared from England in the reign of Henry VII, from Scotland in 1680, and from Ireland in 1766. Cf. *Windsor-Forest*, 72*n.* In *Guardian* 40 Pope ridicules Ambrose Philips, his rival in pastoral poetry, by saying: "*Philips* hath with great Judgment described *Wolves* in *England* in his first Pastoral." Cf. Philips, *The First Pastoral*, 19–21.

80. *And Winds shall waft*] *Partem aliquam, venti, divum referatis ad aures!* Virg. ⟨*Ecl.* III 73⟩ [P. *1736a–51.*]

Wakefield compares Dryden's tr., 113: "Winds on your Wings to Heav'n her Accents bear." Creech translates (90): "Winds bear their Musick to the Gods above."

The wondring Forests soon shou'd dance again,
The moving Mountains hear the pow'rful Call,
And headlong Streams hang list'ning in their Fall!
But see, the Shepherds shun the Noon-day Heat, 85
The lowing Herds to murm'ring Brooks retreat,
To closer Shades the panting Flocks remove,
Ye Gods! and is there no Relief for Love?
But soon the Sun with milder Rays descends
To the cool Ocean, where his Journey ends; 90
On me Love's fiercer Flames for ever prey,
By Night he scorches, as he burns by Day.

---

82. *shou'd dance again*] Cf. Virgil, *Ecl.* III 46: "Orpheaque in medio posuit silvasque sequentis." Creech, 60–1, has:

> *Orpheus* within, and following wood, around
> With bended Tops, seem listning to the sound.

Ogilby, 49, has "Where *Orpheus* 'midst the dancing woods is set", and Dryden, 69–70, has:

> Where *Orpheus* on his Lyre laments his Love,
> With Beasts encompass'd, and a dancing Grove.

84. *And headlong Streams*] Wakefield cites Lucan, VI 472–3: "De rupe pependit / abscisa fixus torrens. . ."; and also Congreve, *The Tears of Amaryllis*, 19; Marvell, *A Dialogue Between the Resolved Soul, and Created Pleasure*, 40; Milton, *Comus*, 493–4. Bowles cites Oldham, *Bion*, 40.

85–92. Cf. Virgil, *Ecl.* II 68*ff.*, and Dryden's tr., 95*ff.*: "See from afar the Fields no longer smoke. . ." The conceit at l. 92 has no example in Virgil, but may have been suggested by Dryden's amplification, 101–2, of the line cited by Pope (88*n*):

> I wish for balmy Sleep, but wish in vain:
> Love has no bounds in Pleasure, or in Pain.

88. *Me tamen urit amor, quis enim modus adsit amori?* Id. ⟨Virgil, *Ecl.* II 68⟩ [P. *1736a–51*.]
Wakefield cites Dryden's tr., 99–100:

> Cool Breezes now the raging Heats remove;
> Ah, cruel Heaven! that made no Cure for Love!

Pope marked the last line with a comma in his copy of Dryden.

91. *Me love inflames, nor will his fires allay.* [P. *1736a–51*.]

AUTUMN.

The Third Pastoral,

OR

HYLAS and ÆGON.

To Mr. WYCHERLEY.

Beneath the Shade a spreading Beech displays,
   Hylas and *Ægon* sung their Rural Lays;
   This mourn'd a faithless, that an absent Love,
And *Delia*'s Name and *Doris* fill'd the Grove.
Ye *Mantuan* Nymphs, your sacred Succour bring;   5
Hylas and *Ægon*'s Rural Lays I sing.
   Thou, whom the Nine with *Plautus*' Wit inspire,

OR HYLAS and ÆGON.] *Om. 1717–43.*
To Mr. WYCHERLEY.] *To* W. WYCHERLEY, *Esq; 1709–16.*
3–4 To whose Complaints the list'ning Forests bend,
   While one his Mistress mourns, and one his Friend: *1709–17.*

   This Pastoral consists of two parts, like the 8th of *Virgil*: The Scene, a Hill;
the Time, at Sun-set. [P. *1736a–51.*]
   1. *spreading Beech*] Wakefield cites Dryden, *Ecl.* 1 1: "Beneath the Shade which
Beechen Boughs diffuse."
   3–4 var. With the earlier reading of l. 3 EC compare Oldham, *Bion*, 41: "And
Trees lean'd their attentive Branches down." As this and subsequent variants
make clear, Pope in 1736 decided to make Hylas mourn an absent mistress instead of an absent friend. He undoubtedly wished to avoid comparison with
Virgil's *Ecl.* II and its suggestions of a homosexual love. See Intro., p. 46.
   4. *fill'd the Grove*] Wakefield compares Dryden, *Ecl.* 1 5–6:
       While stretch'd at Ease you sing your happy loves;
       And *Amarillis* fills the shady Groves.
Cf. *Summer*, 42n; *Windsor-Forest*, 298.
   7. *Thou, whom the Nine*] Mr. Wycherley, a famous Author of Comedies; of
which the most celebrated were the *Plain-Dealer* and *Country-Wife*. He was a
writer of infinite spirit, satire, and wit. The only objection made to him was that
he had too much. However he was followed in the same way by Mr. Congreve;
tho' with a little more correctness. [P. *1751.*]
   Wycherley's excessive wit was a critical commonplace. Cf. A. Boyer, *Letters of
Wit, Politicks and Morality* (1701), p. 217: "The only Fault that has been found

The Art of *Terence*, and *Menander*'s Fire;
Whose Sense instructs us, and whose Humour charms,
Whose Judgment sways us, and whose Spirit warms!   10
Oh, skill'd in Nature! see the Hearts of Swains,
Their artless Passions, and their tender Pains.
    Now setting *Phœbus* shone serenely bright,
And fleecy Clouds were streak'd with Purple Light;
When tuneful *Hylas* with melodious Moan   15

10 Spirit] Rapture *1709–17*.
11–12   Attend the Muse, tho' low her Numbers be,
              She sings of Friendship, and she sings to thee. *1709–17*.
13 Now setting *Phœbus*] The setting Sun now *1709–16*.

---

in it [*The Plain-Dealer*], is its being too full of *Wit*; a Fault which few Authors can be guilty of." Cf. *Ess. on Crit.*, 80–1n.

8. *Menander's Fire*] "This line evidently alludes to that famous Character given of Terence, by Cæsar,

> *Tu quoque, tu in summis,* o dimidiate Menander,
> *Poneris, et merito, puri sermonis amator;*
> *Lenibus atque utinam scriptis adjuncta foret* vis
> Comica.

So that the judicious critic sees he should have said—*with Menander's fire*. For what the Poet meant, in this line, was, that his Friend had joined to Terence's art what Cæsar thought wanting in Terence, namely the *vis comica* of Menander. Besides, ——*and Menander's fire* is making that the Characteristic of Menander which was not. His character was the having art and *comic spirit* in perfect conjunction, of which Terence having only the first, he is called the *half of Menander*." [Warburton] The Latin passage, attributed to Julius Caesar, is quoted by Suetonius at the end of his Life of Terence. Cf. Dryden (*Essays*, 1 42).

10 var. A happy emendation. It is possible to speak of Wycherley's sense, of his humour, his judgment, his spirit, but hardly of his "rapture".

11. *skill'd in Nature*] I.e., Wycherley knew *human nature*; hence the interest he could take in the passions and pains of Pope's shepherds. Lansdowne, in his *A Character of Mr. Wycherley* (in Boyer's *Letters of Wit, Politicks and Morality*, 1701, p. 255), had praised Wycherley's "strickt Enquiries into Nature", and his "close Observations upon the several Humours, Manners, Sentiments, and Affections of Men."

14. *fleecy Clouds*] Cf. *Il Penseroso*, 72: "Stooping through a fleecy cloud".

15 f. Wakefield compares Waller, *To my Lord Admiral*, 11–12,
> *Eurydice*, for whom his num'rous Moan
> Makes list'ning Trees, and salvage Mountains groan,

Taught Rocks to weep, and made the *Mountains* groan.
   Go gentle Gales, and bear my Sighs away!
To *Delia*'s Ear the tender Notes convey!
As some sad Turtle his lost Love deplores,
And with deep Murmurs fills the sounding Shores;   20
Thus, far from *Delia*, to the Winds I mourn,
Alike unheard, unpity'd, and forlorn.
   Go gentle Gales, and bear my Sighs along!
For her, the feather'd Quires neglect their Song;
For her, the Lymes their pleasing Shades deny;   25
For her, the Lillies hang their heads and dye.
Ye Flow'rs that droop, forsaken by the Spring,
Ye Birds, that left by Summer, cease to sing,
Ye Trees that fade when Autumn-Heats remove,
Say, is not Absence Death to those who love?   30
   Go gentle Gales, and bear my Sighs away!
Curs'd be the Fields that cause my *Delia*'s Stay:
Fade ev'ry Blossom, wither ev'ry Tree,
Dye ev'ry Flow'r, and perish All, but She.
What have I said?—where-e'er my *Delia* flies,   35
Let Spring attend, and sudden Flow'rs arise;

18 *Delia*'s] *Thyrsis 1709–17.*   21 *Delia*,] *Thyrsis, 1709–17.*
24, 25, 26 her,] him *1709–17.*   32 *Delia*'s] *Thyrsis' 1709–17.*
34 She.] He. *1709–17.*   35 *Delia*] *Thyrsis 1709–17.*

and his *Thirsis, Galatea,* 44–6; Virgil, *Ecl.* ii 4–5 (and the trs. by Ogilby and Dryden).

   17. The opening phrase of this and the following stanzas is evidently indebted to Waller's *Go, lovely Rose.*

   19*f.* "It was a time-honoured fancy that the 'moan' of the turtle-dove was a lament for the loss of its mate. *Turtur,* the Latin name for the bird, is a correct representation of its monotonous note" [EC].

   30. Wakefield compares Sidney, *Arcadia,* Bk iii, ll. 93–4 of the poem, "The Lad Philisides":

        Say all and I with them
          Absence is death or worse, to them that love.

   33. EC cite Congreve, *The Mourning Muse of Alexis,* 80: "Fade all ye Flowers, and wither all ye Woods."

Let opening Roses knotted Oaks adorn,
And liquid Amber drop from ev'ry Thorn.
  Go gentle Gales, and bear my Sighs along!
The Birds shall cease to tune their Ev'ning Song,   40
The Winds to breathe, the waving Woods to move,
And Streams to murmur, e'er I cease to love.
Not bubling Fountains to the thirsty Swain,
Not balmy Sleep to Lab'rers faint with Pain,
Not Show'rs to Larks, or Sunshine to the Bee,   45
Are half so charming as thy Sight to me.
  Go gentle Gales, and bear my Sighs away!
Come, *Delia*, come; ah why this long Delay?
Thro' Rocks and Caves the Name of *Delia* sounds,
Delia, each Cave and ecchoing Rock rebounds.   50
Ye Pow'rs, what pleasing Frensie sooths my Mind!

45 or] nor *1709–16.*   48, 49, 50 Delia] *Thyrsis 1709–17.*

---

37.   ——————————————*Aurea duræ*
        Mala ferant quercus, narcisso floreat alnus,
        Pinguia corticibus sudent electra myricæ.
                        Virg. Ecl. 8 ⟨52–4⟩ [P. *1736a–51.*]
Wakefield compares Bowles's tr. of Theocritus's *Idyll* 1 182–3 (in *Sylvæ*, vol. 11
of *Miscellany Poems*):
        On Brambles now let Violets be born,
        And op'ning Roses blush on ev'ry Thorn;
Walsh's *Eclogue* 111: *Damon,* 51–2:
        Upon hard Oaks let blushing Peaches grow,
        And from the Brambles, liquid Amber flow;
Ogilby's tr. of Virgil, *Ecl.* v111 59: "And purest Amber flow from every tree";
Virgil's *Ecl.* 1v 29–30, and Dryden's tr., 33–6:
        Unlabour'd Harvests shall the Fields adorn,
        And cluster'd Grapes shall blush on every Thorn.
        And knotted Oaks shall show'rs of Honey weep,
        And through the Matted Grass the liquid Gold shall creep.
43 *ff.*]   *Quale sopor fessis in gramine, quale per æstum*
        Dulcis aquæ saliente sitim restinguere rivo.
                ⟨Virgil⟩ Ecl. 5. ⟨46–7⟩ [P. *1736a–51.*]
Wakefield compares Drummond, *Forth Feasting,* 71–4.
44. Pain] Labour, toil.
51. *pleasing Frensie*] Wakefield cites Horace, *Carm.* 111 iv 5–6: "amabilis in-
sania".

Do Lovers dream, or is my *Delia* kind?
She comes, my *Delia* comes!—Now cease my Lay,
And cease ye Gales to bear my Sighs away!
 Next *Ægon* sung, while *Windsor* Groves admir'd;   55
Rehearse, ye Muses, what your selves inspir'd.
 Resound ye Hills, resound my mournful Strain!
Of perjur'd *Doris*, dying I complain:
Here where the *Mountains* less'ning as they rise,
Lose the low Vales, and steal into the Skies.   60
While lab'ring Oxen, spent with Toil and Heat,
In their loose Traces from the Field retreat;
While curling Smokes from Village-Tops are seen,

52 *Delia*] Shepherd *1709–17.*
53 She comes, my *Delia* comes!] He comes, my Shepherd comes!
                                                              1709–17.
58 I] I'll *1709–16.*

---

    52. *An qui amant, ipsi sibi somnia fingunt?* Ecl. 8. ⟨108⟩ [P. *1736a–51.*]
    53. EC cite Virgil, *Ecl.* viii 109, "parcite, ab urbe venit, iam parcite, carmina, Daphnis", and also Stafford's tr., 101–2, in Tonson's *Miscellany Poems* (1684), vol. 1:

                         cease, cease, my Charms,
         My *Daphnis* comes, he comes, he flies into my Arms.

    58. Wakefield compares Virgil, *Ecl.* viii 20, "extrema moriens tamen adloquor hora", and Dryden's tr., 26, 29:

         While I my *Nisa*'s perjur'd Faith deplore. . .
         Yet shall my dying Breath to Heav'n complain.

61–2. Wakefield cites *Comus*, 290–1:

         Two such I saw, what time the labour'd Oxe
         In his loose traces from the furrow came.

Ll. 61–4 recall Dryden, *Ecl.* ii 95–8:

         See from afar the Fields no longer smoke,
         The sweating Steers unharnass'd from the Yoke,
         Bring, as in Triumph, back the crooked Plough;
         The Shadows lengthen as the Sun goes Low.

    63. Wakefield cites Virgil, *Ecl.* i 82–3:

         et iam summa procul villarum culmina fumant
         maioresque cadunt altis de montibus umbrae.

Cf. the tr. of this eclogue by John Caryll (1625–1711), uncle to Pope's friend, in vol. 1 of *Miscellany Poems* (1684): "And curling smoak from Village tops ascends."

And the fleet Shades glide o'er the dusky Green.
   Resound ye Hills, resound my mournful Lay!   65
Beneath yon Poplar oft we past the Day:
Oft on the Rind I carv'd her Am'rous Vows,
While She with Garlands hung the bending Boughs:
The Garlands fade, the Vows are worn away;
So dies her Love, and so my Hopes decay.   70
   Resound ye Hills, resound my mournful Strain!
Now bright *Arcturus* glads the teeming Grain,
Now Golden Fruits on loaded Branches shine,
And grateful Clusters swell with floods of Wine;
Now blushing Berries paint the yellow Grove;   75
Just Gods! shall all things yield Returns but Love?
   Resound ye Hills, resound my mournful Lay!
The Shepherds cry, "Thy Flocks are left a Prey—"
Ah! what avails it me, the Flocks to keep,

68 hung] grac'd *1709–17*.   75 yellow] fertile *1709–16*.

---

64. *And the fleet shades fly gliding o'er the green.* [P. *1736a–43.*]
67 f. EC recall Garth, *Dispensary*, VI 203–4:
> Their wounded Bark records some broken Vow,
> And Willough Garlands hang on ev'ry Bough.

Wakefield compares Virgil, *Ecl.* X 53–4, "tenerisque meos incidere amores / arboribus", and Dryden's tr.: "The Rind of ev'ry Plant her Name shall know." Cf. Stafford's tr. (in Tonson's *Miscellany Poems*, 1684, vol. I), 69: "On smoothest rinds of Trees, I'le carve my woe."

72. "According to the ancients, the weather was stormy for a few days when Arcturus rose with the sun, which took place in September, and Pope apparently means that rain at this crisis was beneficial to the standing corn. The harvest at the beginning of the last century was not so early as it is now" [EC]. Cf. *Georgics* I 68, 204.

74. *grateful Clusters*] Grapes were successfully cultivated in England. Pope planted a vineyard in his garden at Twickenham, and Sir William Temple in his essay *Of Gardening* had described his own success with various kinds of grapes. Cf. this passage from *Pomona* (1729), by Batty Langley of Twickenham (pp. 110–11): ". . . the Vines now growing in the Garden of Mr. *Warner* at *Rotherhith* . . . by his judicious Management . . . annually produce great Quantities of the *Burgundy*, and, if I mistake not, the Claret-Grape also, with which he makes chearful Nector for the Accommodation of his Friends."

Who lost my Heart while I preserv'd my Sheep.   80
Pan came, and ask'd, what Magick caus'd my Smart,
Or what *Ill Eyes* malignant Glances dart?
What Eyes but hers, alas, have Pow'r to move!
And is there Magick but what dwells in Love?
 Resound ye Hills, resound my mournful Strains!   85
I'll fly from Shepherds, Flocks, and flow'ry Plains.—
From Shepherds, Flocks, and Plains, I may remove,
Forsake Mankind, and all the World—but Love!
I know thee Love! on foreign Mountains bred,
Wolves gave thee suck, and savage Tygers fed.   90
Thou wert from *Ætna*'s burning Entrails torn,

83 to move!] on me! *1709–16.*
84 Oh mighty Love, what Magick is like thee! *1709–16.*
89 on foreign Mountains bred,] wild as the raging Main, *1709–43.*
90 More fell than Tygers on the *Lybian* Plain; *1709–43.*

---

81. Wakefield compares Virgil, *Ecl.* x 26, "Pan deus Arcadiae venit", and 21: "omnes 'unde amor iste' rogant 'tibi?'"

82. *Or what Ill Eyes*] *Nescio quis teneros oculus mihi fascinat agnos.* ⟨Virgil, *Ecl.* III 103⟩ [P. *1736a–51.*]
Wakefield cites Dryden's tr., 158–9:
   What magick has bewitch'd the woolly Dams,
   And what ill Eyes beheld the tender Lambs?
83.   *What eyes but hers, alas, have pow'r on me!*
   Oh mighty Love! what magic is like thee! [P. *1736a–43.*]
89. *Nunc scio quid sit amor, duris in cotibus illum,* &c. ⟨Virgil, *Ecl.* VIII 43⟩ [P. *1736a–51.*]
Wakefield compares Stafford's tr. (in *Miscellany Poems*, vol. I, 1684):
   I know thee Love, on Mountains thou wert bred,
   And *Thracian* Rocks thy infant fury fed;
and also Dryden's, 60–1:
   I know thee, Love; in Desarts thou wert bred;
   And at the Dugs of Salvage Tygers fed.
Cf. also Denham, *The Passion of Dido for Æneas*, 80–1; Walsh, *Eclogue* III: *Damon*, 41–2; Dryden, *Æn.*, IV 524–5. The image goes back to Theocritus, *Idyll* III 15–17.
91*f*. Wakefield cites Dryden's tr. of Ovid, *Dido to Æneas*, 37–40:
   From hardn'd Oak, or from a Rock's cold Womb,
   At least thou art from some fierce Tygress come,
   Or, on rough Seas, from their foundation torn,
   Got by the winds, and in a Tempest born.

Got by fierce Whirlwinds, and in Thunder born!
 Resound ye Hills, resound my mournful Lay!
Farewell ye Woods! adieu the Light of Day!
One Leap from yonder Cliff shall end my Pains.   95
No more ye Hills, no more resound my Strains!
 Thus sung the Shepherds till th'Approach of Night,
The Skies yet blushing with departing Light,
When falling Dews with Spangles deck'd the Glade,
And the low Sun had lengthen'd ev'ry Shade.   100

---

95 *f.* Wakefield cites Virgil, *Ecl.* VIII 58–60,

> vivite silvae;
> praeceps aërii specula de montis in undas
> deferar;

and Dryden's tr., 84, 86:

> From yon high Cliff I plunge into the Main. . .
> And cease, my silent Flute, the sweet *Mænalian* Strain.

Cf. also Walsh, *Eclogue* III: *Damon*, 63–4:

> This Leap shall put an end to all my Pains.
> *Now cease, my Muse, now cease th*' Arcadian *Strains.*

100. Wakefield cites Virgil, *Ecl.* II 67, and Dryden's tr., 98: "The Shadows lengthen as the Sun goes Low."

WINTER.

The Fourth Pastoral,

OR

DAPHNE.

To the Memory of Mrs. TEMPEST.

LYCIDAS.

THyrsis, the Musick of that murm'ring Spring
Is not so mournful as the Strains you sing,
Nor Rivers winding thro' the Vales below,

OR DAPHNE.] *Om. 1717–43.*
Mrs. TEMPEST.] a Fair Young Lady. *1709–16.*

WINTER.] "This was the Poet's favourite Pastoral" [Warburton]. But Spence, p. 312, says that "The Messiah was his favourite above all others."

Mrs. Tempest] This Lady was of an ancient family in Yorkshire, and ⟨of . . . and *add. 1751*⟩ particularly admired by the Author's friend Mr. *Walsh,* who having celebrated her in a Pastoral Elegy, desired his friend to do the same, as appears from one of his Letters, dated Sept. 9, 1706. "Your last Eclogue being on the same subject with mine on Mrs. Tempest's death, I should take it very kindly in you to give it a little turn as if it were to the memory of the same lady." ⟨as appears . . . lady." *add. 1751*⟩ Her death having happened ⟨death happening *1736a–43*⟩ on the night of the great storm in 1703, ⟨1702, *1736a–43*⟩ gave a propriety to this eclogue, which in its general turn alludes to it. The Scene of the ⟨this *1736a–43*⟩ Pastoral lies in a grove, the Time at midnight. [P. *1736a–51.*]

"Miss Tempest was the daughter of Henry Tempest, of Newton Grange, York, and grand-daughter of Sir John Tempest, Bart. She died unmarried" [Croker]. Neither Warton nor following commentators were able to find any allusion, in the "general turn" of this pastoral, to the great storm of 1703. But the allusion is probably to be understood as a general recollection of the lady's death, of the season when it occurred, and of Walsh's poem, entitled *Delia, A Pastoral Eclogue; Lamenting the Death of Mrs. Tempest, Who dy'd upon the Day of the Late Storm.* See also ll. 27–8*n.* below.

Maitland, *The History of London* (1756), 1 504, describes the storm thus: "*On Friday,* the twenty-sixth *November* [1703], happened the greatest and most dreadful Storm of Wind that perhaps ever was known in any Age or Nation. . . Many Persons were buried in the Ruins, many of whom being killed out-right, and great Numbers grievously mangled."

So sweetly warble, or so smoothly flow.
Now sleeping Flocks on their soft Fleeces lye,   5
The Moon, serene in Glory, mounts the Sky,
While silent Birds forget their tuneful Lays,
Oh sing of *Daphne*'s Fate, and *Daphne*'s Praise!

THYRSIS.

Behold the *Groves* that shine with silver Frost,
Their Beauty wither'd, and their Verdure lost.   10
Here shall I try the sweet *Alexis*' Strain,
That call'd the list'ning *Dryads* to the Plain?
Thames heard the Numbers as he flow'd along,
And bade his Willows learn the moving Song.

LYCIDAS.

So may kind Rains their vital Moisture yield,   15
And swell the future Harvest of the Field!

16 the Field!] thy Field! *1709–36b*.

---

1. *Thyrsis, the Musick*] Warburton compares Theocritus, *Idyll* i i. Cf. *Spring*, in.
Wakefield cites Creech's tr. of Theocritus, *Idyll* i 9–10:
> And, *Sheapherd*, sweeter Notes thy Pipe do fill
> Than murmuring springs that roul from yonder hill.

3. Wakefield compares Virgil, *Ecl.* v 83–4, and Dryden's tr., 131: "Nor
winding Streams that through the Valley glide."

5 *f.*   *In the warm folds the tender flocks remain,*
> *The cattle slumber on the silent plain,*
> *While silent birds neglect their tuneful lays,*
> *Let us, dear* Thyrsis, *sing of* Daphne'*s praise.* [P. *1736a–43.*]

11. *the sweet Alexis' Strain*] An allusion, as EC note, to Congreve's poem, *The
Mourning Muse of Alexis, A Pastoral Lamenting the Death of . . . Queen Mary.* EC also
note that the couplet is closely modelled (no doubt to make the allusion clearer)
on Garth's *Dispensary*, IV 215–16:
> As tuneful *Congreve* trys his rural Strains,
> *Pan* quits the Woods, the list'ning Fawns the Plains.

EC also cite Dryden, *Ecl.* vi 100: "And call'd the Mountain Ashes to the Plain."

13. Thames *heard*] *Audiit Eurotas, jussitque ediscere lauros.* Virg. ⟨*Ecl.* vi 83⟩ [P.
1736a–51.]

Pope used the willows of England (the symbol of grief) instead of the laurels
of the Greek Eurotas.

Begin; this Charge the dying *Daphne* gave,
And said; "Ye Shepherds, sing around my Grave!"
Sing, while beside the shaded Tomb I mourn,
And with fresh Bays her Rural Shrine adorn.   20

THYRSIS.

Ye gentle *Muses* leave your Crystal Spring,
Let *Nymphs* and *Sylvans* Cypress Garlands bring;
Ye weeping *Loves*, the Stream with Myrtles hide,
And break your Bows, as when *Adonis* dy'd;
And with your Golden Darts, now useless grown,   25
Inscribe a Verse on this relenting Stone:
"Let Nature change, let Heav'n and Earth deplore,

---

18 Grave!"] Grave. *1709–16;* grave! *1717–43.*

---

17. *this Charge*] EC cite Virgil, *Ecl.* v 41: "mandat fieri sibi talia Daphnis".
21. Cf. the refrain of Oldham's *Bion:*

> *Come all ye* Muses, *come, adorn the Shepherd's Herse,*
> *With never-fading Garlands, never-dying Verse.*

22. *Cypress Garlands*] Cf. Spenser, *Nouember,* 143–5:

> The water Nymphs, that wont with her to sing and daunce,
> And for her girlond Oliue braunches beare,
> Now balefull boughes of Cypres doen aduaunce.

23 *ff.*   ——*Inducite fontibus umbras*——
> *Et tumulum facite, & tumulo superaddite carmen.*

⟨Virgil, *Ecl.* v 40, 42⟩ [P. *1736a–51.*]
    As Wakefield notes, the idea of the stream being hid under myrtles was sug-
gested by Dryden's tr. of the Virgil, 61–2:

> With Cypress Boughs the Crystal Fountains hide,
> And softly let the running Waters glide.

24. *break your Bows*] Wakefield compares Ovid, *Amores,* III ix 7–8, and Bion,
Idyll I 80–2. Cf. Oldham, *The Lamentation for Adonis, Imitated out of the Greek of
Bion of Smyrna,* 166–70:

> In purple wrapt, *Adonis* lies in state,
> A Troop of mourning Loves about him wait;
> Each does some mark of their kind sorrow show,
> One breaks his Shafts, t'other unstrings his Bow,
> A third upon his Quiver wreaks his hate . . .

27 *f.* Wakefield compares Walsh's *Delia, A Pastoral Eclogue; Lamenting the
Death of Mrs. Tempest,* 67–8:

"Fair *Daphne*'s dead, and Love is now no more!"
    'Tis done, and Nature's various Charms decay;
See gloomy Clouds obscure the chearful Day!   30
Now hung with Pearls the dropping Trees appear,
Their faded Honours scatter'd on her Bier.
See, where on Earth the flow'ry Glories lye,
With her they flourish'd, and with her they dye.
Ah what avail the Beauties Nature wore?   35
Fair *Daphne*'s dead, and Beauty is no more!
    For her, the Flocks refuse their verdant Food,
The thirsty Heifers shun the gliding Flood.
The silver Swans her hapless Fate bemoan,

28 more!"] more! *1709–51.*
36 Beauty is] Beauty's now *1709–16.*
38 The thirsty Heifers shun] Nor thirsty Heifers seek *1709–43.*

    Now, Shepherds, now lament! and now deplore!
    Delia is dead, and Beauty is no more!
Perhaps in this refrain Pope gave his poem the "little turn" which linked it with
Walsh's poem. But see introductory note on Mrs Tempest. Cf. also Congreve,
The Mourning Muse of Alexis, 167–8:
    All Nature Mourns; the Flouds and Rocks deplore,
    And cry with me, PASTORA is no more!
    31. *hung with Pearls*] Wakefield cites Dryden, *On the Death of Amyntas*, 1–2:
    'Twas on a Joyless and a Gloomy Morn,
    Wet was the Grass, and hung with Pearls the Thorn.
Cf. also Virgil, *Ecl.* x 13, and Dryden's tr., 20: "And hung with humid Pearls
the lowly Shrub appears." Cf. *Dryope*, 65 (p. 388, below).
    32. *scatter'd on her Bier*] Cf. Oldham, *Bion*, 64: "Trees drop their Leaves to
dress thy Funeral." As Wakefield notes, many of the "topics in this *pastoral* are
found originally in the pathetic elegy of *Moschus* on the death of *Bion*" [*Idyll* III].
    34. *with her they dye*] Wakefield cites Oldham, *Bion*, 66:
    Each Flower fades, and hangs its wither'd head,
    And scorns to thrive, or live now thou art dead.
    38.   For her the flocks the dewy herbs disdain,
    Nor hungry heifers graze the tender plain. [P. *1736a–43.*]
Wakefield recalls *Colin Clouts come home againe*, 26; EC cite Spenser's *Nouember*,
133, and Dryden, *Ecl.* v 38–9.
    39*f.* Wakefield cites Oldham, *Bion*, 25, 27–8:

In Notes more sad than when they sing their own.   40
In hollow Caves sweet *Echo* silent lies,
Silent, or only to her Name replies,
Her Name with Pleasure once she taught the Shore,
Now *Daphne*'s dead, and Pleasure is no more!
No grateful Dews descend from Ev'ning Skies,   45
Nor Morning Odours from the Flow'rs arise.
No rich Perfumes refresh the fruitful Field,
Nor fragrant Herbs their native Incense yield.
The balmy *Zephyrs*, silent since her Death,
Lament the Ceasing of a sweeter Breath.   50
Th'industrious Bees neglect their Golden Store;
Fair *Daphne*'s dead, and Sweetness is no more!
No more the mounting Larks, while *Daphne* sings,

40 In Notes more sad] In sadder Notes *1709–17*.
41–2   *Eccho* no more the rural Song rebounds,
          Her Name alone the mournful *Eccho* sounds, *1709–17*.

Ye gentle Swans . . .
In doleful notes the heavy loss bewail,
Such as you sing at your own Funeral.
 41. *sweet Echo*] Wakefield cites *Comus*, 229, "*Sweet Echo, sweetest Nymph that liv'st unseen*"; Cowley, *Eccho*, 5–6:
Ah gentle *Nymph* who lik'st so well,
In hollow, *solitary Caves* to dwell;
and Oldham, *Bion*, 60: "Sad *Eccho* too does in deep Silence moan." The idea that Echo lives in caves goes back to Ovid, *Met.*, III 394: "solis . . . vivit in antris".
 42. *her Name*] Daphne.
 50. *Lament the Ceasing*] Wakefield compares Oldham, *Bion*, 115–16:
Fair *Galatea* too laments thy death,
Laments the ceasing of thy tuneful breath.
Johnson (*Life of Pope*) wishes "that his fondness [for this Pastoral] had not overlooked a line in which the *Zephyrs* are made *to lament in silence*." Cf. Spenser, *Colin Clouts come home againe*, 24: "And all their birds with silence to complaine".
 51. Wakefield cites Oldham, *Bion*, 69: "The painful Bees neglect their wonted Toil".
 52. *Sweetness is no more*] Wakefield cites Oldham, *Bion*, 70, 72:
Alas! what boots it now their Hives to store . . .
When thou that wast all Sweetness art no more?

Shall list'ning in mid Air suspend their Wings;
No more the Birds shall imitate her Lays,   55
Or hush'd with Wonder, hearken from the Sprays:
No more the Streams their Murmurs shall forbear,
A sweeter Musick than their own to hear,
But tell the Reeds, and tell the vocal Shore,
Fair *Daphne*'s dead, and Musick is no more!   60
    Her Fate is whisper'd by the gentle Breeze,
And told in Sighs to all the trembling Trees;
The trembling Trees, in ev'ry Plain and Wood,
Her Fate remurmur to the silver Flood;
The silver Flood, so lately calm, appears   65
Swell'd with new Passion, and o'erflows with Tears;
The Winds and Trees and Floods her Death deplore,
Daphne, our Grief! our Glory now no more!
    But see! where *Daphne* wondring mounts on high,

55 Birds shall imitate] Nightingales repeat *1709–43*.

---

55 var. EC conjecture that Pope replaced *Nightingales* with *Birds* to avoid comparison with Philips's *Fifth Pastoral*, which recounts a competition in song between a shepherd and a nightingale. Pope praised Philips's poem in a letter to Cromwell of Oct. 28, 1710 (*Corr.*, I 100), but pointed out in *Guardian* 40 and in another letter to Cromwell of Nov. 11, 1710 (*Corr.*, I 103) that Philips had imitated closely some verses of Famianus Strada (see *Prolusiones Academicae*, Bk II, Prol. vi). EC's conjecture seems unlikely, for in 1751, when the new reading first occurs, no one would have thought of comparing Philips and Pope.

61*f*. For comment on the rhyme words in this couplet, see *Ess. on Crit.*, note to ll. 350–3 (p. 279, below).

64. *remurmur*] Wakefield cites Dryden, *Æn.*, VII 1041–2:
        Yet his untimely Fate, th' *Angitian* Woods
        In sighs remurmur'd, to the *Fucine* Floods.
Cf. also XI 695.

65*f*. Wakefield cites Ovid, *Met.*, XI 47–8: "lacrimis quoque flumina dicunt / increvisse suis . . ." Also Oldham, *The Lamentation for Adonis*, 64–5; Sedley, *A Pastoral Dialogue*, 7–8; Fenton, *Florelio*, 8; Duke's tr. of Virgil, *Ecl.* v 32.

69. "In Spenser's November, and in . . . Lycidas, is the same beautiful change of circumstances" [Warburton]. EC point out that such ascents to heaven were commonplaces of elegiac poetry and were ridiculed in *Guardian* 40.

69*ff*.   ——*miratur limen Olympi*,

Above the Clouds, above the Starry Sky.   70
Eternal Beauties grace the shining Scene,
Fields ever fresh, and Groves for ever green!
There, while You rest in *Amaranthine* Bow'rs,
Or from those Meads select unfading Flow'rs,
Behold us kindly who your Name implore,   75
Daphne, our Goddess, and our Grief no more!

LYCIDAS.

How all things listen, while thy Muse complains!
Such Silence waits on *Philomela*'s Strains,
In some still Ev'ning, when the whisp'ring Breeze
Pants on the Leaves, and dies upon the Trees.   80
To thee, bright Goddess, oft a Lamb shall bleed,
If teeming Ewes encrease my fleecy Breed.
While Plants their Shade, or Flow'rs their Odours give,
Thy Name, thy Honour, and thy Praise shall live!

Sub pedibusque vidit nubes & sydera Daphnis.

Virg. ⟨*Ecl.* v 56–7⟩ [P. *1736a–51.*]

Wakefield notes Dryden's tr., 86–7:

> *Daphnis*, the Guest of Heav'n, with wondring Eyes,
> Views in the Milky Way, the starry Skies.

73 *f.* The amaranth flower was reputed never to fade. Cf. *Par. Lost*, XI 78–9:
". . . thir blissful Bowrs / Of *Amarantin* Shade . . ."

81.   ————————*illius aram*

Sæpe tener nostris ab ovilibus imbuet agnus.

Virg. ⟨*Ecl.* I 7–8⟩ [P. *1736a–51.*]

Wakefield cites Dryden's tr., 9–10:

> The tender Firstlings of my Woolly breed
> Shall on his holy Altar often bleed.

In Virgil, *Ecl.* v, Daphnis is to be worshipped as a god, and offered libations of milk, oil, and wine.

84. *thy Praise shall live*] Virgil, *Ecl.* v 76–8:

> dum juga montis aper, fluvios dum piscis amabit,
> dumque thymo pascentur apes, dum rore cicadae,
> semper honos, nomenque tuum, laudesque manebunt.

Cf. *Rape of the Lock*, III 163 *ff.*

THYRSIS.

But see, *Orion* sheds unwholsome Dews,   85
Arise, the Pines a noxious Shade diffuse;
Sharp *Boreas* blows, and Nature feels Decay,
Time conquers All, and We must Time obey.
Adieu ye *Vales*, ye *Mountains, Streams* and *Groves*,
Adieu ye Shepherd's rural *Lays* and *Loves*,   90
Adieu my Flocks, farewell ye *Sylvan* Crew,
Daphne farewell, and all the World adieu!

FINIS.

85 But see, *Orion*] See pale *Orion 1709–43*.

---

85. The rising and setting of the constellation Orion was thought to bring storm and rain.

86.   ——*solet esse gravis cantantibus umbra,*
        Juniperi gravis umbra——
                        Virg. ⟨*Ecl.* x 75–6⟩ [*P. 1736a–51*.]
To this and l. 85 Wakefield compares Dryden's tr., 110–12:
                for hoarsness oft invades
        The Singer's Voice, who sings beneath the Shades.
        From Juniper, unwholesom Dews distill . . .

88. Warburton compares Virgil, *Ecl.* x 69: "omnia vincit Amor: et nos cedamus Amori"; and says, "Vid. etiam Sannazarii Ecl. et Spencer's Calendar." The allusion may not be to a precise quotation from Spenser or Sannazaro, but rather to such "Emblemes" or verse tags as are to be found at the end of the poems in *The Shepherd's Calendar*.

89 *ff.* These four last lines allude to the several *Subjects* of the four Pastorals, and to the several *Scenes* of them, particularized before in each. [*P. 1736a–51*.]
Cf. the conclusion of the *Shep. Cal.*, where E. K. remarks that the last six verses are a "conclusion of all", and that in them the poet "comprehendeth briefly all that was touched in this booke."

91. *Adieu my Flocks*] Wakefield compares Dryden, *Ecl.* I 111–12:
        No more my Song shall please the Rural Crue:
        Adieu, my tuneful Pipe! and all the World, adieu;
and Walsh, *Eclogue III: Damon*, 57–8:
            Adieu, ye Flocks, no more shall I pursue!
            Adieu, ye Groves, a long, a long Adieu!

MESSIAH

INTRODUCTION

I

THE *Messiah* was first published in the *Spectator* for May 14, 1712. It was introduced by a few lines describing the author as a "great Genius, a Friend of mine, in the Country; who is not ashamed to employ his Wit in the Praise of his Maker." This particular *Spectator* was signed with the initial "T", which stood for Steele, but there was nothing to show by whom the poem was written. Pope's authorship was revealed on November 12, when the Spectator, answering, or pretending to answer, the inquiry of a reader, said: ". . . that excellent Piece is Mr. *Pope*'s."

Pope's correspondence offers little information about the poem's composition. A letter from Caryll of May 23, 1712, shows that Pope had discussed with his friend the idea for the poem. Caryll says, "I hope your health permitted you to execute your design of giving us an imitation of *Pollio*."[1] Pope replied to Caryll on May 28 by saying that the "eclogue on the Messiah in imitation of Pollio, I had transcribed a week since with design to send it to you; but finding it printed in the *Spectator* of the fourteenth (which paper I know is constantly sent down to you) I gave it to Mr Englefield."[2] The dates of these letters suggest that the poem was conceived and written in a rather short space of time, while Pope's needless transcription for Caryll suggests that it was printed sooner than he had expected.

Caryll's particular interest in the *Messiah* was no doubt due to the poem's religious subject.[3] Before he had read the poem he wrote to Pope: "I am satisfy'd 'twill be doubly *Divine* and I shall long to see it. I ever thought church-musick the most ravishing of all harmonious compositions, and must also believe sacred subjects, well handled, the most inspiring of all Poetry."[4] At this time Pope was

---

1. *Corr.*, I 142.   2. Ibid., I 144.

3. Caryll's uncle, John Lord Caryll (1625–1711), from whom Caryll inherited the title, had published in 1700 an English version of the Psalms. After Lord Caryll's death Pope sent to the nephew and heir an epitaph which was evidently not used. See *Corr.*, I 133.

4. *Corr.*, I 142.

perhaps in the position he soon afterwards described to Martha
Blount: "Every one values Mr Pope, but every one for a different
reason. One for his firm adherence to the Catholic Faith, another
for his Neglect of Popish Superstition, one for his grave behavior,
another for his Whymsicalness. Mr Tydcomb for his pretty Atheis-
tical Jests, Mr Caryll for his moral and christian Sentences . . ."[1]
Pope had lately shown his "Neglect of Popish Superstition" in certain passages of the *Essay on Criticism*, thereby scandalizing some of
his co-religionists. One may suppose the *Messiah* to have pleased the
poet's family and to have been welcomed by his Roman Catholic
neighbours.

The poem was certainly agreeable to Steele, author of *The Christian Hero* and champion of morals and religion. On June 1, 1712,
Steele wrote to Pope that he had "turn'd to every verse and chapter, and think you have preserv'd the sublime heavenly spirit
throughout the whole, especially at —— *Hark a glad voice* —— and
—— *The lamb with wolves shall graze* —— There is but one line which
I think below the original,

> He wipes the tears for ever from our eyes.

You have express'd it with a good and pious, but not with so
exalted and poetical a spirit as the prophet . . . If you agree with me
in this, alter it by way of paraphrase or otherwise . . . Your Poem is
already better than the *Pollio*."[2]

II

In the collected *Works* of 1717 the *Messiah* followed the four *Pastorals*, the whole group being preceded by the hitherto unpublished
Discourse on Pastoral Poetry. In spite of its position, however, there
seems little reason to apply to *Messiah* the rules set forth by Pope in
his *Discourse*. The *Messiah* does follow the precept that would have
pastoral poetry be "an image" of the Golden Age, though in it of
course the Golden Age is not one of the past, but of the future. At
the same time, Pope was doing that for which he had criticized
Spenser, treating "matters of religion in a pastoral style". He was
also invoking the precedence and authority of an eclogue by Virgil

---

1. Ibid., 1 269.
2. Ibid., 1 146. Pope subsequently did alter the line. See 46*n*.

that, in Pope's own words, had been "given up" as a true pastoral by "the Criticks in general".[1]

In his fourth *Eclogue*, dedicated to Pollio, Virgil had foretold the birth of an infant whose reign over the earth would see the return of the Golden Age of Saturn. The similarity of certain verses to passages in Isaiah and the use of the word *Virgo*, which doubtless stands for Astraea or Justice, but which might be made to apply to the Mother of Christ, explain why this Eclogue should have passed, even in the early days of Christianity, and among others with St Augustine, for a poem of divine inspiration heralding the coming of the Messiah. In his poem Virgil referred to the Sibyl of Cumae, and thus the *Dies irae*, whenever it was written, links together in its first stanza the names of two prophets, David and the Sibyl. Throughout the Middle Ages Virgil was thought to have revealed in his poetry a spirit of great piety and sweetness and to have prepared in some way for the advent of Christ on earth. These considerations, among others, explain Dante's use of him as a guide through the dark wood at the opening of his great poem.

Even in our own time scholars have thought that the Sibylline books may have contained fragments of Jewish prophecy, gathered in when the Romans scoured their domains for oracular utterances of all kinds, and that Virgil may have been influenced by such material when he wrote the poem which was to be given meanings he could not have foreseen.[2] Pope's speculation apparently did not extend so far. In the Advertisement preceding the *Messiah* he says that he was struck by the "remarkable parity" he had found "between many of the thoughts" in Isaiah and Virgil, and the explanation he gives is merely that the "Eclogue was taken from a *Sybilline* prophecy on the same subject." And Pope adds: "One may judge that *Virgil* did not copy it line by line, but selected such Ideas as best agreed with the nature of pastoral poetry, and disposed them in that manner which serv'd most to beautify his piece." This procedure Pope follows also, selecting from the Bible, as Virgil did from the Sibylline books, those passages which fitted his theme and "disposing" them in a new unity.

---

1. See *Guardian* 40.
2. See Joseph B. Mayor, 'Sources of the Fourth Eclogue', in *Virgil's Messianic Eclogue*, three studies by Joseph B. Mayor, W. W. Fowler, R. S. Conway (1907).

From the beginning Pope indicated by chapter and verse the passages of Isaiah on which he had drawn. In 1717 he was more circumstantial: five passages from Virgil were quoted along with their Biblical parallels. These latter he took from the Authorized Version, but in many instances Pope's poetic text does not correspond with this version. The explanation for this is that the Bible used in Pope's Roman Catholic family must have been one of the available editions of the Douai Bible.[1] Thus in l. 82, for example, Pope uses the term "Basilisk", taken from the "basiliscus" of the Douai version, instead of the corresponding "viper" of the Authorized Version.[2] Again, l. 56, Pope speaks of the "promis'd Father of the future Age": the Douai has "Father of the world to come", while the Authorized Version has "the everlasting Father". Often of course the two versions are much alike, but Pope would appear to have searched them both to find the word or phrase which would most "beautify his piece".

III

Pope's *Messiah* has aroused a great deal of indignant criticism, usually in the form of invidious comparisons of its polished verse to what is called the "simple strength" of the Biblical "original".[3] Warton was fairer than most when he said that the *Messiah* "incontestably surpasses the Pollio of Virgil: although perhaps the dignity, the energy, and the simplicity of the original are in a few passages weakened and diminished by florid epithets, and useless circumlocutions."[4] Wordsworth singled out the poem as an example of "poetic diction" which was both "extravagant and absurd",[5] while Elwin suggested that the poem "is framed from first

---

1. The Old and New Testaments of the Rheims and Douai Bible were printed separately. The New Testament was first published from Rheims in 1582; a second printing was made at Antwerp in 1600. The Old Testament was first printed in two volumes at Douai in 1609 and 1610; another edition appeared from Rouen in 1635. These appear to be the only editions Pope could have used. It should be noted that the Douai Bible was much revised shortly after Pope's death, and that this revised edition is not a reliable guide to the poet's practice.
2. See l. 82n.
3. By the "original" most critics seem to mean the Authorized Version.
4. *An Essay on the Genius and Writings of Pope*, 1 11.
5. Appendix to the Preface to *Lyrical Ballads*, 1802.

to last upon the mistaken principle that the original would be embellished by amplifications, by a profusion of epithets, and by a
gaudier diction."[1] The tendency in our own time is to suggest that
the very polish of the poem shows Pope to be lacking in religious
"sincerity" or "intensity".[2]

Much of such criticism seems irrelevant to a judgment of Pope's
success in his poem. As his Advertisement shows, Pope was under
no illusion as to the superiority of the Prophet to both Virgil and
himself. He certainly did not set himself in competition with Isaiah,
but merely tried (as he was later to try with Homer) to cast the
words of a mighty ancient into a form and idiom for his own age.
He could no more write like Isaiah than he could write like Homer,
and so he did not make the attempt. His differences from one or
another translation of Isaiah are therefore hardly a test of his art,
while the assumption that the Messiah can be honoured "sincere-
ly" only in a diction of rugged simplicity scarcely merits consideration.

The original and full title of the poem as it appeared in the *Spectator* was "Messiah. A sacred Eclogue, *compos'd of several Passages of
Isaiah the Prophet.* Written in Imitation of Virgil's Pollio." The portion of the title here italicized was dropped in 1717, but it suggests
how little Pope claimed for himself. In addition, we should note
that his use of the Bible was restricted, as he says in the Advertisement, to those passages which best suited his purpose. In his notes
to the poem he refers the reader to twenty-seven different passages,
taken from sixteen different chapters of Isaiah, and anyone who
has traversed the length and breadth of Isaiah and observed the
variety of its contents will easily understand how selective he was.
Such a reader will also appreciate how Pope harmonized in the
new whole of his eclogue the materials he took from one end of
Isaiah to the other. The original has its own kind of development
and coherence, but this fact need not blind us to the new unity into
which some of the richest passages of the original have been "disposed" by Pope, nor to the virtues of the new music to which he set
the old words.

1. EC, 1 307.
2. See, for one example, R. K. Root, *The Poetical Career of Alexander Pope*
(1941), p. 60.

One of the most striking features about the *Messiah* is the new use
Pope makes of the couplet form. Typically, critics have taken the
balance of lines 3 and 4 as representative of Pope's procedure in the
poem, overlooking the fact that these two lines stand for the pastoral mode which the poet has rejected, along with pagan inspiration,
in favour of "sublimer Strains". This rejection is indicated clearly
by the break in the couplet as it occurs in l. 5:

> The Mossie Fountains and the Sylvan Shades,
> The Dreams of *Pindus* and th'*Aonian* Maids,
> Delight no more —— O Thou my Voice inspire
> Who touch'd *Isaiah*'s hallow'd Lips with Fire!

The more typical mode of the *Messiah* is not one of poised balance
or antithesis, but rather one of straightforward surge and crescen-
do, as in these lines:

> Swift fly the Years, and rise th'expected Morn!
> Oh spring to Light, Auspicious Babe, be born!
> See Nature hasts her earliest Wreaths to bring,
> With all the Incence of the breathing Spring:
> See lofty *Lebanon* his Head advance,
> See nodding Forests on the Mountains dance,
> See spicy Clouds from lowly *Saron* rise,
> And *Carmel*'s flow'ry Top perfumes the Skies!
> Hark! a glad Voice the lonely Desert chears:
> Prepare the Way! A God, a God appears.

One does find of course the kind of couplet which places epithets
and nouns in antithesis, but such lines usually have precise functions. These, for example, serve to juxtapose the iron age of the
world with the new heaven and earth of the Messiah's reign:

> To leaf-less Shrubs the flow'ring Palms succeed,
> And od'rous Myrtle to the noisome Weed.

But such couplets do not prevail in the poem; they are dominated,
rather, by the run-on developments in such a passage as this:

> No more the rising *Sun* shall gild the Morn,
> Nor Evening *Cynthia* fill her silver Horn,[1]

---

1. Pope has been severely criticized for the introduction of a pagan deity into
the Christian context of this line. It would seem obvious, however, that the poet

But lost, dissolv'd in thy superior Rays;
One Tyde of Glory, one unclouded Blaze,
O'erflow thy Courts: The LIGHT HIMSELF shall shine
Reveal'd; and *God*'s eternal Day be thine!

Much of the wrath expended on the *Messiah* has been directed
at Pope's use of epithets, and it is true that he often places epithets
where none exist in the original. But there are several justifications
for his practice. One is the fact that intrinsically there is nothing
wrong with the use of epithets: they are of the very substance of
English poetry[1] (if not of the original Hebrew), and may impart to
a line all of its suggestive value, as in l. 33 of the *Messiah*:

Lo Earth receives him from the bending Skies!

In this instance, Pope is building upon the example of Virgil's
aspice convexo nutantem pondere mundum (*Ecl.* IV 50), and it is well to
remember that Pope, though following the substance of Isaiah, was
imitating the manner of Virgil. The *Pollio* abounds in epithets
(*errantes hederae, rubens uva, durae quercus*), and Pope undoubtedly
was guided by Virgil's usage. At the same time, it should be noted
that epithets are an almost inevitable consequence of the antithetic
decasyllable, and it is in such lines, when they do occur in the
Messiah, that the epithets may seem most obtrusive.

Recent critics have noticed the tendency of Pope's epithets to
sum up the "essence or essential property of an object in an appropriate and apt word",[2] as in "noisome Weed", "healing Plant",
"thirsty Wilds". Joseph Spence attempted to describe the practice
a few years after Pope had written his *Pastorals*, his *Messiah*, and his
Windsor-Forest: ". . . one single Epithet gives us the Idea of any
Object, which has been common and familiar to us. Meadows,
Fields, Woods, Rivers, and the Sea itself, are often imag'd by one

---

is merely saying that the pagan past must give way to the Christian future, that
the light offered by Cynthia will be blotted out by the Light of God.

1. For an informative account of the use of epithets by both Pope and the
Romantics, see Ann Winslow, 'Re-evaluation of Pope's Treatment of Nature',
University of Wyoming Publications, IV (July, 1938), pp. 21–43.

2. See Edward L. Surtz, 'Epithets in Pope's *Messiah*', *PQ*, XXVII (1948), p.
215, and George Sherburn, 'Pope and "The Great Shew of Nature",' in *The
Seventeenth Century*, by R. F. Jones (and Others Writing in His Honor), 1951,
pp. 306–7.

E

well-chosen word. Thus in that beautiful Description of *Calypso*'s
Bower, you see the Groves *of living Green*; the Alders *ever quivering*;
the *nodding* Cyprus, and its high Branches, *waving* with the Storm:
'Tis by Epithets that the ancient Poets paint their *Elysian Groves*:
and the Modern, their *Windsor-Forests*."[1] In his practice Pope neglects realistic detail in favour of the epithet which will fix, often
with special human relevance, the qualities of an object: "lonely
Desert", "od'rous Myrtle", "harmless Serpents". Such epithets
bring man and nature into an intimate relationship, and in the
Messiah they record the changes in status in both man and nature
as the earth is transformed by Divine Grace.

On several occasions in the poem Pope employs a kind of "prophetic perfect" tense, a device by which a future event is vividly
depicted as already present. The two following couplets illustrate
this usage most dramatically, for in them Pope shifts from the
simple future of "See" (the context suggests the meaning of "shall
see") to the sharp immediacy of "Starts":[2]

> The Swain in barren Desarts with surprize
> See Lillies spring, and sudden Verdure rise;
> And Starts, amidst the thirsty Wilds, to hear
> New Falls of Water murm'ring in his Ear.

The dramatic immediacy of the passage is re-enforced by such an
epithet as "sudden" in the second line, and other epithets, like
"unfolding" in l. 42, serve a similar purpose. Ultimately these epithets, and the "prophetic perfect" usage, contribute to the sense of
a joyful spontaneity of response in both man and nature at the
coming of the Lord. There is a gaiety in the occasion which sets
mountains nodding, the lame exulting, portals sparkling. Amidst
the universal celebrations, when valleys rise and mountains sink
down, when steers and lions meet at one crib, there seems little justification for the mockery so often directed at the line that has
flowery bands of youths leading tigers, or perhaps it is that youths
lead tigers by flowery bands. There is a sublime and tender play-
fulness in both nature and man which is an essential part of the

---

1. *An Essay on Pope's Odyssey* (1726), pt II 18. This passage is quoted by Sherburn, *The Seventeenth Century*, p. 307.
2. See Note on the Text, p. 110.

whole scene, and to miss the part played by the epithets in creating this effect is to miss the spirit of the occasion and of the poem.

The *Messiah* was written, one should remember, after the *Essay on Criticism,* and one cannot afford, if one is to recognize Pope's poetic development, to overlook the care with which he organized this poem or the departure from his earlier couplet practice which it reveals. The *Messiah,* unlike other early poems by Pope, never contained examples of the expletive "do", and there are no triplets. There are three Alexandrines, but they are the reverse of "need-less". They mark the climaxes of the successive crescendos created by the couplets of this poem. The first introduces the prophecy of l. 8, "A *Virgin* shall conceive, A *Virgin* bear a Son", setting it off from the rejected pastoral mode and from the invocation to a new muse. The second, at l. 84, completes the picture of the joyful trans-formation the earth shall undergo, while the third, "Thy *Realm* for ever lasts! thy own *Messiah* reigns", is the sustained note which brings this cantata to its triumphant close.

MESSIAH.

A
Sacred Eclogue,
In imitation of VIRGIL's POLLIO.

NOTE ON THE TEXT

Pope's *Messiah* first appeared on May 14, 1712, in the *Spectator*, No. 378. Except for its subsequent appearance in editions of the *Spectator*, the poem was not reprinted until the *Works* of 1717. After 1717 it appeared in the various editions of *Miscellaneous Poems and Translations*, in the fourth edition of *Windsor-Forest*, and in the *Works* from 1736 on.

Only three of the variant readings seem out of the ordinary. They are the eccentric readings at ll. 58 and 59 introduced into two editions of *Miscellaneous Poems and Translations*, and the change of "Sees" to "See" at l. 68. This last change may have been the result of a misprint, but it has the authority of all editions after the first. Because of this authority, and also because it seems likely that in the context Pope was making a dramatic shift from the simple future to the "prophetic perfect" tense (see Introduction, p. 106), the later reading has been accepted.

The text printed here observes the revisions of later editions, but follows the spelling, punctuation, and typography of the first edition.

KEY TO THE CRITICAL APPARATUS

1712 = First edition, The Spectator, No. 378, Griffith 5.
1717 = Works, quarto, Griffith 79.
1720*a* = Miscellaneous Poems and Translations, vol. 1, duodecimo, Griffith 124.
1720*b* = Windsor-Forest, fourth edition, octavo, Griffith 125.
1722 = Miscellaneous Poems and Translations, vol. 1, duodecimo, Griffith 135.
1727 = Miscellany Poems, vol. 1, duodecimo, Griffith 192.
1732 = Miscellany Poems, vol. 1, duodecimo, Griffith 273.
1736*a* = Works, vol. 1, octavo, Griffith 413.
1736*b* = Works, vol. 1, octavo, Griffith 414.
1740 = Works, vol. 1, part 1, octavo, Griffith 510.
1743 = Works, vol. 1, part 1, octavo, Griffith 582.
1751 = Works, ed. Warburton, vol. 1, octavo, Griffith 643.

ADVERTISEMENT.

IN reading several passages of the Prophet *Isaiah*, which foretell the coming of Christ and the felicities attending it, I could not but observe a remarkable parity between many of the thoughts, and those in the *Pollio* of *Virgil*. This will not seem surprizing when we reflect, that the Eclogue was taken from a *Sybilline* prophecy on the same subject. One may judge that *Virgil* did not copy it line by line, but selected such Ideas as best agreed with the nature of pastoral poetry, and disposed them in that manner which serv'd most to beautify his piece. I have endeavour'd the same in this imitation of him, tho' without admitting any thing of my own; since it was written with this particular view, that the reader by comparing the several thoughts might see how far the images and descriptions of the Prophet are superior to those of the Poet. But as I fear I have prejudiced them by my management, I shall subjoin the passages of *Isaiah*, and those of *Virgil*, under the same disadvantage of a literal translation. [P. *1717, 1720b, 1736a–51.*]

ADVERTISEMENT.] This advertisement did not appear in the various editions of *Miscellaneous Poems and Translations*. It followed the text of the poem in *1717* and *1720b*; it preceded the poem in *1736a–51*.

MESSIAH.

A

Sacred Eclogue,

In imitation of VIRGIL'*s* POLLIO.

Y E Nymphs of *Solyma!* begin the Song:
To heav'nly Themes sublimer Strains belong.
The Mossie Fountains and the Sylvan Shades,
The Dreams of *Pindus* and th'*Aonian* Maids,
Delight no more—O Thou my Voice inspire   5
Who touch'd *Isaiah*'s hallow'd Lips with Fire!

Title] *1712 has:* MESSIAH./*A sacred Eclogue, compos'd of several Pas-/sages of* Isaiah *the Prophet./Written in Imitation of* Virgil's POLLIO.
6 hallow'd] hollow'd *1712.*

The *Spectator* prefaces the poem with this statement: "I Will make no Apology for entertaining the Reader with the following Poem, which is written by a great Genius, a Friend of mine, in the Country; who is not ashamed to employ his Wit in the Praise of his Maker."

1. *Solyma*] "Solyma is the latter part of the Greek name for Jerusalem, Ἱεροσόλυμα" [EC]. Cf. below, l. 85*n*.

1–5. *begin the Song . . . Delight no more*] Wakefield cites Dryden, *Ecl.* IV 1–3:
> *Sicilian* Muse begin a loftier strain!
> Though lowly Shrubs and Trees that shade the Plain,
> Delight not all . . .
Bowles suggests that the pause after *more* derives from Dryden's lines.

3. Cf. *Summer*, 72 (p. 77, above).

4. *Dreams*] "The poets of antiquity were thought to receive inspired dreams by sleeping on the poetic mountains. So *Persius* in his *prologue* [2–3]:
> nec in bicipiti somniasse Parnaso
> memini" [Wakefield].

Pindus] A mountain in Thessaly regarded as a seat of the Muses.

Aonian Maids] Aonia was another name for Boeotia. The Muses, who frequented Mt Helicon in Boeotia, were called Aonides, the Aonian Maidens.

6. *hallow'd Lips*] Isaiah, 6:6–7 (DB) reads: "And one of the Seraphims flewe to me, & in his hand an hote cole. . . And he touched my mouth, and said: Behold this hath touched thy lippes. . ." The Authorized Version is very similar.

Rapt into future Times, the Bard begun;
A *Virgin* shall conceive, a *Virgin* bear a Son!
From *Jesse*'s Root behold a Branch arise,
Whose sacred Flow'r with Fragrance fills the Skies.   10
Th'Æthereal Spirit o'er its Leaves shall move,
And on its Top descends the Mystic Dove.

Wakefield compares Milton, *On the Morning of Christs Nativity*, 28: "From out his
secret Altar toucht with hallow'd fire."

7. *Rapt*] "Carried away *in spirit*, without bodily removal" (OED).
begun] The form was common in Pope's time.

8. *A Virgin shall conceive*———*All Crimes shall cease, &c.*] VIRG. E. 4. v. 6.

Jam redit & Virgo, redeunt Saturnia regna,
Jam nova progenies cælo demittitur alto——
Te duce, si qua manent sceleris vestigia nostri,
Irrita perpetua solvent formidine terras——
Pacatumque reget patriis virtutibus orbem.

Now the Virgin returns, now the kingdom of Saturn *returns, now a new Progeny is sent
down from high heaven. By means of thee, whatever reliques of our crimes remain, shall be
wip'd away, and free the world from perpetual fears. He shall govern the earth in peace,
with the virtues of his Father.*

ISAIAH, Ch. 7. v. 14. *Behold a Virgin shall conceive, and bear a Son*—Ch. 9. v. 6, 7.
*Unto us a Child is born, unto us a Son is given; The Prince of Peace: of the increase of his
government, and of his Peace, there shall be no end: Upon the Throne of* David, *and upon
his Kingdom, to order and to stablish it, with judgment, and with justice, for ever and ever.*

[P. *1717, 1720b, 1736a–51.*]

In classical mythology Astraea, or Justice, left the earth at the end of the
Golden Age and was placed in the Zodiac as the constellation called the Virgin.
Cf. *Georgics* II 473–4:

extrema per illos [agricolas]
Justitia excedens terris vestigia fecit.

Pope's quotations of Isaiah are from AV. But see Intro., p. 102.

9. *Jesse's Root*] Isaiah, Ch. 11. v. 1. [P. *1712–51.*]
DB reads: "And a rod shal come forth of the roote of Iesse, and a flowre
shal rise vp out of his roote." AV has *Branch* instead of *flowre*; Pope seems to
have combined the two versions.

The marginal references by Pope were written in various ways for the different editions: e.g., Cap. 11. v[erse]. 1.; Chap. 11. v. 1. The form of editions
1736a–43 is followed here. Pope identified Isaiah only in his first reference;
chapter and verse references attributed to Pope in these notes should be understood as referring to it unless otherwise identified.

12. *the Mystic Dove*] The line recalls not only Isaiah 11:2 (DB), "And the
Spirite of our Lord shal rest vpon him. . .", but also Matthew 3:16 (DB): "And

Ye Heav'ns! from high the dewy Nectar pour,
And in soft Silence shed the kindly Show'r!
The Sick and Weak the healing Plant shall aid;   15
From Storms a Shelter, and from Heat a Shade.
All Crimes shall cease, and ancient Fraud shall fail;
Returning Justice lift aloft her Scale;
Peace o'er the World her Olive-Wand extend,
And white-roab'd Innocence from Heav'n descend.   20
Swift fly the Years, and rise th'expected Morn!
Oh spring to Light, Auspicious Babe, be born!
See Nature hasts her earliest Wreaths to bring,

Iesvs being baptized . . . he saw the Spirit of God descending as a doue, &
coming vpon him."

13. *dewy Nectar*] Ch. 45. v. 8. [P. *1712–51*.]
DB reads: "Droppe dew ye heauens from aboue, and let the cloudes rayne
the iust. . ." There is no mention of dew in AV.

14. Wakefield compares Dryden, *Don Sebastian* (near end of Act v): "But shed
from nature, like a kindly shower", and also Virgil, *Ecl.* VII 60.

15. *The Sick and Weak*] Ch. 25. v. 4. [P. *1712–51*.]
In this couplet Pope seems to follow AV: "For thou hast been a strength to the
poor, a strength to the needy in his distress, a refuge from the storm, a shadow
from the heat."

17. *ancient Fraud*] The "fraud of the Serpent", according to Warburton, who
perhaps recalled *Par. Lost*, IX 643: "So glister'd the dire Snake, and into fraud /
Led Eve . . ." Wakefield compares Virgil, *Ecl.* IV 31, "priscae vestigia fraudis",
and Dryden's tr., 37: "Yet, of old Fraud some footsteps shall remain."

18. *Returning Justice*] Ch. 9. v. 7. [P. *1712–51*.]
DB reads: ". . . he shal sit vpon the throne of Dauid . . . that he may confirme
it, and strengthen it in iudgement and iustice . . ." Cf. 8*n*. The reappearance of
Justice on the earth was to be the first sign of the return of the Golden Age. Cf.
Dunciad A, I 50.

21. *Swift fly the Years*] Wakefield compares Virgil, *Ecl.* IV 46–7:
        "Talia saecla" suis dixerunt "currite" fusis
        concordes stabili fatorum numine Parcae.

22. *Babe, be born*] "This seems a palpable imitation of *Callimachus*, but where
our poet fell upon it, I cannot discover: Hymn. Del. 214" [Wakefield].

23. *See Nature hasts*, &c.] VIRG. E. 4. v. 18.
        At tibi prima, puer, nullo munuscula cultu,
        Errantes hedæras passim cum baccare tellus,
        Mixtaque ridenti colocasia fundet acantho——
        Ipsa tibi blandos fundent cunabula flores.

With all the Incence of the breathing Spring:
See lofty *Lebanon* his Head advance,   25
See nodding Forests on the Mountains dance,
See spicy Clouds from lowly *Saron* rise,
And *Carmel*'s flow'ry Top perfumes the Skies!
Hark! a glad Voice the lonely Desert chears:

*For thee, O Child, shall the earth, without being tilled, produce her early ⟨produce early
1717, 1720b⟩ offerings; winding Ivy, mixed with ⟨Ivy, with 1717, 1720b⟩ Baccar, and
Colocasia with ⟨Colocasia mixed with 1717, 1720b⟩ smiling Acanthus. Thy Cradle
shall pour forth pleasing flowers about thee.*

Isaiah, Ch. 35. v. 1. *The wilderness and the solitary place shall be glad, and the
desert shall rejoice and blossom as the rose.* Ch. 60. v. 13. *The glory of* Lebanon *shall
come unto thee, the firr-tree, the pine-tree, and the box together, to beautify the place of thy
Sanctuary.* [P. *1717, 1720b, 1736a–51*.]

24. *Incence . . . breathing*] Pope seems to combine in "Incence" the suggestions
of a flower's perfume and also those of religious homage (OED, senses 3, 4).
Breathing: emitting fragrance. Cf. *Par. Lost*, IX 193–5:

the humid Flow'rs, that breath'd
Thir morning incense, when all things that breathe
From th'Earth's great Altar send up silent praise. . .

25. *lofty Lebanon*] Ch. 35. v. 2. [P. *1712–51*.]
DB reads: "Springing it shal spring, & shal reioyce ioyful and praising: the
glorie of Libanus is giuen to it, the beautie of Carmel, & Saron, they shal see
the glorie of our Lord, and the beautie of our God." *Saron* is the DB form for AV
Sharon.

26. *nodding Forests*] Wakefield recalls Virgil, *Ecl.* VI 27–8, and Dryden's tr.,
44–5:

And Sylvan Fauns, and Savage Beasts advanc'd,
And nodding Forrests to the Numbers danc'd.

29. *Hark! a glad Voice, &c.*] VIRG. E. 4. v. 46 ⟨48–9⟩.

Aggredere ô magnos, aderit jam tempus, honores,
Cara deûm soboles, magnum Jovis incrementum——
Ipsi lætitia voces ad sydera jactant
Intonsi montes, ipsæ jam carmina rupes,
Ipsa sonant arbusta, Deus, deus ille Menalca!

E. 5. v. 62.

*Oh come and receive the mighty honours: The time draws nigh, O beloved offspring of
the Gods, O great encrease of* Jove! *The uncultivated mountains send shouts of joy to the
stars, the very rocks sing in verse, the very shrubs cry out, A God, a God!*

Isaiah, Ch. 40. v. 3, 4. *The voice of him that crieth in the wilderness, Prepare ye the
way of the Lord! make strait in the desert a high way for our God! Every valley shall be
exalted, and every mountain and hill shall be made low, and the crooked shall be made*

Prepare the Way! a God, a God appears.   30
A God, a God! the vocal Hills reply,
The Rocks proclaim th'approaching Deity.
Lo Earth receives him from the bending Skies!
Sink down ye Mountains, and ye Vallies rise:
With Heads declin'd, ye Cedars, Homage pay;   35
Be smooth ye Rocks, ye rapid Floods give way!
The SAVIOR comes! by ancient Bards foretold:
Hear him ye Deaf, and all ye Blind behold!
He from thick Films shall purge the visual Ray,
And on the sightless Eye-ball pour the Day.   40
'Tis he th'obstructed Paths of Sound shall clear,
And bid new Musick charm th'unfolding Ear.
The Dumb shall sing, the Lame his Crutch foregoe,
And leap exulting like the bounding Roe.

---

strait, and the rough places plain. Ch. 44. v. 23. *Break forth into singing, ye mountains!*
O forest, and every tree therein! for the Lord hath redeemed Israel. [*P. 1717, 1720b,*
1736a–51.]

30. In addition to the note of Pope to l. 29, all editions give to l. 30 the marginal reference: Ch. 40. v. 3, 4.

31. *vocal Hills*] Cf. *Par. Lost*, v 203–4:
      ... Hill, or Valley, Fountain, or fresh shade
      Made vocal by my Song, and taught his praise.

33. Wakefield cites Virgil, *Ecl.* IV 50: "aspice convexo nutantem pondere
mundum".

35. Wakefield cites *Par. Lost*, v 193–4:
      and wave your tops, ye Pines,
      With every Plant, in sign of Worship wave.

38*ff.* Ch. 42. v. 18. Ch. 35. v. 5, 6. [*P. 1712–51. 1712 omits reference to Ch. 35.*]
DB (42:18) reads: "Heare ye deafe, and ye blind behold to see." Ch. 35:5–6,
is as follows: "Then shal the eies of the blind be opened, and the eares of the
deafe shal be open. Then shal the lame leape as an hart, and the tongue of the
dumme shal be opened . . ."

39. *visual Ray*] Wakefield compares the "visual ray" of *Par. Lost*, III 620, and
the "visual beam" of *Samson Agonistes*, 163. Warburton approves the figure
"which calls the *instrument* of vision [the eye] by the name of the cause [the ray],"
but he objects, as do EC, to the "thick Films" which "agree only with the thing
to which it is applied, namely to the *sight* or eye; and not to that from which it
is taken, namely a *ray of light* coming to the eye."

44. Cf. Song of Solomon, 2:8–9.

No Sigh, no Murmur the wide World shall hear,   45
From ev'ry Face he wipes off ev'ry Tear.
In adamantine Chains shall Death be bound,
And Hell's grim Tyrant feel th'eternal Wound.
As the good Shepherd tends his fleecy Care,
Seeks freshest Pasture and the purest Air,   50
Explores the lost, the wand'ring Sheep directs,
By Day o'ersees them, and by Night protects;
The tender Lambs he raises in his Arms,
Feeds from his Hand, and in his Bosom warms:
Thus shall Mankind his Guardian Care ingage,   55
The promis'd Father of the future Age.
No more shall Nation against Nation rise,

45–8   Before him Death, the grisly Tyrant, flies;
         He wipes the Tears for ever from our Eyes. *1712.*
50 Pasture] Pastures, *1712.*
55 Thus shall Mankind] Mankind shall thus *1712.*

---

46. *From ev'ry Face*] Steele objected to the first reading (see Intro., p. 100). In his revision Pope followed AV, 25:8: ". . . the Lord God will wipe away tears from off all faces." To the first reading Wakefield compared *Lycidas*, 181: "And wipe the tears for ever from his eyes." Cf. *Epil. to the Satires*, Dial. 1 102; also *Od.*, xvii 14.

47. Ch. 25. v. 8. [P. *1712–51.*]
Wakefield cites *Par. Lost*, 1 48: "In Adamantine Chains and penal Fire."

48. *eternal Wound*] Wakefield compares Lucretius, *De Rerum Natura*, ii 638, "aeternumque daret matri sub pectore volnus"; and Cowley, *Davideis*, 1 17: "And *Hells* black *Tyrant* . . ."

51. *Explores*] "To search for; to find by searching" (OED). Cf. *Ep. to Arb.*, 412.

53. Ch. 40. v. 11. [P. *1712–51.*]
DB and AV are much alike.

56. *The promis'd Father*] Ch. 9. v. 6. [P. *1712–51.*]
The line appears inspired by DB: ". . . and his name shal be called, Meruelous, Counseler, God, Strong, Father of the world to come, the Prince of peace." AV has "the everlasting Father". Wakefield says that Pope's "good sense led him to correct . . . the monstrous absurdity of our common translation at this passage of *Isaiah*, which applies the phrase EVERLASTING FATHER to *a son of man.*"

57. Ch. 2. v. 4. [P. *1712–51.*]

Nor ardent Warriors meet with hateful Eyes,
Nor Fields with gleaming Steel be cover'd o'er;
The Brazen Trumpets kindle Rage no more: 60
But useless Lances into Scythes shall bend,
And the broad Faulchion in a Plow-share end.
Then Palaces shall rise; the joyful Son
Shall finish what his short-liv'd Sire begun;
Their Vines a Shadow to their Race shall yield; 65
And the same Hand that sow'd, shall reap the Field.
The Swain in barren Desarts with surprize

58 Nor] Or *1727–32*. 59 Nor] Or *1727–32*.

---

60. Wakefield compares *Aen.*, VI 165, and Dryden's tr., 245: "With breathing Brass to kindle fierce Alarms."

61. *Scythes*] DB (Is., 2:4) has "they shal turne . . . their spears into siethes." AV has "pruning-hooks".

62. *Plow-share*] Here Pope follows AV, which has (Is., 2:4): ". . . and they shal beat their swords into plow-shares." DB has: ". . . they shal turne their swordes into culters."

63. *the joyful Son*] Ch. 65. v. 21, 22. [P. *1712–51*.] AV and DB are much alike.

64. Wakefield compares Dryden, *Britannia Rediviva*, 40: "And finish what thy Godlike Sire begins."

66. Wakefield compares Callimachus, Hymn VI 137; Dryden, *Ecl.* I 101; St John, 4:37.

67. *The Swain in barren Desarts*, &c.] VIRG. E. 4. v. 28.

    Molli paulatim flavescet campus arista,
    Incultisque rubens pendebit sentibus uva,
    Et duræ quercus sudabunt roscida mella.

The field shall grow yellow with ripen'd ears, and the red grape shall hang upon the wild brambles, and the hard Oaks shall distill honey like dew.

ISAIAH, Ch. 35. v. 7. *The parched ground shall become a pool, and the thirsty land springs of water: In the habitations where dragons lay, shall be grass, and reeds and rushes.* Ch. 55. v. 13. *Instead of the thorn shall come up the firr-tree, and instead of the briar shall come up the myrtle-tree.* [P. *1717, 1720b, 1736a–51*.]

DB reads: "And that which was drie land, shal be as a poole, and the thirstie ground as fountaines of waters. In the dennes wherein dragons dwelt before, shal spring vp the greennes of reede and bulrush" (35:7). "For the shrubbe shal come vp the firre tree, and for the nettle, shal grow the myrtle tree" (55:13).

67*ff.* Ch. 35. v. 1, 7. [P. *1712–51*.]

See Lillies spring, and sudden Verdure rise;
And Starts, amidst the thirsty Wilds, to hear
New Falls of Water murm'ring in his Ear: 70
On rifted Rocks, the Dragon's late Abodes,
The green Reed trembles, and the Bulrush nods.
Waste sandy Vallies, once perplex'd with Thorn,
The spiry Firr and shapely Box adorn;
To leaf-less Shrubs the flow'ring Palms succeed,   75
And od'rous Myrtle to the noisome Weed.
The Lambs with Wolves shall graze the verdant Mead,
And Boys in flow'ry Bands the Tyger lead;
The Steer and Lion at one Crib shall meet;

68 See] Sees *1712*.

DB (35:1) reads: "The desert and the land without passage shal be glad, & the wildernes shal reioyce & shal florish as the lilie." AV mentions only the rose. For verse 7, see preceding note.

Wakefield notes that this "part of the poem is highly animated and picturesque, to which the use of the *present tense* essentially contributes: and the effect of an unexpected circumstance is admirably pointed out by the word *starts* in verse sixty-nine." See Intro., p. 106.

71. Cf. *Comus*, 517: "rifted Rocks whose entrance leads to hell."

73. *sandy Vallies*] Ch. 41. v. 19. *and* Ch. 55. v. 13. [P. *1712–51*.]

perplex'd] Intricate, entangled. Cf. Dryden, *Sigismonda and Guiscardo*, 143: "the wood perplex'd with thorns".

77. *The Lambs with Wolves*, &c.] VIRG. E. 4. v. 21.

> Ipsæ lacte domum referent distenta capellæ
> Ubera, nec magnos metuent armenta leones——
> Occidet & serpens, & fallax herba veneni
> Occidet.———

The goats shall bear to the fold their udders distended with milk: nor shall the herds be afraid of the greatest lions. The serpents shall die, and the herb that conceals poison shall die.

ISAIAH, Ch. 11. v. 6 ⟨v. 16 *1717*, *1720b*, *1736a–51*, an obvious misprint.⟩ &c. *The wolf shall dwell with the lamb, and the leopard shall lie down with the kid, and the calf and the young lion and the fatling together; and a little child shall lead them——And the lion shall eat straw like the ox. And the sucking child shall play on the hole of the asp, and the weaned child shall put his hand on the den of the cockatrice.* [P. *1717*, *1720b*, *1736a–51*.]

77. *The Lambs*] Ch. 11. v. 6, 7, 8. [P. *1712–51*.]

And harmless Serpents lick the Pilgrim's Feet.   80
The smiling Infant in his Hand shall take
The crested Basilisk and speckled Snake;
Pleas'd, the green Lustre of the Scales survey,
And with their forky Tongue shall innocently play.
Rise, crown'd with Light, Imperial *Salem* rise!   85
Exalt thy Tow'ry Head, and lift thy Eyes!

84 Tongue shall innocently play.] Tongue, and pointless Sting
shall play. *1712–32.*

---

80. Ch. 65, v. 25. [P. *1717–51.*]
DB reads: "The wulfe and the lambe shal feede together, the lion and the
oxe shal eate straw: & to the serpent dust shal be his bread: they shal not
hurt . . ." EC recall the transformation of Cadmus and his wife into mild and
harmless snakes (Ovid, *Met.*, IV 505, 602).

82. *Basilisk*] A fabulous reptile (Lat. *basiliscus*) characterized by a crest on its
head. DB (30:6) has *basiliscus*, AV has *viper*. The words *Basilisk* and *Cockatrice*
were often used interchangeably, and both AV and DB use *cockatrice* at 11:8.

84. An Alexandrine. Wakefield conjectures that Pope altered the line when
he learned that the sting of a serpent is not in its tail. Pope may have been misled by Dryden. Cf. *Æn.*, XI 1112: "And shoots her forky Tongue, and whisks
her threat'ning Tail". Wakefield also compares the new reading to Dryden's
Palamon and Arcite, III 98: "And Troops of Lions innocently play." Cf. Pope's
version of Psalm XCI, 16 (vol. VI, p. 69).

85. *Rise, crown'd with Light, &c.*] The thoughts of *Isaiah*, which compose the
latter part ⟨thoughts that follow to the end *1717, 1720b*⟩ of the Poem, are
wonderfully elevated, and much above those general exclamations of *Virgil*
which make the loftiest parts of his *Pollio*.

> *Magnus ab integro sæclorum nascitur ordo!*
> ————*toto surget gens aurea mundo!*
> ————*incipient magni procedere menses!*
> *Aspice, venturo lætentur ut omnia sæclo! &c.*
>
> ⟨ll. 5, 9, 12, 52⟩

The reader needs only turn ⟨to turn *1751*⟩ to the passages of *Isaiah*, here cited
⟨as they are cited in the margins of the preceding Eclogue. *1717, 1720b*⟩.

[P. *1717, 1720b, 1736a–51.*]

85. *Rise, crown'd*] Ch. 60. v. 1. [P. *1712–51.*]
AV and DB are very similar.
Salem] Σαλήμ was thought to be an ancient name of Jerusalem.

86. *thy Eyes*] Wakefield objects to the "open vowel". Both AV and DB (see
Isaiah, 60:4) have "thine".

See, a long Race thy spatious Courts adorn;
See future Sons, and Daughters yet unborn
In crowding Ranks on ev'ry Side arise,
Demanding Life, impatient for the Skies!   90
See barb'rous Nations at thy Gates attend,
Walk in thy Light, and in thy Temple bend.
See thy bright Altars throng'd with prostrate Kings,
And heap'd with Products of *Sabæan* Springs!
For thee, *Idume*'s spicy Forests blow;   95
And Seeds of Gold in *Ophyr*'s Mountains glow.
See Heav'n its sparkling Portals wide display,
And break upon thee in a Flood of Day!
No more the rising *Sun* shall gild the Morn,

---

87. *a long Race*] Ch. 60. v. 4. [P. *1712–51*.]
In the immediately following lines Pope is closer to DB: "Lift vp thine eies round about, and see al these are gathered together, they are come to thee: thy sonnes shal come from a farre, & thy daughters shal rise from the side." AV has: ". . . thy daughters shall be nursed at thy side."
90. Wakefield cites *Aen.*, vi 749–51:
> Lethaeum ad fluvium deus evocat agmine magno,
> scilicet immemores supera ut convexa revisant,
> rursus et incipiant in corpora velle reverti,
and Pope's parody of the same lines in *Dunciad* A, iii 21–2 (vol. v, p. 152).
91*f.* Ch. 60. v. 3. ⟨Ibid. v. 3. *1712.*⟩ [P. *1712–51*.]
DB has: "And the Gentiles shal walke in thy light, and kings in the brightnes of thy rising." AV has: ". . . come to thy light".
94. *Sabæan Springs*] Ch. 60. v. 6. ⟨Ibid. v. 6. *1712.*⟩ [P. *1712–51*.]
DB reads: ". . . al of Saba shal come, bringing gold and frakincense [sic]: and shewing forth prayse to our Lord." Saba (Sheba in AV) was famous for its gold and incense. Wakefield compares Dryden, *Aureng-Zebe*, iv 102: "What Sweets soe'er *Sabean* Springs disclose."
95. *Idume*] The Greek equivalent of Edom, a region to the south of Palestine. There seems to be no reference to it in the Bible as a place where spicy forests were to be found. Virgil's "molles sua tura Sabaei" (*Georgics* i 57) is translated by Dryden, l. 86: "And soft *Idume* weeps her od'rous Tears."
96. *Ophyr*] A place celebrated in antiquity for its gold, but whether it was in Africa, Arabia, or the Far East remains uncertain. Gold was popularly believed to ripen, plant-like, within the earth.
99. *No more the rising Sun*] Ch. 60. v. 19, 20 ⟨Ibid. v. 19. 20. *1712.*⟩ [P. *1712–51*.]
AV and DB are much alike.

Nor Evening *Cynthia* fill her silver Horn,   100
But lost, dissolv'd in thy superior Rays;
One Tyde of Glory, one unclouded Blaze,
O'erflow thy Courts: The LIGHT HIMSELF shall shine
Reveal'd; and *God*'s eternal Day be thine!
The Seas shall waste; the Skies in Smoke decay;   105
Rocks fall to Dust, and Mountains melt away;
But fix'd *His* Word, *His* saving Pow'r remains:
Thy *Realm* for ever lasts! thy own *Messiah* reigns!

---

99 *f.* Wakefield compares Ovid's description of the beginning of the world (*Met.*, I 10–11),

> nullus adhuc mundo praebebat lumina Titan,
> nec nova crescendo reparabat cornua Phoebe,

and Sandys's tr., 10: "Now waxing *Phœbe* fill'd her waned hornes."

104. *eternal Day be thine*] Wakefield compares Dryden, *To the pious Memory of . . . Mrs. Anne Killigrew*, 14–15:

> Thou wilt have time enough for Hymns Divine,
> Since Heaven's Eternal Year is thine.

106. *melt away*] Ch. 51. v. 6. *and* Ch. 54. v. 10. [P. *1712–51.*]
The word *melt* suggests that Pope used DB (51:6): ". . . the heauens shal melt as smoke, and the earth shal be worne away as a garment . . . but my saluation shal be for euer, and my iustice shal not faile." AV has: "the heavens shall vanish away like smoke. . ."

108. *thy own Messiah reigns*] Virgil, *Ecl.* IV 10: "tuus iam regnat Apollo."

WINDSOR-FOREST

INTRODUCTION

I: PERIOD OF COMPOSITION

ON February 23, 1713, the publisher Bernard Lintot paid Pope the sum of £32 5s. od. for his *Windsor-Forest*,[1] and two weeks later, on March 7, the poem was published. One of several poems written in celebration of the eagerly-awaited Peace, *Windsor-Forest* made its appearance only a few weeks before the treaties of peace were signed at Utrecht on April 11.

Over twenty years later, in a note to l. 1 of the poem in the 1736 edition of his *Works*, Pope stated that *Windsor-Forest* "was written at two different times: the first part of it which relates to the country, in the year 1704, at the same time with the Pastorals: the latter part was not added till the year 1710, in which it was publish'd." 1710 as the year of publication was an obvious error, yet it was not until the Warburton edition of 1751 that the date for the "latter part" of the poem was changed to 1713.

A MS of the poem which differs in many ways from the first printed text, and which dates from 1712, still exists.[2] It contains the following memorandum, written by Pope in a hand apparently later than that of the poetic text: "This Poem ⟨was writ mostly in ye year⟩ was written just after ye Pastorals as appears by ye last verse of it. ⟨The author was then⟩ That was in ye year when ye author was   years of age. But the last hundred lines ⟨beginning with⟩ including ye Celebration of ye Peace, were added in ye year
1   soon after ye Ratification of ye Treaty at Utrecht —— It was

---

1. John Nichols, *Literary Anecdotes of the Eighteenth Century* (1814), VIII 300.

2. The MS is reproduced in facsimile in Robert M. Schmitz's *Pope's Windsor Forest 1712, A Study of the Washington University Holograph* (1952). The MS was given by Pope to Jonathan Richardson the younger, and was later used by Warburton and EC. According to EC (I 323–4), Richardson transcribed variant readings from the MS into his copy of the 1717 quarto along with this note: "Altered from the first copy of the author's own hand, written out beautifully, as usual, for the perusal and criticism of his friends". Even in Richardson's time the MS was incomplete, ending, as it still does, at l. 386. Before the publication of his own study, Dr Schmitz very kindly lent a photograph of the MS to the editors of the present volume.

first printed in folio in 1   Again in folio yᵉ same year, & ⟨after-
wards⟩ in Octavo yᵉ next."[1] The hesitations here show plainly that
when Pope wrote the memorandum, probably as a first draft of the
note for l. 1 of the 1736 edition, his recollection of dates and events
was far from certain. In the note as it was finally printed, he assigned part of the poem to 1704, the "same time" as the *Pastorals*, while
the MS memorandum places the poem "after yᵉ Pastorals". In the
printed note he ascribed the latter part of the poem to 1710, before
the signing of the Treaty; in the MS he dates this part of the poem
"soon after" the Treaty. The hesitations, and the contradictions
revealed in the different versions of the note, make it impossible for
one to accept completely Pope's own testimony about the composition of his poem.

We do know that the poem existed in some form in 1707, before
the *Pastorals* were published. On October 28, 1707, the Rev. Ralph
Bridges wrote to his uncle, Sir William Trumbull, that Pope intended to print his *Pastorals* the following spring,[2] and that one of
them was to be dedicated to Sir William. If not one of these, adds
Bridges, "the verses upon Windsor Forest are to be dedicated to
you."[3] The dedication of *Windsor-Forest* to Trumbull would certainly have been appropriate, for after the poem was published Sir
William wrote to Bridges that he "had long since put him [Pope]
upon this subject."[4]

---

1. The two folio editions of 1713 are Griffith 9 and 10. As for the octavo edition of 1714, Griffith (1 i 33) wonders whether Pope refers to the 2nd edn of
Lintot's *Miscellany* (1714, Griffith 32), or to an unknown edition of the poem.

2. The *Pastorals* were finally published in May, 1709.

3. *Hist. MSS Comm.: Report on the MSS of the Marquess of Downshire*, 1 ii 853.

4. The full context of this statement, preserved in a transcript of a portion of
Trumbull's letter (in the Bodleian Library, MS Eng. letters d. 59), is interesting.
Dated May 12, 1713, the transcription reads: "As to our friend Mr. Pope, I
should have commended his Poem on Windsor Forest much more, if he had not
servᵈ. me a slippery Trick. For you must know, I had long since put him upon
this subject, gave severall hints & at last wⁿ. he brought it & read it, & made
some little Alterations &c. not one word of putting in my Name 'till I found it
in Print." If Trumbull is disturbed here, it would seem to be because he was
mentioned, without his permission, in *Windsor-Forest*, not because it was dedicated to another man. A copy of the transcript of his letter was made available
to the editors by the kindness of Professor George Sherburn. See "New Anecdotes about Alexander Pope", *N & Q*, N.S., v (Aug., 1958), pp. 343–8.

Having dedicated *Spring* to Trumbull when he published his *Pastorals*, Pope must have felt that he had done his duty by his old friend. Even so, Trumbull's memory remains inseparable from *Windsor-Forest* and the early history of its composition. Around 1700, when Pope was twelve years old, the poet's family left London to settle in the small village of Binfield, in the district known as Windsor Forest. Shortly before this, Trumbull had retired to his family estate at Easthampstead Park, which lay only a mile or so from the Pope household. It is impossible to say exactly when the friendship between the old statesman and the young poet began, but many years later Pope printed a letter dated 1705 in which Trumbull thanked him for the loan of a volume of Milton's poems.[1] The boy became Trumbull's favourite companion, and was called by him, with affectionate irony, his "little neighbour, but a great Poet".[2] Later in life Pope told Spence that "It was while I lived in the Forest, that I got so well acquainted with Sir William Trumbull, who loved very much to read and talk of the classics in his retirement. We used to take a ride out together, three or four days in the week, and at last, almost every day".[3]

It may have been on one of these jaunts that Trumbull suggested to Pope a poem on the Forest, perhaps in the manner of *Cooper's Hill*. Certainly Trumbull was in a position to supply Pope with valuable information about the Forest and the Forest Laws, for he held the office of verderer, and the "forest trees and underwood" in Windsor Forest were therefore under his care. Too, it was perhaps in Sir William's library that Pope gained access to some of the old chronicles which were of great use to his poem.[4]

We know nothing at all of the version of the poem which may have existed, on the evidence of Pope's note, in 1704, or of the version which Bridges mentions in 1707, and in view of the extent and kind of revision normally practised by Pope, attempts to reconstruct such an early version appear to be ill-advised and useless. Scholars have been led by Pope's 1736 note to assume that during the year preceding the Peace the poet suddenly recalled his juvenile work on the Forest, and then hastily decided to attach to its "pas-

---

1. *Corr.*, I 10.
2. *Hist. MSS Comm.: Report on the MSS of the Marquess of Downshire*, I ii 852.
3. Spence, p. 194. 4. See notes to ll. 43.*ff.*

toral simplicity" a politically inspired conclusion. In the light of
all the evidence, including that of the MS, such an explanation of
the poem's development seems much too simple.

On May 20, 1712, Lintot advertised in the *Spectator* a volume
entitled *Miscellaneous Poems and Translations, by Several Hands*. It now
seems clear that Pope was the anonymous editor of the volume,[1]
but of more immediate concern is the fact that in the first edition
of this miscellany thirty-two pages (321–52), signatures Y and Z,
are omitted. In the second edition of 1714 the missing pages are restored, taken up with *Windsor-Forest* and the *Ode for Musick*, but
they differ from the other pages in the volume in that they have
two or three more lines to each page. A reasonable, if by no means
certain, conclusion appears to be that at some time prior to the
spring of 1712 Pope had prepared a version of *Windsor-Forest* for
publication. From what we know of his practice, this was probably
an extensively revised version of the poem on the Forest he said he
wrote near the time of the *Pastorals*. Shortly before publication of
the miscellany, but after both *Windsor-Forest* and the *Ode for Musick*
had been printed on the missing sheets, Pope may have been persuaded either by political or financial considerations, perhaps both,
to adapt his poem to the circumstances of the approaching Peace
and to give it, and the *Ode for Musick*, separate publication in folio.
Then when the second edition of the miscellany was printed the
two poems were apparently restored to their original places, but
with some crowding of the lines on each page because of the additions that Pope had made to *Windsor-Forest*.

If the above circumstances are correctly explained it would appear that throughout the greater part of 1712[2] Pope was busy with
revisions and additions to a version of *Windsor-Forest* which had
been prepared (again, probably, with much revision and addition)
for publication during the previous year. In October of 1712
Thomas Tickell published his poem *On the Prospect of Peace*, and in
a letter to Caryll on November 29 Pope commends the poem for
its versification. He mentions several passages, and quotes one (ll.

---

1. The evidence for this, and the argument of this paragraph as a whole, is to
be found in N. Ault's *New Light on Pope* (1949), chap. II.

2. From May, when the miscellany was published, to February, 1713, when
the poem was sent to Lintot.

194–201) in which is found the "description of the several parts of the world in regard to our trade: which had interfered with some lines of my own in the poem called Windsor Forrest, tho' written before I saw his". He asks for Caryll's "sincere judgment whether I ought not to strike out mine, either as they seem too like his, or as they are inferior".[1] The letter suggests that by this time Pope had written a draft at least of the latter portion of his poem, even the last paragraph of it.

Caryll must have seen an earlier version of the poem, perhaps the one prepared for the miscellany of May, 1712, for on December 5 Pope writes that "*Windsor Forest* has undergone many alterations, and received many additions since you saw it, but has not yet been out of my hands to any man . . ."[2] Two weeks later he tells Caryll that in the midst of a winter which sets his "very imagination a shivering, I am endeavouring to raise up round about me a painted scene of woods and forests in verdure and beauty, trees springing, fields flowering, Nature laughing", and he adds that he does not yet know when *Windsor-Forest* "will come out".[3] Finally, some time in February,[4] he tells Caryll "I have just sent the poem of *Windsor Forest* to the press", and mentions again a version of the poem seen by Caryll at some previous time.

The MS that has come down to us appears to date from late 1712 or early 1713. It is an example of Pope's superb craftsmanship in lettering, and probably was carefully prepared for circulation among literary friends and patrons. The care lavished on it would seem to indicate that it was prepared after the work of revision and addition Pope described to Caryll during the months of November and December. Even so, the poet had not finished his labours. The fine writing of the MS is marred, in the earlier as well as later portions of the poem, by interlinear additions and substitutions, by erasures and deletions. There are, moreover, so many differences

---

1. *Corr.*, 1 157.

2. *Corr.*, 1 162. Cf. Pope's statement (*Corr.*, 1 173) to Caryll that he "was at the same time both glad and ashamed to find (when we were at Old Windsor) that you had more lines than one of that poem [*Windsor-Forest*] by heart." The date of the meeting at Old Windsor has not been determined.

3. *Corr.*, 1 168. One supposes, though perhaps wrongly, that "painted scene" refers to *Windsor-Forest*.

4. *Corr.*, 1 173.

between the MS and the first printed text that we must conclude that Pope either sent an even later MS to the printer, or made extensive corrections (adding over twenty completely new lines, and dropping over thirty lines[1]) in proof stage. One may recall that Pope said of himself, "I corrected because it was as pleasant to me to correct as to write."[2]

Pope told Spence that George Granville, Lord Lansdowne, "insisted on my publishing my Windsor Forest, and the motto (*non injussa cano*), shows it."[3] One may suppose from this that it was Lansdowne who encouraged Pope to give his poem its final form, and that Pope therefore felt he had good reason to dedicate *Windsor-Forest* to him rather than to Trumbull. Lansdowne had been interested in Pope for several years, perhaps since 1706, the date of a fragmentary letter in which he speaks of Pope as "a young Poet, newly inspir'd", who "promises Miracles".[4] In addition, Pope had made in his *Pastorals* (*Spring*, l. 46) a flattering allusion to "*Granville*'s moving Lays".[5] Since the early days of their acquaintance Granville had risen rapidly in the political world. He had replaced Walpole in 1710 as Secretary for War, and he was one of the twelve new peers created on January 1, 1712, by Queen Anne in the stroke that saved the Tory ministry and the Peace. Pope must have felt that the dedication of *Windsor-Forest* belonged to the man who had "commanded" a poem on the Peace, and who indeed was a member of the ministry that had negotiated that Peace.

On January 10, 1713, Pope wrote to Lansdowne to thank him for the permission given to dedicate the poem to him,[6] and two months later *Windsor-Forest* was published. It did not enjoy the immediate popularity of Tickell's *On the Prospect of Peace*,[7] perhaps

---

1. See Schmitz, op. cit., p. 62.

2. See Pope's *Preface*, p. 6, above. In his *Lives of the English Poets* (ed. G. B. Hill, 1905, III 218), Johnson noted of Pope that to "make verses was his first labour, and to mend them was his last."

3. Spence, p. 202. Cf. l. 5 of the poem.

4. Lansdowne, *Works* (1732), I 437.

5. Lansdowne is one of those mentioned by Pope as having seen the MS of the *Pastorals*. See Intro. to the *Pastorals*, p. 38, above.

6. *Corr.*, I 172.

7. Six editions of Tickell's poem were issued within two years of publication; *Windsor-Forest* went into three editions in its first two years.

because the latter was praised by Addison in *Spectator* 523 (Oct. 30, 1712). Yet there can be no doubt as to the superior merit of Pope's poem, and there were those who at the time recognized its value. Two days after the poem appeared, Swift wrote to Stella: "Mr Pope has publishd a fine Poem calld Windsor Forrest; read it."[1]

II: THE POEM AND ITS BACKGROUND

I

A critical commonplace that has blighted most discussions of *Windsor-Forest*[2] is the notion that the poem is composed of two distinct and maladjusted parts. In this view the first portion of the poem, down to about l. 290, is essentially a juvenile work of "pastoral simplicity", one to which Pope, in 1712, attached a conclusion that is little more than a piece of Tory political propaganda.

The inspiration for such a view of *Windsor-Forest* has been Pope himself, for when he said in his 1736 note that he had written the poem at two different times, in 1704 and 1710, and that the first part related "to the country", he both suggested and seemed to justify ideas of the poem's disunity, especially to critics who did not inquire very deeply into the principles of its composition or into the sources and models used by Pope. As we have seen, however, all the evidence relating to the composition of the poem, including that of the MS, points to comprehensive revision of the poem, throughout its entire length, down to the very moment of publication. We know too that a "date of composition" for a poem by Pope is nearly always a highly relative and tentative matter: with him creation was usually a continuing process that might extend over a period of several years and endure numerous interruptions.[3] Nothing, in fact, that we do know of the poet who about this time was making the additions to the *Rape of the Lock* would suggest that Pope did not endeavour to make *Windsor-Forest* all of a piece. In all probability, Pope in the note merely indulged, as he did so often, his desire to

---

1. *Journal to Stella*, ed. Sir Harold Williams (1948), II 635.
2. But see the discussions by Maynard Mack, in *College English*, VII (1945–6), pp. 263–73, and by Earl Wasserman, in *The Subtler Language* (1959), chap. IV.
3. See Intro. to *An Essay on Criticism*, pp. 197–202, below.

appear to have been remarkably precocious. Any other interpretation of his words seems clearly denied by the relationship in which
Windsor-Forest stands to other poems of the same kind.

In the creation of *Windsor-Forest* Pope drew upon a particularly
rich and various background of both classical and native materials.
The *Georgics* and *Pollio* of Virgil, the *Mosella* of Ausonius, the *Metamorphoses* of Ovid, are used to impart to the poem a sense of "glades,
fables, and hexameters",[1] while the Bible, Spenser, Drayton, Denham, Waller, Milton, along with Camden and the Anglo-Saxon
chronicler, are used to impart to the poem suggestions not only of
English landscape and history, but also those of Christian tradition
and prophecy. Like the England it celebrates, the poem is sustained
by a rich and far-flung commerce.

With all its rich remembrance of things past, however, *Windsor-
Forest* is yet a poem of a distinct type, the nearest analogies for
which are to be found in Virgil's *Georgics* and Denham's *Cooper's
Hill*. That Pope's poem stands in some relationship to these works
has long been recognized, but what does not seem to have been
grasped is the way in which *Windsor-Forest* unites the native materials of *Cooper's Hill* to the themes and strategies of Virgil's poem.
The movement of Pope's poem from the shades and glades of Windsor Forest to the villas and public buildings of London and to the
"Golden Days" inaugurated by Queen Anne is nothing less than
a direct imitation of the way Virgil in the *Georgics* moves "from
crops to towns and from the works of men to the men themselves,
the older heroes and the hero [Augustus] of the age, in which the
golden days of Saturn have come again."[2] Pope's subject, too, is
the same as Virgil's: his country's "need of peace, well typified by
the simplicity of rural life."[3]

Denham's *Cooper's Hill* is a species of "local poetry", full of description and topography. It is also full of English political history,
for the discussion of which the scenery serves mainly as an inspiration. Because of this, it is the more surprising that those who find
the early portion of *Windsor-Forest* to be "pure pastoral" also find
the model for this portion to be *Cooper's Hill*. Moral and political
reflection on Henry VIII's destruction of monastic life is as much

---

1. Geoffrey Tillotson, *On the Poetry of Pope* (1950), p. 89.
2. E. K. Rand, *The Magical Art of Virgil* (1931), p. 235.   3. Ibid., p. 220.

a part of Denham's poem as the stag hunt (itself in great part a fable of the course of political life), while the conclusion of the poem is as direct a sample of political moralizing as one might hope to find. And if Denham's blend of politics and poetry were not example enough, Pope could have found, and evidently did find, further precedent in such poems as Waller's *On St. James's Park* and Otway's *Windsor Castle*.

It is not simply by precedent alone, however, that Pope's fusion of the scenic, the moral, and the political is to be understood and justified. Pope was writing in a time when a vast system of analogical correspondences between God and man and nature was still in force. This system "assumed that God, expressing Himself in all creation", had "made the physical, moral, and spiritual levels analogous to each other and to Himself."[1] And because this was felt to be true, man, when he scanned the book of creation, could there discover analogues to his own moral and political experiences. Because all the links in the Chain of Being were similar, "joy and grief" could be "read in trees and plants", and "precepts of morality" could be "insinuated by reference to 'those Faculties in the Souls of Brutes, which bear an Analogy to the Will and Passions . . .' "[2] This analogous relationship between all things enabled the imagination to discover, rather than merely to fabricate, similitudes between the natural world on the one hand, and the moral and political worlds on the other. In a poem like *Windsor-Forest* one cannot expect, nor does one often find, purely descriptive scenes of nature: the setting of the poem is always offering its analogue to human experience. It is not simply that the poem offers one a scene from nature and then injects into it a moral or ethical prescription; the two elements are rather fused in the one act of perception, for the poet in this instance is discovering meanings inherent in nature, not adding one thing to another.

In the light of this view of nature it is irrelevant, and a complete misunderstanding of *Windsor-Forest*, to praise Pope for having written something called "pure pastoral" down to l. 290 of his poem,

1. Earl R. Wasserman, 'Nature Moralized: The Divine Analogy in the Eighteenth Century', *ELH*, xx (1953), p. 40.
2. Ibid., p. 42. The discussion in this paragraph is indebted to Professor Wasserman's essay.

and then to scold him for having spoiled it all by adding a syco-
phantic political conclusion. As any close study of the poem will
reveal, the early descriptions of the "nature" about Windsor are
always reflecting the divine or human orders of existence: the first
long verse paragraph, ll. 7–42, reflects not only the order and variety
of a cosmos governed by God, but also the peace and plenty of a
kingdom governed by a Stuart queen. Because the moral and political realms are implicit in the poem from its start, it is rather pointless to speak of them as being "added" at the end. The poem does
move from the country to the court, from the rural world of "Sylvan
War" to the political world of warring nations, but it is a movement
upward through a chain of hierarchical correspondences, the lowest link of which is represented by the country life about Windsor,
and the highest by the political life of the nation and the world at
large.

We shall better understand the kind of poetry Pope wrote in the
earlier portion of *Windsor-Forest*, and also the relation of this portion to the poem's conclusion, if we approach it in terms of Pope's
own understanding of the "Art" of *Cooper's Hill*. Speaking, in the
notes to his translation of the *Iliad*, of Homer's "indirect and oblique manner of introducing moral Sentences and Instructions . . .
even in Descriptions and poetical Parts, where one naturally expects only Painting and Amusement", Pope goes on: "I must do a
noble *English* Poet the justice to observe, that it is this particular
Art that is the very distinguishing Excellence of *Cooper's-Hill*:
throughout which, the Descriptions of Places, and Images rais'd
by the Poet, are still tending to some Hint, or leading into some
Reflection, upon moral Life or political Institution: Much in the
same manner as the real Sight of such Scenes and Prospects is apt
to give the Mind a compos'd Turn, and incline it to Thoughts and
Contemplations that have a Relation to the Object."[1]

1. *Iliad*, Bk XVI, 466*n*. One should perhaps note also the following observation
from Spence, pp. 281–3: "At the end of his Cooper's Hill, (edition of 1709) Mr.
Pope had written the following note.—'This poem was first printed without the
author's name, in 1643. In that edition a great number of verses are to be found,
since entirely omitted; and very many others, since corrected and improved.
Some few, the author afterwards added: and in particular the four celebrated
lines on the Thames . . . all with admirable judgment; and the whole read together is a very strong proof of what Mr. Waller says:

It was not in *Cooper's Hill* alone, however, that Pope discovered the art he was to make the "distinguishing Excellence" of his own poem. An art similar to that described by Pope was thought by many in the age to characterize Virgil's *Georgics*, the poem that moved, as *Windsor-Forest* was to move, from long "descriptions" of the "country" to soaring celebrations of a contemporary ruler and a national destiny. In an essay Pope could not have failed to read, the *Essay on Virgil's Georgics* to be found in all contemporary editions of Dryden's *Virgil*, Addison had described the art of the *Georgics* in these words: "But this kind of Poetry . . . addresses it self wholly to the imagination. . . It raises in our minds a pleasing variety of scenes and landscapes, whilst it teaches us; and makes the dryest of its precepts look like a description. . . This way of writing . . . is particularly practised by *Virgil*, who loves to suggest a truth indirectly, and without giving us a full and open view of it, to let us see just so much as will naturally lead the imagination into all the parts that lie concealed."[1]

II

In selecting the "Scenes and Prospects" about Windsor as the geographical foundation of his poem Pope provided himself with an area rich in the kind of associations which might lead the mind to reflections "upon moral Life or political Institutions". When Edward III reconstructed Windsor Castle as a meeting place for his newly established Order of Knights of the Garter, he was governed in his choice of the site by an ancient legend which held that it was on this spot that King Arthur sat with his Knights of the Round Table. The very conception of a "forest", stressed as it is in the poem and its title, is important, for, as Pope must have known, the word did not mean merely a "wood". It was a legal rather than a topographical term, and referred specifically to land outside (*foris*) the common law. Such land was subject to a special law which aimed at setting aside and preserving certain territory

---

> Poets lose half the praise they should have got,
> Could it be known what they discreetly blot'."

Pope's words might easily stand as an account of his own successive revisions in *Windsor-Forest*.

1. Dryden's *Virgil* (2nd edn, 1698), pp. 97–8.

for the king's recreation, whether by the chase or otherwise. This territory would contain not merely woods, but lawns and fruitful pastures and green retreats. Most important, however, was the position that Windsor and its Castle occupied as the centre of much of English history, and as the repository, second only to Westminster Abbey, for the bodies of those monarchs who made that history. With these associations Windsor Forest could serve to mirror England and its national life, recall its past, and perhaps suggest its future.

The political tenor his poem is to have is announced by Pope in the first two lines: the groves and green retreats of Windsor are "At once the Monarch's and the Muse's Seats". The emphasis designed here is made clearer when we know that the lines directly imitate, with one significant difference, the opening lines of Charles Hopkins's sequence of amatory pieces, *The History of Love* (1695):

> Ye Woods, and Wilds, serene and blest retreats,
> At once the Lovers, and the Muses seats.

By so terse a change as "Monarch's" for "Lovers" Pope suggests clearly the way his poem diverges from typical pieces of pastoral courtship. Indeed, he goes further, for in the next two lines, with his command to the sylvan nymphs to "Unlock [their] Springs", he associates his poem directly with a crucial passage in the second Georgic, where Virgil announces that he will dare to unseal the sacred founts and sing the praises of Italy, the "land of Saturn, great mother of earth's fruits, great mother of men".[1]

Immediately following the invocation Pope presents a generalized picture of England which suggests that, under the reign of Anne, a kind of Golden Age has been achieved, one very like the one Virgil celebrates in his account of Italy under Augustus. Here the literary associations, both Christian and pagan, are particularly rich. Eden is recalled, with all the wealth and order in variety that God had placed in it and Milton had celebrated.[2] Windsor

---

1. Ll. 173–6. The editors follow the translation by H. R. Fairclough in the Loeb Classical Library edn of Virgil, 1 129.

2. Pope's celebration of England in terms of Eden and the golden age is discussed by Maynard Mack, 'On Reading Pope', *College English*, VII, pp. 263 ff. The editors wish to acknowledge a general debt to Professor Mack's essay.

Forest becomes an analogue for England, and also a microcosm of the larger world, and all things exist in it in a harmonious profusion. Even the weeping amber and balmy trees of India, "borne" on the "Oaks" of English shipping, are to be found here. This is Pope's ingenious conversion of lines taken from Virgil's account of the Golden Age in the *Pollio*, where it is said that the "stubborn oak shall distil dewy honey" and that "every land shall bear all fruits".[1] Pan and Pomona are here, not as deities of a creed outworn, but as they are exemplified in their blessings, the flocks and fruits. But though the waving grain and the fruit "tempt the joyful Reaper's Hand", the picture is not one of an Eden or Golden Age perfectly re-achieved, where toil would be totally absent. It is rather the golden age depicted in the *Georgics*, one achieved by peaceful and industrious toil, a conception Virgil took from Hesiod. Pope therefore concludes his picture of England at peace with an image of Industry, an Industry which "sits smiling on the Plains".

Pope concludes this first long paragraph with the statement that all this "Peace and Plenty tell, a STUART reigns." The full political implications of this line, as indeed of the whole paragraph, are often completely ignored. They may be illuminated by the fact that in 1607 James I, the first Stuart, set before his Parliament a vision of an era of "Peace, Plenty, Love", an era to be achieved as the result of a union of the two great nations of England and Scotland.[2] A hundred years later, in 1707, another Stuart, Queen Anne, had given the royal assent to the Act which did unite the two countries, and thereby realized, one may suppose, the era prophesied so long before. In any event, the resemblance of the whole paragraph to the *Georgics*, II 136–76, leaves little doubt that Pope is celebrating here the rule of Anne as Virgil had celebrated that of Augustus and, in the fourth Eclogue, the consulship of Pollio. In the Tory bias of the whole passage there is as much political propaganda, if such it must be called, as in any passage in the last hundred lines of *Windsor-Forest*.

From the green and pleasant land of contemporary England as it is imaged in Windsor Forest Pope turns, in his next paragraph,

---

1. Eclogue IV, ll. 30, 39, Loeb trans.
2. See *Journals of the House of Commons*, I 360. Professor Geoffrey Tillotson directed the editors to this speech by James I.

F

to a grim England of the past. The events of this passage are all associated with another geographical area: the scene here, it is important to note, is not the Forest of Windsor, but the New Forest of Hampshire. In this new setting Pope presents the Iron Age of England, a portrait of an era that is quite the reverse of any conception of "pastoral simplicity". Here again the landscape reflects the character of its rulers. It is an age of the sword rather than of the plough, and the land teems, not with harvests and flocks, but with weeds and wild beasts. The association of the Norman kings with Nimrod, King of Babylon, the first hunter and type of the tyrant, recalls the period after the Flood when violence and cruelty prevailed over the earth. The whole passage also reflects closely the curse laid upon Babylon by God in chapter 13 of Isaiah: "But wild beasts of the desert shall lie there; and their houses shall be full of doleful creatures; and owls shall dwell there. . . And the wild beasts of the islands shall cry in their desolate houses, and dragons in their pleasant palaces." Yet amidst the cruel violence in the waste land here described an element of divine justice is to be found. For Pope, following his sources in Camden and the Anglo-Saxon chronicler, sees the deaths of William's sons as acts of divine vengeance: those who live by the sword are shown to die by it.[1]

The dark and gloomy past of England under the Norman kings has its counterpart too in the past of Rome as it is presented in the *Georgics*. When great Caesar died, lofty cities echoed "all the night with the howl of wolves",[2] and the country was plunged into civil war. Pope seems indebted also to the great plague scene at the end of the third Georgic, where men are shown as reduced to the status of beasts, and deer are said to stray about the houses.[3] But while Virgil looks back upon civil war and implores Augustus to restore peace to a chaotic world,[4] Pope can say, in the conclusion of this paragraph, that in England the face and character of the land have been restored to order by monarchs who "heard the Subjects Cries", and by a Queen who, in the role of "Fair *Liberty*", leads in the "golden Years" of a Peace she herself has ordained.

In the *Georgics* Virgil arranges a number of scenes in vivid counterpoint, concluding Georgic I, for example, with a picture of war and chaos, and Georgic II with an account of the simple, yet pro-

---

1. See ll. 79–84*n*.   2. I 485–6, Loeb trans.   3. III 534–40.   4. I 461–end.

found, pleasures of rural peace. Pope adopts the same procedure, and also follows Virgil's art of transferring "significant details from one context to its opposite for the sake of contrast."[1] For the bleak violence of the hunting scenes in the New Forest he therefore fashions a companion piece, the more happy hunting scenes in Windsor Forest which immediately follow. The contexts are different, but the activities—those of the hunt and the chase—are the same, and the similarities are as important as the differences. We should be much mistaken if we looked upon the hunting scenes of Windsor as examples of innocent pastoral exuberance, for throughout these seasonal scenes Pope tries repeatedly to reveal the likeness of the passions of the chase to the passions of war, and to show how the violence of the one is an analogue for the violence of the other. The Normans turned, like Nimrod, from the pursuit of the beasts to the pursuit of men, and then like beasts they themselves were shot down. In the scenes of country sport about Windsor the pattern is merely reversed. The age-old inclinations to violence and cruelty are not shown as having departed from men: they are merely pictured as contained, and expended, within the bounds of activities to which Pope gives the name, at l. 148, of "Sylvan War". The excitements of the chase are here shown as providing man with a "moral substitute for war",[2] and it is this fact that explains the many military metaphors with which these hunting scenes abound. Thus, for the simple pastime of netting partridges, Pope provides the reader with a simile that recalls the siege and capture of some rich, and peaceful, city by British troops:

> Thus (if small Things we may with great compare)
> When *Albion* sends her eager Sons to War,
> Some thoughtless Town, with Ease and Plenty blest,
> Near, and more near, the closing Lines invest;
> Sudden they seize th'amaz'd, defenceless Prize,
> And high in Air *Britannia*'s Standard flies.

The analogy between these two kinds of "war", and the poem's

---

1. Rand, op. cit., p. 218.
2. The idea that men had the need of a "moral substitute for war", and that this need could be met by maintaining preserves of game on which men might expend their urges to violence, was voiced by others in Pope's time. See A. O. Lovejoy, *The Great Chain of Being* (1948), p. 187.

suggestion that "peace" can be served by the substitution of one for the other, are clearly revealed in the hope voiced by Father Thames near the end of the poem:

> The shady Empire shall retain no Trace
> Of War or Blood, but in the Sylvan Chace,
> The Trumpets sleep, while chearful Horns are blown,
> And Arms employ'd on Birds and Beasts alone.

The themes of "war" and "peace" which unite the scenes of rural sport to the "sports" of the Norman tyrants, and which ultimately form the subject of the whole poem, are continued in the Lodona passage, the episode so often dismissed as a puerile Ovidian excrescence. Lodona, Pope emphasizes, is a huntress too, one who scorns the "Praise of Beauty" for the pleasure of wounding the flying deer with her darts. In the midst of such a hunt, when she is "eager of the Chace", she becomes herself the hunted creature, pursued by Pan. The episode is a renewal of the pattern established earlier, when the Norman Rufus became "At once the Chaser and at once the Prey". It is another reminder of how easily the passions of men turn against themselves, another example of how "small Things we may with great compare", and it has its place, as do all the other scenes of "Sylvan War", in the poem Pope wrote in celebration of the peace his country needed.

From the scenes of the Forest under the sway of Anne (who, like Diana, protects the "Sylvan Reign" and is also "Empress of the Main"), Pope moves, by way of the Lodona episode, to the Thames. The Thames itself serves as the topographical feature by which Pope connects the Forest to the Castle and Court of Windsor situated on its banks, to the City and Port of London, and ultimately to the ends of the earth. The river connects analogous "worlds", for the peace and plenty which a Stuart queen had previously established amidst the "Oaks" of her "Sylvan Reign" is soon to have its correspondence in the peace and plenty this same Stuart queen establishes, by means of these same "Oaks", throughout the entire earth.[1]

---

1. Pope reminds the reader on three separate occasions (ll. 29–32, 221–2, 385ff.) that England has achieved dominion over the other nations of the world by means of ships and navies constructed from "Oaks" such are to be found in the "country" his poem celebrates.

In the midst of the transition provided by the Thames, at ll. 235–58, one finds Pope's statement of the theme of rural retirement, which imitates particularly the long passage at the end of Georgic II where Virgil praises country life as conducive to the highest thought and the deepest peace. Next, the celebration of the scenes through which the Thames moves allows Pope to recall other poets who have made the region "venerable", among them Lansdowne, who had celebrated James II and his queen as "gods", and who, after the Revolution of 1688, had gone, like an Atticus, a Scipio, or a Trumbull, into political retirement. Lansdowne, then, as poet and politician, and more especially as one of the architects of the Peace, is called upon to sing the blessings and glories of England. The implications are all complimentary, but not without their special relevance to the subject of Pope's poem.

It is in this area, at l. 290, that a division is supposed to occur in *Windsor-Forest*. This supposition is based not only on the note Pope in 1736 supplied to l. 1,[1] but also on a note he supplied at the same time to l. 290: "All the lines that follow till within eight of the conclusion, were not added to the poem till the year 1710." 1710 is again probably a mistake: 1712 would seem to be the time for the additions to the poem. It is doubtless true also that this note, like the note to l. 1, gives a vastly oversimplified account of the way Pope "added" to his poem. Certainly there seems little justification in the note for the view that Pope at this point did violence to his poem by attaching a mere bit of politics to its original "pastoral simplicity". Such a view is not supported by the essentially ambiguous words in either of the two notes, nor is it supported by the poem itself.

What we do have throughout this transitional passage is Pope's wish that Lansdowne will also celebrate in verse England's rich history. In the course of this suggestion Pope gives himself an opportunity to create another perspective on the past in which, as in the hunting scenes, "blended lie th' Oppressor and th' Opprest", and to speak of the day when Anne, in the divine majesty of her queenship, brings to England and to the world the peace and order that the poet, in the first long paragraph of his poem, had shown the "world" of Windsor Forest to possess:

1. See above, pp. 125–6.

> At length great *ANNA* said – – – Let Discord cease!
> She said, the World obey'd, and all was *Peace*!

An approach to monarchy in the metaphoric terms of divinity was widespread in the 17th century, reflecting, perhaps, one side of the intense debate over the question of "Divine Right". There is Cowley, who says that in "Kings we see / The liveliest Image of the Deity",[1] and Dryden, who compares the word of James II to the Word of God:

> Thus Britain's basis on a word is laid,
> As by a word the world itself was made.[2]

Such language may often seem a mere indulgence in fulsome court compliment, but in *Windsor-Forest* it is made to carry a weightier burden, primarily because of the connections the last one hundred lines of the poem have with the *Georgics*, and also with the *Pollio* and Isaiah.

In a famous passage in the second Georgic, ll. 136–76, Virgil moves from his account of the olives, vines, and herds of Italy's rich landscape to a celebration of the noble towns and cities which line the sides of Italian rivers, then to the heroic figures of the past, the Decii, the Marii, the Camilli, the Scipios, and to the hero of the present, the greatest of all men, Augustus, who had made Roman arms victorious to the earth's farthest bounds, and under whose reign Saturnian days of gold will return to Italy. Pope's poem moves in the same manner from the trees of the country about Windsor to the stately villas and cities which line the Thames, from the heroes of the past such as Edward III, Henry VI, Edward IV, and Charles I, to the great figure of the present, Anne, whose armies and fleets have won world-wide dominion, and whose ministers have brought about a Peace to which Pope attributes all the blessings of a Saturnian age of gold. Like Virgil too, Pope attributes to the monarch of his poem the virtues and powers of a deity, in whose hands lies the salvation, or ruination, of the land.

With the celebration of Italy as a land in which the golden age is to be restored Virgil surges into a higher rhetoric, a procedure Pope follows in giving to Father Thames lines of resounding eloquence with which to speak of England's mythic future. Here too

---

1. See l. 425*n*.   2. Epil. to *Albion and Albanius*, 33–4.

the language gathers together fragments from Old Testament prophecy and from the *Pollio*. The identification of the seat of empire as the "World's great Oracle" where, in times to come, "Kings shall sue, and suppliant States be seen", can hardly fail to recall the passages in Isaiah where the gentiles converge upon Israel to acknowledge the glory and light of the Lord that resides there: "And the Gentiles shall come to thy light, and kings to the brightness of thy rising. . . The sons also of them that afflicted thee shall come bending unto thee; and all they that despised thee shall bow themselves down at the soles of thy feet."[1] The same chapter of Isaiah also hovers behind the long paragraph in which Pope speaks of the riches of the world which will converge upon England: ". . . the abundance of the sea shall be converted unto thee, the forces of the Gentiles shall come unto thee. . . Therefore thy gates shall be open continually; they shall not be shut day nor night;[2] that men may bring unto thee the forces of the Gentiles, and that their kings may be brought." One should recall too that only the previous year Pope had written and published his *Messiah*, an amalgam of Virgil and Isaiah in which occur such lines as these:

> See barb'rous Nations at thy Gates attend,
> Walk in thy Light, and in thy Temple bend.
> See thy bright Altars throng'd with prostrate Kings,
> And heap'd with Products of *Sabæan* Springs!

Near the conclusion of his poem Pope makes it clear that the peace he celebrates is one that would banish to "deepest Hell", in a way a mere political peace could not, such passions and vices as Pride, Ambition, and Envy. The immediate source of the conception here seems to be the third Georgic, where Virgil describes the triumphs of Augustus and says that "Envy shall cower before the Furies and the stern stream of Cocytus, Ixion's twisted snakes and monstrous wheel".[3] Yet Pope so expands the Virgilian original as to extend even further the moral and mythical dimension he has

---

1. Chap. 60. The parallels from Isaiah cited here are cited by Mack, *College English*, VII 267–8.

2. Cf. Pope's note to l. 398, where he expresses "A wish that London may be made a FREE PORT."

3. Ll. 37–9, Loeb trans.

given to the political occasion of his poem. The implications of renewal and regeneration which he has gathered from both Christian
and pagan prophecy and with which he had informed *Windsor-
Forest* from the beginning are made at the conclusion of the poem
to suggest, at least half-seriously, the transformation which the
earth, in the fulness of time, shall undergo. By these means Pope
creates a poem which celebrates not only the destiny of a nation,
but also that of a world.

WINDSOR-FOREST.

To the Right Honourable
GEORGE Lord *LANSDOWN.*

Non injuſſa cano: Te noſtræ, Vare, *Myricæ*
Te Nemus omne canet; nec Phœbo gratior ulla eſt
Quam ſibi quæ Vari *præſcripſit Pagina nomen.*
VIRG.

NOTE ON THE TEXT

Windsor-Forest was first published, in folio, on March 7, 1713. A second edition, again in folio, was published the following month, and in 1714 the poem appeared among the works by Pope printed in *Miscellaneous Poems and Translations* (see pp. 128–9, above). Pope made a large number of revisions for the *Works* of 1717, and subsequently new readings appear mainly in the *Works* of 1736 and 1751. Through the years the poem also continued to appear, sometimes with minor variants, in editions of *Miscellaneous Poems and Translations*. A fourth edition of the poem, printed in octavo along with *Messiah*, appeared in 1720. Pope, in the MS of the poem which has survived (see pp. 125–6 and note), mentions a third edition of 1714, in octavo, but it is possible that he here refers, as Griffith notes (*Alexander Pope, A Bibliography*, 1 i 33), to the 1714 edition of *Miscellaneous Poems and Translations*.

There are a few eccentricities revealed in the collation. At l. 121, for example, a minor change occurred in the miscellany editions of 1720 and 1722. At ll. 79, 165, 262, the miscellany editions of 1727 and 1732 introduce minor variants, or perhaps misprints. Warburton in his edition of the *Works* in 1751 perpetuated three misprints which first appeared in the *Works* of 1740 and 1743.

In three instances, at ll. 49–50, 261, and 324, revisions which Pope made in punctuation have been followed in the text printed here, and Lodona's speech has been closed with inverted commas at l. 202. Otherwise the text follows the spelling, punctuation, and typography of the first edition, but observes the new readings introduced into later editions.

KEY TO THE CRITICAL APPARATUS

1713*a* = Windsor-Forest, First Edition, folio, Griffith 9.

1713*b* = Windsor-Forest, Second Edition, folio, Griffith 10.

1714 = Miscellaneous Poems and Translations, octavo, Griffith 32.

1717 = Works, quarto, Griffith 79.

1720*a* = Miscellaneous Poems and Translations, vol. 1, duodecimo, Griffith 124.

1720*b* = Windsor-Forest, Fourth Edition, octavo, Griffith 125.

1722 = Miscellaneous Poems and Translations, vol. 1, duodecimo, Griffith 135.

1727 = Miscellany Poems, vol. 1, duodecimo, Griffith 192.

1732 = Miscellany Poems, vol. 1, duodecimo, Griffith 273.

1736*a* = Works, vol. 1, octavo, Griffith 413.

1736*b* = Works, vol. 1, octavo, Griffith 414.

1740 = Works, vol. 1, part 1, octavo, Griffith 510.

1743 = Works, vol. 1, part 1, octavo, Griffith 582.

1751 = Works, ed. Warburton, vol. 1, octavo, Griffith 643.

WINDSOR-FOREST.

To the Right Honourable
GEORGE Lord *LANSDOWN*.

THY Forests, *Windsor*! and thy green Retreats,
    At once the Monarch's and the Muse's Seats,
    Invite my Lays. Be present, Sylvan Maids!
Unlock your Springs, and open all your Shades.
Granville commands: Your Aid O Muses bring!   5
What Muse for *Granville* can refuse to sing?
    The Groves of *Eden*, vanish'd now so long,

---

1. This poem was written at two different times: the first part of it which relates to the country, in the year 1704, at the same time with the Pastorals: the
latter part was not added till the year 1713, ⟨1710, *1736a–43*⟩ in which it was
publish'd. [P. *1736a–51*.]
    According to Pope the "first part" ended at l. 290 (see 290*n*). For the first
draft of Pope's note above, see Intro., pp. 125–6.
    1*f.* Wakefield compares Charles Hopkins, *The History of Love* (1695), 1–2:
           Ye Woods, and Wilds, serene and blest retreats,
           At once the Lovers, and the Muses seats.
Cf. *Summer*, 71 (p. 77, above), and Intro., p. 136.
    3, &c. originally thus,
          ——————*Chaste Goddess of the woods,*
          Nymphs of the Vales, and Naiads of the floods,
          Lead me thro' arching bow'rs, and glimm'ring glades.
          ⟨Unlock your springs— *Add. 1751*⟩   [P. *1736a–51*.]
    4. Wakefield cites Dryden, *Georgics* II 245, "Once more unlock for thee the
sacred Spring", and observes that "*open all your shades*, is the *pandite nunc Helicona,
Deae*", of *Aen.*, VII 641. Virgil repeats the phrase at *Aen.*, X 163, and Dryden
translates: "Now sacred Sisters open all your Springs." See Intro., p. 136.
    5. *Granville*] See Intro., p. 130, and vol. IV, p. 363.
    6. *refuse to sing*] Warburton cites Virgil, *Ecl.* X 3: "Neget quis carmina
Gallo?" Wakefield cites *Lycidas*, 10: "Who would not sing for *Lycidas*?"
    7*ff.* Pope's lines undoubtedly allude to the "Eden" so marvellously re-created
in *Par. Lost.* Wakefield noted that the lines are "an adumbration of the introductory lines" to Waller's *On St. James's Park*:
          Of the first Paradice there's nothing found,
          Plants set by Heav'n are vanisht, & the ground;

Live in Description, and look green in Song:
These, were my Breast inspir'd with equal Flame,
Like them in Beauty, should be like in Fame.   10
Here Hills and Vales, the Woodland and the Plain,
Here Earth and Water seem to strive again,
Not *Chaos*-like together crush'd and bruis'd,
But as the World, harmoniously confus'd:
Where Order in Variety we see,   15

Yet the description lasts; who knows the fate
Of lines that shall this Paradice relate?

Wakefield also notes two passages from Addison's *A Letter from Italy* (1704), 31–6, 51–4:

Sometimes, misguided by the tuneful throng,
I look for streams immortaliz'd in song,
That lost in silence and oblivion lye,
(Dumb are their fountains and their channels dry)
Yet run for-ever by the Muse's skill,
And in the smooth description murmur still. . .
Oh cou'd the Muse my ravish'd breast inspire
With warmth like yours, and raise an equal fire,
Unnumber'd beauties in my verse shou'd shine,
And *Virgil*'s *Italy* shou'd yield to mine!

(*Miscellaneous Works*, ed. A. C. Guthkelch, 1914, vol. 1). See Intro., pp. 136–7, above.

10. *like in Fame*] Bowles noted the resemblance to the couplet (ll. 71–2) in *Cooper's Hill* which suggests that the original builder of Windsor Castle is as doubtful as the birth-place of Homer:

(Like him in birth, thou should'st be like in fame,
As thine his fate, if mine had been his Flame).

Pope of course alludes to Milton.

13 f. Wakefield cites Waller, *Of her passing through a crowd of People*, 1–2:

As in old *Chaos* Heaven with Earth confus'd,
And Stars with Rocks, together crush'd and bruis'd;

and suggests that Pope recalled "the *concors discordia*, *the friendly discord* of *Ovid* [*Met.*, 1 433]." Ovid's actual words are "discors concordia". See the discussion of this concept in the poem by Earl Wasserman, *The Subtler Language* (1959), chap. IV.

15 ff. Warton compares *Cooper's Hill*, 197 ff.:

Here Nature, whether more intent to please
Us or her self, with strange varieties . . .
Wisely she knew, the harmony of things,
As well as that of sounds, from discord springs.

And where, tho' all things differ, all agree.
Here waving Groves a checquer'd Scene display,
And part admit and part exclude the Day;
As some coy Nymph her Lover's warm Address
Nor quite indulges, nor can quite repress.   20
There, interspers'd in Lawns and opening Glades,
Thin Trees arise that shun each others Shades.
Here in full Light the russet Plains extend;
There wrapt in Clouds the blueish Hills ascend:
Ev'n the wild Heath displays her Purple Dies,   25
And 'midst the Desart fruitful Fields arise,
That crown'd with tufted Trees and springing Corn,
Like verdant Isles the sable Waste adorn.

Such was the discord, which did first disperse
Form, order, beauty through the Universe.
See Intro., pp. 136–7, above.

17. Cf. Milton, *L'Allegro*, 96: "Dancing in the Chequer'd shade".

21. *Lawns*] An open space between woods; a glade (OED). Cf. ll. 81, 149.

22. Cf. Dryden, *Annus Mirabilis*, st. 126:
Where the thin scatt'ring Trees admit the light,
And shun each others shadows as they grow.

23. *russet*] Of a reddish-brown colour (OED). Cf. *L'Allegro*, 70: "Russet Lawns and Fallows Gray". The painterly composition of this and neighbouring lines should be noted. See Ault, *New Light on Pope* (1949), pp. 87*ff.*

24. *blueish*] Cf. Dryden, *Æn.*, III 684–5:
When we from far, like bluish Mists, descry
The Hills, and then the Plains of *Italy*.

25.   *Why should I sing our better suns or air,*
           Whose vital draughts prevent the leach's care,
           While thro' fresh fields th'enliv'ning odours breathe,
           Or spread with vernal blooms the purple heath. [P. *1736a–51.*]

EC compare Dryden, *To my Honour'd Kinsman, John Driden*, 115–16:
He scapes the best, who Nature to repair,
Draws Phisick from the Fields, in Draughts of Vital Air.
Cf. ll. 241*ff.*, below.

27. *tufted Trees*] OED defines *tuft* as a "small group of trees or bushes; a clump." Cf. *L'Allegro*, 78: "Boosom'd high in tufted Trees"; and Dryden, *Æn.*, III 300.

28. *sable*] Cf. l. 410*n*, below.

Let *India* boast her Plants, nor envy we
The weeping Amber or the balmy Tree,   30
While by our Oaks the precious Loads are born,
And Realms commanded which those Trees adorn.
Not proud *Olympus* yields a nobler Sight,
Tho' Gods assembled grace his tow'ring Height,
Than what more humble Mountains offer here,   35
Where, in their Blessings, all those Gods appear.
See *Pan* with Flocks, with Fruits *Pomona* crown'd,
Here blushing *Flora* paints th'enamel'd Ground,

29–42. This whole passage should be compared with Virgil, *Georgics* II 136–76. See Intro., p. 137.

29–32. Cf. Virgil, *Ecl.* IV 30, 39: ". . . et durae quercus sudabunt roscida mella", and "omnis feret omnia tellus". See Intro., p. 137.

30. *weeping Amber*] Cf. Sandys, Ovid, *Met.*, II 401–2:
> From these cleere dropping trees, tears yearly flow:
> They, hardned by the Sunne, to Amber grow;

and *Par. Lost*, IV 248: "Groves whose rich Trees wept odorous Gumms and Balme." EC recall the Ovidian myths of Myrrha (*Met.*, x 500) and of the sisters of Phaethon (*Met.*, II 364). Cf. *Spring*, 62n, p. 67, above.

31. *Oaks*] Alluding to the ships built of English oak which "bore" valuable spices to England and enabled her to rule over the lands whence they came. Cf. ll. 385–8, below. For the thought of this and neighbouring lines, cf. Waller, *A Panegyrick to my Lord Protector*, 57–64:
> The Taste of hot *Arabia*'s Spice we know,
> Free from the scorching Sun that makes it grow;
> Without the Worm, in *Persian* Silks we shine,
> And without Planting drink of ev'ry Vine. . .
> Ours is the Harvest where the *Indians* mow,
> We plough the Deep, and reap what others sow.

Cf. also Waller's *Of a War with Spain*, 29–30:
> Our Oaks secure, as if they there took root,
> We tread on billows with a steady foot.

See Intro., pp. 137, 140.

33*f*. Warburton compares *Cooper's Hill*, 51–2:
> Than which, a nobler weight no Mountain bears,
> But *Atlas* only, that supports the Sphears.

38. *enamel'd Ground*] A technical phrase, referring to the process "of entirely covering metals with enamel, to form a ground for painting in vitrifiable colours . . ." (OED). The *ground* is in painting the "main surface or first coating of colour, serving as a support for other colours or a background for designs . . ."

Here *Ceres'* Gifts in waving Prospect stand,
And nodding tempt the joyful Reaper's Hand,   40
Rich Industry sits smiling on the Plains,
And Peace and Plenty tell, a STUART reigns.
    Not thus the Land appear'd in Ages past,

(OED). For a discussion of this passage, see M. Mack, "On Reading Pope", *College English*, VII (Oct., 1945–May, 1946), pp. 263–73.

42. For the political import of this line, see Intro., p. 137. Here, and in the ensuing lines on William the Conqueror, Pope implicitly criticizes the reign of William III. See J. R. Moore, "*Windsor Forest* and William III", *MLN*, 66 (1951), pp. 451–4.

43 *ff.* This portion of the poem re-creates the traditional view of the tyrannies exercised by the Norman kings, especially as they were illustrated in the formation of the New Forest as a royal hunting ground by William I. The fact that so many members of the Conqueror's family met their death in the New Forest led commentators into the mythical view that these deaths were examples of divine vengeance, taken because of the wickedness involved in the creation of the royal preserve, and this is an essential element in Pope's version. There is reason to doubt that William I was guilty of many of the excesses attributed to him by the myth and by Pope (see G. B. Adams, *The History of England from the Norman Conquest to the Death of John*, 1905, *Polit. Hist. Eng.*, II 58–9; also F. H. M. Parker, "The Forest Laws and the Death of William Rufus", *Eng. Hist. Rev.*, XXVII (1912), pp. 26–38). William II seems to have been far more vicious than his father in his plunderings, his oppressions of the poor and the Church, his open and blasphemous defiance of God, and many of Pope's lines could therefore be more aptly applied to him. In terms of the myth, however, the precise distribution of blame is unimportant.

Pope had almost surely read the account (see l. 65*n*) in *Camden's Britannia* (1695, p. 115) of William I's creation of the New Forest: "On the east-side of this river [the Avon], William the Conqueror destroy'd all the towns, villages, and churches; and turning out the poor inhabitants, made a forest for wild beasts of more than thirty miles in circuit, which the English in that age call'd *Ytene*, we at this day *New Forest*; of which, Walter Mapes, who liv'd in the next age, writes thus: *The Conqueror took away much land from God and men, and converted it to the use of wild beasts, and the sport of his dogs; by which he demolish'd 36 Mother-Churches, and drove away the poor inhabitants.* This he did either to make a more easie access for his Normans into England (for it lies opposite to Normandy) in case there should be a new insurrection in this Island after his suppos'd Conquest of it; or to indulge himself in hunting; or to raise money by methods tho' never so unjust. For he, more merciful to beasts than to mankind, appointed a most grievous pecuniary mulct, and other more severe penalties, to be inflicted on those who should trespass on his game." See Intro., pp. 138–9.

A dreary Desart and a gloomy Waste,
To Savage Beasts and Savage Laws a Prey,   45
And Kings more furious and severe than they:
Who claim'd the Skies, dispeopled Air and Floods,
The lonely Lords of empty Wilds and Woods.
Cities laid waste, they storm'd the Dens and Caves,
(For wiser Brutes were backward to be Slaves.)   50
What could be free, when lawless Beasts obey'd,
And ev'n the Elements a Tyrant sway'd?

49 Caves,] Caves *1713a–14.*
50 Slaves.)] Slaves) *1713a–14.*

44. *gloomy Waste*] EC site Dryden, Ovid, *Met.*, 1 473: "A dismal Desart, and a silent Waste."

45. *Savage Laws*] *The Forest Laws.* [P. *1713a–51.*]
"With the Norman Conquest, the forest law and the forest courts of Normandy were introduced into England, and they resulted in a rapid and violent extension of 'forest' land—that is, land outside (*foris*) the common law and subject to a special law, whose object was the preservation of the king's hunting. The word 'forest' was thus a legal and not a geographical term. At their widest extent, the forests must have included much land that was neither wooded nor waste. . . Of the Conqueror, the [Anglo-Saxon] chronicler wrote under the year 1087: 'He made large forests for deer and enacted laws therewith, so that whoever killed a hart or a hind should be blinded. As he forbade killing the deer, so also the boars. . . He also appointed concerning the hares that they should go free. The rich complained and the poor murmured but he was so sturdy that he recked nought of them.' " See H. C. Darby, "The Economic Geography of England, A.D. 1000–1250", in *An Historical Geography of England Before A.D. 1800* (1936), ed. H. C. Darby. The forest laws were among the grievances which led to Magna Carta. After the Revolution of 1688 they fell into disuse.

46. Wakefield compares Waller, *Upon the Death of my Lady Rich*, 3–4:
> Prove all a Desart, and none there make stay,
> But savage Beasts, or men as wilde as they.

EC compare Temple's description (*Upon the Approach of the Shore at Harwich*, 38–40) of the European forests which
> give a shade
> To savage beasts, who on the weaker prey,
> Or human savages more wild than they.

52. *Elements*] "Pope puts 'the elements' for the creatures which inhabited them" [EC].

In vain kind Seasons swell'd the teeming Grain,
Soft Show'rs distill'd, and Suns grew warm in vain;
The Swain with Tears his frustrate Labour yields,   55
And famish'd dies amidst his ripen'd Fields.
What wonder then, a Beast or Subject slain
Were equal Crimes in a Despotick Reign;
Both doom'd alike for sportive Tyrants bled,
But while the Subject starv'd, the Beast was fed.   60

55 his frustrate Labour] to Beasts his Labour *1713a–32.*
57 No wonder Savages or Subjects slain *1713a–32.*
60 But Subjects starv'd while Savages were fed. *1713a–32;*
    But that the subject starv'd, the beast was fed. *1736a–43.*

---

53. *teeming Grain*] Cf. Dryden, *Georgics* 1 156: "With pregnant Streams, to swell the teeming Grain."

55. EC note that the first reading made it clearer that the crops were ravaged by the strictly protected game and suggest that Pope changed "the expression to avoid the recurrence of the same word when he introduced 'beast' into the next couplet."

56. *famish'd dies*] Wakefield compares Addison, *A Letter from Italy*, 113–18, where the miseries of the Italian peasant, starving amidst plenty, are described:

> The poor inhabitant beholds in vain
> The red'ning Orange and the swelling grain:
> Joyless he sees the growing Oils and Wines,
> And in the Myrtle's fragrant shade repines:
> Starves, in the midst of nature's bounty curst,
> And in the loaden vineyard dies for thirst.

Pope told Spence (p. 316): "I used formerly to like Mr. Addison's Letter from Italy extremely, and still like it the most of all his poems."

ripen'd Fields] Cf. Tickell, *On the Prospect of Peace*, 113–14:

> Curst by the Hind, when to the Spoil he yields
> His Year's whole Sweat, and vainly ripen'd Fields.

57, &c.   *No wonder savages or subjects slain—*
           But subjects starv'd while savages were fed.

It was originally thus, but the word Savages is not ⟨not so *1736a–43*⟩ properly apply'd to beasts but to ⟨as to *1736a–43*⟩ men; which occasion'd the alteration. [P. *1736a–51.*]

Pope repeatedly applied the word to beasts in his *Iliad*: e.g., XIII 144; XVII 815; XVIII 373. It was used in the same sense by Macaulay as late as 1831 (see OED). The change made by Pope led to the alteration of l. 55, which was clearer in the first reading.

Proud *Nimrod* first the bloody Chace began,
A mighty Hunter, and his Prey was Man.
Our haughty *Norman* boasts that barb'rous Name,
And makes his trembling Slaves the Royal Game.
The Fields are ravish'd from th'industrious Swains,   65

61f. The text of Genesis speaks of Nimrod only as a hunter, but commentators make it clear that he was regarded as the type of the despot: "To this Nemrod the sonne of Chus, first builder and King of Babylon . . . generally al ancient writers ascribe the first tyrannie, and first setting vp of an earthlie citie opposit to the Citie of God after the floud. He was a *Valiant*, or rather a *Violent hunter*, a giant hunter . . . who by falshood and force brought manie vnder his dominion" (commentary in Douay Bible, 1609 and 1635, p. 39). Cf. also: "Who according to Nemrods heresie (not thinking themselues beholding to God for temporal happines, but to their owne forces) tyrannized ouer the weaker, and manie wicked banning together extreamly oppressed the more peaceable, especially the Church and true seruants of God (Ibid., p. 46). Cf. Waller, *Of the late Invasion and Defeat of the Turks, &c.*, 1–4:

> The Modern *Nimrod*, with a false Delight
> Pursuing Beasts, that save themselves by Flight,
> Grown proud, and weary of his wonted Game,
> Wou'd Christians chase, and sacrifice to Fame.

See Intro., pp. 138–9, above.

65. *The fields are ravish'd etc.*] *Alluding to the destruction made in the* New Forest ⟨*Alluding to the* New Forest, *1713a–43*⟩, *and the Tyrannies exercis'd there by* William I ⟨*the First. 1713a–43*⟩. [P. *1713a–51*.]

65. *The Fields . . . Fanes*] Translated from,
> *Templa adimit divis, fora civibus, arva colonis,*
an old monkish writer, I forget who. [P. *1751*.]

Pope's forgotten source was *Camden's Britannia (Newly Translated into English: With Large Additions and Improvements*. . . London, 1695, p. 115), where it is said of the New Forest ". . . there are extant some Verses of *John White* [1510–1560] Bishop of Winchester; which though they falsely attribute the making of this Forest to William Rufus, yet because many readers are pleased with them, I am content to insert them in this place.

> *Templa adimit Divis, fora civibus, arva colonis*
> *Rufus, & instituit Beaulensi in rure forestam:*
> *Rex cervum insequitur, Regem vindicta, Tirellus*
> *Non bene provisum transfixit acumine ferri.*

> Towns, Fields, and Churchs, took from God and Men,
> A spatious forest made in *Beaulieu*-plain:
> The King a Hart, Vengeance the King pursu'd,
> And *Tirrel*'s arrow drunk his guilty blood."

From Men their Cities, and from Gods their Fanes:
The levell'd Towns with Weeds lie cover'd o'er,
The hollow Winds thro' naked Temples roar;
Round broken Columns clasping Ivy twin'd;
O'er Heaps of Ruin stalk'd the stately Hind;   70
The Fox obscene to gaping Tombs retires,
And savage Howlings fill the sacred Quires.

70 Ruin] Ruins *1713a–14*.
72 And savage Howlings] And Wolves with Howling *1713a–32*.

67*ff*. Cf. Isaiah, 13: 21–2: "But wild beasts of the desert shall lie there; and
their houses shall be full of doleful creatures. . . And the wild beasts of the
islands shall cry in their desolate houses . . .'' See Intro., pp. 138–9.

67. *cover'd o'er*] EC cite Addison, *The Campaign* (1705), 91–2:
        O'er prostrate Towns and Palaces they pass,
        (Now cover'd o'er with Weeds, and hid in Grass).
Wakefield cites Ovid, *Heroides*, 1 56 (Penelope to Ulysses): "ruinosas occulit
herba domos''.

68*ff*. The "Temples'', "broken Columns'', and "Quires'', EC note, "suppose
a much statelier architecture than belonged to the rude village churches of the
Saxons.'' Pope probably hints at the destruction of the abbeys at the time of the
Reformation, but he also suggests *all* ravages, whenever they occur. Cf. *Cooper's
Hill*, 111–56, where Denham condemns the religious policy of Henry VIII. Cf.
Donne, *Satyre* 11, 60: "Then when winds in our ruin'd Abbeyes rore.''

69. Cf. *El. to Abel.*, 243 (vol. 11, p. 318): "Where round some mould'ring tow'r
pale ivy creeps''.

70. Cf. Virgil, *Georgics* 111 539–40:
                timidi dammae cervique fugaces
        nunc interque canes et circum tecta vagantur.

70*ff*. Speaking of the New Forest as an area which William I "had appropriated for the nurture and refuge of wild beasts'', William of Malmesbury comments: ". . . a dreadful spectacle, indeed, that where before had existed human
intercourse and the worship of God, there deer, and goats, and other animals of
that kind, should now range unrestrained, and these not subjected to the general
service of mankind'' (*Chronicle of the Kings of England*, ed. J. A. Giles, 1847, p.
306).

71. *The Fox obscene*] Cf. *Georgics* 1 470–1: "obscenaeque canes importunaeque
volucres / signa dabant.''

72 var. *And wolves with howling fill, &c.*] The Author thought this an error,
wolves not being common in *England* at the time of the Conqueror. [P. *1736a–
51*.]
    Cf. *Summer*, 79*n*, where it is noted that wolves are said to have disappeared

Aw'd by his Nobles, by his Commons curst,
Th' Oppressor rul'd Tyrannick where he *durst*,
Stretch'd o'er the Poor, and Church, his Iron Rod,   75
And serv'd alike his Vassals and his God.
Whom ev'n the *Saxon* spar'd, and bloody *Dane*,
The wanton Victims of his *Sport* remain.
But see the Man who spacious Regions gave
A Waste for Beasts, himself deny'd a Grave!   80

76 serv'd] treats *1713a–32.*
79 who] whose *1727–32.*

in England in the reign of Henry VII. Pope may have remembered *Georgics* I
485–6: "et altae / per noctem resonare lupis ululantibus urbes."

79–84. The element of divine justice implied in these lines is explicitly stated
in *Camden's Britannia* (1695), p. 115: "But divine vengeance was not long wanting to this impious project of the King's [William's afforestation of the land and
his severe punishment of trespassers]: for Richard his second son and William
Rufus King of England another of his sons, both lost their lives in this Forest;
the latter being casually shot with an arrow by *Walter Tirrel*; and the other
poisoned by a pestilential blast. And *Henry* his grandchild by Robert his eldest
son, while he was here eagerly pursuing his sport, was caught by the head in
the boughs, and there ended his life; to teach us that the crimes of parents are
often punish'd upon their children's children." Drayton (*Poly-Olbion*, Song XVII,
l. 120n) says that the deaths of Richard and William Rufus "have been thought
as divine revenges on *William* the first, who destroy'd in *Hantshire* XXXVI. parish
Churches to make dens for wild beasts."

The deaths of both William I and William III were hastened by falls from
horses while hunting, and an element of divine justice was attributed to both
accidents by opponents of William III. Throughout this whole passage Pope
seems to imply a parallel between the reigns of the two kings. See J. R. Moore,
"*Windsor Forest* and William III", *MLN*, 66 (1951), pp. 451–4, and Earl Wasserman, *The Subtler Language* (1959), chap. IV.

80. *deny'd a Grave*] William of Malmesbury thus describes William I's burial:
"The body, embalmed after royal custom, was brought down the river Seine to
Caen, and there consigned to the earth, a large assembly of the clergy attending,
but few of the laity. Here might be seen the wretchedness of earthly vicissitude;
for that man who was formerly the glory of all Europe, and more powerful than
any of his predecessors, could not find a place of everlasting rest, without con-
tention. For a certain knight, to whose patrimony the place pertained, loudly
exclaiming at the robbery, forbade his burial; saying, that the ground belonged
to himself by paternal right; and that the king had no claim to rest in a place

Stretch'd on the Lawn his second Hope survey,
At once the Chaser and at once the Prey.
Lo *Rufus*, tugging at the deadly Dart,
Bleeds in the Forest, like a wounded Hart.
Succeeding Monarchs heard the Subjects Cries,   85
Nor saw displeas'd the peaceful Cottage rise.
Then gath'ring Flocks on unknown Mountains fed,
O'er sandy Wilds were yellow Harvests spread,
The Forests wonder'd at th'unusual Grain,

which he had forcibly invaded. Whereupon, at the desire of Henry, the only one of his sons who was present, a hundred pounds of silver were paid to this brawler, and quieted his audacious claim" (*Chronicle of the Kings of England*, 1847, p. 311).

81. *second Hope*] Richard, *second Son of* William *the Conqueror*. [P. *1713a–51.*]
1720a, 1722, 1727, 1732 substitute *William Rufus* for *Richard* in the above note.

82. *the Prey*] Wakefield cites Denham, *The Destruction of Troy*, 58: "At once the Taker, and at once the Prey."

83. William of Malmesbury (*Chronicle of the Kings of England*, 1847, p. 345) describes the death of William Rufus: "After dinner he went into the forest, attended by few persons; of whom the most intimate with him was Walter, surnamed Tirel. . . This man alone had remained with him, while the others, employed in the chase, were dispersed as chance directed. The sun was now declining, when the king, drawing his bow and letting fly an arrow, slightly wounded a stag which passed before him; and, keenly gazing, followed it, still running, a long time with his eyes, holding up his hand to keep off the power of the sun's rays. At this instant Walter, conceiving a noble exploit, which was while the king's attention was otherwise occupied to transfix another stag which by chance came near him, unknowingly, and without power to prevent, Oh, gracious God! pierced his breast with a fatal arrow. On receiving the wound, the king uttered not a word; but breaking off the shaft of the weapon where it projected from his body, fell upon the wound, by which he accelerated his death."

87. *on unknown Mountains fed*] Mountains hitherto unknown to the flocks, now for the first time permitted to feed there [EC]. Cf. Roscommon's tr. of Virgil's *Ecl.* VI 57 (in *Miscellany Poems*, 1684): "Till when, few wandring Beasts on unknown Mountains fed". See *Spring*, 21*n*, p. 62, above; also *The Arrival of Ulysses in Ithaca*, 67, p. 468, below.

89. *th'unusual Grain*] Warburton compares *Georgics* II 82: "miraturque novas frondes et non sua poma." EC note that Virgil is "treating of grafts, and says that the parent stock, when the slips grow, wonders at leaves and fruit not its own."

And secret Transport touch'd the conscious Swain.   90
Fair *Liberty, Britannia*'s Goddess, rears
Her chearful Head, and leads the golden Years.
    Ye vig'rous Swains! while Youth ferments your Blood,
And purer Spirits swell the sprightly Flood,
Now range the Hills, the gameful Woods beset,   95
Wind the shrill Horn, or spread the waving Net.
When milder Autumn Summer's Heat succeeds,

90 Transport] Transports *1713a–14.*
95 gameful] thickest *1713a–43.*

---

90. *secret Transport*] Wakefield cites *Aen.*, I 502, "Latonae tacitum pertemptant gaudia pectus", and EC cite Dryden's tr., I 706: "And feeds with secret Joy her silent Breast."

conscious] OED gives this as the first instance of the word in the sense of knowing, witting, well-aware. But cf. Dryden, *Sigismonda and Guiscardo*, 151: "The conscious Priest . . ."

91.   *Oh may no more a foreign master's rage*
               With wrongs yet legal, curse a future age!
               Still spread, fair Liberty! thy heav'nly wings,
               Breath plenty on the fields, and fragrance on the springs.
                                              [P. *1736a–51.*]

Pope may have suppressed the first couplet because it was too pointed an allusion to William III. As a matter of fact Charles I, not William III, revived the "yet legal" forest laws, primarily to raise money independently of parliament. See *Enc. Brit.*, 11th ed., s.v. Forest Laws. For the bias against William III in these and preceding lines, see J. R. Moore, "*Windsor Forest* and William III", *MLN*, 66 (1951), pp. 451–4. "Fair *Liberty, Britannia*'s Goddess", is perhaps to be identified with Queen Anne.

93. *ferments your Blood*] See Kersey, *Dictionarium Anglo-Britannicum* (1708), s.v. *Fermentation*: "In *Physick*, any gentle Motion of the Parts of the Blood or Juices in the Body, a kind of bubbling up, rais'd by the Spirits that endeavour to get out of a Mixt Body." See l. 94*n.*

94. *sprightly Flood*] EC cite Addison, *The Campaign*, 107–8:
               Their Courage dwells not in a troubl'd Flood
               Of mounting Spirits, and fermenting Blood.
The allusion is to the animal spirits which were supposed to move in the blood. See l. 93*n.*

97.   *When yellow autumn summer's heat succeeds,*
               And into wine the purple harvest bleeds,
               The partridge feeding in the new-shorn fields

And in the new-shorn Field the Partridge feeds,
Before his Lord the ready Spaniel bounds,
Panting with Hope, he tries the furrow'd Grounds,   100
But when the tainted Gales the Game betray,
Couch'd close he lyes, and meditates the Prey;
Secure they trust th'unfaithful Field, beset,
Till hov'ring o'er 'em sweeps the swelling Net.
Thus (if small Things we may with great compare)   105

Both morning sports and ev'ning pleasures yields. [P. *1736a–51.*]
As an explanation of the rejection of some of these lines, the following note, signed P., appeared in *1751*: "Perhaps the Author thought it not allowable to describe the season by a circumstance not proper to our climate, the vintage." But see *Autumn*, 74*n*, p. 85, above.

98. *new-shorn Field*] "The places they [partridges] most delight in are the Corn-fields, especially whilst the Corn grows; for under that covert they shelter, ingender and breed. Neither are these places unfrequented by them when the Corn is cut down, by reason of the Grain they find therein, especially in Wheat-stubble; and the height thereof they delight in, being to them as a covert or a shelter" (N. Cox, *The Gentleman's Recreation*, 4th ed., 1697, pt III 39–40).

99 *ff.* "There is no Art of taking *Partridges* so excellent and pleasant as by the help of a Setting-dog. . . If in your Dog's ranging you perceive him to stop on the sudden, or stand still, you must then make in to him, (for without doubt he hath set the *Partridge*). . . Then commanding the Dog to lie still, draw forth your Net, and prick one end to the ground [with a stake], and spread your Net all open, and so cover as many of the *Partridges* as you can; which done, make in with a Noise, and spring up the *Partridges*; which shall no sooner rise, but they will be entangled in the Net" (Cox, *The Gentleman's Recreation*, 1697, pt III 44–5). Perhaps the net was sometimes cast, rather than spread, over the birds (cf. l. 96 with l. 104). At any rate, the success of the method evidently depended upon the partridges (called "cowardly, fearful, simple, and foolish" by Cox) responding to the presence of the dog by cowering immobile amidst the stubble.

101. *tainted*] "Imbued with the scent of an animal" (OED).

102. *meditates*] "To fix one's attention upon, to observe with interest or intentness" (OED). Wakefield compares Dryden, *Sigismonda and Guiscardo*, 244: "So, like a Lion . . . / With inward Rage he meditates his Prey." Cf. *The Episode of Sarpedon*, 23 (p. 450, below).

103. Cf. *Cooper's Hill*, 257 (of the stag): "Betray'd in all his strengths, the wood beset."

105. *with great compare*] Wakefield cites Virgil, *Georgics* IV 176: "si parva licet componere magnis"; and Dryden's tr., 256: "If little things with great we may compare." Cf. also *Par. Lost*, II 921–2, VI 310–11; Dryden, *Met.*, I 727; Sandys, *Met.*, V 417.

When *Albion* sends her eager Sons to War,
Some thoughtless Town, with Ease and Plenty blest,
Near, and more near, the closing Lines invest;
Sudden they seize th'amaz'd, defenceless Prize,
And high in Air *Britannia*'s Standard flies.   110
   See! from the Brake the whirring Pheasant springs,
And mounts exulting on triumphant Wings;
Short is his Joy! he feels the fiery Wound,
Flutters in Blood, and panting beats the Ground.
Ah! what avail his glossie, varying Dyes,   115
His Purple Crest, and Scarlet-circled Eyes,
The vivid Green his shining Plumes unfold;
His painted Wings, and Breast that flames with Gold?
   Nor yet, when moist *Arcturus* clouds the Sky,
The Woods and Fields their pleasing Toils deny.   120
To Plains with well-breath'd Beagles we repair,

107–9 Pleas'd, in the Gen'ral's Sight, the Host lye down
     Sudden, before some unsuspecting Town,
     The Young, the Old, [The captive Race, *1717–32*] one In-
     stant makes our Prize, *1713a–32*.
121 well-breath'd] well-bred *1720a, 1722*.

---

110. These lines may have been inspired by the capture of Gibraltar in 1704 [Ward]. See Intro., p. 139, above.

111. *Brake*] Thicket.

115. Warburton cites *Aen.*, II 429–30: "nec te tua plurima, Panthu, / labentem pietas nec Apollinis infula texit." Warton (in his *Essay on . . . Pope*) cites Virgil on the ox dying of the plague (*Georgics* III 525):
        quid labor aut benefacta iuvant? quid vomere terras
        invertisse gravis?

116. Jonson, *To Penshurst*, 28, had previously celebrated "The purpled pheasant with the speckled side".

118. *painted Wings*] Wakefield compares Virgil, *Georgics* III 243: "pictaeque volucres". EC cite *Par. Lost*, VII 434, where birds spread "thir painted wings".

119.   *When hoary winter cloaths the year in white,*
      The woods and fields to pleasing toils invite.   [P. *1736a–43*.]

119. See *Autumn*, 72n (p. 85, above).

121. Cf. Dryden, *To My Honour'd Kinsman, John Driden*, 52: "With well-breath'd Beagles, you surround the Wood".

And trace the Mazes of the circling Hare.
(Beasts, urg'd by us, their Fellow Beasts pursue,
And learn of Man each other to undo.)
With slaught'ring Guns th'unweary'd Fowler roves, 125
When Frosts have whiten'd all the naked Groves;
Where Doves in Flocks the leafless Trees o'ershade,
And lonely Woodcocks haunt the watry Glade.
He lifts the Tube, and levels with his Eye;
Strait a short Thunder breaks the frozen Sky.   130
Oft, as in Airy Rings they skim the Heath,
The clam'rous Lapwings feel the Leaden Death:
Oft as the mounting Larks their Notes prepare,
They fall, and leave their little Lives in Air.
     In genial Spring, beneath the quiv'ring Shade   135

123 urg'd] taught *1713a–32.*
132 Lapwings] Plovers *1713a–43.*

---

122. Cf. Cowley, *Horat. Epodon.* (see *Of Agriculture,* in *Several Discourses by way of Essays*), 35: "He runs the *Mazes* of the nimble Hare."
125*ff.* Cf. J. Philips, *Cyder* (1708), II 169–76:

Now the Fowler, warn'd
By these good Omens, with swift early Steps
Treads the crimp Earth, ranging thro' Fields and Glades
Offensive to the Birds, sulphureous Death
Checques their mid Flight, and heedless while they strain
Their tuneful Throats, the tow'ring, heavy Lead
O'er-takes their Speed; they leave their little Lives
Above the Clouds, præcipitant to Earth.

129. *The fowler lifts his level'd tube on high.* [P. *1736a–51.*]
EC cite Dryden, *Georgics* II 744: "And bends his Bow, and levels with his Eyes." Pope placed a comma against Dryden's line in the margin of his copy (Brit. Mus. shelf mark C. 28. f. 6).
132 var. Lapwings and plovers are closely related, and the two names in practice often have been interchanged. The description of the bird's flight and cry is appropriate to the lapwing.
134. Warburton compares Virgil, *Georgics* III 547: "praecipites alta vitam sub nube relinquunt." Cf. Dryden's tr., 815: "From Clouds they fall, and leave their Souls above". Cf. also Dryden, *Æn.,* v 683. Ault (*Pope's Own Miscellany,* p. xxxviii) points out that Pope quotes himself in *Il.,* XXIII 1041.
135. *quiv'ring Shade*] See *Summer,* 4n (p. 71, above).

Where cooling Vapours breathe along the Mead,
The patient Fisher takes his silent Stand
Intent, his Angle trembling in his Hand;
With Looks unmov'd, he hopes the Scaly Breed,
And eyes the dancing Cork and bending Reed.   140
Our plenteous Streams a various Race supply;
The bright-ey'd Perch with Fins of *Tyrian* Dye,
The silver Eel, in shining Volumes roll'd,
The yellow Carp, in Scales bedrop'd with Gold,
Swift Trouts, diversify'd with Crimson Stains,   145
And Pykes, the Tyrants of the watry Plains.
    Now *Cancer* glows with *Phœbus*' fiery Car;

135–46. Pope's catalogue of fishes imitates that given by Ausonius in *Mosella*,
85 *ff.*

137 *f.* Cf. the opening lines of *Windsor* (attributed to Rochester in *Poems on
Affairs of State*, vol. 1):
        Methinks I see our mighty Monarch stand,
        His pliant Angle trembling in his hand.
Cf. *Vertumnus and Pomona*, 42 (p. 379, below). Wakefield cites Ovid, *Art. Am.*, II
77: ". . . tremula dum captat arundine pisces". Cf. also *Met.*, VIII 217, and
Waller, *Upon a Lady*'s Fishing . . . , 11.

143. *Volumes*] Coils, folds, convolutions, especially of a serpent (OED).

144. *Scales bedrop'd with Gold*] Wakefield cites *Par. Lost*, VII 406: "thir wav'd
coats dropt with Gold". Cf. Philips, *Cerealia* (1706), 91: "Spires bedropt with
Gold".

145. *Crimson Stains*] Wakefield compares Drayton, *Poly-Olbion*, XXVI 240: "The
Trout by Nature markt with many a Crimson spot". Cf. Ausonius, *Mosella*, 88:
"purpureisque salar stellatus tergora guttis".

146. *Pykes, the Tyrants*] Wakefield cites Drayton, *Poly-Olbion*, XXVI 244–5:
"The *Chub* . . . / Food to the Tyrant *Pyke*". The epithet was common. Cf. *The
Compleat Angler*, ch. VIII: "The mighty *Luce* or *Pike* is taken to be the Tyrant (as
the *Salmon* is the King) of the fresh waters."

watry Plains] Wakefield cites *Aen.*, VI 724: "principio caelum ac terras campos-
que liquentis". Cf. Dryden, *Georgics* II 625: "And all for Keels of Ships, that
scour the watry Plains."

147.   But when bright Phœbus *from the twins invites*
            Our active genius to more free delights,
            With springing day we range the lawns around.
                                    [P. *1736a–43.*]
The sun (Phoebus's car) is in the constellation of the Twins (the zodiacal sign

The Youth rush eager to the Sylvan War;
Swarm o'er the Lawns, the Forest Walks surround,
Rowze the fleet Hart, and chear the opening Hound. 150
Th'impatient Courser pants in ev'ry Vein,
And pawing, seems to beat the distant Plain,
Hills, Vales, and Floods appear already crost,
And ere he starts, a thousand Steps are lost.
See! the bold Youth strain up the threatning Steep,   155
Rush thro' the Thickets, down the Vallies sweep,
Hang o'er their Coursers Heads with eager Speed,
And Earth rolls back beneath the flying Steed.
Let old *Arcadia* boast her ample Plain,
Th' Immortal Huntress, and her Virgin Train;   160
Nor envy *Windsor*! since thy Shades have seen
As bright a Goddess, and as chast a Queen;

159 ample] spacious *1713a–14*.

---

of Gemini) from about May 21 to June 22. It enters the constellation of the
Crab (the zodiacal sign of Cancer) at the summer solstice, June 22.
   This passage seems closely related to the opening of the hunt episode in *Aen.*,
IV 129–35.
   150. *Rowze*] A technical hunting term. Cf. Kersey, *Dictionarium Anglo-Britannicum*: "To Rouse a Hart, is to raise him from his Harbour". Denham had described a royal stag-hunt at length in *Cooper's Hill*, 241–322.
   opening] Giving tongue.
   151*ff.* "Translated from Statius [*Theb.*, VI 400–1],
                    Stare adeo miserum est, pereunt vestigia mille
                    Ante fugam, absentemque ferit gravis ungula campum.
These lines Mr. Dryden, in his preface to his translation of Fresnoy's Art of
painting, calls *wonderfully fine*, and says *they would cost him an hour, if he had the
leisure to translate them, there is so much of beauty in the original*; which was the reason,
I suppose, why Mr. P. tried his strength with them" [Warburton]. Pope may
have been inspired by the whole passage; thus l. 151 seems to echo Statius, 395:
"Concurrit summos animosum frigus in artus". Wakefield cites Virgil, *Georgics*
III 83–4:
                    tum, si qua sonum procul arma dedere,
                stare loco nescit, micat auribus et tremit artus.
   151–4. Cf. *Ess. on Crit.*, 225–8.
   162. Wakefield noted the application "of the offices and attributes of *Diana* as
goddess of the *woods*, the *luminary* of the *night*, and the chief agent in the produc-

Whose Care, like hers, protects the Sylvan Reign,
The Earth's fair Light, and Empress of the Main.
    Here too, 'tis sung, of old *Diana* stray'd,   165
And *Cynthus'* Top forsook for *Windsor* Shade;
Here was she seen o'er Airy Wastes to rove,
Seek the clear Spring, or haunt the pathless Grove;
Here arm'd with Silver Bows, in early Dawn,
Her buskin'd Virgins trac'd the Dewy Lawn.   170
    Above the rest a rural Nymph was fam'd,
Thy Offspring, *Thames*! the fair *Lodona* nam'd,
(*Lodona*'s Fate, in long Oblivion cast,

165–6 Here, as old Bards have sung, *Diana* stray'd,
    Bath'd in the Springs, [spring, *1727–32*] or sought the cool-
    ing Shade; *1713a–43*.
167–8 *Add. 1751.*   171 *No new paragraph 1713a–32.*

tion of the *tides*, to Queen *Anne.*" EC compare Congreve, *Prologue to the Queen*
[Mary], 9–10:

    For never was in *Rome*, nor *Athens*, seen
    So fair a Circle, and so bright a Queen.

See Intro., p. 140, above.
   163. An allusion to the interest taken by Anne in hunting. Cf. Swift, *Journal
to Stella*, July 31, 1711: "The queen was abroad to-day in order to hunt . . . she
hunts in a chaise with one horse, which she drives herself, and drives furiously,
like Jehu, and is a mighty hunter, like Nimrod."
   165.   *Yet here, 'tis sung, of old* Diana *stray'd:*
                  And Cynthus' *top forsook for* Windsor *shade.*
                  Here was she seen o'er sunny heaths to rove,
                  Seek the clear spring, or haunt the pathless grove.
                               [P. *1736a–43*.]
    These variant lines noted by Pope were finally incorporated into the 1751
text. See textual variant.
   170. *trac'd*] I.e., trod or traversed.
   171. In the following Ovidian episode of Lodona, Pope made use of several
sources, including perhaps an anonymous translation of Ovid, *Met.*, v 572–641,
attributed to him by Ault (*New Light on Pope*, 1949, pp. 38–48), and published
in Lintot's *Miscellany* (1712) with the title, *The Story of Arethusa*. See Intro., p. 140,
above.
   173. *long Oblivion*] Wakefield cites Virgil, *Aen.*, vi 715: "securos latices et
longa oblivia potant". Dryden, vi 968, has "long oblivion".

The Muse shall sing, and what she sings shall last)
Scarce could the Goddess from her Nymph be known,
But by the Crescent and the golden Zone,   176
She scorn'd the Praise of Beauty, and the Care;
A Belt her Waste, a Fillet binds her Hair,
A painted Quiver on her Shoulder sounds,
And with her Dart the flying Deer she wounds.   180
It chanc'd, as eager of the Chace the Maid
Beyond the Forest's verdant Limits stray'd,
Pan saw and lov'd, and burning with Desire

183 burning] furious *1713a–14.*

175*f.* Cf. Sandys, *Met.,* I 736–40 (Syrinx episode):

> In exercises, and in chaste desire,
> *Diana*-like: and such in her attire.
> You either in each other might behold:
> Her Bowe was Horne; *Diana's* was of Gold:
> Yet oft mistooke.

EC compare Dryden, *Met.,* I 961–2.

176. *Crescent*] The crescent moon, emblem of Diana.
Zone] A girdle or belt. Cf. l. 178*n.*

177. Cf. Ovid, *Met.,* v 580–2 (Arethusa episode):

> sed quamvis formae numquam mihi fama petita est,
> quamvis fortis eram, formosae nomen habebam,
> nec mea me facies nimium laudata iuvabat.

178. Warburton cites Ovid, *Met.,* II 412–13 (Callisto episode):

> nec positu variare comas; ubi fibula vestem,
> vitta coercuerat neglectos alba capillos.

Cf. Sandys, *Met.,* II 451–5:

> 'Twas not her Art to spin, nor with much care
> And fine varietie to trick her haire;
> But, with a zone, her looser garments bound,
> And her rude tresses in a fillet wound:
> Now armed with a Dart, now with a Bowe.

a Fillet binds] Cf. Ovid, *Met.,* I 477 (Daphne episode): "vitta coercebat positos sine lege capillos". Cf. Sandys, *Met.,* I 497; Dryden, *Met.,* I 640.

179. *painted Quiver*] Cf. Ovid, *Met.,* II 421, "pictam . . . pharetram", tr. by Sandys (II 464) as "painted Quiuer". Cf. Dryden, *Æn.,* I 466.

on her Shoulder sounds] Wakefield compares Dryden, *Æn.,* XI 968: "*Diana's* Arms upon her Shoulder sound". EC compare XI 1140: "A guilded Quiver from his Shoulder sounds".

183. *burning with Desire*] EC compare Dryden, *Æn.,* XII 108–9:

Pursu'd her Flight; her Flight increas'd his Fire.
Not half so swift the trembling Doves can fly,   185
When the fierce Eagle cleaves the liquid Sky;
Not half so swiftly the fierce Eagle moves,
When thro' the Clouds he drives the trembling Doves;
As from the God she flew with furious Pace,
Or as the God, more furious, urg'd the Chace.   190
Now fainting, sinking, pale, the Nymph appears;

189–90 As from the God with fearful Speed she flew,
　　　　As did the God with equal Speed pursue. *1713a–14.*

　　　　The Lover gaz'd, and burning with desire,
　　　　The more he look'd, the more he fed the Fire.
Cf. also Ovid, *Met.*, II 410.
　　184. Cf. Sandys, *Met.*, v 603: "The faster followed he, the more did burne."
　　185. Warburton compares Ovid, *Met.*, v 605–6:
　　　　ut fugere accipitrem penna trepidante columbae,
　　　　ut solet accipiter trepidas urgere columbas.
EC cite Sandys's tr., v 698–9:
　　　　As trembling Doues the eger Hawkes exchew;
　　　　So eger Hawkes the trembling Doues persew.
　　186. *liquid Sky*] Latin *liquidus,* i.e., clear, transparent. Cf. Dryden, *Georgics* III 378: ". . . but they / That wing the liquid Air . . ." Cf. *The Arrival of Ulysses in Ithaca,* 14 (p. 466, below).
　　189. Cf. Dryden, *Met.*, I 709 (Daphne episode): ". . . so furiously she flies."
　　190 var. Note the alteration of this line in 1717, to remove the only expletive in the poem.
　　191–6. Warburton cites Ovid, *Met.*, v 614–17:
　　　　sol erat a tergo: vidi praecedere longam
　　　　ante pedes umbram, nisi si timor illa videbat;
　　　　sed certe sonitusque pedum terrebat et ingens
　　　　crinales vittas adflabat anhelitus oris.
Wakefield compares Sandys's tr., v 708–11:
　　　　The Sunne was at our backs: before my feet
　　　　I saw his shadow; or my feare did see't.
　　　　How-ere his sounding steps, and thick-drawne breath
　　　　That fann'd my haire, affrighted me to death;
and also Ovid, *Met.*, I 540–44 (Daphne episode):
　　　　qui tamen insequitur pennis adiutus Amoris,
　　　　ocior est requiemque negat tergoque fugacis

Now close behind his sounding Steps she hears;
And now his Shadow reach'd her as she run,
(His Shadow lengthen'd by the setting Sun)
And now his shorter Breath with sultry Air   195
Pants on her Neck, and fans her parting Hair.
In vain on Father *Thames* she calls for Aid,
Nor could *Diana* help her injur'd Maid.
Faint, breathless, thus she pray'd, nor pray'd in vain;
"Ah *Cynthia*! ah—tho' banish'd from thy Train,   200
"Let me, O let me, to the Shades repair,
"My native Shades—there weep, and murmur there."
She said, and melting as in Tears she lay,
In a soft, silver Stream dissolv'd away.
The silver Stream her Virgin Coldness keeps,   205
For ever murmurs, and for ever weeps;
Still bears the Name the hapless Virgin bore,
And bathes the Forest where she rang'd before.

---

194 *No parentheses 1736a–51.*   197 calls] call'd *1736a–43.*
202 there."] there. *1713a–51.*

---

                inminet et crinem sparsum cervicibus adflat.
                viribus absumptis expalluit illa citaeque
                victa labore fugae. . .
Cf. *The Story of Arethusa*, 50–1.
    200. "*Ah Cynthia*] Wakefield compares Daphne's prayer to her father Peneus
in Ovid, *Met.*, I 545. Cf. also Arethusa's cry to Diana in *Met.*, v 618.
    203 *ff.* Wakefield compares Claudian, *Rape of Proserpine*, III 250–3:
                illa nihil, tacito sed laesa veneno
           solvitur in laticem: subrepit crinibus umor;
           liquitur in roremque pedes et brachia manant
           nostraque mox lambit vestigia perspicuus fons.
Cf. the transformation of Arethusa into a stream in Ovid, *Met.*, v 632 *ff.*
    207. *Still bears the Name*] *The River* Loddon. [P. *1713a–51.*]
  As the river Loddon flows into the Thames near Binfield, Pope perhaps knew
it better than the other tributaries he mentions later. The idea of using the
Loddon may have been suggested by the fact that the river in Arcadia where
Syrinx met her fate (Ovid, *Met.*, I 702) was called the Ladon. Cf. Dryden's tr.
of the Syrinx episode, l. 988: "They still retain the Name of his Ungrateful
Fair".

In her chast Current oft the Goddess laves,
And with Celestial Tears augments the Waves.   210
Oft in her Glass the musing Shepherd spies
The headlong Mountains and the downward Skies,
The watry Landskip of the pendant Woods,
And absent Trees that tremble in the Floods;
In the clear azure Gleam the Flocks are seen,   215
And floating Forests paint the Waves with Green.
Thro' the fair Scene rowl slow the lingring Streams,
Then foaming pour along, and rush into the *Thames*.
   Thou too, great Father of the *British* Floods!
With joyful Pride survey'st our lofty Woods,   220

220 survey'st] survey *1717–32*.

210. *augments the Waves*] EC cite Dryden's tr. of Ovid, *Art of Love*, I 599: "Her briny Tears augment the briny Flood." Cf. *Sapho to Phaon*, 185*n* (p. 401, below).

211–16. These six lines were added after the first writing of this poem. [P. *1751*.]

Pope imitates Ausonius, *Mosella*, 189–99:

> Illa fruenda palam species, cum glaucus opaco
> respondet colli fluvius, frondere videntur
> fluminei latices et palmite consitus amnis.
> quis color ille vadis, seras cum propulit umbras
> Hesperus et viridi perfundit monte Mosellam!
> tota natant crispis iuga motibus et *tremit absens*
> *pampinus* et vitreis vindemia turget in undis.
> adnumerat virides derisus navita vites,
> navita caudiceo fluitans super aequora lembo
> per medium, qua sese amni confundit imago
> collis et umbrarum confinia conserit amnis.

Italics added. Cf. also Vida, *Poetica*, III 64–9.

212. Cf. Ausonius, *Mosella*, 223–4:

> reddit nautales vitreo sub gurgite formas
> et redigit pandas *inversi corporis* umbras.

Italics added. Wakefield compares Dryden, *The State of Innocence*, II 171–2:

> What's here? another Firmament below,
> Spread wide, and other Trees that downward grow?

For *Mountains* in this line, see above, 87*n*.

219. Wakefield cites Dryden, *Æn.*, VIII 46: ". . . the Father of the *Roman* Flood."

G

Where tow'ring Oaks their growing Honours rear,
And future Navies on thy Shores appear.
Not *Neptune*'s self from all his Streams receives
A wealthier Tribute, than to thine he gives.
No Seas so rich, so gay no Banks appear,   225
No Lake so gentle, and no Spring so clear.
Nor *Po* so swells the fabling Poet's Lays,
While led along the Skies his Current strays,
As thine, which visits *Windsor*'s fam'd Abodes,
To grace the Mansion of our earthly Gods.   230
Nor all his Stars above a Lustre show,
Like the bright Beauties on thy Banks below;
Where *Jove*, subdu'd by mortal Passion still,
Might change *Olympus* for a nobler Hill.

221 growing] spreading *1713a–43*.
222 Shores] Banks *1713a–32*.
223 his Streams] his Floods *1713a–32*; her streams *1740–51*.
225 so gay no Banks appear,] so full no Streams appear, *1713a–32*.
227–8 Not fabled *Po* more swells the Poets Lays,
      While thro' the Skies his shining Current strays, *1713a–43*.
229 As] Than *1713a–43*.
231–3 Nor all his Stars a brighter Lustre show,
      Than the fair Nymphs that gild [grace *1736a–43*] thy Shore
      [side *1736a–43*] below;
      Here *Jove* himself, subdu'd by Beauty still, *1713a–43*.

226. Cf. Denham's famous lines on the Thames, *Cooper's Hill*, 191–2:
      Though deep, yet clear, though gentle, yet not dull,
      Strong without rage, without ore-flowing full.
  228. Virgil (*Georgics* I 482, IV 372) and Ovid (*Met.*, II 372) gave to the river
Po the name of Eridanus, a constellation of the southern hemisphere which has
the form of a winding river. EC compare *Cooper's Hill*, 193–6:
      Heaven her *Eridanus* no more shall boast,
      Whose Fame in thine, like lesser Currents lost,
      Thy Nobler streams shall visit *Jove*'s aboads,
      To shine amongst the Stars, and bath the Gods.
  229. *As thine*] The Thames, especially as it was celebrated in *Cooper's Hill*.

Happy the Man whom this bright Court approves,
His Sov'reign favours, and his Country loves;   236
Happy next him who to these Shades retires,
Whom Nature charms, and whom the Muse inspires,
Whom humbler Joys of home-felt Quiet please,
Successive Study, Exercise and Ease.   240
He gathers Health from Herbs the Forest yields,
And of their fragrant Physick spoils the Fields:
With Chymic Art exalts the Min'ral Pow'rs,
And draws the Aromatick Souls of Flow'rs.
Now marks the Course of rolling Orbs on high;   245

235.   *Happy the man who to the shades retires,*
            But doubly happy, if the Muse inspires!
            Blest whom the sweets of home-felt quiet please;
            But far more blest, who study joins with ease. [P. *1736a–51.*]

If these early lines refer to Trumbull's retirement in the Forest, the words
"whom the Muse inspires" are puzzling, for there is no evidence that Trumbull
attempted poetry. He wrote to Pope on April 9, 1708 (*Corr.*, I 45), that he could
not "pretend to judge of Poetry", for he had never been "practic'd in the Art."
See also his letter to Pope of Jan. 19, 1716 (*Corr.*, I 327).

235–58. Pope is primarily indebted here to Virgil's praise of country retirement in *Georgics* II 458*ff*. (but see also Horace, *Epode* II). The opening phrase,
"Happy the Man", seems to have introduced innumerable English poems on
the same theme, including an early version of Pope's *Ode on Solitude* (*Corr.*, I 68).
See Maren-Sofie Røstvig, *The Happy Man* (1954–8), 2 vols.

241*ff*. Cf. J. Philips, *Cyder*, I 754–64:
                        he to his Labours hies
            Gladsome, intent on somewhat that may ease
            Unhealthy Mortals, and with curious Search
            Examines all the Properties of Herbs,
            Fossils and Minerals . . .
                                    Or else his Thoughts
            Are exercis'd with Speculations deep
            Of Good, and Just, and Meet, and th'wholesome Rules
            Of Temperance, and aught that may improve
            The moral Life. . .

242. Cf. Dryden, *To My Honour'd Kinsman, John Driden*, 116: "Draws Phisick
from the Fields, in Draughts of Vital Air."

243. *exalts*] "In Alchemy and early Chemistry: To raise (a substance or its
qualities) to a higher 'degree' . . . to intensify, render more powerful" (OED).

244. *draws*] To inhale, or perhaps to extract by suction or distillation.

O'er figur'd Worlds now travels with his Eye.
Of ancient Writ unlocks the learned Store,
Consults the Dead, and lives past Ages o'er.
Or wandring thoughtful in the silent Wood,
Attends the Duties of the Wise and Good,   250
T'observe a Mean, be to himself a Friend,
To follow Nature, and regard his End.
Or looks on Heav'n with more than mortal Eyes,
Bids his free Soul expatiate in the Skies,
Amid her Kindred Stars familiar roam,   255
Survey the Region, and confess her Home!
Such was the Life great *Scipio* once admir'd,
Thus *Atticus*, and *Trumbal* thus retir'd.

255 Amid] Amidst *1713a–22*.

246. *figur'd Worlds*] Perhaps the Zodiac, or a globe of the world. To figure is
to portray or represent, and OED cites Addison, *Dialogues Upon Ancient Medals*:
"The Emperor . . . holds a Globe in his hand, to figure out the Earth. . ." Cf.
l. 335*n*, below.
   250. *the Wise and Good*] Wakefield cites Horace, *Ep.* i iv 4:
           an tacitum silvas inter reptare salubris,
           curantem quidquid dignum sapiente bonoque est?
EC cite Creech's tr. (in *Odes, Satyrs and Epistles*, 1684):
           Or dost thou gravely walk the healthy Wood,
           Considering what befits the Wise and Good?
   252. *regard his End*] Warton compares Lucan, ii 381–2:
                   . . . servare modum finemque tenere
           naturamque sequi.
The lines express the stoical principles of Cato.
   254.*ff*. Cf. *An Essay on Man*, i 97–8 (vol. iii i, p. 26).
   255. *Kindred Stars*] Wakefield cites Ovid, *Met.*, i 81: "cognati caeli".
   257. After his victory over Hannibal and the Carthaginians in the second
Punic War, Scipio Africanus declined the various political distinctions offered
to him. When, many years later, his enemies succeeded in bringing him to trial
on charges of misconduct, he reminded the people of Rome of his past services,
set the laws at defiance, and retired to his country seat at Liternum. He never
returned to Rome, but passed his life cultivating his estate.
   Cf. *Temple of Fame*, 163–4 (vol. ii, pp. 254–5).
   258. *Atticus*] Titus Pomponius, the friend and correspondent of Cicero, refused to sue for public honour or to become engaged in political controversy.

Ye sacred Nine! that all my Soul possess,
Whose Raptures fire mc, and whose Visions bless, 260
Bear me, oh bear me to sequester'd Scenes,
The Bow'ry Mazes and surrounding Greens;
To *Thames*'s Banks which fragrant Breezes fill,
Or where ye Muses sport on *Cooper*'s Hill.
(On *Cooper*'s Hill eternal Wreaths shall grow, 265
While lasts the Mountain, or while *Thames* shall flow)
I seem thro' consecrated Walks to rove,
I hear soft Musick dye along the Grove;
Led by the Sound I roam from Shade to Shade,
By God-like Poets Venerable made: 270
Here his first Lays Majestick *Denham* sung;
There the last Numbers flow'd from *Cowley*'s Tongue.

261 Scenes,] Scenes *1713a–14*.
262 The] Of *1713a–22*; To *1727–32*.   268 I] And *1713a–32*.

Instead he withdrew from Rome to Athens and devoted himself to a life of study.
He was called Atticus because of his long residence in Athens.

259. *Ye sacred Nine*] Wakefield compares *Georgics* II 475, and Dryden's tr.,
673–4:

> Ye sacred Muses, with whose Beauty fir'd,
> My Soul is ravish'd, and my Brain inspir'd.

261–4. Cf. *Georgics* II 486–9, and Dryden's tr., 692–5:

> Some God conduct me to the sacred Shades,
> Where Bacchanals are sung by *Spartan* Maids.
> Or lift me high to *Hemus* hilly Crown;
> Or in the Plains of *Tempe* lay me down.

266. *Mountain*] Cooper's Hill. But see above, l. 87*n*.
270. *Venerable made*] EC compare Philips, *Cyder*, II 6–8:

> or what,
> Unrival'd Authors by their Presence, made
> For ever venerable, rural Seats . . .

271. *first Lays*] Before the opening of the Civil War in 1642, Denham had
written *The Destruction of Troy* (a translation of *Aeneid* II), the first draft of *Cooper's
Hill*, and *The Sophy*. His house in Egham, near Windsor, was confiscated by the
Parliamentary forces in 1643. See Denham's *Poetical Works*, ed. T. H. Banks
(1928), pp. 6, 11. For the epithet *majestic* see *Ess. on Crit.*, 361*n*.

272. *Mr.* Cowley died at Chertsey, *on the Borders of the Forest, and was from thence
convey'd to* Westminster. [P. *1713a–51*.]

O early lost! what Tears the River shed
When the sad Pomp along his Banks was led?
His drooping Swans on ev'ry Note expire,   275
And on his Willows hung each Muse's Lyre.
    Since Fate relentless stop'd their Heav'nly Voice,
No more the Forests ring, or Groves rejoice;
Who now shall charm the Shades where *Cowley* strung
His living Harp, and lofty *Denham* sung?   280
But hark! the Groves rejoice, the Forest rings!
Are these reviv'd? or is it *Granville* sings?
    'Tis yours, my Lord, to bless our soft Retreats,
And call the Muses to their ancient Seats,
To paint anew the flow'ry Sylvan Scenes,   285
To crown the Forests with Immortal Greens,
Make *Windsor* Hills in lofty Numbers rise,

---

273. *O early lost*] Cowley died in 1667, at the age of 49. Cf. Walsh, *Delia*, 87:
"Oh, early lost!"
    273*f.* Wakefield cites Virgil, *Aen.*, VI 869-70, 873-4:
          ostendent terris hunc tantum fata, nec ultra
          esse sinent . . .
                              . . . vel quae, Tiberine, videbis
          funera, cum tumulum praeterlabere recentem!
See Dryden's tr., VI 1208: "What Fun'ral Pomp shall floating *Tiber* see."
    Cowley's body was floated down the river from Chertsey to London. The
pomp is not exaggerated, for Evelyn, who attended the funeral, says (*Diary*,
August 3, 1667) that Cowley was "conveyed to Westminster Abbey in a hearse
with six horses . . . near a hundred coaches of noblemen and persons of quality
following." Pope may have had in mind these words from Cowley's epitaph in
Westminster Abbey: "Excessit e vita Anno Ætatis suae 49; et honorifica pompa
elatus ex Ædibus Buckingamianis, Viris illustribus omnium Ordinum exsequias
celebrantibus sepultus est. . ."
    275.   *What sighs, what murmurs fill'd the vocal shore!*
                  His tuneful swans were heard to sing no more.
                                                    [P. *1736a-51.*]
    276. *each Muse's Lyre*] Cowley attempted many poetical genres. In his epitaph
in Westminster Abbey, he is called *Anglorum Pindarus, Flaccus, Maro.* As Wakefield notes, Pope's line recalls Psalm CXXXVI 2 (Douay, 1635 edn): "On the
willowes in the middes therof, we hanged vp our instruments."
    280. *living Harp*] Appropriately, Pope seems to take the phrase from Cowley
himself, *The Resurrection*, st. 2: "Begin the *Song*, and strike the *Living Lyre*".

And lift her Turrets nearer to the Skies;
To sing those Honours you deserve to wear,
And add new Lustre to her Silver *Star*.   290
   Here noble *Surrey* felt the sacred Rage,
Surrey, the *Granville* of a former Age:
Matchless his Pen, victorious was his Lance;

290. All the lines that follow ⟨till within eight of the conclusion, *1736a–43*⟩ were not added to the poem till the year 1710. ⟨The 425th verse, *My Humble Muse in unambitious strains*, &c. immediately follow'd this. *1736a–43.*⟩ ⟨*1751 adds:*⟩ What immediately followed this, and made the Conclusion, were these,

> My humble Muse in unambitious strains
> Paints the green forests and the flow'ry plains;
> Where I obscurely pass my careless days,
> Pleas'd in the silent shade with empty praise,
> Enough for me that to the list'ning swains
> First in these fields I sung the sylvan strains.

[P. 1736a–51.]

For 1710 one should perhaps read 1712 or 1713 (see Intro., pp. 125–30). The lines quoted in the note, with slight alterations, still serve as a conclusion to the poem. Cf. 427 *ff*.

290. *Silver Star*] The Star of the Order of the Garter, instituted at Windsor Castle by Edward III. It was to provide a meeting-place for the Order that Edward reconstructed Windsor Castle.

Granville in his *The Progress of Beauty* (in *Poems Upon Several Occasions*, 1712), 150–9, had already "sung the Honours" of the Order. Cf. these lines alluding to the well-known anecdote of the garter of the Countess of Salisbury:

> But *Salisbury*'s Garter shall for ever last,
> Which thro' the World by living Monarchs worn,
> Adds Grace to Scepters, and does Crowns adorn.

Denham alluded to the Order in *Cooper's Hill*, 83 *ff*. In spite of Pope's l. 289, Granville was never admitted to the Order.

291. *Surrey*] Henry Howard, *Earl of* Surrey, *one of the first Refiners of the* English *Poetry*; ⟨*famous in the Time of* Henry *the* VIII*th for his Sonnets, the Scene of many of which is laid at* Windsor. *1713a–14*⟩ *who flourish'd in the time of* Henry *the* VIIIth ⟨*who . . . the* VIII [th]. *1717–51*⟩. [P. *1713a–51*.]

293 *f*. In their compliment these lines appear to echo a poem sent to Granville by his cousin Elizabeth Higgons (see the verses *Sent the Author into the Country*, in *Poems Upon Several Occasions*, 1712, pp. 94–6), which opens by remarking upon Granville's self-imposed retirement to the "Shades", and then recalls to him the time when, at a tournament in Paris, his

victorious Lance

Bore the disputed Prize from all the Youth of *France*,

Bold in the Lists, and graceful in the Dance:
In the same Shades the *Cupids* tun'd his Lyre,   295
To the same Notes, of Love, and soft Desire:
Fair *Geraldine*, bright Object of his Vow,
Then fill'd the Groves, as heav'nly *Myra* now.
 Oh wou'dst thou sing what Heroes *Windsor* bore,
What Kings first breath'd upon her winding Shore, 300

In the first Trials that are made for Fame.
The lady also compliments Granville as one who succeeded in all he did, whe-
ther with "graceful Art" he led
 The fiery Barb, or with as graceful Motion tread
 In shining Balls, where all agree
 To give the highest Praise and the first Place to thee.
 297. *Fair Geraldine*] Lady Elizabeth Fitzgerald (1528?–89), youngest daugh-
ter of the Earl of Kildare. Surrey's love poems were long supposed to have been
addressed to her. In 1537 he wrote the sonnet, *Description and praise of his loue
Geraldine*, in which occur the lines:
 Hampton me taught to wishe her first for mine:
 And Windsor, alas, dothe chase me from her sight.
Surrey was confined at Windsor in 1537 for striking a courtier in the royal
grounds of Hampton Court. It is admitted that this was the only poem written
for this lady: she was only nine years old at the time. But later, with Nashe's
novel *The Unfortunate Traveller*, which gives a fanciful account of Surrey's travels
on the continent, and Drayton's Heroicall Epistle, *Henry Howard, Earle of Surrey,
to the Lady Geraldine* (1598), there grew up a legend in which Surrey and Geraldine became the English Dante and Beatrice. Pope followed the accepted tradition, and ll. 293–8 of his poem seem to echo these written by Surrey during his
confinement in Windsor Castle (*Prisoned in windsor, he recounteth his pleasure there
passed*):
 The secrete groues, which oft we made resounde
 Of pleasaunt playnt, and of our ladies prayse . . .
 298. *fill'd the Groves*] See *Autumn*, 4n (above, p. 80).
 Myra] The name Granville bestowed in his songs, first upon Mary of Modena,
then upon Frances Brudenal, Countess of Newburgh, when the latter became
his mistress. See E. Handasyde, *Granville the Polite* (1933), 21*ff*.
 299. Cf. *Georgics* II 167–72, where Virgil celebrates heroes of the Roman past.
See Intro., p. 142, above. Pope's lines also recall a similar roll-call of noble
names in *Cooper's Hill*, 61*ff*.:
 she [Cybele] cannot boast . . .
 More *Hero's* than can *Windsor*. . .
 300. *What Kings*] Bowles compares *Cooper's Hill*, 75–6:

Or raise old Warriors whose ador'd Remains
In weeping Vaults her hallow'd Earth contains!
With *Edward*'s Acts adorn the shining Page,
Stretch his long Triumphs down thro' ev'ry Age,
Draw Monarchs chain'd, and *Cressi*'s glorious Field, 305

305 Monarchs chain'd,] Kings enchain'd; *1713a–14.*

> Not to recount those several Kings, to whom
> It gave a Cradle, or to whom a Tombe.

Edward III and Henry VI were born at Windsor, the first in 1312, the second in 1421. Edward IV, Henry VIII, and Charles I were buried there.

winding Shore] Perhaps Pope knew the etymological meaning of the word *Windsor* as given in *Camden's Britannia* (1695), p. 151: "Next, the Thames goes to *Windsor*, call'd in Saxon Windesoure, Windlesora, and also Windlesofra, from the *winding banks*, ofre in that language signifying a *bank* or *shore*." But compare Dryden, *Æn.*, 1 809: "The Ports and Creeks of ev'ry winding Shore".

302. *weeping Vaults*] Wakefield says, "A puerile conceit, from the dew, which runs down stone and metals in damp weather", and cites Virgil, *Georgics* 1 480: "et maestum inlacrimat templis ebur aeraque sudant." Cf. *El. to Abel.*, 22 (vol. II, p. 300). See below, l. 313*n.*

303. Edward III. *born here.* [P. *1713a–51.*]

303. *adorn the shining Page*] Otway, *Windsor Castle* (1685), 348–50, describes, much as does Pope, the paintings by Verrio in St George's Hall:

> Describe that lofty monumental Hall,
> Where *England*'s Triumphs grace the shining Wall,
> When she led captive Kings from conquer'd *Gaul.*

303–10. Verrio had represented in St George's Hall at Windsor the triumphal procession in which King John of France was led captive by the Black Prince. There is a description by George Bickham, quoted by W. H. St John Hope in *Windsor Castle* (1913), I 338.

Antonio Verrio, born at Lecce in 1639, was called from France to England by Charles II, who employed him to paint the ceilings in Windsor Castle. He was retained by James II, but for some time he was unwilling to work for William III. He later agreed to decorate Hampton Court for William and died there in 1707. As Wakefield noted, Pope was not always so complimentary to Verrio. See *Epistle* IV (*To Burlington*), 146.

305. *Monarchs chain'd*] An allusion to David II, King of Scotland, taken prisoner (according to popular belief by Queen Philippa, the consort of Edward III) at the battle of Neville's Cross in 1346 and released in 1357; and to Jean le Bon, King of France, whom the Black Prince defeated and captured at Poitiers in 1356. King John was brought to Windsor and at one time was allowed to go to France to raise his ransom of three million gold crowns. As he was unable to

The Lillies blazing on the Regal Shield.
Then, from her Roofs when *Verrio*'s Colours fall,
And leave inanimate the naked Wall;
Still in thy Song shou'd vanquish'd *France* appear,

---

collect the entire sum, he returned to captivity and died at the Savoy Palace in
1364. The phrase "Monarchs chain'd" is figurative, for both princes enjoyed
considerable liberty.

Otway, *Windsor Castle*, 359–63, describes Verrio's portrayal of the Black
Prince's Triumph thus:

> Here may they see how good old *Edward* sate
> And did his Glorious Son's Arrival wait,
> When from the Fields of vanquish'd *France* he came,
> Follow'd by Spoils, and usher'd in by Fame.
> In Golden Chains he their Quell'd Monarch led.

Denham, *Cooper's Hill*, 79–82, addressed Edward III thus:

> And thy *Bellona*, who the Consort came
> Not only to thy Bed, but to thy Fame,
> She to thy Triumph led one Captive King,
> And brought that son, which did the second bring.

Bellona here is Queen Philippa. Even Granville, *The Progress of Beauty*, 150–1,
had recalled these heroic events:

> Of *Scots*, and *Gauls* defeated, and their Kings
> Thy Captives, *Edward*, Fame for ever sings.

306. *The Lillies*] EC cite *Cooper's Hill*, 77–8:

> But thee (great *Edward*) and thy greater son,
> (The lillies which his Father wore, he won),

the "greater son" being Edward, the Black Prince. On Jan. 26, 1340, Edward
III "assumed the title of king of France, and quartered the lilies of France with
the leopards of England" (DNB).

307. *Then, from her Roofs*] An allusion to some of the ceilings painted by Verrio. Cf. the description of the Queen's Guard-Chamber, where Verrio represented "*Britannia*, in all her Glory, seated on a Globe; and *Europe*, *Asia*, *Africa*,
and *America*, paying their Court to her" (George Bickham, *Deliciae Britannicae*,
1742, quoted by W. H. St John Hope in *Windsor Castle*, 1913, 1 337). Also this
description of the King's Bedchamber: "On the Cieling is delineated King
Charles the IId, seated on his Throne in his Robes of State, with a Figure, drest
in a Mantle, embroider'd with *Flower-de-luces*, representing *France*, as an humble
Supplicant, kneeling at his Feet" (Ibid., 1 339).

Colours fall] Describing (1724) Verrio's paintings in *A Tour Thro the whole
Island of Great Britain* (ed. G. D. H. Cole, 1927, 1 307), Defoe speaks of the "Salts
of the Lime in the Wall, having work'd out, and spoiled a great Piece of the
Paint."

And bleed for ever under *Britain*'s Spear.   310
   Let softer Strains Ill-fated *Henry* mourn,
And Palms Eternal flourish round his Urn.
Here o'er the Martyr-King the Marble weeps,
And fast beside him, once-fear'd *Edward* sleeps:
Whom not th'extended *Albion* could contain,   315
From old *Belerium* to the *Northern* Main,
The Grave unites; where ev'n the Great find Rest,
And blended lie th' Oppressor and th' Opprest!

316 *Northern*] *German 1713a–14.*

310. *And bleed for ever*] Wakefield compares the couplet in Halifax's *An Epistle to . . . Dorset* (1690), which describes ironically all the fuss the French would have made if Louis had been victorious and wounded in the arm as William III was in 1690 at the battle of the Boyne. The Gobelins, Halifax says, would cover the walls of the palaces with pictures of the King's victory:
       The wounded Arm wou'd furnish all their Rooms,
       And bleed for ever Scarlet in the Looms.
The phrase is parodied in *Dunciad* A, II 148 (vol. v, p. 119).
   311. *Henry*] Henry VI. [P. *1713a–51.*]
   Edward, duke of York, proclaimed himself king under the title of Edward IV in 1461. Henry VI was a fugitive in the North until he was taken prisoner in 1465. From October, 1470, to April, 1471, Henry was restored to the throne, and Edward took flight. Henry's allies were defeated at Barnet, April 14, 1471, and Henry was probably murdered on May 21. His body was transferred from its grave in Chertsey Abbey to Windsor in 1484. He was buried in St George's chapel, not far from Edward IV, who had been buried there in 1483. DNB notes that Henry VI was revered after his death by Yorkshiremen "as a saint and martyr, and many miracles attested his holiness." His formal canonization was sought for. Hence the phrase in l. 312, *palms eternal*, which are not those of victory, but of martyrdom.
   313. Cf. Congreve, *The Mourning Muse of Alexis*, 85: "The Marble weeps . . ." See above, l. 302n.
   314. *Edward*] Edward IV. [P. *1713a–51.*]
   316. *old Belerium*] *Belerium* (or *Bolerium*) *promontorium* was the Latin name for Land's End in Cornwall. Cf. *Lycidas*, 159–60: "Or whether thou . . . Sleep'st by the fable of *Bellerus* old"; and also Diodorus Siculus, v xxi 3. Cf. Cowley, *Plantarum Liber Sextus*, 667: "*Belerii* extremis a cornibus *Orcadas* usque."
   Northern Main] Wakefield compares Dryden's tr. of Juvenal, *Sat.*, x 236–7:
       Whom *Affrick* was not able to contain,
       Whose length runs Level with th'*Atlantick* main.

Make sacred *Charles*'s Tomb for ever known,
(Obscure the Place, and uninscrib'd the Stone)   320
Oh Fact accurst! What Tears has *Albion* shed,
Heav'ns! what new Wounds, and how her old have bled?
She saw her Sons with purple Deaths expire,
Her sacred Domes involv'd in rolling Fire,
A dreadful Series of Intestine Wars,   325
Inglorious Triumphs, and dishonest Scars.

324 Fire,] Fire. *1713a–22.*

319. *Charles's Tomb*] The body of Charles I was buried in St George's Chapel, in the same tomb as Henry VIII, and without any service. The coffin was identified in 1813. In 1678, at the command of Charles II, Sir Christopher Wren drew up plans for a mausoleum and monument; these are preserved in the library of All Souls' College, Oxford, but the project was never carried out. See Hope, *Windsor Castle*, I 342*ff.*

Wakefield compares Chetwood, *To the Earl of Roscommon*, 61: "Make *Warlike James*'s *peaceful* Virtues known".

321. *Oh Fact accurst*] Cf. Philips, *Cyder*, II 508–9: "O Fact / Unparallel'd! O *Charles*! O best of Kings!"

322. Cf. Denham, *The Destruction of Troy*, 4: ". . . you make our old wounds bleed anew."

323*ff.* The MS makes clear that Pope in this passage originally intended the Great Plague (1665), the Great Fire (1666), and the Revolution of 1688 to be regarded as evil consequences of the execution of Charles I. In this light it is possible to see the lines as revealing a marked Jacobite bias; but many persons, irrespective of political loyalties, thought the Plague and Fire to be evidence of the wrath of God.

323. *purple Deaths*] Pope probably alludes to the deaths resulting from the Great Plague. *Purple* was a term used for the "bubo of the plague" or of a "disease characterized by an eruption of purplish pustules" (OED). Cf. Dryden, *Æn.*, XII 1090 (of the death of a stag): "The Purple Death is pitch'd along the Strand". Wakefield compares *Iliad*, v 83: πορφύρεος θάνατος. Cf. l. 417, below: "purple *Vengeance*".

324. *Domes*] A stately building, a mansion (OED). Wakefield compares *Aen.*, IV 670–1: "flammaeque furentes / culmina perque hominum volvantur perque deorum."

326. *dishonest*] Shameful (OED). EC recall Creech's tr. of Horace, *Carm.*, I xxxv:

> I blush at the dishonest show,
> I die to see the Wounds and Scars,
> Those Glories of our Civil Wars . . .

At length great *ANNA* said—Let Discord cease!
She said, the World obey'd, and all was *Peace*!
In that blest Moment, from his Oozy Bed
Old Father *Thames* advanc'd his rev'rend Head.   330

In his *Iliad* Pope often used the word to describe a wound received in the back;
e.g., VIII 120. Cf. Dryden, *Æn.*, XI 84, 646.

327. Pope's imitation of the divine fiat in this line was more explicit in MS,
i.e., "*Let there be Peace*". In *Cyder*, II 637 *ff.*, after a long review of dissensions in
English history, Philips had concluded with this allusion to the union between
England and Scotland:

> neither Fear, nor Hope,
> Nor the sweet Prospect of a mutual Gain,
> Cou'd ought avail, 'till prudent *ANNA* said
> *Let there be UNION*; strait with Reverence due
> To Her Command, they willingly unite. . .

See Intro., pp. 141–2, above.

330 *ff.* Pope here echoes descriptions of sea and river deities in various authors.
Wakefield compares the description of "th' auncient Thame" in *F.Q.*, IV xi 25:

> With head all hoary, and his beard all gray,
> Deawed with siluer drops, that trickled downe alway;

and also Claudian's description of the Eridanus (*de Sexto Consulatu Honorii*,
159 *ff.*), tr. by Addison in *Remarks on Several Parts of Italy* (1705), pp. 440–1:

> His Head above the Floods he gently rear'd,
> And as he rose his golden Horns appear'd,
> That on the Forehead shone divinely bright,
> And o'er the Banks diffus'd a yellow Light. . .
> Beneath his Arm an Urn supported lyes,
> With Stars embellish'd, and fictitious Skies.

"Fictitious Skies" perhaps suggested the "fictitious stars" of the variant cited
in l. 330*n*. Cf. *Aen.*, VIII 31–4.

330. Between Verse 328 ⟨330⟩ and 329 ⟨331⟩ originally stood these lines,

> *From shore to shore exulting shouts he heard,*
> *O'er all his banks a lambent light appear'd,*
> *With sparkling flames heav'ns glowing concave shone,*
> *Fictitious stars, and glories not her own.*
> *He saw, and gently rose above the stream;*
> *His shining horns diffus'd a golden gleam:*
> *With pearl and gold his tow'ry front was drest,*
> *The tributes of the distant East and West.*   [P. *1736a–51*.]

1740–51 have *diffuse* instead of *diffus'd*.

Wakefield compares Dryden, *Annus Mirabilis*, st. 232: "Old Father *Thames*
rais'd up his reverend head"; and also *Threnodia Augustalis*, 513–14:

His Tresses dropt with Dews, and o'er the Stream
His shining Horns diffus'd a golden Gleam:
Grav'd on his Urn appear'd the Moon, that guides
His swelling Waters, and alternate Tydes;
The figur'd Streams in Waves of Silver roll'd,   335
And on their Banks *Augusta* rose in Gold.
Around his Throne the Sea-born Brothers stood,

While starting from his Oozy Bed,
Th'asserted Ocean rears his reverend Head.

EC note that the "gods of rivers are invariably represented as old men."

As we do not know when the variant lines were written, it is impossible to say whether ll. 3 and 4 allude to actual festivities on the occasion of the proclamation of peace, or anticipate them. In July, 1713, "a General Thanksgiving for the Peace was celebrated with the greatest Solemnity . . . and at Night two Fireworks were made, one on the River *Thames*, and the other in *West-Smithfield*" (W. Maitland, *The History of London*, 1756, 1 512). Similar festivities were arranged on the accession of Queen Anne, in 1702: the Queen "returned to her Palace of St. *James*'s, amidst . . . Illuminations that vied with the Sun in Glory" (Maitland, 1 503). And again: ". . . the Night concluded with the Ringing of Bells, Bonfires, Fire-works, Illuminations" (1 504). Bonfires and illuminations would explain Pope's allusion to the "lambent light" over the banks of the Thames, and the fireworks would explain the "fictitious stars".

332. *shining Horns*] "The River-gods . . . were often given the head or horns of a bull, indicative of their roaring or winding, of their strength or of their influence on agriculture. . . A bull was the sacrifice to them, as to Poseidon" (T. Keightley, *The Mythology of Ancient Greece and Italy*, ed. L. Schmitz, 1912, p. 220). Wakefield cites *Georgics* IV 371–2: "et gemina auratus taurino cornua voltu / Eridanus."

335. *figur'd*] Shaped into a figure, represented by figures (OED). Cf. l. 246*n*, above.

336. *Augusta*] The name given at one time to London by the Romans.

337. *Sea-born Brothers*] The legend was that all rivers were born of Oceanus and Tethys [EC]. Cf. Spenser, *F.Q.*, IV xi 18:

Next came the aged *Ocean*, and his Dame,
Old *Tethys*, th'oldest two of all the rest,
For all the rest of those two parents came,
Which afterwards both sea and land possest;

and *Cooper's Hill*, 161–2:

Thames, the most lov'd of all the Oceans sons,
By his old Sire . . .

Who swell with Tributary Urns his Flood.
First the fam'd Authors of his ancient Name,
The winding *Isis*, and the fruitful *Tame*:   340
The *Kennet* swift, for silver Eels renown'd;
The *Loddon* slow, with verdant Alders crown'd:
Cole, whose dark Streams his flow'ry Islands lave;
And chalky *Wey*, that rolls a milky Wave:
The blue, transparent *Vandalis* appears;   345

338 Who] That *1713a–32*.   343 dark] clear *1713a–43*.

339–48. Pope's catalogue of rivers resembles closely that found in Ausonius, *Mosella*, 349–74. The lines are also indebted to Spenser, *F.Q.*, IV xi; to Milton, *At a Vacation Exercise*; and to Drayton, *Poly-Olbion*, Song XVII.

339. *fam'd Authors*] The Thames (Tamesis) was thought to be the offspring of the Thame and the Isis. Thus Spenser, *F.Q.*, IV xi 24:

> Soone after whom the louely Bridegroome came,
> The noble Thamis, with all his goodly traine,
> But him before there went, as best became,
> His auncient parents, namely th'auncient Thame.
> But much more aged was his wife than he,
> The Ouze, whom men doe Isis rightly name . . .

In *Poly-Olbion*, Song XV, Drayton also describes the wedding of the Thame and the Isis and the birth of their offspring the *Tames*.

341. *Kennet swift*] Spenser (*F.Q.*, IV xi 29) calls the Kennet "chaulky"; Drayton (*Poly-Olbion*, XV 290) calls it "cleere".

renown'd] Bowles cites Drayton, *Ideas Mirrour*, Amour 24: "The christall Trent, for Foords & fishe renowned."

342. *verdant Alders crown'd*] EC compare Addison, *Remarks on Several Parts of Italy*, p. 191: "Where Silver Lakes, with verdant Shadows crown'd . . ."

343. *Cole*] The river Colne. About 20 miles before it falls into the Thames at Staines, the Colne traverses a flat valley and divides into several channels, hence the allusion to its islands.

343 var. *clear*] Drayton, *Poly-Olbion*, Song XVI, has "Crystall *Colne*" (l. 3) and "transparent *Colne*" (l. 9). The epithet *dark* perhaps suggested itself to Pope because of the river's name, i.e., Cole⟩ coal.

344. *chalky Wey*] Drayton, *Poly-Olbion*, XVII 21, has "cleere *Wey*". Spenser, *F.Q.*, IV xi 29, has "chaulky Kenet".

milky] Perhaps a fanciful etymology suggested itself to Pope: *whey* for *Wey*.

345. *transparent Vandalis*] The Wandle. Cf. Drayton, *Poly-Olbion*, XVII 73:

> Then *Wandal* commeth in, the *Moles* beloved mate,
> So amiable, faire, so pure, so delicate,
> So plump, so full, so fresh, her eyes so wondrous cleer.

The gulphy *Lee* his sedgy Tresses rears:
And sullen *Mole*, that hides his diving Flood;
And silent *Darent*, stain'd with *Danish* Blood.
    High in the midst, upon his Urn reclin'd,
(His Sea-green Mantle waving with the Wind)   350
The God appear'd; he turn'd his azure Eyes
Where *Windsor*-Domes and pompous Turrets rise,
Then bow'd and spoke; the Winds forget to roar,
And the hush'd Waves glide softly to the Shore.

The epithets, EC suggest, Pope may have borrowed from one of Addison's translations of Claudian in his *Remarks on Several Parts of Italy*, p. 56:
> Her dropping Locks the Silver *Tessin* rears,
> The blue transparent *Adda* next appears.

346. *gulphy Lee . . . sedgy Tresses*] EC recall that Milton, *At a Vacation Exercise*, has (l. 92) "gulphie *Dun*" and (l. 97) "Sedgie *Lee*". *Gulfy* suggests a stream full of "eddies and whirlpools" (OED).

347. *sullen Mole*] Cf. Milton, *At a Vacation Exercise*, 95, "Or sullen *Mole* that runneth underneath"; and also Drayton, *Poly-Olbion*, XVII 59–60; Spenser, *F.Q.*, IV xi 32. In *A Tour Thro' the whole Island of Great Britain* (ed. G. D. H. Cole, 1927) I 148, Defoe gives a long account of this river which, he says, is "called the *Mole*, from its remarkable sinking into the Earth, *at the Foot of* Box-Hill, *near a Village call'd* Mickleham, and working its way under Ground like a *Mole*, rising again at or near this Town of *Leatherhead*."

348. *silent Darent*] Spenser, *F.Q.*, IV xi 29, has "still Darent". In st. 44 Spenser speaks of the "balefull Oure, late staind with English blood". Bowles cites Drayton, *Ideas Mirrour*, Amour 24: "And old *Legea* brags of *Danish* blood." Pope's allusion may be explained in *Camden's Britannia* (1695), p. 190: "The *Thames* afterwards growing narrower, is met by the river *Darent*, which coming out of Surrey, flows with a gentle chanel not far from *Seven-oke* . . . and so to . . . *Otford*, famous for a bloody defeat of the Danes in the year 1016." Cf. *Statius*, 57–8n (p. 412, below).

350. *Sea-green Mantle*] Cf. the description of the Tiber, *Aen.*, VIII 33–4: "eum tenuis glauco velabat amictu / carbasus . . ." The mantles of marine deities were of a glaucous (green-blue) colour. Cf. again *Aen.*, XII 885 (speaking of Juturna): "tantum effata caput glauco contexit amictu"; and Dryden's tr., 1281: "But in her Azure Mantle wrap'd her Head."

353. *Then bow'd*] A gesture common from minor to greater gods in classical poetry. Cf. Dryden, Ovid, *Met.*, XII 788 (Apollo to Neptune): "*Apollo* bows to the superior Throne . . ."

354. *hush'd Waves*] Wakefield compares Dryden, *Æn.*, X 157–8:
> the Winds their Breath restrain;

Hail Sacred *Peace*! hail long-expected Days,   355
That *Thames*'s Glory to the Stars shall raise!
Tho' *Tyber*'s Streams immortal *Rome* behold,
Tho' foaming *Hermus* swells with Tydes of Gold,
From Heav'n it self tho' sev'nfold *Nilus* flows,
And Harvests on a hundred Realms bestows;   360
These now no more shall be the Muse's Themes,
Lost in my Fame, as in the Sea their Streams.

356 That] Which *1713a–14*.

And the hush'd Waves lie flatted on the Main.
EC compare Charles Hopkins, *White-hall* (1698), 259–60:
    Unrowling waves steal softly to the shore,
    They know their Soveraign, and they fear to roar.
  355. The preliminaries to the Treaty of Utrecht were signed in London in October, 1711. The main treaties were signed at Utrecht on April 11, 1713. The war of the Spanish Succession had begun in 1701.
  357–62. Cf. Ausonius, *Mosella*, 374–7:
                quod si tibi, dia Mosella,
    Smyrna suum vatem vel Mantua clara dedisset,
    cederet Iliacis Simois memoratus in oris
    nec praeferre suos auderet Thybris honores.
See also Horace, *Carm.*, I vii 1–4:
    Laudabunt alii claram Rhodon aut Mytilenen
      aut Ephesum bimarisue Corinthi
    moenia vel Baccho Thebas vel Apolline Delphos
      insignes aut Thessala Tempe.
  357. Enumerating the rivers which were dried up by the fall of Phaethon, Ovid (*Met.*, II 259) speaks of the Tiber as having been promised the empire of the world: "cuique fuit rerum promissa potentia, Thybrin."
  358. *foaming Hermus*] EC cite *Georgics* II 137: "auro turbidus Hermus". Cf. *Cooper's Hill*, 165–6 (of the Thames):
    Though with those streams he no resemblance hold,
    Whose foam is Amber, and their Gravel Gold.
  359. *sev'nfold Nilus*] Wakefield compares Ovid, *Met.*, I 422–3, "septemfluus ... Nilus", and also Homer, *Il.*, XVI 174, and Catullus, XI 7–8.
  360. *on a hundred Realms*] Wakefield compares Bathurst, *On the Death of* . . . *Selden* (in *Examen Poeticum*, 1693), 71–4:
    As when old *Nilus* who with bounteous flows
    Waters an hundred Nations as he goes,
    Scattering rich Harvest keeps his Sacred Head
    Amongst the Clouds still undiscovered.

Let *Volga*'s Banks with Iron Squadrons shine,
And Groves of Lances glitter on the *Rhine*,
Let barb'rous *Ganges* arm a servile Train;   365
Be mine the Blessings of a peaceful Reign.
No more my Sons shall dye with *British* Blood
Red *Iber*'s Sands, or *Ister*'s foaming Flood;
Safe on my Shore each unmolested Swain
Shall tend the Flocks, or reap the bearded Grain;   370
The shady Empire shall retain no Trace

363. *Volga's Banks*] An allusion to the war of Charles XII of Sweden against Russia. Charles was defeated, however, at Poltawa, some 500 miles west of the Volga in 1709. Cf. Philips, *Blenheim* (1705), 405–10:

> See, with what Outrage from the frosty North,
> The early Valiant *Swede* draws forth his Wings
> In Battailous Array, while *Volga*'s Stream
> Sends Opposite, in shaggy Armor clad,
> Her Borderers; on mutual Slaughter bent,
> They rend their Countries.

Iron Squadrons] Wakefield compares *Aen.*, VII 703: "aeratas acies".

364. *Groves of Lances*] Cf. Dryden, *Æn.*, X 1009: "And shakes a Grove of Lances from his Side." Cf. Pope, *Il.*, II 991; IV 322*ff.*; *Sarpedon*, 181 (p. 456, below).

365. *Ganges*] An allusion to the wars waged by the Moghul Emperor Aurangzeb against the rising Maratha powers. He died in 1707. Cf. Dryden, *Abs. and Achit.*, I 331–2:

> Let haughty Pharaoh curse with such a reign
> His fruitful Nile, and yoke a servile train.

366. "This fine panegyric on *peace*, in opposition to the horrors and devastations of war, was in part occasioned, I presume, by our author's politics; by his hostility to the name of *Marlborough*, and an uneasiness at the glory of his victories" [Wakefield].

368. *Iber's Sands*] Iberus or Hiberus, the modern Ebro. An allusion to the Allies' campaign in Spain in 1710 and to the victory gained at Saragossa on August 19, in which Lord James Stanhope took a leading part. The word "sands" may refer to the arid country through which the Allies marched in great distress for want of water before they gained the Ebro.

Ister's foaming Flood] The Danube. The campaign of 1704 there ended with Marlborough's famous victory at Blenheim. Cf. *Georgics* III 350: "turbidus . . . Hister". Also Philips, *Cerealia*, 23: ". . . th'Ensanguin'd *Ister*'s reeking Flood".

370. *bearded Grain*] Cf. *Par. Lost*, IV 981–2: ". . . *Ceres* ripe for harvest waving bends / Her bearded Grove of ears"; Dryden, *Georgics* II 746: "A full return of bearded Harvest yield".

Of War or Blood, but in the Sylvan Chace,
The Trumpets sleep, while chearful Horns are blown,
And Arms employ'd on Birds and Beasts alone.
Behold! th'ascending *Villa's* on my Side   375
Project long Shadows o'er the Chrystal Tyde.
Behold! *Augusta's* glitt'ring Spires increase,
And Temples rise, the beauteous Works of Peace.
I see, I see where two fair Cities bend

373 Trumpets] Trumpet *1743–51.*

---

374. Wakefield compares Cowley, *Horat. Epodon.*, 41–2 (see Cowley's *Essay 4, Of Agriculture*):

> And all his malice, all his craft is shown
> In innocent wars, on beasts and birds alone.

See Intro., pp. 139-40.

375. *Villa's*] An early instance of the use of *villa* to describe English homes (the first instance recorded by OED is 1711), though it had been used of Roman and continental houses by English writers in the 17th century. Defoe notes in his *Tour* (1724–7; ed. Cole, I 167) that ". . . in a few Years fine Gardens, and fine Houses began to grow up in every corner . . . but no where more than in the two Counties of *Middlesex* and *Surrey*, as they border on the River *Thames*." Wakefield compares *Poly-Olbion*, Song xvii, 81–6:

> But now this mighty Flood, upon his voiage prest
> (That found how with his strength, his beauties still increast,
> From where, brave *Windsor* stood on tip-toe to behold
> The faire and goodly *Tames*, so farre as ere he could,
> With Kingly houses Crown'd, of more then earthly pride,
> Upon his either Banks, as he along doth glide).

375–80. Wakefield compares Hopkins, *White-hall* (1698), 1–6:

> Above that Bridge, which lofty Turrets Crown,
> Joyning two Cities; of it self a Town,
> As far as fair *Augusta's* Buildings reach,
> Bent like a Bow, along a peaceful beach.
> Her guilded Spires the Royal Palace show,
> Towring to Clouds, and fix'd in Floods below.

378. *Temples rise*] The fifty new Churches. [P. *1751.*] They were built at the recommendation of Queen Anne to meet the requirements of the growing population of London. See *Sat.* ii ii 119n (vol. iv, pp. 62–3).

379. *two fair Cities bend*] London and Westminster, at that time two distinct towns. EC recall Cowley, *On the Queens Repairing Somerset House*, 47–8:

> And here, Behold, in a long bending Row,
> How two joynt Cities make one glorious Bow.

See ll. 375–80n.

Their ample Bow, a new *White-Hall* ascend!　　　380
There mighty Nations shall inquire their Doom,
The World's great Oracle in Times to come;
There Kings shall sue, and suppliant States be seen

---

380. *a new White-Hall*] Whitehall Palace was at various times the residence of English monarchs till it was burned down in 1698. Inigo Jones's Banqueting Hall alone survived. Defoe (*A Tour . . .* , Letter v) describes at length the projected reconstruction to which Pope alludes. It was never carried out. EC note that Whitehall "is just above that circular sweep of the Thames in the midst of which the cities of London and Westminster unite." Cf. *Sat.* II ii 120*n* (vol. IV, p. 63), also *Dunciad* A, III 324, and Pope's note (vol. v, p. 189).

381–422. The pervasive influence of Isaiah, chap. 60, is discernible throughout this entire passage. See M. Mack, 'On Reading Pope', *College English*, VII (1945–6), pp. 263–73, and also Intro., pp. 142–4.

381. EC compare Addison's tr. (in *Remarks on Several Parts of Italy*, p. 334) of a passage in Claudian (*de Sexto Consulatu Honorii*, 35 *ff.*) on the imperial palace at Rome:

> Thither the Kingdoms and the Nations come,
> In supplicating Crouds to learn their Doom;
> To *Delphi* less th'enquiring Worlds repair.

Cf. Waller, *A Panegyrick to my Lord Protector*, 15–16:

> The Seat of Empire, where the *Irish* come,
> And the unwilling *Scotch*, to fetch their Doom;

and Hopkins, *White-hall*, 9–10:

> Thither all Nations of the Earth resort,
> Not only *England*'s now, but *Europe*'s Court.

Ver. 383, &c. were originally thus;

> *Now shall our fleets the bloody Cross display*
> *To the rich regions of the rising day,*
> *Or those green isles, where headlong* Titan *steeps*
> *His hissing axle in th'*Atlantic *deeps.*
> *Tempt icy seas*, &c.　　　　　　　[P. *1736a–51.*]

Pope quoted the above lines to Caryll (*Corr.*, I 156), the fourth line having "chariot" instead of "axle", and asked his "sincere judgment" as to whether or not they were inferior to some Tickell had written in *On the Prospect of Peace*. Bowles suggested that Pope rejected the last two lines because they too nearly resembled *Comus*, 95–7:

> And the gilded Car of Day,
> His glowing Axle doth allay
> In the steep *Atlantick* stream. . .

383. *Kings shall sue*] Cf. Isaiah, 60: 3: "And the Gentiles shall come to thy light, and kings to the brightness of thy rising."

Once more to bend before a *British* QUEEN.

Thy Trees, fair *Windsor*! now shall leave their Woods,
And half thy Forests rush into my Floods,   386
Bear *Britain*'s Thunder, and her Cross display,
To the bright Regions of the rising Day;
Tempt Icy Seas, where scarce the Waters roll,
Where clearer Flames glow round the frozen Pole;   390
Or under Southern Skies exalt their Sails,

386 my] thy *1740, 1751. An evident misprint.*

384. *Once more*] The allusion is to those occasions, in 1575 and 1585, when the sovereignty of the United Provinces was offered to Queen Elizabeth and her aid was solicited in the struggles of the Dutch against Philip of Spain [Wakefield].

386. The trees of Windsor Forest, turned into ships, will carry British power and commerce all over the world. See Intro., p. 140. Pope may have recalled Waller, *A Panegyrick to my Lord Protector*, 41–2:

> Lords of the Worlds great waste, the *Ocean*, we
> Whole Forrests send to Reign upon the Sea.

Cf. also Ovid, *Met.*, I 94–5:

> nondum caesa suis, peregrinum ut viseret orbem,
> montibus in liquidas pinus descenderat undas.

Cf. ll. 31*n*, 222.

387. *her Cross*] The red cross of St George on the Union Jack. Pope quotes a slightly different version of this and following lines in his letter to Caryll of Nov. 29, 1712 (*Corr.*, I 156).

388. EC cite Waller, *Of Tea*, 5: "To the fair Region, where the Sun does rise".

389. *Tempt Icy Seas*] EC note that "to tempt the seas" is a "classical expression, significant of hazard and resolution". OED cites this line in its definition of *tempt*, sense 2c: "To adventure oneself in or upon; to risk the perils of." Wakefield compares Dryden, *The First Book of Homer's Ilias*, 85–6: "What now remains, / But that once more we tempt the watry Plains."

390–1. EC compare Addison, *A Poem to his Majesty* [King William III], (1695), 115–22:

> Where-e'er the Waves in restless errors rowle,
> The Sea lies open now to either Pole:
> Now we may safely use the *Northern* gales,
> And in the *Polar Circle* spread our sails;
> Or deep in *Southern* climes, Secure from wars,
> New Lands explore, and sail by Other stars;
> Fetch Uncontroll'd each labour of the Sun,
> And make the product of the World our own.

Led by new Stars, and born by spicy Gales!
For me the Balm shall bleed, and Amber flow,
The Coral redden, and the Ruby glow,
The Pearly Shell its lucid Globe infold,   395
And *Phœbus* warm the ripening Ore to Gold.
The Time shall come, when free as Seas or Wind

392. Wakefield compares Waller, *The Night-Piece*, 39–42:

> So we th' *Arabian* Coast do know
> At distance, when the Spices blow,
> By the rich Odour taught to steer,
> Tho' neither Day nor Stars appear;

and also *Par. Lost*, IV 161–3.

393 *ff.* Cf. Isaiah, 60:5: ". . . because the abundance of the sea shall be converted unto thee, the forces of the Gentiles shall come unto thee." See succeeding verses also. Dryden, *Annus Mirabilis*, st. 3, says of the Dutch:

> For them alone the Heav'ns had kindly heat,
>   In Eastern Quarries ripening precious Dew:
> For them the *Idumæan* Balm did sweat,
>   And in hot *Ceilon* Spicy Forrests grew.

Cf. Philips, *Cyder*, II 652–7:

> uncontrol'd
> The *British* Navy thro' the Ocean vast
> Shall wave her double Cross, t'extreamest Climes
> Terrific, and return with odorous Spoils
> Of *Araby* well fraught, or *Indus*' Wealth,
> Pearl, and Barbaric Gold.

393. *Balm shall bleed*] From the wound inflicted on the bark to draw off the juices of the tree [Wakefield]. Cf. Dryden, *Georgics* II 165–6:

> Balm slowly tiickles thro' the bleeding Veins
> Of happy shrubs in *Idumæan* Plains.

396. *ripening Ore*] An allusion to the belief that gold and precious stones were "ripened" into maturity by the sun. EC compare Tickell, *On the Prospect of Peace*, 202, 204:

> Here nearer Suns prepare the rip'ning Gemm . . .
> And here the Ore . . .

In Act II of *Three Hours after Marriage* Plotwell says: "I need not acquaint de illustrious Doctor *Fossile*, dat all de Metals be but unripe Gold."

397. *free as Seas or Wind*] Wakefield compares *Cooper's Hill*, 179–80:

> Nor are his Blessings to his Banks confin'd,
> But free, and common as the Sea or Wind.

Cf. also ll. 181–8:

> When he to boast, or to disperse his stores

Unbounded *Thames* shall flow for all Mankind,
Whole Nations enter with each swelling Tyde,
And Seas but join the Regions they divide;   400
Earth's distant Ends our Glory shall behold,
And the new World launch forth to seek the Old.
Then Ships of uncouth Form shall stem the Tyde,
And Feather'd People crowd my wealthy Side,

400 And Oceans join whom they did first divide; *1713a–14.*

       Full of the tributes of his grateful shores,
       Visits the world, and in his flying towers
       Brings home to us, and makes both *Indies* ours;
       Finds wealth where 'tis, bestows it where it wants,
       Cities in deserts, woods in Cities plants.
       So that to us no thing, no place is strange,
       While his fair bosom is the worlds exchange.

398. *Unbounded Thames*] A wish that London may be made a FREE PORT [P. *1751.*]
    That such a wish was current at the time nothing shows better than the name given by Addison to the representative of moneyed interests in the Spectator Club, that "Merchant of great Eminence in the City of *London*", Sir Andrew Freeport (*Spectator*, March 2, 1711). Roger Coke in his *Treatise* (1671) had proposed to substitute an excise in place of customs duties in order to increase the carrying trade and thus make England "an universal storehouse" (E. Lipson, *The Economic History of England*, 1943, III 144). His proposal had been adopted in 1709, when a duty on coal exported in British bottoms was abolished; but it was reimposed the following year (cf. Lipson, II 117).
    Cf. Isaiah, 60:11: "Therefore thy gates shall be open continually; they shall not be shut day nor night; that men may bring unto thee the forces of the Gentiles, and that their kings may be brought." See Intro., pp. 143–4, above.
    400. Wakefield compares Waller, *A Panegyrick to my Lord Protector*, 99–100:
       While by your Valour and your bounteous mind
       Nations divided by the Sea are joyn'd.
    404 *ff.* Apparently an allusion to the four Iroquois Indian chiefs who visited England in April, 1710, and who were granted a public audience with Queen Anne. The sachems were a sensational success with the London populace, and inspired comment in prose and verse. Addison wrote an amusing essay in the *Spectator* (April 27, 1711) on the ideas which the Indians must have conceived of the English. He makes fun, in particular, of English dress, and this may have suggested Pope's couplet, ll. 405–6. Indeed, the visit of the kings may well have provided Pope with the type of regal reception he here foresees accorded by Britain to all the nations of the earth. See R. P. Bond, *Queen Anne's American*

And naked Youths and painted Chiefs admire   405
Our Speech, our Colour, and our strange Attire!
Oh stretch thy Reign, fair *Peace!* from Shore to Shore,
Till Conquest cease, and Slav'ry be no more:
Till the freed *Indians* in their native Groves
Reap their own Fruits, and woo their Sable Loves,   410
Peru once more a Race of Kings behold,
And other *Mexico's* be <u>roof'd with Gold.</u>
Exil'd by Thee from Earth to deepest Hell,

405 And naked Youths] While naked Youth *1713a–14*; Whose
naked Youth *1717–32.*

Kings (1952), pp. 74–5. Tickell had alluded to the chiefs in *On the Prospect of
Peace,* 180–1:

Did not the Painted Kings of *India* greet
Our Queen, and yield their Sceptres at Her Feet!

With *my wealthy Side,* cf. Isaiah, 60: 4: "Lift up thine eyesr ound about and
see: all they gather themselves together, they come to thee: thy sons shall come
from far, and thy daughters shall be nursed at thy side." See also *Messiah,* 91–4
(p. 121, above), and Intro., pp. 143–4.

408. *Slav'ry be no more*] One cannot help remembering that the Anglo-Spanish
treaty signed at Utrecht "accorded to Great Britain and the British South Sea
Company . . . for a term of thirty years the sole right of importing negroes into
Spanish America" (*The Cambridge Modern History,* v 445), and that Pope put
some of his money into the company.

409. *freed Indians*] From the tyranny of Spain.

410. *Reap their own Fruits*] Cf. *Messiah,* 66 (p. 118, above).

Sable] Warton objected to *sable,* saying, "they are not negroes". Kersey, *Dictionarium Anglo-Britannicum* (1708), defines sable as a "rich Fur, of Colour between Black and Brown". Cf. l. 28, above.

411*f.* ". . . as Peru was particularly famous for its long succession of Incas,
and Mexico for many magnificent works of massy gold, there is great propriety
in fixing the restoration of the grandeur of each to that object, for which each
was once so remarkable" (Warton, *An Essay on . . . Pope,* 1 28–9).

412. *roof'd with Gold*] Cf. Dryden, *Æn.,* vi 16–17: ". . . and now behold, / And
enter now, the Temple roof'd with Gold." Pope's lines may refer particularly to
the richly-adorned cathedral of Mexico City. Allusions to the wealth of Mexico
were frequent in literature of the time. Cf. Dryden, *Annus Mirabilis,* st. 293:

Rich as the Town which gives the *Indies* name,
With Silver pav'd, and all divine with Gold.

In a note to the word *Indies* Dryden makes clear that he is referring to Mexico.

413*ff.* Discord was expelled from Heaven by Jupiter. In these lines, as Wake-

In Brazen Bonds shall barb'rous *Discord* dwell:
Gigantick *Pride*, pale *Terror*, gloomy *Care*,   415
And mad *Ambition*, shall attend her there.
There purple *Vengeance* bath'd in Gore retires,
Her Weapons blunted, and extinct her Fires:
There hateful *Envy* her own Snakes shall feel,
And *Persecution* mourn her broken Wheel: 420
There *Faction* roar, *Rebellion* bite her Chain,
And gasping Furies thirst for Blood in vain.
    Here cease thy Flight, nor with unhallow'd Lays
Touch the fair Fame of *Albion*'s Golden Days.
The Thoughts of Gods let *Granville*'s Verse recite,   425

421 roar,] roars, *1713a–32*.   bite] bites *1713a–32*.

field notes, Pope was indebted to two passages in Virgil: *Georgics* III 37–9,
          Invidia infelix furias amnemque severum
          Cocyti metuet tortosque Ixionis anguis
          immanemque rotam et non exsuperabile saxum;
and *Aen.*, I 293–6:
                    dirae ferro et compagibus artis
          claudentur Belli portae; Furor impius intus
          saeva sedens super arma et centum vinctus aënis
          post tergum nodis fremet horridus ore cruento.
    419. *her own Snakes*] Pope perhaps recalled Ovid, *Met.*, II, where Envy is de-
scribed, ll. 768–9, as devouring snakes, "edentem / vipereas carnes, vitiorum ali-
menta suorum", and, ll. 781–2, inflicting on herself the torments she inflicts on
others: "carpitque et carpitur una / suppliciumque suum est." See Intro., pp.
143–4, above.
    420. *broken Wheel*] Persons bound to the wheel for torture had their arms and
legs broken by blows from an iron bar. Pope suggests an appropriate fate for the
wheel itself. See preceding line.
    421. *bite her Chain*] EC compare Sir John Beaumont, *Bosworth-Field* (1629),
117–18:
          Beneath his feete pale Enuie bites her chaine,
          And snaky Discord whets her sting in vaine.
    425. *The Thoughts of Gods*] Warburton cites Horace, *Carm.* III iii 70–2:
          quo, Musa, tendis? desine pervicax
          referre sermones deorum et
          magna modis tenuare parvis,
and EC recall Addison's tr., 124–5:

And bring the Scenes of opening Fate to Light.
My humble Muse, in unambitious Strains,   ⎫
Paints the green Forests and the flow'ry Plains,   ⎰
Where Peace descending bids her Olives spring,   ⎫
And scatters Blessings from her Dove-like Wing.   ⎰   430
Ev'n I more sweetly pass my careless Days,   ⎫
Pleas'd in the silent Shade with empty Praise;   ⎰
Enough for me, that to the listning Swains   ⎫
First in these Fields I sung the Sylvan Strains.   ⎰

FINIS.

> But hold, my Muse, forbear thy towering flight,
> Nor bring the secrets of the Gods to light.

The word *Gods* refers, as in ll. 162, 230, to the Queen and her court (see Intro., pp. 141–2), and Pope's lines are not merely an expression of modesty and flattery: they allude to the fact that Granville enjoyed the particular favour of Queen Anne and also recall that Granville had often celebrated, in his earlier poetry, James II as the British Jove and Mary of Modena as a goddess worthy of such a divinity. Such comparisons of royalty to gods were usual at the time. Cf. Cowley, *On the Queens Repairing Somerset House*, 39–40: "... for as in Kings we see / The liveliest Image of the Deity".

427. These lines, with the exception of the couplet at 429–30, came originally after l. 290. See note to l. 290, and also Intro., pp. 131–2.

428*ff.* "He adopted one or two hints, and especially the turn of the compliment to Lord Lansdowne, from the conclusion of Addison's Letter to Lord Halifax [*A Letter from Italy*, 163–8]:

> But I've already troubled you too long,
> Nor dare attempt a more advent'rous song.
> My humble verse demands a softer theme,
> A painted meadow, or a purling stream;
> Unfit for Heroes; whom immortal lays,
> And lines like *Virgil*'s, or like yours, shou'd praise" [EC].

431*ff.* Pope's conclusion was modelled on that of the *Georgics*. Wakefield compares Dryden's tr., IV 815–16:

> While I at *Naples* pass my peaceful Days,
> Affecting Studies of less noisy Praise.

As Virgil closed his *Georgics* with the first line of his *Eclogues*, so Pope's final couplet echoes the opening line of *Spring*.

AN ESSAY ON CRITICISM

INTRODUCTION

I: PERIOD OF COMPOSITION

I

An Essay on Criticism was published anonymously in the middle of May, 1711.[1] The date or period of the poem's composition, however, cannot be precisely established, for the evidence we possess is vague and contradictory. The title page of Pope's manuscript preserved in the Bodleian Library bears the words "Written in the Year 1709", but in an ink different from that used in the poetic text. When Pope printed the *Essay* with his other works in the 1717 quarto the same words appeared on the poem's half-title, and appeared there in all subsequent editions. To this announcement on the half-title of his own copy of the 1717 quarto Jonathan Richardson the younger appended these words: "Mr. Pope told me himself that the Essay on Criticism was, indeed, written 1707, though said 1709 by mistake".[2] If 1709 was a mistake, it is strange that Pope permitted it to stand as printed in later editions.

Warburton, perhaps prompted by Pope himself, perhaps accommodating himself to one of Pope's small vanities, concludes his notes to the *Essay* by calling the attention of the reader to the fact that "it was the work of an Author who had not attained the twentieth year of his age".[3] This of course would suggest that the poem was largely written by 1708. Pope himself printed different, and vaguely ambiguous, notes about the poem in the editions of his *Letters* published in 1735 and 1737. In 1735 the note to the last letter he addressed to Walsh said: "Mr. *Walsh* died at 49 Years old, in the Year 1708. The Year after, Mr. Pope writ the *Essay on Criticism*. . ."[4] In 1737 the note ran: "Mr. Walsh died at 49 years old, in the year 1708, the year before the Essay on Criticism was print-

---

1. *Spectator* 65, May 15, 1711: "This Day is publish'd, An Essay on Criticism."
2. EC, II 10. See I xviii: "Richardson's interlined copy of the first quarto volume of Pope's poetry passed into the hands of Malone, and was ultimately bought by Mr. Croker."
3. *Works*, 1751, I 209.
4. *Corr.*, I 25n (letter of Oct. 22, 1706). See also EC, II 11.

ed. . . ." The shift from "writ" to "printed", and the differing punctuation in the notes, may be viewed as part of a deliberate plan to
confuse the issue; on the other hand, they may represent nothing
more than an erroneous memory of events which occurred nearly
thirty years before.

The *Anecdotes* of Spence, recording Pope's utterances over a num-
ber of years, are also contradictory. Thus Pope once said, "My
Essay on Criticism was written in 1709; and published in 1711;
which is as little time as ever I let any thing of mine lay by me."[1]
But at another time he said: "I was with him [Walsh] at his seat in
Worcestershire, for a good part of the summer of 1705, and showed
him my Essay on Criticism in 1706. Walsh died the year after."[2]
Walsh died on March 15, 1708. It is very doubtful, moreover, that
Pope was at Abberley in 1705; he was certainly there in the late
summer of 1707.[3] In addition, one may wonder how this last statement fits in with what Pope says in the poem, ll. 735–8, that he took
to the "low Numbers" of didactic poetry because he no longer had
the guidance of Walsh, his "Judge and Friend".[4]

Pope's correspondence is of no greater help in fixing the period
of the poem's composition. The correspondence with Cromwell,
which began in 1707 and continued until December, 1711, alludes
to the poem only after its publication. This is true also of the correspondence with Caryll, yet it is certain that Pope showed his
poem in MS to Caryll when he visited him at Ladyholt.[5] And this
was presumably late in 1710 or early in 1711, for Pope says he
would have altered certain lines objected to by Caryll "but for the
haste of the press."

In his letter of November 25, 1710,[6] Pope does communicate to
Cromwell "a few Thoughts" about versification, many of which
form a part of the *Essay*, ll. 337*ff*.: the poet should use the hiatus
with caution; he should avoid expletives, monosyllabic lines, the
repetition of rhymes, and "needless Alexandrines"; and he should
strive to make the sound "seem an *Eccho* to the *Sense*". These same

---

1. Spence, 170. Cf. also p. 270: "I wrote the Essay on Criticism, two or three
years before it was printed."
2. Ibid., 194.   3. See *Corr.*, 1 29*n*. See also p. 201, below.
4. EC, II 11.   5. See Pope's letter of June 25, 1711 (*Corr.*, 1 121).
6. *Corr.*, 1 106–8.

remarks are to be found in a letter to Walsh of October 22, 1706, but this letter is of doubtful authenticity.[1] If Pope set himself these rules as early as 1706, we should expect him to follow them from that date. A glance at the variant readings of the poem itself will show, however, that the expletive "do" was not suppressed until the 1717 quarto, and this is true of the same fault in other poems included in that edition. The lines in the early editions of the *Essay* which violated Pope's own rules would seem to belong to one period of composition, while the rules themselves would appear to belong to another, and later, period. Perhaps it was only in late 1710 that Pope, thinking of introducing such rules into the *Essay*, resolved to try them out on Cromwell, from whom he asked a long letter "in answer to these Notions concerning Versification."[2]

In the face of the contradictions and uncertainties offered by Pope's own recollections and correspondence an editor may well feel himself to be in the following rather comic state of perplexity: "a biographer may assert, on equal authority, that the Essay was written in 1706, or 1707, or 1709,—that Pope kept it by him in MS for one or two or more years,—that it was written off hand, and printed when written, in 1709, that it was shown to Walsh in 1706, or 1707,—or not shown to him at all, and not written till after his death."[3]

II

A few pieces of internal evidence may have some bearing on the date of the poem's composition. One of these is the line, "But *Appius* reddens at each Word you speak", which would seem limited by the date of the production—and failure—of Dennis's play, *Appius and Virginia*, that is, February 5, 1709. The value of the allusion is destroyed, however, by the evidence of the MS, which shows that "D——" was first written, then crossed out and replaced by "Appius". The MS of the poem is the one Pope sent to the printer,[4] but the original line suggesting Dennis's name could have been written

1. Ibid., I 22n, 106n.
2. Cromwell in reply told Pope that "among the moderns, I find your Practice the Prosodia of your Rules." See letter of Dec. 5, 1710 (*Corr.*, I 109).
3. C. W. Dilke, *The Papers of a Critic* (1875), I 223.
4. As Percy Simpson has demonstrated, in *Proof-Reading in the Sixteenth Seventeenth and Eighteenth Centuries* (1935), pp. 99–104.

prior to the production of *Appius and Virginia*, and altered at any time before the MS went to press.

Another possibly helpful topical allusion is to be found in the MS in a passage which was struck out by Pope and partly printed later in a note.[1] The whole passage in MS reports the banishment of anagrams, acrostics, and puns to the *"Hibernian* Shore" and includes the following allusion to the opera, so despised by Pope and others of his day:

> And thither soon soft *Op'ra* shall repair,
> Convey'd by *Sw——y* to his native Air,
> There languishing a while prolong its Breath,
> Till, like a Swan, it *sings* itself to Death.

Owen Swiney came to London from Ireland in 1706 and worked under Christopher Rich, manager of Drury Lane and the Haymarket Theatre. On October 15, 1706, Swiney became sole manager of the Haymarket, which on December 31, 1707, was reserved for opera by the Lord Chamberlain. In 1708 opera was such a success that it brought Swiney profits which Colley Cibber compared to "a moderate younger brother's fortune".[2] In the next year William Collier took over the management of Drury Lane. Tempted by Swiney's profits, Collier intrigued successfully to get him transferred to Drury Lane and to take over the Haymarket himself. But the tide of public taste had turned, at least momentarily, and Collier's opera season was a failure. He thereupon resumed the management of Drury Lane and sent Swiney back to the Haymarket, where, Cibber says, he found the opera in a "sinking condition".

Pope's allusion in the MS would seem to refer not to the years when opera was a success, but to the period of its apparent decline in 1709 and 1710.

One other allusion which may be considered is that suspected in ll. 550–1:

> *Pulpits* their *Sacred Satire* learn'd to spare,
> And Vice *admir'd* to find a *Flatt'rer there!*

---

1. See l. 447*n*.

2. *An Apology For His Life*, Everyman edn, p. 200. For some account of these events, see F. Dorothy Senior, *The Life and Times of Colley Cibber* (1928), pp. 49–56.

The lines are thought to refer to a sermon preached by Dr White Kennett on September 5, 1707, at the funeral of the first Duke of Devonshire. The sermon became notorious, the more so when it was followed by Kennett's preferment in February, 1708.[1] If Pope does allude to this episode, the most one can say is that these lines, at least, were not written before the end of 1707.

III

Pope's official, or public, statements about the date of the poem's composition refer us, as we have seen, to the year 1709. It is in his private conversations with friends such as Richardson and Spence that conflicting testimony about an earlier date is given. Because of this it is unreasonable to stress an attempt to gain admiration for precocity; certainly Pope is not engaged in an elaborate scheme to win public admiration. In addition, the very contradictions of the evidence suggest what is perhaps the only reasonable conception of the poem's composition. The varying dates offered by Pope at different times indicate that the poem was formed over a number of years, and that Pope, when asked about the matter years later, found it impossible to attribute the composition to any one year.

What we know of Pope's early years supports such a view. He told Spence that in his "great reading period", which occurred evidently between his fourteenth and twentieth years,[2] he "went through all the best critics".[3] In all probability he took notes on these critics, some of which may have come to hand when, as he told Spence, he "had digested all the matter" of the *Essay on Criticism* in prose, before he "began upon it in verse."[4] By early 1706 he was working at the revision of Wycherley's poems (facing in very practical terms some of the issues he was later to treat in the *Essay*[5]), and he had also formed his friendship with Walsh. He was most likely mistaken when he said that he visited Walsh at Abberley in 1705; he probably had in mind the visit he made in 1707, the evidence of which is presented in two letters between Sir William Trumbull and his nephew Ralph Bridges. On August 5, 1707, Trumbull

---

1. For details of this affair see the notes to ll. 547*ff*.   2. Spence, 274–5.
3. Ibid., 278–9. Pope mentions (Spence, 193–4) Rapin, Le Bossu, and Quintilian among authors he read early.
4. Ibid., 142.   5. See the Pope–Wycherley correspondence.

H

writes: "... our little Poet ... is gone a dreadful long Journey into Worcestershire, to M^r. Walsh, from whence I never expect to see the poor Creature return: He look'd, & really was no more than a shaddow... If ever I see him again, he will come full-freighted with new Criticisms..."[1] Pope returned from Walsh's by September 18,[2] and here he is a few weeks later, sketched by Bridges in a letter to Trumbull: "Near the Temple met 'little Pope.' He would walk with me from thence to the farther end of St. James's Park, and all that way he plied me with criticisms and scraps of poetry..."[3]

Quite apart from any reference to the *Essay on Criticism*, Pope told Spence that, "About fifteen, I got acquainted with Mr. Walsh."[4] This suggests that Pope met Walsh in 1703, but a survey of the evidence seems to show that the two met, at the earliest, in 1705.[5] It is scarcely credible that in such statements as this the poet consciously tried to deceive a friend. Such statements rather support the picture of a man who, some thirty years later, recalls as best he can a youthful span of crowded years spent in the company of great men and in a zestful search for literary principles.

Throughout the years from 1705 to 1709 it is likely that Pope was consciously gathering in various ways the materials which ultimately found their way into the *Essay*. His early reading of the critics, his conversations about poetic theory with Walsh, his struggles to "improve" the work of Wycherley, all must have contributed, over a number of years, to the formation of a fund which, in 1709 or 1710, stood "fit for Use, and ready at Command". The fair copy of the MS which was sent to the printer may have been, and probably was, preceded by any number of working drafts. In the face of such circumstances as these, how is anyone, even the poet, to say "when" a poem was written?

---

1. From a transcription of Trumbull's letter made by Bishop Thomas Percy. The transcriptions are preserved in the Bodleian Library (MS Eng. letters d. 59), and were made available to the editors by the kindness of Professor George Sherburn. See *N & Q*, N.S., v (Aug., 1958), pp. 343–8.

2. Trumbull says he has "return'd from M^r. Walsh's" in a letter dated Sept. 18, 1707 (Bodleian Library, MS Eng. letters d. 59). See previous note.

3. Oct. 28, 1707. See *Hist. MSS Comm., Report on the Manuscripts of the Marquess of Downshire*, 1 ii 853.

4. Spence, 280.   5. *Early Career*, p. 55.

AN
ESSAY
ON
CRITICISM.

Si quid novisti rectius istis
Candidus imperti; si non, his utere mecum. Hor.

'TIS hard to say, if greater Want of Skill
    Appear in *Writing* or in *Judging* ill;
But, of the two, less dang'rous is th' *Offence*,
To tire our *Patience*, than mislead our *Sense*:
Some *few* in *that*, but *Numbers* err in *this*,
Ten censure wrong for one who writes amiss;
A *Fool* might ~~simply~~ once *himself* alone *expose*,
Now *One* in *Verse* makes many more in *Prose*.]

    'Tis with our *Judgments* as our *Watches*, none
Go just *alike*, yet each believes his *own*.
In *Poets* as true *Genius* is but rare,
True *Taste* as seldome is the *Critick's* share;
Both must alike from *Heav'n* derive their *Light*,
These ~~han~~ to judge, as well as those to write.

        Let

PASTORAL POETRY
The first page of the autograph manuscript of An Essay on Criticism

II: PUBLICATION AND EARLY HISTORY

I

We are on more obviously safe ground with the history of the poem's publication and early reception. The MS sent to the printer preserves instructions for pagination, and also Pope's instructions for the deletion of certain passages. It was kept by Pope and used for the 1736 *Works*, where suppressed passages were printed as notes, no doubt under the direction of Pope, who alone could decide what he wished to be preserved. The MS does not represent, however, the last step before publication, for the first printed text contains lines, or versions of lines, which are not in the MS. We must assume therefore that correction or alteration occurred in printed proofs. One may suspect that the printer at times simply failed through carelessness to italicize as in the MS, but in view of the care with which Pope is known to have corrected his work the editors have not thought best to correct the 1711 text by the MS, even in such matters as the use of italics and punctuation.[1]

According to Pope,[2] the printer drew off a "thousand copies in his first impression" of the *Essay*, and Pope told Caryll he did not expect the poem to run to a second edition. Not that he doubted the value of his work; he rather thought it a treatise "which not one gentleman in three score even of a liberal education can understand".

But the tradition that the *Essay* attracted little attention when first published is not wholly to be trusted.[3] It certainly attracted enough attention to engage the poet, within five weeks of its publication, in a serious dispute with some of his co-religionists about certain allusions which could be interpreted as reflecting upon Roman Catholicism. Pope learned of the objections to his poem from his friends Thomas Southcote, a priest, and John Caryll, and his letters to the latter record an earnest, if sometimes devious, defence of what he had written.

The "alarms" and "clamor" which Pope says his poem aroused seem to have focused on three or four passages considered to be heterodox. One of these is the simile of wit and faith,

---

1. See General Note on the Texts, pp. xv–xvi, above.
2. Letter of July 19, 1711 (*Corr.*, I 128).   3. *Early Career*, pp. 86–7.

> Thus *Wit*, like *Faith*, by each Man is apply'd
> To *one small Sect*, and All are *damn'd beside*,

where the poet seemed to reduce every Church to a sect, and at the same time sharply to attack the Roman Catholic doctrine of salvation. Pope pleaded in a letter to Caryll[1] that the punctuation of the lines clearly showed the simile to be a parenthetical construction, and to enforce this quality of the couplet, in later editions, he set it off by parentheses. His temper aroused, however, by the continuing scandal his poem had given, Pope, in a second defence of the couplet,[2] told Caryll frankly that he had been glad of an opportunity to introduce, by a casual similitude, a repudiation of views often wrongly attributed to the Catholic Church by the uninformed.

Pope never changed this couplet, but he did make a concession in another. He had written:

> So Schismatics the *dull Believers* quit,
> And are but damn'd for having *too much Wit*.

Pope told Caryll that "an ordinary man would imagine the author plainly declared against these schismatics for quitting the true faith out of contempt of the understanding of some few of its believers. But these believers are called *Dull*, and because I say that *These schismatics think some believers dull*, therefore these charitable well-disposed interpreters of my meaning say that *I think all believers dull*."[3] He had earlier said that "if the alteration of a word or two will gratify any man of sound faith tho' of weak understanding, I will, (tho' it were from no other principle than that of common good nature) comply with it".[4] So, no doubt with tongue in cheek, he altered "dull" into "plain" believers.

When he was charged with praising Erasmus at the expense of the Monks of the Middle Ages, however, Pope refused to give way to those he called the "holy Vandals" of his day. He took up the defence of Erasmus with vigour: ". . . I would advise them [his Catholic critics] to suffer the mention of him to pass unregarded least I should be forced to do that for his reputation which I would never do for my own, I mean to vindicate so great a light of our

---

1. June 18, 1711 (*Corr.*, 1 118).   2. July 19, 1711 (*Corr.*, 1 126).
3. Ibid., 1 127.   4. June 18, 1711 (*Corr.*, 1 118).

Church from the malice of past times and the ignorance of the present, in a language which may extend farther than that in which the trifle about criticism is written."[1] This would seem to mean that he was prepared to write a defence of Erasmus in Latin.

The charges of heterodoxy brought against the *Essay* seem to have taken Pope wholly by surprise, yet there is that in his life and poetic method which was almost certain to arouse religious criticism of a kind. An early disposition to a rather free perspective in religion is revealed by Pope himself. He wrote to Atterbury that when he was a boy he read over the religious controversies of James II's time, and the consequence was that he found himself "a Papist and a Protestant by turns, according to the last book" he read.[2] In addition, he was aligned, by instinct and association, in a witty tradition with poets who often played fast and loose with sacred themes. The collocation of the pagan and the Christian, the sacred and the profane, which so often finds expression in English poetry before Pope, also reveals itself, though often only delicately, in the *Essay on Criticism*.[3]

II

The criticism Pope received from his Roman Catholic neighbours was of a private, and seemingly unexpected, character. Not so an attack launched from another quarter. Pope could not have expected that his thrust at John Dennis, "But *Appius* reddens at each Word you speak", would go unanswered, and indeed, Dennis's reply came in June,[4] little more than a month after the publication of the *Essay*. In a letter to Cromwell of June 25, Pope says that Lintot has favoured him with a copy of Dennis's pamphlet before publication, and in another letter of the same date Pope tells Caryll that he is sending him Dennis's attack, with a "few observations in my hand in the margin".[5] Some of these observations are perhaps preserved in a short MS memorandum which accompanies the MS of the poem, and on which Pope has jotted down

---

1. Ibid., I 118–19.   2. Nov. 20, 1717 (*Corr.*, I 453–4).
3. In such descriptions in the *Essay* of the Ancients as "Patriarch-Wits"; in the MS Homer's work is called "Sacred Writ".
4. It was advertised in *The Daily Courant*, June 21, 1711, as "just publish'd".
5. *Corr.*, I 125, 121.

several lines and suggestions for amendment. A number of these jottings were obviously provoked by Dennis's criticisms: thus ll. 566–7 are copied out with the note, "Dennis, p. 21" and "alter yᵉ Inconsistency".[1] The fact that Pope alters three passages objected to by Dennis indicates his willingness to apply his own maxim: "Make use of ev'ry *Friend*—and ev'ry *Foe*". Pope, indeed, told Caryll that, "to give this man his due, he has objected to one or two lines with reason, and I will alter them in case of another edition: I will make my enemy do me a kindness where he meant an injury, and so serve instead of a friend."[2]

The full title of Dennis's pamphlet is *Reflections Critical and Satyrical, upon a late Rhapsody, call'd, an Essay upon Criticism*. Having been "attack'd" in his "Person", in a "clandestine manner with the utmost Falshood and Calumny", and "without any manner of Provocation", Dennis states in his Preface that he feels justified in hitting back, making amends, he adds, for "the Ill-nature of my Criticism, by the Allurements of my *Satyr*."[3]

Dennis was a man of rough and ready temper, a staunch individualist whose very real contributions to literary criticism are often obscured by the violence of his passion. Thus if he objects to several passages in the *Essay* with reason, his attack is nevertheless disqualified by the heavy-handed abuse which he employs throughout. At the same time, he reveals an extreme literalness of mind which completely fails to grasp the graceful ambivalence of much of the poem. Among other things, he accuses Pope of a "servile Deference" to the Ancients, yet Pope, as his *Essay* reveals, was no more a servile admirer of the Ancients than was Dennis himself. Indeed, the irony of the whole quarrel between the two men is the fact that, despite their differing temperaments and talents, they so largely shared similar critical standards and principles. There was, of course, much in which they differed, and not only in the realm of literary values. Dennis was strongly Protestant and an enthusiastic supporter of William III. He strongly resents the allusions in the *Essay* to the "Foreign Reign" and its Socinian trend. He guesses, or pretends to guess, that the anonymous author of the *Essay* must be "by Politicks a *Jacobite*" and "derive his Religion from St. *Omer's*,

---

1. The MS memorandum is reproduced in Appendix B (pp. 482–4, below).
2. Letter of June 25, 1711 (*Corr.*, 1 121).   3. Hooker, 1 396–7.

as he seems to have done his Humanity and his Criticism". He suggests that Pope awaits the "coming over of the Pretender, which by his Insolence he seems to believe approaching".[1] The gravity of such remarks can be realized only if one remembers the political situation of 1711, and the suspicions attached to Catholics.

The reasons why Pope had attacked Dennis in the poem are not precisely known. There is no evidence for the tradition that Dennis had spoken ill of Pope's *Pastorals*.[2] If the lines that caricature Dennis in the poem recall an actual incident, this must have been an occasion when Pope had seen Dennis respond irascibly to reproof or criticism.[3] Yet during several years prior to 1711 Dennis had been an occasional object of ridicule by the wits, and Pope may have intended no more than another stroke at a stock figure. In 1702 Dennis had "aligned himself with the critics and against the wits".[4] For doing so he was promptly assigned, and at times he proved himself eminently qualified to assume, the traditional qualities thought to exist inalienably in all critics: ill-nature, pride, passion. Since Pope's whole poem is an attempt to define what a true critic and criticism should be, he probably introduced Dennis, with whatever injustice, as a mere illustration of faults he believed typical in the critics of his day.

III

We have seen that the *Essay* achieved at least a kind of early notoriety.[5] Status of a different kind was awarded it on December 20, 1711, when Addison gave a long account of it in the *Spectator*, No. 253. The effect of this notice seems to have been immediate, for in less than two weeks, about January 1, 1712, a second "issue" of the first edition was printed.[6] Addison gave the poem high praise.

---

1. Ibid., I 415.   2. *Early Career*, pp. 88–9.

3. Dennis said he was "about thrice in Company" with Pope. See Hooker, II 370.

4. Hooker, II liii.

5. Dennis in his attack speaks of the "Approbation" the *Essay* "has met with". See Hooker, I 396.

6. Griffith uses the term "issue" to distinguish publication of the *Essay* at this time from the "Second Edition" published in November, 1712. See Griffith nos. 3 and 8.

He admired particularly the beautiful way in which Pope described the characters of the Latin critics and, like Longinus, "exemplified several of his Precepts in the very Precepts themselves." He dwelt at length on the theme so well expounded and illustrated by Pope, that the "*Sound* must seem an *Eccho* to the *Sense*". And Addison concluded his paper by placing the *Essay on Criticism* on a par with two other "Master-pieces" of the same kind: Roscommon's *Essay on Translated Verse*, and Sheffield's *Essay upon Poetry*.

The two rival Essays soon faded, or had already faded, into relative insignificance. The reputation of Pope's poem for a while increased. It received perhaps its highest praise from Johnson, who said that, if Pope had written nothing else, the *Essay* would have placed him "among the first cricks and the first poets".[1] After Johnson the reputation of the *Essay* steadily declined. Warton, who at first praised the poem highly,[2] by the end of the century introduced a notable qualification of Johnson's words: "It may fairly entitle . . . [Pope] to the character of being one of the first of critics, though surely not of poets. . ."[3] Not too much later one finds De Quincey saying that the *Essay* "is the feeblest and least interesting of Pope's writings,—being substantially a mere versification, like a metrical multiplication-table, of commonplaces the most mouldy with which criticism has baited its rat-traps."[4] And near the end of the 19th century Elwin says that De Quincey had not rated the "matter" of the *Essay* "below its value".[5]

The reputation of the *Essay* had spread to the continent almost at once. A letter of October 10, 1713,[6] from Pope to Anthony Hamilton, shows that the author of the famous *Mémoires du Comte de Grammont* sent Pope a verse translation he had made of the *Essay*. It was never published, but it probably was passed about in French literary circles. It was followed in 1717 by another verse translation by Robethon, private secretary to King George I, and also by Du Resnel's verse translation of 1730. This last, in which Voltaire was supposed to have had a hand, was re-issued in 1736 together with

---

1. *Lives of the English Poets*, ed. G. B. Hill (1905), III 228.
2. In *An Essay on the Writings and Genius of Pope* (1756).
3. See Warton's edn of Pope's *Works* (1797), I 173.
4. *Collected Writings*, ed. David Masson (1890), XI 29–30.   5. EC, II 19.
6. See *Corr.*, I 192–3, and Pope's notes to the letter.

a verse translation of *An Essay on Man* under the title of *Les Principes de la Morale et du Goût*. For a time the *Essay on Criticism* was overshadowed by the *Essay on Man*, until both lost favour in the gradual triumph of Romanticism.

III: THE *ESSAY* AS A CRITICAL DOCUMENT

"I admired", said Lady Mary Wortley Montagu, "Mr. Pope's Essay on Criticism at first, very much, because I had not then read any of the antient critics, and did not know that it was all stolen."[1] This objection to the poem has persisted since Pope's own time, and it is invariably the sign of a lack of understanding of the contemporary literary situation and of Pope's purposes in writing the poem. The objection records only part of the truth, for Pope's "borrowings" were not solely or even mainly from the Ancients; and it seldom, or never, realizes the significance of the truth. Along with this perennial objection have endured certain related ones: that Pope is a slave to a narrow and dogmatic classicism, and paradoxically, that he is loose and contradictory in his treatment of such central terms as "Nature" and "Wit". As these objections verge upon one another, so do the answers to them.

The development of "neo-classical" literary theory in 17th-century England was neither straightforward nor uniform in character. In this period nearly all the moods of criticism are either strongly or fitfully represented,[2] and the main course of development is not toward the utter elimination of one or another of these moods, but towards a precarious and delicate reconciliation of all of them together. The end, indeed, towards which this development moved is precisely represented by the kind of critical synthesis one finds formulated in the *Essay on Criticism*. Pope's poem is the logical culmination of nearly a century's effort to harmonize the extremes and variables of critical thinking. But it was the culmination, for the reconciliation of conflicting critical moods which it attempts could neither be more delicately stated nor could such a finely wrought balance endure.

In the development of "neo-classical" theory in England one may perhaps distinguish, though only roughly and vaguely, three

---

1. Spence, 234.   2. See Spingarn, 1 cvi.

stages, or phases, of progression.[1] The first phase might be said to
cover roughly the period between 1650 and 1670, and represents
English attempts to assimilate early French influences and to guide
contemporary literature along correct lines. Here the main influences are those of such French writers as Godeau, Chapelain, and
Corneille, and the opinions expressed range from Cowley's on Pin-
daric odes and Dryden's on the Unities to those of the Royal
Society on the reform of language. The second phase covers, again
only roughly, the last quarter of the century, a period marked by
the influence of French "neo-classical" thought of a more sophisticated character, and by the discussion of literary problems of a
more fundamental and general kind. At this time were published,
and frequently translated into English almost immediately, such
works as Bouhours's *Les Entretiens D'Ariste et D'Eugène* (1671) and
Manière de bien penser (1687), Boileau's *Art Poétique* (1674) and translation of Longinus (1674), Rapin's *Réflexions sur la Poétique* (1674),
Le Bossu's *Traité du Poëme épique* (1675), Dacier's translation of Aristotle's *Poetics* (1692). Here speculation was concerned with the imitation of Nature and the Rules, and also with Taste, the *je ne sais
quoi*, and the Sublime. The third phase occurs during the opening
years of the 18th century, and is marked by the general, but by no
means uncritical, acceptance of "neo-classical" doctrine as an or-
thodoxy. At this time there was a preoccupation with the methods
and principles of criticism itself and with the improvement of public taste.

But the important point to be noted is that in none of these
"phases" is there a general acceptance of a rigid "neo-classical"
doctrine. Only perhaps in a writer such as Rymer is "neo-classical"
theory carried to a logical, and thoroughly ridiculous, conclusion.
But against Rymer's rigid application of the rules of decorum and
his sneer at *Paradise Lost* ("which some are pleas'd to call a Poem"[2]),
there is to be set Dryden's understanding of dramatic character and
his view that Milton's poem was one of the "greatest, most noble,
and most sublime"[3] of poems. Dryden's very use of the word "sub-

---

1. J. W. H. Atkins, *English Literary Criticism: 17th and 18th Centuries* (1951),
distinguishes three such phases of development.
2. *The Tragedies of the Last Age* (1678), in Spingarn, II 208.
3. *The Author's Apology for Heroic Poetry*, in *Essays*, I 179.

lime" in his praise is recognition of an element in art which may be
more grand than correct, and reveals the influence of Longinus.
Against Rymer too there is to be set the characteristic struggle of
the age to reconcile all the opposing principles and values with
which, in one guise or another, it was presented. Thus, though
there is a general acceptance of the truths of Nature as being eternal
and immutable, there is also a recognition that the circumstances
which produced the classics of Greece and Rome do not exist in
England, and that works of art which reflect an English society are
possible. Against French influences there are posed the special features of English character and the native literary tradition: if Pope
pretends to despise the "brave *Britons*" who reject the "Rules", he
"contrives still more to despise the French for keeping them".[1]
Against submission to Reason and the Rules is set the assertion that
"Some Beauties yet, no Precepts can declare", an assertion that reflects the complications of 17th-century literary history by echoing
both Bacon (beauty is achieved by a "kind of felicity . . . and not by
rule"[2]) and Rapin ("There are no precepts, to teach the hidden
graces . . . of Poetry"[3]). Against the rationalistic formulae, the "receipts" of literature of a Rymer or a Le Bossu, are set those echoes
of Boileau (the "*brave Disorder*" which parts from "*vulgar Bounds*"[4]),
of Rapin (the graces which gain "The *Heart*" and all their "End *at
once*" attain[5]), of Davenant ("For there's a *Happiness* as well as
Care"[6]).

In the formulation of a "neo-classical" position, the best minds
of the period roam freely, in the manner of Swift's (or perhaps of
Ben Jonson's[7]) famous bee, over a broad and fertile field, selecting
(or "borrowing" and "stealing") from a variety of sources those
ingredients which appear most sweet and wholesome for literature.
These minds were contemptuous of those who, like the spider, spun
out of themselves a narrow rationalistic dogma. And what emerges
from the writings of men like Dryden and Pope is not so much a

---

1. See William Empson, 'Wit in the Essay on Criticism', *The Hudson Review*,
II (1950), p. 577. Also in *The Structure of Complex Words* (1951), pp. 84–100.

2. See *n* to ll. 141–4.   3. See *n* to l. 144.

4. See *n* to l. 154.   5. See *n* to l. 144.

6. See *n* to l. 142.

7. See *Timber, or Discoveries*, in Spingarn, I 54 (also Spingarn's note on the
passage, I 228).

system as a highly eclectic set of values, in substance an attempt to harmonize apparently opposing attitudes. This was bound to appear at times vague and paradoxical. Only by vagueness and paradox, however, could the essentially flexible nature of the position be maintained.

This set of values, so eclectically derived, and so pervaded with antithetical elements, was not the product of critical naïveté or of a bland indifference to incompatibles, nor was it one which was, or could be, maintained with a sense of comfortable complacency. The rival claims of wit and judgment, of the head and the heart, were not to be reconciled easily and neatly, if at all. Yet Dryden, Pope, and others preferred to maintain, whatever the apparent contradictions in which they became involved, the complications rather than the simplifications of artistic truth. The result of such a preference is a poem like *An Essay on Criticism*, where the antithetical reality is not obscured but emphasized. Thus Pope's use of italics and capitals carefully stresses the complicated truth about art:

> For there's a *Happiness* as well as *Care*.
>
> The *Whole* at once is *Bold*, and *Regular*.
>
> *Nature*, like *Liberty*, is but restrain'd
> By the same Laws which first *herself* ordain'd.
>
> Great Wits sometimes may *gloriously offend*,
> And *rise* to *Faults* true Criticks *dare not mend*.

The same refusal to oversimplify is illustrated by a couplet which has exasperated critics and editors from the beginning. From 1711 to 1743, ll. 80–1 read thus:

> There are whom Heav'n has blest with store of Wit,
> Yet want as much again to manage it.

The context of these lines, and the apparent sources for them, make it clear that Pope is here refusing to separate wit and judgment cleanly, and for his refusal he received a full blast of scorn from Dennis,[1] and another from Matthew Concanen, who said: "*Wit* to manage *Wit*, is full as good as one Tongue's tiring another. Any one may perceive that the Writer meant *Judgment* should manage *Wit*;

---

1. See Hooker, 1 404.

but as it stands, it's *Pert*, and that's to be preferr'd to all other Considerations."[1] Pope was evidently willing, however, to pay a price for the paradox he had enunciated in his couplet, and so, even in the face of such ridicule, he maintained the studied ambiguity of the lines; even when, some thirty years after Dennis's attack, he revised the couplet, he carefully preserved its equivocal character:

> Some to whom Heav'n in Wit has been profuse,
> Want as much more, to turn it to its use.

To understand Pope's refusal to separate wit and judgment cleanly is to be led into some of the most complex and pressing issues of the contemporary literary scene,[2] and perhaps the best way to illuminate his position as it is illustrated in the two versions of his couplet is to cite a passage from one of his favourite classical authors. In Book III of his *Institutio Oratoria*, in a discussion of the five parts of oratory (invention, arrangement, expression, memory, and delivery), Quintilian says: "Some have added a sixth department, subjoining *judgment* to *invention*, on the ground that it is necessary first to *invent* and then to *exercise our judgment*. For my own part I do not believe that *invention* can exist apart from *judgment*, since we do not say that a speaker has *invented* inconsistent, two-edged or foolish arguments, but merely that he has failed to avoid them. It is true that Cicero in his Rhetorica includes *judgment* under *invention*; but in my opinion *judgment* is so inextricably mingled with the first three departments of rhetoric (for without *judgment* neither *expression* nor *arrangement* are possible), that I think that even delivery owes much to it."[3]

---

1. *A Supplement to the Profound* (1728), p. 11.

2. E. N. Hooker has previously explored the issues raised by Pope's refusal to separate wit and judgment. See 'Pope on Wit: The *Essay on Criticism*', in *The Seventeenth Century ... By Richard Foster Jones and Others Writing in His Honor* (1951), pp. 225–46.

3. III iii 5–7 (Loeb Classical Library edn, tr. by H. E. Butler). The original reads: "His adiecerunt quidam sextam partem, ita ut inventioni iudicium subnecterent, quia primum esset invenire, deinde iudicare. Ego porro ne invenisse quidem credo eum, qui non iudicavit; neque enim contraria, communia, stulta invenisse dicitur quisquam, sed non vitasse. Et Cicero quidem in Rhetoricis iudicium subiecit inventioni; mihi autem adeo tribus primis partibus videtur esse permixtum (nam neque dispositio sine eo neque elocutio fuerit), ut pronuntiationem quoque vel plurimum ex eo mutuari putem."

The intimate relationship in which rhetoric and poetry stood to one another in the Renaissance is well known, and any close reading of the *Essay* will reveal that for Pope the role of wit (in some of the more important senses of the term as it is used in his poem) is one which corresponds closely to Quintilian's "invention". Wit in the *Essay* is at times *the* inventive, imaginative, faculty, and in its most exalted sense the term is not one which suggests a wild fancy or a merely extravagant imagination in need of the curb of judgment or good sense: it is rather a term which suggests the ability of the imagination to pierce into and illuminate the most profound truths of human experience. It has all the suggestions revealed in this passage from La Rochefoucauld, a passage which seems to bear closely on Pope's ambiguous couplets and which he must have read about the time he was composing the first of them:

> The making a Difference between *Wit* and *Judgment*, is a *Vulgar Error*. *Judgment* is nothing else but the *exceeding Brightness* of *Wit*, which, like *Light*, pierces into the very *Bottom of Things*, observes all that ought to be observed there, and discovers what seemed to be past any bodies finding out: From whence we must conclude, that the *Energy* and *Extension* of this *Light* of the *Wit*, is the very Thing that produces all those Effects, usually ascrib'd to the *Judgment*.[1]

To appreciate the full significance of the line of thought represented by the passages from Quintilian and La Rochefoucauld,[2] and by Pope's couplets, we must now glance at another line of thought which threatened to dominate literary discussion in Pope's time. Here we may begin with the work of the French logician Peter Ramus, a figure of great influence during the 16th and 17th centuries, one of whose main efforts had been directed towards a

---

1. *Moral Maxims and Reflections*, 2nd edn (1706), Maxim xcviii; quoted by Hooker, *The Seventeenth Century*, pp. 240–1. In a letter to Wycherley of Nov. 29, 1707 (*Corr.*, 1 34), Pope refuses to accept the notion that Wit means "no more than *Fancy* or *Conceit*", and advises that it would be to Wycherley's advantage to reduce much of his poetry "into *single Thoughts in Prose*, like *Rochfoucault*, as I have more than once hinted to you." The same advice is given to Wycherley again in a letter of May 2, 1710 (*Corr.*, 1 86).

2. Hooker, *The Seventeenth Century*, cites other examples in this line of thought.

"radical reassignment of the anciently established five parts of the art of rhetoric".[1] In direct opposition to the thought of a writer of Quintilian's position, Ramus took invention, arrangement, and memory away from rhetoric and gave them to be the sole concern of dialectic, leaving to rhetoric only expression (style) and delivery. It is difficult to weigh exactly the full effects of this division wrought by Ramus between the matter or content of a discourse and its style or ornamentation, but that it did tend to reduce the function of rhetoric to a concern with the mere ornamentation of truths that logic was happy enough to discover seems certain.[2] This tendency, moreover, was strengthened greatly by other developments in the 17th century, and these we can trace in terms which relate very closely to the wording of Pope's ambiguous couplets.

In one of the most famous passages in his *Timber, or Discoveries*, Ben Jonson applies to Shakespeare words that Seneca the elder had applied to the Latin poet Haterius: "His wit was in his owne power; would the rule of it had beene so too."[3] There may be no direct connection between the two, but Jonson's words have at least some resemblance to these of Thomas Sprat on Cowley: "His Fancy flow'd with great speed, and therefore it was very fortunate to him that his Judgment was equal to manage it."[4] Whatever Jonson's turn of phrase may have implied, it would certainly seem that Sprat's words reflect the intervening influence of Thomas Hobbes, who in such statements about wit as the following had clearly distinguished, for many Englishmen at least, the difference between Fancy (or Wit) and Judgment: ". . . those that observe their similitudes, in case they be such as are but rarely observed by others, are said to have a *good wit*; by which, in this occasion, is meant a *good fancy*. But they that observe their differences, and dissimilitudes; which is called *distinguishing*, and *discerning*, and *judging* between

1. See William K. Wimsatt, Jr, and Cleanth Brooks, *Literary Criticism: A Short History* (1957), pp. 222*ff.*, for a survey of Ramist influence in English literary criticism.

2. Ibid., pp. 225-6.

3. See Spingarn, I 19. Seneca (*Excerpta Controversiarum*, IV, Proem. 8) says: "In sua potestate habebat ingenium, in aliena modum."

4. See Sprat's *Account of the Life and Writings of . . . Cowley* (in Spingarn, II 130).

thing and thing; in case, such discerning be not easy, are said to have a *good judgment*. . ."[1]

The thought of Hobbes on wit undergoes curious changes.[2] At an early stage in his career Wit seems to embrace both the faculty (Fancy) which perceives similarities and also that (Judgment) which perceives dissimilarities.[3] Later on, however, he seems to identify Wit with Fancy alone, or at least he reveals to us the tendency in the age to do so: "For men more generally affect and admire Fancie than they do either Judgment, or Reason, or Memory, or any other intellectual Virtue; and for the pleasantness of it, give to it alone the name of Wit, accounting Reason and Judgment but for a dull entertainment."[4] And in a comment which at least recalls the divisive spirit of Ramistic efforts, he says: "Judgment begets the strength and structure, and Fancy begets the ornaments of a Poem."[5]

The important consequence of such speculation about the nature and function of Wit was the tendency (re-enforced by the efforts of the Royal Society to achieve a severely scientific way of speech) to associate wit, which for La Rochefoucauld had pierced "into the very *Bottom* of *Things*", with the merely pleasing, ornamental, fanciful, impetuous, and insubstantial. To this tendency Locke lent his authority in his *Essay Concerning Human Understanding*:

Since wit and fancy find easier entertainment in the world than dry truth and real knowledge, figurative speeches and allusion in language will hardly be admitted as an imperfection or abuse of it. I confess, in discourses where we seek rather pleasure and delight than information and improvement, such ornaments as are borrowed from them can scarce pass for faults. But yet if we would speak of things as they are, we must allow that all the art of rhetoric, besides order and clearness; all the artificial and figurative applications of words eloquence hath invented, are

1. *Leviathan*, Part i, chap. viii.

2. See W. L. Ustick and H. H. Hudson, 'Wit, "Mixt Wit," and the Bee in Amber', *Huntington Library Bulletin*, VIII (Oct., 1935), especially pp. 108*ff*.

3. See *Humane Nature*, 2nd edn (1651), chap. x: "And both *Fancie* and *Judgement* are commonly comprehended under the name of *Wit*. . ." Cited by Ustick and Hudson, p. 108.

4. Preface to *Homer's Odysses* (1675), in Spingarn, II 70.

5. *The Answer . . . to . . . D'Avenant's Preface* (1650), in Spingarn, II 59.

for nothing else but to insinuate wrong ideas, move the passions, and thereby mislead the judgment; and so indeed are perfect cheats...[1]

The ultimate effect of such a line of thought as this would be the trivialization of poetry itself: the faculty of Wit and the figurative language it inspires are seen as unrelated to truth and real knowledge, to "things as they are". Since figurative language is of the essence of poetry, the denial of its ability to express truth is the denial of the value and dignity of poetry. At best, the main role of Wit or of poetry becomes (as in Ramistic theory) the mere ornamentation of those truths provided for it by the judgment, and it is scarcely conceivable that Pope, for whom Wit in the *Essay* is synonymous on occasion with Genius and Art itself, would or could share in assumptions so prejudicial to his art.[2]

Nor did he. We have only to look at two other apparent sources of his paradoxical couplets to see how self-consciously and deliberately he must have tried, in these instances, to blur distinctions between Wit and Judgment. In 1674 a poem by Charles Cotton appeared which contained these lines:

> Nor is it *all*, to have a share of *Wit*,
> There must be *Judgment too* to manage it.[3]

A few years later, in 1687, a poem by John Cutts formulated the relationship between Wit and Judgment in very much the same terms:

> Nature to some has giv'n an active Wit,
> But hardly Sense enough to manage it.[4]

Both couplets follow closely Sprat's words about Cowley, and both

---

1. Bk III, chap. x, par. 34. Cf. Warburton's note, *Works* (1751), I 172: "Mr. *Locke* had defined *Wit* to consist *in the assemblage of ideas, and putting those together, with quickness and variety, wherein can be found any resemblance or congruity, whereby to make up pleasant pictures and agreeable visions in the fancy.* But that great Philosopher, in separating *Wit* from *Judgment*..."
2. See Hooker's essay, *passim*, in *The Seventeenth Century.*
3. See Cotton's recommendatory poem, ll. 12–13, prefixed to Thomas Flatman's *Poems and Songs.* This volume went into several editions; a 4th edn had appeared by 1685.
4. Ll. 10–11 of *To the Dutchess of Monmouth*, in *Poetical Exercises* (1687).

amount to what had become traditional formulations of a critical literary question. Most important for our purposes, however, is the fact that the two versions of Pope's couplet, verbally so closely related to these traditional formulations in all other respects, depart from them only in insisting that Wit, rather than Judgment or Sense, can manage Wit. Wit thus becomes not only a faculty which provides quickness of insight and liveliness of expression, but also a controlling and ordering faculty. Wit and Judgment seem to be, on this crucial occasion in the poem, differing aspects of the same faculty.

Pope's equivocal couplet opens a way into only a few of the meanings and issues suggested by his use of the term "Wit", for in the *Essay* the word is used in a variety of other carefully shaded senses. Dennis responded to the multiplicity of meaning given to Wit in the poem by saying that Pope, whenever he spoke of Wit, was "sure to say something . . . very foolish",[1] and later critics too have felt that Pope used the term "with a perplexing want of precision".[2] It now seems clear not only that Pope's usage accurately reflects the varied senses the term possessed in his time, but that by employing these varied senses he informed his poem with the bright and social tone of easy conversation.[3] By playing over the scale of the word's meaning Pope, to adapt a sentence from Shaftesbury about the "Hero" of "Philosophical Writings", maintains "a certain exquisite and refin'd Raillery which belong'd to his Manner, and by virtue of which he cou'd treat the highest Subjects, and those of the commonest Capacity both together, and render 'em explanatory of each other."[4]

Faced with the linguistic fact of a word which could mean anything from a mere jester or "witling" like D'Urfey to a "Patriarch-Wit" such as Homer, from mere knowledge to the highest poetic genius and power, a word for which there was apparently no substitute in the critical vocabulary of his time, Pope refuses to falsify the term by a simplification of its meaning. He rather puts the word's multiplicity of meaning to use, and gains thereby a special

---

1. Hooker, I 411.   2. EC, II 25.

3. See Empson, 'Wit in the Essay on Criticism', *The Hudson Review*, II 559–77; also in *The Structure of Complex Words* (1951), pp. 84–100.

4. *Characteristicks of Men, Manners, Opinions, Times,* 5th edn (1732), I 194–5.

kind of unity. In such couplets, moreover, as this most famous one,

> *True Wit* is *Nature* to Advantage drest,
> What oft was *Thought*, but ne'r so well *Exprest*,

Pope, by his emphatic linking of "Wit" with "Nature", manages to enclose the word in the body of his doctrine, if "doctrine" it can be called, and insists that Wit, in its most exalted sense, is conformable to that which is permanent and universal in human experience.

This "Nature" is the ultimate authority in the *Essay*, and it has been, like Wit, the subject of much complaint since Pope's time. Thus Dennis, who throughout his *Reflections* seems determined to misapprehend Pope's most commonplace assertions and whose views have been echoed down to our own time, said that Pope should have said "what he means by Nature, and what it is to write or to judge according to Nature".[1] A proper answer to this might be that Pope would have thought it as unnecessary to define Nature, in so many words, as it was to define Truth and Reason, terms for which, in fact, Nature was a satisfactory equivalent.[2] Throughout the *Essay* Pope is working with a set of assumptions which, if they are not entirely clear from the poem alone, are easily recoverable from other contemporary writings. These assumptions suggest, moreover, a body of thought which conforms closely to Dennis's own thinking about Nature as it is revealed in that critic's work.[3]

Fundamental to "neo-classical" thought about Nature is the conception of a cosmos which, in its order and regularity and harmony, reflects the order and harmony in the Divine Mind of its Creator. "Nature", says Davenant, "is the onely visible power and operation of God".[4] Man can perceive this order and rule in Nature because he has a rational soul made in the image of that Nature's Creator. "The Law of Nature", says Robert South, "I take to be nothing else, but the mind of God, signified to a Rational Agent by the bare discourse of his Reason."[5] In the view which prevails in the

---

1. Hooker, I 403.
2. For the many and varied meanings of "Nature", see A. O. Lovejoy, '"Nature" as Aesthetic Norm', in *Essays in the History of Ideas* (1955), pp. 69–77.
3. See Hooker, I 202, 335.   4. Preface to *Gondibert* (in Spingarn, II 7).
5. *Twelve Sermons Preached Upon Several Occasions*, 3rd edn (1704), I 458–9.

period "Nature" is the manifestation in the visible creation of the Order and Reason behind all things, a reflection of the medieval view that the likeness of God is imprinted in the very matter and organization of the universe. Or as Dennis himself explains: "As Nature is Order and Rule, and Harmony in the visible World, so Reason is the very same throughout the invisible Creation", and "both Nature and Reason" are, "in a larger Acceptation . . . Nature".[1] The reason in man thus faces the Reason in Nature, and ideally one should mirror the other. Or, as Pope says in the *Essay*, a true work of wit will give us Nature to advantage dressed,

> *Something*, whose Truth convinc'd at Sight we find,
> That gives us back the Image of our Mind.

Whatever influence Descartes may have had on this view of Nature, and however it may have been appropriated to Deism, its roots lie deep in the pagan and Christian past, nourished by the Stoic doctrine of the Logos and by traditional Christian contemplation of God as mirrored in His creation. The attitude toward Nature which underlies most "neo-classical" art is not so much related to the mechanical universe of Hobbes and others as to a conception "as old as Stoicism", and which had "for centuries been a familiar and guiding principle in ethics and law". To the Stoics, "Nature meant a kind of world-order, an order perceived by the enlightened and disciplined soul, which in turn found within itself a noble capacity for conforming to this ideal world-order, and thus raising itself above sordidness and vice. The Nature which is imitated by art is also of this ideal and normative kind, the Unerring Nature . . . of Pope's *Essay on Criticism*."[2] It is against this background that one may best comprehend the reverence for Nature which is so visible in the writings of Pope and others, and understand too their conviction that, in "following Nature", they were giving expression to all that gave the universe and human life its meaning and dignity.

The primary, though not the only, meaning of "Nature"[3] as the

---

1. Hooker, 1 202.

2. See Louis I. Bredvold, 'The Tendency Toward Platonism in Neo-Classical Esthetics', *ELH*, 1 (1934), pp. 98–9.

3. Other meanings of the term as it is used in the poem can be found in Lovejoy's essay cited above, p. 219, and note.

term appears in the *Essay on Criticism* can best be seen in these famous lines:

> First follow NATURE, and your Judgment frame
> By her just Standard, which is still the same:
> *Unerring Nature*, still divinely bright,
> One *clear*, *unchang'd*, and *Universal* Light,
> Life, Force, and Beauty, must to all impart,
> At once the *Source*, and *End*, and *Test* of *Art*.

The scarcely veiled analogy here is one between Nature and God:
the attributions and formulae used are those traditionally reserved
for the First Cause. Nature is one, eternal, immutable, and the
source and end of all things. There is of course no suggestion of pan-
theism here. Instead, this is Pope's statement of the old idea that as
God gives being to beings, so He makes causes to be causes, and thus
grants to them the ability to participate in His power.[1] That Nature
which from one point of view may seem to have merely *received* the
laws and order of its being, may from another be seen, by its participation in causality, as *conferring* these qualities. Pope is here concerned with a Nature which has a mysterious analogy to its Source
in all its functioning. If "neo-classical" speculation so often seems
to be an exercise in abstract reasoning, there is yet a sense, as here,
in which it touches the heart of a mystery.

Dennis, in reproving Pope for not saying what it means to "follow
Nature", set out his own views in a special appendix to his *Reflections*. Dennis was not a Platonist, though his phrasing partakes of
the Platonic colouration common in attempts to state the idealism
inherent in the age's aesthetic.[2] To "follow Nature", he said, "in
giving a draught of human Life, and of the manners of Men . . . [is]
to consult that innate Original, and that universal Idea, which the
Creator has fix'd in the minds of ev'ry reasonable Creature, and so
to make a true and a just Draught."[3] But Pope had said no less
himself:

> So when the faithful *Pencil* has design'd
> Some *bright Idea* of the Master's Mind,
> Where a *new World* leaps out at his command,
> And ready Nature waits upon his Hand . . .

---

1. See Etienne Gilson, *The Spirit of Medieval Philosophy* (1940), p. 100.
2. See Bredvold, *ELH*, I 106–7.   3. Hooker, I 418.

Pope of course understood the difficulties involved in any attempt to mirror "Nature" in art. The light of Nature might be one and universal, but the judgments of men (prompted, paradoxically, by Nature again)[1] are as their watches: none "Go just *alike*, yet each believes his own." As a check, then, to the eccentricities of the individual, he gave assent, as did most in his age, to the Rules. This assent, however, was not unqualified, nor was it in any way an assent to arbitrary authority. The Rules were accepted because they were based on Reason, a reason which discovered in Nature herself a *regularity* and order. Even the human mind had its laws, against which it might not transgress without lessening its own reason.[2] The Rules were thus defended on rational grounds and had their metaphysical foundation in the order of things. Mere regularity, moreover, was not to be sought: for in the luxuriance of Nature, the source of the Rules, were to be found those objects, the "shapeless *Rock*, or hanging *Precipice*" which "*out of* Nature's *common Order* rise". Pope expresses his contempt for those who "Write dull *Receits* how Poems may be made", and emphasizes the *je ne sais quoi* of the school of taste, the "*nameless Graces* which no Methods teach". Against those works which are "*Correctly cold*, and *regularly low*", he sets those in which "*Nature moves*, and *Rapture warms* the Mind". The poet who was to stress in the Preface to his translation of the *Iliad* his admiration for Homer's poetic fire also addressed the same poet in his *Essay*:

Oh may some Spark of *your* Cœlestial Fire,
The last, the meanest of your Sons inspire.

Throughout the *Essay* one is aware of Pope's indebtedness above all to Dryden. It is Dryden rather than Walsh who was Pope's master in criticism. And more important than Pope's use of Dryden as a source for particular critical ideas is the way in which the *Essay* reflects Dryden's broad capacity for synthesis of the best that was thought and felt in his time, and his capacity to express the judgments of the head and the heart in memorable language. The wit and good sense of Dryden, who, more than any one else of his time,

---

1. See the discussion of Nature by J. M. Cameron in "Mr Tillotson and Mr Pope", *The Dublin Review*, No. 480 (1959), pp. 153–70.
2. Hooker, I 202.

guided the formation of English "neo-classical" thought, also guided the young poet who gave that thought its finest expression.

The extent of Pope's "borrowings" from Ancient and Modern writers is revealed in the notes to this edition. The very variety of the sources which lie behind the poem is the best evidence that the *Essay* represents no narrow or exclusive doctrine. At the same time the poem cannot be reduced to its scattered sources, for Pope has brought them together and given their union a special new life and grace. The *Essay* is the best illustration of Pope's own view that writers who "borrow" are like "Trees which of themselves wou'd produce only one sort of Fruit, but by being grafted upon others, may yield variety. A mutual commerce makes Poetry flourish. . ."[1]

IV: THE DESIGN OF THE *ESSAY*

I

The analytical summary which first preceded the *Essay on Criticism* in the 1736 *Works* implied that Pope was not, amidst his poem's maze of critical observations, without some kind of plan. And Warburton was to emphasize the poem's regularity of "method".[2] On the other hand, Pope's friend Richardson maintained that there was no such "regularity"; for Pope, "when often speaking of [the *Essay*], (before he so much as knew *Warburton*) spoke of it always, as an 'irregular collection of thoughts, thrown together as they offered themselves, as *Horace's Art of Poetry* was,' he said, 'and written in imitation of that irregularity,' which he even admired, and said was beautiful."[3] Addison too considered that the thoughts of the poem "follow one another like those in *Horace's Art of Poetry*, without that methodical Regularity which would have been requisite in a Prose Author."[4]

The observations in the *Essay* do not, of course, follow one another in a strictly methodical or logical fashion, but then it is also

---

1. Letter to Walsh, July 2, 1706 (*Corr.*, I 19–20).

2. See Warburton's edn of the *Works* (1751), I 137–8.

3. *Richardsoniana* (1776), p. 264. Professor R. H. Griffith has suggested that the analytical summary prefixed to the poem in 1736 was the work of Richardson himself (see 'Pope Editing Pope', *University of Texas, Studies in English*, 1944, p. 7).

4. *Spectator* 253.

wrong to say that they exhibit no order or dependency whatever. Pope eschewed the pedantic and regular division and sub-division which characterized such treatises as Le Bossu's on the epic. He preferred to assume, as we have seen, the urbane and apparently effortless manner of the drawing-room, and to glide naturally and easily from point to point. The connections are there, though the effort of his art has been to conceal them.

The very first of Pope's observations recorded in Spence's *Anecdotes* runs as follows: "Most little poems should be written by a plan: this method is evident in Tibullus, and Ovid's Elegies, and almost all the pieces of the ancients.—Horace's Art of Poetry was probably only fragments of what he designed; it wants the regularity that flows from the following a plan; and there are several passages in it that are hints only of a larger design." These words were spoken, of course, long after the event of Pope's own "little poem". Taken with the ways in which the *Essay* reflects some of the more significant features of the contemporary scene, however, they perhaps suggest that Pope may have tried to give his poem, not a "regularity of method", but that "larger design" he felt Horace only partially achieved in his.

II

"The great Design of Arts is to restore the Decays that happen'd to human Nature by the Fall, by restoring Order". These words appear (significantly, perhaps, in the light of the title of Pope's poem) in Dennis's *The Grounds of Criticism in Poetry* (1704), and they assert, with special relevance for art, the commonplace idea of the time[1] that the Fall had presented man with a great task of reformation and restoration. Dennis states clearly that his own "Design . . . is the Re-establishment of Poetry", and that he is to "Attempt to restore and re-establish the noblest Art in every Branch of it: an Art, that by the Barbarity of the Times, is fallen and sunk in them all, and has been driven and banish'd from every Country excepting *England* alone; and is even here so miserably fallen for the most part by the Extravagance of its Professors, and by the Unskilfulness of its Admirers. . ." Throughout the whole discussion Dennis dwells

---

1. Cf. Milton, *Of Education*: "The end then of learning is to repair the ruins of our first parents. . ."

on the imperfections and confusions which entered the world once man departed from his "Primitive State, by transgressing Order", and dwells also on the use of poetry "to instruct and reform the World".[1]

The concept to which Dennis here gives such explicit expression did not, of course, imply a restoration to the state of original perfection. There was, however, a widespread assumption that man's efforts should be directed at restoring a semblance of his primitive state. This theme, and the historical perspective which necessarily frames it, can be traced throughout the *Essay on Criticism*; it is the theme which provides the poem with its "larger design": the restoration of the decays in Critics, and in Criticism.

Divisions, both grand and petty, characterized the "Peace" of the Augustans. The Quarrel between the Ancients and Moderns had by no means subsided; Swift's *Battle of the Books* was published in 1704, and the Quarrel had still a course to run during Pope's lifetime. The turn of the century had seen violent conflict between Sir Richard Blackmore and the Wits, a conflict which had involved serious questions about the relationship between wit and poetry and morality, and which had settled none of them.[2] This conflict contained, moreover, a large amount of class antagonism: middle-class "men of sense" were arrayed against aristocratic "men of wit", the City against the West End.[3] Men such as Wycherley and Dennis, survivors from a previous era, were unable to adjust to the new climate of the age of Anne, and brought their own special kinds of irritation to the scene. Differences about the relative value of wit and judgment prevailed, the coffee-houses provided their cliques and claques, political considerations were beginning to exert their pressures upon literature, poet scorned poet, and both together scorned the critic.

Of special importance for the *Essay on Criticism*, however, is the

---

1. See Hooker, 1 334*ff.*

2. See R. C. Boys, *Sir Richard Blackmore and the Wits*, The University of Michigan Contributions in Modern Philology, No. 13, 1949. See also Hooker, 'Pope on Wit: The *Essay on Criticism*', in *The Seventeenth Century*, pp. 225–46.

3. See R. M. Krapp, 'Class Analysis of a Literary Controversy: Wit and Sense in Seventeenth Century English Literature', *Science and Society*, x (1946), pp. 80–92.

bitter contemporary attitude toward Critics and all their works. We "are fallen", Dryden had said in a statement which may well be considered as another proper starting point for an understanding of the *Essay*, "into an age of illiterate, censorious, and detracting people, who, thus qualified, set up for critics."[1] And such is the view that prevailed throughout the opening years of the 18th century. Thus Swift, in the *Battle of the Books*, describes Criticism as a malignant deity on whose right hand sat Ignorance, her father and husband, and on whose left sat Pride, her mother. "About her played her children, Noise and Impudence, Dulness and Vanity, Positiveness, Pedantry, and Ill-Manners." Typical also are the words of Samuel Cobb, who echoes Dryden: "Criticism, which was formerly the Art of judging well, is now become the pure Effect of Spleen, Passion and Self-conceit."[2]

The *Essay on Criticism* was conceived and written in awareness of such antagonisms as these, and in the awareness too of all the human imperfections which inspired most of them: folly, malice, pride. We have seen that, in the critical position it formulates, the *Essay* is essentially a compromise, an effort to bring into harmonious accord the various, and sometimes opposing, principles of its sources. This effort at an inner reconciliation of artistic principles is very accurately oriented toward the contemporary literary scene. For Pope endeavours to bring about a literary peace in his own time, not only by providing his age with a broad and flexible critical position on which all can in some measure agree, but also by providing it with a reminder of a great and glorious past from which it has fallen, an insight into the sources of its own difficulties, and a programme for its own reformation. This is the great and noble design of the *Essay on Criticism*, but it is not a design Pope had to invent for himself. He rather found it at hand in such statements as those of John Dennis about the need, in a degenerate age, for a reformation and restoration of the art of poetry. Dennis's programme for restoration in its turn conforms almost exactly to a programme for the restoration of the art of poetry enunciated many years before by Henry Reynolds. Having severely

1. *The Author's Apology for Heroic Poetry*, in *Essays*, I 179.
2. *A Discourse on Criticism* (1707), in The Augustan Reprint Series, No. 1 (1946), A^v.

chastised the poets of his own time for their failings, Reynolds went on to say this: "Let mee leaue them, and looke backe to the neuer-enough honoured Auncients; and set them before our eyes. . . To the end wee may, if in this declining state of the world we cannot rectify our oblique one by their perfect and strait line, yet in-deauour it; and in the meane time giue the awefull reuerence due to them, for the many regions of distance between their knowledges and ours. And this that wee may the better doe, let vs paralell them with the Poets (if I may so call them) of our times . . . and so carry along together their strait and our crooked line, for our better knowledge of them, and reformation of our selues."[1] Pope's *Essay on Criticism* is an exhortation to an age, one which parallels almost exactly, in the sequence of its three parts, such traditional exhortations to reformation and restoration as those of Dennis and Reynolds. Only perhaps when the poem's kinship with such earlier exhortations is clearly recognized can one fully comprehend the *Essay*, not only as a great critical document, but also as a rich and complex poem with its own grand design.

III

The historical perspective in which events are viewed within the *Essay on Criticism* can best be opened with the idea thus expressed by Vasari in the Preface to his *Lives of the Painters*: ". . . the first men, being less removed from their divine origin, were more perfect, possessing a brighter intelligence, and . . . with Nature as a guide, a pure intellect for master, and the lovely world as a model, they originated these noble arts, and by gradually improving them brought them at length, from small beginnings, to perfection."[2] Vasari's words are a formulation of a special aspect of the doctrine of primitivism, and it was to this doctrine Pope turned in order "to place 'authority' behind his treatise". Pope's "doctrine was that the world of Man was created perfect in Adam; since the Fall of Man . . . his world has been in a process of progressive decay; it follows therefore that ancient men who lived nearer the state of perfec-

---

1. *Mythomystes* (in Spingarn, I 149). The original edition of this work is un-dated, but it was entered on the Stationers' Registers Aug. 12, 1632, and Spin-garn (see note, I 244) assigns it a publication date of 1633.

2. Everyman edn, I 5–6.

tion could be and make things more nearly perfect than any modern. . ."[1] Homer's greatness, in this perspective, is due to the "brighter intelligence" by which he perceived, and could therefore better "follow" or "imitate", the more lovely Nature he had for a model. It is because Homer was able to see so clearly this Nature in her original splendour, and thereby mirror her so faithfully in his work, that Pope can say that "*Nature* and *Homer* were . . . the *same*". There was simply a great advantage given to the genius born among the pristine glories of Nature, and it followed that succeeding writers, including Virgil, could improve their vision by a study of the Homeric texts.

It is in the first part of his poem that Pope in the main establishes this image of a golden past in art. After a beginning which inquires into the limitations under which men at present write and judge, he introduces us abruptly to that "Nature" which, in its universality and brightness, is always ready to supply the light by which man sees and yet also always reveals the limitations of his perceptions:

> *Unerring Nature*, still divinely bright,
> One *clear, unchang'd*, and *Universal* Light. . .

Immediately after this celebration of "Nature", Pope turns the attention of the reader (ll. 92*ff.*) to an ancient past, to an age when men more fully comprehended this "Nature". In this golden time, a personified Greece was able to derive those precepts from her poets which they, in their turn, "deriv'd from *Heav'n*". The implication that the Ancients, like Adam before the Fall, enjoyed a direct infusion of knowledge "from *Heav'n*" seems unmistakable.

The triumphant bards born in those "*happier Days*" enjoyed other advantages which Pope then proceeds to contrast sharply with the contemporary state of affairs. Chief among these was the peace and harmony which characterized relations between poets and critics. In the golden age of art

> The gen'rous Critick *fann'd* the *Poet's Fire*,
> And taught the World, *with Reason* to *Admire*.

---

1. R. H. Griffith, 'Pope Editing Pope', *University of Texas, Studies in English* (1944), pp. 8–9. See also Lovejoy, 'The Parallel of Deism and Classicism', *Essays in the History of Ideas* (1955), especially pp. 86–90, 96–7.

> Then Criticism the Muse's Handmaid prov'd,
> To dress her Charms, and make her more belov'd.

But:

> following Wits from that Intention stray'd;
> Who cou'd not win the Mistress, woo'd the Maid;
> Against the Poets *their own Arms* they turn'd,
> Sure to hate most the Men from whom they *learn'd*.

The first part of the *Essay* concludes with a celebration of the Ancients which scarcely disguises the religious nature of its veneration. Here, in worship before a common altar, divisions and sects and quarrels in criticism are forgotten as men unite in a single congregation. The learned from all climes and ages bring, like the wise men of old, their incense to a common shrine, and *"all Tongues"* are joined in one mighty hymn of praise. Pope's verse, echoing with Christian and Longinian associations,[1] rises in full response to the inspiration his age received from a glorious past, a past which was both an inspiration, and a reproach, to the present:

> Still green with Bays each *ancient* Altar stands,
> Above the reach of *Sacrilegious* Hands,
> Secure from *Flames*, from *Envy's* fiercer Rage,
> Destructive *War*, and all-involving *Age*.
> See, from *each Clime* the Learn'd their Incense bring;
> Hear, in *all Tongues* consenting *Pæans* ring!
> In Praise so just, let ev'ry Voice be join'd,
> And fill the *Gen'ral Chorus* of *Mankind*!
> Hail *Bards Triumphant*! born in *happier Days*;
> *Immortal* Heirs of *Universal* Praise!
> Whose Honours with Increase of Ages *grow*,
> As Streams roll down, *enlarging* as they flow!
> Nations *unborn* your mighty Names shall sound,
> And Worlds applaud that must not yet be *found*!

In the second part of the *Essay* Pope turns mainly to his own carping and distracted times and reveals in various ways how it has fallen away:

> No longer now that Golden Age appears,
> When *Patriarch-Wits* surviv'd a *thousand Years*. . .

---

1. See notes to ll. 181*ff*.

> *Now*, they who reach *Parnassus'* lofty Crown,
> Employ their Pains to spurn some others down...

Against the glorious background of the past are now displayed in full vigour the divisions, blindnesses, and failings of his own and preceding ages. The opening lines of this part, furthermore, continue the primitivistic perspective in their emphasis on Pride, the cause of the original Fall and therefore the source of all the decays in human nature and in the arts. The light of Nature, divinely bright, is still present, but the capacity of men to perceive it or to be guided by it has weakened: some pervert and distort the light and produce works which are "One *glaring Chaos* and *wild Heap* of *Wit*"; others ignore it completely: "The Face of Nature we no more Survey". The dissensions which have prevailed in religion over the centuries as a result of man's pride and folly have also prevailed throughout the history of art.[1]

> Some *foreign* Writers, some our *own* despise;
> The *Ancients* only, or the *Moderns* prize:
> (Thus *Wit*, like *Faith*, by each Man is apply'd
> To *one small Sect*, and All are *damn'd beside*.)
> Meanly they seek the Blessing to confine,
> And force *that Sun* but on a *Part* to Shine;
> Which not alone the *Southern Wit* sublimes,
> But ripens Spirits in cold *Northern Climes*;
> Which from the first has shone on *Ages past*,
> Enlights the *present*, and shall warm the *last*...

Having revealed in the second part of his poem the degeneracy of his own age in the light of the past, Pope turns in the third part to the means of reformation and to the restoration of some kind of peace and order in art. The heavy moral cast of this part, which is declared in the opening line, "Learn then what MORALS Criticks ought to show", is the natural conclusion to the vision of human

---

1. Compare with Pope's lines this passage from Rapin, *The Whole Critical Works* (1706), I 10 (speaking of the Egyptians): "And as their Apprehensions of things were more conformable to the Simplicity of Nature, as not yet Corrupted by a multitude of different Opinions, nor Biass'd by the Partiality of particular Sects; so was their Insight more clear and pure, their Notions less abstracted, and their views less Circumscrib'd."

history which marked the programmes of Dennis and Reynolds and which pervades the whole of Pope's poem. The ruin which entered the larger world, and inevitably invaded the world of art, was the result of moral failure. Restoration of the decays in critics and in criticism must be based, then, on moral reformation. Without such reformation the genius of a critic may always be used for petty and malicious ends. The connection of literary failings with ethical and moral failings is stressed throughout the *Essay*: "*Pride, Malice, Folly*, against *Dryden* rose, / In various Shapes of *Parsons, Criticks, Beaus*". Taste and good sense, then, are not enough:

> For 'tis but *half* a *Judge's Task*, to *Know*.
> 'Tis not enough, Taste, Judgment, Learning, join;
> In all you speak, let Truth and Candor shine. . .

What was needed was not only more learning, but more humility; not only more intelligence, but more charity. It is this idea which accounts for the occurrence throughout the poem of such lines as, "So *vast* is Art, so *narrow* Human Wit", and "To Err is *Humane*; to Forgive, *Divine*". It is in this respect too that the "design" of the *Essay* conforms fully and precisely to the designs for reformation and restoration formulated previously by Reynolds and Dennis. Reynolds too, it will be remembered, had "set . . . before our eyes" the "neuer-enough honoured Auncients", in order that we might "carry along together their strait and our crooked line, for our better knowledge of them, and reformation of our selues."

Throughout the last part of the poem Pope is, of course, in touch with the concept of the *honnête homme*, the honest man and the accomplished gentleman. But perhaps more fundamental is the concept which is basic to the *Institutio Oratoria* of his beloved Quintilian, the concept that the orator must be a good man. Pope's conviction, however lightly we may regard the idea today, is that the Critic too must be a good man: one should never, he insists, "in the *Critick* let the *Man* be lost".

Pope concludes his *Essay* with a historical survey which derives most of its dignity and weight from its participation in the ancient idea of *translatio studii*, the idea of a transmission of cultural treasure from country to country and from age to age.[1] Moving general'v

---

1. See Aubrey Williams, *Pope's Dunciad* (1955), pp. 42*ff.*

from east to west the light of Nature illuminated first the critics of Greece and Rome. Then, after what Pope regarded as being the darkness and ignorance of the middle ages, civilization and the arts next shone brightly in Italy, then faded there to rise again in France and England. The argument is perhaps not without the urgency suggested by Dennis in speaking of Poetry: "an Art, that by the Barbarity of the Times, is fallen and sunk . . . and has been driven and banish'd from every Country excepting *England* alone; and is even here so miserably fallen . . ."[1] It is an argument by which Pope suggests that, throughout the course of time and despite time's deteriorations, there have been great, and good, critics whom the men of his own age might propose to themselves as patterns for "imitation".

1. Hooker, 1 334.

AN
ESSAY
ON
CRITICISM.

——————Si quid novifti rectius iftis,
Candidus imperti ; fi non, his utere mecum.
HORAT.

NOTE ON THE TEXT

An Essay on Criticism was first published on May 15, 1711, and some seven months later, about January 1, 1712, a second issue of this first edition appeared. The title pages of the two issues vary slightly, and there is some disagreement as to which appeared first. The texts of the two issues are identical, however, and they have been treated here as one edition, *1711*. By 1722 the poem had been printed separately in seven editions, and had also appeared in the *Works* of 1717 and in several editions of *Miscellaneous Poems and Translations*. Subsequently it appeared in *Miscellany Poems*, edition of 1727 and 1732, and in the editions of the *Works* from 1736 on. In 1744 the poem was published in quarto, and in 1749 in octavo, "With the Commentary and Notes of W. Warburton, A. M." For our purposes the poem's textual history ends with its appearance in the 1751 edition of the *Works* published by Warburton.

The text printed here follows the spelling, punctuation, and typography of the first edition, but observes the new readings introduced into later editions. A few modifications in punctuation have been made to avoid confusion. Thus Pope's use of the genitive singular to indicate the genitive plural has been altered to conform to modern practice. Two or three minor revisions in punctuation which Pope himself made have also been followed. Changes of this kind are recorded in the textual apparatus, but obvious misprints have been corrected silently.

In two instances variant readings which first appear in editions in which Warburton had a hand have been rejected. One of these, at l. 148, may be a misprint; at any rate, the original reading has the authority of all editions, including those of 1744 and 1749, prior to that of 1751. The other change which has been rejected is the displacement of ll. 152–3. In 1744 this couplet was made to follow l. 160. As R. H. Griffith has pointed out, however, Warburton himself later, in 1764, reverted to the original sequence. Griffith's argument (see "Early Warburton? Or late Warburton?", *University of Texas Studies in English*, 1940, pp. 123–31) for the use of the original sequence has seemed incontestable.

A number of editions of the poem appearing in Pope's lifetime have been ignored. These are the "Dublin" editions and two editions printed by T. Johnson. Collation of these texts revealed them as being erratic and unreliable. Collation of the texts appearing in the various editions of *Miscellany Poems*, on the other hand, revealed genuinely new readings (see ll. 30–1, 116, 270, 420, 573). These last were apparently an effort to persuade the public that these volumes offered new and "revised" editions of the poem.

Extensive revision of the poem is revealed mainly in four editions. Variants in the second edition of 1713 suggest that Pope combed the poem for minor failures in precision of statement, such as those which were corrected in ll. 45, 123, 199, 495. Here too were considered objections to the poem raised by John Dennis and Roman Catholics (see, for examples, the notes to ll. 428 var., 502–4, 567 var., 648 var.). In the 1717 *Works*, the major change is the careful removal of instances of the expletive *do* (see ll. 74–5, 92, 137, 219, etc.), but there is also an effort made to gain more precision and balance (see ll. 259, 265, 502). In the 1736 *Works* further effort at polish and precision is made (as at ll. 30–1, 374, 449), and this effort is continued in the last of the editions personally supervised by Pope, the 1744 quarto. Brief comment on all of these revisions can be found in R. H. Griffith's essay, "Pope Editing Pope", *University of Texas Studies in English* (1944), pp. 37–49.

KEY TO THE CRITICAL APPARATUS

1711 = An Essay on Criticism, First Edition, quarto, Griffith 2.

1713a = Second Edition, octavo, Griffith 8.

1713b = Third Edition, octavo, Griffith 26.

1713c = Fourth Edition, octavo, Griffith 27.

1714 = Miscellaneous Poems and Translations, octavo, Griffith 32.

1716 = Fifth Edition, octavo, Griffith 71.

1717 = Works, quarto, Griffith 79.

1719 = Sixth Edition, octavo, Griffith 107.

1720 = Miscellaneous Poems and Translations, vol. 1, duodecimo, Griffith 124.

1722a = Seventh Edition, octavo, Griffith 129.

1722b = Miscellaneous Poems and Translations, vol. 1, duodecimo, Griffith 135.

1727 = Miscellany Poems, vol. 1, duodecimo, Griffith 192.

1732 = Miscellany Poems, vol. 1, duodecimo, Griffith 273.

1736a = Works, vol. 1, octavo, Griffith 413.

1736b = Works, vol. 1, octavo, Griffith 414.

1740 = Works, vol. 1, part 1, octavo, Griffith 510.

1743 = Works, vol. 1, part 1, octavo, Griffith 582.

1744 = An Essay on Criticism, quarto, Griffith 590.

1749 = An Essay on Criticism, octavo, Griffith 635.

1751 = Works, ed. Warburton, vol. 1, octavo, Griffith 643.

CONTENTS

OF THE

ESSAY ON CRITICISM.

1 *Introduction.*] *Add. 1751.*

3 The variety of men's Tastes; of a true Taste, how rare to be found. *1736a–43.*

16 PART II. Ver. 203, &c.] PART II. Ver. 204, &c. *1736a–43.*

CONTENTS] This table first appeared in the *Works* of 1736, but the version printed here is that of *1744–51.* In the earlier versions the sections of Part I are numbered 1 to 11. The verse numbers following the sections in each Part were not added until *1744,* and they do not always designate accurately the lines referred to.

305. 339, &c. 4. *Being too hard to please, or too apt to admire,* v 384.   20
5. Partiality—*too much Love to a* Sect,—*to the* Ancients *or* Moderns, v 394. 6. Prejudice *or* Prevention, v 408. 7. Singularity,
v 424. 8. Inconstancy, v 430. 9. Party Spirit, v 452, &c. 10.
Envy, v 466. *Against Envy, and in praise of Good-nature,* v 508,
&c. *When Severity is chiefly to be used by Critics,* v 526, &c.   25

PART III. Ver. 560, &c.

Rules for the Conduct *of* Manners *in a Critic,* 1. Candour, v 563.
Modesty, v 566. Good-breeding, v 572. Sincerity, *and* Freedom *of Advice,* v 578. 2. *When one's Counsel is to be restrained,*
v 584. *Character of an* incorrigible Poet, v 600. *And of an* imper-   30
tinent Critic, v 610, &c. *Character of a* good Critic, v 629. *The*
History *of* Criticism, *and Characters of the best Critics,* Aristotle,
v 645. Horace, v 653. Dionysius, v 665. Petronius, v 667.
Quintilian, v 670. Longinus, v 675. *Of the Decay of Criticism,
and its Revival.* Erasmus, v 693. Vida, v 705. Boileau, v 714.   35
Lord Roscommon, &c. v 725. *Conclusion.*

21 Partiality—*too much*] Too much *1736a–43.*
23 Party Spirit,] Partiality. *1736a–43.*
25 *Add. 1736a–43:* Against Immorality and Obscenity.
26 PART III. Ver. 560, &c.] PART III. Ver. 565, &c. *1736a–43.*
31 *Character of*] The Character of *1736a–43.*

AN

ESSAY

ON

CRITICISM.

'TIS hard to say, if greater Want of Skill
    Appear in *Writing* or in *Judging* ill;
    But, of the two, less dang'rous is th' Offence,
To tire our *Patience*, than mis-lead our *Sense*:
Some few in *that*, but Numbers err in *this*,   5
Ten Censure wrong for one who Writes amiss;
A *Fool* might once *himself* alone expose,
Now *One* in *Verse* makes many more in *Prose*.
    'Tis with our *Judgments* as our *Watches*, none

An Essay] A long introductory note in the 1744 edn, written apparently by Warburton, opens with this description of the poem: "The Poem is in one Book, but divided into three principal *parts* or members. The first [to v. 201.] gives rules for the *Study of the Art of Criticism*: the second [from thence to v. 560.] exposes the *Causes of wrong Judgment*: and the third [from thence to the end] prescribes the *Morals of the Critic*."

    2. Cf. Sheffield, *Ess. upon Poetry*, 1–2:

        Of Things in which Mankind does most excell,
        Nature's chief Master-piece is writing well.

Cf. l. 724, below; also Dryden, *The Author's Apology for Heroic Poetry* (*Essays*, 1 179): "Criticism, as it was first instituted by Aristotle, was meant a standard of judging well. . ."

    8. EC cite Dryden, Epil. to *All for Love*, 5–6:

        We wonder how the Devil this diff'rence grows,
        Betwixt our Fools in Verse, and yours in Prose.

The idea that critics in England had become more numerous and tiresome with the passage of time is expressed by Rymer in his Pref. to the tr. of Rapin's *Refl. on Aristotle's Treatise of Poesie* (Spingarn, II 164): ". . . till of late years *England* was as free from Criticks as it is from *Wolves*, that a harmless well-meaning Book might pass without any danger. But now this priviledge, whatever extraordinary Talent it requires, is usurped by the most ignorant; and they who are least acquainted with the game are aptest to bark at every thing that comes in their way." See Intro., p. 226, above.

    9. *as our Watches*] West, Collins, cite Suckling, Epil. to *Aglaura*, 6–8:

239

Go just *alike*, yet each believes his own.   10
In *Poets* as true *Genius* is but rare,
True *Taste* as seldom is the *Critick*'s Share;
Both must alike from Heav'n derive their Light,
These *born* to Judge, as well as those to Write.
Let such teach others who themselves excell,   15

---

15 *New paragraph 1727–32.*

But as when an authentick Watch is shown,
Each Man winds up, and rectifies his own,
So in our very Judgments.

"He observes first, that the Judgments of the multitude, like *the artificial measures of Time*, go different, and yet, each relies upon his own. But *Taste* in the Critic, is as rare as Genius in the Poet: both are derived from Heaven, and like the sun (the *natural measure of Time*) always constant and equal" [Warbu.ton].

12. *True Taste*] Cf. Saint-Évremond, *Some Observations upon the Tast and Judgment of the French* (*Works*, 1700, I 166): "Since good Judges are as rare as good Authors; since 'tis as difficult to find Judgment in one, as Genius in the other..." Cf. La Bruyère, *Characters*, 4th edn, (1705), p. 7: "As there is in Nature, so there is in Art, a point of Perfection. He who is sensible of it, and is toucht with it, has a good taste ... [but] there are few Men whose Wit is attended with a solid Taste, and a judicious Criticism." See Spingarn, I lxxxviii–cv.

13. *derive their Light*] Cf. the English tr. of Roger de Piles, *The Art of Painting* (1706), pp. 9–10: "*Genius therefore is that Light of the Mind, which conducts us to the end by the most easy Means.* 'Tis a Present which Nature makes to a Man at the hour of his Birth." Cf. also Temple, *Of Poetry* (Spingarn, III 80): "From this [poetic inspiration] arises that Elevation of Genius which can never be produced by any Art or study, by Pains or by Industry, which cannot be taught by Precepts or Examples, and therefore is agreed by all to be the pure and free Gift of Heaven or of Nature, and to be a Fire kindled out of some hidden spark of the very first Conception." Cf. l. 21, below.

13f. Cf. Gildon, *Letters and Essays on several Subjects* (1696), p. 14: "... a Poet derives the honor of that Name from his *Nature* and *Genius*, not from his *Art*; *This* every Scholar has, *That* none but the Darlings of Heav'n and Nature. This may be acquir'd by a Studious Pedant, That must be born ... for *Poeta nascitur non fit.*"

15. *Qui scribit artificiosè, ab aliis commodè scripta facile intelligere poterit.* Cic. ad Herenn. lib. 4 ⟨cap. 4⟩. [P. *1713a–51.*]

De Pictore, Sculptore, Fictore, nisi Artifex judicare non potest. Pliny ⟨*Ep.* I 10⟩. [P. *1711, 1744–51.*]

EC compare *Tatler* 239 (Oct. 19, 1710): "It is ridiculous for any man to criticize on the works of another, who has not distinguished himself by his own

And *censure freely* who have *written well*.
Authors are partial to their *Wit*, 'tis true,
But are not *Criticks* to their *Judgment* too?
   Yet if we look more closely, we shall find
Most have the *Seeds* of Judgment in their Mind;   20
Nature affords at least a *glimm'ring Light*;
The *Lines*, tho' touch'd but faintly, are drawn right.
But as the slightest Sketch, if justly trac'd, ⎫
Is by ill *Colouring* but the more disgrac'd,   ⎬
So by *false Learning* is *good Sense* defac'd; ⎭   25

performances." Cf. Dryden, Pref. to *All for Love* (*Essays*, I 195): "Poets themselves are the most proper, though I conclude not the only critics." But Dennis
sanely observed (Hooker, I 398–9) that Aristotle and many other critics were
not poets.

   The attribution of the *Rhetorica ad Herennium* to Cicero, though traditional in
Pope's time, is not acceptable to modern scholars.

   17. Cf. Dryden's Persius, *Sat.* I 110: "All Authors, to their own defects, are
blind."

   20. *Omnes tacito quodam sensu, sine ulla arte, aut ratione, quæ sint in artibus ac
rationibus recta ac prava dijudicant.* Cic. de Orat. lib. 3 ⟨50⟩. [P. *1711–51.*]

   Cf. Dryden, *A Disc. conc. . . . . Sat.* (*Essays*, II 45): "Mankind, even the most
barbarous, have the seeds of poetry implanted in them."

   22–5. Wakefield cites Aristotle, *Poetics*, 1450b. Cf. the anonymous English tr.
of 1705, p. 73: ". . . it is absolutely [in tragedy] as in Painting. For, if the finest
Colours were mix't on a Cloath confusedly and without order, it would not give
so much pleasure, as the simple Sketches of a Draught." In these lines we find
the first of many parallels drawn by Pope between the "sister arts" of poetry
and painting. The analogies reveal the continuing influence of Horace's phrase
"ut pictura poesis". For other examples, see below, ll. 171–4, 245–6, 293*ff.*,
484*ff.*

   25. *Plus sine doctrina prudentia, quam sine prudentia valet doctrina.* Quint. ⟨*Inst.
Orat.*, VI v 11⟩. [P. *1744–51.*]

   This quotation is in the MS, but struck out. There was another quotation in
the MS which was never printed: "Adolescentulos existimo in scholis stultissi-
mos fieri, qui nil ex his quæ in usu habemus, aut audiunt, aut vident. Petronius."
See *Satyricon*, I i. The correct and complete quotation from Quintilian reads:
"Illud dicere satis habeo, nihil esse non modo in orando, sed in omni vita prius
consilio, frustraque sine eo tradi ceteras artes, plusque vel sine doctrina pruden-
tiam quam sine prudentia facere doctrinam."

   25. Between Verse 25 and 26 were these lines, ⟨since omitted by the author:
1744–51⟩

Some are bewilder'd in the Maze of Schools,
And some made *Coxcombs* Nature meant but *Fools*.
In search of *Wit* these lose their *common Sense*,
And then turn Criticks in their own Defence.
Each burns alike, who can, or cannot write,   30
Or with a *Rival*'s, or an *Eunuch*'s spite.

30–1 Those [Some *1727–32*] hate as *Rivals* all that write; and
    others
    But envy *Wits*, as *Eunuchs* envy *Lovers*. *1711–32*.

> *Many are spoil'd by that* pedantic *throng*,
> *Who with great pains teach youth to reason wrong.*
> Tutors, *like* Virtuoso's, *oft inclin'd*
> *By strange* transfusion *to improve the mind*,
> *Draw off the sense we have, to pour in* new;
> *Which yet, with all their skill, they ne'er could do.*
>   [P. *1736a–51*.]

As Wakefield noted, "The *transfusion* spoken of in the *fourth* verse of this variation is the transfusion of one *animal's blood* into another: concerning which practice *Sprat* says in his *history of the Royal Society* [London, 1667, p. 317], that Dr.
Christopher Wren (the celebrated architect) 'was the first author of the noble
anatomical experiment of injecting liquors into the veins of animals'..."
    27. *meant but Fools*] Warburton cites Rochester, *A Letter from Artemisa*, 159–60:
> God never made a Coxcomb worth a Groat.
> We owe that Name to Industry and Arts.

EC cite Dryden, *The Hind and the Panther*, III 1107: "For Fools are double Fools,
endeav'ring to be wise." The thought is common. Ault (*Prose Works*, I xliv)
compares *Spectator* 404 (June 13, 1712): "[Nature] ... has sometimes made a
Fool, but a Coxcomb is always of a Man's own making, by applying his Talents
otherwise than Nature designed..." See Dryden, Epil. to *The Man of Mode*, 1–2.
    29. *in their own Defence*] EC cite Dryden, *The Medal*, 51: "The Wretch turn'd
loyal in his own defence." Cf. Prol. to *Amphytrion*, 14–15:
> The Blockhead stands excus'd, for wanting Sense;
> And Wits turn Blockheads in their own defence.

    31. *Eunuch's spite*] Cf. Rochester, Epil. to *Circe*, 14 *ff.*:
> 'Twas Impotence did first this Vice begin,
> Fooles censure Wit, as Old men raile of Sin,
> Who envy Pleasure which they cannot tast ...

EC cite Dryden, Prol. to the Second Part of *The Conquest of Granada*, 1–2:
> They who write Ill, and they who ne'r durst write,
> Turn Critiques, out of meer Revenge and Spight.

All *Fools* have still an Itching to deride,
And fain *wou'd* be upon the *Laughing Side*:
If *Mævius* Scribble in *Apollo*'s spight,
There are, who *judge* still *worse* than he can *write*.   35
    Some have at first for *Wits*, then *Poets* past,
Turn'd *Criticks* next, and prov'd plain *Fools* at last;
Some neither can for *Wits* nor *Criticks* pass,
As heavy Mules are neither *Horse* nor *Ass*.
Those half-learn'd Witlings, num'rous in our Isle,   40
As half-form'd Insects on the Banks of *Nile*;
Unfinish'd Things, one knows not what to call,
Their Generation's so *equivocal*:

32 *Fools*] such *1717–32*.

---

34. *in Apollo's spight*] EC cite Dryden's Persius, *Sat.* 1 95–6:
      Such little Elegies as Nobles Write;
      Who wou'd be Poets, in *Apollo*'s spight.
Maevius was a scribbling contemporary of Virgil and Horace, known only by their contemptuous allusions to him, in *Ecl.* III 90 and in *Epode* x.

36f. Perhaps a hit at Dennis, as Pope himself suggested when he wrote in *The Narrative of Dr. Robert Norris* (*Prose Works*, 1 166) "That the said Mr. *John Denn*[is] on the 27th of *March*, 1712. finding on the said Mr. *Lintott*'s Counter a Book called an *Essay on Criticism*, just then publish'd, he read a Page or two with much Frowning and Gesticulation, till coming to these two Lines. . . He flung down the Book in a terrible Fury, and cried out, *By G— he means Me.*" Cf. Dryden, Dedic. of *Examen Poeticum* (*Essays*, II 2–3): "Ill writers are usually the sharpest censors. . . Thus the corruption of a poet is the generation of a critic."

39. *heavy Mules*] The simile has a double import: the "witlings" are neither one thing nor the other, and besides, like mules, they are barren [Collins]. Cf. Dryden, *The Hind and the Panther*, II 265 ff.:
      But you [the Panther] . . .
      Are like a *Mule* made up of diff'ring seed,
      And that's the Reason why you never breed.

41. *Insects*] The word was applied to earth-worms, snails, and even frogs, and also to insignificant and despicable persons. Cf. Dryden, Dedic. to *Examen Poeticum* (*Essays*, II 5), speaking of critics: "But there is another sort of insects, more venomous than the former. . ."
half-form'd] See l. 43n.

43. *equivocal*] "Equivocal generation: the (supposed) production of plants and animals without parents; spontaneous generation" (OED). This allusion to the birth of insects as a consequence of the flooding of the Nile is found frequently

> To tell 'em, wou'd a *hundred Tongues* require,
> Or *one vain Wit's*, that might a hundred tire.   45
>   But *you* who seek to *give* and *merit* Fame,
> And just bear a Critick's noble Name,
> Be sure *your self* and your own *Reach* to know,
>   How far your *Genius*, *Taste*, and *Learning* go;
>   Launch not beyond your Depth, but be discreet,   50
> And mark *that Point* where Sense and Dulness *meet*.
>   Nature to all things fix'd the Limits fit,

45 might] wou'd *1711*.   52 *No new paragraph 1711–43*.

---

in authors with whom Pope was conversant. EC cite Dryden, *Dedic. of the Æn.*
(*Essays*, II 231): "I am confident . . . that you will look on those half lines here-
after as the imperfect products of a hasty Muse; like the frogs and serpents in
the Nile; part of them kindled into life, and part a lump of unformed unani-
mated mud." The ultimate source of all such allusions is evidently, as Wakefield noted, Ovid's *Met.*, I 423 *ff.* Cf. Dorset, *A Faithful Catalogue of our most Eminent Ninnies*, 178–9:

> With foul Corruption sure he first was fed,
> And by Equivocal Generation bred.

45. *a hundred tire*] EC cite Dryden's Persius, *Sat.* v 36–7:

> For this a hundred Voices I desire;
> To tell thee what an hundred Tongues wou'd tire.

Cf. also Denham, *The Progress of Learning*, 161–2. The phrase is a stock one deriving, with cumulative effect, from Homer: *Il.*, II 489, "ten tongues"; *Aen.*, VI
625, "one hundred"; Pope, *Il.*, II 580, "a thousand": "To count them all, demands a thousand tongues."

48*f.* Cf. Horace, *Ars Poet.*, 38–40:

> Sumite materiam vestris, qui scribitis, aequam
> viribus, et versate diu quid ferre recusent,
> quid valeant humeri;

also Vida, *De Arte Poet.*, I 39–40:

> Tu vero ipse humeros explorans consule primum,
> atque tuis prudens genus elige viribus aptum;

and Boileau, *L'Art Poét.*, I 12: "Et consultez longtemps votre esprit et vos forces."

52–67. Commentators have taken pains to refute the thought of these lines,
but Pope is merely giving expression to a common idea of his time: proud man
must learn to recognize his limitations. Cf. Temple, *Essay Upon the Ancient and
Modern Learning* (Spingarn, III 60–1): "One Man or one Country at a certain
Time runs a great Length in some certain Kinds of Knowledge, but lose as
much Ground in others that were perhaps as useful and as valuable. There is
a certain Degree of Capacity in the greatest Vessel, and when 'tis full, if you

And wisely curb'd proud Man's pretending Wit:
As on the *Land* while *here* the *Ocean* gains,
In *other Parts* it leaves wide sandy Plains;   55
Thus in the *Soul* while *Memory* prevails,
The solid Pow'r of *Understanding* fails;
Where Beams of warm *Imagination* play,
The *Memory*'s soft Figures melt away.
One *Science* only will one *Genius* fit;   60

pour in still, it must run out some way or other; and the more it runs out on one side, the less runs out at the other. So the greatest Memory, after a certain Degree, as it learns or retains more of some Things or Words, loses and forgets as much of others. The largest and deepest Reach of Thought, the more it pursues some certain Subjects, the more it neglects others. Besides, few men or none excel in all Faculties of Mind. A great Memory may fail of Invention, both may want Judgment to Digest or Apply what they Remember or Invent. Great Courage may want Caution, great Prudence may want Vigour, yet all are necessary to make a great Commander. But how can a man hope to excel in all qualities, when some are produced by the heat, others by the coldness, of Brain and Temper?" Cf. also Montaigne (*Essais*, ɪ ix): ". . . il se voit par expérience plustost au rebours, que les mémoires excellentes se joignent volontiers aux jugements débiles." Locke (*An Essay on Human Understanding*, ɪɪ xi 2) remarks on that "common observation,—that men who have a great deal of wit, and prompt memories, have not always the clearest judgment or deepest reason."

54.f. Cf. Addison's tr. of Lucan (*De Bello Civili*, ɪ 409–11) in *Remarks on . . . Italy* (1705), p. 115:
> Wash'd with successive Seas, the doubtful Strand
> By turns is Ocean, and by turns is Land.

See also Donne, *Elegie on the Lady Marckham*, 29.

58. Wakefield cites Dryden, *The Character of a Good Parson*, 36: "But, when the milder Beams of Mercy play . . ."

59. *soft*] "The epithet seems to be proleptic, the metaphor being taken from waxen figures melting in the sunshine" [Sargeaunt].

60ff. Cf. Bolingbroke's recommendatory poem prefixed to Dryden's *Virgil*:
> No undisputed Monarch Govern'd yet
> With Universal Sway, the Realms of Wit:
> Nature cou'd never such Expence afford,
> Each several Province own'd a several Lord.

Pope may have remembered Virgil, *Ecl.* vɪɪɪ 63: "non omnia possumus omnes." Cf. Sheffield, *Ess. upon Poetry*, 342: "Who can all Sciences exactly know?" Ll. 60–4 were criticized by Dennis (Hooker, ɪ 403): "Is not this a rare Pretender to Poetry and Criticism, who talks at this rate, when all the World knows that 'tis

So *vast* is Art, so *narrow* Human Wit:
Not only bounded to *peculiar Arts*,
But oft in *those*, confin'd to *single Parts*.
Like Kings we lose the Conquests gain'd before,
By vain Ambition still to make them more: 65
Each might his *sev'ral Province* well command,
Wou'd all but *stoop* to what they *understand*.
    First follow NATURE, and your Judgment frame
By her just Standard, which is still the same:
Unerring Nature, still divinely bright,   70

63 oft] ev'n *1711*.   65 to make] t'extend *1711–16*.

---

impossible for a Man with only one Science to be either Poet or Critick?" Pope
was perturbed, for he wrote the first words of each line in his MS memorandum
(see Appendix B, pp. 482–4, below), the last one beginning "But oft in those",
showing the emendation adopted in 1713.

    61. *So vast is Art*] Possibly suggested, as Wakefield notes, by the famous maxim
which opens the *Aphorisms* of Hippocrates. Ὁ Βίος Βραχύς, ἡ δὲ τέχνη μακρή:
"Life is short, but art is long."

    Art] Scholarship, learning, science (OED).

    64–7. If there is an allusion in these lines to any particular king, it may be
Charles XII of Sweden, whose amazing career was checked by his defeat at
Poltawa in 1709. But cf. Dryden, *Astraea Redux*, 9–12, referring to Charles X of
Sweden:

            Th' Ambitious *Swede* like restless Billowes tost,
            On this hand gaining what on that he lost,
            Though in his life he Blood and Ruine breath'd,
            To his now guideless Kingdome Peace bequeath'd.

    68. *First follow* NATURE] For the meaning of "Nature", and the principle of
"following" it, see Intro., pp. 219–22, above. For the phrasing of this and the
following lines, cf. Dryden, *A Paral. of Poet. and Paint.* (*Essays*, II 134): "The way
to please being to imitate Nature, both the poets and the painters in ancient
times, and in the best ages, have studied her. . . For Nature is still the same in
all ages, and can never be contrary to herself." Wakefield compares Vida, *De
Arte Poet.*, II 455–8:

            Praeterea haud lateat te nil conarier artem,
            naturam nisi ut assimulet, propiusque sequatur.
            Hanc unam vates sibi proposuere magistram:
            quicquid agunt, hujus semper vestigia servant.

And *A.P.*, III 358: "To study Nature be your only care".

    70. Wakefield cites Roscommon, *Ess. on Tr. Verse*, 193–4:

One *clear, unchang'd,* and *Universal* Light,
Life, Force, and Beauty, must to all impart,
At once the *Source,* and *End,* and *Test* of *Art.*
Art from that Fund each *just Supply* provides,
Works *without Show,* and *without Pomp* presides: 75
In some fair Body thus th' informing Soul

74-5   That *Art* is best which most resembles *Her*;
Which still *presides,* yet never does *Appear*; *1711–16.*
76 th' informing] the sprightly *1711–16*; the secret *1717–32.*

Truth still is One; Truth is Divinely bright;
No cloudy Doubts obscure her Native light.

71. Cf. Bouhours, *Les Entretiens D'Ariste et D'Eugène* (Paris, 1671), p. 242, comparing the *je ne sais quoi* (see ll. 76–9n) to the "light" of Nature: "Cet agrément, ce charme, cet air ressemble à la lumière qui embellit toute la nature, & qui se fait voir à tout le monde, sans que nous sçachions ce que c'est; de sorte qu'on n'en peut mieux parler à mon gré, qu'en disant qu'on ne peut ni l'expliquer, ni le concevoir."

72. *Life, Force, and Beauty*] EC cite *A.P.,* I 37-8:

Love Reason then: and let what e're you Write
Borrow from her its Beauty, Force, and Light.

73. Cf. Longinus on "Nature", as translated by Boileau (*Oeuvres Diverses,* 1701, p. 18 of *Traité du Sublime*): ". . . dans toutes nos productions il la faut toûjours supposer comme la baze, le principe, & le premier fondement."

74 var. *That Art is best*] Cf. Dryden, *A Paral. of Poet. and Paint.* (*Essays,* II 136): "To imitate Nature well in whatsoever subject, is the perfection of both arts; and that picture, and that poem, which comes nearest to the resemblance of Nature, is the best." Dennis criticized the whole couplet for expressing nothing but *Ars est celare artem,* "the common Subject that Pedants give their Boys to make Themes and Declamations upon" (Hooker, I 404), but Pope probably altered the lines to remove the expletive *does.*

76. *informing*] Endowing with a form, or essential character; permeating as an animating and characterizing quality.

76 var. Pope may have altered *sprightly* to *informing* to avoid the pleonasm of "sprightly Soul", or to avoid the repetition caused by *Spirits* in the next line.

76-9. Cf. Sheffield, *Ess. upon Poetry,* 20ff.:

Without a Genius too, for that's the Soul,—
A Spirit which inspires the work throughout,
As that of Nature moves this World about:
A heat that glows in every word that's writ,
That's something of Divine, and more than Wit;
It self unseen, yet all things by it shown.

"It self unseen" in this passage and in l. 79 recalls the aphorism, "Ars est celare

With Spirits feeds, with Vigour fills the whole,
Each Motion guides, and ev'ry Nerve sustains;
It self unseen, but in th' *Effects*, remains.
Some, to whom Heav'n in Wit has been profuse,   80
Want as much more, to turn it to its use;
For *Wit* and *Judgment* often are at strife,
Tho' meant each other's Aid, like *Man* and *Wife*.
'Tis more to *guide* than *spur* the Muse's Steed;

80–1 There are whom Heav'n has blest with store of Wit,
      Yet want as much again to manage it; *1711–43*.
82 often] ever *1711–43*.

---

artem". Pope seems to join the concept of "hidden art" to that of *je ne sais quoi*, as had Bouhours (*Les Entretiens*, 1671, p. 253): "Ce qui nous charme . . . dans ces peintures & dans ces statuës, c'est vn je ne sçay quoy inexplicable. Aussi les grands maistres qui ont découvert que rien ne plaist davantage dans la nature, que ce qui plaist sans qu'on sçache bien pourquoy, ont tasché toûjours de donner de l'agrément à leurs ouvrages, en cachant leur art avec beaucoup de soin, & d'artifice." Cf. l. *71n*.

77. *fills the whole*] Wakefield cites Dryden, *Æn.*, vi 983–4: ". . . one Common Soul / Inspires, and feeds, and animates the whole."

79. Cf. this description of the *je ne sais quoi* in art (Bouhours, *Les Entretiens*, 1671, p. 244): "Quoy qu'il en soit . . . il est certain que le je ne sçay quoy est de la nature de ces choses qu'on ne connoist que par les effets qu'elles produisent." Wakefield cites Ovid, *Met.*, iv 287: "causa latet, vis est notissima fontis." Cf. ll. 155–7*n*.

80–4. An assertion of the complementary relationship of wit and judgment against those who set them apart as opposed faculties (see Intro., pp. 212–19, above).

82*f*. Cf. Rapin, *Refl. on Aristotle's Treatise of Poesie* (1674), ch. II, p. 2: ". . . as Judgment without Wit is cold and heavy, so Wit without Judgment is blind and extravagant".

84–7. Cf. Longinus, as translated by Boileau (*Oeuvres Diverses*, 1701, *Traité du Sublime*, ch. 2): "Nôtre esprit assez souvent n'a pas moins besoin de bride que d'éperon." See also Quintilian, *Inst. Orat.*, x iii 10: "Sed tum maxime, cum facultas illa contigerit, resistamus ut provideamus et efferentes equos frenis quibusdam coerceamus; quod non tam moram faciet quam novos impetus dabit." Jonson, *Timber, or Discoveries* (Spingarn, I 32), in a passage apparently directly inspired by Quintilian, perhaps suggested the wording of l. 87: "Yet when wee thinke wee have got the faculty [of good writing], it is even then good to resist it, as to give a Horse a check sometimes with bit, which does not so much stop his course as stirre his mettle."

Restrain his Fury, than provoke his Speed;   85
The winged Courser, like a gen'rous Horse,
Shows most true Mettle when you *check* his Course.
   Those RULES of old *discover'd*, not *devis'd*,
Are *Nature* still, but *Nature Methodiz'd*;
Nature, like *Liberty*, is but restrain'd   90
By the same Laws which first *herself* ordain'd.

90 *Liberty*,] *Monarchy*, *1711–43*.

86. *The winged Courser*] Wakefield compares Waller, *Upon the Earl of Roscommon's Translation of Horace De Arte Poetica*, 11–12:
> Direct us how to back the winged Horse,
> Favour his flight, and moderate his force.

gen'rous] Applied to animals means *spirited*.

88*f.* For the doctrine of the "Rules" see Intro., pp. 219–20, above. Pope's lines echo the Pref. to *Troilus and Cressida* (*Essays*, I 228) where Dryden is quoting, almost verbatim, from Rymer's tr. of Rapin's *Refl. on Aristotle's Treatise of Poesie* (1674), p. 16: "If the rules be well considered, we shall find them to be made only to reduce Nature into method, to trace her step by step, and not to suffer the least mark of her to escape us: 'tis only by these, that probability in fiction is maintained, which is the soul of poetry. They are founded upon good sense, and sound reason, rather than on authority. . ." Rapin had also said (p. 16) that "*Aristotle* drew the platform [*le plan*] of these Rules from the Poems of *Homer*, and other Poets of his Time, by the Reflections he had a long time made on their Works." In other words, the Rules were not invented (devised), but actually discovered in Homer and Nature. Rapin was also echoed by Dennis (Hooker, I 39): "The Rules of *Aristotle* are nothing but Nature and Good Sence reduc'd to a method."

90*f.* var. The original reading may have been suggested by Cowley, *Inconstancy*, 20–1:
> *Constant*, in *Nature* were *Inconstancy*;
> For 'twere to break the *Laws* her self has made. . .

The change of *Monarchy* to *Liberty* may have been due, as suggested by Griffith (*Univ. of Texas, Studies in English*, xx, 1940), to Warburton if it is he who wrote the note to *Dunciad* iv, 181–2 (vol. v, p. 359), signed "Scriblerus", in which l. 91 was misquoted (or improved), "By the same Laws herself at first ordain'd", and the correction *Liberty* for *Monarchy* advanced. The original version, which expressed the conception of an old-fashioned Stuart monarchy, would have lost some of its pertinence by 1743. The correction is quite understandable without the interventi_n of Warburton. Cf. l. 162, and also Dryden, *The Medal*, 139*f.*:
> Already they [Kings] have lost their best defence,
> The benefit of Laws, which they dispence.

Hear how learn'd *Greece* her useful Rules indites,
When to repress, and when indulge our Flights:
High on *Parnassus'* Top her Sons she show'd,
And pointed out those arduous Paths they trod,   95
Held from afar, aloft, th' Immortal Prize,
And urg'd the rest by equal Steps to rise;
Just *Precepts* thus from great *Examples* giv'n,
She drew from *them* what they deriv'd from *Heav'n*.
The gen'rous Critick *fann'd* the *Poet's Fire*,   100
And taught the World, *with Reason* to *Admire*.

92 First Learned *Greece* just Precepts did indite, *1711–16.*
93 Flights:] Flight: *1711–16.*
98 From great *Examples useful Rules* were giv'n; *1711–16.*

96. *th'Immortal Prize*] Wakefield cites *A.P.*, IV 229: "And afar off hold up the glorious Prize."

98. *Nec enim artibus editis factum est ut argumenta inveniremus, sed dicta sunt omnia antequam præciperentur, mox ea scriptores observata & collecta ediderunt.* Quintil. ⟨*Inst. Orat.* V x 120⟩. [P. *1717–51.*]

Precepts replaced *rules*, as a consequence of the change in l. 92. Cf. Dryden, *The Author's Apology for Heroic Poetry* (*Essays*, I 183): "Aristotle raised the fabric of his *Poetry* from observation of those things in which Euripides, Sophocles, and Aeschylus pleased: he considered how they raised the passions, and thence has drawn rules for our imitation."

99. Cf. l. 13*n*, above.

100*ff.* Wakefield compares Dryden, Dedic. of *Examen Poeticum* (*Essays*, II 3): ". . . formerly they [critics] were quite another species of men. They were defenders of poets, and commentators on their works; to illustrate obscure beauties; to place some passages in a better light; to redeem others from malicious interpretations. . . . But neither Zoilus, nor he who endeavoured to defame Virgil, were ever adopted into the name of critics by the Ancients; what their reputation was then, we know; and their successors in this age deserve no better. Are our auxiliary forces turned our enemies? are they, who at best are but wits of the second order, and whose only credit amongst readers is what they obtained by being subservient to the fame of writers, are these become rebels, of slaves, and usurpers, of subjects?" Dryden and Pope emphasize a criticism of "beauties" as opposed to a criticism of "faults". By a "fault" was usually meant a departure from the "Rules"; but interest was centring on the elements of charm (see l. 103) in a work of art, and strengthening the "claims of charm and power at the expense of regularity and imitation" (Spingarn, I xcviii–c).

Then Criticism the Muse's Handmaid prov'd,
To dress her Charms, and make her more belov'd;
But following Wits from that Intention stray'd;
Who cou'd not win the Mistress, woo'd the Maid;   105
Against the Poets *their own Arms* they turn'd,
Sure to hate most the Men from whom they *learn'd.*
So modern *Pothecaries*, taught the Art
By *Doctor's Bills* to play the *Doctor's Part*,
Bold in the Practice of *mistaken Rules*,   110
Prescribe, apply, and call their *Masters Fools*.
Some on the Leaves of ancient Authors prey,

102 Muse's] Muses *1711–16, 1727–51.*
105 *Add. 1711–32:*
        Set up themselves, and drove a *sep'rate* Trade:

---

102. *Muse's Handmaid*] A clever turn on *Philosophia Theologiae ancilla.* Cf. Dryden, *Annus Mirabilis*, st. 155: "Nature's Handmaid Art".

107. A monosyllabic line. Cf. l. 347.

108–11. A reference to the controversy about the relation of the apothecary to the physician. Though they lacked formal medical training, the apothecaries frequently seem to have learned enough from the medical prescriptions handed to them by doctors to usurp, especially among the poor, the doctor's role. Because of the high fees charged for their drugs, as also by their illegal medical practice, many apothecaries prospered exceedingly and aroused the antagonism of many physicians. The College of Physicians proposed a plan for giving free medical advice to the poor, but even so the poor were found unable to pay the apothecaries for medicines prescribed. A dispensary was therefore opened by the College in 1696, and there drugs were sold at cost. The apothecaries charged that this was a mere device to get the profits of the drug trade into the physicians' hands. Dr Samuel Garth sided with the physicians who supported the plan, and wrote *The Dispensary* as an attack on the apothecaries and on those doctors who allied with them.

109. *Bills*] Medical prescriptions or recipes.

111. *Prescribe, apply*] Cf. Garth, *Dispensary*, ii 107 *f.*:
        Long has he been of that amphibious Fry,
        Bold to Prescribe, and busie to Apply.

112–17. Pope alludes first (ll. 112–13) to the commentators who emend poetic texts; next (ll. 114–15), to critics who offer, in mechanical fashion, rules for writing a poem. In the first instance, he may have been thinking of Bentley; in the second, of Le Bossu, whose treatise on the epic he parodied in *Guardian* 78 (June 10, 1713) and in *Peri Bathous*, ch. xv. Warburton says that Pope's allusion

Nor Time nor Moths e'er spoil'd so much as they:
Some dryly plain, without Invention's Aid,
Write dull *Receits* how Poems may be made: 115
These leave the Sense, their Learning to display,
And those explain the Meaning quite away.
 You then whose Judgment the right Course wou'd steer,
Know well each ANCIENT's proper *Character*,
His *Fable, Subject, Scope* in ev'ry Page,   120
Religion, Country, Genius of his *Age*:
Without all these at once before your Eyes,
Cavil you may, but never *Criticize*.

116 leave] lost *1711–32*; lose *1736a–43*.   the] their *1727–32*.
117 explain] explain'd *1711–32*.
123 *Cavil* you may,] You may *Confound, 1711*.

---

in ll. 114–15 was to "the *plagiaries* from the *French*, who had made some admirable Commentaries on the ancient critics". These plagiaries would include men
such as Oldmixon and Gildon.
    118. Wakefield compares Boileau, *L'Art Poét.*, 1 7: "O vous donc qui, brûlant
d'une ardeur périlleuse..."
    119. *proper Character*] Cf. the English tr. of Roger de Piles, *The Art of Painting*
(1706), p. 52: "There is one Thing, which is as the Salt of a *Design* that seasons
it, and gives it its relish, without which 'tis worth little or nothing, and which I
can't express better than by the Word Character. This Character consists then
in the manner in which the Painter thinks Things. 'Tis the Seal that distinguishes his Works from those of other Men, and which imprints on them the
lively Image of his Mind. 'Tis this Character that agitates our Imagination, and
'tis by this that Skilful Painters, after having Study'd under good Masters, or
after the Works of others, feel themselves constrain'd by a Secret Violence, to let
their Genius loose, and fly with their proper Wings." EC compare *A.P.*, III 110:
                Keep to each man his proper Character.
                Of Countryes and of Times the humors know;
                From diff'rent Climates, diff'ring Customs grow.
Pope here reflects the increasing interest in the historical method in criticism.
See R. Wellek, *The Rise of English Literary History* (1941), and R. L. Brett, 'The
Aesthetic Sense and Taste in the Literary Criticism of the Early Eighteenth
Century', *RES*, XX (1944), pp. 199–213.
    123. *Cavil you may but never criticise*] The author after this verse originally in-
serted the following, which he has however omitted in all the editions ⟨Between
Verse 124 and 125; *1736a–43*⟩:
                Zoilus, *had these been known, without a name*

Be *Homer*'s Works your *Study,* and *Delight,*
Read them by Day, and meditate by Night,   125
Thence form your Judgment, thence your Maxims bring,
And trace the Muses *upward* to their *Spring;*
Still with *It self compar'd,* his *Text* peruse;

126 Maxims] Notions *1711–43.*

> *Had dy'd, and* Perault *ne'er been damn'd to fame;*
> *The sense of sound Antiquity had reign'd,*
> *And sacred* Homer *yet been unprophan'd.*
> *None e'er had thought his comprehensive mind* ⎫
> *To modern Customs, modern Rules confin'd;*   ⎬
> *Who for all Ages writ and all Mankind.*   ⎭
>
> [P. *1736a–51.*]

An allusion to the *Parallèle des Anciens et des Modernes,* in which Perrault put the modern writers above the ancient and criticized Homer severely. This was the beginning of a new phase in the long-standing quarrel between the Ancients and Moderns, in which Boileau sided naturally with the Ancients and "damn'd" Perrault "to fame". The last line of Pope's variant reading echoes Ben Jonson, *To the memory of . . . William Shakespeare,* 43: "He was not of an age, but for all time!"

123. *Cavil you may*] Cf. Dryden, Pref. to *Sylvæ* (*Essays,* I 264): ". . . to arraign a man is one thing, and to cavil at him is another."

123 var. EC cite Roscommon, *Essay on Tr. Verse,* 195–6:
> While in your *Thoughts* you find the *least* debate,
> You may *Confound,* but *never* can *Translate.*

124–7. Cf. Vida, *De Arte Poet.,* I 409–11:
> Nulla dies tamen interea tibi, nulla abeat nox,
> quin aliquid vatum sacrorum e fontibus almis
> hauseris, ac dulcem labris admoveris amnem.

Wakefield cites Horace, *Ars Poet.,* 268–9: "Vos exemplaria Graeca / nocturna versate manu, versate diurna"; also Roscommon's tr., 294–5:
> Consider well the *Greek* Originals,
> Read them by Day, and think of them by Night;

and Tate and Brady's version of Psalm I:
> But makes the perfect Law of God
>   his Business and Delight;
> Devoutly reads therein by Day,
>   and meditates by Night.

127. Wakefield cites Dryden, *Georgics* IV 408: "And upward follow Fame's immortal Spring."

128. EC cite Roscommon, *Essay on Tr. Verse,* 186: "Consult your *Author,* with *Himself* compar'd."

And let your *Comment* be the *Mantuan Muse*.
　When first young *Maro* in his boundless Mind   130
A Work t'outlast Immortal *Rome* design'd,
Perhaps he seem'd *above* the Critick's Law,
And but from *Nature's Fountains* scorn'd to draw:
But when t'examine ev'ry Part he came,

129 And] Or *1736a–43*.   130 young] great *1711*.
130–1   When first young *Maro* sung of *Kings* and *Wars*,
　　Ere warning *Phœbus* touch'd his trembling Ears, *1713a–43*.

---

129. *Mantuan Muse*] Virgil, born near Mantua.
130*f.* Virgil, Eclog. 6. *Cum canerem Reges & Prœlia, Cynthius aurem Vellit*——
[P. *1713a–51*.]
　In *1744* Pope added: "It is a tradition preserved by *Servius*, that *Virgil* began with writing a poem of the *Alban* and *Roman* affairs; which he found above his years, and descended first to imitate *Theocritus* on rural subjects, and afterwards to copy *Homer* in Heroic poetry." He told Spence (p. *278*): "My next work, after my Epic, was my Pastorals; so that I did exactly what Virgil says of himself.—'Cum canerem reges' . . .'" Servius comments on *Ecl.* VI 3: "Et significat aut Aeneidem, aut gesta regum Albanorum, quae coepta omisit, nominum asperitate deterritus."
　The couplet quoted as a variant in *1736a–43* may have been altered as a result of strictures by Dennis, who criticized (Hooker, I 402) the passage because it seemed to imply that Virgil "designed to write his *Æneis* without Art", and also because of the contradiction in the idea of "*Maro*'s designing a Work to outlast immortal *Rome*". In his MS memorandum (see Appendix B, pp. *482–4*, below) Pope quoted the first words of l. 130 and noted: "alter yᵉ seeming Inconsistency". But in *1744* he returned to the *1711* version, substituting *young* for *great*. Dennis's criticism was exaggerated, and Pope may have decided to be pleased with his hyperbole. As EC note, "The phrase only expresses the double fact that the city was destroyed, and that its fame was durable." The variant lines reflect Dryden, *Ecl.* VI 3–5, where Virgil is made to say of his Muse:

> But when I try'd her tender Voice, too young,
> And fighting Kings, and bloody Battels sung,
> *Apollo* check'd my pride . . .

Carruthers remarked that the variant couplet contained "not only a bad rhyme, but a theft from Milton" [*Lycidas*, 77]: "*Phoebus* repli'd, and touch'd my trembling ears".
　132. Cf. Addison on Milton (*An Account of the Greatest English Poets*, 1694, 66–7):

> Bold, and sublime, my whole attention draws,
> And seems above the critick's nicer laws.

Nature and *Homer* were, he found, the *same*:   135
Convinc'd, amaz'd, he checks the bold Design, ⎫
And Rules as strict his labour'd Work confine, ⎬
As if the *Stagyrite* o'erlook'd each Line.   ⎭
Learn hence for Ancient *Rules* a just Esteem;
To copy *Nature* is to copy *Them*.   140
    Some Beauties yet, no Precepts can declare,
For there's a *Happiness* as well as *Care*.

136 checks] checkt *1711–16*.
137 And did his Work to Rules as strict confine, *1711–16*.

---

136. Cf. Dryden, Prol. to *The Tempest*, 7–8 (of Shakespeare):
        He Monarch-like gave those his subjects law,
        And is that Nature which they paint and draw.
Cf. l. 140, below.

137. The earlier reading was noted in the editions from 1736 to 1743.

138. *Stagyrite*] Aristotle, born at Stagira in 384 B.C.

141–80. The influence of Longinus and the School of Taste is apparent throughout. The belief that irregular genius is preferable to a cold and flat correctness, that there is a criticism by *taste* as well as by *rules*, that the success of a work of art may depend upon a quality difficult to define, a *je ne sais quoi*, that a criticism of *beauties* is preferable to a criticism of *faults*, that departures from poetic rules are like irregular but pleasing objects in the natural world, is emphatic in the lines, and declares the lack of rigour with which Pope adhered to the "Rules". By and large Longinus was introduced into England by way of Rapin, who cited him frequently and whose *Réflexions sur la Poétique d'Aristote* was published in 1674 and translated by Rymer almost immediately, and by Boileau, who in the same year, 1674, published his translation of Longinus, and also his *L'Art Poétique*, in which the influence of Longinus is immediately perceptible. See Intro., pp. 210–11. For helpful discussions of the influence of Longinus in England, see S. H. Monk, *The Sublime: A Study of Critical Theories in XVIII-Century England* (1935); A. F. B. Clark, *Boileau and the French Classical Critics in England* (1925); and A. Warren, *Alexander Pope as Critic and Humanist* (1929). For a useful account of the native, English, tradition in which Pope was writing, see also Monk, "'A Grace Beyond the Reach of Art'", *Journal of the History of Ideas*, V (1944), pp. 131–50.

141–4. Warton cites Bacon, *Essay* XLIII, "Of Beauty": "There is no excellent beauty that hath not some strangeness in the proportion . . . a painter may make a better face than ever was; but he must do it by a kind of felicity, (as a musician that maketh an excellent air in music,) and not by rule."

142. *a Happiness as well as Care*] Cf. Davenant, Pref. to *Gondibert* (Spingarn, II 20): "*Wit* is the laborious and the lucky resultances of thought, having towards

Musick resembles *Poetry*, in each ⎫
Are *nameless Graces* which no Methods teach, ⎬
And which a *Master-Hand* alone can reach. ⎭   145
If, where the *Rules* not far enough extend,
(Since Rules were made but to promote their End)
Some Lucky LICENCE answers to the full
Th' Intent propos'd, *that Licence* is a *Rule*.

148 answers] answer *1751*.

---

its excellence, as we say of the strokes of Painting, as well a happinesse as care."
The original of the phrase is probably the "curiosa felicitas" attributed to
Horace by Petronius (*Satyricon*, 118), and referred to by Dryden in the Pref. to
Sylvæ (*Essays*, 1 267), *A Disc. conc. . . . Sat.* (id., 11 40), *A Paral. of Poet. and Paint.*
(id., 11 151).

144. *nameless Graces*] Here again Pope touches upon the *je ne sais quoi*. Cf.
Rapin, *Reflections* (1674), p. 57: "Yet is there in *Poetry*, as in other Arts, certain
things that *cannot be expressed*, which are (as it were) *mysteries*. There are no precepts, to teach the hidden *graces*, the insensible *charms*, and all that secret *power*
of *Poetry* which passes to the heart. . ." Perhaps Leibnitz should be recalled
(*Thoughts on Knowledge, Truth and Ideas* (1684), in *The Philosophical Works of Leibnitz*, tr. by G. M. Duncan, 1890, p. 28): "Just so we often see painters or other
artists who judge very correctly that a work is good or defective, without being
able to account for their judgment, and who reply to those who ask their opinion, that that of which they disapprove, lacks something, *I know not what*."

146. *If, where the rules, &c.*] *Neque enim rogationibus plebisue scitis sancta* ⟨*Neque
tam sancta 1711–43*⟩ *sunt ista Præcepta, sed hoc quicquid est, Utilitas excogitavit; Non
negabo autem sic utile esse plerumque;* ⟨*alioqui nec scriberem;*⟩ *verum si eadem illa
nobis aliud suadebit utilitas, hanc, relictis magistrorum autoritatibus* [sic], *sequemur.*
Quintil. lib. ii. cap. 13 ⟨6–7⟩. [P. *1711–51*.]

148. LICENCE] Cf. the English tr. of Roger de Piles, *The Art of Painting* (1706),
p. 39: "The *Licences* are so necessary, that all Arts admit of them; they are
Literally against the *Rules*, but when we come to explain our selves, we shall
shew they assist them, if they are made use of *à Propos*. Every Man of sense thinks
they are to the purpose, when the Piece in which they are imploy'd, has the
greater Effect by them, and when, by their means, the Painter reaches the end
he aims at, which is to impose on the sight; but 'tis not every Painter that can
make an advantageous use of them. There are none but great *Genius*'s who are
above Rules, and who know when to make use ingeniously of the *Licences*. . ."

149. *Licence is a Rule*] Boileau, *Discours sur L'Ode*, quotes from his *Art Poétique*,
11 71–2,

> Son stile impétueux souvent marche au hasard;
> Chez elle un beau désordre est un effet de l'art,

Thus *Pegasus*, a nearer way to take,   150
May boldly deviate from the common Track.
Great Wits sometimes may *gloriously offend*,
And *rise* to *Faults* true Criticks *dare not mend*;
From *vulgar Bounds* with *brave Disorder* part,

152–3 *This couplet follows l. 160 in 1744–51.*

and goes on to say: "Ce précepte effectivement qui donne pour règle de ne point garder quelquefois de règles, est un mystère de l'Art, qu'il n'est pas aisé de faire entendre à un Homme sans aucun goust, qui croit que la Clélie & nos Opéras sont les modèles du Genre sublime; qui trouve Térence fade, Virgile froid, Homère de mauvais sens . . ." See l. 154*n*.

152*f. 1744* placed this couplet after l. 160. It remained there until 1764, when Warburton, as a result of criticism advanced by Warton, returned to the original sequence. See Note on the Text, p. 234, above.

152. "This phrase itself, *gloriously offend*, has a happy boldness, which successfully exemplifies the very rule, which it is employed to enforce. Like that of *Horace, splendide mendax, illustriously deceitful.* So our poet himself in his *Elegy* [l. 14]: 'The glorious fault of angels and of gods.' And of *Homer*, in his *Temple of Fame* [l. 195]: 'And here and there disclos'd a brave neglect'" [Wakefield]. Wakefield also notes Dryden, *Aureng-Zebe*, IV i 115: "Mean Soul! and dar'st not gloriously offend?"

153. *rise to Faults*] Cf. Dryden, *The Author's Apology for Heroic Poetry* (*Essays*, I 179–80): ". . . Longinus, who was undoubtedly, after Aristotle, the greatest critic amongst the Greeks, in his twenty-seventh chapter ΠΕΡΙ ΎΨΟΥΣ, has judiciously preferred the sublime genius that sometimes errs, to the middling or indifferent one, which makes few faults, but seldom or never rises to any excellence. . . I could, says my author [Longinus], find out some blemishes in Homer; and am perhaps as naturally inclined to be disgusted at a fault as another man; but, after all, to speak impartially, his failings are such, as are only marks of human frailty: they are little mistakes, or rather negligences, which have escaped his pen in the fervour of his writing; the sublimity of his spirit carries it with me against his carelessness. . ." Cf. Addison on Milton, *n* to l. 132, above. Cf. also *Spectators* 160 and 591.

154. *brave Disorder part*] Wakefield cites *A.P.*, II 76–7:
        Her generous stile at random oft will part,
        And by a brave disorder shows her Art;
and also IV 76–9:
        'Tis he will tell you, to what noble height
        A generous Muse may sometimes take her flight;
        When, too much fetter'd with the Rules of Art,
        May from his stricter Bounds and Limits part.

And *snatch* a *Grace* beyond the Reach of Art,   155
Which, without passing thro' the *Judgment*, gains
The *Heart*, and all its End *at once* attains.
In *Prospects*, thus, some *Objects* please our Eyes, ⎫
Which *out of* Nature's *common Order* rise,   ⎬
The shapeless *Rock*, or hanging *Precipice*.   ⎭ 160

160 *Add. 1711–43:*
              But Care in Poetry must still be had,
              It asks *Discretion* ev'n in *running Mad*;

155–7. Cf. the English tr. of Roger de Piles's *The Art of Painting* (1706), p. 8:
"*Grace* must season the parts we have spoken of, and every where follow *Genius*;
Grace supports and perfects it, but it is not to be so throughly acquir'd as by any
Rules to be demonstrated. A Painter has it from Nature only, and does not
know that he has it, nor in what degree, nor how he communicates it to his
Works. It surprises the Spectator, who feels the effect without penetrating into
the true Cause of it; but this Grace does not touch him otherwise, than according to the Disposition wherein he finds it. We may define it thus. *'Tis what
pleases, and gains the Heart, without concerning it self with the Understanding.* Grace
and Beauty are two different things, Beauty pleases by the Rules only, and
Grace without them." As de Piles's last sentence makes clear, he has removed
"grace beyond the reach of art". See S. H. Monk, "'A Grace Beyond the Reach
of Art'", *Journal of the History of Ideas*, v (1944), pp. 131–50, for a discussion of
these lines, and for a history of the term "grace" in English criticism. See also
the same author's *The Sublime*, p. 171. Cf. l. 144*n*, above.

158–60. The approval of the wilder and more irregular aspects of nature suggests the influence of Longinus. Pope, as EC note, closely echoes Sprat, *An
Account of the Life and Writings of . . . Cowley* (Spingarn, ii 129): "He knew that
in diverting mens minds there should be the same variety observ'd as in the
prospects of their Eyes, where a Rock, a Precipice, or a rising Wave is often
more delightful than a smooth, even ground or a calm Sea." See the qualification Dennis introduces into a discussion of the order necessary to poetry (Hooker, i 202–3): "But, as in some of the numberless Parts, which constitute this
beauteous All, there are some appearing Irregularities, which Parts, notwithstanding, contribute with the rest, to compleat the Harmony of Universal
Nature . . . so, if we may compare great Things with small, in the Creation of
the accomplish'd Poem, some Things may at first Sight be seemingly against
Reason, which yet, at the Bottom, are perfectly regular, because they are indis-
pensably necessary to the admirable Conduct of a great and just Design." Cf.
also Davenant, Pref. to *Gondibert* (Spingarn, ii 3).

160 var. *running Mad*] Cf. Rapin, *Reflections* (1674), ch. v, p. 6: " 'Tis in no wise
true, what most believe, That some little mixture of Madness goes to make up

But tho' the *Ancients* thus their *Rules* invade,
(As *Kings* dispense with *Laws* Themselves have made)
Moderns, beware! Or if you must offend
Against the *Precept,* ne'er transgress its *End,*
Let it be *seldom,* and *compell'd by Need,*   165
And have, at least, *Their Precedent* to plead.
The Critick else proceeds without Remorse,
Seizes your Fame, and puts his Laws in force.
    I know there are, to whose presumptuous Thoughts

161 But] And *1711–43.*

the character of a Poet: for though his Discourse ought in some manner to resemble that of one inspir'd: yet his mind must always be serene, that he may
discern when to *let his Muse run mad,* and when to govern his Transports." Wakefield recalls ". . . the *insanire cum ratione* taken from *Terence* [*Eun.,* I i 18] by
Horace, at Sat. II 3. 271."
    162. Cf. Cowley, *Inconstancy,* 21: "For 'twere to break the *Laws* her self has
made." EC cite Dryden, *Dedic. of the Æn.* (*Essays,* II 194): ". . . he [Virgil] might
make this anachronism, by superseding the mechanic rules of poetry, for the
same reason that a monarch may dispense with or suspend his own laws, when
he finds it necessary so to do, especially if those laws are not altogether fundamental." Cf. Chetwood's statement in Pref. to the *Pastorals* (prefixed to Dryden's *Virgil*): "*But extraordinary* Genius*'s have a sort of Prerogative, which may dispense them from Laws, binding to* Subject-Wits."
    163–4. Cf. l. 148*n,* above.
    165. Cf. Horace, *Ars Poet.,* 51–3:
                        dabiturque licentia sumpta pudenter:
            et nova fictaque nuper habebunt verba fidem, si
            Graeco fonte cadent parce detorta.
    168. *Seizes*] Here used probably in the legal sense: "to take possession of . . .
in pursuance of a judicial order" (OED).
    169 *ff.* Cf. Rapin, *Reflections* (1674), pp. 66–7: "[The poet must] know al-
wayes, that in great works he may be *negligent* in certain places, which regularly
ought to be *neglected;* that all may not be *finish'd* alike, and what is *finish'd* may
appear so the more, among the studied *negligences.* These *strokes* less perfect then
the rest, and these *inequalities* of expression which Art requires, are as necessary
to *Poesie,* as the *shades* to a *Painter,* which serve to give *lustre* to the other parts of
his work." Pope wrote to Walsh (*Corr.,* I 18–19): ". . . in Poetry as in Painting,
a Man may lay Colours one upon another, till they stiffen and deaden the
Piece. Besides to bestow heightening on every part is monstrous: Some parts
ought to be lower than the rest; and nothing looks more ridiculous, than a Work,
where the Thoughts, however different in their own nature, seem all on a

Those *Freer Beauties*, ev'n in *Them*, seem Faults: 170
Some Figures *monstrous* and *mis-shap'd* appear,
Consider'd *singly*, or beheld too *near*,
Which, but *proportion'd* to their *Light*, or *Place*,
Due Distance *reconciles* to Form and Grace.
A prudent Chief not always must display   175
His Pow'rs in *equal Ranks*, and *fair Array*,

---

level. . . I believe too that sometimes our first Thoughts are the best. . ." Cf. also
Dryden, *The Author's Apology for Heroic Poetry* (*Essays*, 1 179–80).

169 *f*. The rhyme *Thoughts–Faults* is not an instance of false rhyme, for, as
much contemporary spelling attests, the *l* in *fault* was evidently not sounded in
Pope's time. Cf. Roscommon, *Essay on Tr. Verse*, 324–5:

> Absur'd Expressions, crude, Abortive Thoughts,
> All the lewd *Legion* of *Exploded fau'ts*.

See ll. 422–3, below.

170. For the criticism of "beauties" versus the criticism of "faults", see note
to ll. 100*ff*., above.

171–4. Cf. the anonymous English tr. of Longinus, *An Essay Upon Sublime*
(1698), pp. 82–3: "'Tis just so with a Discourse, as 'tis with a natural Body,
whose beauty rises from the union, and just proportion of every part: and tho'
each limb by it self has nothing graceful, yet jointed together they form a most
beauteous frame. Thus the parts of *Sublime*, when they are pull'd asunder, the
sublimity is quite lost. . ."

173. EC cite Horace, *Ars Poet.*, 361–3:

> Ut pictura poesis: erit quae, si propius stes,
> te capiat magis, et quaedam, si longius abstes;
> haec amat obscurum; volet haec sub luce videri . . .;

and also *A.P.*, 1 177–8:

> Each Object must be fix'd in the due place,
> And diff'ring parts have Corresponding Grace. . .

Cf. the passage from Dennis, ll. 158–60*n*.

175. *A prudent Chief*] Warburton quotes Dionysius of Halicarnassus, *De Struc-
tura Orationis*, sec. xii, but Pope evidently imitated Quintilian, *Inst. Orat.*, II xiii
3: "Quid si enim praecipias imperatori, quotiens aciem instruat, derigat fron-
tem, cornua utrinque promoveat, equites pro cornibus locet? erit haec quidem
rectissima fortasse ratio, quotiens licebit; sed mutabitur natura loci, si mons
occurret, si flumen obstabit, collibus, silvis, asperitate alia prohibebitur; mutabit hostium genus, mutabit praesentis condicio discriminis; nunc acie directa
nunc cuneis, nunc auxiliis nunc legione pugnabitur, nonnunquam terga etiam
dedisse simulata fuga proderit." See also VI iv 18.

176. *equal Ranks, and fair Array*] Cf. Oldham, *A Letter from the Country to a
Friend in Town*, 194–5:

But with th' *Occasion* and the *Place* comply,
Conceal his Force, nay seem sometimes to *Fly*.
Those oft are *Stratagems* which *Errors* seem,
Nor is it *Homer Nods*, but *We* that *Dream*.   180
    Still green with Bays each *ancient* Altar stands,
Above the reach of *Sacrilegious* Hands,
Secure from *Flames*, from *Envy's* fiercer Rage,

178 *Conceal*] Oft *hide 1711*.   179 oft are] are but *1711*.
181 *No new paragraph 1711*.

        . . . the conduct of my words, when they
        March in due ranks, are set in just array.
179. Wakefield cites Roscommon, *Essay on Tr. Verse*, 330–1:
        For I mistake, or far the greatest Part
        Of what some call *Neglect* was *study'd* Art.
    180. *Modeste, & circumspecto judicio de tantis viris pronunciandum est, ne quod (quod plerisque accidit) damnent quod non intelligunt. Ac si necesse est in alteram errare partem, omnia eorum legentibus placere, quam multa displicere maluerim.* Quintil. ⟨lib. x i 26.⟩ [P. *1744–51*.]
    Pope alludes to Horace, *Ars Poet.*, 359: "indignor quandoque bonus dormitat Homerus". Cf. Dryden, *The Author's Apology for Heroic Poetry* (*Essays*, 1 182): "Ought they not rather, in modesty, to doubt of their own judgments, when they think this or that expression in Homer, Virgil, Tasso, or Milton's *Paradise*, to be too far strained, than positively to conclude that 'tis all fustion, and mere nonsense?"
    181–200. In this climactic paragraph Pope not only expresses a religious veneration of the ancients but also offers his own illustration of "sublimity" and of the "way to the sublime". Cf. the following passage, which also describes the "way to the sublime", from the anonymous English translation of Longinus, *An Essay Upon Sublime* (1698), p. 33: "'Tis an Imitation, or Emulation of those great Poets and Masters, who have liv'd before us. . . And certainly we may often see Men, who are raptur'd and inspir'd by another's Spirit, like the Priestess of *Apollo*. . . Thus the Majesty of the Old Writers is breath'd from their works, like Celestial blasts from so many *Tripods*, into the Souls of their Imitators. And the very dullest, and most unfit for Inspiration, are transported by a Prophetick Spirit, which is none of their own." Cf. l. 183*n*. Cf. the conclusion to Vida's *De Arte Poetica*. See Intro., pp. 210–11.
    182. *Sacrilegious Hands*] Wakefield cites Roscommon, Epil. to *Alexander the Great*, 11–12:
        Secur'd by higher Pow'rs, exalted stands
        Above the reach of Sacrilegious Hands.
    183 *ff*. Pope seems to have in mind throughout Longinus, ch. 36. Cf. the ano-

Destructive *War*, and all-involving *Age*.
See, from *each Clime* the Learn'd their Incense bring;
Hear, in *all Tongues* consenting *Pæans* ring!   186
In Praise so just, let ev'ry Voice be join'd,
And fill the *Gen'ral Chorus* of *Mankind*!
Hail *Bards Triumphant*! born in *happier Days*;
Immortal Heirs of *Universal* Praise!   190

184 all-involving] all-devouring *1711–43*.
186 consenting] Triumphant *1711*.

---

nymous tr. 1698 (pp. 76–7, referring to the ancient writers): "These extraordinary writers oftentimes by one noble beauty, one *sublime* flight, attone for
all their faults. . . And this is the reason, that envy and malice themselves cannot
hinder them from bearing away the prize, which they keep still, and are like to
maintain to all eternity.

> *While Rivers in their oozy Channels flow.*
> *And circl'ing Springs on Groves fresh Youth bestow.*"

   184. *all-involving Age*] The four great causes of the ravage amongst ancient
writings are here alluded to: The destruction of the *Alexandrine* and *Palatine*
libraries by fire; the fiercer rage of *Zoilus* and *Mævius* and their followers against
Wit; the irruption of the *Barbarians* into the empire; and the long reign of Ignorance and Superstition in the cloisters. [W. *1744*.]
   Pope ultimately preferred "all-involving", no doubt because if age had
been "all-devouring" nothing would have been left of Homer or Virgil. But
cf. *Ep. to Addison*, 1 (vol. VI, p. 202): "See the wild Waste of all-devouring
years!"
   186. *consenting*] In harmony, in concord; unanimous. Pope, as his MS memorandum indicates, altered the original reading because of the repetition of
"triumphant" three lines later. See Appendix B, p. 483, below.
   Pæans] Songs of triumph, praise, or joy addressed to Apollo.
   189. *Hail Bards Triumphant!*] Wakefield cites Cowley, *On the Death of Mr.
Crashaw*, 59–60:

> Hail, *Bard Triumphant!* and some care bestow
> On us, the *Poets Militant* Below!

Also *Aen.*, VI 649: "Magnanimi heroes, nati melioribus annis". EC cite Dryden,
Religio Laici, 80: "Those Gyant Wits, in happyer Ages born." Cf. Sheffield,
Es. upon Poetry, 321–4:

> So those Gigantick souls, amaz'd, we find
> As much above the rest of humane kind.
> Nature's whole strength united! endless fame,
> And universal shouts attend their name!

Cf. Vida, *De Arte Poet.*, III 286: "Autoresque alii nati felicibus annis".

Whose Honours with Increase of Ages *grow*,
As Streams roll down, *enlarging* as they flow!
Nations *unborn* your mighty Names shall sound,
And Worlds applaud that must not yet be *found*!
Oh may some Spark of *your* Cœlestial Fire   195
The last, the meanest of your Sons inspire,
(That on weak Wings, from far, pursues your Flights;
Glows while he *reads*, but *trembles* as he *writes*)
To teach vain Wits a Science *little known*,
T' *admire* Superior Sense, and *doubt* their own!   200

OF all the Causes which conspire to blind
Man's erring Judgment, and misguide the Mind,
What the weak Head with strongest Byass rules,

197 on] with *1711*.   199 a] that *1711*.

191*f.* Pope told Spence (p. 277) that this couplet came unaltered from his youthful epic, *Alcander, Prince of Rhodes*.

194. *And Worlds applaud*] Wakefield cites Cowley, *Davideis*, II 833:
> Round the whole Earth his dreaded Name shall sound,
> And reach to Worlds, that must not yet be found.

195. *Cœlestial Fire*] Wakefield cites Dryden, *Æn.*, VII 52:
> Now, *Erato*, thy Poet's Mind inspire,
> And fill his Soul with thy Cœlestial Fire.
Cf. Roscommon, *Essay on Tr. Verse*, 173–6.

197. "Here he seems to have had in view, what *Statius*, at the end of the *Thebaid* [XII 817], says of himself with reference to *Virgil*: 'Sed longe sequere et vestigia semper adora'" [Wakefield].

201. "The allusion to that caelestial maxim *Know thyself*, with which the *first* division of this poem concluded, introduces us, by a very natural and easy transition, to these exquisite remarks on *pride*, or 'an absurd persuasion of our own powers and attainments,' with which the *second* divison opens" [Wakefield]. See Intro., p. 230, above, and V. M. Hamm, 'Pope and Malebranche: A Note on the *Essay on Criticism*: Part II', *PQ*, XXIV (1945), pp. 65–70.

203. *Byass*] A term in bowls: the construction of a bowl which imparts an oblique motion. See *Mac Flecknoe*, 189–90:
> This is that boasted Byas of thy mind,
> By which, one way, to dullness, 'tis inclined.
Also *Dunciad* A, I 148 (vol. v, p. 81).

Is *Pride*, the *never-failing Vice of Fools*.
Whatever Nature has in *Worth* deny'd,   205
She gives in large Recruits of *needful Pride*;
For as in *Bodies*, thus in *Souls*, we find
What wants in *Blood* and *Spirits*, swell'd with *Wind*;
Pride, where Wit fails, steps in to our Defence,
And fills up all the *mighty Void* of *Sense*!   210
If once right Reason drives *that Cloud* away,
Truth breaks upon us with *resistless Day*;
Trust not your self; but your Defects to know,
Make use of ev'ry *Friend*—and ev'ry *Foe*.

A *little Learning* is a dang'rous Thing;   215
Drink deep, or taste not the *Pierian* Spring:
There *shallow Draughts* intoxicate the Brain,

---

205 *f*. EC cite Oldham, *Elegies*, II x 33: "What Nature has in Bulk to me denied. . ." Cf. Temple, *Upon the Ancient and Modern Learning* (Spingarn, III 62):
". . . [Man's] Pride is greater than his ignorance; and what he wants in Knowledge he supplies by Sufficiency." See also *E. on Man*, II 286 (vol. III i, p. 89).
    206. *Recruits*] Additional supplies.
    207 *ff*. The image is derived from the ancient theory that nature abhors a
void, and also from the physiology of Pope's time which supposed that the blood
and chief organs of the body were permeated by "one or other of certain subtle
highly-refined substances or fluids" (see OED, s.v. *spirit*, IV 16).
    209 *f*. Cf. Roscommon, *Essay on Tr. Verse*, 161–2:
            Pride, of all others the most *dangerous* Fau't,
            Proceeds from want of *Sense* or want of *Thought*.
    212. Cf. *Messiah*, 98 (p. 121, above): "And break upon thee in a Flood of
Day!"
    214. Cf. *A.P.*, I 186–8:
            But find You faithful Friends that will reprove,
            That on your Works may look with careful Eyes,
            And of your Faults be zealous Enemies.
Pope's own use of his enemy John Dennis is attested by his MS memorandum,
printed in Appendix B (pp. 482–4, below).
    215. Cf. Pope's *Thoughts on Various Subjects* (EC, x 550): "Learning is like
mercury, one of the most powerful and excellent things in the world in skilful
hands; in unskilful, the most mischievous."
    216. *Pierian Spring*] A spring sacred to the Pierides, a surname of the Muses,
which they derive from Pieria, near Mt Olympus, where they were first worshipped by the Thracians.
    217 *f*. Warburton suggests that the thought was taken from Bacon, "who ap-

And drinking *largely* sobers us again.
Fir'd at first Sight with what the *Muse* imparts,
In *fearless Youth* we tempt the Heights of Arts,   220
While from the bounded *Level* of our Mind,
Short Views we take, nor see the *Lengths behind*,
But *more advanc'd*, behold with strange Surprize
New, distant Scenes of *endless* Science rise!
So pleas'd at first, the towring *Alps* we try,   225
Mount o'er the Vales, and seem to tread the Sky;
Th' Eternal Snows appear already past,
And the first *Clouds* and *Mountains* seem the last:
But *those attain'd*, we tremble to survey
The growing Labours of the lengthen'd Way,   230
Th' *increasing* Prospect *tires* our wandring Eyes,
Hills peep o'er Hills, and *Alps* on *Alps* arise!

219 Fir'd with the Charms fair *Science* does impart, *1711–16*.
220 Arts,] Art; *1711–16*.   223 behold] survey *1711*.

---

plies it to more serious enquiries". See *Essay* xvi, "Of Atheism": "It is true, that
a little philosophy inclineth man's mind to atheism; but depth in philosophy
bringeth men's minds about to religion."

220. In *fearless Youth*] Wakefield cites Virgil, *Georgics* iv 565: "audax juventa".
tempt] Attempt. Wakefield cites Dryden, *State of Innocence*, i i 139: "Nor need
we tempt those heights which Angels keep."

225.   *So pleas'd at first the tow'ring* Alps *to try,*
        Fill'd with ideas of fair Italy,
        The traveller beholds with chearful eyes
        The less'ning vales, and seems to tread the skies.
                        [P. *1736a–43, 1751*.]
Pope used the first couplet in *Ep. to Jervas*, 25–6 (vol. vi, p. 157).
226. A monosyllabic line. Cf. l. 347.
232. Warton suggests that this simile ("the best that English poetry can
shew", said Dr Johnson) was imitated from Drummond, *An Hymn of the Fairest
Faire*, 149–56:
        Ah! as a Pilgrime who the *Alpes* doth passe,
        Or *Atlas* Temples crown'd with winters glasse,
        The ayrie *Caucasus*, the *Apennine*,
        Pyrenès cliftes where Sunne doth neuer shine,
        When hee some heapes of Hilles hath ouer-went,
        Beginnes to thinke on rest, his Iourney spent,

K

A perfect Judge will *read* each Work of Wit
With the same Spirit that its Author *writ*,
Survey the *Whole*, nor seek slight Faults to find,   235
Where *Nature moves*, and *Rapture warms* the Mind;

235 find,] find; *1711–13a*; find *1736a–51*.

Till mounting some tall Mountaine hee doe finde,
More hights before him than hee left behinde.

Pope may have recalled Drummond, but as Warburton hinted (in a note to
l. 216, where a young author is said to engage "in an undertaking as arduous
almost as that of Hannibal"), and as Wakefield suggested, it is more likely that
Pope imitated a passage in Silius Italicus which he must have seen quoted and
translated in Addison's *Remarks on . . . Italy* (1705), pp. 426–7. Addison describes
the passage from Florence to Bologna through the Apennines: "It gave me a
lively Idea of *Silius Italicus's* Description of *Hannibal's* March.

Quoque magis subiere jugo atque evadere nisi
Erexere gradum, crescit labor, ardua supra
Sese aperit fessis, & nascitur altera moles.

From Steep to Steep the Troops advanc'd with Pain,
In hopes at last the topmost Cliff to gain;
But still by new Ascents the Mountain grew,
And a fresh Toil presented to their View."

The passage from Silius Italicus goes on, III *528ff.*:

unde nec edomitos exsudatosque labores
respexisse libet; tanta formidine plana
exterrent repetita oculis; atque una pruinae
canentis, quacumque datur promittere visus,
ingeritur facies.

Cf. also Vida, *De Arte Poet.*, II *66ff.*

"The redundancy of expression in this verse is happily illustrative of the circumstance described, and leaves the mind fully possessed with the idea of
fatigue and disappointment" [Wakefield].

233*ff. Diligenter legendum est, ac pæne ad scribendi sollicitudinem: Nec per partes
modo scrutanda sunt omnia, sed perlectus liber utique ex integro resumendus.* Quintilian.
⟨*Inst. Orat.*, x i 20.⟩ [P. *1711–51*.]

235. *Survey the Whole*] Cf. Dryden, Pref. to *Sylvæ* (*Essays*, I 264): "True judgment in Poetry, like that in Painting, takes a view of the whole together, whether it be good or not; and where the beauties are more than the faults, concludes for the poet against the little judge. . ." Also Prol. to *Tyrannick Love*, 9–11:

So hopes [our Poet] . . .
You equal Judges of the whole will be:
They judge but half who only faults will see.

See note to ll. 100*ff.*, above.

Nor lose, for that malignant dull Delight,
The *gen'rous Pleasure* to be charm'd with Wit.
But in such Lays as neither *ebb*, nor *flow*,
Correctly cold, and *regularly low*,   240
That shunning Faults, one quiet *Tenour* keep;
We cannot *blame* indeed—but we may *sleep*.
In Wit, as Nature, what affects our Hearts
Is not th' Exactness of peculiar Parts;
'Tis not a *Lip*, or *Eye*, we Beauty call,   245

---

239 *ff*. Wakefield compares Horace, *Ars Poet.*, 267–8: "Vitavi denique culpam, / non laudem merui." EC cite *A.P.*, 1 71–2:

> A frozen Stile, that neither Ebs or Flows,
> Instead of pleasing, makes us gape and doze.

240. *Correctly cold*] Wakefield compares lines from the anonymous *On the Death of Mr. Oldham* (in *Sylvæ*, 1685, pp. 468–74):

> Yet Art he us'd, where Art cou'd useful be,
> But sweated not to be correctly dull.

241–2. Cf. the anonymous *A New Session of the Poets* (1700), p. 6 (of Blackmore):

> In which thy Rhymes a constant Cadence keep,
> At once they make us smile, and make us sleep.

245 *f*. The imagery here is traditional, especially as an illustration of the *je ne sais quoi* in art. Cf. Bouhours, *Les Entretiens* (1671), p. 251: "La physionomie ingenieuse est vn autre je ne sçay quoy: car si l'on se donne la peine de chercher ce qui fait qu'vn homme d'esprit se reconnoist d'ordinaire à la seule veüe, on trouvera que ce n'est ni la largeur du front, ni le brillant & le feu des yeux, ni la delicatesse & la regularité des traits, ni la forme & la couleur du visage; que c'est quelque chose qui resulte de tout cela [cf. Pope's "full Result of all"], ou plûtost que ce n'est rien de tout cela." Cf. C. Codrington's dedicatory poem prefixed to Garth's *Dispensary*:

> I wou'd a Poet, like a Mistress, try,
> Not by her Hair, her Hand, her Nose, her Eye;
> But by some Nameless Pow'r, to give me Joy.

Cf. Denham, *Out of an Epigram of Martial*, 8: "'Tis not Cheeks, nor Lips nor Eyes, / That I prize . . ." EC compare Dryden, *Eleonora*, 156–7:

> Nor this part Musk or Civet can we call,
> Or Amber, but a rich Result of all.

In *An Ess. of Dram. Poesy* (*Essays*, 1 47–8), Dryden had said: ". . . the characters are indeed the imitations of Nature, but so narrow, as if they had imitated only an eye or an hand, and did not dare to venture on lines of a face, or the proportion of a body." Cf. also Dryden, *Ep. to Sir Godfrey Kneller*, 71; Horace, *Ars Poet.*, 32–7; Boileau, *A.P.*, 1 175–80.

But the joint Force and full *Result* of *all*.
Thus when we view some well-proportion'd Dome,
(The *World*'s just Wonder, and ev'n *thine* O *Rome*!)
No single Parts unequally surprize;
All comes *united* to th' admiring Eyes;   250
No monstrous Height, or Breadth, or Length appear;
The *Whole* at once is *Bold*, and *Regular*.
    Whoever thinks a faultless Piece to see,
Thinks what ne'er was, nor is, nor e'er shall be.
In ev'ry Work regard the *Writer's End*,   255
Since none can compass more than they *Intend*;

---

247 *ff*. Cf. Addison (*Remarks on . . . Italy*, pp. 174–7): "The Proportions are
so very well observ'd, that nothing appears to an Advantage, or distinguishes
it self above the rest. It seems neither extreamly high, nor long, nor broad, because it is all of 'em in a just Equality. As on the contrary in our *Gothic* Cathe-
drals, the Narrowness of the Arch makes it rise in Height, or run out in Length;
the Lowness often opens it in Breadth, or the Defectiveness of some other Particular makes any single Part appear in greater Perfection." Speaking of the
dome of St Peter's, Addison remarks: "Tho' every thing in this Church is admirable, the most astonishing part of it is the Cupola. . . Nor is it easie to conceive a more glorious Show in Architecture, than what a Man meets with in
St. *Peters*, when he stands under the Dome."
    252. Cf. Wycherley, *To Mr. Pope, on his Pastorals*, 19: "Your Strains are regu-
larly bold. . ."
    253. Cf. Sheffield, *Es. upon Poetry*, 232–5:
        Reject that vulgar error which appears
        So fair, of making perfect characters;
        There's no such thing in Nature, and you'll draw
        A faultless Monster which the world ne're saw.
Cf. Boileau, *L'Art Poét.*, III 107–8:
        A ces petits défauts marqués dans sa peinture,
        L'esprit avec plaisir reconnoît la nature.
La Bruyère, *Characters* (4th edn, London, 1705), p. 13, has: "What a prodigious
difference is there between a fine Piece, and one that's Regular and Perfect!
I question whether there is any of the last kind, it being less difficult for a rare
Genius to hit upon the Great and Sublime, than to avoid all Errors."
    254. Wakefield cites Dryden, Ovid, *Met.*, xv 654: "Greater than what e'er
was, or is, or e'er shall be."
    256. Cf. Postscript to the *Od.*, where Pope says "the first principle of criti-
cism" is "to consider the nature of the Piece, and the intent of its author."

And if the *Means* be just, the *Conduct* true,
Applause, in spite of trivial Faults, is due.
As Men of Breeding, sometimes Men of Wit,
T' avoid *great Errors*, must the *less* commit,   260
Neglect the Rules each *Verbal Critick* lays,
For *not* to know some Trifles, is a Praise.
Most Criticks, fond of some subservient Art,
Still make the *Whole* depend upon a *Part*,

259 sometimes] oft the *1711–16*.
263 Criticks,] Criticks *1711–16*.

---

257 *f*. Cf. Dryden, *The Author's Apology for Heroic Poetry* (*Essays*, I 179) : "If the design, the conduct, the thoughts, and the expressions of a poem, be generally such as proceed from a true genius of Poetry, the critic ought to pass his judgment in favour of the author. 'Tis malicious and unmannerly to snarl at the little lapses of a pen, from which Virgil himself stands not exempted." Also Prol. to *Tyrannick Love*, II : "They judge but half who only faults will see." EC cite Horace, *Ars Poet.*, 351 : "verum ubi plura nitent in carmine, non ego paucis/ offendar maculis . . .''

259 *f*. Cf. Horace, *Ars Poet.*, 31 : "in vitium ducit culpae fuga, si caret arte."

261. *Verbal Critick*] OED cites this couplet in its definition of a verbal critic as one "interested . . . in the mere words of a literary composition". Rymer in his Pref. to his tr. of Rapin's *Reflections on Aristotle's Treatise of Poesie* (1674), distinguishes between true and verbal criticism by saying of his own remarks that "What has been noted, rather concerns the Niceties of *Poetry*, than any the little trifles of *Grammar*". Gildon (*The Complete Art of Poetry*, 1718, I 115) says that true critics "dwell not on the meer *grammatical Criticisms* on Words, but penetrate farther into the *Reasons*, and *Sense*, and *Judgment* of the Authors. . ." In 1751 Warburton said that "verbal critic" was not here "used in its common signification, of one who retails the sense of single words; but of one who deals in large cargo's of them without any sense at all". The context suggests critics who pay too much attention to detail, and sacrifice the spirit to the letter of the rules. For a portrait of a verbal critic, see *Dunciad* IV 203–38 (vol. v, pp. 362 *ff*.).

262. "To the same effect *Quintilian*, lib. i [viii 21]. *Ex quo mihi inter virtutes grammatici habebitur, aliqua nescire*. On which account I shall esteem it one excellence of a grammarian, *to be ignorant of some things*" [Wakefield].

263. "These introductory lines and the story, for which they so happily prepare the reader, are conducted exactly after the manner of *Horace* in his epistles: and for sprightliness of humour, an unaffected ease of narrative, and an elegant facility of the purest diction, may be compared with the most successful efforts of that admirable writer" [Wakefield].

They talk of *Principles*, but Notions prize,   265
And All to one lov'd Folly Sacrifice.
    Once on a time, *La Mancha*'s Knight, they say,
A certain *Bard* encountring on the Way,
Discours'd in Terms as just, with Looks as Sage,
As e'er cou'd *Dennis*, of the *Grecian* Stage;   270
Concluding all were desp'rate Sots and Fools,
Who durst depart from *Aristotle*'s Rules.
Our Author, happy in a Judge so nice,
Produc'd his Play, and beg'd the Knight's Advice,
Made him observe the *Subject* and the *Plot*,   275

265 Notions] Parts they *1711–16*.
270 *Dennis*] D——s, *1711–16*.
    of the *Grecian* Stage;] of the Laws o' th' Stage; *1711–22b*,
    1736a–43; of th' *Athenian* stage; *1727–32*.
272 Who] That *1711–32*.

---

267. Pope found the episode in *A Continuation of the Comical History Of the most Ingenious Knight, Don Quixote De la Mancha*, chap. x, bk III, written under the name of Don Alonzo Fernandez de Avellaneda, and translated by Captain John Stevens in 1705. For the portion of the episode used by Pope see Appendix C, pp. 484-6, below.

270. The first version ("of the Laws o' th' Stage") reflects the contemporary view that Dennis was a critic "excessively given to judging by the Rules", and one who "lifted his Rules and the jargon of criticism from the French critics" (Hooker, II lxi). Dennis argued consistently for "Regularity" in drama and poetry, for "the bringing some Rules into Practice" (Hooker, I 200). The later versions ("Of th' *Athenian* stage" and "of the *Grecian* Stage") reflect Dennis's preoccupation throughout his work with the excellencies of Greek drama. Cf. *The Grounds of Criticism in Poetry* (Hooker, I 332): "And here we make it our business to shew how much the present *English* Stage is degenerated from the Virtue and Greatness of the Ancient Tragedy, and what is to be done to restore Modern Tragedy first to the Innocence, and secondly to the Greatness of the *Grecian* Stage."

271*f*. Dennis believed the "Rules of *Aristotle* . . . nothing but Nature and Good Sence reduc'd to a Method" (Hooker, I 39), and constantly employed them as a standard for the stage. But his regard for the rules was not inflexible. He praised Milton for resolving to "break thro' the Rules of Aristotle", and thought *Paradise Lost* not so much "against the Rules" as "above them all" (Hooker, I 333).

The *Manners, Passions, Unities,* what not?
All which, exact to *Rule* were brought about,
Were but a *Combate in the Lists* left out.
What! Leave the Combate out? Exclaims the Knight;
Yes, or we must renounce the *Stagyrite.*   280
Not so by Heav'n (he answers in a Rage)
Knights, Squires, and Steeds, must enter on the Stage.
So vast a Throng the Stage can ne'er contain.
Then build a New, or act it in a Plain.
    Thus Criticks, of less *Judgment* than *Caprice,*   285
Curious, not *Knowing,* not *exact,* but *nice,*
Form *short Ideas;* and offend in *Arts*
(As most in *Manners*) by a *Love to Parts.*
    Some to *Conceit* alone their Taste confine,
And glitt'ring Thoughts struck out at ev'ry Line;   290

283 The Stage can ne'er so vast a Throng contain. *1711–43.*
289 *No new paragraph 1711, 1717–22b.*

286. *Curious, not Knowing*] Pope wrote in his MS, and then struck out, the passage from Petronius (*Sat.,* xlvi 6) which had inspired him: "Est et alter, non quidem Doctus, sed Curiosus, qui plus docet quam scit."

289. *Some to Conceit*] Cf. Pope's letter to Walsh, July 2, 1706 (*Corr.,* I 19): "People seek for what they call *Wit,* on all subjects, and in all places; not considering that Nature loves Truth so well, that it hardly ever admits of flourishing: *Conceit* is to Nature what *Paint* is to Beauty; it is not only needless, but impairs what it wou'd improve." Walsh replied on Sept. 9, 1706 (*Corr.,* I 21): "They [some who pass for great critics] scan their Verses upon their Fingers; run after Conceits and glaring Thoughts; their Poems are all made up of Couplets, of which the first may be last, or the last first, without any sort of prejudice to their Works; in which there is no Design, or Method, or any thing Natural or Just. For you are certainly in the right, that in all Writings whatsoever . . . *Nature* is to be follow'd; and we shou'd be jealous of our selves for being fond of *Similies, Conceits,* and what they call saying *Fine Things.*"

290ff. *And glitt'ring Thoughts*] Pope here sets forth some of the objections his age had to much poetry of the Metaphysical School. Cf. his account of Crashaw's verse (*Corr.,* I 110): ". . . only pretty conceptions, fine metaphors, glitt'ring expressions, and something of a neat cast of Verse, (which are properly the dress, gems, or loose ornaments of Poetry) may be found in these verses. . . And (to express my self like a Painter) their *Colouring* entertains the sight, but the *Lines* and *Life* of the Picture are not to be inspected too narrowly." Addison

Pleas'd with a Work where nothing's just or fit;
One *glaring Chaos* and *wild Heap* of *Wit*:
Poets like Painters, thus, unskill'd to trace
The *naked Nature* and the *living Grace*,
With *Gold* and *Jewels* cover ev'ry Part,   295
And hide with *Ornaments* their *Want of Art*.
True Wit is *Nature* to Advantage drest,

(*An Account of the Greatest English Poets*, 1694) had previously commented on
Cowley thus (ll. 36–7):

> One glittering thought no sooner strikes our eyes
> With silent wonder, but new wonders rise.

See further A. Warren, 'The Reputation of Crashaw in the Seventeenth and
Eighteenth Centuries', *SP*, xxxi (1934), pp. 385–407; W. L. Ustick and H. H.
Hudson, 'Wit, "Mixt Wit," and the Bee in Amber', *Huntington Library Bulletin*,
viii (1935), pp. 103–30.

293 *ff.* The analogy between the efforts of poets and painters to express the
"living Grace" in their arts was traditional; so was the repudiation of affectation and excessive ornament in achieving this "grace". See S. H. Monk, ' "A
Grace Beyond the Reach of Art" ', *Journal of the History of Ideas*, v (1944), pp.
131–50. One should recall Ben Jonson, *Still to Be Neat*:

> Give me a look, give me a face
> That makes simplicity a grace;
> Robes loosely flowing, hayre as free:
> Such sweet neglect more taketh me
> Than all th' adulteries of art;
> They strike mine eyes, but not my heart.

Cf. Cowley, *Of Wit*, st. 5:

> Yet 'tis not to adorn and gild each part;
> That shows more Cost, then Art.
> *Jewels* at *Nose* and *Lips* but ill appear;
> Rather than *all things Wit*, let *none* be there.

The whole passage recalls Dryden, *A Paral. of Poet. and Paint.* (*Essays*, ii 147–8):
"Expression, and all that belongs to words, is that in a poem which colouring
is in a picture. . . If [the design] be vicious . . . the cost of colouring is thrown
away upon it: 'tis an ugly woman in a rich habit set out with jewels. . ."

297 *ff. True Wit*] *Naturam intueamur, hanc sequamur: id facillimè accipiunt animi
quod agnoscunt.* Quintil. lib. viii. c. 3 ⟨71⟩. [P. *1711–51.*]

For the relationship between "Wit" and "Nature", and the poetic power and
dignity accorded to "Wit", see Intro., pp. 212–22, above. Pope's words recall
Davenant, who in his Pref. to *Gondibert* (Spingarn, ii 23) had said that his endeavour was to bring truth home to men "by representing Nature, though not
in an affected, yet in an unusual dress." Dryden (*The Author's Apology for Heroic*

What oft was *Thought*, but ne'er so well *Exprest*,
Something, whose Truth convinc'd at Sight we find,
That gives us back the Image of our Mind: 300
As Shades more sweetly recommend the Light,
So modest Plainness sets off sprightly Wit:

298 so well] before *1711*.

Poetry, in *Essays*, I 90) had defined wit as a "propriety of thoughts and words; or, in other terms, thoughts and words elegantly adapted to the subject." Pope wrote to Wycherley on Dec. 26, 1704 (*Corr.*, I 2) that "True Wit I believe, may be defin'd a Justness of Thought, and a Facility of Expression; or (in the Mid-wives phrase) a perfect Conception, with an easy Delivery." Walsh, in a letter of Sept. 9, 1706 (*Corr.*, I 22), said to Pope: "As for what you say of Expression: 'tis indeed the same thing to Wit, as Dress is to Beauty".

298 and var. Cf. Pope's letter to Walsh of July 2, 1706 (*Corr.*, I 19): ". . . it seems not so much the Perfection of Sense, to say things that have *never* been said before, as to express those *best* that have been said *oftenest*". EC cite Boileau, Pref. to *Oeuvres Diverses* (1701): "Qu'est-ce qu'une pensée neuve, brillante, ex-traordinaire? Ce n'est point, comme se le persuadent les Ignorans, une pensée que personne n'a jamais euë, ni dû avoir. C'est au contraire une pensée qui a dû venir à tout le monde, & que quelqu'un s'avise le premier d'exprimer. Un bon mot n'est bon mot qu'en ce qu'il dit une chose que chacun pensoit, & qu'il la dit d'une manière vive, fine & nouvelle." In Ozell's tr. of Boileau's *Works*, 1712 (I iii), the last sentence is rendered: "*Wit* is not *Wit*, but as it says some-thing every Body thought of, and that in a lively, delicate, and New Manner." In *Spectator* 253, which he devoted to discussion of Pope's *Essay*, Addison re-marked: "And here give me leave to mention what Monsieur *Boileau* has so very well enlarged upon in the Preface to his Works, that Wit and fine Writing doth not consist so much in advancing Things that are new, as in giving Things that are known an agreeable Turn. It is impossible for us, who live in the latter Ages of the World, to make Observations in Criticism, Morality, or any Art or Science, which have not been touched upon by others. We have little else left us, but to represent the common Sense of Mankind in more strong, more beau-tiful, or more uncommon Lights."

300. Cf. de Piles, *The Art of Painting*, p. I: ". . . the Painter must regard *Visible Nature* as his object. He must have an Image of her in his Mind, not only as he happens to see her in particular Subjects, but as she ought to be in her self, and as she would be, were she not hinder'd by certain accidents." See Intro., pp. 219-22, above.

301. Cf. quotation from Rapin in the note to ll. 169 *ff*.

302. Cf. Roscommon, *Essay on Tr. Verse*, 219: "For truth shines brightest through the plainest dress."

For *Works* may have more *Wit* than does 'em good,
As *Bodies* perish through Excess of *Blood*.

    Others for *Language* all their Care express,   305
And value *Books*, as Women *Men*, for *Dress*:
Their Praise is still—*The Stile is excellent*:
The *Sense*, they humbly take upon Content.
Words are like *Leaves*; and where they most abound,
Much *Fruit* of *Sense* beneath is rarely found.   310
False Eloquence, like the *Prismatic Glass*,
Its gawdy Colours spreads on *ev'ry place*;
The Face of Nature we no more Survey,
All glares *alike*, without *Distinction* gay:
But true *Expression*, like th' unchanging *Sun*,   315
Clears, and *improves* whate'er it shines upon,
It *gilds* all Objects, but it *alters* none.
Expression is the *Dress* of *Thought*, and still
Appears more *decent* as more *suitable*;

---

303. Wakefield recalls *Hamlet*, IV vii 118–19: "For goodness, growing to a plurisy, / Dies in his own too-much"; and also Ascham, *The Schoolmaster* (London, 1711), p. 136: "For twenty to one, offend more in writing too much, than too little: even as twenty to one, fall into Sickness, rather by over much Fulness, than by any Lack, or Emptiness."

308. *take upon Content*] To accept without question or examination.

309. *Words are like Leaves*] Cf. Quintilian, *Inst. Orat.*, VIII Pr. 23: "Sed evenit plerumque ut in hac diligentia deterior etiam fiat oratio, primum, quia sunt optima minime arcessita et simplicibus atque ab ipsa veritate profectis similia. Nam illa, quae curam fatentur et ficta atque composita videri etiam volunt, nec gratiam consequuntur et fidem amittunt propter id quod sensus obumbrantur et velut laeto gramine sata strangulantur." In his MS Pope cites Quintilian (VIII ii 17): "Est etiam in quibusdam turba inanium verborum, qui, dum communem loquendi morem reformidant, ducti specie nitoris circumeunt omnia copiosa loquacitate". Cf. Horace, *Ars Poet.*, 60*ff.* For possible sources of the image in medieval theological writings, see J. M. Morse, 'Pope's "Words are like Leaves" ', *N & Q*, CCI (Oct., 1956), pp. 430–1.

315. Cf. Sheffield, *Ess. upon Poetry*, 12: "True Wit is everlasting, like the Sun."

318*f.* EC cite Dryden, Pref. to *All for Love* (*Essays*, I 193): ". . . expressions . . . are a modest clothing of our thoughts, as breeches and petticoats are of our bodies." Cf. also *A Paral. of Poet. and Paint.* (*Essays*, II 152): "As the words, &c., are evidently shown to be the clothing of the thought, in the same sense as colours are the clothing of the design, so the painter and the poet ought to judge

A vile Conceit in pompous Words exprest,   320
Is like a Clown in regal Purple drest;
For diff'rent *Styles* with diff'rent *Subjects* sort,
As several Garbs with Country, Town, and Court.
Some by *Old Words* to Fame have made Pretence;
Ancients in *Phrase*, meer Moderns in their *Sense*!   325
Such *labour'd Nothings*, in so *strange* a Style,
Amaze th'unlearn'd, and make the Learned *Smile*.
Unlucky, as *Fungoso* in the Play,   ⎫
These Sparks with aukward Vanity display   ⎬
What the Fine Gentleman wore *Yesterday*!   ⎭   330

320 Words] Style *1711*.   324 *New paragraph 1727–32*.
330 Gentleman] Gentlemen *1711–32*.

---

exactly, when the colouring and expressions are perfect, and then to think their
work is truly finished." Cf. note to ll. 297 *ff*., above.

322. Cf. Wycherley, *To Mr. Pope, on his Pastorals*, 30–1:
                And the true measure of the shepherd's wit
                Should, like his garb, be for the Country fit.

322 *f*. The subjects appropriate to "Country, Town, and Court" are perhaps,
respectively, pastoral, satire or comedy, and epic. Cf. Hobbes, *Answer . . . to . . .
Davenant* (Spingarn, II 55): "As Philosophers have divided the Universe . . . into
three Regions . . . so the Poets . . . have lodg'd themselves in the three Regions
of mankinde, *Court, City*, and *Country*. . . From hence have proceeded three sorts
of Poesy, *Heroique, Scommatique*, and *Pastorall*."

324. *Abolita & abrogata retinere, insolentiæ cujusdam est, & frivolæ in parvis jactan-
tiæ*. Quintil. lib. i. c. 6 ⟨20⟩.

*Opus est ut verba à vetustate repetita neque crebra sint, neque manifesta, quia nil est
odiosius affectatione, nec utique ab ultimis repetita temporibus. Oratio cujus summa virtus
est perspicuitas, quam sit vitiosa, si egeat interprete? Ergo ut novorum optima erunt maximè
vetera, ita veterum maximè nova*. Idem ⟨39–41⟩. [P. *1711–51*.]

Pope has modified Quintilian to suit his own purposes. In the second quotation he omits a first sentence in which Quintilian speaks of the pleasing majesty
given to style by the use of old words, and of which the sentence quoted by Pope
is merely a qualification.

324 *ff*. Pope may here glance at Ambrose Philips, who had revived archaic
or Spenserian dialect in his *Pastorals* and whose practice Pope satirized in *Guardian* 40 (see Intro. to *Discourse on Pastoral Poetry*, pp. 17–18, above).

328. *—unlucky as* Fungoso] See ⟨*1744–51*⟩ Ben. Johnson's *Every Man in his
Humour*. [P. *1711–51*.]

The allusion is to *Every Man out of his Humour*. Pope's information, as EC note,

And but so mimick ancient Wits at best,
As Apes our Grandsires in their *Doublets drest.*
In *Words*, as *Fashions*, the same Rule will hold;
Alike Fantastick, if *too New*, or *Old*;
Be not the *first* by whom the *New* are try'd,   335
Nor yet the *last* to lay the *Old* aside.
But most by *Numbers* judge a Poet's Song,

---

may have been confined to Dryden's allusion in the Dedic. to *The Assignation*:
". . . he is only like *Fungoso* in the Play, who follows the Fashion at a distance."
It is surprising that the correction was not made in the later editions.

332. Monkeys dressed in mock finery were part of the show put on by moun-
tebanks, as they continued to be of organ-grinders till the beginning of the
20th century. Doublets had ceased to be worn in the days of Charles II. Cf.
Pepys, *Diary*, Oct. 15, 1666, where the new fashion brought in by the king is
recorded.

335*f.* "This", said Dennis (Hooker, I 407), "being directed to all without
Exception, and deliver'd without Limitation or Restriction, is another flat Contradiction of *Horace*" (*Ars Poet.*, 48–53):

Si forte necesse est
indiciis monstrare recentibus abdita rerum,
fingere cinctutis non exaudita Cethegis
continget, dabiturque licentia sumpta pudenter;
et nova fictaque nuper habebunt verba fidem, si
Graeco fonte cadent, parce detorta.

Dennis termed the couplet a "Libel upon the memory of Mr. *Dryden* whom he
pretends to admire; for never any one was a greater Coiner than he. . ." But
Pope is repeating opinions expressed by Dryden on several occasions. Cf. *An Ess.
on the Dram. Poet. of the Last Age* (*Essays*, I 170): "They, who have lately written
with most care, have, I believe, taken the rule of Horace for their guide; that is,
not to be too hasty in receiving of words, but rather to stay till custom has made
them familiar to us." Cf. also in *A Disc. conc. . . . Sat.* (*Essays*, II 29) the passage
on Milton, which concludes: "unnecessary coinage, as well as unnecessary revival, runs into affectation; a fault to be avoided on either hand." Pope returns
to the subject in *Ep.* II ii 167 (vol. IV, p. 177).

337.   *Quis populi sermo est? quis enim? nisi carmina molli*
              Nunc demum numero fluere, ut per læve severos
              Effundat junctura ungues: scit tendere versum,
              Non secus ac si oculo rubricam dirigat uno.

Persius, Sat. I ⟨63–6⟩. [P. *1711–51.*]

In *1711–22a*, *1732–43*, l. 3 has *Effugit* for *Effundat.*

337*f.* The discussion falls into two parts, the first (to l. 357) dismissing con-

And *smooth* or *rough*, with them, is *right* or *wrong*;
In the bright *Muse* tho' thousand *Charms* conspire,
Her *Voice* is all these tuneful Fools admire,   340
Who haunt *Parnassus* but to please their Ear, ⎫
Not mend their Minds; as some to *Church* repair, ⎬
Not for the *Doctrine*, but the *Musick* there. ⎭
These *Equal Syllables* alone require,

338 them,] such, *1711–16*.

temptuously those poets who insist rigorously on "harmonious numbers" as the
essential element of the poet's art. D. T. Mace has shown ('The Doctrine of
Sound and Sense in Augustan Poetic Theory', *RES*, n.s. II (1951), pp. 129–39),
that Pope was attacking here a doctrine which would have abandoned meaning
as the core of poetry, led to a subordination of the rational to the irrational in
poetry, and made poetry an art aimed almost entirely at the senses. In the
second part Pope treats sound not as the "sole delight of the senses", but as an
"integral part of word-meaning itself". He "sought to resolve the irrational and
the rational into an indissoluble poetic unity, from which no part could be justi-
fiably shorn away" (Mace, pp. 138–9). It is in this context that one should read
l. 365, "The *Sound* must seem an *Eccho* to the *Sense*". See l. 365*n*.
    344. *Equal Syllables*] Pope may have had Cowley, *The Resurrection*, st. 2, in
mind:

> Lo how the *Years to come* . . .
> All hand in hand do decently advance,
> And in my *Song* with smooth and equal measures *dance*.
> Whilst the *dance* lasts, how long so e're it be,
> My *Musicks* voyce shall bear it companie.

Cowley placed great emphasis on the "numbers" of poetry, as his notes to his
poems reveal. His phrase "equal measures" is the nearest equivalent found to
Pope's "Equal Syllables", and the line in which the phrase appears is followed,
as is Pope's phrase, by open vowels: "so e're it be". The expletive *do* in Cowley's second line would certainly make the whole passage a good example of
many of the faults Pope is describing. Cf. also Roscommon, *Essay on Tr. Verse*,
226*ff.*:

> Affected *Noise* is the most *wretched* Thing
> That to *Contempt* can *Empty Scriblers* bring.
> *Vowels* and *Accents*, *Regularly plac'd*
> On *even Syllables*, and still the *Last*,
> Tho gross, innumerable *Faults* abound,
> In spight of non sense never *fail* of *Sound*.

See notes to ll. 337–83, 357.

Tho' oft the Ear the *open Vowels* tire,   345
While *Expletives* their feeble Aid *do* join,
And ten low Words oft creep in one dull Line,
While they ring round the same *unvary'd Chimes*,

---

345. *Fugiemus crebras vocalium concursiones, quæ vastam atque hiantem orationem reddunt.* Cic. ad Heren. lib. iv ⟨12⟩. *Vide etiam* Quintil. lib. ix. c. 4 ⟨33: Tum vocalium concursus; quod cum accidit, hiat et intersistit et quasi laborat oratio. Pessime longae, quae easdem inter se litteras committunt, sonabunt. Praecipuus tamen erit hiatus earum, quae cavo aut patulo maxime ore efferuntur⟩. [P. *1711–51.*]

Cf. Dryden, Dedic. of *Examen Poeticum* (*Essays*, II 11). The Latin passages, with two more from Cicero, are quoted by Pope in his letter to Walsh of Oct. 22, 1706 (*Corr.*, I 24 5). In this letter, and the one to Cromwell of Nov. 25, 1710 (*Corr.*, I 106–8), Pope discusses the questions of prosody taken up here in the *Essay*. There is doubt that the letter of Oct. 22 is altogether authentic. Note that in this line Pope gives three instances of hiatus.

346. *While Expletives*] Cf. Pope's letter to Cromwell of Nov. 25, 1710 (*Corr.*, I 107): "I wou'd except against all Expletives in Verse, as Do before Verbs plural, or ev'n too frequent use of Did & Does, to change the Termination of the Rhime; all these being against the usual manner of Speech & meer fillers up of unnecessary syllables." Pope also discusses expletives in his letter to Walsh of Oct. 22, 1706 (*Corr.*, I 23), but if he had formulated his rule on this point so early it is strange that he should have used so many expletives in the first edition of his *Essay* (see Note on the Text, pp. 234–5, above). In this line the expletive is introduced deliberately as an example to be avoided. See the quotation from Dryden, next note.

347. *ten low Words*] Cf. Dryden, *An Ess. of Dram. Poes.* (*Essays*, I 31–2): ". . . he is a very Leveller in Poetry: he creeps along with ten little words in every line, and helps out his numbers with *For to*, and *Unto*, and all the pretty expletives he can find, till he drags them to the end of another line; while the sense is left tired half way behind it." Cf. also *Dedic. of the Æn.* (*Essays*, II 226): "'Tis possible, I confess, though it rarely happens, that a verse of monosyllables may sound harmoniously. . ." Pope did not object to monosyllabic lines altogether, for they occur occasionally in his own verse. In his letter to Cromwell of Nov. 25, 1710 (*Corr.*, I 107), he said: "Monosyllable-Lines, unless very artfully manag'd, are stiff languishing, & hard." Warton compares Quintilian (*Inst. Orat.*, IX iv 42): "Etiam monosyllaba, si plura sunt, male continuabuntur, quia necesse est compositio multis clausulis concisa subsultet."

348f. Cf. Pope to Cromwell, Nov. 25, 1710 (*Corr.*, I 107): "I wou'd except against . . . the Repeating the Same Rhimes within 4 or 6 lines of each other: which tire the Ear with too much of the like Sound." Cf. Atterbury's Pref. to *The Second Part of Mr. Waller's Poems* (1690): "He [Waller] had a fine Ear, and knew

With sure *Returns* of still *expected Rhymes*.
Where-e'er you find *the cooling Western Breeze*,   350
In the next Line, it *whispers thro' the Trees*;
If *Chrystal Streams with pleasing Murmurs creep*,
The Reader's threaten'd (not in vain) with *Sleep*.
Then, at the *last*, and *only* Couplet fraught
With some *unmeaning* Thing they call a *Thought*,   355

---

how quickly that Sense was cloy'd by the same round of chiming Words still returning upon it."

350*f*. Wakefield compares Dryden, *Æn.*, VI 954-5:
> A sep'rate Grove, thro' which a gentle Breeze
> Plays with a passing Breath, and whispers thro' the Trees.

Holt White suggested to Wakefield that Garth took the allusion as being to a
couplet in *The Dispensary*, II 1-2:
> Soon as with gentle Sighs the ev'ning Breeze
> Begun to whisper thro' the murm'ring Trees,

and that, as a result, Garth altered the couplet in the next (7th) edn of his
poem to: Soon as the Ev'ning veil'd the Mountains Heads,
> And Winds lay hush'd in subterranean Beds.

350*ff*. *Western Breeze . . . with Sleep*] Wakefield cites C. Hopkins's tr. of Ovid,
Met., XI (description of the God of Sleep and his Palace):
> No tame, nor savage Beast dwells there, no Breeze
> Shakes the still Boughs, or whispers through the Trees . . .
> Here easie Streams with pleasing Murmurs creep,
> At once inviting, and assisting sleep.

Croker notes that "Pope uses these trite ideas and 'unvaried chimes' himself. In
the fourth Pastoral [ll. 61-2, 79-80] we have 'gentle breeze, trembling trees,
whispering breeze, dies upon the trees', and in Eloisa [ll. 159-60] we have 'the
curling breeze, panting on the trees'." Cf. also Wycherley, *To Mr. Pope, on his
Pastorals*:   So purling Streams with even Murmurs creep,
> And hush the heavy Hearers into Sleep.

EC note that "Pope took the idea from Boileau" (*Satire* II 37-42):
> Si je loüois Philis, *En miracles féconde;*
> Je trouverois bientost, *À nulle autre seconde.*
> Si je voulois vanter un objet *Nompareil;*
> Je mettrois à l'instant, *Plus beau que le Soleil.*
> Enfin parlant toûjours d'*Astres* & de *Merveilles*,
> De *Chefs-d'oeuvre des Cieux*, de *Beautez sans pareilles*. . .

Cf. Dryden, *Æn.*, VI 954-5.

355. ". . . an instance of the figure of speech called oxymoron, a contradiction in terms. . . Notice Pope's contemptuous 'they call', and the happy alliteration . . . all the happier because its art is concealed" [West].

A *needless Alexandrine* ends the Song,
That like a wounded Snake, drags its slow length along.
Leave such to tune their own dull Rhimes, and know
What's *roundly smooth*, or *languishingly slow*;
And praise the *Easie Vigor* of a Line,   360
Where *Denham*'s Strength, and *Waller*'s Sweetness join.

---

357. *a wounded Snake*] Wakefield compares Dryden, *Annus Mirabilis*, st. 123:
        So glides some trodden Serpent on the Grass,
        And long behind his wounded Volume trails.
West compares *Georgics* III 423-4:
        cum medii nexus extremaeque agmina caudae
        solvuntur, tardosque trahit sinus ultimus orbis.
Cf. Cowley's note 25 to *Davideis*, bk 1: "I am sorry that it is necessary to ad-
monish the most part of *Readers*, that it is not by *negligence* that this verse ["Nor
can the glory contain it self in th'endless space"] is so loose, long, and as it were,
Vast; it is to paint in the number the nature of the thing which it describes. . .
The thing is, that the disposition of words and numbers should be such, as that
out of the order and sound of them, the things themselves may be represented."
The Alexandrine which Pope uses to drive home his point in this line is apparently to be contrasted with the one he employs at l. 373. See notes to ll. 337-83,
344.

358. *own dull Rhimes*] EC cite *A.P.*, IV 52: "Those Tuneful Readers of their
own dull Rhymes."

360*ff.* That *ease* and *art* were qualities brought by Waller into English poetry
was asserted in *A.P.*, I 131*ff.*:
        Waller came last, but was the first whose Art
        Just Weight and Measure did to Verse impart;
        That of a well-plac'd Word could teach the force,
        And shew'd for Poetry a nobler Course:
        His happy Genius did our Tongue Refine,
        And easie Words with pleasing Numbers joyn:
        His Verses to good method did apply,
        And chang'd harsh Discord to Soft Harmony.

361. *Denham's Strength*] Cf. Dryden, *Epistle Dedicatory of the Rival Ladies* (*Essays*,
I 7): "This sweetness of Mr. Waller's lyric poesy was afterwards followed in the
epic by Sir John Denham, in his *Cooper's Hill*, a poem which your Lordship
knows for the majesty of the style." Again, in *An Ess. of Dram. Poes.* (*Essays*, I
34-5): ". . . they [the Elizabethans] can produce . . . nothing so even, sweet, and
flowing, as Mr. Waller; nothing so majestic, so correct, as Sir John Denham."
Cf. *Windsor-Forest*, 271, 280.

Waller's Sweetness] Pope told Spence, p. 24: "In versification there is a sensible

True Ease in Writing comes from Art, not Chance,
As those move easiest who have learn'd to dance.
'Tis not enough no Harshness gives Offence,
The *Sound* must seem an *Eccho* to the *Sense*.   365

362–3 *Add. 1717–51.*

---

difference between softness and sweetness that I could distinguish from a boy.
Thus on the same points, Dryden will be found to be softer, and Waller sweeter.
It is the same with Ovid and Virgil; and Virgil's Eclogues, in particular, are
the sweetest poems in the world." Cf. Henry Hall, *To the Memory of John Dryden*
(in *Luctus Britannici*, 1700), 75: "More smooth than *Waller*, or than *Denham*
strong!"

362f. Pope quotes this couplet, with slight modification, in *Ep.* II ii 178–9 (vol.
IV, p. 177).

364ff. Perhaps an expansion upon Garth, *Dispensary*, IV 204–5:
          Harsh words, tho' pertinent, uncouth appear,
          None please the Fancy, who offend the Ear.
Garth had merely echoed Boileau, *L'Art Poét.*, I 112:
          Le vers le mieux rempli, la plus noble pensée
          Ne peut plaire à l'esprit quand l'oreille est blessée.
Cf. Pope's letter to Cromwell, l. 365n.

365. Cf. Roscommon, *Essay on Tr. Verse*, 345: "The *sound* is still a *Comment* to
the *Sense*." Dryden says of Virgil (Pref. to *Sylvæ*, in *Essays*, I 255): "His verse is
everywhere sounding the very thing in your ears, whose sense it bears." Cf. also
Pref. to *Albion and Albanius* (*Essays*, I 277): "The chief secret is the choice of
words; and, by this choice, I do not here mean elegancy of expression, but propriety of sound, to be varied according to the nature of the subject." Pope states
his own theory in a letter to Cromwell of Nov. 25, 1710 (*Corr.*, I 107): "It is not
enough that nothing offends the Ear, that the Verse be (as the French call it)
Coulante [sic]; but a good Poet will adapt the very Sounds, as well as Words, to
the Things he treats of. So that there is (if one may express it so) a Style of
Sound: As in describing a gliding stream the Numbers shou'd run easy & flowing, in describing a rough Torrent or Deluge, sonorous & swelling. & so of the
rest. This is evident ev'ry where in Homer and Virgill, and no where else that I
know of to any observable degree. The following Examples will make this very
plain, which I have taken from Vida." See Vida, *De Arte Poetica*, III 367ff. Cf.
Wycherley, *Lines to Mr. Pope, on his Pastorals*, 5–6:
                    in your verse are found
          Art strength'ning Nature, Sense improv'd by Sound.
In the lines following Pope illustrates his precept. For an analysis of Pope's
practice, see C. M. Lotspeich, 'The Metrical Technique of Pope's Illustrative
Couplets', *JEGP*, XXVI (1927), pp. 471–4.

Soft is the Strain when *Zephyr* gently blows,
And the *smooth Stream* in *smoother Numbers* flows;
But when loud Surges lash the sounding Shore,
The *hoarse, rough Verse* shou'd like the *Torrent* roar.
When *Ajax* strives, some Rock's vast Weight to throw,
The Line too *labours*, and the Words move *slow*;   371
Not so, when swift *Camilla* scours the Plain,

368 Surges] billows *1717–32*.

366*f.* Warburton compares Vida, *De Arte Poet.*, III 403 *f.*:
> Tum, si laeta canunt, hilari quoque carmina vultu
> incedunt, laetumque sonant haud segnia verba . . .

366*ff.* Pope's lines recall, though with different emphasis, *A.P.*, I 167 70:
> More pleas'd we are to see a River lead
> His gentle Streams along a flow'ry Mead,
> Than from high Banks to hear loud Torrents roar,
> With foamy Waters on a Muddy Shore.

368*f.* Warburton compares Vida, *De Arte Poet.*, III 388*ff.*:
> Tunc longe sale saxa sonant, tunc et freta ventis
> incipiunt agitata tumescere: littore fluctus
> illidunt rauco, atque refracta remurmurat unda
> ad scopulos, cumulo insequitur praeruptus aquae mons.

Cf. Milton, *Par. Lost*, II 661: "that Parts / *Calabria* from the hoarse *Trinacrian* shore." Garth, *Dispensary*, v 5, has: "The Surges gently dash against the Shoar".

370*f.* Warburton compares Vida, *De Arte Poet.*, III 415 *ff.*:
> Atque adeo, siquid geritur molimine magno,
> adde moram, et pariter tecum quoque verba laborent
> segnia . . .

Warburton also cites III 420, "At mora si fuerit damno, properare jubebo", but III 375 *f.* seem more appropriate:
> ille autem membris, ac mole ignavus ingens
> incedit tardo molimine subsidendo.

For Pope's allusion to Ajax, see *The Episode of Sarpedon*, 99 *ff.*, p. 453, below.

372*f.* Cf. Vida, *De Arte Poet.*, III 373 *f.*:
> Hic melior motuque pedum, et pernicibus alis,
> molle viam tacito lapsu per levia radit;

and Virgil, *Aen.*, VII 808 *ff.*:
> illa vel intactae segetis per summa volaret
> gramina nec teneras cursu laesisset aristas,
> vel mare per medium fluctu suspensa tumenti
> ferret iter celeris nec tingueret aequore plantas.

Wakefield remarks that Pope here follows Dryden in fastening "on *Virgil* a most

Flies o'er th'unbending Corn, and skims along the Main.
Hear how *Timotheus'* vary'd Lays surprize,
And bid Alternate Passions fall and rise!   375
While, at each Change, the Son of *Lybian Jove*
Now *burns* with Glory, and then *melts* with Love;
Now his *fierce Eyes* with *sparkling Fury* glow;
Now *Sighs* steal out, and *Tears begin to flow*:
Persians and *Greeks* like *Turns of Nature* found,   380

374 vary'd] various *1711–32.*

---

insufferable absurdity, which no poetical *hyperbole* whatsoever will justify; namely, the reality of these wonderful performances. . . Whereas *Virgil* only puts the
supposition, and speaks of her extraordinary velocity in the way of comparison,
with a degree of extravagance indulged to the poets, that she seemed capable of
accomplishing so much, had she made the attempt. She *could fly*, if she had
chosen. . ." Dryden (VII 1100–3) says that Camilla

> Outstripp'd the winds in speed upon the plain,
> Flew o'er the field, nor hurt the bearded grain:
> She swept the seas, and, as she skimm'd along,
> Her flying feet unbathed in billows hung.

Cf. l. 357*n.*

374. *See* ⟨*1744–51*⟩ Alexander's Feast, *or* the Power of Music; *an Ode by Mr.*
Dryden. [P. *1711–51.*]

Dryden introduces into his ode the Theban musician Timotheus, who

> to his breathing Flute,
> And sounding Lyre,
> Cou'd swell the Soul to rage, or kindle soft Desire.

In his letter to Cromwell of Nov. 25, 1710 (*Corr.*, I 108), Pope mentions Dryden's
ode as being "One excellent Example" of the adaptation of the sounds to the
things treated.

375. Cf. Prior, *Presented to the King At His Arrival in Holland* (in *Poems on Several
Occasions*, 1709), 4: "And bid alternate Empires rise and fall." Wakefield compares J. Hughes, *The Court of Neptune* (1700), 46: "Beholds th' alternate Billows
fall and rise."

376. *Libyan Jove*] When Alexander visited the oracle of Zeus Ammon in the
oasis of Siwah in Libya, he was proclaimed son of the god. Cf. Milton, *Par. Lost*,
IV 276*f.*: ". . . where old *Cham*, / Whom Gentiles *Ammon* call and *Lybian Jove* . . ."

377. Cf. the passage from Dryden quoted in l. 374*n.*

379. *begin to flow*] Cf. *Alexander's Feast*, 87*f.*:

> And, now and then, a Sigh he stole;
> And Tears began to flow.

And the *World's Victor* stood subdu'd by *Sound*!
The Pow'r of Musick all our Hearts allow;
And what *Timotheus* was, is *Dryden* now.

Avoid *Extreams*; and shun the Fault of such,
Who still are pleas'd *too little*, or *too much*.   385
At ev'ry Trifle scorn to take Offence,
That always shows *Great Pride*, or *Little Sense*;
Those *Heads* as *Stomachs* are not sure the best
Which nauseate all, and nothing can digest.
Yet let not each gay *Turn* thy Rapture move,   390
For Fools *Admire*, but Men of Sense *Approve*;

390 *New paragraph 1727–32.*

---

381. *the World's Victor*] Cf. *Alexander's Feast*, 115: "The vanquish'd Victor sunk
upon her Breast."

383. *Timotheus . . . Dryden*] The comparison of Dryden to his own figure of
Timotheus (and a similar employment of antithetical verse structure in the con-
text) had been made in the anonymous *To the Memory of . . . John Dryden* (in
Luctus Britannici, 1700, pp. 13–15), st. 4:

> Not Fam'd *Timotheus* could with greater ease
> Command our Anger, or our Wrath appease:
> True Measure with *his* [Dryden's] Verse, our Passions kept,
> And as *He* Pleas'd, we either Smil'd, or Wept.

386–9. Cf. the passage from Dryden quoted at l. 153*n*.

390. *Turn*] An iterative or echoing pattern of words. See Dryden's discussion
in his *Disc. conc. . . . Sat.* (*Essays*, II 108*ff*., and Ker's note, II 288–9), and the
Intro. to the Translations, pp. 344–5, below.

391. EC cite Horace, *Ars Poet.*, 455–6,

> fugientque poetam
> qui sapiunt; agitant pueri incautique sequuntur,

and Creech's tr., 665–6:

> Men of Sense retire,
> The Boys abuse, and only Fools admire.

Cf. the English tr. of La Bruyère, *Characters* (4th edn, 1705), p. 15: "An Author
endeavours in vain to make himself admir'd by his Productions. A Fool may
sometimes admire him, but then 'tis but a Fool: And a Man of Sense has in him
the Seeds of all Truths and all Sentiments, nothing is new to him. He admires
little; He approves." According to Aaron Hill (see *The Corr. of Samuel Richardson*,
1804, I 112), Pope was very fond of this line, and would often repeat it. Cf. also
Horace, *Ep.* I vi 1–2, and Pope's "imitation" of it (vol. IV, pp. 236–7).

As things seem *large* which we thro' *Mists* descry,
Dulness is ever apt to *Magnify.*
    Some *foreign* Writers, some our *own* despise;
The *Ancients* only, or the *Moderns* prize: 395
(Thus *Wit*, like *Faith*, by each Man is apply'd
To *one small Sect*, and All are *damn'd beside.*)

394 *foreign*] the *French 1711–43.*
396–7 *Parentheses omitted 1711, 1744–51.*

392*f.* Cf. Sir R. Howard, Pref. to *The Great Favourite* (Spingarn, II 111), speaking of the sun: "But when descended and grown low, its oblique shining renders the shadow larger than the substance, and gives the deceiv'd person a wrong measure of his own proportion." Cf. *Dunciad* A, I 78, 218 (vol. v, pp. 68, 89).

394. var. The original reading reflects the period of 1711, when there was more discussion of Boileau and the French critics and of Corneille and Racine. Pope may have had in mind Dryden's *An Ess. of Dram. Poesy*, where the relative merits of Ancient, Modern, and French writers are discussed.

396. *Thus Wit, like Faith*] Cf. Cowley, *To Sir William Davenant*, 27–8:
        Some men their *Fancies* like their *Faith* derive,
        And think all Ill but that which *Rome* does give.
The idea that divisions in arts and sciences had their parallel in the divisions of religious history was common. Cf. Rapin, *Critical Works* (1706), I 10 (speaking of the Egyptians): "And as their Apprehensions of things were more conformable to the Simplicity of Nature, as not yet Corrupted by a multitude of different Opinions, nor Biass'd by the Partiality of particular Sects; so was their Insight more clear and pure, their Notions less abstracted, and their views less Circumscrib'd." See Intro., pp. 230–1, above. For MS variants of these lines, see vol. VI, pp. 234–5.

396*f.* This couplet was taken by some of Pope's co-religionists as a criticism of Roman Catholics (see Intro., pp. 203–4, above). Pope vindicated the lines in a letter to Caryll of July 19, 1711 (*Corr.*, I 126): "Nothing has been so much a scarecrow to them [enemies of Roman Catholicism] as the too peremptory and seemingly uncharitable assertion of an utter impossibility of salvation to all but ourselves, invincible ignorance excepted, which indeed some people define under so great limitations and with such exclusions, that it seems as if that word were rather invented as a salvo or expedient . . . than as a real exceptive to almost universal damnation. . . Therefore I own to you I was glad of any opportunity to express our dislike of so shocking a sentiment as those of the religion I profess are charged with, and hoped a slight insinuation, introduced so easily, of a casual similitude only could never have given offense. . ." Some Roman Catholics seem to have taken to themselves the couplet "Meanly they seek",

Meanly they seek the Blessing to confine,
And force *that Sun* but on a *Part* to Shine;
Which not alone the *Southern Wit* sublimes,   400
But ripens Spirits in cold *Northern Climes*;
Which from the first has shone on *Ages past*,
Enlights the *present*, and shall warm the *last*:

which followed the simile, but, as EC note, "Pope pointed out [letter to Caryll, June 18, 1711, *Corr.*, 1 117] that the plural 'some' [l. 394], and not the singular 'each man' [l. 396], was the antecedent to 'they' [l. 398]." Pope emphasized in this letter that the "simile of wit and faith . . . plainly concludes at the second line, where stands a full stop; and what follows, *meanly they seek &c.*, speaks only of wit. . . Now the word *They* refers (as I'm sure I meant it and as I thought every one must have known) to those cricks there spoken of [l. 394], who are partial to some particular set of writers, to the prejudice of all others, and the very simile itself . . . if read twice may convince them that the censure of damning here lies not on our Church unless they will call our Church one small sect." It seems obvious that Pope, when in 1713 he revised the poem, added the parentheses around the offending simile in order further to suggest that it was not logically or syntactically a necessary part of the thought of the whole passage and in order further to disengage the simile from the "they" of l. 398. Pope recorded briefly in a MS memorandum (see Appendix B, pp. 482–4, below) his decision to ignore his co-religionists' objections: "Wit & Faith   nihili."

399. *on a Part to Shine*] "A beauty derived from that glorious passage in *Matthew's* Gospel, v. 45. 'That ye may be the children of your father, which is in heaven: for *he maketh his sun to rise on the evil and on the good*, and sendeth rain on the just and on the unjust'" [Wakefield]. Pope here repudiates the ancient idea that climate might impose limitations on the minds and works of men. Cf. Milton, *Par. Lost*, IX 41–6:

> Mee of these
> Nor skill'd nor studious, higher Argument
> Remains, sufficient of itself to raise
> That name, unless an age too late, or cold
> Climate, or Years damp my intended wing
> Deprest . . .

See Spingarn, 1 ci–cii.

400. *sublimes*] To exalt, but also perhaps, in the context of "ripens" in the next line, to "cause (the juices of a plant)to rise, and thereby rarefy and purify them" (OED).

401. Cf. Dryden, Prol. to *Aureng-Zebe*, 33–4:

> And Wit in Northern Climates will not blow,
> Except, like *Orange-Trees*, 'tis Hous'd from Snow.

(Tho' *each* may feel *Increases* and *Decays*,
And see now *clearer* and now *darker Days*)   405
Regard not then if Wit be *Old* or *New*,
But blame the *False*, and value still the *True*.
    Some ne'er advance a Judgment of their own,
But *catch* the *spreading Notion* of the Town;
They reason and conclude by *Precedent*,   410
And own *stale Nonsense* which they ne'er invent.
Some judge of Authors' *Names*, not *Works*, and then
Nor praise nor blame the *Writings*, but the *Men*.
Of all this *Servile Herd* the worst is He
That in *proud Dulness* joins with *Quality*,   415
A constant Critick at the Great-man's Board,
To *fetch and carry* Nonsense for my Lord.
What *woful stuff* this Madrigal wou'd be,
In some starv'd Hackny Sonneteer, or me?
But let a *Lord* once own the *happy Lines*,   420

404–5 *Parentheses omitted 1744–51.*
412 Authors'] Author's *1711–16*; authors *1717–51.*
413 blame] damn *1711–16.*   414 *New paragraph 1727–32.*
420 a *Lord* once] his Lordship *1727–32.*

---

404. EC cite Sir R. Howard, *Against the Fear of Death*, 12: "And neither gives Encrease, nor brings Decay."

409. "The colour of expression in this verse, delineated from an *infectious epidemic*, is happily employed to represent this *malady* of criticism. So in his *prologue* to the *Satires* [*Ep. to Dr Arbuth.*, 224]: 'To spread about the itch of verse and praise' " [Wakefield].

414. *Servile Herd*] Cf. Horace, *Ep.* I xix 19: "o imitatores, servum pecus . . ."

417. Cf. *Ep. to Dr Arbuth.*, 225*f.* (vol. IV, p. 112), and *Sandys's Ghost*, 18*f.* (vol. VI, p. 171).

419. *Hackny*] OED cites this line: "Doing or ready to do work for hire, hireling."

Sonneteer] Not a writer of sonnets, but a "minor or indifferent poet" (OED). Cf. Dryden, Pref. to *All for Love* (*Essays*, I 195): "Our little sonneteers . . . have too narrow souls to judge of Poetry."

420–3. Cf. Horace, *Ars Poet.*, 382–4:

    qui nescit versus tamen audet fingere. quidni?
    liber et ingenuus, praesertim census equestrem
    summam nummorum vitioque remotus ab omni,

How the *Wit brightens*! How the *Style refines*!
Before *his* sacred Name flies ev'ry Fault,
And each *exalted* Stanza *teems* with *Thought*!
    The *Vulgar* thus through *Imitation* err;
As oft the *Learn'd* by being *Singular*;   425
So much they scorn the Crowd, that if the Throng
By *Chance* go right, they *purposely* go wrong;
So Schismatics the *plain Believers* quit,
And are but damn'd for having *too much Wit*.
    Some praise at Morning what they blame at Night;
But always think the *last* Opinion *right*.   431
A Muse by these is like a Mistress us'd,
This hour she's *idoliz'd*, the next *abus'd*,
While their weak Heads, like Towns unfortify'd,
'Twixt Sense and Nonsense daily change their Side.   435
Ask them the Cause; *They're wiser still*, they say;
And still to Morrow's wiser than to Day.
We think our *Fathers* Fools, so *wise* we grow;
Our *wiser Sons*, no doubt, will think *us* so.
Once *School-Divines* this zealous Isle o'erspread;   440
Who knew most *Sentences* was *deepest read*;

428 *plain*] *dull 1711*.   440 this] our *1711*.

424. Cf. l. 414*n*.
425-7. Cf. Jonson, *Timber, or Discoveries* (Spingarn, I 21): "These men erre not by chance, but knowingly and willingly; they are like men that affect a fashion by themselves, have some singularity in a Ruffe, Cloake, or Hat-band... and set a marke upon themselves."
428 var. For the offence given by this line to some of Pope's co-religionists see Intro., p. 204, above.
430*f*. Cf. Garth, *Dispensary*, III 33-4:
        New Passions, new Opinions still excite,
        And what they like at Noon, despise at Night.
436*f*. Cf. Hobbes, *Answer ... to ... Davenant* (Spingarn, II 66): "... there is no reason for any man to think himself wiser to day then yesterday, which does not equally convince he shall be wiser to morrow then to day."
441. *Sentences*] An allusion to such works as Peter Lombard's *Libri quattuor sententiarum*. Lombard's work was designed "to place before the student, in as strictly logical a form as practicable, the views (*sententiae*) of the fathers and all

Faith, Gospel, All, seem'd made to be *disputed*,
And none had *Sense enough to be Confuted.*
Scotists and *Thomists,* now, in Peace remain,
Amidst their *kindred Cobwebs* in *Duck-Lane.*   445
If *Faith* it self has *diff'rent Dresses* worn,
What wonder *Modes* in *Wit* shou'd take their Turn?

---

the great doctors of the church upon the chief and most difficult points in the Christian belief. Conceived with the purpose of allaying and preventing, it really stimulated, controversy" (*Encycl. Brit.,* 11th edn, s.v. *Universities*).

444. *Scotists and Thomists*] Conflicts between followers of the Franciscan Duns Scotus (1265 or 1275–1308), Doctor Subtilis, and the Dominican Thomas Aquinas (c. 1227–1274), Doctor Angelicus, dominated the intellectual life of the 14th century. In the Renaissance Duns Scotus became for humanists the symbol of an utter misuse of the human reason. From his name derives the word *dunce* and, ultimately, the title of Pope's *Dunciad.* See next note.

445. *Cobwebs in Duck-Lane*] A place where old and second-hand books were sold formerly, near *Smithfield.* [P. *1736a–51.*]

Cf. Cowley, *Life and Fame,* 4–6:

> In all the *Cobwebs* of the *Schoolmans* trade,
> We no such nice *Distinction* woven see . . .

Cowley explains the simile, a traditional one, in a note: "The Distinctions of the *Schoolmen* may be likened to *Cobwebs* . . . either because of the too much fineness of the work which makes it slight, and able to catch only little Creatures; or because they take not the materials from *Nature,* but spin it out of *Themselves.*" The "kindred" cobwebs are those spun by actual spiders across books long untouched.

447. Between Verse 449 and 450 ⟨447 and 448⟩:

> *The rhyming Clowns that gladded* Shakespear's *age,*
> *No more with crambo entertain the stage.*
> *Who now in Anagrams their Patron praise*
> *Or sing their Mistress in Acrostic lays?*
> *Ev'n pulpits pleas'd with merry puns of yore;*
> *Now all are banish'd to the* Hibernian *shore!*
> *Thus leaving what was natural and fit,*
> *The current folly prov'd their ready wit;*
> *And authors thought their reputation safe,*
> *Which liv'd as long as fools were pleas'd to laugh.*
>   [P. *1736a–43, 1751.*]

EC suggest that the "whole passage was probably written after the poem was first published, since the topics seem to have been suggested by Addison's papers upon false wit in the *Spectator* of May, 1711, where [see No. 63, May 12] the anagrams, acrostics, and punning sermons of the reign of James I. are all enu-

Oft, leaving what is Natural and fit,
The *current Folly* proves the *ready Wit*,
And Authors think their Reputation safe,   450
Which lives as long as *Fools* are pleas'd to *Laugh*.
   Some valuing those of their own *Side*, or *Mind*,
Still make themselves the measure of Mankind;
Fondly we think we honour Merit then,
When we but praise *Our selves* in *Other Men*.   455
Parties in *Wit* attend on those of *State*,
And publick Faction doubles private Hate.
Pride, Malice, Folly, against *Dryden* rose,

449 the *ready*] our *ready 1711–32*.

---

merated." Addison also mentions a "Game of *Crambo*" and a "Party of *Punns*".
But the fact that the lines are to be found in the MS which was used for the 1711
edition makes EC's suggestion untenable. It is likely that Pope remembered
Cowley, *Of Wit*, st. 6:

> In which who finds out *Wit*, the same may see
> In *An'grams* and *Acrostiques Poetrie*;

or Dryden, *MacFlecknoe*, 203–6:

> Thy Genius calls theee not to purchase fame
> In keen Iambicks, but mild Anagram:
> Leave writing Plays, and chuse for thy command
> Some peaceful Province in Acrostick Land.

OED defines "crambo" as a game "in which one player gives a word or line
of verse to which each of the others has to find a rime". For a survey of the
"Modes in Wit" Pope probably had in mind in l. 447, see W. L. Ustick and
H. H. Hudson, 'Wit, "Mixt Wit," and the Bee in Amber', *Huntington Library
Bulletin*, VIII (Oct., 1935), pp. 103–130; and also E. N. Hooker, 'Pope on Wit:
The *Essay on Criticism*', in *The Seventeenth Century* (1951), pp. 225–46.
   450*f*. Cf. *To Mr. Dryden on his Religio Laici* (in *Miscellany Poems*, 1684), 30–1:

> Whose Reputation shall last as long,
> As Fops and Ladies sing the amorous Song.

   456*f*. As the succeeding couplet shows, Pope had Dryden in mind. Cf. his
letter to Wycherley of Dec. 26, 1704 (*Corr.*, I 1), where, speaking of the attacks
against Dryden, he says: "I suppose those Injuries were begun by the Violence
of Party . . ." Cf. Dryden's Prol. and Epil. to *The Loyal Brother*.
   458*f*. Warton (*The Adventurer* 63) compared Boileau, *Ep*. VII 23–5, about
Molière:

> L'Ignorance & l'Erreur à ses naissantes Pièces,
> En habits de Marquis, en robes de Comtesses,
> Venoient pour diffamer son chef-d'oeuvre nouveau.

In various Shapes of *Parsons, Criticks, Beaus*;
But *Sense* surviv'd, when *merry Jests* were past;   460
For rising Merit will *buoy up* at last.
Might he return, and bless once more our Eyes,
New *Blackmores* and new *Milbourns* must arise;

463 *Blackmores*] *Bl——s 1711; S——s 1713a–16.*
    Milbourns] *M——s 1711; M——ns 1713a–16; Milbournes
    1727–32.*

459. *Parsons, Criticks, Beaus*] The parsons were the Rev. Jeremy Collier who, in his *A Short View of the Profaneness and Immorality of the English Stage* (1698), accused Dryden of profanity, lewdness, and blasphemy, and the Rev. Luke Milbourne, whose *Notes on Dryden's Virgil* (1698) was full of tedious and carping criticisms against Dryden's tr. of Virgil's *Eclogues* and *Georgics*. Among the more important contemporary "critics" were Thomas Shadwell, who engaged in a bitter feud with Dryden in the 1680's; Elkanah Settle, who initiated an attack on Dryden in 1674; Sir Richard Blackmore, who attacked Dryden in his *A Satyr Against Wit* and in *Prince Arthur*, bk VI; Gerard Langbaine, who was hostile to Dryden in his *An Account of the English Dramatic Poets*. The "beaus" included George Villiers, Duke of Buckingham, one of the authors of *The Rehearsal* (1671), and John Wilmot, Earl of Rochester, who satirized Dryden in his *An Allusion to Horace. The 10th Satyr of the 1st Book.*
   462. Wakefield compares Dryden, *Georgics* IV 729: "But she return'd no more, to bless his longing Eyes."
   463. *Blackmores . . . Milbourns*] The two names in this context were suggested by Dryden's own words in the Pref. to the *Fables*, which concludes: "As for the rest of those who have written against me, they are such scoundrels, that they deserve not the least notice to be taken of them. B—— and M—— are only distinguished from the crowd by being remembered to their infamy. . ." Earlier in the same essay (*Essays*, II 266) Dryden had written: "lest some future Milbourne should arise. . ." Wakefield recalls Martial, VIII lvi 5:
        "Sint Maecenates, non deerunt, Flacce, Marones:
        'New *Virgils* with *Maecenas* would appear'."
Note that Pope replaced Bl[ackmore]s with S[hadwell]s in the editions from 1713–16. During this interval he was apparently on good terms with Blackmore, for he asked John Hughes, in a letter of April 19, 1714 (*Corr.*, I 218), to make his "most humble service acceptable" to Blackmore. But in 1716 Blackmore, in *Essays upon Several Subjects*, vol. I, attacked Swift as an "impious Buffoon" (p. 217), and in vol. II (1717) referred to Pope as the "godless Author" who "burlesqu'd the *First Psalm* of David in so obscene and profane a manner" (p. 270). These circumstances undoubtedly led Pope to reintroduce Blackmore's name, this time in full. This interpretation of the variant reading of this line is based

Nay shou'd great *Homer* lift his awful Head,
Zoilus again would start up from the Dead.   465
Envy will *Merit* as its *Shade* pursue,
But like a Shadow, proves the *Substance* true;
For envy'd Wit, like *Sol* Eclips'd, makes known
Th' *opposing Body's* Grossness, not its *own*.
When first that Sun too powerful Beams displays,   470
It draws up Vapours which obscure its Rays;
But ev'n those Clouds at last adorn its Way,
Reflect new Glories, and augment the Day.
    Be thou the *first* true Merit to befriend;
His Praise is lost, who stays till *All* commend;   475
Short is the Date, alas, of *Modern Rhymes*;
And 'tis but just to let 'em live *betimes*.

467 true;] too; *1711–16*.

on Ault's account of the Pope–Blackmore quarrel in *New Light on Pope* (1949), chap. xv.

  464*f*. EC cite *A.P.*, iv 195–6:

> Let mighty *Spencer* raise his reverend Head,
> *Cowley* and *Denham* start up from the dead.

  465. Zoilus, a Greek grammarian of the 3rd or 4th century B.C., known for his severe and captious criticisms of Homer. Cf. the account of him in Vitruvius, *De Architectura*, pref. to bk VII: "Insequentibus annis a Macedonia Zoilus, qui adoptavit cognomen, ut Homeromastix vocitaretur, Alexandriam venit suaque scripta contra Iliadem et Odyssean comparata regi recitavit. Ptolomaeus vero, cum animadvertisset poetarum parentem philologiaeque omnis ducem absentem vexari et, cuius ab cunctis gentibus scripta suspicerentur, ab eo vituperari, indignans nullum ei dedit responsum." Dryden, Dedic. of *Examen Poeticum* (*Essays*, II 3), says that Zoilus was never adopted into the name of critic by the ancients, and that his "successors in this age deserve no better." Cf. notes to ll. 100*ff*., 123, above.

  468–74. Cf Sheffield, *Ess. upon Poetry*, 12–14:

> True Wit is everlasting, like the Sun,
> Which though sometimes beneath a cloud retir'd,
> Breaks out again, and is by all admir'd.

  475. Cf. the saying (quoted by Erasmus, *Adagia*): "Bis dat qui cito dat." Erasmus cites Seneca, *De Beneficiis*, II i 2: "Ingratum est beneficium quod diu inter dantis manus haesit . . ."

  476. Cf. Dryden, *Abs. and Achit.*, 1 847: "Short is the date of all immoderate fame". Cf. also *Episode of Sarpedon*, 239 (p. 458, below).

No longer now that Golden Age appears,
When *Patriarch-Wits* surviv'd a *thousand Years*;
Now Length of *Fame* (our *second* Life) is lost,   480
And bare Threescore is all ev'n That can boast:
Our Sons their Fathers' *failing Language* see,
And such as *Chaucer* is, shall *Dryden* be.
So when the faithful *Pencil* has design'd

---

482 Fathers'] Father's *1711–32*; fathers *1736a–51*.

---

479. "A very elegant and pleasing allusion to the longevity of the Antedilu-
vians, as recorded in the book of Genesis" [Wakefield].

480. *our second Life*] Cf. *Temple of Fame*, 505 (vol. ii, p. 271); *Ess. on Man*, iv
237 (vol. iii i, p. 149).

480*f*. Cf. Waller, *Of English Verse*, sts. 2, 5:

> But who can hope his Lines should long
> Last in a daily changing Tongue?
> While they are new, Envy prevails;
> And as that dies, our Language fails.
> . . . . . .
> *Chaucer* his Sense can only boast
> The glory of his Numbers lost.

Cf. also Temple, *On Ancient and Modern Learning* (Spingarn, iii 63). The imper-
manent nature of the English language was a common complaint in Pope's time.
See Pope's Preface (p. 7, above). Cf. also Horace, *Ars Poet.*, 68*ff*.

481. Dennis (Hooker, i 410) pounced upon the evident exaggeration in this
line and apparently provoked Pope to attempt a change, noted thus in his MS
memorandum (see Appendix B, pp. 482–4, below): "bare threescore, wch if it
were, & threescore years is all". The words are crossed out in the memorandum.

483. *shall Dryden be*] Pope's line recalls a statement Dryden had made in connection with his "modernization" of Chaucer in Pref. to the *Fables* (*Essays*, ii
265): "Another poet, in another age, may take the same liberty with my writings." Perhaps as a result of criticism by Dennis of these lines (Hooker, i 410),
Pope attempted another version in his MS memorandum (see Appendix B,
pp. 482–4, below): "Such as Chaucer is, may *Dryden* be." The words were
subsequently crossed out.

484*ff*. Warton, *Ess. on Pope* (1806), i 149, compares Dryden, *To Sir Godfrey
Kneller*, 174–81:

> More cannot be by Mortal Art exprest;
> But venerable Age shall add the rest.
> For Time shall with his ready Pencil stand:
> Retouch your Figures, with his ripening Hand,

Some *bright Idea* of the Master's Mind,   485
Where a *new World* leaps out at his command,
And ready Nature waits upon his Hand;
When the ripe Colours *soften* and *unite*,
And sweetly *melt* into just Shade and Light,
When mellowing Years their full Perfection give,   490
And each Bold Figure just begins to *Live*;
The *treach'rous Colours* the fair Art betray,
And all the bright Creation fades away!
    Unhappy *Wit*, like most mistaken Things,
Attones not for that *Envy* which it brings.   495
In *Youth* alone its empty Praise we boast,
But soon the Short-liv'd Vanity is lost!
Like some fair *Flow'r* the early *Spring* supplies,
That gaily Blooms, but ev'n in blooming *Dies*.
What is this *Wit* which must our Cares employ?   500
The *Owner's Wife*, that *other Men* enjoy,

485 *bright*] *fair 1711–16.*
490 Years their] Time does *1711–16.*
492 the fair Art betray,] in few Years decay, *1711–16.*
495 Attones not for] Repays not half *1711.*
498 the early *Spring* supplies,] that in the *Spring* does rise, *1711–16.*
499 That] And *1711–16.*
500 which must] that does *1711*; which does *1713a–16.*

Mellow your Colours, and imbrown the Teint;
Add every Grace, which Time alone can grant:
To future Ages shall your Fame convey;
And give more Beauties, than he takes away.
492 var. In *1736a–43* Pope quotes the earlier reading in a note.
493. Pope here recalls Addison's lines on the decays wrought by time in the works of Chaucer and Spenser (*An Account of the Greatest English Poets*, 1694). Cf. particularly ll. 30–1:
But when we look too near, the shades decay,
And all the pleasing landscape fades away.
498 var. In its original form, say EC, "This line was an example both of the 'feeble expletive' and of the 'ten low words'." Pope noted the earlier reading in *1736a–43.*

Then most our *Trouble* still when most *admir'd*,
And still the more we *give*, the more *requir'd*;
Whose Fame with *Pains* we guard, but lose with *Ease*,
Sure *some* to *vex*, but never *all* to *please*;   505
'Tis what the *Vicious fear*, the *Virtuous shun*;
By *Fools* 'tis *hated*, and by *Knaves undone*!
    If *Wit* so much from *Ign'rance* undergo,
Ah let not *Learning* too commence its Foe!
Of old, those met *Rewards* who cou'd *excel*,   510
And such were *Prais'd* who but *endeavour'd well*:

502 The more his *Trouble* as the more *admir'd*; *1711*;
     'Tis most our *Trouble* when 'tis most *admir'd*; *1713a–16*;
     Still most our trouble when the most admir'd; *1717–32*;
     The most our trouble still when most admir'd; *1736a–43*.
503–4 Where *wanted*, scorn'd, and envy'd where *acquir'd*;
     Maintain'd with *Pains*, but forfeited with *Ease*; *1711*;
     The more we *give*, the more is still *requir'd*:
     The Fame with Pains we gain, but lose with ease;
                                  1713a–43.
508 If *Wit* so much] Too much does *Wit 1711–16*.
510 met] found *1711*.   511 who] as *1713a–16*.

502–4. These lines gave Pope much trouble. They were attacked (as they stood in the first edn) by Dennis (Hooker, I 411): ". . . how can Wit be scorn'd where it is not? Is not this a Figure frequently employ'd in *Hibernian* Land?" Pope admitted the "palpable hit" and wrote in the MS memorandum (see Appendix B, pp. 482–4, below): "where wanted scornd—of Wit (yᵉ 2 lines left out—to be alterd—See Dennis p. 20". See Intro., pp. 205–7, above.

509. In his *Satyr against Wit* Sir R. Blackmore tried to set learning in opposition to wit:

        The *Mob* of Wits is up to storm the Town,
        To pull all Virtue and right Reason down. . .
        Against all Springs of Learning they declare. . .
        For next to Virtue, Learning they abhor. . .
        Wit does our Schools and Colleges invade,
        And has of Letters vast Destruction made.

510*f.* EC compare Dryden, *Prologue, To the University of Oxford*, 27–8:
        Be kind to Wit, which but endeavours well,
        And, where you judge, presumes not to excel.

Tho' *Triumphs* were to *Gen'rals* only due,
Crowns were reserv'd to grace the *Soldiers* too.
Now, they who reach *Parnassus'* lofty Crown,
Employ their Pains to spurn some others down;   515
And while Self-Love each jealous Writer rules,
Contending Wits become the *Sport of Fools*:
But still the *Worst* with most Regret commend,
For each *Ill Author* is as bad a *Friend*.
To what base Ends, and by what abject Ways,   520
Are Mortals urg'd thro' *Sacred Lust of Praise*!

514 they who] those that *1711*.   519 For] And *1711*.
521 thro'] by *1711–16*.   *Praise*!] *Praise*? *1711–16*.

513–15. *Crowns*] Crowns of various kinds were awarded, at the time of a general's triumph, to soldiers who had distinguished themselves in the field: the *corona civica* to one who had saved a fellow-soldier's life, the golden *corona muralis* to the first man to storm an enemy wall, and the golden *corona castrensis* or *vallaris* for mounting an enemy wall, or for penetration into an enemy camp. Cf. Aulus Gellius, *Noctes Atticae*, v vi 16–17. Pope seems to apply the ideas of both the *corona civica* and the *corona muralis* to poets in an almost literal (and highly ironic) way in ll. 514 *f*.: those poets who scale the heights of Parnassus gain its "crown"; but then, instead of saving or aiding (like soldiers in an assault) those behind them, they rather kick them down the heights.

514–23. EC compare *A.P.*, IV 110–21:

> But above all, base Jealousies avoid,
> In which detracting Poets are employ'd:
> A noble Wit dares lib'rally commend;
> And scorns to grudge at his deserving Friend.
> Base Rivals, who true Wit and Merit hate,
> Caballing still against it with the Great,
> Maliciously aspire to gain Renown
> By standing up, and pulling others down.
> Never debase your self by Treacherous ways,
> Nor by such abject methods seek for praise:
> Let not your only bus'ness be to write;
> Be Virtuous, Just, and in your Friends delight.

521*f*. *Sacred Lust . . . dire a Thirst*] EC cite Virgil, *Aen.*, III 56–7, "quid non mortalia pectora cogis, / auri sacra fames", and *Georgics* I 37: "nec tibi regnandi veniat tam dira cupido". The second of these examples is tr. by Dryden, l. 53, as "Nor let so dire a thirst of empire move." The latinism *sacred* means *accursed*. Cf. *Temple of Fame*, 522 (vol. II, p. 272), and *Statius*, 178 (p. 417, below).

Ah ne'er so *dire* a *Thirst of Glory* boast,
Nor in the *Critick* let the *Man* be lost!
Good-Nature and *Good-Sense* must ever join;
To Err is *Humane*; to Forgive, *Divine*.   525
    But if in Noble Minds some Dregs remain,
Not yet purg'd off, of Spleen and sow'r Disdain,
Discharge that Rage on more Provoking Crimes,
Nor fear a Dearth in these Flagitious Times.
No Pardon vile *Obscenity* should find,   530
Tho' *Wit* and *Art* conspire to move your Mind;
But *Dulness* with *Obscenity* must prove
As Shameful sure as *Impotence* in *Love*.
In the fat Age of Pleasure, Wealth, and Ease,
Sprung the rank Weed, and thriv'd with large Increase;

---

526 *No new paragraph 1711–22b.*

---

524. Cf. Dryden, *A Disc. conc. . . . Sat.* (*Essays*, ii 17): "Good sense and good nature are never separated, though the ignorant world has thought otherwise."

525. *Humane*] A common earlier spelling of "human". OED cites this line and says: "Belonging or relative to man as distinguished from God or superhuman beings; pertaining to the sphere or faculties of man (with implication of limitation or inferiority)."

530*f.* Wakefield compares Waller, *Upon the Earl of Roscommon's Translation of Horace*, 17–18:

> Chaste moral writing we may learn from hence;
> Neglect of which no Wit can recompence.

Sheffield, in his *Ess. upon Poetry*, 80*ff.*, rebuked the taste for "Bawdry barefac'd, that poor pretence to Wit", in the age of Charles II, and Roscommon continued the campaign against indecency in *Ess. on Tr. Verse*, saying (ll. 113–14):

> *Immodest words* admit of no defence,
> For want of *Decency* is want of *Sense*.

See Spingarn, i xlviii.

535. *rank Weed*] Dryden, *Threnodia Augustalis*, 354, speaks of England as being "With rank Geneva weeds run o'er", referring to Calvinism. Bowles quotes *Hamlet*, i v 32: "And duller shouldst thou be than the fat weed". Cf. also, with special reference to obscenity and licence, iii iv 151–2: "And do not spread the compost on the weeds / To make them ranker." Cf. also Roscommon, *Ess. on Tr. Verse*, 66: "*rank Pedantick Weeds*".

L

When *Love* was all an easie Monarch's Care;   536
Seldom at *Council*, never in a *War*:
Jilts rul'd the State, and Statesmen *Farces* writ;
Nay *Wits* had *Pensions*, and *young Lords* had *Wit*:

536. *easie Monarch's*] Charles II. Dryden, Epil. to Fletcher's *The Pilgrim*, 5*ff.*, presents a similar view of the responsibility of the Court:
> But sure, a banish'd court, with lewdness fraught,
> The seeds of open vice, returning, brought . . .
> Thus did the thriving malady prevail,
> The court its head, the poets but the tail.

537. *never in a War*] Charles commanded an army which was defeated at the Battle of Worcester, Sept. 3, 1651. His behaviour in this battle was celebrated by Dryden in these terms (*Astræa Redux*, 73–4):
> For when his early valor Heav'n had cross'd,
> And all at Worc'ster but the honor lost . . .

538. *Jilts rul'd the State*] A "jilt" here means a "kept mistress" (OED). Although Charles II had many mistresses, two only exerted any great influence on his policies: Barbara Villiers (afterwards Palmer), Lady Castlemaine, Duchess of Cleveland, and Louise de Kéroualle, Duchess of Portsmouth. The former worked against Clarendon, the latter for Louis XIV's interests (see *From the Restoration to the Death of William III*, ed. Richard Lodge, 1910, vol. XII of *Polit. Hist. Eng.*, pp. 65, 106).

Statesmen Farces writ] The allusion is to the Duke of Buckingham's part in the writing of *The Rehearsal* (1671). DNB (s.v. Villiers) relates the amusing anecdote in which Louis XIV is said to have asked his minister Colbert "when he would write him a play". When Colbert excused "his want of talents that way to serve him, the king told him he would be out of fashion, for the chief minister of state in England had gotten a great deal of honour by writing a farce."

539. *Wits had Pensions*] Dennis pointed out (Hooker, 1 413) that this was a somewhat unfortunate remark: "*Butler* was starv'd at the same time that the King had his Book in his Pocket. Another great Wit [Wycherley] lay seven Years in Prison for an inconsiderable Debt, and *Otway* dar'd not to shew his Head for fear of the same Fate."

young Lords had Wit] In *A Large Account of the Taste in Poetry, and the Causes of the Degeneracy of It* (1702), Dennis had spoken (Hooker, 1 279) of "all those men of extraordinary parts, who were the Ornaments of that Court [Charles II's]; as the late Duke of *Buckingham*, my Lord *Normanby*, my Lord *Dorset*, my late Lord *Rochester*, Sir *Charles Sidley* . . ." Dennis had maintained that the taste of the public had degenerated, at least as far as comedy and tragedy were concerned, since the time of Charles II. He seems to come to the defence of Charles's Court in his remark upon this line (Hooker, 1 413): "If the looking favourably upon young Persons of Quality who had Wit, may be imputed as Scandal to the Court of King *Charles* the Second, that Court was certainly the most scandalous one in

The Fair sate panting at a *Courtier's Play*,   540
And not a Mask went *un-improv'd* away:
The modest Fan was lifted up no more,
And Virgins *smil'd* at what they *blush'd* before—

Europe." Further on (Hooker, 1 414) Dennis teaches Pope another lesson: "I hope, I may without offence, gently put young Mr. *Bays* in mind, that the Subordination which is absolutely necessary to the Government of the World requires that Respect should be paid to Persons of Quality. . . For I know very few People of Quality who have applied themselves to Poetry, who have not succeeded. . ." In his letter to Caryll of June 25, 1711 (*Corr.*, 1 123), Pope alludes to this remark of Dennis. Speaking of Lord Petre, who was to become the "Baron" of *The Rape of the Lock*, he says: "I hope my lord will not, from what Mr Dennis is pleased to say, look upon me as a despiser of Men of Quality." Pope concludes by calling Lord Petre "one of those young lords that have wit in our days!"

540. *a Courtier's Play*] A reference to such courtiers as Sir Charles Sedley, the undoubted author of at least three plays (see *Poetical and Dramatic Works*, ed. V. de S. Pinto, 1928, 1 xxx): *The Mulberry Garden* (1668), *Antony and Cleopatra* (1677), and *Bellamira* (1687). Such a play as the last of these might be supposed to have caused the "Fair" to breathe more quickly. In view of the notorious amount of dalliance between the sexes in the theatrical audiences of the Restoration period, there may be another sense intended for *play*: "amorous disport" (OED). See next note.

541. *Mask* here means a woman wearing one of the masks which came into fashion during the reign of Charles II. Cf. Pepys, June 12, 1663: ". . . when the House began to fill she [Lady Mary Cromwell] put on her vizard, and so kept it on all the play: which of late is become a great fashion among the ladies, which hides their whole face. So to the Exchange, to buy things with my wife; among others, a vizard for herself." While the mask was worn by ladies of quality immediately after the Restoration, a few years later it apparently was given over, owing to its convenience for intrigue, to women of the town, and it soon came to pass that there was "no commoner term for a whore than 'vizard-mask' or 'mask' " (M. Summers, *The Restoration Theatre*, 1934, p. 85). The "masks" contributed greatly to violence and indecency among the audiences in the theatres, and shortly after the turn of the century (on Jan. 17, 1704), as part of the reaction to abuses associated with the stage, Queen Anne issued an edict which "forbade and straitly banned for the future any use of vizard masks by the audiences" in the theatres (Summers, p. 90).

The sense of "un-improv'd" in Pope's line seems ambiguous. If by "mask" the poet refers to harlots who frequented the theatres, then the word perhaps suggests that they "profited" from a play in a way not designed by the author. Perhaps the inference is that no woman could leave the theatre uninstructed in some kind of viciousness.

The following Licence of a Foreign Reign
Did all the Dregs of bold *Socinus* drain;   545
Then Unbelieving Priests reform'd the Nation,

545 *Add. 1711–32:*
      Then *first* the *Belgian Morals* were extoll'd;
      We their *Religion* had, and they our *Gold*:

---

544. The "Foreign Reign" is that of William III. This was clearer in the 1711 edn (cf. *n* to l. 545 var.). In the context the word "Licence" may admit of both general and particular reference. In general, it may glance at the policy of increased toleration, especially toward the Nonconformists, which characterized William's reign. In 1689 was passed the Toleration Act, which allowed Nonconformists to have their own places of worship provided they believed in the Trinity, met with unlocked doors, and certified their places of meeting with proper authorities. The more particular reference of the line may be to the fact that the Licensing Act of 1663 was allowed to lapse, thereby permitting the publication of books Pope and others would regard as heretical and blasphemous. Cf. G. M. Trevelyan, *English Social History* (1946), p. 262: "The first Licensing Act, passed in 1663 by the Cavalier Parliament, aimed at preventing the publication of seditious and heretical works—meaning in the first instance Roundhead and Puritan writings. The Act was periodically renewed, except during the period of the Whig Houses of Commons and the years without a Parliament that followed (1679–85). Revived by the Parliament of James II, the Licensing Act was finally allowed to expire in the more liberal age ushered in by the Revolution. After 1696 an Englishman was permitted to print and publish whatever he chose, without consulting any authority in Church or State; only he could be called to account for it on a charge of libel or sedition before a jury of his countrymen." Compare with Pope's lines the following charge from *The Belgic Heroe Unmasked* (in *Miscellaneous Works . . . by . . . George, Late Duke of Buckingham*, 1704), pp. 252–3: "To the eternal Honour of his [William's] Reign be it observ'd, All the *Socinian* Treatises, that stole into the World in the late accursed times of Licentiousness and Disorder, were fairly reprinted, and these, together with the modern Improvements of *Deism*, sold in the Face of the Sun, without the least check or discountenance from any at the Helm. 'Twas come to that pitch at last, that a Man might better call the Divinity of our Saviour into question, than the Legality of the Revolution. . ."

545. *bold Socinus*] Laelius Socinus (Lelio Sozzini, 1525–62) conceived the doctrine which was completed and systematized by his nephew, Fausto Sozzini (1539–1604). Socinians rejected the doctrines of the divinity of Christ and of the atonement or satisfaction for sin by Christ. Socinianism made considerable progress in England during the latter part of the 17th century, developing into English Unitarianism. The spread of Socinian ideas inspired fear and outrage among Englishmen of a conservative and high-church point of view, and also

inspired, in part, the great Trinitarian controversy of the last decade of the 17th century. The "press teemed" at this time "with pamphlets setting forth with more or less ability the usual arguments against the Trinity" (C. J. Abbey and J. H. Overton, *The English Church in the Eighteenth Century*, 1878, I 488). Socinianism was, in addition, "an influential factor in the rise of English Latitudinarianism" (H. J. McLachlan, *Socinianism in Seventeenth-Century England*, 1951, p. 338), and the two were associated by their opponents, including Pope. The aversion aroused by the two movements among conservative members of the Church of England is easily illustrated. Thus the famous *Letter to a Convocation Man* (1697) p. 6: "Indeed, to be plain, there seems to be an universal Conspiracy amongst a sort of Men, under the Style of Deists, Socinians, Latitudinarians, Deniers of Mysteries, and pretending Explainers of them, to undermine and overthrow the Catholick Faith." And thus the even more famous sermon in which Henry Sacheverell attacked those within the Church whom he regarded as too liberal in their theology and politics and for which he was impeached (*The Perils of False Brethren, both in Church, and State*, 1709, pp. 14–15): "These FALSE BRETHREN in Our *Government*, do not *Singly* and in *Private* spread their *Poyson*, but . . . are suffer'd to combine into *Bodies*, and *Seminaries*, wherein *Atheism*, *Deism*, *Tritheism*, *Socinianism*, with all the *Hellish Principles* of *Fanaticism*, *Regicide*, and *Anarchy*, are openly *Profess'd*, and *Taught*, to *Corrupt* and *Debauch* the *Youth* of the *Nation*. . . Certainly the *Toleration* was never intended to *Indulge*, and *Cherish* such *Monsters*, in our Bosom. . ." The epithet "bold" had been applied to Socinians by Dryden, *Religio Laici*, 311.

545. *The Author has omitted two lines which stood here, as containing a* National Reflection, *which in his stricter judgment he could not but disapprove, on any People whatever. [P. 1736a–51.]*

545 var. "Belgian" here designates the Netherlands. The lines recall the traditional trade rivalry between the Dutch and English, and suggest that an unfavourable balance of trade has been established whereby good English wealth is exchanged for the kind of Dutch latitudinarianism so abhorred by Pope and many others of his age. Pope also seems to point to the Netherlands as the source of the spreading Socinianism in 17th-century England (see the chapter entitled 'Holland, the Gateway for Socinianism into England', in McLachlan, *Socinianism in Seventeenth-Century England*). In addition, Pope's lines reflect the feeling which existed among many Englishmen that William III unduly favoured and rewarded an inner circle of Dutch advisers and favourites, among them Willem Bentinck, whom he made Duke of Portland, and Arnold Joost van Keppel, whom he made Earl of Albemarle. Large grants of land by the king to such favourites were protested by Parliament. Partisan arguments were advanced that William's closest political supporters had "squandered great sums which might have been used for paying the expenses of the war" with France (G. N. Clark, *The Later Stuarts*, 1949, p. 182).

546. *Unbelieving Priests*] In this line, according to Pope's contemporary John Jortin (*Tracts, Philological, Critical, and Miscellaneous*, 1790, II 523), the poet had Gilbert Burnet "in view, and his History of the Reformation". Burnet (1643–

And taught more *Pleasant* Methods of Salvation;
Where Heav'ns Free Subjects might their *Rights* dispute,
Lest God himself shou'd seem too *Absolute*.
Pulpits their *Sacred Satire* learn'd to spare,   550

1715) was Bishop of Salisbury, an active supporter of William III, an opponent of Jacobites and Roman Catholics, and tolerant towards nonjurors and presbyterians. He was the most prominent Latitudinarian, and charges of Socinianism were often made against him. "Reforming the nation" may be a glance, as Jortin suggests, at his *History of the Reformation of the Church of England*. Charges of distortion were brought against the work, and Pope might therefore claim that Burnet had "reformed" history. Or the line may refer to the active part Burnet played in Whig politics; he was an important figure in the negotiations which led William to the English throne. Here again, he could be said to have "reform'd the Nation", that is, to have replaced the strongly Catholic flavour of the reign of James II with the staunch Protestantism of William. Another "Unbelieving Priest" may have been John Tillotson (1630–94), Archbishop of Canterbury. Tillotson and Burnet were frequently linked together as "freethinkers", atheists, Socinians (cf. Abbey and Overton, *The English Church in the Eighteenth Century*, 1878, I 300–1). Of Pope's animus Jortin remarks (II 522): ". . . this ingenious and religious author [Pope] seems to have had two particular antipathies; one to grammatical and verbal criticism, the other to false doctrine and heresy. . . To the second, we will impute his pious zeal against those divines of King William's time, whom he supposed to be infected with the Infidel, or the Socinian, or the Latitudinarian spirit. . ." Pope's knowledge of the complex religious issues of the late 17th century is suggested by his letter to Atterbury of Nov. 20, 1717 (*Corr.*, I 453–4): "Your Lordship has formerly advis'd me to read the best controversies between the Churches. Shall I tell you a secret? I did so at fourteen years old, (for I loved reading, and my father had no other books) there was a collection of all that had been written on both sides in the reign of King James the second: I warm'd my head with them, and the consequence was, that I found my self a Papist and a Protestant by turns, according to the last book I read."

547. *more Pleasant Methods*] The allusion, according to Jortin (*Tracts*, II 523), was to Dr (later Bishop) White Kennett, who "was accused of having said, in a funeral sermon on some nobleman, that converted sinners, if they were men of parts, repented more speedily and effectually than dull rascals". Jortin refers to Kennett's *Sermon Preach'd at the Funeral Of the Right Noble William Duke of Devonshire . . . On Friday Septemb. 5th. MDCCVII* (1708), but his comment misses the point of Pope's jibe. The verse is directed specifically toward that portion of the sermon which seemed to look too complacently upon a death-bed repentance after a life of vice. The sermon was the more susceptible to such a construction because Kennett ignored the notorious sins of Devonshire's life and seemed to imply that men of quality were more apt to repent at death than men

of lesser birth. It is possible to see the sermon as being innocent of the charges made against it, but portions of its argument are so ineptly presented as to invite attack. A portion of the famous sermon for which Henry Sacheverell was impeached (*The Perils of False Brethren*, 1709, p. 10) seems aimed at Kennett's sermon, and may have provided the inspiration for Pope's line: "If to *Flatter* both the *Dead* and the *Living* in their *Vices*, and to tell the World, that if they have *Wit*, and *Money* enough they need no *Repentance*, and that only *Fools* and *Beggers* can be *Damn'd*; If these, I say, are the *Modish*, and Fashionable *Criterions* of a *True-Church-Man*, God deliver *Us All from such* FALSE BRETHREN."

548*f*. Pope means, as West pointed out, that the "unbelieving priests", usually Whigs in their politics, "taught that the government of God, like that of the king, was a limited, not an absolute monarchy, and that men were free to yield or to withhold their allegiance". Pope's couplet thus bears directly on contemporary disputes over the doctrines of divine right and of non-resistance and passive obedience to the "Supreme Power". The issues were complicated by the fact that from a High Church or "Tory" point of view the "Supreme Power" was not merely the state power, but was rather the state power as an embodiment of the Divine Will. Disputes with the sovereign over the rights of subjects could thus be seen as disputes with God. See Sacheverell's famous sermon (*The Perils of False Brethren*, p. 12): "But this *Fundamental Doctrin* [of absolute, unconditional obedience to the Supreme Power (the state presumably here, though at his trial Sacheverell maintained that he intended the "Supreme Power" in this passage to refer to God) in all things lawful], notwithstanding it's *Divine Sanction* in the *Express Command* of *God* in *Scripture*, and without which, it is impossible any *Government* of any *Kind*, or *Denomination* in the World, should *subsist* with Safety . . . is now, it seems, quite *Exploded*, and *Redicul'd* out of Countenance, as an *Unfashionable*, *Superannuated*, nay . . . as a *Dangerous Tenet*, utterly *Inconsistent* with the *Right Liberty*, and *Property* of the PEOPLE; who as our *New Preachers*, and *New Politicians* teach us, (I suppose by a *New*, and *Unheard* of *Gospel*, as well as *Laws*) have in Contradiction to *Both*, the *Power* Invested in *Them*, the Fountain and *Original* of it, to *Cancel* their *Allegiance* at pleasure, and call their *Sovereign* to account for *High Treason* against his *Supream Subjects*, forsooth! nay to *Dethrone*, and *Murder* Him for a Criminal, as they did the *Royal Martyr* by a *Judiciary* Sentence." Cf. also Sacheverell's dedication of the sermon to the Lord Mayor of London: "*Moses*, and the *Prophets*, may with *Christ*, and his *Apostles*, be *Banish'd* Our *Synagogues*, when Truth must be Oppress'd by *Number*, and *Noise*, and *Rebellious Appeals* to the *People*, as the only Judges of *Right*, and *Wrong*, and *Dernier Resort* of *Justice*, and *Dominion*."

550–1. In his funeral sermon (see l. 547*n*) Kennett had ignored the obvious sins of the first Duke of Devonshire and had closed with a eulogy of the deceased Duke's successor. As the DNB observes, "Kennett's subsequent preferment [he was installed in the deanery of Peterborough on Feb. 21, 1707–8] was naturally connected by his enemies with the strain of adulatory reference to the second duke with which the sermon concludes." Cf. Pope's allusion to the second Duke of Devonshire in *Ep.* II ii 220–5 (vol. IV, p. 181, l. 220*n*).

And Vice *admir'd* to find a *Flatt'rer there*!
Encourag'd thus, Witt's *Titans* brav'd the Skies,
And the Press groan'd with Licenc'd *Blasphemies*—
These Monsters, Criticks! with your Darts engage,
Here point your Thunder, and exhaust your Rage!   555
Yet shun their Fault, who, *Scandalously nice*,
Will needs *mistake* an Author *into Vice*;
All seems Infected that th' Infected spy,
As all looks yellow to the Jaundic'd Eye.

LEARN then what MORALS Criticks ought to show,
For 'tis but *half* a *Judge's Task*, to *Know*.   561

---

552. *Witt's Titans*] The allusion is to the deistic writers, who at times passed for atheists. Cf. James Drake, *To Dr. Garth* (in *Commendatory Verses on the Author of the Two Arthurs*, 1700, pp. 20–1), 10: "Whose tow'ring Non-sense braves the very Skies."

553. *Licenc'd Blasphemies*] The Commons having refused in 1695 to renew the licensing Act of 1663, authors were free to publish anything they chose. As a result Pope could say that deistical and Socinian writings, which he would regard as blasphemous, were condoned, or "licenc'd" by the administration of William III. One of the most famous and controversial of such writings, published in 1696, was Toland's *Christianity not Mysterious: or, A Treatise Shewing, That there is nothing in the Gospel Contrary to Reason, Nor Above it: And that no Christian Doctrine can be properly call'd a Mystery*. The Licensing Act had limited the number of master-printers in England to twenty, and had restricted printing presses to the cities of London, Oxford, and Cambridge. When Pope states that the "Press groan'd" with heterodox publications, he refers to the great increase in printing presses and in printed matter which occurred when restrictions were lifted. See l. 544n.

557. *mistake an Author*] OED cites this couplet: "To misunderstand the meaning of (a person); to attach a wrong meaning to the sayings or doings of (a person)." Pope may have recalled Collier's attacks on Dryden. Cf. Dryden, Pref. to the *Fables* (*Essays*, II 272): ". . . in many places he has perverted my meaning by his glosses, and interpreted my words into blasphemy and bawdry, of which they were not guilty."

559. *As all looks yellow*] Wakefield cites Dryden, Dedic. of *Examen Poeticum* (*Essays*, II 2): "There is too often a jaundice in the eyes of great men; they see not those whom they raise in the same colours with other men. All whom they affect look golden to them, when the gilding is only in their own distempered sight." EC compare Lucretius, IV 332–3: "lurida praeterea fiunt quaecumque tuentur / arquati"; and Creech's tr.:

'Tis not enough, Taste, Judgment, Learning, join;
In all you speak, let Truth and Candor shine:
That not alone what to your *Sense* is due,
All may allow; but seek your *Friendship* too.   565
 Be *silent* always when you *doubt* your Sense;
And *speak*, tho' *sure*, with *seeming Diffidence*:
Some positive persisting Fops we know,
Who, if *once wrong*, will needs be *always so*;
But you, with Pleasure own your Errors past,   570
And make each Day a *Critick* on the last.
 'Tis not enough your Counsel still be *true*,

562 Taste . . . join;] Wit, Art, and Learning join; *1711–43*.
564 *Sense* is] *Judgment's 1711–43*.
567 *Speak* when you're *sure*, yet speak with *Diffidence*; *1711*.
569 Who,] That, *1711–43*.

  Besides, whatever *Jaundice* Eyes do view,
  Look pale as well as those, and yellow too.

 562. var. The reason for the change seems clear: wit (inspiration) and art apply more to the poet; taste and judgment more to the critic. But having introduced the word *judgment* Pope replaced the same word in l. 564 by *sense*. He does not seem to have been troubled about the use of *sense* two lines farther on, but in a new paragraph.

 563. *Candor*] Here probably means "sweetness of temper, openness or kindness of mind". See M. C. Randolph, '"Candour" in xviiith-Century Satire', *RES*, xx (1944), pp. 45–62.

 567 var. Dennis (Hooker, I 411) objected to this line in the first edn: "But what can be more wrong or more absurd than the latter Verse of the Couplet? . . . Now I should think that when a man is sure, 'tis his Duty to speak with a modest Assurance; since in doing otherwise he betrays the Truth, especially when he speaks to those who are guided more by Imagination than they are by Judgment. . ." In his MS memorandum (see Appendix B, pp. 482–4, below) Pope copied the couplet and wrote in the margin: "Dennis p. 21. alter y[e] Inconsi[stenc]y".

 571. *a Critick on the last*] That is, a *criticism*. Wakefield compares *A.P.*, I 183–4:
  The publick Censure for your Writings fear,
  And to your self be Critic most severe.
Cf. Pope's letter to Cromwell of July 20, 1710 (*Corr.*, I 92): ". . . the more a man advances in understanding, he becomes the more every day a critic upon himself".

> *Blunt Truths* more Mischief than *nice Falshoods* do;
> Men must be *taught* as if you taught them *not*;
> And Things *unknown* propos'd as Things *forgot*:   575
> Without *Good Breeding, Truth* is disapprov'd;
> *That* only makes *Superior* Sense *belov'd*.
>   Be Niggards of Advice on no Pretence;
> For the *worst Avarice* is that of *Sense*:
> With mean Complacence ne'er betray your Trust,   580
> Nor be so *Civil* as to prove *Unjust*;
> Fear not the Anger of the Wise to raise;
> Those best can *bear Reproof*, who *merit Praise*.
>   'Twere well, might Criticks still this Freedom take;
> But *Appius* reddens at each Word you speak,   585
> And *stares, Tremendous*! with a *threatning Eye*,

573 Mischief] mischiefs *1727–32*.
575 *unknown*] *ne'er known 1711–16*.
576 disapprov'd;] not approv'd, *1711–16*.

576. *Good Breeding*] Cf. *n* to l. 640, below.
586. *This picture was taken to himself by* John Dennis, *a furious old Critic by profession, who, upon no other provocation, wrote against this Essay and its author, in a manner perfectly lunatic: For, as to the mention made of him in ver. 270. he took it as a Compliment, and said it was treacherously meant to cause him to overlook this* Abuse *of his* Person. [P. *1744–51*.]
Pope applied to Dennis the name of one of the characters in his tragedy *Appius and Virginia* (Drury Lane, Feb. 5, 1709), who was as sensitive to criticism as his creator (*N & Q*, N.S., VII (Aug., 1960), pp. 292–4). The play was withdrawn after a run of four nights, a failure which made Pope's allusion to Appius all the more stinging. In his suggestion that Dennis wrote in a "lunatic" manner against the *Essay* Pope appears to be exploiting further an idea he had treated in *The Narrative of Dr. Robert Norris, Concerning the strange and deplorable frenzy of Mr. John Dennis* (1713).
586. *stares, Tremendous!*] EC note that the "stare was one of [Dennis's] characteristics" and quote Steele (*The Theatre* 12, Feb. 9, 1719–20): ". . . he starts, stares, and looks round him at every promotion, or rather jerk of his person forward." The epithet "tremendous" also had peculiar propriety, for Dennis's fondness for the word had already inspired satiric comment. T. Cheek, in his Prol. to Boyer's *Achilles* (1700), states that Boyer's muse, unlike that of Dennis, "in Nature's Majesty appears, / She has no Sounds *Tremendous* to the Ears." EC note the remark by the author (perhaps Gildon) of *A Comparison Between the Two*

Like some *fierce Tyrant* in *Old Tapestry*!
Fear most to tax an *Honourable* Fool,
Whose Right it is, *uncensur'd* to be dull;
Such without *Wit* are Poets when they please,   590
As without *Learning* they can take *Degrees*.
Leave dang'rous *Truths* to unsuccessful *Satyrs*,
And *Flattery* to fulsome *Dedicators*,
Whom, when they *Praise*, the World believes no more,
Than when they promise to give *Scribling* o'er.   595

588 *New paragraph 1727–32.*

Stages (1702), p. 37, that very few persons at the time knew what to make of Dennis's *Iphigenia*, "tho' there were many TREMENDOUS things in't; but if there be any thing of Tragedy in't it lies in that word, for he is so fond of it, he had rather use it in every Page, than slay his belov'd *Iphigenia*." In *Three Hours after Marriage* (1717), Pope, Gay, and Arbuthnot introduced Dennis as Sir Tremendous, "the greatest *Critick* of our Age".

587. *in Old Tapestry*] Wakefield compares Donne, *Satyre* IIII, 225–6: "And though his face be as ill / As theirs, which in old hangings whip Christ". According to Dennis himself it was the personal allusion in these lines of Pope which drove him to publish his *Reflections Critical and Satyrical, Upon . . . An Essay Upon Criticism* (Hooker, 1 396).

588*ff*. Cf. Roscommon's tr. of ll. 382–4 of Horace's *Ars Poet.* (cited in the *n* to ll. 420–23, above):

> Some thinking that th'Omnipotence of Wealth
> Can turn them into Poets when they please.

588–91. *Honourable . . . Degrees*] Degrees could be conferred upon "privy councillors, bishops, peers, and the sons of peers without requiring them to fulfil any of the conditions of time, exercises or examination" imposed upon other candidates. In 1578 this privilege had been extended to "persons related to the sovereign by consanguinity or affinity, provided they were such as were commonly styled 'honourable personages', and to the eldest sons of such persons" (D. A. Winstanley, *Unreformed Cambridge*, 1935, p. 79). The crown could issue letters mandatory for a degree to be granted to unqualified persons, and in the reign of Charles II it seems that such degrees were "more frequently granted than they ever had been before" (Winstanley, *The University of Cambridge in the Eighteenth Century*, 1922, p. 160).

593. *fulsome Dedicators*] Those whose dedications were little more than servile appeals for patronage. As Beljame (*Le Public et les Hommes de Lettres en Angleterre au Dix-huitième Siècle*, 1883) has shown, Pope was the first man of letters to achieve financial independence as a result of the sale of his work through publishers.

'Tis best sometimes your Censure to restrain,
And *charitably* let the Dull be *vain*:
Your Silence there is better than your *Spite*,
For who can *rail* so long as they can *write*?
Still humming on, their drowzy Course they keep,   600
And *lash'd* so long, like *Tops*, are lash'd *asleep*.
False Steps but help them to renew the Race,
As after *Stumbling*, Jades will *mend* their Pace.
What Crouds of these, impenitently bold,
In *Sounds* and jingling *Syllables* grown old,   605
Still *run on* Poets in a raging Vein,
Ev'n to the Dregs and *Squeezings* of the *Brain*;
Strain out the last, dull droppings of their Sense,
And Rhyme with all the *Rage* of *Impotence*!

597 the Dull] dull Fools *1711*.   600 drowzy] old dull *1711*.
606 raging] frantick *1713b–16*.

---

599. *who can rail*] EC compare Sheffield, *Ess. upon Satire*, 71: "But who can rail so long as he can sleep?"

601. *are lash'd asleep*] EC compare the *Epil. written by a Person of Honour* to Dryden's *Secret Love*, 38–41:

> But 'tother day I heard this Rhyming Fop
> Say Criticks were the Whips, and he the Top;
> For, as a Top spins best the more you baste her,
> So ev'ry lash you give, he writes the faster.

Cf. this passage near the conclusion of Congreve's *The Old Bachelor*: "Should he seem to rouse, 'tis but well lashing him, and he will sleep like a Top." According to OED (s.v. *sleep*, v., 3 c), "A top sleeps when it moves with such velocity, and spins so smoothly, that its motion is imperceptible."

603. *mend their Pace*] Travel faster (OED, s.v. *mend*).

607*f*. Cf. Oldham, *Satyrs upon the Jesuits*, II 25: "With all the *dregs*, and *squeesings* of his rage." Wakefield cites Dryden, *Aureng-Zebe*, II i 230: "The dregs and droppings of enervate Love."

609. *Rage of Impotence*] Warton, Bowles, and EC suggest that Pope was alluding to Wycherley in these lines. For the image, cf. Dryden, Epil. to the First Part of *The Conq. of Gran.*, 14–16:

> But elder wits are like old Lovers curst;
> Who, when the vigor of their youth is spent,
> Still grow more fond as they grow impotent.

Such shameless *Bards* we have; and yet 'tis true,   610
There are as mad, abandon'd *Criticks* too.
The Bookful Blockhead, ignorantly read,
With *Loads* of *Learned Lumber* in his Head,
With his own Tongue still edifies his Ears,
And always *List'ning to Himself* appears.   615
All Books he reads, and all he reads assails,
From *Dryden*'s *Fables* down to *Durfey*'s *Tales*.
With *him*, most Authors steal their Works, or buy;
Garth did not write his own *Dispensary*.
Name a new *Play*, and *he's* the Poet's *Friend*,   620
Nay show'd his Faults—but when wou'd Poets mend?

617 *Durfey*'s] *D——y*'s *1711–22b*.

Wakefield cites Virgil, *Georgics* III 99: "ut quondam in stipulis magnus sine viribus ignis, / incassum furit"; and adds: "The expression is happy: for *rage*, though violent, is the result of *imbecility*, and of incapacity to govern the mind. Hence *impotentia* in the Latin . . . means indiscriminately, *weakness* or *impetuosity*."

612. *The Bookful Blockhead*] *Nihil pejus est iis, qui paullum aliquid ultra primas litteras progressi, falsam sibi scientiæ persuasionem induerunt: Nam & cedere præcipiendi peritis indignantur, & velut jure quodam potestatis, quo ferè hoc hominum genus intumescit, imperiosi, atque interim sævientes, Stultitiam suam perdocent.* Quintil. lib. i. ch. i ⟨8⟩. [P. *1711–16*.]

613. *Lumber*] "Useless or cumbrous material" (OED).

617. *Durfey's Tales*] Cf. Blackmore, *A Satyr Against Wit*, 180: "From *D——fy*'s, or from Poet *D——n—*'s Plays." In his *Fables* (1700), Dryden renovated certain tales of Ovid, Boccaccio, and Chaucer. Thomas D'Urfey (1653–1723) published his *Tales Tragical and Comical* in 1704 and his *Stories, Moral and Comical* in 1706. D'Urfey's tales were adaptations of continental writings, "with large Additions and Embellishments".

619. A common slander at that time in prejudice of that deserving author. Our poet did him this justice, when that slander most prevail'd; and it is now (perhaps the sooner for this very verse) dead and forgotten. [P. *1744–51*.]

This may allude to an accusation perhaps brought against Garth that *The Dispensary* was closely modelled upon the *Lutrin*. Cf. Blackmore, *A Satyr Against Wit*, 315–16:

Felonious *G——* pursuing this Design,
Smuggles *French* Wit, as others Silks and Wine.

An anonymous author, in *Letters of Wit, Politicks and Morality* (1701), p. 221, says that the Witlings call "*Garth* a Copier".

No Place so Sacred from such Fops is barr'd,
Nor is *Paul's Church* more safe than *Paul's Church-yard*:
Nay, fly to *Altars*; *there* they'll talk you dead;
For *Fools* rush in where *Angels* fear to tread.   625
Distrustful *Sense* with modest Caution speaks; ⎫
It still *looks home*, and *short Excursions* makes; ⎬
But *ratling Nonsense* in full *Vollies* breaks; ⎭
And never shock'd, and never turn'd aside,
Bursts out, resistless, with a thundring Tyde!   630
But where's the Man, who Counsel *can* bestow,

624 fly] run *1711*.

---

623. Between Verse 625 and 626 ⟨623 and 624⟩;
          In vain you shrug, and sweat, and strive to fly,
          These know no Manners, but in Poetry:
          They'll stop a hungry Chaplain in his Grace,
          To treat of Unities *of* Time *and* Place.

                                        [P. *1736a–43, 1751*.]
     623. Pope's statement is literally true, for in the 17th century St Paul's
Cathedral "was used regularly as a meeting-place to transact business. . . The
aisles . . . were the recognized haunts of loiterers, needy adventurers, and broken-
down gallants" (Stow's *Survey of London*, ed. C. L. Kingsford, 1908, II 349). Such
abuse of the Cathedral precincts had not altogether disappeared in the poet's
own time. Paul's Churchyard was the booksellers' quarter round the Cathedral.
Arber's *Term Catalogues* locates at least sixteen booksellers there in 1709. Their
places of business were of two kinds: houses which bordered the churchyards,
and booths and stalls which clustered round the walls and at the doors of the
Cathedral itself.
     624. "Horace [*Ars Poet.*, 475] says, occiditque legendo, *reads you dead*" [Wake-
field].
     625. *where Angels fear to tread*] Warton cites Boileau, *L'Art Poét.*, IV 53–8:
          Gardez-vous d'imiter ce rimeur furieux,
          Qui, de ses vains écrits lecteur harmonieux,
          Aborde en récitant quiconque le salue,
          Et poursuit de ses vers les passans dans la rue.
          Il n'est temple si saint, des anges respecté,
          Qui soit contre sa muse un lieu de sûreté.
A.P. does not translate "des anges respecté"; this perhaps suggests that Pope
was familiar with the French original.
     627. *short Excursions makes*] Wakefield compares Virgil, *Georgics* IV 194: "ex-
cursusque brevis temptant"; and Dryden's tr., 283: "Nor Forrage far, but short
Excursions make." Cf. l. 738*n*.

Still *pleas'd* to *teach,* and yet not *proud* to *know* ?
Unbiass'd, or by *Favour* or by *Spite*;
Not *dully prepossest,* nor *blindly right*;
Tho' Learn'd, well-bred; and tho' well-bred, sincere;
Modestly bold, and Humanly severe?   636
Who to a *Friend* his Faults can freely show,
And gladly praise the Merit of a *Foe*?
Blest with a *Taste* exact, yet unconfin'd;
A *Knowledge* both of *Books* and *Humankind*;   640
Gen'rous Converse; a *Soul* exempt from *Pride*;
And *Love to Praise,* with *Reason* on his Side?
    Such once were *Criticks,* such the Happy *Few*,
Athens and *Rome* in better Ages knew.
The mighty *Stagyrite* first left the Shore,   645

634 nor] or *1711–43*.

635. Cf. Roscommon, *Ess. on Tr. Verse,* 69*f.*:
> For none have been with *Admiration* read,
> But who, beside their *Learning,* were *Well-bred.*

Cf. also Pope's eulogy of Voiture, *Ep. to Miss Blount,* 7*f.* (vol. vi, p. 62). See *n* to l. 640, below.

637. *Who to a Friend*] Wakefield notes *A.P.,* 1 200:
> A Faithful Friend is careful of your Fame,
> And freely will your heedless Errors blame.

Cf. also Horace, *Ars Poet.,* 450*ff.*

640. *and Humankind*] Pope's conception of the ideal critic is closely related to that of the "poète honnête homme" in Boileau, *L'Art Poét.,* IV 121–4:
> Que les vers ne soient pas votre éternel emploi;
> Cultivez vos amis, soyez homme de foi.
> C'est peu d'être agréable et charmant dans un livre,
> Il faut savoir encore et converser et vivre.

641. *Gen'rous Converse*] Well-bred intercourse. The advantage of writing in an age marked by polite conversation is discussed by Dryden in his *Defence of the Epilogue* (*Essays,* 1 175–6). Cf. Knightly Chetwood's praise of Roscommon, *To the Earl of Roscommon,* 33–4:
> *Wit, Reading, Judgment, Conversation, Art,*
> A *Head* well *ballanc'd,* and a *generous Heart.*

645–8. "It is not improbable . . . that our poet, who wanted no dexterity to turn the hints even of inferior writers to his own advantage, and so improved what he borrowed as to give it all the air and merit of an original; might take

> Spread all his Sails, and durst the Deeps explore;
> He steer'd securely, and discover'd far,
> *Led* by the Light of the *Mæonian Star.*

648 *Add. 1711:*

> Not only *Nature* did his Laws obey,
> But *Fancy's* boundless Empire own'd his Sway.

up a suggestion from *Roscommon's Essay* [the following lines are really from Chetwood, *To the Earl of Roscommon*, 51–2]:

> Hoist Sail, bold Writers, *search, discover far,*
> You have a *Compass* for a *Polar-Star*" [Wakefield].

648. Between Verse 650 and 651 ⟨648 and 649⟩;

> *He when all Nature was subdu'd before,*
> *Like his great pupil, sigh'd, and long'd for more:*
> *Fancy's wild regions yet unvanquish'd lay,*
> *A boundless empire, and that own'd no sway.*
> *Poets, &c.*   [P. *1736a–43.*]

From 1744 to 1751 the note appeared in Warburton's commentary as follows: "Between v. 646 and 647. I found the following lines, since supprest by the author:

> *That bold* Columbus *of the realms of wit,*
> *Whose first discov'ry's not exceeded yet.*
> *Led by the light of the Mæonian Star,*
> *He steer'd securely, and discover'd far.*
> *He, when . . .*" [and so on as in Pope's note above].

The metaphor of philosophic or poetic "exploration" is frequently encountered in the 17th century. Cf. Cowley, *To Mr. Hobs*, st. 4: "Thou great *Columbus* of the *Golden Lands* of *new Philosophies*"; and Oldham, *Upon the Works of Ben. Johnson*, st. 1:

> By that we may Wit's vast, and trackless Ocean try,
> Content no longer, as before,
> Dully to coast along the shore . . .

The reference to Aristotle's "great pupil", Alexander the Great, may have been inspired by Cowley, *Tentanda via est, &c.,* 27–30:

> Welcome, great *Stagirite*, and teach me now
> All I was born to know.
> Thy *Scholars vict'ries* thou dost far out-do;
> *He* conquer'd the *Earth*, the whole *World you.*

Mæonian Star] Homer. Maeonia was the name often given to Lydia, where Homer was supposed to have been born. Cf. Milton, *Par. Lost*, III 35: "blind *Mæonides*".

648 var. Pope may have omitted this early couplet because of Dennis's objection that the "Expression in the first Verse is not only absurd, but blasphe-

Poets, a *Race* long unconfin'd and free,
Still fond and proud of *Savage Liberty*,   650
Receiv'd his Laws, and stood convinc'd 'twas fit
Who conquer'd *Nature*, shou'd preside o'er *Wit*.
    Horace still charms with graceful Negligence,
And without Method *talks* us into Sense,

651 Laws,] Rules, *1711*.

---

mous. The Laws of Nature are unalterable and indispensable but by God himself" (Hooker, I 412). But it is difficult to understand why Pope should yield to
this criticism, for his language is merely hyperbolical and metaphorical. As EC
note, Aristotle "presided over wit by his Rhetoric and Poetics, and gave proofs
by his Physics that he had 'conquered nature'." Speaking of the title of Homer
and Virgil to the "supream Dominion" in poetry, Temple in his essay *Of Poetry*
(Spingarn, III 82) had said that these two writers were those "from whom, as
the great Law-givers as well as Princes, all the Laws and Orders of it are or may
be derived." Perhaps Pope removed the couplet merely because it contained
the expletive *did*.

    651. *Laws*] The line read *Rules* in 1711 apparently because Pope had employed
Laws in the couplet he suppressed (l. 648 var.).

    652. See *n* to l. 648 var.

    653. *graceful Negligence*] Wakefield quotes Dryden, *Palamon and Arcite*, III 72–3:
                His Amber-colour'd Locks in Ringlets run,
                With graceful Negligence . . . ;
and also Oldham, *A Letter from the Country*, 48–9:
                Each strain of yours so easie does appear,
                Each such a graceful Negligence does wear . . .
Cf. *n* to ll. 293 *ff*.

    654. *without Method*] Cf. Dryden, *Dedic. of the Æn.* (*Essays*, II 164), where he
says that he writes in "a loose epistolary way . . . after the example of Horace,
in his . . . *Art of Poetry*; in . . . which he observes no method that I can trace,
whatever Scaliger . . . may have seen. . ." Dryden must have misunderstood
Scaliger, who had said (see the Pref. to *Poetices libri septem*): "Nam & Horatius
artem quum inscripsit, adeo sine vlla docet arte, vt Satyræ propius totum opus
illud esse videatur." Peacham, *Compleat Gentleman*, ch. 10 (Spingarn, I 127), repeats Scaliger in these terms: Horace's *Poetica* is "his worst peece; for while he
teacheth the Art, he goeth vnartificially to worke, euen in the verie beginning."
Cf. Dryden again, in his tr. of Persius, *Sat.* I 227–8:
                Unlike [Lucilius] in method, with conceal'd design,
                Did crafty Horace his low numbers join.
See J. W. H. Atkins, *Literary Criticism in Antiquity* (1934), II 70*ff*. See Intro., pp.
223–4, above.

Will like a *Friend* familarly convey   655
The *truest Notions* in the *easiest way*.
He, who Supream in Judgment, as in Wit,
Might boldly censure, as he boldly writ,
Yet *judg'd* with *Coolness* tho' he sung with *Fire*;
His *Precepts* teach but what his *Works* inspire.   660
Our Criticks take a contrary Extream,
They *judge* with *Fury*, but they *write* with *Fle'me*:
Nor suffers *Horace* more in wrong *Translations*
By *Wits*, than *Criticks* in as wrong *Quotations*.
　　See *Dionysius Homer*'s Thoughts refine,   665

655 Will] Does *1711–16*.　　665–6 *Add. 1713a–51*.

656. *easiest*] In the smoothest and most flowing style (OED, s.v. *easy*).

657. *Supream in Judgment*] Cf. Dryden, Prol. to *Oedipus*, 4 (of Socrates and Sophocles): "Supreme in Wisdom one, and one in Wit."

659. *judg'd with Coolness*] Dennis (Hooker, 1 409) said of this line: "Before he goes ten Lines farther, he forgets himself, and commends *Longinus* for the very contrary Quality for which he commended *Horace*, and for the very same thing for which he condemns his Contemporaries. . . He commends *Horace* for judging coolly in Verse, and extols *Longinus* for criticizing with Fire in Prose." The criticism apparently disturbed Pope. In the MS memorandum (see Appendix B, pp. 482–4, below) he recorded and struck out the following attempts:

　　Horace judgd wth Coolness & Longin wth Fire.
　　Supreme alike in Judgmt—
　　He boldly censurd & he boldly writ
　　He judgd wth Spirit as he sung.

He finally wrote in the margin: "not to be alterd".

662*f*. Dennis noted (Hooker, 1 409) that this couplet was modelled on Roscommon, *Ess. on Tr. Verse*, 301*f*.,

　　　　Thus make the *proper Use* of each *Extream*,
　　　　And *write* with *Fury*, but *correct* with *Phleam*,

and added: "But what is a perspicuous sensible Precept in my Lord *Roscommon*, as soon as this Essayer handles it, becomes a gross Absurdity and a palpable Contradiction." It would appear that Pope actually twisted Roscommon's verse into a criticism of just such critics as Dennis.

664. *than Criticks*] Than by critics.

665. Dionysius *of* Halicarnassus. [P. *1713a–43, 1751*.]

Speaking, in the Pref. to his *Iliad*, of the frequent agreement of sound and sense in Homer, Pope says that Dionysius "has pointed out many of our Author's beauties in this kind, in his treatise of the *Composition of Words*." Cf. also

And call new Beauties forth from ev'ry Line!
Fancy and Art in gay *Petronius* please,
The *Scholar's Learning*, with the *Courtier's Ease*.
In grave *Quintilian*'s copious Work we find
The justest *Rules*, and clearest *Method* join'd;   670
Thus *useful Arms* in Magazines we place,
All rang'd in *Order*, and dispos'd with *Grace*,

667 please,] meet, *1736a–43*.
668 with] and *1711*.   *Ease*.] wit. *1736a–43*.

Pope's letter to Addison, Oct. 10, 1714 (*Corr.*, I 264). Wakefield compares
Rochester, *An Allusion to the Tenth Satyr*, 101–2:

> Compare each Phrase, examine ev'ry Line,
> Weigh ev'ry Word, and ev'ry thought refine.

667. *Petronius*] Pope was censured by Warton for mentioning this "dissolute
and effeminate writer" among good critics. Pope apparently agreed with Dryden, who had called Petronius "the greatest wit perhaps of all the Romans"
(Dedic. of *Examen Poeticum*, in *Essays*, II 3) and also the "most elegant, and one
of the most judicious authors of the Latin tongue" (*An Essay of Heroic Plays*, in
Essays, I 152). Saint-Évremond (*Works*, 1700, I 223) regarded Petronius as
"rather a nice Courtier", and said (I 229) that he was "to be admired throughout, for the Purity of his Stile, and the Delicacy of his Thoughts. . ." The Advertisement to Rapin's *Reflections* (1674) says: "*Petronius* . . . amongst the Or-
dures of his *Satyre*, gives certain precepts for Poetry that are admirable. . . Nothing more judicious was writ in those dayes, yet himself had not that ease and
natural way, which he requires so much in others. He gives the best Rules in
the world against *affectation*, which he never observes himself. . ." Swift (*An En-
quiry into the Behaviour of the Queen's last Ministry*) says that Bolingbroke had a
great respect for "the Characters of Alcibiades and Petronius, especially the
latter, whom he would gladly be thought to resemble" (see *Political Tracts*,
1713–1719, ed. by H. Davis and I. Ehrenpreis, 1953, pp. 134–5).

667 *f.* var. Pope altered the *please–Ease* rhyme here apparently because the
same rhyme occurred, in the earlier editions, only four lines later. When he re-
wrote the couplet at ll. 673 *f.* it was possible for him to revert to the earlier
reading.

671*ff.* Here Pope applies to Quintilian one of that writer's own favourite comparisons. See *Inst. Orat.*, II i 12; VII x 14. The lines also describe Pope's own procedure, for as his notes show, he had read Quintilian carefully and noted passages for future use. Cf. also Vida, *De Arte Poet.*, I 63–5:

> tibi digna supellex
> verborum rerumque paranda est, proque videnda
> instant multa prius, quorum vatum indiget usus.

But less to please the Eye, than arm the Hand,
Still fit for Use, and ready at Command.
    Thee, bold *Longinus*! all the Nine inspire,   675
And bless *their Critick* with a *Poet's Fire.*
An ardent *Judge*, who Zealous in his Trust,
With *Warmth* gives Sentence, yet is always *Just*;
Whose *own Example* strengthens all his Laws,
And *Is himself* that great *Sublime* he draws.   680
    Thus long succeeding Criticks justly reign'd,
Licence repress'd, and *useful Laws* ordain'd;

673–4 Nor thus alone the Curious Eye to please,
      But to be *found*, when Need requires, with Ease. *1711–43.*
675 The *Muses* sure *Longinus* did inspire, *1711–16.*
676 bless] blest *1711–16.*   677 who] that *1711.*

---

    675. *Thee, bold Longinus*] "This abrupt address to Longinus is more spirited and striking, and more suitable to the character of the person addressed, than if he had coldly spoken of him in the third person, as it stood in the first edition" [Warton]. The line is an interesting instance of an improvement produced apparently by Pope's desire to conform to his own precept in suppressing the expletive *did*. Pope quotes the earlier reading in his notes to *1736a–43*. The reputation of Longinus was probably at its highest point in England between 1735 and 1740 (see S. H. Monk, *The Sublime*, p. 24). Little known in England before the 1670's, he became a potent force in English criticism about 1700, as is well illustrated in the writings of Dennis and in Pope's *Essay* (see notes to ll. 141*ff.*).
    679. Cf. Dryden, Prol. to *Love Triumphant*, 50: "Who by his own Examples damns his Rules" (*N & Q*, ccv (March, 1960), p. 115).
    680. *And Is himself*] Wakefield compares a passage in Boileau's Pref. to his tr. of Longinus (*Oeuvres Diverses*, 1701, pp. 3–4 of Pref.): ". . . Longin ne s'est pas contenté, comme Aristote & Hermogene, de nous donner des préceptes tous secs & dépoüillés d'ornemens. . . En traitant des beautez de l'Elocution, il a employé toutes les finesses de l'Elocution. Souvent il fait la figure qu'il enseigne; & en parlant du Sublime, il est lui-mesme très-sublime." Wakefield also compares Dryden, Prol. to *The Tempest*, 7–8:

        He [Shakespeare] Monarch-like gave those his subjects law,
        And is that Nature which they paint and draw.

Cf. Sheffield, *Ess. upon Poetry*, 46 (of Horace): "That mighty Master and Example too".
    681*f.* Cf. Chetwood, *To the Earl of Roscommon*, 19*f.*:

        There wanted one who *License* cou'd restrain,
        Make *Civil Laws* o'er *Barbarous Usage* reign.

Learning and *Rome* alike in Empire grew,
And *Arts* still *follow'd* where her *Eagles flew*;
From the same Foes, at last, both felt their Doom,   685
And the same Age saw *Learning* fall, and *Rome*.
With *Tyranny*, then *Superstitition* join'd,
As that the *Body*, this enslav'd the *Mind*;
Much was *Believ'd*, but little *understood*,
And to be *dull* was constru'd to be *good*;   690
A *second* Deluge Learning thus o'er-run,

689 Much] All *1711*.   little] nothing *1711*.

---

684. *Eagles flew*] The Eagles carried as standards by the Roman armies. Cf. Denham, *The Progress of Learning*, 51*f.*:

> Then wheresoe're her Conquering Eagles fled,
> Arts, Learning, and Civility were spread.

In the Pref. to his *Miscellanies in Verse and Prose* (1693), Dennis remarked (Hooker, I 10) that "Arts and Empire in Civiliz'd Nations have generally flourish'd together." See Intro., pp. 231-2, above.

686. *Rome*] Pope here uses an older pronunciation of the word *Rome*, to rhyme with *Doom*. The modern pronunciation of the word derives from the French, but it had been used by Dryden and Cowley, and elsewhere in the *Essay* by Pope himself (see l. 248). See H. C. Wyld, *Studies in English Rhymes from Surrey to Pope* (1923), p. 128.

687 *ff.* These were among the lines which caused discontent among Pope's co-religionists. He answered their objections in three letters to Caryll (June 18, 25, July 19, 1711; *Corr.*, I 117*ff.*) and altered l. 689. Of l. 687 he wrote to Caryll (*Corr.*, I 127): ". . . I took occasion to mention the superstition of some ages after the subversion of the Roman Empire, which is too manifest a truth to be denied, and does in no sort reflect upon the present Catholics, who are free from it. Our silence in these points may with some reason make our adversaries think we allow and persist in those bigotries, which in reality all good and sensible men despise, tho' they are persuaded not to speak against them. . ." Cf. *Ess. on Man*, III 246*ff.* (vol. III i, p. 117).

689 var. Pope quoted the variant reading in *1736a-43*. Cf. l. 687*n.*

690. Between Verse 690 and 691 ⟨the author omitted these two, *1744-51*⟩:

> *Vain Wits and Critics were no more allow'd,*
> *When none but Saints had Licence to be proud.*

[P. *1736a-51*.]

dull] Cf. *n* to l. 428 var.

691*f.* In a letter to Caryll of June 25, 1711 (*Corr.*, I 122) Pope speaks of the objections raised to these lines by his priestly friend Thomas Southcote: "The only difference between us in relation to the monks is, that he thinks most sorts

> And the *Monks* finish'd what the *Goths* begun.
> At length, *Erasmus*, that *great, injur'd* Name,
> (The *Glory* of the Priesthood, and the *Shame*!)

of learning *flourish'd* among 'em, and I am of opinion that only some sort of learning was barely *kept alive* by 'em. He believes the most natural and obvious sense of that line [691] . . . will be thought meant of learning in general, and I fancy it will be understood only, as 'tis meant, of polite learning, criticism, poetry, &c., which is the only learning concerned in the subject of the *Essay*." Cf. Dryden, *To the Earl of Roscommon*, 15–16:

> But *Italy* reviving from the trance
> Of *Vandal, Goth*, and *Monkish* ignorance . . .

Wakefield compares Roscommon, *Ess. on Tr. Verse*, 370–1:

> And by Succession of unlearned Times,
> As *Bards began*, so *Monks Rung on* the *Chimes*.

Cf. *Dunciad* A, III 75*ff.* (vol. v, pp. 156–7).

693. Erasmus (1466–1536) traditionally has occupied an ambiguous position in the history of religious controversy. Although ordained a priest, he attacked the abuses of the clergy and influenced in important respects the course of the Reformation. Congenial as he was to the Protestant and humanist spirit of his time, he yet remained loyal to the Roman Catholic Church. Considerable indignation seems to have been aroused among Pope's co-religionists by this passage. Perhaps the high praise awarded to one whom they had come to regard as being, in some sense, an enemy of the Church seemed, in this context, to be gratuitous; it may have seemed that Erasmus was not a critic of the same order as Horace and Vida, and therefore that his inclusion here was an arbitrary act. Pope's letters to Caryll (June 18 and July 19, 1711) show that he was not ready to give way on this point. In the second letter, speaking of those who had attacked him, he says (*Corr.*, I 128): "What these . . . are really angry at is that a man whom their tribe oppressed and persecuted (Erasmus by name) should be vindicated after a whole age of obloquy, by one of their own people who is free and bold enough to utter a generous truth in behalf of the dead, whom no man sure will flatter, and few do justice to." Pope alludes to Erasmus as his model in *Imit. Hor., Sat.* II i 66–7 (vol. IV, p. 11):

> Like good *Erasmus* in an honest Mean,
> In Moderation placing all my Glory . . .

In his will Pope bequeathed, together with his own *Works* and translation of Homer, "the eleven volumes of those of Erasmus" to Bolingbroke.

694. *The Glory . . . and the Shame*] Wakefield cites Oldham, *A Satyr . . . Dissuading . . . from the Study of Poetry*, 175–6:

> On *Butler* who can think without just Rage,
> The Glory and the Scandal of the Age?

Erasmus was the "glory" of the priesthood because of his learning, and its "shame" because of the treatment he received at its hands.

Stemm'd the *wild Torrent* of a *barb'rous Age*,   695
And drove those *Holy Vandals* off the Stage.
   But see! each *Muse*, in *Leo*'s Golden Days,
Starts from her Trance, and trims her wither'd Bays!
Rome's ancient *Genius*, o'er its *Ruins* spread,
Shakes off the *Dust*, and rears his rev'rend Head!   700
Then *Sculpture* and her *Sister-Arts* revive;
Stones leap'd to *Form*, and *Rocks* began to *live*;

---

697. *Leo's Golden Days*] *Saecla Leonis, Saecla Aurea.* The election of Leo X to
the Papal throne was hailed by humanists on all sides as the end of an iron age
and as a return to a Golden Age of art and learning. Thus Castiglione in his
Cleopatra wrote,

> At tu magne Leo, Divum genus, aurea sub quo
> Saecula & antiquae redierunt laudis honores,

translated by Pope (vol. VI, p. 67):

> But thou great *Leo*! in whose *golden* days
> Revive the honours of *Rome*'s ancient praise . . .

Leo X was Pope from 1513 to 1521. His age was "golden" in the sense that he
squandered the papal resources on artists of the time and on his own amuse-
ments, and also in the sense that the Italian Renaissance reached its zenith in
Rome under his reign. He was patron to such scholars, poets, and artists as
Lascaris, Bembo, Raphael, Michelangelo, Bramante. The humanist tradition
in which Pope wrote exaggerated heavily the very real praise due to Leo X's
patronage of art. Much that his predecessors initiated and accomplished was
credited to Leo's reign (Pastor, *History of the Popes*, 1908, VIII 375 ff.). This portion of Pope's poem recalls, as Wakefield noted, Dryden, *To Sir Godfrey Kneller*,
45–9, 57–60:

> *Rome* rais'd not Art, but barely kept alive;
> And with Old *Greece*, unequally did strive:
> Till *Goths* and *Vandals*, a rude *Northern* Race,
> Did all the matchless Monuments deface.
> Then all the Muses in one ruine lye. . .
>   Long time the Sister Arts, in Iron sleep,
> A heavy Sabbath did supinely keep;
> At length, in *Raphael*'s Age, at once they rise;
> Stretch all their Limbs, and open all their Eyes.

Cf. also l. 95: "And *Raphael* did with *Leo*'s Gold abound."
   698. *Starts from her Trance*] Cf. the quotation from Dryden, ll. 691n.
trims] Perhaps here means *restores* (OED).
   700. Cf. Dryden, *Threnodia Augustalis*, 514: "Th' asserted Ocean rears his
reverend Head".
   702 ff. This whole paragraph recalls the myth of Amphion, who moved the

With *sweeter Notes* each *rising Temple* rung;
A *Raphael* painted, and a *Vida* sung!
Immortal *Vida*! on whose honour'd Brow   705
The Poet's *Bays* and Critick's *Ivy* grow:

stones of Thebes into place by the music of his lyre. Pope may merely echo
Horace, *Ars Poet.*, 394–6, but considering the idea of *translatio studii* (see Intro.,
pp. 231–2, above) which informs this portion of the poem, it is more likely that
he is imitating the passage in Ovid (*Met.*, xv 418–35) which recalls Amphion
and also describes the transfer of glory from ancient city to ancient city, and
finally suggests that Rome is to be the capital of the world. Cf. also Boileau,
L'Art Poét., IV 149–50.

With *leap'd to Form* Wakefield compares Dryden, *Religio Laici*, 18–19: "Or
various Atoms interfering Dance / Leapt into Form"; and Addison, *A Letter
from Italy*, 144: "Or teach their animated rocks to live."

703. *sweeter Notes*] Pastor, *History of the Popes*, VIII 144–8, mentions Leo's fana-
tical love of music; but it may be that Pope was thinking of the revival and reform of church music in Rome which took place much later, largely under the
direction of Palestrina, as a result of the Council of Trent (1563).

each rising Temple] Leo's reign was not characterized by any remarkable new
buildings. The financial difficulties into which he plunged himself by his extravagance effectively prevented the completion of several architectural projects
begun by his predecessor, Julius II.

704. *Raphael*] For many in Pope's age Raphael Santi (1483–1520) was pre-
eminently "sublime" in his genius. As de Piles stated (*Art of Painting*, p. 27), in
speaking of the revival of the art of painting in Italy, many persons considered
"all the Perfection of Painting is to be found in the works of *Raphael*." Raphael
went to Rome in 1508, and there executed his famous frescoes in the Vatican
at the command of Julius II. Many of his greatest paintings were done in the
pontificate of Leo X. For references to Raphael in a similar context, see the
passages from Dryden, l. 697*n.*

705. *Immortal Vida*] M. Hieronymus Vida, ⟨*of* Cremona, *1713b–16*⟩ *an excellent* Latin *Poet, who writ an Art of Poetry in Verse* ⟨*1711–43*⟩*. He flourish'd in the
time of* Leo *the Tenth* ⟨*1713a–43*⟩*.* [P. *1711–43*.]

Vida (1490?–1566) wrote didactic poems in Latin, and Pope (see notes to
ll. 365 *ff.*) had carefully studied his *Poetica*. The game of Ombre in *The Rape of
the Lock* had a measure of debt to Vida's *Game of Chess*, and Pope included several
of Vida's poems in his two-volume edition of the Latin poems of Italian poets
(*Selecta Poemata Italorum Qui Latine Scripserunt*, 1740). Leo X treated Vida with
marked favour, and he was praised by Dryden and Boileau.

706. *Critick's Ivy*] Pope seems to have been the first to crown a critic with ivy,
though his notion of doing so seems also to have been a logical development of
previous associations held by the plant. In *Ecl.* VIII 11–13, Virgil had said:

accipe iussis
carmina coepta tuis atque hanc sine tempora circum
inter victrices hederam tibi serpere laurus.

Virgil's image (see also *Ecl.* VII 25) became widely popular, particularly in contexts involving questions of literary fame. It suggested the humility of the poet (ivy) in presenting his work to an *imperator* (bay), while also suggesting a time-honoured connexion between them. Later, especially from the 15th to the 17th centuries, ivy was associated not only with poets but with learned men. This association of ivy with learning seems due to a number of causes, chief among them the extension of the meaning of *doctus* from *skilled* to *erudite*, and the generalized wish to emphasize the congenial notion of the learned labour which the Renaissance in particular felt to be inseparable from the practice of literature. In addition to the Virgilian source, there was also a Horatian source in *Carm.*. I 29-30:

me doctarum hederae praemia frontium
dis miscent superis . . .

On the Horatian passage the early commentators are silent, except to remark that ivy is the poet's crown. Here the first to stress the notion of learning, or skill in many disciplines, is Cristoforo Landino in 1482, who was copied by all his successors as late as the 18th century. The emblem writers then take up the notion of ivy and learning, and their commentators, intent on increasing the number of applications, emphasize the connexion. Whether Pope knew the emblem writers is not certain, but he must have known Andrea Alciati's emblem *De hedera*: the verses, without commentary, are quoted in a note to *Ecl.* VII 25 in Ogilby's *Virgil* (1654). Piero Valeriano (*Hieroglyphica*, 1556) remarks that poets are crowned with laurel and ivy mixed to signify that they excel both in *ingenium* and *ars* (in Apollonian inspiration and in the industry to turn it to account), and the crown of mixed ivy and bay makes its appearance in academic laureation ceremonies during the 16th and 17th centuries. The poet's bays owe their popularity to other causes than their use in crowning victors at the Pythian games. Classical poets had unflaggingly pointed out that bay was the prerogative of *triumphatores* and *imperatores*, on whom poets alone could confer lasting fame. But Petrarch allows that poets were anciently crowned with bay, ivy, or myrtle, and he insisted on bay for himself. Crowned with bay on April 8, 1341, he was more responsible than any other post-classical author for standardizing bay as the poet's garland. In Virgil's lines the laurel is the reward of conquerors, the ivy of poets, because, in Cowley's words (*Davideis*, II, note 5), "*Ivy* is always *green*, and requires the support of some stronger *Tree*, as *Learning* does of *Princes* and great men." Hence, perhaps, Pope's extension of the idea: if laurel (bay), the tree sacred to Apollo, is the reward of poets, ivy can appertain to critics, who could not exist if there were no poets. Or perhaps his usage was suggested by Dryden, Dedic. of *Examen Poeticum* (*Essays*, II 3). Speaking of critics who have become the enemies of poets, he says: ". . . are they from our seconds become principals against us? Does the ivy undermine the oak which supports its weakness?" That Pope's usage was something of a new departure

Cremona now shall ever boast thy Name,
As next in Place to *Mantua,* next in Fame!
   But soon by Impious Arms from *Latium* chas'd,
Their *ancient Bounds* the banish'd Muses past;   710
Thence Arts o'er all the *Northern World* advance;
But *Critic Learning* flourish'd most in *France.*
The *Rules,* a Nation born to serve, obeys,

---

is suggested by Matthew Concanen, who attacks Pope (*A Supplement to the Pro-found,* 1729, p. 13) in these terms: ". . . the Ancients always gave Ivy to the Poets . . . nor was it ever apply'd to Patrons or Criticks . . . by any but this in-genious Author." Pope's compliment to Vida is the more graceful for its Vir-gilian form. Not only was his poetry strongly influenced by Virgil's, and widely held to rival it, but Vida himself was a native of Cremona, next in place to Mantua, Virgil's childhood home. Vida apparently was never laureated, though he is sometimes referred to as *laureato,* and frequently so represented in his por-traits. Pope uses the same image on other occasions: *Summer,* 10 (p. 72, above), *Dunciad* A, III 45–6, and *Dunciad* B, I 303–4 (vol. v, pp. 154, 291). Cf. also Waller, *To my Lord of Falkland,* 13–15; and Dryden, *To the Memory of Mr. Old-ham,* 24. (Note kindly contributed by Mr J. B. Trapp.)

707–8. Warburton cites Virgil, *Ecl.* IX 28: "Mantua vae miserae nimium vicina Cremonae." Warton pointed out that the application had been made by Basil Kennett in the preface to his edition of Vida's *Poetica* (1701): "Quos inter recognoscere gavisa est civem suum (ipsius beneficio, aemula ferè vicinae *Man-tuae*) *Cremona.*" Wakefield cites Denham, *Cooper's Hill,* 71: "Like him in birth, thou should'st be like in fame."

709. *Impious Arms*] As Warburton noted, the reference is to the Sack of Rome in 1527 by the troops of the Emperor Charles V under the leadership of the Duke of Bourbon. The spoliation of the city by the German and Spanish troops was so great that "More than one contemporary declared that the deeds of the Vandals, Goths, and Turks were outdone" (Pastor, *History of the Popes,* VII 42).

710. *banish'd Muses*] Cf. Vida, *De Arte Poet.,* I 185–6:
   Pierides donec Romam, et Tyberina fluenta
   Deseruere, Italis expulsae protinus oris.

712. An allusion to the French critics of the reign of Louis XIV (see Intro., pp. 210–11, above). Cf. Dryden, *Dedic. of the Æn. (Essays,* II 178): "For, impar-tially speaking, the French are as much better critics than the English, as they are worse poets."

713. "A reflexion on the servility of the French, who submitted to the despotic government of Louis XIV., as contrasted with the independence of the 'brave Britons', who had within the limits of half-a-century cut off the head of one king and expelled another" [West]. Cf. Dryden, Dedic. of *Examen Poeticum (Essays,* II 7): "They [the French] follow the ancients too servilely in the mechanic rules,

And *Boileau* still in Right of *Horace* sways.
But *we*, brave *Britons, Foreign Laws* despis'd,   715
And kept *unconquer'd*, and *unciviliz'd*,
Fierce for the *Liberties of Wit*, and bold,
We still defy'd the *Romans*, as *of old*.
Yet *some* there were, among the *sounder Few*
Of those who *less presum'd*, and *better knew*,   720
Who durst assert the *juster Ancient Cause*,
And here *restor'd* Wit's *Fundamental Laws*.
Such was the Muse, whose Rules and Practice tell,
Nature's chief Master-piece is writing well.

---

715 *New paragraph 1727–32.*   *Britons,*] *Britains, 1711–16.*
723–4 *Add. 1717–51.*

---

and we assume too much licence to ourselves, in keeping them only in view at too great a distance." Gildon, *Letters and Essays* (1696), p. 91, says: ". . . the *French*, whose *Genius*, as well as Language, is not strong enough to rise to the Majesty of Poetry, are easier reduc'd within the Discipline of Rules, and have perhaps of late Years, more exactly observ'd 'em. Yet I never yet met with any Englishman, who wou'd preferr their Poetry to ours." The influence of Longinus is perhaps not totally absent from this passage. Cf. Monk, *The Sublime*, p. 26: "In the last section of his treatise, Longinus accounts for the decline of genius in his age on the grounds that liberty no longer existed, and that only in a state of freedom can great art be produced—an opinion that would naturally commend itself to the English in an age when they complacently contrasted their own constitutional monarchy with the despotism that prevailed on the Continent, and when they prided themselves on the prevalence of individual liberty in the body politic." See also S. Kliger, 'Whig Aesthetics: A Phase of Eighteenth-Century Taste', *ELH*, xvi (1949), especially pp. 144 *ff.*

714. Boileau claimed to be the pupil of Horace. Cf. the conclusion to *L'Art Poét.*, where he says that all he pretends to do is:

Vous offrir ces leçons que ma muse au Parnasse
Rapporta, jeune encore, du commerce d'Horace.

Cf. Dryden, *A Disc. conc. . . . Sat.* (*Essays*, II 26): ". . . if I would only cross the seas, I might find in France a living Horace and a Juvenal, in the person of the admirable Boileau. . ."

722. *Wit's Fundamental Laws*] Cf. Dryden, *Dedic. of the Æn.* (*Essays*, II 162): "A native of Parnassus, and bred up in the studies of its fundamental laws, may receive new lights from his contemporaries. . ."

724. *Essay on Poetry, by the Duke of* Buckingham ⟨*1717–43, 1751*⟩. Our Poet is

Such was *Roscomon*—not more *learn'd* than *good*,   725
With Manners gen'rous as his Noble Blood;
To him the Wit of *Greece* and *Rome* was known,

---

not the only one of his time who complimented this *Essay*, and its noble Author.
Mr. Dryden had done it very largely in the Dedication to his translation of the
Æneid; and Dr. Garth in the first Edition of his Dispensary says,

> *The Tyber now no courtly Gallus sees,*
> *But smiling Thames enjoys his Normanbys.* ⟨IV 217–18⟩

Tho' afterwards omitted ⟨the lines were omitted in editions after the fifth
(1703)⟩, when parties were carried so high in the reign of Queen Anne, as to
allow no commendation to an opposite in Politics. The Duke was all his life a
steady adherent to the Church of England-Party, yet an enemy to the extravagant measures of the Court in the reign of Charles II. On which account after
having strongly patronized Mr. Dryden, a coolness succeeded between them on
that poet's absolute attachment to the Court, which carried him some lengths
beyond what the Duke could approve of. This Nobleman's true character had
been very well marked by Mr. Dryden before,

> *the Muse's friend,*
> *Himself a Muse. In Sanadrin's debate*
> *True to his prince, but not a slave of state.*
>   Abs. and Achit. ⟨I 877–9⟩

Our Author was more happy, he was honour'd very young with his friendship,
and it continued till his death in all the circumstances of a familiar esteem.
[P. *1751*.]

John Sheffield, Duke of Buckingham and Normanby, was said by Pope to
have been one of those who had seen his *Pastorals* in manuscript. He wrote a
recommendatory poem printed by Pope in the 1717 *Works*, the volume in which
appeared for the first time ll. 723–4 of the *Essay*. L. 724 is a direct quotation
from Sheffield's *Ess. upon Poetry*, 2.

725. *Roscomon*] Wentworth Dillon, fourth Earl of Roscommon (1633?–85),
translated Horace's *Art of Poetry* (1680) and wrote *An Essay on Translated Verse*
(1684), in the second edn (1685) of which he was one of the first publicly to
praise Milton's *Par. Lost*. Cf. Pope's eulogy of him in *Ep.* II i 213–14 (vol. IV,
p. 213). Cf. J. Cutts, *To Her Royal Highness the Princess of Orange* (in *Poetical Exer-*
cises, 1687), 4: "There flows a Spirit not more Great, than Good."

727. *the Wit of Greece and Rome*] Cf. Dryden, *To the Earl of Roscommon*, 26–31:

> The Wit of *Greece*, the Gravity of *Rome*,
> Appear exalted in the *British* Loome;
> The Muses Empire is restor'd agen,
> In *Charles* his Reign, and by *Roscomon*'s Pen.
> Yet modestly he does his Work survey,
> And calls a finish'd Poem an ESSAY . . .

And ev'ry Author's *Merit,* but his own.
Such late was *Walsh,*—the Muse's Judge and Friend,
Who justly knew to blame or to commend;   730
To Failings *mild,* but *zealous* for Desert;
The *clearest Head,* and the *sincerest Heart.*
This humble Praise, lamented *Shade!* receive,
This Praise at least a grateful Muse may give!
The Muse, whose early Voice you taught to Sing,   735
Prescrib'd her Heights, and prun'd her tender Wing,
(Her Guide now lost) no more attempts to *rise,*

729 Muse's] Muses *1711–16.*

728. EC cite Rochester, *A Letter from Artemisa,* 164–5: "to her was known /
Ev'ry one's Fault, or Merit, but her own."

729. *Walsh*] Noting that the persons cited by Pope in these concluding lines
of the poem were all poets as well as critics in verse, Warburton (*1744–51*) adds:
"It is true, the last instance is of one who was no eminent poet, the late Mr.
Walsh. This small deviation might be well over-looked, was it only for its being
a pious offering [office *1751*] to the memory of his friend: But it may be farther
justified as it was an homage paid in particular to the MORALS of the Critic,
nothing being more amiable than the character here drawn of this excellent
person. He being our Author's Judge and Censor, as well as Friend, it gives him
a graceful opportunity to add *himself* to the number of the later Critics; and
with a *character of himself,* sustained by that *modesty* and *dignity* which it is so
difficult to make consistent, this performance concludes."

733. *This humble Praise*] A letter from Pope to Caryll of July 19, 1711 (*Corr.,*
I 128), shows that he was criticized by some of his Catholic friends for praising
Walsh: "Others you know, were as angry that I mentioned Mr. Walsh with
honour, who, as he never refused to any one of merit, of any party, the praise
due to him, so honestly deserved it from all others of never so different interests
or sentiments." Walsh sat in Parliament, and supported the Protestant succession and the Whig war policy.

734. Wakefield compares Virgil, *Aen.,* VI 885: "his saltem accumulem do-
nis . . .''

734.*f. Muse*] Pope himself. Cf. Dryden, *Abs. and Achit.,* I 877–8.

735.*f.* Cf. Welsted, *To the Duke of Buckingham, on his Essay on Poetry,* 1–2:
        Here the Young Muse instructed how to sing,
        Forms for the distant Flight her tender Wing.
The date of Welsted's poem is uncertain. It may have been 1709. See *N & Q,* CC
(Nov., 1955), pp. 485–6.

736. *prun'd*] "To trim or dress the feathers with the beak" (OED).

But in low Numbers short Excursions tries:
Content, if hence th' Unlearn'd their Wants may view,
The Learn'd reflect on what before they knew: 740
Careless of *Censure*, nor too fond of *Fame*,
Still pleas'd to *praise*, yet not afraid to *blame*,
Averse alike to *Flatter*, or *Offend*,
Not *free* from Faults, nor yet too vain to *mend*.

FINIS.

741 nor] not *1736b–43*.

---

738. *low Numbers*] Here perhaps Pope associates his poem with Horace's *Ars Poetica*, especially as that poem had been described by Dryden in his tr. of Persius, *Sat.* 1 227–8:

Unlike [Lucilius] in method, with conceal'd design,
Did crafty Horace his low numbers join.

short Excursions] Under "excursion. 1 ", Johnson in his *Dictionary* cites this passage and gives this definition: "The act of deviating from the stated or settled path; a ramble." See l. 627*n*. Cf. Dryden, Prol. to *Circe*, 11–14:

Your Ben and Fletcher, in their first young flight,
Did no *Volpone*, no *Arbaces* write;
But hopp'd about, and short excursions made
From bough to bough, as if they were afraid.

741*ff*. Warton says: "These concluding lines bear a great resemblance to Boileau's conclusion of his Art of Poetry, but are perhaps superior.

Censeur un peu fâcheux, mais souvent nécessaire,
Plus enclin à blâmer que savant à bien faire."

The Soames-Dryden version:

Apter to blame, than knowing how to mend;
A sharp, but yet a necessary Friend.

741–2. "So *Pindar* of himself, Nem. viii. 64.

... ἐγὼ δ' ἀστοῖς ἁδὼν καὶ χθονὶ γυῖα καλύψαιμ',
αἰνέων αἰνητά, μομφὰν δ' ἐπισπείρων ἀλιτροῖς.

Lov'd by my friends may I pass through my days;
Where due, give censure; and where due, give praise"

[Wakefield].

EC cite Dryden, *Religio Laici*, 452: "Yet neither Praise expect, nor Censure fear".

TRANSLATIONS

INTRODUCTION

I: GENERAL BACKGROUND

IN the Advertisement to the third volume of his *Works* in 1736 Pope introduced his translations of Ovid and Statius, and also those of Chaucer, in this manner: "The following Translations were selected from many others done by the Author in his Youth; for the most part indeed but a sort of *Exercises*, while he was improving himself in the Languages, and carried by his early Bent to *Poetry* to perform them rather in Verse than Prose." According to Warburton's Advertisement in his edition of the *Works* in 1751, Pope never intended to include these early translations in a final edition of his work, "on account of the levity of some, the freedom of others, and the little importance of any."

Whatever the diffidence with which Pope regarded his "Juvenile translations", for the student of his work they are of considerable interest. From the beginning Pope was known as a translator as well as a poet, and it was as a translator, indeed, that he won the financial independence that enabled him to pursue his career unhampered by material considerations. In these early translations are to be found, moreover, the most striking evidences of the formation of his style and art, and of his progress from translation to imitation, from imitation to creation.

Pope's knowledge of Greek and Latin has often been censured, and critics have deplored his lack of formal training in these languages under the rule of sound scholars and stern pedagogues. No doubt his education was singularly irregular and erratic, but there were good reasons for it being so. The poet was, first of all, the sickly, only child of aging parents. He was also a Roman Catholic in the anxious period after the Revolution of 1688, when the movements and activities of Catholics were hindered by many restrictions.[1] Yet whatever the disadvantages of his early training, it would be a mistake to underestimate his ability to read and understand the classical originals. He was not, and never pretended to be,

---

1. On anti-Catholic legislation, see vol. IV, pp. 168–9*n*.

a classical scholar in the strict sense of the term, yet to Spence and others he seemed to have become, by virtue of his own most assiduous and enthusiastic private efforts, the equal in scholarship to men from the universities.[1]

Our knowledge of Pope's early education derives mainly from the reminiscences collected by Spence from the poet himself and from his relatives and friends. According to these, Pope received some early instruction at home from a priest who started him in Greek and Latin.[2] When he was eight he went for a year to school at Twyford, near Winchester. He left Twyford after being severely punished for writing a satire on his master,[3] and went to school in London under Thomas Deane, first in Marylebone and later near Hyde Park Corner.[4] He may have studied under Deane for several years, perhaps until he was twelve, the age at which he moved to Binfield and again received instruction at home, for "a few months", from another priest.[5] From this early schooling, lasting in all about four years, Pope said he learned very little.[6] Thenceforth he undertook his own education. Thus, the Rev. William Mannock told Spence, he "set to learning Latin and Greek by himself, about twelve; and when he was about fifteen he resolved that he would go up to London and learn French and Italian."[7] Pope himself told Spence that he "continued in this close pursuit of pleasure and languages, till nineteen or twenty."[8]

The early translations which have come down to us should be seen as deriving from this private discipline the poet imposed upon himself. They were, in truth, what he called them, "a sort of *Exercises*", though later improved, no doubt, for publication. He felt he had taught himself Latin, Greek, and French, and that in all three his "chief way of getting them" was by making translations.[9] He had been familiar with translations of the classics by others from an

---

1. *Early Career*, p. 40.   2. Spence, pp. 259, 269, 283.
3. Ibid., pp. 25, 206, 259.   4. Ibid., pp. 192, 259.
5. Ibid., pp. 192–3.   6. Ibid.
7. Ibid., p. 25.
8. Ibid., p. 270. The "five or six years" spent in reading and "getting" the languages Pope later described to Spence (p. 193) "as the happiest part" of his life.
9. Ibid., p. 270.

early age: he read Ogilby's Homer when he was eight, and from it was led to Sandys's Ovid and to Thomas Stephens's translation of a "part of Statius".[1] When, in his later period of study at Binfield, he met "a passage, or story" that pleased him "more than ordinary", he endeavoured, he said,[2] to "imitate it, or translate it into English". In the "scattered lessons" he thus set himself, he "translated above a quarter of the Metamorphoses, and that part of Statius which was afterwards printed".[3] A quarter of the *Metamorphoses* represents about three thousand lines and an astonishing industry. When one considers that he had also written, before he was fifteen, an epic poem in four cantos of a thousand lines each, and that he undertook, about the age of sixteen, the writing of the *Pastorals*, it is little wonder than when he was about seventeen he fell ill, and received from a wise doctor the advice "to apply less".[4] He was also advised to ride out every day in the Forest, an exercise in which he was joined by Sir William Trumbull, the retired statesman and former Fellow of All Souls who would seem to have served as his last, and perhaps best, tutor in the classics.[5]

Of the many episodes in the *Metamorphoses* apparently translated by Pope, only three have come down to us. Two of these were published by Pope, *Vertumnus and Pomona* in 1712, the *Fable of Dryope* in 1717. The third episode, *Polyphemus and Acis*, was published posthumously in 1749 and has not since been reprinted. Other translations from the Latin that have survived are Ovid's epistle of *Sappho to Phaon*, published in 1712, and the *First Book of Statius His Thebais*, also published in 1712. Lastly, from the *Iliad* there is the *Episode of Sarpedon*, published in 1709, and from the *Odyssey*, the *Arrival of Ulysses in Ithaca*, published in 1713.[6] With the publication of these Homeric fragments Pope advanced his first claim to the epic works of translation which were to establish his fame and make his fortune.

1. Ibid., p. 276.   2. Ibid., p. 193.
3. Ibid., p. 278.   4. Ibid., pp. 7, 278–9.
5. See *Corr.*, 1 10n.
6. A third fragment of early Homeric translation, *The Gardens of Alcinous*, is to be found in vol. VI, pp. 103–4.

II: TRANSLATIONS FROM
THE *METAMORPHOSES*

I

Speaking of the period when Pope "got into the way of teaching himself, and applied so close to it in the Forest", Spence recorded that "some of his first exercises were imitations of the stories that pleased him most in Ovid", and added: "I have one of these original exercises now by me, in his own hand. It is the story of Acis and Galatea, from Ovid; and was translated when he was but fourteen years old. The title-page to this, (from his manner of learning to write), is so like print, that it requires a good eye and nice regard to distinguish it."[1]

This early translation, of an episode in Book XIII of the *Metamorphoses*, was first published, perhaps by Spence himself, in the *London Magazine* of December, 1749. It then bore the title of *Polyphemus and Acis*, and the author was not identified until the July, 1751, issue of the same magazine, when it was said that Pope had written the piece at the age of fourteen. Published first, no doubt, as a literary curiosity, and as a proof of Pope's precocity, the poem now gives us an opportunity to inspect an authentic piece of juvenile work which the poet, in all probability, never touched up, at some later stage of his career, for publication. If he had polished the piece for the press, we should have expected him to remove, as he ultimately did in other poems, the seven instances of the expletive *did* which are to be found in it.

For this translation Pope, as the notes to this edition show, studied closely the version of two great predecessors, Sandys and Dryden. Sandys's beautiful edition of the complete *Metamorphoses* had first appeared in 1626, and was followed in 1632 by an even more elaborate edition, with revisions and the addition of a prose commentary. Pope evidently used both of these editions, though he seems most often to have followed that of 1626. When neither edition provided him with the inspiration he sought, he had recourse to Dryden, who had also admired Sandys and whose use of him provided an example Pope was quick to follow.

Though he did avail himself of Sandys and Dryden, he did not

1. Spence, p. 283*n*.

follow either of them slavishly. He is not, furthermore, so crabbed
and elliptical as Sandys often is, nor is he so *galant* and diffuse as
Dryden. Sandys attempts to follow his original almost word by
word, while Dryden amplifies and invents: where Ovid and Sandys
take two lines, Dryden takes four. Pope seems to aim at a mean between these two procedures. He does not attempt, as does Sandys,
to crowd a host of details into a single line: he omits a detail, or cap-
tures it allusively. Neither does he expatiate in the manner of Dryden: he aims rather at the nice and pointed and clear expression of
the substance of the original.[1] The following versions by the three
poets of the same passage will indicate the ways in which Pope both
follows and differs from his predecessors. Here is the original:[2]

> Telemus interea Siculam delatus ad Aetnen,
> Telemus Eurymides, quem nulla fefellerat ales,
> terribilem Polyphemon adit 'lumen' que, 'quod unum
> fronte geris media, rapiet tibi' dixit 'Ulixes.'
> risit et 'o vatum stolidissime, falleris,' inquit,
> 'altera iam rapuit.'

Sandys follows closely in six lines:

> When *Telemus* came from *Sicilian* Seas,
> Augurious[3] *Telemus Eurymides*,
> And said to *Polypheme*, Thy browes large sight
> Shall by *Vlysses* be depriu'd of light.
> O foole, he laughing said, thou tell'st a lye;
> A female hath alreadie stolne that eye.

Dryden amplifies into ten lines:

> The prophet *Telemus* (arriv'd by chance
> Where *Ætna*'s Summet's to the Seas advance,
> Who mark'd the Tracts of every Bird that flew,
> And sure Presages from their flying drew,)
> Foretold the *Cyclops* that Ulysses' hand
> In his broad eye should thrust a flaming brand.

---

1. To translate Ovid's 148 lines, Sandys used 160, Dryden 233, Pope 164.
Pope, however, did omit two lines, and abridged another passage (see l. 65*n*).
2. Book XIII 770–5.
3. In 1632 "Augurious" became "The Augur".

> The giant, with a scornful grin, replied:
> "Vain augur, thou hast falsely prophesied;
> Already Love his flaming brand has toss'd;
> Looking on two fair eyes, my sight I lost."[1]

Pope uses only six lines, but it is clear that he is influenced by Dryden as well as by Sandys:

> It chanc'd prophetick Telemus, who knew
> The flight of birds, and thence presages drew,
> Arriving then by Ætna's steepy height,
> Foretold the Cyclops he shou'd lose his sight.
> The laughing Cyclops gave the bard the lye,
> And said, a charming female stole that eye.

Ovid's Polyphemus is not the dread figure of the *Odyssey*: he rather derives from the grotesque lover of Theocritus's eleventh *Idyll*, and thus is made to comb his hair with a rake and to shave with a scythe. Dryden makes him more grotesque still: the one-eyed monster is made to "kneel" before the "nymph" whom he "adores". Pope's version retains the portrait of a buffoon in love, yet his piece is more "polite" than that of Sandys, more subdued than that of Dryden. In Sandys, Polyphemus threatens Acis thus: "His guts I would extract, squeaze out his brains". Pope's version goes thus: "I'll from his bleeding breast his entrails tear". Where Dryden says that Polyphemus looks in the "crystal stream"

> to try
> His simagres, and rolls his glaring eye,

Pope avoids the exotic "simagres" (affected air) and the exaggeration of "glaring eye":

> while in the crystal brook
> He views and practices a milder look.

In the Dedication to *Examen Poeticum* Dryden had described Sandys as one of those who ran to the "extreme of a literal and close translation, where the poet is confin'd so straitly to his author's words, that he wants elbow-room to express his elegancies." By such a method, Ovid was made "obscure" and reduced to "prose",

---

1. *The Fable of Acis, Polyphemus, and Galatea,* 34–43.

and Dryden declares that such "translations want to be translated into English."[1] At the same time Dryden is critical of Ovid for a certain luxuriant fancy and expression, and admitted that in his own translations he had perhaps imitated this "character" of Ovid further than he should have done, even to "his very faults".[2]

Such observations as these doubtless guided Pope to the method of translation he adopted. He seems to have recognized early that a translation utterly faithful to the original was impossible, and that the attempt to produce such a translation would inevitably result in a poetic failure on his part:[3] utter fidelity involved a sacrifice, or a distortion, of the graces of the English language itself. In the order of time Pope was perhaps a translator before he was a poet, but in any other order he was first a poet, and therefore could not sacrifice the form and spirit of his own utterance to a literalness of meaning which was, in the last analysis, impossible to achieve.[4] This is not to say that he did not labour to achieve a faithful version of the original: as we shall see, all the evidence shows that he went to great pains to do so. In *Polyphemus and Acis* he does not permit himself the freedom of Dryden, yet he was soon, like Dryden, to follow his author even into "his very faults". More important, perhaps, is the fact that even thus early he is seen aiming at that "correctness" which imparted to all his verse the qualities of simplicity, clarity, and conciseness. Other elements were soon to be added that would complicate, but never destroy, these qualities so soon established in it.

II

The Fable of Vertumnus and Pomona, Pope's translation of an episode in the fourteenth book of the *Metamorphoses*, appeared for the first time in 1712, in *Miscellaneous Poems and Translations, By Several Hands*, a volume for which Pope himself seems to have served as

1. Ker, *Essays*, II 9–10.
2. Ibid., II 9. Cf. also Dryden's criticisms of Ovid in the Preface to the *Fables* (*Essays*, II 256*ff.*).
3. In the Preface to the *Iliad* Pope says: "It is certain no literal Translation can be just to an excellent Original in a superior Language."
4. See the Preface to the *Iliad*: "I know no Liberties one ought to take, but those which are necessary for transfusing the Spirit of the Original, and supporting the Poetical Style of the Translation."

editor.[1] There is no evidence as to the date the translation was made, though it may stem from the same period as *Polyphemus and Acis*.[2] In all probability, Pope revised the poem before publication, yet the revision would seem to have occurred before 1711, the year in which he published the *Essay on Criticism* and publicly condemned the use of expletives.[3] In *Vertumnus and Pomona* there occur, in the texts of 1712 and 1714, three instances of *did*, all of which were removed from the poem when it appeared in the *Works* of 1717.

Whether it is due to a later date of composition, or to revision for publication, *Vertumnus and Pomona* represents an advance over *Polyphemus and Acis*. Its verse is more smooth and flowing, and the translation is less literal. Pope is more inclined to embellishment and amplification in the manner of Dryden, as is indicated by the fact that he took 123 lines to translate seventy-nine of the original.[4] He again avoids the more rough and elliptical qualities of Sandys's version, and is altogether less indebted to him than he was in *Polyphemus and Acis*.

The difference in quality between Pope's version and that of Sandys is easily illustrated. In the original Ovid begins the episode thus, ll. 623–5:

> Rege sub hoc Pomona fuit, qua nulla Latinas
> inter hamadryadas coluit sollertius hortos
> nec fuit arborei studiosior altera fetus.

Sandys translates thus:

> *Pomona* flourisht in those times of ease:
> Of all the *Latian Hamadryades*,
> None fruitfull Hort-yards held in more repute;
> Or tooke more care to propagate their fruit.

---

1. N. Ault, *New Light on Pope* (1949), pp. 27*ff.*

2. Pope refers to the characters of Vertumnus and Pomona in a letter to Cromwell of April 25, 1708 (*Corr.*, I 47), but there is nothing to connect his reference to his translation.

3. Pope of course set forth his rules on expletives and other matters in his letter to Cromwell of Nov. 25, 1710 (*Corr.*, I 105*ff.*). The translation therefore may have been revised some time before then.

4. See *Metamorphoses*, Book XIV 623 *ff.* Pope did not translate, as Sandys did, the long episode of Iphis.

Here is Pope:

> The fair *Pomona* flourish'd in his Reign;
> Of all the Virgins of the Sylvan Train,
> None taught the Trees a nobler Race to bear,
> Or more improv'd the Vegetable Care.

Pope is indebted to Sandys for the structure of his lines, but he is also, here and elsewhere, both more and less faithful than Sandys to the original. His first line is thus closer to Ovid than that of Sandys, yet in the second he substitutes "Sylvan Train" for the non-English of "*Latian Hamadryades*". Pope also "humanizes" his plants, in a way that Sandys does not, by the coupling of epithets and nouns in such phrases as "nobler Race" and "Vegetable Care"; yet it might be argued that Pope has the better succeeded in capturing the tender zeal in pastoral care which is attributed to Pomona, at least by implication, in the original. Of course Pope must have learned the use of such phrases, in part, from Sandys himself. They were a means of saying a great deal in little, and thereby a means of reproducing, in a near-equivalent number of words, the classical original.[1] By using even more of them than Sandys, Pope was able to smooth out his lines and, at the same time, retain the substance of the original.

The additions Pope makes to his text are mainly ones of small detail, and they are obviously introduced to support the "Poetical Style of the Translation";[2] he is making a poem as well as a translation. Thus when Ovid describes Vertumnus as *piscator harundine sumpta*, translated by Sandys as "an Angler with his rod", Pope brings the original to life thus: "A Fisher next, his trembling Angle bears". He adds to Vertumnus's disguise as a farm labourer by giving him "Sun-burnt Temples", and both he and his steers are described as "sweating". The love of gardening which Pope formed so early and maintained throughout his life must not only have influenced his choice of this Ovidian episode for one of his exercises; it must also have made him acquainted with the details by which he was to vivify the original for English readers.

---

1. See Tillotson, *On the Poetry of Pope*, pp. 63 *ff.*, and also Intro. to *Messiah*, pp. 104–6, above.

2. See above, p. 335*n.*

III

The third of Pope's translations from the *Metamorphoses, The Fable of Dryope*, from Book IX, appeared for the first time in the *Works* of 1717. Like the other two, it dates, presumably, from the youthful period when Pope exercised himself in translation. It contains, however, no examples of the expletive *did*, which suggests that the poem was revised, if not written, at some period after he had formulated his rules on this point. There are no other indications as to the time of its composition.

Like *Vertumnus and Pomona, The Fable of Dryope* represents an advance over the apparently unrevised *Polyphemus and Acis*. Pope is more confident and free in his verse, more ready to heighten his original. In addition, while he is more smooth and fluent than Sandys, he also succeeds, occasionally at least, in preserving better than Sandys some of the more subtle effects of the Ovidian text. This last is seen particularly in Pope's efforts to preserve the subtleties of Dryope's metamorphosis, the evolution in the course of which Ovid first mixes the life of the woman and the life of the tree, and then absorbs the terms of the one into the terms of the other. Sandys, for example, translates l. 375 of Ovid, *hunc tamen infantem maternis demite ramis*, in this way: "This Infant from his dying mother beare". Pope realizes the possibilities of *ramis* (branches, limbs) in this fashion: "But from my branching arms this infant bear". Immediately afterwards Ovid writes: *nostraque sub arbore saepe | lac facitote bibat, nostraque sub arbore ludat*. Sandys translates: ". . . and often let him here / Be fed with milke; oft in my shaddow play". Pope preserves what Wakefield called the "beautiful repetition of his author" even more closely:

> And to his mother let him oft' be led,
> Sport in her shades, and in her shades be fed.

Portions of this episode seem to indicate clearly that Pope used both the 1626 and 1632 editions of Sandys's Ovid. In the first of these Sandys had translated ll. 354-5 of Ovid thus:

> she thought t'haue torne her haire: her hand
> She fils with leaues.

He then revised thus:

> she thought t'haue torne her haire: but teares
> Leaues from their twigs.

Pope follows the more dramatic, and more literal, version of 1626:

> her trembling hand she heaves
> To rend her hair; her hand is fill'd with leaves.

On another occasion, however, Pope seems closer to the 1632 edition. Thus l. 89 of his poem, "If in your breast or love or pity
dwell", seems closer to "If in your gentle hearts compassion dwell",
from 1632, than to "Since you I know in piety excell", from 1626.

Pope appears to take every opportunity to support the dramatic
and pathetic effect of his translation, and if he occasionally alters
the letter, he rarely distorts the spirit of his author. One more example will illustrate, and perhaps justify, his procedure. Near the
end of her transformation Dryope says: *nam iam per candida mollis/
colla liber serpit, summoque cacumine condor*. Pope's version goes thus:

> the creeping rind invades
> My closing lips, and hides my head in shades.

In the original Dryope certainly becomes hidden in the foliage of
her tree, but Pope's choice of the word "shades" not only conveys
this meaning: it also suggests those other "shades", those of another
world, into which Dryope is dying. Such touches as these came
from the hand of a translator who was "true to his poet's sense, but
truer to his fame".[1]

III: *SAPHO TO PHAON*

I

In 1680 Jacob Tonson published for the first time the volume of
translations entitled *Ovid's Epistles*. Containing a preface by Dryden, who also translated three of the epistles, the volume opened
with a translation of *Sappho to Phaon*[2] (the fifteenth epistle in the
Latin text) by Sir Carr Scrope, and other epistles were the work of
such writers as Mulgrave (with Dryden), Tate, Rymer, Settle, Ot-

---

1. The words are adapted from Denham's *To Sir Richard Fanshaw Upon His
Translation of Pastor Fido*, 24.

2. Scrope and Pope both use the spelling "Sapho" (though the 1751 edition
of Pope's *Works* uses "Sappho"), and this spelling is retained here when speaking of their translations. When speaking of the lady herself, or of the Latin original, the spelling "Sappho" is used.

way, Aphra Behn. The success of the collection was such that it
reached its seventh edition in 1705, and still another edition was
called for in 1712.[1] In an advertisement in this last edition the publisher said that because Scrope had omitted to translate the greater
part of *Sappho to Phaon*, he had "sollicited an entire new Version of
that Epistle, to render the whole Book compleat." He then added:
"The Author of it will have me acquaint the Reader, that it was
undertaken on that account only, and not out of any suppos'd de-
fect in what that Gentleman [Scrope] had done." Thus, directly
after Scrope's, came Mr Pope's translation.

The manuscript of Pope's *Sapho to Phaon* is still extant.[2] It was
seen by Richardson, who appended this note to the poem in his
copy of the 1717 *Works*: "Corrected by the first copy, written out
elegantly (as all his MSS) to show friends, with their remarks in
the margin; the present reading for the most part the effect of
them."[3] Elwin and Courthope used the manuscript, citing in their
notes a few of the variant readings it contains. They also noted that
the remarks to be found in the margin of the manuscript, for the
most part exclamations such as *Pulchrè, Bené, Bellè*, and so on, recall those that Cromwell had written, according to Pope,[4] on the
manuscript of the translation from Statius. The obvious, if by no
means certain, conclusion is that *Sapho to Phaon* was also submitted
to Cromwell for criticism.

The manuscript would appear to date from late 1711 or early
1712, for it conforms closely, in its corrected state, to the first printed text. There are differences, but fewer than appear between the
manuscripts of the *Essay on Criticism* and *Windsor-Forest* and the first
printed texts of these poems. Further evidence of the lateness of the
manuscript is provided by the fact that it bears, under the title, the
phrase "Wholly Translated", which corresponds to the title in the
first printed text and suggests the contrast with Scrope's version.
There is also what appears to be a preliminary page-count on the
left margin of the text. The notations occur, with the exception of
the count for the first page, at intervals of eighteen or nineteen lines,

1. It was advertised in the *Spectator* of March 18.
2. It is in the Pierpont Morgan Library, the trustees of which have kindly
consented to its use by the editors.
3. EC, 1 90.   4. *Corr.*, 1 63.

and by the side of several of the page numbers, written as (11), (12), and so on, there appears the phrase "19 lines". The page-count on the manuscript does not conform to the pages of the first printed text, but it is perhaps significant that Scrope's version in 1705 contained an average of nineteen lines on a full page, and Pope, or someone else, may have used Scrope's text as a guide to an estimation of the number of pages to be occupied by Pope's. It is conceivable that this is the manuscript sent to the printer, for the corrections on it are not too difficult to decipher. If it were sent to the printer, then the variations between it and the first printed text suggest that Pope made further corrections, as he did with the *Essay on Criticism*, in proof stage. In any event, Cromwell's remarks (if so they may be ascribed) and Pope's attempts to work out definitive readings make the manuscript of more than ordinary interest.

On the separate title page of the manuscript there occur the words, in Pope's own hand, "Written first 1707". There may be a conflict here with Tonson's statement that Pope undertook the translation at his request, though it is possible that Pope revised for Tonson a version he had made some years earlier. It is unlikely that Tonson commissioned Pope to write it five years before its publication, at a time when Pope, in spite of his budding reputation, was not a poet of any real standing.

There is no definite reference to the poem in Pope's correspondence. There is a letter of December 15, 1709, in which he thanks Cromwell for "reviewing the Papers I sent you", and says that Sir William Trumbull is anxious "for a sight of that Translation", but the work referred to may have been the translation of Statius, or something else.[1] In the last surviving letter (December 21, 1711) of their early friendship, Pope warns Cromwell that he designs a new task for him, the "reviewing a Piece of mine that may better deserve Criticisme".[2] If this were *Sapho to Phaon* Cromwell must have been expeditious in his aid, for three months later the poem was published.

---

1. Ibid., 1 76–7. The only direct reference to Ovid's epistle occurs in a letter of Oct. 12, 1710 (*Corr.*, 1 100), when it is cited in connection with a living lady to whom Cromwell gave the name "Sapho".

2. Ibid., 1 139.

II

Cromwell's remarks on the manuscript are in Latin, and generally express approval: *Pulcherrimè, Bellissimè, Pulchrum epiphonema et
rectum*. There are also, however, instances of the phrase *haud liquet*,
i.e., "this is obscure". Cromwell notes phrases in Ovid that have
been omitted, but he does not insist on a literal translation. Indeed,
there are many instances of the phrase *Bella Paraphrasis*, and there
even occurs the advice to abridge or subdue a passage (the lines in
which Sappho recalls her "criminal loves") for reasons of propriety.

Most of the remarks are based on a comparison of Pope's version
with that of Scrope. This, after all, was the easiest way to criticize,
and it is noticeable that when the material for comparison fails him,
in passages Scrope did not translate, Cromwell has little to say.
More often he approves Pope: *Magis Poeticè quam Scrope*; *Bené—
melius quam Scroop*. Sometimes he considers Scrope the better: *Scroop
melius hic*. Pope certainly took these remarks into account, for more
than a few passages seem corrected as a result of them. Yet he did
not submit blindly, and he consulted at least one other person who
is designated in the manuscript by an "X". Thus besides Cromwell's remark at ll. 13–14, *Pulchrè—at rectius Scroop*, Pope notes that
"X thinks mine best", and leaves the couplet unchanged. The identity of "X" is not known. He may have been Trumbull, to whom
Pope seems to have submitted several of his early poems, or Caryll,
whom he consulted about the *Essay on Criticism*.

Cromwell's remarks were an anticipation, no doubt, of the kind
of comparative examination the two versions would receive from
the public, and they thus must have served to put Pope on his
mettle. As the following lines from Scrope reveal, Pope was to measure his skill against that of a translator who was not without his
own fluency and elegance:

> A Thousand tender things to Mind I call,
> For they who truly love remember all.
> Delighted with the Musick of my Tongue, ⎫
> Upon my Words with silent Joy he hung,   ⎬
> And snatching Kisses, stopp'd me as I sung. ⎭
> Kisses, whose melting touch, his Soul did move,
> The Earnest of the coming Joys of Love.
> Then tender Words, short Sighs, and thousand Charms

> Of wanton Arts endear'd me to his Arms;
> 'Till both expiring with Tumultous Joys,
> A gentle Faintness did our Limbs surprize.

Scrope did not hesitate to make innovations in his version. He thus inserts a degree of tender melancholy into Sappho's memories that is equalled neither in Ovid nor in Pope, though it was to appear later in *Eloisa to Abelard*.[1] At the same time, Scrope's translation is far from complete. He omitted whole passages, he severely abridged others, and the conclusion of the poem is so ruthlessly curtailed that it is difficult to recognize the original.[2] Scrope's poem is more an adaptation, or a summation, than a full-scale translation, and it therefore provided a young and ambitious poet with the opportunity of surpassing it.

III

In his Preface to the volume in which the translation by Scrope, and later that by Pope, appeared, Dryden states that all translation may be reduced to three categories. First, "that of Metaphrase, or turning an Author Word by Word, and Line by Line, from one Language into another." This, as we have seen, was the method adopted by Sandys. Second is "that of Paraphrase, or Translation with Latitude, where the Author is kept in view by the Translator, so as never to be lost, but his Words are not so strictly followed as his Sense, and that too is admitted to be amplified, but not alter'd." The third is "that of Imitation, where the Translator (if now he has not lost that name) assumes the liberty not only to vary from the Words and Sense, but to forsake them both as he sees Occasion." This last was Scrope's procedure, but in Dryden's view the "two Extreams" of metaphrase and imitation were to be avoided, and the "Mean betwixt them", the way of paraphrase, adopted.[3] As

---

1. Cf. ll. 70–3 of Scrope:
> with Grief I throw me on the Ground,
> And view the melancholy *Grotto* round,
> Whose hanging Roof of Moss and craggy Stone
> Delights my Eyes above the brightest Throne.

2. Scrope reduces the 220 lines of the Latin to 97 lines. Pope's version contains 259 lines.

3. The passage is to be found in Ker, *Essays*, I 237*ff.*

Sapho to Phaon clearly shows, this was an opinion shared by Pope.

The best indication of Pope's efforts to retain both the sense and the spirit of his author is to be found in his attempts to reproduce Ovid's "turns", the "darling sin" of the Latin poet as well as of Dryden and Pope.[1] Dryden had said that in the use of the turn "Ovid particularly excels all poets",[2] and had also stated that in his own translations of Ovid he had "given him his own turns . . . which I cannot say are inimitable, because I have copied them, and so may others, if they use the same diligence".[3] Scrope did not trouble much with turns, but Pope uses this iterative figure frequently. His purpose in this is perhaps best revealed in a comment he made on Trapp's translation of Ovid, a comment made before his own *Sapho to Phaon* was published:[4] "I think he has nothing of the main Characteristick of his Author, a graceful Easiness. For let the Sense be never so exactly rendered, unless an Author looks like himself in his Air, Habit, and Manner, tis a Disguise and not a Translation."

On some occasions Pope follows a turn of Ovid closely, as in his translation of *et semper causa est, cur ego semper amem* by "Still is there cause for *Sapho* still to love".[5] Elsewhere the words of his turn differ from those of the original. Thus when Sappho says to the Sicilian women, *quae dicit vobis, dixerat ante mihi*,[6] Pope answers to his author with a more elaborate repetition:

> Nor be with all those tempting Words abus'd,
> Those tempting Words were all to *Sapho* us'd.

The deliberate pursuit of these turns is clearly revealed in the manuscript. In the original poem Ovid had used the phrase *ales Ityn* in successive lines (154–5), and Pope's first attempt on the passage went thus:

> All, but the mournful Nightingale and I;
> With her I wake, with her I joyn my Strain.

---

1. See Tillotson, *On the Poetry of Pope*, pp. 98–9.
2. Preface to the *Fables* (*Essays*, II 257).
3. Dedication of *Examen Poeticum* (*Essays*, II 10).
4. Letter to Cromwell, Nov. 25, 1710 (*Corr.*, I 106).
5. See l. 90n.   6. Line 56.

Borrowing the word "Philomel" from Scrope, from whom he had already taken "mournful", Pope then alters the lines to

> All, but the mournful *Philomel* and I;
> With mournful *Philomel* I join my Strain.[1]

In this poem again there are those occasions when, for one reason or another, Pope departs from the strict sense of his author. He prefers, for example, to crown Bacchus "with Ivy" rather than with "horns",[2] and he omits mention of Ovid's "bird of green", the parrot.[3] He softens or abridges two or three of the more frank and realistic passages of the original, and he omits, but only rarely, an entire line. On the other hand, he occasionally heightens his own version by the addition of a new detail, as in this couplet, the second line of which is entirely his own:

> *Farewel my* Lesbian *Love!* you might have said,
> Or coldly thus, *Farewel oh* Lesbian *Maid!*

To heighten the dramatic effect of a passage he may also alter the sequence of Ovid's lines. Thus when Sappho says, ll. 121–2:

> non veniunt in idem pudor atque amor. omne videbat
> vulgus; eram lacero pectus aperta sinu,

Pope, who got the hint for his new line structure from Scrope,[4] translates:

> Stung with my Love, and furious with Despair,
> All torn my Garments, and my Bosom bare,
> My Woes, thy Crimes, I to the World proclaim;
> Such inconsistent things are Love and Shame!

It is in the conclusion to his poem, however, that one may best find revealed the way in which Pope follows the sense and spirit, if not the actual words, of Ovid:

> O launch thy Bark, nor fear the watry Plain,
> *Venus* for thee shall smooth her native Main.
> O launch thy Bark, secure of prosp'rous Gales,
> *Cupid* for thee shall spread the swelling Sails.

---

1. For additional comment on these lines, see 175–8*n*.
2. See l. 25*n*.   3. See ll. 43–4*n*.   4. See ll. 139–42*n*.

> If you will fly—(yet ah! what Cause can be,
> Too cruel Youth, that you shou'd fly from me?)
> If not from *Phaon* I must hope for Ease,
> Ah let me seek it from the raging Seas:
> To raging Seas unpity'd I'll remove,
> And either cease to live, or cease to love!

As in the original, there are here apostrophes, exclamations, parentheses, and, above all, iterations. Some of these last ("launch thy Bark . . . launch thy Bark"; "If you will fly . . . that you shou'd fly") are present in Ovid, while others ("raging Seas . . . raging Seas"; "for thee . . . for thee") are of Pope's own invention. He has reduced to a single line Ovid's description of Cupid at the helm of the ship that is to restore Phaon to Sappho, but it is doubtless so as not to break the flow that culminates in the final lines, where he adds another iteration in the form of a culminating antithesis:

> And either cease to live, or cease to love!

While being careful to respect the characteristics of his author, Pope displays a technical virtuosity and ease which show plainly how far he has advanced from the stage represented by *Polyphemus and Acis*. Even so, greater skill was to come, for *Sapho to Phaon* is only the forerunner of *Eloisa to Abelard*.

IV: *THE FIRST BOOK OF STATIUS*

I

On May 20, 1712, Pope's translation of *The First Book of Statius His Thebais* was published for the first time by Lintot in *Miscellaneous Poems and Translations, By Several Hands*. At the end of the prose "Argument" prefixed to the poem Pope said, rather ambiguously, that he hoped he need "not apologize for his Choice of this Piece, which was made almost in his Childhood." He then added that he had been "prevail'd upon" a "few Years afterwards" to give it "some Correction". Five years later, on the half-title page of the poem in the 1717 *Works*, he specified that it had been "Translated in 1703", and in 1735, in a note to his printed correspondence, he said that the translation was made when he was "but 14 Years old",[1] that is, in 1702 or 1703.

---

1. See *Corr.*, 1 36, *n*3.

He apparently had been introduced to Statius early, for he told Spence[1] that he had been led, when he was "about eight years old", to Sandys's Ovid and to a "translation of part of Statius, by some very bad hand". The very bad hand was that of Thomas Stephens, but Pope liked "extremely" both his and Sandys's translations. He also informed Spence that the epic poem he wrote at the age of twelve contained imitations of various poets, among them Statius.[2] In his "great reading period" he read Statius and liked him, "next to Virgil", better than "all the Latin poets".[3]

It was during the period when he set himself "scattered lessons" in the languages, he told Spence, that he translated "that part of Statius which was afterwards printed with the corrections of Walsh".[4] This is the only indication that Walsh, who died in March, 1708, advised Pope on the translation. The time of his death presents no obstacle, especially if a date of January 19, 1708, is accepted for the letter to Cromwell in which Pope enclosed his translation for criticism.[5] Here Pope asks Cromwell for advice about the "Accuracy" and "fidelity" of his work, which he says he has not had time "to Compare of Late with its Original". This last suggests that he speaks of a translation made some time before, and his explanation that he had omitted "in this Copy" a passage he had previously translated also suggests that he had revised, at least in part, an earlier version. In any event, the translation was not at this time complete, for the letter states that he has left out, for various reasons, ll. 128–43, 167–310,[6] 408–81.

If a date of January 19, 1708, is allowed to the above letter, it was over a year later that Pope again submitted the poem to Cromwell. On May 7, 1709,[7] he writes to say that he is sending his "Continuation of the Version of Statius". This "Continuation" was apparently the very manuscript Cromwell had already seen and criticized, plus at least some portions not previously translated. For Pope not only says he has had an "extraordinary Flux of Rhyme" upon him

---

1. Spence, p. 276.   2. Ibid., p. 277.   3. Ibid., p. 279.
4. Ibid., p. 278.
5. In his printed correspondence Pope, whose memory was often faulty, gave the letter a date of Jan. 22, 1708–9. A contemporary transcript of the letter bears the date of Jan. 19, 1707–8, and Professor Sherburn argues for its validity. See *Corr.*, I 36, *n*2.
6. Actually, ll. 168–311.   7. *Corr.*, I 56–8.

for three days, "in which time all the Verses you see added, have been written", but adds: "If you will please to begin where you left off last, & mark the Margins as you have done in the pages immediately before, (which you will find corrected to your Sense since your last perusal) you will extreamly oblige me, and improve my Translation." About a month later, on June 10,[1] he writes to thank Cromwell for his remarks, "which I think to be just, except where you cry out (like one in *Horace*'s *Art of Poetry*) *Pulchrè, bené, recté!*" By the end of the summer he must have considered his work of correction nearly finished, for Sir William Trumbull wrote to his nephew Ralph Bridges on October 31, 1709, that "Little Pope" is "copying fairly his Translat^n. of the 1st. Book of Statius' Theb."[2] On November 30 Pope says that Cromwell has "reason to make some delay" with some "Faults" then under his examination,[3] and on December 15 he thanks him for "reviewing" some papers which Trumbull has repeatedly asked to see, but which he has deferred showing to him "till I coud supply the Blank Spaces I left in the fair Copy by your Approbation."[4] The identity of the work discussed in these last two letters is not certain: it may have been the first book of Statius, it may have been *Sapho to Phaon*. On April 10, 1710, however, another specific reference occurs, for Pope says he is sending "these Arguments in Prose to the Thebaid", which suggests that, instead of the one "Argument" now prefixed to the poem, Pope had written several, perhaps as summaries of those portions of the poem he did not translate.[5] On June 24 he asks to have the "Arguments to Statius" returned, "with any Remarks you may have made on that Author."[6]

---

1. *Corr.*, I 63.

2. From the Bishop Percy transcripts in the Bodleian Library (MS Eng. letters d. 59), made available to the editors through the kindness of Professor Sherburn. The transcripts also contain the following fragment, dated 18 Oct. 1708, of a letter from Trumbull to Bridges: "If Monsieur Vaillant knows of Statius in French by Monsieur Saumaise, you will favour me to send me word of it." Was the request for the book on Pope's behalf? On Dec. 1, 1708, Trumbull again requests the book, and on Jan. 12, 1709, Bridges replies that he cannot purchase it. See *Hist. MSS Comm.*, *Report on the MSS of the Marquess of Downshire*, I ii 864, 868; *N & Q*, N.S., v (Aug., 1958), pp. 343–8.

3. *Corr.*, I 76.   4. Ibid., I 76–7.   5. Ibid., I 82, *n*1.
6. Ibid., I 91.

The letters exchanged between Pope and Cromwell indicate that
Pope worked intermittently on a revision of an early version of his
poem over a period of at least eighteen months, and probably over a
period of nearly three years.[1] We do not know precisely when he
considered the poem to be finished, but the evidence suggests that it
was before he imposed upon himself those rules in which he condemns the use of expletives and of needless Alexandrines. One supposes that he finished work on the poem before the letter to Cromwell of November 25, 1710, in which these rules are formulated,[2]
and that he subsequently sent the poem, containing thirteen examples of *did* and nine Alexandrines, to the press without further
revision. He turned to these faults later, however, for ten of the expletives and three of the Alexandrines were removed from the poem
when it appeared in the 1717 *Works*.

II

In 1648 Thomas Stephens published *An Essay upon Statius: or,
The Five First Books of Publ. Papinius Statius his Thebais, Done into
English Verse*. The translation is singularly uncouth and halting
and, as the author admitted in his preface "To the ingenuous
Reader", without any real literary pretensions: "Thou art here
presented with a piece of *Statius* metaphrased. . . The translation
was meditated, midst all the clamour and imployments of a publike
Schoole; and so, cannot be so accomplish'd as might be expected
from a vacant retirednesse. And, when I shall tell thee, that it was
intended for a help to my scholars, for understanding the Poet, thou
wilt not wonder at my marginall explications of the Poetick story."

Like Sandys, Stephens represented to Pope an outmoded style of
translation, the way of metaphrase which Dryden rejected in his
Preface to *Ovid's Epistles* and which Pope never practised. Yet Pope
consulted Stephens's translation, as he had Sandys's, and it might
be said that he honoured the old schoolmaster posthumously by
becoming his brightest pupil. The happiest instance of Stephens's
influence derives from ll. 419–26 of his translation:

1. The time depends on which date, 1708 or 1709, is assigned to the letter in
which Pope first discusses Statius with Cromwell. See p. 347, *n* 5, above.

2. As early as May, 1709, however, Pope had agreed with Cromwell's strictures on the use of the hiatus. See *Corr.*, I 57.

By this time had the Moon begun her station,
And *Sol*, tir'd out with's last perambulation,
VVas gone to bed. The silent world does view
Her Ayery charriot, pearld with drops of dew.
No beasts doe roare, no birds doe chatter, sleep
Or'e mans desires, and careful thoughts does creep:
And nodding through the aire, brings down in hast,
A sweet forgetfulness of labour past.

Out of this and the original Pope created these shining lines:

'Twas now the Time when *Phœbus* yields to Night,
And rising *Cynthia* sheds her silver Light,
Wide o'er the World in solemn Pomp she drew
Her airy Chariot, hung with Pearly Dew;
All Birds and Beasts lye hush'd; Sleep steals away
The wild Desires of Men, and Toils of Day,
And brings, descending thro' the silent Air,
A sweet Forgetfulness of Human Care.

In these lines Pope not only exhibits that skill in correcting and improving which led Broome, his partner in the translation of the *Odyssey*, to say that he "turns everything he touches into gold";[1] he is also often closer (in the fifth and last lines, for example) to the original.

The influence of Stephens was not, however, very great. As the notes to this edition show, Pope's borrowings were very rare, and often confined to a single word. When he first attempted Statius in his early youth he may have relied on Stephens as a guide to the meaning, but in the finished piece he is markedly different from him in style and language. Thus when Adrastus says, in his prayer to Apollo, ll. 703–5,

tela tibi longeque feros lentandus in hostes
arcus, et aetherii dono cessere parentes
aeternum florere genas . . . ,

Stephens translates almost word for word:

The Quiver's thine, and bow stiffe-bent, to quell

---

1. See *Corr.*, II 150.

> Thy daring foes: Eternal youth does dwell
> Upon thy cheeks.

Pope's translation is confined within a couplet,

> By thee the Bow and mortal Shafts are born,
> Eternal Charms thy blooming Youth adorn.

and he suppresses certain details: the destruction of savage foes is summed up in "mortal Shafts", and "cheeks" is replaced by "Charms" and "blooming Youth". Yet this tendency towards simplification is checked, if not halted, by the more pointed way in which Pope's couplet juxtaposes Apollo's beauteous form against his death-dealing character, his "Eternal Charms" against his "mortal Shafts".

In his correspondence with Cromwell Pope's concern to reflect the original closely is seen clearly in his request that his friend be "very free" of his remarks on the accuracy and fidelity of the translation, and also in these words: "I desire you to be the more severe as it is much more Criminal for me to make another speak Nonsense than to do it in my own proper Person."[1] The letters also make clear, however, that he was determined not to follow his author into what he considered faults of decorum. Thus he refused to the last to preserve ll. 408–81 of Statius, which he considered "an odd account of an Unmannerly Batle at fistycuffs between the *two Princes* [Polynices and Tydeus] on a Very slight Occasion, & at a time when one would think the fatigue of their Journy in so Tempestuous a Night might have renderd 'em Very unfit for such a Scuffle."[2] When Statius emphasizes that the prize for which the brothers fight is not a realm of wealth and great palaces, but only a poor kingdom, Pope translates a portion of the passage with remarkable brilliance.[3] In order to safeguard, however, what he considered to be the dignity of an epic poem, he objects to what he calls Statius's "Mean Opinion" of the prize,[4] and therefore omits the lines which contain one of the major ironies of the conflict:

---

1. Ibid., 1 36.
2. Ibid., 1 37. Pope translated the passage, but refused to transmit it to Cromwell or to print it.
3. Ll. 200–9.   4. *Corr.*, 1 37.

> sed nuda potestas
> armavit fratres, pugna est de paupere regno.[1]

He refuses to follow Statius into what he considers instances of bathos,[2] or of extravagant hyperbole and geographical error,[3] and tells Cromwell that "there are numberless particulars blameworthy in our Author, which I have try'd to soften."[4]

Throughout his poem Pope seems to have remembered Virgil, particularly as he had been translated by Dryden. He also, in the turns and ingenuities of his language, often recalls Ovid, yet, as the notes reveal, he is attempting at the same time to capture some of the epic breadth and vigour he discovered in Milton. His task is no longer limited to the reproduction of the easy, flowing graces of the *Metamorphoses* or of the elegiac passion of Sappho. He is trying his hand at vast pictures, like that of the Council of the Gods with its grandiose speeches, at epic comparisons and descriptions such as are required in the flight of Mercury "down the Steep of Heav'n". In a word, he is preparing to become the translator of Homer.

V: TRANSLATIONS FROM HOMER

I

The Episode of Sarpedon, taken from the twelfth and sixteenth books of the *Iliad*, was the first of Pope's translations from the classics to be published. It appeared, along with the *Pastorals* and his version of Chaucer's *Merchant's Tale*, in *Poetical Miscellanies, The Sixth Part*, in 1709. Pope's receipt for the sum paid to him for the translation still exists,[5] and reads thus: "Jan. 13. 1708/9. Receivd of Mr Tonson 3 Guineas for a Translation of the Episode of Sarpedon, printed in ye 6th p^t of Miscellany Poems. A. Pope."

---

1. Ll. 150–1.   2. *Corr.*, I 37.   3. Ibid., I 64.

4. Ibid. The letters show that Pope had read, or was reading, the French critics, particularly Le Bossu's *Traité du poëme épique*. He reproaches Statius for extending his story beyond the duration of a year, and is surprised that Le Bossu had not observed this. He apparently had not noticed that Le Bossu (bk II, ch. xviii) regarded the action of an epic poem as limited neither in time nor in space.

5. It is in the Pierpont Morgan Library. See *Early Career*, facing p. 85, for a reproduction of the receipt.

The poet was yet a child when he discovered Homer. "Ogilby's translation of Homer was one of the first large poems that ever Mr. Pope read", reports Spence; "and he still spoke of the pleasure it then gave him, with a sort of rapture, only in reflecting on it.—'It was that great edition with pictures, I was then about eight years old'."[1] He must have made his early translations of Ovid and Statius before he attempted Homer, yet he had advanced upon the Greek by 1707, the year of a letter (dated September 18) from Trumbull to his nephew Ralph Bridges: "Little Pope is returned from Mr. Walsh's; and resolves to go on with translating of Homer. He has begun with some Pieces taken out here & there according to his Fancy; and what I have seen, I think (but 'tis no matter what I think) they are very well don. The little Creature is my darling more and more."[2]

Some months later, on March 3, 1708, Pope himself seems to have written to Bridges, to ask if he might wait upon him, on a day when he is "like to be much at leisure", to confer on "some private business".[3] This business may have been a request that Bridges consent to read and criticize the Homer translations, for a month later, on April 5, 1708, Pope writes to thank him for his "Remarks" and to explain that he had been led into some of his "deviations from the Greek" by the translations of Chapman and Hobbes.[4] In the meantime, it seems, Pope had submitted his manuscript to Trumbull, for on April 9 the latter writes that his nephew had sent him his critical observations but that he had not had time to consult them. As for his own opinion, he writes: "I entirely approve of your Translation of those Pieces of *Homer*, both as to the versification and the true sense that shines thro' the whole." He reminds Pope that he had urged him repeatedly to translate the whole of Homer, and entreats him to add the present pieces to the "Miscellanies", saying "I hope it will come time enough for that purpose."[5] Trumbull's words indicate that Pope had already sent his *Pastorals* and his version of Chaucer to Tonson, a fact confirmed by the differing dates on Pope's receipts for his first poetical earnings: the receipt of the *Pastorals* is dated March 4, 1708, that of the *Episode of Sarpedon*

1. Spence, p. 276.
2. From the Percy transcripts in the Bodleian Library (MS Eng. letters d. 59).
3. See *Corr.*, I 41 and *n*2.   4. Ibid., I 43–4.   5. Ibid., I 45–6.

nearly a year later. In the event there was, as it proved, time enough, for the "Miscellanies", considerably overdue, did not come out until May, 1709.

The record of the critical interchange between Bridges and Pope concerning the meaning and translation of passages in the Sarpedon episode still exists, bound with the manuscripts of Pope's translation of the *Iliad* in the British Museum.[1] It occurs just before the fair copy of the episode the poet must have made subsequent to Bridges's criticisms, and which he later made use of, with only slight revision, in his translation of the rest of the *Iliad*. The record was published by an anonymous writer in the *European Magazine and London Review* (vol. XI, June, 1787), but has not since been reproduced.

These notes now exist in the form of a colloquy, and are written on what once may have formed a wide margin to the translation submitted to Bridges. One suspects that Pope indicated by an "X" next to his text those passages he particularly wished Bridges to examine. At one point, for example, there occurs a notation in Pope's hand which apparently refers to l. 232 of the printed text: "X Impending Fate". Bridges says: "I see no reason for any alteration there"; and then Pope replies: "(Twas markd only on acc^t of having been us'd in another place, & is to remain here)". As an example of the help Bridges gave, one may cite the exchange concerning ll. 119–20. First occurs (though it may have been written after Bridges's remark) in Pope's hand, after an "X", what must have been the reading on the manuscript sent to Bridges:

> With deep regret the Lycian King beheld
> His Friend retreating, *and his Troops repelld.*[2]

Then occurs Bridges's comment: "It does not appear in Homer that Glaucus' Troops retreated with him . . . I rather believe ye contrary." Below this Pope writes: "Altred thus.

---

1. Add. MSS 4807–9.

2. One is inclined to think Pope transferred to the margins, above Bridges's comments, the lines to which his comments referred, and that then the margins (if so wide a space can be so described) were cut from the manuscript. This is guess-work, however: the comments of Bridges may have been written on loose sheets.

> With deep Regret the Lycian King beheld
> Disabled Glaucus slowly quit the Field."

The altered reading is found in the fair copy of the manuscript, but then Pope there revised the first line of the couplet to give the reading of the first printed text. Again, there is, in Pope's hand, a reference to *Iliad*, xii 406, under which is this comment by Bridges: "Then turning to his Lycian troops he thus encourages them.— That's what Homer says.—By all means alter those lines." Then Pope writes: "The lines objected to were these:

> With his own Fires his fainting Troops he warms,
> Revives their Rage, and animates their Arms.

Will the following do?

> Then rais'd with Hope, and fir'd with Glory's Charms,
> His fainting Squadrons with these Words he warms, &c.[1]

(For you will find Homer mentioning in this place the Hopes Sarpedon had of gaining Glory in this Battle.—ἐπεί οἱ θυμὸς ἐέλπετο κῦδος ἀρέσθαι.[2])."

According to the anonymous writer who first published in the *European Magazine* the exchange between Pope and Bridges, there were at that time, in 1787, in the possession of the Rev. Brook Bridges, nephew of Ralph Bridges, "Many curious letters of Sir William Trumbull (some of them relating to Mr. Pope) and some original letters of Mr. Pope himself to the aforesaid Mr. Ralph Bridges."[3] In one of these letters, the writer was informed, "Mr. Pope confesses his ignorance of the Greek language; but at the same time asserts the possibility of making a good version of Homer, by aid of the Latin and English translators, without understanding a

---

1. Cf. ll. 143–4. The lines given here by Pope are close to the reading of the fair copy, which is identical with the reading of the first printed text.
2. XII 407.
3. The Percy transcripts recently discovered by Professor Sherburn in the Bodleian Library may derive from this collection of letters. A transcript of the Percy transcripts was made at one time by C. W. Dilke, who recorded them in a manuscript volume he entitled *Pope Chronology* (Brit. Mus. shelf mark 12274. i. 13). See *n* 2, p. 348, above.

word of the original."[1] The truth of this report is dubious, particularly when set against Pope's citation of the Greek, as in the above paragraph, in his defence, or against Trumbull's earnest urgings that he undertake to translate the whole of Homer.[2] There is no doubt that Bridges was able to find fault with Pope's lines: he points out errors in meaning, or departures from Homeric "simplicity", or possible obscurities in the translation. On occasion Pope justifies his expression by the example of Dryden but it is clear that he took Bridges's criticisms to heart and corrected his lines accordingly. Bridges, on his part, must have studied the translation fairly closely, at least the first part of it,[3] and yet on the whole there are few instances of his remark, "By all means change that Verse." And against these remarks it is only fair to set this one, on an unspecified passage: "You need not alter this. To do you Justice here, once for all. You have an admirable Talent in turning Homer's Speeches, wch I always thought the best & most difficult part of Him."

Pope did seek aid from translators who preceded him, as he avows in his notes to Bridges and in the letter in which he thanks him for his remarks.[4] He used, he said, "the Cambridge Editors of the large Homer, in Greek and Latin", and also Chapman and Hobbes. The "Authority" of these personages, "join'd to the knowledge" of his "own imperfectness in the Language", often led him, he says, into errors he would otherwise have avoided. He followed Chapman and Hobbes at times because they "are (it seems) as much celebrated for their knowledge of the Original, as they are decryd, for the baldness of their Translations." Here he seems to echo Dryden, for whom the "incredible pleasure and extreme transport" with which the Earl of Mulgrave and Waller read Chapman

---

1. P. 390. This statement may be a mere distortion of Pope's words cited in the next paragraph.

2. The Percy transcripts make it clear that Trumbull encouraged Pope in the project of translating Homer, and also that Pope was on very good terms with Bridges for several years after the period in which he sought criticism of the Sarpedon episode.

3. At one point in the record, near l. 283, Pope says: "Sir, I observe you have made very few Remarks on this second Part of the Episode of Sarpedon, & fear it was want of Time, not want of seeing the faults, that caus'd it to pass wth fewer blots than the other."

4. *Corr.*, 1 43-4.

could only proceed from Homer himself, and not from the translator who "has thrown him down as low as harsh numbers, improper English, and a monstrous length of verse could carry him."[1]
And then Dryden asked the question which perhaps encouraged
Pope to make his own attempt on Homer: "What then would he
appear in the harmonious version of one of the best writers,[2] living
in a much better age than was the last? I mean for versification, and
the art of numbers. . ."

Efforts to achieve such a "harmonious version" were made long
before Pope undertook the task: Dryden himself translated the first
book of the *Iliad*. The most important of these, for our purposes, is
the translation by John Denham of the very passage, Sarpedon's
famous speech to Glaucus, that is so central to the whole of Pope's
chosen episode. Comparison of Denham's version of the speech
with that of Chapman reveals how completely Denham departed
from his predecessor and, in so doing, gave to Pope the example he
needed. These lines of Chapman, for example,

> and every way we go,
> Gaze on us as we were their Gods,

become, in the couplet used by Denham:

> Why as we pass, do those on *Xanthus* shore,
> As Gods behold us, and as Gods adore?[3]

Where Chapman's lines are halting,

> But since we must go, though not here; and that besides the
>   chance
> Proposd now, there are infinite fates, of other sorts in death,
> Which (neither to be fled nor scapt) a man must sinke
>   beneath:
> Come, trie we, if this sort be ours: and either render thus,
> Glorie to others, or make them, resigne the like to us,

Denham is smooth and pointed:

> But since with Fortune Nature doth conspire,

---

1. Dedication of *Examen Poeticum* (*Essays*, II 14).
2. Dryden seems to have had Congreve in mind.
3. *Sarpedon's Speech to Glaucus in the 12th of Homer*, 10–11.

Since Age, Disease, or some less noble End,
Though not less certain, doth our days attend;
Since 'tis decreed, and to this period lead,
A thousand ways the noblest path we'll tread;
And bravely on, till they, or we, or all,
A common Sacrifice to Honour fall.

One has only to read Denham's and Pope's translations of Sarpedon's speech side by side (which is what Pope wanted Bridges to do[1]) to realize an important source of Pope's inspiration. That the public might be sure of his model Pope included in "The Argument" to the first printed text a notice of Denham's translation, and later he made more specific acknowledgement: ". . . this speech of Sarpedon is excellently translated by Sir John Denham, and if I have done it with any spirit, it is partly owing to him."[2]

II

The Arrival of Ulysses in Ithaca, from Book XIII of the *Odyssey*, appeared for the first time, along with several other pieces by Pope, in the volume that Steele published in December, 1713, under the title of *Poetical Miscellanies*. According to a receipt, dated October 5, 1713, Pope received fifteen guineas from Jacob Tonson for this translation and his *The Wife of Bath Her Prologue*.[3] There is no certain evidence of the date of composition of the poem, but it did contain, in its early printings, two instances of the expletive *did*, an indication that it was written before Pope's formulation of rules against such usage and that he did not revise it before sending it to the printer. It may date from the period in 1707–8 in which he translated the *Episode of Sarpedon*, or there may be a hidden reference to the poem in the letter from Trumbull to Bridges of October

1. In one of his manuscript notes to Bridges, Pope says: "I wish you had read S^r. John Denham's Translation of this Speech wth mine (wch is printed in his Poem). Do you think it will be not necessary I shou'd make some Apology to ye World, in ye Argument or otherwise, for attempting the speech after that Author?"

2. See *Iliad*, Bk XII 387n.

3. The receipt is in the Berg Collection of the New York Public Library. See the letter from Tonson to Pope of Oct. 5, 1713 (*Corr.*, I 191–2) and Sherburn's note 8, I. 191.

31, 1709, where it is said that Pope is recopying his Statius: "But for Homer, he desists; his frequent pains in his Head, disable yᵉ poore Creature; which I am griev'd at."[1] Ultimately the episode was included, with very few modifications, in the complete translation of the *Odyssey*.

In his Postscript to the *Odyssey*, published many years after this early fragment, Pope placed himself in the long tradition of those who regarded Homer's poem as a "moral and political work, instructive to all degrees of men". Even at the time of this early translation, however, he seems to have regarded the *Odyssey* as offering exceptional opportunities for "moral sentences" of the type so honoured by French critics such as Le Bossu, and therefore he has Ulysses say of the Phaeacians, when he thinks himself abandoned by them in a strange land, such words as these·

> Oh righteous Gods! of all the Great, how few
> Are just to Heav'n, and to their Promise true!

Or again, when Pallas informs Ulysses that he must "Yield to the Force of unresisted Fate, / And bear unmov'd the Wrongs of base Mankind", Pope is inspired to describe such an attitude of self-denial as the "last and hardest Conquest of the Mind".

Pope departs from literalistic fidelity to Homer in other ways too. He omits to mention cauldrons as being among the presents Ulysses received from the Phaeacians, or he has Ulysses "beat his careful Breast" rather than, as Homer has it, "slap his thighs". These were matters of "decorum", yet under that term lay pressing issues for a translator. In a strictly literal translation which makes no claims to being poetic in its own right, a translator assumes no responsibility for those elements in his author which, in a different language and to a different age, may appear grotesque or bathetic. As the maker of a poem as well as of a translation, Pope could not adopt such an attitude, and he was therefore willing, in order to preserve what he regarded as the inherent dignity of an epic poem, to omit a detail or change a gesture.

In the Preface to his *Iliad* Pope felt it a "great Loss to the Poetical World" that Dryden did not translate Homer, and declared that he would not have undertaken his own translation if he had. If this

---

1. From the Percy transcripts in the Bodleian Library.

is true, the loss cannot be one of great regret, for it became the
occasion for Pope to give to his own age as noble and spirited a
translation of Homer as Dryden had given, of Virgil, to his. True,
the translations of both were attacked in their own time, as they
have been since, and the charges made against Dryden were also
made against Pope, who, indeed, found cause for glory in the
parallel.[1] In their achievements as well, perhaps, as in what have
come to be regarded as their faults, the two poets seem fully com-
parable. Yet how great is the contrast between the translator of
Virgil, struggling against age and sickness and clamorous sub-
scribers,[2] and the young poet who, from the outset of his career, was
to find, thanks to his Homer, friends, fame, and fortune.

---

1. See *A Parallel of the Characters of Mr. Dryden and Mr. Pope*, appended to the
Dunciad (vol. v, pp. 230*ff.*).
2. See the *Dedication of the Æneis* (*Essays*, ii 216, 240).

ADVERTISEMENT.

THE following Translations were selected from many others done by the Author in his Youth; for the most part indeed but a sort of *Exercises*, while he was improving himself in the Languages, and carried by his early Bent to *Poetry* to perform them rather in Verse than Prose. Mr. 5 *Dryden*'s *Fables* came out about that time, which occasion'd the Translations from *Chaucer*. They were first separately printed in Miscellanies by *J. Tonson* and *B. Lintot*, and afterwards collected in the Quarto Edition of 1717. The *Imitations* of *English Authors* which are added at the end, were done as early, some 10 of them at fourteen or fifteen Years old; but having also got into Miscellanies, we have put them here together to complete this Juvenile Volume.

ADVERTISEMENT.] This Advertisement appeared in editions of the *Works* from 1736 to 1751. It is placed here even though some of the following translations did not appear in these editions.

7. *Translations from Chaucer*] See Vol. II.
9–10. *Imitations of English Authors*] See Vol. VI.

POLYPHEMUS

AND

ACIS.

NOTE ON THE TEXT

The text of *Polyphemus and Acis* was first published in *The London Magazine: Or Gentleman's Monthly Intelligencer*, in the issue of December, 1749. It has not been reprinted since. In its first appearance there was no identification of its author, but the July, 1751, issue of the *London Magazine*, p. 320, states that Pope "At 14 . . . wrote his Polyphemus and Acis, out of the 13th book of Ovid's Metamorphoses; which our readers may see in our Magazine for 1749, p. 568." Spence relates, p. 283*n*, that some of Pope's "first exercises were imitations of the stories that pleased him most in Ovid . . . I have one of these original exercises now by me, in his own hand. It is the story of Acis and Galatea, from Ovid; and was translated when he was but fourteen years old."

POLYPHEMUS *and* ACIS.

Out of the thirteenth Book *of*
OVID'S METAMORPHOSES.

Connexion *of the* FABLE.

On occasion of Æneas's Passage by Scylla *and* Charybdis, *the Poet introduces an Account of the former; who was, before her Transformation, an Attendant of* Galatea. *As she is employed in dressing her Mistress, she relates to her the following Story of her Amours with* Acis, *and the Love of* Polyphemus.

FROM fair Symæthis and her Faunus came
A lovely youth, and Acis was his name;
His parents joy, who did a comfort prove
To them by nature, but to me by love:
To me the boy did an affection bear,   5
His only pleasure, and his early care.
E'er sixteen passing years had overlaid
His downy cheeks with a beginning shade,
Acis I lov'd, and Polyphemus too
With equal ardour did my love pursue;   10
Nor knew I then which passion greater prov'd,
If most I hated, or if most I lov'd.

1–3. Cf. Dryden (*The Fable of Acis, Polyphemus, and Galatea*, 1–2):
> Acis, the Lovely Youth, whose loss I mourn,
> From *Faunus* and the Nymph *Symethis* born;

and Sandys, 845–6:
> The Nymph *Simethis* bore a louely Boy
> To *Faunus*, *Acis* cald; to them a ioy.

Symaethis was the daughter of the Sicilian river-god Symaethus.

Throughout these notes the 1626 edn of Sandys's Ovid is used. Cf. *Fable of Dryope*, 7–8n (pp. 385–6, below).

5. Sandys, 848: "To me an innocent affection bare".

8. Dryden, 8: "And doubtful Down, began to shade his Chin"; and Sandys, 850: "And signe his cheekes with scarce-appearing downe".

10. Sandys, 851:
> As I the gentle boy, so *Polypheme*
> My loue persude . . .

Great queen of love! how boundless is thy sway;
Which monsters wild, and savages obey!
Thy force the barb'rous Polyphemus try'd,   15
The proud despiser of all heav'n beside;
Ev'n he, the terror of his native grove,
Dismiss'd his fierceness, and cou'd learn to love!
    Now all neglected, he forgets his home,
His flocks at random round the forest roam: 20
While nice, and anxious in his new disease,
He vainly studies every art to please:
To trim his beard, th'unweildy scythe prepares;
And combs with rakes, his rough, disorder'd hairs:
Adjusts his shapes; while in the crystal brook   25
He views and practises a milder look.
Love makes him all his cruelty forego,
And ships, in safety, wander to and fro.
    It chanc'd prophetick Telemus, who knew
The flight of birds, and thence presages drew,   30
Arriving then by Ætna's steepy height,
Foretold the Cyclops he shou'd lose his sight.
The laughing Cyclops gave the bard the lye,
And said, a charming female stole that eye.
Thus scorning prophecy, and warn'd in vain,   35
With heavy steps he sinks the sandy plain;
Then weary grown, to shady grotts retires,
But finds no shelter from his raging fires.

---

13. Dryden, 16 (of Venus): ". . . and boundless is thy Sway".
17. Dryden, 19: "The Terrour of the Woods . . ."
25. *shapes*] Appearance, perhaps, or attitude and dress.
25–6. See Intro., p. 334.
27–8. Sandys, 868: "Lesse cruell now: ships come and goe in peace."
29*ff.* See Intro., pp. 333–4.
33 *f.* See Intro., pp. 333–4.
35. Dryden, 44: "Thus, warn'd in vain, with stalking pace he strode".
36. *sinks*, which is neither in Sandys nor in Dryden, translates Latin *degravat*.
38. This line is not in Ovid, at least not in this place. Pope may be anticipating the thought of Ovid's ll. 868–9. See l. 131*n*, below.

Far in the main a promontory grows,
Around whose rocky sides the water flows: 40
High in the midst, upon this airy steep
He sate, pursu'd by all his flocks of sheep.
Before his feet his pondrous staff he cast;
A pine which ships might challenge for a mast:
His whistle (which a hundred reeds compose)   45
With all his strength the giant-lover blows;
The neighbouring mountains, and resounding main
Shook, and return'd the dreadful blast again.
Hid in a rock, and by my Acis laid,
The boist'rous musick did my ears invade;   50
While to his reeds he sung his amorous pains,
In words like these, which still my mind retains.
    Oh! lovely nymph, and more than lilies fair, ⎫
More sweet than winter's sun, or summer's air, ⎬
And smooth as shells that gliding waters wear; ⎭   55
Not ice or crystal equal splendor yield,
O far more pleasing than the flow'ry field!
Wanton as kids; and more delicious far,
Than grapes mature, or blushing apples are;
More strait than alders, taller than the planes;   60
And soft as down upon the breast of swans:

40–2. Dryden, 50–2:
> On either side, below, the water flows;
> This airy walk, the Giant Lover chose.
> Here, on the midst he sate . . .

43–4. Sandys, 883–4:
> His staffe, a well-growne Pine, before him cast,
> Sufficient for a yard-supporting mast.

45. Dryden, 57–8: ". . . his Whistle while he try'd. / A hundred Reeds . . ."

54–5. Sandys, 892–3:
> Smoother then shels whereon the surges driue,
> More wisht then winters Sun, or Summers aire.

58. Dryden, 70: "More wanton than a Kid . . ."

60. *taller than the planes*] This *sounds* absurd. Ovid, 794, has "platano conspectior alta". Sandys, 895, has "More seemely then tall Planes".

60–1. The rhyme *planes–swans* is found in both Sandys and Dryden.

As gardens fresh, where running rivers stray,
But, ah! like rivers, swift to glide away;
And what alone must all my hopes remove,
Swift as the wind before pursuing love;   65
    Yet know, coy maid, and curse your long delay,
Know from whose arms you fly so fast away.
Behold the rocky caverns where I dwell,
Which summer suns, and winter frosts expel.
See how my fruits the loaded branches bend,   70
And grapes in clusters from the vine depend;
These bright, like gold, and those with purple shine;
And these and those, my dearest, shall be thine.
Here cornels rise, and in the shady grove
Grow scarlet strawberries to feast my love: 75
The chesnut, wilding, plum, and every tree,
For thee shall bear their fruits, and offer all to thee!
    These flocks are mine, and more are pen'd at home,
Range in the woods, and in the vallies roam:
So great the tale, I scarce can count them o'er;   80
The poorest shepherd best may tell his store.
Believe not me, but come and witness here,
How, scarce, my ewes their strutting udders bear;
What tender lambkins here my folds contain,

62-3. Dryden, 78-9:
                or running Streams, that stray
        Through Garden Plots, but ah more swift than they.
65. Pope, unlike Sandys and Dryden, has abridged the original at this point.
66. *curse your long delay*] Sandys, 910: "Curse thy delay . . ."
71. Dryden, 107: "And Grapes in clusters . . ."
73. Dryden, 109: "And these and those, are all reserv'd for you."
75. *scarlet strawberries*] Dryden, 110, has "Red Strawberries". Ovid, 816, has "mollia fraga", and Sandys, no epithet.
78-9. Sandys, 920-1:
        These flocks are ours: in vallies many stray,
        Woods many shade, at home as many stay.
82. Sandys, 926: "Belieue not me, but credit your owne eyes".
84. Dryden, 129: "In the warm Folds, their tender Lambkins lye."

And there what kids of equal age remain. 85
Nor boast we only common dainties here,
But roes and lev'rets, and the fallow deer;
The goat, the hare, with ev'ry forest beast;
And turtles taken from their airy nest.
Two cubs I have, as like as twins can be; 90
And these, dear nymph, are kept to play with thee:
Two little bears, I found them, and did please
Myself to think, my mistress shou'd have these.
    Come Galatea, from the sea arise,
And see my presents, nor the gifts despise. 95
I'm not so monst'rous; I my face did view
In yon clear lake, and thought it handsome too:
How great I look'd! of what a godlike size!
Not Jove himself (your Jove that sways the skies)
Is half so mighty, half so large, my love; 100
Your beauty charms a greater man than Jove.

---

85. *of equal age*] Ovid, 828: "par aetas". Not in Sandys and Dryden. Note
two lines in Ovid, 829–30, which were translated by Sandys and Dryden, but
omitted by Pope:

> lac mihi semper adest niveum: pars inde bibenda
> servatur, partem liquefacta coagula durant.

86. Dryden, 133: "Nor are these House-hold Dainties all my Store."
87. *lev'rets*] Young hares, in their first year.
89. Dryden, 137: "A pair of Turtles taken from the Nest."
90–3. Sandys, 935–8:

> A rugged Beares rough twins I found vpon
> The mountaine late, scarce from each other knowne,
> For thee to play with: finding these, I said,
> My Mistris you shall serue.

94. *Come Galatea*] Sandys, 939–40:

> Come *Galatea*, from the surges rise,
> Bright as the Morning; nor our gifts despise.

Dryden strikes a different tone:

> Oh raise, fair Nymph, your Beauteous Face above
> The Waves . . .

98–9. Dryden, 149–50:

> Survey my towring Stature, and my Size:
> Not *Jove*, the *Jove* you dream that rules the Skies . . .

Hairs, like a wood, my head and shoulders grace,
And cast a majesty on all my face:
The comely steeds are grac'd with flowing manes;
With fleeces sheep, and birds with plumy trains;   105
Leaves deck the stately trees; and man is fair,
By bearded cheeks, and members rough with hair.
With one large eye my ample front is grac'd,
Round like a shield, and in the middle plac'd:
The sun all objects views beneath the sky,   110
And yet, like me, has but a single eye.
My father o'er your seas presides; and he
Will be your father by your wedding me.
Oh! yeild at last, nor still remain severe;
I worship you, and you alone I fear!   115
Jove's harmless lightning unregarded flies;
No lightning wounds me but your angry eyes.
Nor thy contempt cou'd cause me thus to mourn,
If thou all others didst despise and scorn:
But Acis, Acis is thy dear delight;   120
For his embraces you the Cyclops slight.
Well, he may please himself, and you may share
His pleasures too (tho' that I scarce can bear)
Yet he shall find, wou'd time th'occasion shew,
The strength and fury of a giant foe.   125
I'll from his bleeding breast his entrails tear,

104–5. Dryden, 159–60:
> Foul is the Steed, without a flowing Main:
> And Birds without their Feathers and their Train.

109. Sandys, 954: "Round, like a mightie shield ..."

110–11. Sandys, 955–6:
> The Sun all obiects sees beneath the skie:
> And yet behold, the Sun hath but one eye.

113. *Will be your father*] Ovid, 855, has: "hunc tibi do socerum."

115. Sandys, 960: "To you I onely bow; you onely feare". Dryden, 170: "You I adore; and kneel to you alone."

117. Sandys, 962: "More dread the lightning of thy angrie eyes".

And hurl his mangled carcass in the air;
Or cast his limbs into thy guilty flood,
And mix thy waters with his reeking blood!
For oh! I burn, nor you my flames asswage;   130
And love disdain'd revives with fiercer rage.

Two lines here wanting.

This said, he rose, and frantick with his pain,
Roar'd out for rage, and hurried o'er the plain:
So bulls in forests hunt their absent loves,
And stung with anguish bellow through the groves.
But as around his rowling orb he cast,   136
Myself and Acis he descry'd at last.
These thefts, false nymph, thou shalt enjoy no more,
He cry'd, and Ætna trembled with the roar!
Frighted, beneath my native deeps I fled;   140
Acis too run, and help, oh help! he said,
A wretch undone: O parents help, and deign
T'admit your offspring in your watry reign!

---

129. Sandys, 971-2: ". . . mixe thy waue / With his hot blood . . ."
130-1. Dryden, 185-6:
> For oh I burn with Love, and thy Disdain
> Augments at once my Passion, and my Pain.
131. Pope omitted ll. 868-9 of Ovid:
> cumque suis videor translatam viribus Aetnam
> pectore ferre meo, nec tu, Galatea, moveris.
See l. 38*n*, above.
132. Sandys, 977: "This said, he rose . . ."
133. The word *hurried* is taken evidently from Sandys, 979.
134. *their absent loves*] The tone here recalls Dryden, 193-4:
> Mad as the vanquish'd Bull, when forc'd to yield
> His lovely Mistress . . .
Ovid, 871, has: "ut taurus vacca furibundus adempta . . ." Sandys, 980, has: "Much like a bull that hath his heifer lost." See Intro., p. 333.
141-3. Sandys, 986-8:
> you, o parents, aid
> The vtterly undone; and entertaine
> Your issue in the Empire where you raigne.

The Cyclops follow'd, and a stone he threw,
Torn from the rock, which threatned as it flew;   145
No further speech the thundering rock affords,
O'ertakes the flying boy, and smothers half his words.
Yet what we cou'd, and what no fates deny'd, ⎱
We soon perform'd, and Acis deify'd,   ⎬
To rule in streams to which he was ally'd: ⎭   150
His body press'd beneath the stone, the blood
Flow'd from the marble in a crimson flood;
Which lost its native red; and first appear'd
A troubled stream; the troubled stream was clear'd;
The rock asunder cleav'd, and thro' the chink   155
Long reeds sprung up as on a fountain's brink:
Strait from the hollow cliff, and yawning ground,
Insulting waters yield a murmuring sound:
At last a youth above the waist arose,

144-5. Dryden, 208-9:
　　　The Cyclops follow'd: but he sent before
　　　A Rib, which from the living Rock he tore.
　150. *ally'd*] The grandsire of Acis was Symaethus, the river-god. See ll. 1-3*n*.
　151-7. In this passage Pope made use of Sandys, and borrowed Dryden's
rhymes. Here is Sandys, 993-8:
　　　The purple blood from that depressure fled;
　　　Which presently forsooke the natiue red:
　　　First like a raine-discoloured streame appeares;
　　　Then christaline. The rock in sunder teares:
　　　Whose crannies with vp-starting reeds abound;
　　　And in the breach insulting waues resound.
Here is Dryden, 216-21:
　　　Straight issu'd from the Stone, a Stream of Blood;
　　　Which lost the Purple, mingling with the Flood.
　　　Then, like a troubl'd Torrent, it appear'd:
　　　The Torrent too, in little space was clear'd.
　　　The Stone was cleft, and through the yawning chink,
　　　New Reeds arose on the new River's brink.
　158. *Insulting*] Assaulting. Cf. Sandys, 998.
　159-60. Sandys, 999-1000:
　　　From whence a youth arose aboue the wast;
　　　His horned browes with quiuering reeds imbrac't.

Whose horned temples reedy wreaths inclose; 160
And, but he seem'd a larger bulk to bear,
With looks more azure, Acis might appear;
And Acis was; who now transform'd became
A crystal fountain, and preserv'd the name.

Memorandum. Done at 14 years old.

Cf. also Dryden, 226–7:
    Horns from his Temples rise; and either Horn
    Thick Wreaths of Reeds, (his Native growth) adorn.
For the "horned temples" of river-gods, see *Windsor-Forest*, 332n (p. 182, above).
  164. Sandys, 1004: ". . . which still preserues his name."

THE
FABLE
OF
Vertumnus and *Pomona*;

FROM
The Fourteenth Book of OVID'S
METAMORPHOSES.

Rege sub hoc Pomona fuit————&c.

NOTE ON THE TEXT

The Fable of Vertumnus and Pomona was first printed in Bernard Lintot's *Miscellaneous Poems and Translations, By Several Hands,* 1712. Pope made very few changes in the poem, the only revisions of which appear in the *Works* of 1717. Warburton, by following the text of 1741, perpetuated another misprint, this time at l. 61 (see *The Fable of Dryope*, Note on the Text). The present text incorporates the revisions Pope made, but follows the punctuation, spelling, and typography of the first edition.

In the editions from 1736 on Pope printed the Latin text along with his translation.

KEY TO THE CRITICAL APPARATUS

1712 = Miscellaneous Poems and Translations, octavo, Griffith 6.
1714 = Miscellaneous Poems and Translations, octavo, Griffith 32.
1717 = Works, quarto, Griffith 79.
1720 = Miscellaneous Poems and Translations, duodecimo, Griffith 124.
1722 = Miscellaneous Poems and Translations, duodecimo, Griffith 135.
1736*a* = Works, vol. III, octavo, Griffith 417.
1736*b* = Works, vol. III, octavo, Griffith 418.
1741 = Works, vol. I, part II, octavo, Griffith 521.
1751 = Works, ed. Warburton, vol. II, octavo, Griffith 644.

VERTUMNUS
AND
POMONA.

THE fair *Pomona* flourish'd in his Reign;
   Of all the Virgins of the Sylvan Train,
   None taught the Trees a nobler Race to bear,
Or more improv'd the Vegetable Care.
To her the shady Grove, the flow'ry Field,   5
The Streams and Fountains, no Delights cou'd yield;
'Twas all her Joy the ripening Fruits to tend,
And see the Boughs with happy Burthens bend.
The Hook she bore, instead of *Cynthia*'s Spear,
To lop the Growth of the luxuriant Year,   10
To decent Form the lawless Shoots to bring,
And teach th'obedient Branches where to spring.
Now the cleft Rind inserted Graffs receives,
And yields an Off-spring more than Nature gives;
Now sliding Streams the thirsty Plants renew,   15
And feed their Fibres with reviving Dew.
    These Cares alone her Virgin Breast imploy,
Averse from *Venus* and the Nuptial Joy;
Her private Orchards wall'd on ev'ry side,

Title] *Add. 1717–22:* From the FOURTEENTH BOOK of/*OVID*'s
METAMORPHOSES.
8 see] view *1712–14.*
9 No Dart she wielded, but a Hook did bear, *1712–14.*

---

   1. *his Reign*] The reign of Procas, legendary king of Alba Longa.
   1–4. On the structure of these lines see Intro., pp. 336–7. Citations from
Sandys's Ovid are from the 1626 edn.
   4. *Vegetable Care*] Cf. Dryden, *Georgics* IV 178: "To teach the vegetable
Arts . . ."
   15. *sliding Streams*] Sandys, 688: "soft-sliding Springs".

To lawless Sylvans all Access deny'd.   20
How oft the *Satyrs* and the wanton *Fawns*,
Who haunt the Forests or frequent the Lawns,
The *God* whose Ensign scares the Birds of Prey,
And old *Silenus*, youthful in Decay,
Imploy'd their Wiles and unavailing Care,   25
To pass the Fences, and surprize the Fair?
Like these, *Vertumnus* own'd his faithful Flame,
Like these, rejected by the scornful Dame.
To gain her Sight, a thousand Forms he wears,
And first a Reaper from the Field appears,   30
Sweating he walks, while Loads of golden Grain
O'ercharge the Shoulders of the seeming Swain.
Oft o'er his Back a crooked Scythe is laid,
And Wreaths of Hay his Sun-burnt Temples shade;
Oft in his harden'd Hand a Goad he bears,   35
Like one who late unyok'd the sweating Steers.
Sometimes his Pruning-hook corrects the Vines,
And the loose Straglers to their Ranks confines.
Now gath'ring what the bounteous Year allows,
He pulls ripe Apples from the bending Boughs.   40
A Soldier now, he with his Sword appears;

27–8 But most *Vertumnus* did his Love profess,
     With greater Passion, but with like Success; *1712–14.*

---

23. *The God*] Priapus, the god of fertility in vegetable and animal life. Images of Priapus were placed in gardens as protection against robbers and birds. Cf. Dryden, *Georgics* IV 167–8 (of Priapus):
    Besides, the God obscene, who frights away,
    With his Lath Sword, the Thiefs and Birds of Prey.
27. *Vertumnus*] A deity thought to preside over the seasons and their various productions in the vegetable world. To him gardeners offered their first fruits (cf. l. 96).
35–6. Sandys, 703–4:
    A gode now in his hardned hands he beares,
    And newly seemes to haue vnyok't his Steeres.
37. Sandys, 705–6: "Oft vines and fruit-trees with a pruning hooke / Corrects . . ."

A Fisher next, his trembling Angle bears.
Each Shape he varies, and each Art he tries,
On her bright Charms to feast his longing Eyes.
  A Female Form at last *Vertumnus* wears,   45
With all the Marks of rev'rend Age appears,
His Temples thinly spread with silver Hairs:
Prop'd on his Staff, and stooping as he goes,
A painted Mitre shades his furrow'd Brows.
The God, in this decrepit Form array'd,   50
The Gardens enter'd, and the Fruits survey'd,
And *happy You*! (he thus address'd the Maid)
Whose Charms as far all other Nymphs out-shine,
As other Gardens are excell'd by thine!
Then kiss'd the Fair; (his Kisses warmer grow   55
Than such as Women on their Sex bestow.)
Then plac'd beside her on the flow'ry Ground,
Beheld the Trees with Autumn's Bounty crown'd;
An Elm was near, to whose Embraces led,
The curling Vine her swelling Clusters spread;   60
He view'd their twining Branches with Delight,

61 their] her *1741–51*.

---

42. *trembling Angle*] Sandys, 708, following Ovid, has merely "an Angler with his cane". For Pope's epithet, see *Windsor-Forest*, 137–8n (p. 163, above).

44. *his longing Eyes*] Sandys, 710: "To winne accesse, and please his longing eyes."

49. *painted Mitre*] So Sandys. Ovid, 654, has "picta . . . mitra". The *mitra* was a head-dress worn by women; *picta* means that it was embellished, probably embroidered.

55 f. EC cite Sandys, *Met.*, II 430f. (episode of Calisto and Jupiter):
           His kisses too intemperate grow;
    Not such as Maids on Maidens do bestow.

59–66. Cf. *Par. Lost*, V 215-19:
           . . . or they led the Vine
    To wed her Elm; she spous'd about him twines
    Her marriageable arms, and with her brings
    Her dow'r th' adopted Clusters, to adorn
    His barren leaves.

And prais'd the Beauty of the pleasing Sight.
　　Yet this tall Elm, but for his Vine (he said)
Had stood neglected and a barren shade;
And this fair Vine, but that her Arms surround   65
Her marry'd Elm, had crept along the Ground.
Ah beauteous Maid, let this Example move
Your Mind, averse from all the Joys of Love.
Deign to be lov'd, and ev'ry Heart subdue!
What Nymph cou'd e'er attract such Crowds as you?
Not she whose Beauty urg'd the *Centaur*'s Arms,   71
Ulysses' Queen, nor *Helen*'s fatal Charms.
Ev'n now, when silent Scorn is all they gain,
A thousand court you, tho' they court in vain,
A thousand Sylvans, Demigods, and Gods,   75
That haunt our Mountains and our *Alban* Woods.
But if you'll prosper, mark what I advise,
Whom Age and long Experience render wise,
And one whose tender Care is far above
All that these Lovers ever felt of Love,   80
(Far more than e'er can by your self be guest)
Fix on *Vertumnus*, and reject the rest.
For his firm Faith I dare ingage my own,
Scarce to himself, himself is better known.
To distant Lands *Vertumnus* never roves;   85
Like you, contented with his Native Groves;
Nor at first sight, like most, admires the Fair; ⎫
For you he lives; and you alone shall share   ⎬
His last Affection, as his early Care.   ⎭

71 *Centaur's*] *Centaurs 1717–51.*

66. *crept . . . Ground*] Sandys, 726, has "would creepe vpon the ground".
71. Pope, who is more precise than Ovid here, was remembering the episode
in *Met.*, XII 71*ff.*, where Ovid describes the battle between the Lapithae and the
Centaurs, begun when one of the latter, Eurytus, tried to rape Hippodamia, the
beautiful bride of Pirithous. The reading *Centaur's* of the early texts seems preferable to the indefinite *Centaurs* introduced in *1717*.
87. Sandys, 744: "Nor loues, like common louers, at first sight".

Besides, he's lovely far above the rest,　　　　　　90
With Youth Immortal and with Beauty blest.
Add, that he varies ev'ry Shape with ease,
And tries all Forms, that may *Pomona* please.
But what shou'd most excite a mutual Flame,
Your Rural Cares, and Pleasures, are the same.　　95
To him your Orchards early Fruits are due,
(A pleasing Off'ring when 'tis made by you;)
He values these; but yet (alas) complains,
That still the best and dearest Gift remains.
Not the fair Fruit that on yon' Branches glows　　100
With that ripe red th'Autumnal Sun bestows,
Nor tastful Herbs that in these Gardens rise,
Which the kind Soil with milky Sap supplies;
You, only you, can move the God's Desire:
Oh crown so constant and so pure a Fire!　　　　105
Let soft Compassion touch your gentle Mind;
Think, 'tis *Vertumnus* begs you to be kind!
So may no Frost, when early Buds appear,
Destroy the Promise of the youthful Year;
Nor Winds, when first your florid Orchard blows,　110
Shake the light Blossoms from their blasted Boughs!
　　This when the various God had urg'd in vain,
He strait assum'd his Native Form again;
Such, and so bright an Aspect now he bears,
As when thro' Clouds th'emerging Sun appears,　　115
And thence exerting his refulgent Ray,
Dispels the Darkness and reveals the Day.

95–7. Sandys, 750–2:
　　　　　　　Your delights, the same:
　　　The first-fruits of your Hort-yard are his due;
　　　Which ioyfully he still accepts from you.
　107. Pope here omits the episode of Iphis and Anaxarete, told by Vertumnus (Ovid, 693–762).
　108. Sandys, 834: "So may thy fruits suruiue the Vernall frost".
　112. *various*] Appearing in a variety of forms (OED). Cf. *Od.*, IV 525.

Force he prepar'd, but check'd the rash Design;
For when, appearing in a Form Divine,
The Nymph surveys him, and beholds the Grace   120
Of charming Features and a youthful Face,
In her soft Breast consenting Passions move,
And the warm Maid confess'd a mutual Love.

120 surveys . . . beholds] survey'd . . . beheld *1712–14.*
122 A sudden Passion in her Breast did move, *1712–14.*

118–23. These six lines translate two of Ovid's, 770–1:
            vimque parat: sed vi non est opus, inque figura
            capta dei nympha est et mutua vulnera sensit.
See Intro., p. 336.

THE
FABLE of *DRYOPE*.

From the NINTH BOOK of
OVID's METAMORPHOSES.

NOTE ON THE TEXT

The Fable of Dryope was apparently first printed in the 1717 edition of Pope's *Works*, which appeared on June 3 according to Griffith. A short time later the poem was printed as part of Book IX in Tonson's edition of *Ovid's Metamorphoses*, to which Griffith assigns a date of August 1. The variant readings of this second printing have been recorded. Warburton's edition of the *Works* in 1751 apparently followed the text of the 1741 *Works*, and in doing so may have perpetuated a misprint in that edition (see variant to l. 55). In this instance the more reliable reading of the earlier editions has been preferred. The text printed here follows the text in the 1717 edition of the *Works* in spelling, punctuation, and typography.

In the editions from 1736 on Pope printed the Latin text along with his translation.

KEY TO THE CRITICAL APPARATUS

1717*a* = Works, quarto, Griffith 79.
1717*b* = Ovid's Metamorphoses, folio, Griffith 88.
1736*a* = Works, vol. III, octavo, Griffith 417.
1736*b* = Works, vol. III, octavo, Griffith 418.
1741 = Works, vol. I, part II, octavo, Griffith 521.
1751 = Works, ed. Warburton, vol. II, octavo, Griffith 644.

THE

FABLE

OF

DRYOPE.

Upon occasion of the death of Hercules, *his mother* Alcmena *recounts her misfortunes to* Iole, *who answers with a relation of those of her own family, in particular the transformation of her sister* Dryope, *which is the subject of the ensuing Fable.*

S HE said, and for her lost *Galanthis* sighs,
　　When the fair Consort of her son replies.
　　Since you a servant's ravish'd form bemoan,
And kindly sigh for sorrows not your own;
Let me (if tears and grief permit) relate　　　　　5
A nearer woe, a sister's stranger fate.
　　No nymph of all *Oechalia* could compare
For beauteous form with *Dryope* the fair,

Title] *1717 adds:* From the Ninth Book of/*OVID's META-MORPHOSES.*
Upon occasion . . . Fable.] *Om. 1717b.*
7 *No new paragraph 1736a–51.*

Upon occasion] This introduction does not appear in *1717b*, and it is placed in a note in *1751*.
　1. *She said*] Alcmena has just told the story of Galanthis, one of her maids. Juno sent Lucina, goddess of childbirth, to cause the death of Alcmena by delaying the birth of Hercules, her son by Zeus. Galanthis brought about the delivery of Hercules by outwitting Lucina, but as punishment she was turned into a weasel.
　2. *Consort of her son*] Iole, who was the wife not of Hercules but of Hyllus, his son. The Latin *nurus* applies not only to the wife of a son, but to the wife of a grandson.
　7. *nymph*] The Latin *nympha* can mean either a young woman or a demi-goddess. In this line the word has the former sense, though there is nothing in Ovid to which it corresponds. Elsewhere (ll. 31, 37) Pope uses it to imply semi-divine status.
　7–8. EC compare Sandys, 346–7:

Her tender mother's only hope and pride,
(My self the offspring of a second bride.)   10
This nymph compress'd by him who rules the day,
Whom *Delphi* and the *Delian* isle obey,
Andræmon lov'd; and bless'd in all those charms
That pleas'd a God, succeeded to her arms.

A Lake there was, with shelving banks around,   15
Whose verdant summit fragrant myrtles crown'd.
These shades, unknowing of the fates, she sought,
And to the *Naiads* flow'ry garlands brought,
Her smiling babe (a pleasing charge) she prest
Within her arms, and nourish'd at her breast.   20
Not distant far a watry *Lotos* grows;
The spring was new, and all the verdant boughs
Adorn'd with blossoms, promis'd fruits that vie

---

17 These] Those *1717ab*.   20 Within] Between *1717b*.

Of all the' *Oechalides*
For forme few might with *Dryope* compare.
Oechalia was a city of Euboea, where Dryope's father, Eurytus, reigned.

Sandys's *Ovids Metamorphosis Englished* first appeared complete in 1626. It was revised for publication in 1632. Pope apparently used both editions: the parallel cited in the note to ll. 45–6 could have come only from 1626, while the parallel cited in the note to ll. 88–91 suggests the use of 1632. For purposes of convenience, all parallels, unless otherwise noted, are taken from 1626. See also Intro., pp. 338–9.

11. *compress'd*] Embraced sexually. Cf. Pope's *Od.*, I 95.

14. *succeeded to her arms*] He married her. Cf. Pope's *Il.*, XVI 225.

15–16. Sandys, 353–4:

A Lake there is, which sheluing margents bound,
Much like a shore; with fragrant myrtles crownd.

18. *Naiads*] Ovid and Sandys use the general term *nymphs*, but Pope had used this word above, l. 7.

19. *a pleasing charge*] Ovid, 339, has "dulce . . . onus". Sandys, 357, has "a pleasing burden".

21. *watry Lotos*] Not the well-known Egyptian lotus, a water-lily, but probably the *Zizyphus lotus*, a jujube tree, the fruit of which was esteemed by the ancients. Sandys in his Commentary to the Ninth Book confused the two; Pope probably did the same. Cf. *Sapho to Phaon*, 181–2 (p. 401, below).

In glowing colours with the *Tyrian* dye.
Of these she crop'd, to please her infant son;   25
And I my self the same rash act had done,
But lo! I saw, (as near her side I stood)
The violated blossoms drop with blood;
Upon the tree I cast a frightful look;
The trembling tree with sudden horror shook.   30
Lotis the nymph (if rural tales be true)
As from *Priapus'* lawless lust she flew,
Forsook her form; and fixing here, became
A flow'ry plant, which still preserves her name.
    This change unknown, astonish'd at the sight   35
My trembling sister strove to urge her flight,
And first the pardon of the nymphs implor'd,
And those offended sylvan pow'rs ador'd:
But when she backward wou'd have fled, she found
Her stiff'ning feet were rooted in the ground: 40
In vain to free her fasten'd feet she strove,
And as she struggles, only moves above;
She feels th'encroaching bark around her grow
By quick degrees, and cover all below:
Surpriz'd at this, her trembling hand she heaves   45
To rend her hair; her hand is fill'd with leaves;

37 And] Yet *1717ab*.   40 in] to *1717b*.
44 quick] slow *1717ab*.   cover] covers *1717a*.

25-6. *son . . . done*] Cf. Sandys, 361-2:
        Thence pulling flowers, she gaue them to her son
        To play with all; so was I like t'haue don.
  28. Wakefield compares Dryden, *Æn.*, III 53 (episode of Polydore): "The violated Myrtle ran with Gore".
  32. *Priapus*] See *Vertumnus and Pomona*, 23n (p. 378, above).
  36. *urge her flight*] Cf. *Windsor-Forest*, 190 (p. 167, above), and *Statius*, 558 (p. 433, below).
  42. *only moves above*] Sandys, 371, has "Who onely moues aboue".
  45*f*. See Intro., p. 338. Cf. also the transformation of Phaethon's sisters, *Met.*, II 346*ff*.

Where late was hair, the shooting leaves are seen
To rise, and shade her with a sudden green.
The child *Amphisus*, to her bosom prest,
Perceiv'd a colder and a harder breast,   50
And found the springs that ne'er till then deny'd
Their milky moisture, on a sudden dry'd.
I saw, unhappy! what I now relate,
And stood the helpless witness of thy fate;
Embrac'd thy boughs, the rising bark delay'd,   55
There wish'd to grow, and mingle shade with shade.
    Behold, *Andræmon* and th'unhappy Sire
Appear, and for their *Dryope* enquire;
A springing tree for *Dryope* they find,
And print warm kisses on the panting rind,   60
Prostrate, with tears their kindred plant bedew,
And close embrace, as to the roots they grew.
The face was all that now remain'd of thee,
No more a woman, nor yet quite a tree:
Thy branches hung with humid pearls appear,   65
From ev'ry leaf distills a trickling tear,
And strait a voice, while yet a voice remains,

55 the rising] thy rising *1741–51*.
62 embrace] embrac'd *1717ab*.

57. *th'unhappy Sire*] Eurytus, Dryope's father. He is mentioned in the Latin,
356, as having given Amphissos his name. This Pope omitted, making l. 57
somewhat obscure.
57–8. Sandys, 383–4:
        Behold, *Andræmon* comes; with him, her Sire;
        (Both wretched!) and for *Dryope* inquire.
60. Pope may have recalled *Met.*, I 554, the fable of Daphne, where Apollo
"sentit adhuc trepidare novo sub cortice pectus". and Dryden's tr., 749–50:
        The Tree still panted in th'unfinish'd part:
        Not wholly vegetive, and heav'd her Heart.
64. Wakefield cites Cowley, *Davideis*, III 254: "No more a *Woman*, nor yet
quite a *Stone*."
65. Wakefield cites Dryden, *Ecl.* x 20: "And hung with humid Pearls the
lowly Shrub appears".

Thus thro' the trembling boughs in sighs complains.
   If to the wretched any faith be giv'n,
I swear by all th'unpitying pow'rs of heav'n,   70
No wilful crime this heavy vengeance bred,
In mutual innocence our lives we led:
If this be false, let these new greens decay, ⎱
Let sounding axes lop my limbs away,   ⎰
And crackling flames on all my honours prey. ⎰   75
But from my branching arms this infant bear,
Let some kind nurse supply a mother's care:
And to his mother let him oft' be led,
Sport in her shades, and in her shades be fed;
Teach him, when first his infant voice shall frame   80
Imperfect words, and lisp his mother's name,
To hail this tree; and say, with weeping eyes,
Within this plant my hapless parent lies:
And when in youth he seeks the shady woods,
Oh, let him fly the crystal lakes and floods,   85
Nor touch the fatal flow'rs; but, warn'd by me,
Believe a Goddess shrin'd in ev'ry tree.
My sire, my sister, and my spouse farewell!

76 But] Now *1717ab*.   78 And] Yet *1717ab*.

69–70. EC compare Sandys, 393–4:
      If Credit to the wretched may be giuen;
      I sweare by all the Powres inbowr'd in Heauen . . .
   72. *In mutual innocence*] Warton gives this note "From Mr. Bowyer", the learned printer: "This translation is faulty. . . Nothing is more common in verse
than to use the first plural for the singular: 'Patior sine crimine [poenam.], &
viximus innocuae,' [Ovid, 372–3] is but one and the same person; a testimony
of her own innocence, but not of the mutual concord between her relations."
Sandys, 396, has "innocent my life hath been".
   75. *honours*] Her foliage. The word was frequently used of trees in this sense.
   76. See Intro., p. 338.
   79. See Intro., p. 338.
   87. Sandys, 406: "But think that euery tree inshrines a Powre."
   88–91. Sandys (1632 edn), 407–10:
      Deare Husband, Sister, Father, all farewell,

If in your breasts or love or pity dwell,
Protect your plant, nor let my branches feel   90
The browzing cattel, or the piercing steel.
Farewell! and since I cannot bend to join
My lips to yours, advance at least to mine.
My son, thy mother's parting kiss receive,
While yet thy mother has a kiss to give.   95
I can no more; the creeping rind invades
My closing lips, and hides my head in shades:
Remove your hands, the bark shall soon suffice
Without their aid, to seal these dying eyes.
  She ceas'd at once to speak, and ceas'd to be;   100
And all the nymph was lost within the tree:
Yet latent life thro' her new branches reign'd,
And long the plant a human heat retain'd.

---

100 *No new paragraph 1717b.*

> If in your gentle hearts compassion dwell,
> Suffer no axe to wound my tender boughes;
> Nor on my leaues let hungry cattaile brouse.

For l. 408 Sandys in 1626 had written: "Since you I know in piety excell". See Intro., p. 339.

96–7. Wakefield compares Dryden, *Baucis and Philemon*, 190: "At once the'incroaching Rinds their closing Lips invade."

97. See Intro., p. 339.

98–9. Sandys, 417–18:

> Remoue your hands: with out the helpe of those,
> The wrapping bark my dying eyes will close.

100. *at once*] She ceased to speak and to be at the same instant.

103. *human heat*] Sandys, 419–20:

> Yet humane heat
> In her chang'd body long retain'd a seat.

SAPHO to *PHAON*.

Wholly Translated.

NOTE ON THE TEXT

Sapho to Phaon was first published in the eighth edition of *Ovid's Epistles . . . By Several Hands*, shortly before March 18, 1712. It was revised for publication in the 1717 edition of the *Works*, two of the revisions consisting in the suppression of *does* (l. 36) and *did* (l. 167). Later revisions were introduced into the second issue of the 1736 *Works* (Griffith 418) and into the 1741 *Works*. Some of the revisions of 1736 and 1741 (see ll. 38, 73, 188, 225) are not above suspicion and may be misprints (see the Notes on the Text preceding *The Fable of Dryope*, *Vertumnus and Pomona*, and *The First Book of Statius*).

The text printed here follows the spelling, punctuation, and typography of the first edition, but observes the revisions of later editions. The inverted commas of ll. 198 and 217 have been closed, however, and minor revisions of punctuation which Pope made in ll. 212, 216, and 221 have been followed. Some obvious misprints have been disregarded. From 1736 onwards the Latin text was printed along with Pope's translation.

KEY TO THE CRITICAL APPARATUS

1712 = Ovid's Epistles, eighth edition, octavo, Griffith 4.
1717 = Works, quarto, Griffith 79.
1736*a* = Works, vol. III, octavo, Griffith 417.
1736*b* = Works, vol. III, octavo, Griffith 418.
1741 = Works, vol. I, part II, octavo, Griffith 521.
1751 = Works, ed. Warburton, vol. II, octavo, Griffith 644.

SAPHO
TO
PHAON

S AY, lovely Youth, that dost my Heart command,
 Can *Phaon*'s Eyes forget his *Sapho*'s Hand?
 Must then her Name the wretched Writer prove?
To thy Remembrance lost, as to thy Love!
Ask not the cause that I new Numbers chuse,   5
The Lute neglected, and the Lyric Muse;
Love taught my Tears in sadder Notes to flow,
And tun'd my Heart to Elegies of Woe.
I burn, I burn, as when thro' ripen'd Corn
By driving Winds the spreading Flames are born!   10
Phaon to *Ætna*'s scorching Fields retires,
While I consume with more than *Ætna*'s Fires!
No more my Soul a Charm in Musick finds,
Musick has Charms alone for peaceful Minds:
Soft Scenes of Solitude no more can please,   15

Title] For the spelling *Sapho*, see Intro., p. 339, *n*.

1. For this line, which is not in Ovid, Wakefield compares Aphra Behn, "Say, lovely Youth, why wouldst thou thus betray", l. 231 of *A Paraphrase . . . of Oenone to Paris*, printed in the same volume as Sir Carr Scrope's tr. of *Sapho to Phaon* (see Intro., p. 340). Cf. also Scrope, 11: "Ah lovely Youth! how can'st thou cruel prove".

5. *new Numbers*] An allusion to the elegiac distichs used by Ovid, which differ from the Sapphic metre used by Sappho and named after her.

9–10. Wakefield compares Scrope, 3–4:
> I burn, I burn, like kindled Fields of Corn,
> When by the driving Winds the Flames are born.

11. To avoid Sappho's love, Phaon had fled to Sicily, where Mount Aetna is situated.

13–14. Wakefield compares Scrope, 5–6:
> My Muse and Lute can now no longer please,
> They are th'Employments of a Mind at ease.

15–18. Pope here abridges Ovid's enumeration of Sappho's "guilty loves", ll. 15–19, and introduces a note of solitary melancholy which has no precedent either in Ovid or Scrope.

O   393

Love enters there, and I'm my own Disease:
No more the *Lesbian* Dames my Passion move,
Once the dear Objects of my guilty Love;
All other Loves are lost in only thine,
Ah Youth ungrateful to a Flame like mine!   20
Whom wou'd not all those blooming Charms surprize,
Those heav'nly Looks, and dear deluding Eyes?
The Harp and Bow wou'd you like *Phœbus* bear,
A brighter *Phœbus*, *Phaon* might appear;
Wou'd you with Ivy wreath your flowing Hair,   25
Not *Bacchus'* self with *Phaon* cou'd compare:
Yet *Phœbus* lov'd, and *Bacchus* felt the Flame,
One *Daphne* warm'd, and one the *Cretan* Dame;
Nymphs that in Verse no more cou'd rival me,
Than ev'n those Gods contend in Charms with thee.   30
The Muses teach me all their softest Lays,
And the wide World resounds with *Sapho*'s Praise.
Tho' great *Alcæus* more sublimely sings,
And strikes with bolder Rage the sounding Strings,
No less Renown attends the moving Lyre,   35

26 *Bacchus'*] *Bacchus 1712.*

21. *blooming*] Scrope, 12: "When blooming Years and Beauty bid thee love?"
22. *dear deluding*] Scrope, 64: "The dear deluding Vision to retain".
24. *brighter Phœbus*] Ovid, 23, has: "fies manifestus Apollo".
25. *with Ivy*] Ovid, 24, only speaks of horns, which were characteristic of Bacchus: "accedant capiti cornua—Bacchus eris". See Intro., p. 345.
26. Ovid, 24, has merely "Bacchus eris". The praise was the greater as Bacchus, according to Ovid (*Met.*, IV 18–19), was considered the most beautiful of the gods.
28. *warm'd*] Inspired with love.
the Cretan Dame] Ariadne, daughter of Minos, king of Crete. She was abandoned by Theseus on the island of Naxos, where Bacchus discovered her on his return from India. Ovid tells the story of Apollo and Daphne in *Met.* 1.
29. *Nymphs*] Daphne was a nymph, but Ariadne was not. Here, as in l. 65, the word describes a young and lovely woman. Cf. *Dryope*, 7n (p. 385, above).
33. *Alcæus*] An older contemporary of Sappho, he was also a native of Lesbos. Love and wine, satire and politics, were subjects of his odes, written in the alcaic metre ,so called after him.

Which *Venus* tunes, and all her Loves inspire.
To me what Nature has in Charms deny'd
Is well by Wit's more lasting Flames supply'd.
Tho' short my Stature, yet my Name extends
To Heav'n it self, and Earth's remotest Ends.   40
Brown as I am, an *Æthiopian* Dame
Inspir'd young *Perseus* with a gen'rous Flame.
Turtles and Doves of diff'ring Hues, unite,
And glossy Jett is pair'd with shining White.
If to no Charms thou wilt thy Heart resign,   45
But such as merit, such as equal thine,
By none alas! by none thou can'st be mov'd,
Phaon alone by *Phaon* must be lov'd!
Yet once thy *Sapho* cou'd thy Cares employ,
Once in her Arms you center'd all your Joy: 50

36 Which *Cupid* tunes, and *Venus* does inspire. *1712.*
38 Flames] Charms *1712–36a.*

---

38. *Wit*] Genius, Latin *ingenium*. Compare this couplet with *Ess. on Crit.*,
205–6 (p. 264, above).

41. *Æthiopian Dame*] Andromeda, daughter of Cepheus and Cassiopeia, king
and queen of Ethiopia.

43–4. Ovid, 37–8, has:

> et variis albae iunguntur saepe columbae,
> et niger a viridi turtur amatur ave.

The green bird is the parrot, which Pope may have wished to avoid. See Intro.,
p. 345.

45–8. The Latin original of these lines had been cited by Dryden in *Disc.
conc. . . . Sat. (Essays,* II 110) as an "extraordinary turn upon the words". Ovid,
39–40, has:

> si, nisi quae facie poterit te digna videri,
> nulla futura tua est, nulla futura tua est.

Pope attempted the "turn" in his repetitions: "By none . . . by none", and
"*Phaon . . . Phaon*". The conceit that Phaon, if he was to be loved by his equal
in beauty, could only be loved by himself, is borrowed not from Ovid, but from
Scrope, 13–14:

> If none but equal Charms thy Heart can bind,
> Then to thy self alone thou must be kind.

See Intro., p. 344.

No Time the dear Remembrance can remove,
For oh! how vast a Memory has Love?
My Musick, then, you cou'd for ever hear,
And all my Words were Musick to your Ear.
You stop'd with Kisses my inchanting Tongue,   55
And found my Kisses sweeter than my Song.
In all I pleas'd, but most in what was best;
And the last Joy was dearer than the rest.
Then with each Word, each Glance, each Motion fir'd,
You still enjoy'd, and yet you still desir'd,   60
Till all dissolving in the Trance we lay,
And in tumultuous Raptures dy'd away.
The fair *Sicilians* now thy Soul inflame;
Why was I born, ye Gods, a *Lesbian* Dame?
But ah beware, *Sicilian* Nymphs! nor boast   65
That wandring Heart which I so lately lost;
Nor be with all those tempting Words abus'd,
Those tempting Words were all to *Sapho* us'd.
And you that rule *Sicilia*'s happy Plains,
Have pity, *Venus*, on your Poet's Pains!   70

51 Still all those Joys to my Remembrance move, *1712–36b.*

55. Ovid, 44, has only: "oscula cantanti tu mihi rapta dabas." Pope follows Scrope, 21: "And snatching Kisses, stop'd me as I sung."

57. Ovid, 46, has: "sed tum praecipue, cum fit amoris opus." Pope's line is monosyllabic.

58. Cf. Dryden's tr. of Ovid's *Elegies*, II xix 18: "How every kiss was dearer than the last!"

61–2. Pope is indebted to Scrope, 26–7:
              'Till both expiring with tumultous Joys,
              A gentle Faintness did our Limbs surprize.

63. Ovid, 51, says the Sicilian maids will be "new prey" ("nova praeda") for Phaon.

65–6. Scrope, 28–9:
              Beware, *Sicilian* Ladies, ah! beware
              How you receive my faithless Wanderer.

70. *Venus*] Erycina, a surname of Aphrodite, in the original. There was a temple dedicated to Venus on Mount Eryx in Sicily.

Shall Fortune still in one sad Tenor run,
And still increase the Woes so soon begun?
Enur'd to Sorrow from my tender Years,
My Parent's Ashes drank my early Tears.
My Brother next, neglecting Wealth and Fame,   75
Ignobly burn'd in a destructive Flame.
An Infant Daughter late my Griefs increast,
And all a Mother's Cares distract my Breast.
Alas, what more could Fate it self impose,
But Thee, the last and greatest of my Woes?   80
No more my Robes in waving Purple flow,
Nor on my Hand the sparkling Diamonds glow,
No more my Locks in Ringlets curl'd diffuse
The costly Sweetness of *Arabian* Dews,
Nor Braids of Gold the vary'd Tresses bind,   85
That fly disorder'd with the wanton Wind:
For whom shou'd *Sapho* use such Arts as these?
He's gone, whom only she desir'd to please!
Cupid's light Darts my tender Bosom move,
Still is there cause for *Sapho* still to love: 90
So from my Birth the *Sisters* fix'd my Doom,
And gave to *Venus* all my Life to come;
Or while my Muse in melting Notes complains,

73 Sorrow] Sorrows *1712–36a.*

71. Ault (*Pope's Own Miscellany*, p. xxxix) compares Pope's *Il.*, VI 520.

75–6. Ovid, 63, is more explicit: "arsit iners frater meretricis captus amore". The brother, Charaxus, ransomed a courtesan, Rhodopis, from Egypt. Pope omits Ovid's account, 65–6, of the brother's piracy.

84. *Arabian Dews*] Perfumes, reputed to come from Arabia. Ovid, 76, has "Arabum . . . dona".

87–8. Scrope, 35–6:

> For whom, alas! should now my Art be shown?
> The only Man I car'd to please is gone.

90. Cf. Ovid, 80: "et semper causa est, cur ego semper amem". See Intro., p. 344.

My yielding Heart keeps Measure to my Strains.
By Charms like thine which all my Soul have won,   95
Who might not—ah! who wou'd not be undone?
For those, *Aurora Cephalus* might scorn,
And with fresh Blushes paint the conscious Morn.
For those might *Cynthia* lengthen *Phaon*'s Sleep,
And bid *Endymion* nightly tend his Sheep.   100
Venus for those had rapt thee to the Skies,
But *Mars* on thee might look with *Venus*' Eyes.
O scarce a Youth, yet scarce a tender Boy!
O useful Time for Lovers to employ!
Pride of thy Age, and Glory of thy Race,   105
Come to these Arms, and melt in this Embrace!
The Vows you never will return, receive;
And take at least the Love you will not give.
See, while I write, my Words are lost in Tears;
The less my Sense, the more my Love appears.   110
Sure 'twas not much to bid one kind Adieu,
(At least to feign was never hard to you.)
Farewel my Lesbian *Love!* you might have said,
Or coldly thus, *Farewel oh* Lesbian *Maid!*
No Tear did you, no parting Kiss receive,   115
Nor knew I then how much I was to grieve.
No Lover's Gift your *Sapho* cou'd confer,
And Wrongs and Woes were all you left with her.
No Charge I gave you, and no Charge cou'd give,
But this; *Be mindful of our Loves, and live.*   120

94 My Heart relents, and answers to my Strains. *1712*;
     My beating heart keeps measure to my strains. *1717*.
108 you will] thou wilt *1712*.
117 No ... your] No Gift on thee thy *1712*.

---

97. The hunter Cephalus, faithful husband of Procris, was loved in vain by
Aurora.
98. *conscious*] Sensible of wrong-doing, guilty (OED).
108–9. Two monosyllabic lines.
109. Ovid, 98, has: "adspice, quam sit in hoc multa litura loco!"

Now by the Nine, those Pow'rs ador'd by me,
And Love, the God that ever waits on thee,
When first I heard (from whom I hardly knew)
That you were fled, and all my Joys with you,
Like some sad Statue, speechless, pale, I stood;   125
Grief chill'd my Breast, and stop'd my freezing Blood;
No Sigh to rise, no Tear had pow'r to flow;
Fix'd in a stupid Lethargy of Woe.
But when its way th'impetuous Passion found,
I rend my Tresses, and my Breast I wound,   130
I rave, then weep, I curse, and then complain,
Now swell to Rage, now melt in Tears again.
Not fiercer Pangs distract the mournful Dame,
Whose first-born Infant feeds the Fun'ral Flame.
My scornful Brother with a Smile appears,   135
Insults my Woes, and triumphs in my Tears,
His hated Image ever haunts my Eyes,
And *why this Grief? thy Daughter lives*; he cries.
Stung with my Love, and furious with Despair,
All torn my Garments, and my Bosom bare,   140
My Woes, thy Crimes, I to the World proclaim;
Such inconsistent things are Love and Shame!
'Tis thou art all my Care and my Delight,
My daily Longing, and my Dream by Night:

130 Breast] Breasts *1712*.

125. *sad Statue*] Not in Ovid. Cf. Aphra Behn (*Oenone to Paris*, 216): "I look'd like the sad Statue of Despair".

134. *first-born Infant*] Ovid, 115, has: "nati pia mater". Pope may have been influenced by Scrope, 50: "her only Son".

139–42. Pope changes the order of the original to conclude on the opposition of love and shame. He was led to this by Scrope, 51–3:

> Expos'd to all the World my self I see,
> Forgetting Virtue, Fame, and all but thee;
> So ill, alas! do Love and Shame agree!

See Intro., p. 345.

143–4. EC compare Dryden, *Dido to Æneas*, 28 (in the same volume as Scrope's tr.): "Their daily longing, and their nightly Dream." Cf. also Scrope,

O Night more pleasing than the brightest Day,   145
When Fancy gives what Absence takes away,
And drest in all its visionary Charms,
Restores my fair Deserter to my Arms!
Then round your Neck in wanton Wreaths I twine,
Then you, methinks, as fondly circle mine: 150
A thousand tender Words, I hear and speak;
A thousand melting Kisses, give, and take:
Then fiercer Joys—I blush to mention these,
Yet while I blush, confess how much they please!
But when with Day the sweet Delusions fly,   155
And all things wake to Life and Joy, but I,
As if once more forsaken, I complain,
And close my Eyes, to dream of you again.
Then frantick rise, and like some Fury rove
Thro' lonely Plains, and thro' the silent Grove,   160
As if the silent Grove, and lonely Plains
That knew my Pleasures, cou'd relieve my Pains.
I view the *Grotto*, once the Scene of Love,
The Rocks around, the hanging Roofs above,
That charm'd me more, with Native Moss o'ergrown,
Than *Phrygian* Marble or the *Parian* Stone.   166
I find the Shades that veil'd our Joys before,
But, *Phaon* gone, those Shades delight no more.

165 That] Which *1712*.
167 veil'd . . . before,] did our Joys conceal, *1712*.
168 Not Him, who made me love those Shades so well, *1712*.

54: "'Tis thou alone that art my constant Care." Ault (*Pope's Own Miscellany*, p. xlvi) compares Pope's *Statius*, 445–6 (p. 428, below).

  158. Not in Ovid. It was suggested by Scrope, 64–5:
> The dear deluding Vision to retain,
> I lay me down, and try to sleep again.

  160–1. Ovid, 137, has: "antra nemusque peto, tamquam nemus antraque prosint—".

  166. *Phrygian Marble*] For the Mygdonian marble of the original Pope has substituted marbles equally famous in antiquity.

Here the prest Herbs with bending Tops betray
Where oft entwin'd in am'rous Folds we lay;   170
I kiss that Earth which once was prest by you,
And all with Tears the with'ring Herbs bedew.
For thee the fading Trees appear to mourn,
And Birds defer their Songs till thy Return:
Night shades the Groves, and all in Silence lye,   175
All, but the mournful *Philomel* and I:
With mournful *Philomel* I join my Strain,
Of *Tereus* she, of *Phaon* I complain.

   A Spring there is, whose Silver Waters show,
Clear as a Glass, the shining Sands below;   180
A flow'ry *Lotos* spreads its Arms above,
Shades all the Banks, and seems it self a Grove;
Eternal Greens the mossie Margin grace,
Watch'd by the Sylvan *Genius* of the Place.
Here as I lay, and swell'd with Tears the Flood,   185
Before my Sight a Watry Virgin stood,
She stood and cry'd, "O you that love in vain!

---

173. Scrope, 78–9:
> The Trees are wither'd all since thou art gone,
> As if for thee they put their mourning on.

175–8. Ovid speaks of the bird of Daulis, who sings "Itys", thus alluding not to Philomel (the nightingale), but to her sister Procne (the swallow). The time is not the night; Ovid merely says, l. 156, "ut media cetera nocte silent." Pope was evidently misled by Scrope, 80–3:
> No warbling *Bird* does now with Musick fill
> The Woods, except the mournful *Philomel*.
> With hers my dismal Notes all Night agree,
> Of *Tereus* she complains, and I of thee.

See Intro., pp. 344–5.

  181. *flow'ry Lotos*] Cf. *The Fable of Dryope*, 21*n* (p. 386, above).

  185. *and swell'd with Tears*] Not in Ovid. The conceit was common in the period. Cf. *Windsor-Forest*, 210 (p. 169, above), and also J. Cooper's tr. of *Œnone to Paris*, 45*f*. (in the same volume as Scrope's tr.) :
> You wept, and on my Eyes you gazing stood,
> Whose falling Tears increas'd the briny Flood!

  186. *Watry Virgin*] Ovid, 162, has "Naias una". Cf. Dryden, *Georgics* I 43: "The wat'ry Virgins for thy Bed shall strive "

"Fly hence; and seek the fair *Leucadian* Main;
"There stands a Rock from whose impending Steep
"*Apollo*'s Fane surveys the rolling Deep;   190
"There injur'd Lovers, leaping from above,
"Their Flames extinguish, and forget to love.
"*Deucalion* once with hopeless Fury burn'd,
"In vain he lov'd, relentless *Pyrrha* scorn'd;
"But when from hence he plung'd into the Main,   195
"*Deucalion* scorn'd, and *Pyrrha* lov'd in vain.
"Haste *Sapho*, haste, from high *Leucadia* throw
"Thy wretched Weight, nor dread the Deeps below!"
    She spoke, and vanish'd with the Voice—I rise,
    And silent Tears fall trickling from my Eyes.   200
    I go, ye Nymphs! those Rocks and Seas to prove;
    How much I fear, but ah! how much I love?
    I go, ye Nymphs! where furious Love inspires:
    Let Female Fears submit to Female Fires!
    To Rocks and Seas I fly from *Phaon*'s Hate,   205
    And hope from Seas and Rocks a milder Fate.
    Ye gentle Gales, beneath my Body blow,

188 fair] far *1712–17*.   198 below!"] below! *1712–51*.

188. *Leucadian Main*] Leucadia, now called Leucas, is one of the Ionian islands, off the west coast of Greece. It terminates in a promontory 2,000 feet in
height, on which can still be seen the remains of the temple of Apollo to which
Ovid alludes. It was said that lovers who threw themselves from this headland
into the sea might be cured of their infatuation. The whole passage in Ovid
makes the legend sufficiently clear. Addison (*Spectator* 233, Nov. 27, 1711) gives
a humorous account of this Lover's Leap and of Sappho's end.
    205–6. Ault (*Pope's Own Miscellany*, p. xlv) compares *Palæmon, A Pastoral*, 21–2
(see vol. VI, p. 417):
            There I, retreating from *Amynta*'s hate,
            From wolves and bears expect a milder fate!
    207–8. These two lines have been quoted as being the most smooth and melli-
fluous in our language [Warton]. Wakefield compares Dryden, *Annus Mirabilis*,
st. 304:
            A constant Trade-wind will securely blow,
            And gently lay us on the Spicy shore.

And softly lay me on the Waves below!
And thou, kind *Love*, my sinking Limbs sustain,
Spread thy soft Wings, and waft me o'er the Main, ⎫
Nor let a Lover's Death the guiltless Flood profane! ⎭ 210
On *Phœbus*' Shrine my Harp I'll then bestow,
And this Inscription shall be plac'd below.
"Here She who sung, to Him that did inspire,
"*Sapho* to *Phœbus* consecrates her Lyre,   215
"What suits with *Sapho*, *Phœbus*, suits with thee;
"The Gift, the Giver, and the God agree."
      But why alas, relentless Youth! ah why
To distant Seas must tender *Sapho* fly?
Thy Charms than those may far more pow'rful be,   220
And *Phœbus*' self is less a God to me.
Ah! canst thou doom me to the Rocks and Sea,
O far more faithless and more hard than they?
Ah! canst thou rather see this tender Breast
Dash'd on these Rocks, than to thy Bosom prest?   225
This Breast which once, in vain! you lik'd so well;
Where the *Loves* play'd, and where the *Muses* dwell.—
Alas! the *Muses* now no more inspire,
Untun'd my Lute, and silent is my Lyre,
My languid Numbers have forgot to flow,   230
And Fancy sinks beneath a Weight of Woe.

212 *Phœbus*'] *Phœbus 1712*.   216 *Phœbus*,] *Phœbus 1712–17*.
217 agree."] agree. *1717–41*.   221 *Phœbus*'] *Phœbus 1712*.
225 these] sharp *1712*; those *1717–36a*.

214–17. Ovid, 183–4, has:
            grata lyram posui tibi, Phoebe, poetria Sappho:
            convenit illa mihi, convenit illa tibi.
    223. Ovid, 189, has: "o scopulis undaque ferocior omni". Scrope, 93, has:
"To one more hard than Rocks, more deaf than Seas". Cf. Dryden, *Æn.*, IV
551 (Dido to Aeneas): "The faithless Waves, not half so false as thou".
    224–5. Cf. Scrope, 90–1:
            Thou cou'dst not see this naked Breast of mine
            Dasht against Rocks, rather than join'd to thine.

Ye *Lesbian* Virgins, and ye *Lesbian* Dames,
Themes of my Verse, and Objects of my Flames,
No more your Groves with my glad Songs shall ring,
No more these Hands shall touch the trembling String: 235
My *Phaon*'s fled, and I those Arts resign,
(Wretch that I am, to call that *Phaon* mine!)
Return fair Youth, return, and bring along
Joy to my Soul, and Vigour to my Song:
Absent from thee, the Poet's Flame expires,   240
But ah! how fiercely burn the Lover's Fires?
Gods! can no Pray'rs, no Sighs, no Numbers move
One savage Heart, or teach it how to love?
The Winds my Pray'rs, my Sighs, my Numbers bear,
The flying Winds have lost them all in Air!   245
Oh when, alas! shall more auspicious Gales
To these fond Eyes restore thy welcome Sails?
If you return—ah why these long Delays?
Poor *Sapho* dies while careless *Phaon* stays.
O launch thy Bark, nor fear the watry Plain,   250
Venus for thee shall smooth her native Main.
O launch thy Bark, secure of prosp'rous Gales,
Cupid for thee shall spread the swelling Sails.
If you will fly—(yet ah! what Cause can be,
Too cruel Youth, that you shou'd fly from me?)   255
If not from *Phaon* I must hope for Ease,
Ah let me seek it from the raging Seas:
To raging Seas unpity'd I'll remove,
And either cease to live, or cease to love!

236–7 Since *Phaon* fled, I all those Joys resign,
          Wretch that I am, I'd almost call'd him mine! *1712*.
253 *Cupid* . . . shall] For thee shall *Cupid 1712*.
257 Ah] *1712* has And, *possibly a misprint. MS has* Ah! let . . .
258 To . . . unpity'd] From thee to those, unpity'd, *1712*.

250*ff.* For the concluding line, cf. *The Fable of Dryope*, 100 (p. 390, above).
See Intro. p. 346.

THE
FIRST BOOK
OF
STATIUS
HIS
THEBAIS.

NOTE ON THE TEXT

Pope's translation of Statius was first published in *Miscellaneous Poems and Translations . . . By Several Hands*, on May 20, 1712. A second edition of this volume was published by Lintot in 1714, but Pope made no changes in his poem until the 1717 edition of his *Works*. Of the many variants which appear in 1717, ten were introduced to suppress the expletive *do*.

The 1736 edition of Pope's *Works* appeared in two issues. The second of these, which Griffith regarded as a "close reprint" of the first, introduces a number of problematic readings which are perpetuated in succeeding editions. Some of these readings (at ll. 612 and 736) are obvious misprints; others (at ll. 56, 175, 559) are of such a nature that it is difficult to decide whether or not they are authoritative. In addition, it seems fairly certain from collation that Warburton's text follows the 1741 edition of the *Works*, and perpetuates certain readings found only in that edition (see variants cited at ll. 17, 436, 708). These variant readings introduced into *1736b* and *1741* always involve a single word or letter, and so there is the possibility that they may be simple misprints. Finally, there are three readings (at ll. 394, 723, 775), all involving a single word or letter, which appear only in the Warburton edition of 1751, and which may represent Warburtonian "improvements" on Pope's text. Faced with these dubious readings, the editors have had to rely, in some instances, on the sense of a passage; at other times they have taken the conservative course and printed the earlier readings of *1717* and *1736a*. In any event, all such doubtful variants have been preserved in the textual notes.

In several places Pope used the genitive singular when the plural is obviously required. The editors have modified such words to conform to modern practice, relegating Pope's version to the textual notes. Except for a few instances, which are recorded, the text here printed follows the punctuation, spelling, and typography of the first edition. The revisions of later editions, aside from the doubtful readings mentioned above, are observed.

In the editions from 1736 on, Pope printed the Latin text along with his translation.

KEY TO THE CRITICAL APPARATUS

1712 = Miscellaneous Poems and Translations, octavo, Griffith 6.
1714 = Miscellaneous Poems and Translations, octavo, Griffith 32.
1717 = Works, quarto, Griffith 79.
1736a = Works, vol. III, octavo, Griffith 417.
1736b = Works, vol. III, octavo, Griffith 418.
1741 = Works, vol. I, part II, octavo, Griffith 521.
1751 = Works, ed. Warburton, vol. II, octavo, Griffith 644.

THE ARGUMENT.

OEdipus *King of* Thebes *having by mistake slain his Father* Laius, *and marry'd his Mother* Jocasta, *put out his own Eyes, and resign'd the Realm to his Sons,* Etheocles *and* Polynices. *Being neglected by them, he makes his Prayer to the Fury* Tisiphone, *to sow Debate betwixt the Brothers. They agree at last to Reign singly, each a Year by turns, and the first Lot is obtain'd by* Etheocles. Jupiter, *in a Council of the Gods, declares his Resolution of punishing the* Thebans, *and* Argives *also, by means of a Marriage betwixt* Polynices *and one of the Daughters of* Adrastus *King of* Argos. Juno *opposes, but to no effect; and* Mercury *is sent on a Message to the Shades, to the Ghost of* Laius, *who is to appear to* Etheocles, *and provoke him to break the Agreement.* Polynices *in the mean time departs from* Thebes *by Night, is overtaken by a Storm, and arrives at* Argos; *where he meets with* Tydeus, *who had fled from* Calydon, *having kill'd his Brother.* Adrastus *entertains them, having receiv'd an Oracle from* Apollo *that his Daughters shou'd be marry'd to a Boar and a Lion, which he understands to be meant of these Strangers by whom the Hydes of those Beasts were worn, and who arriv'd at the time when he kept an annual Feast in honour of that God. The Rise of this Solemnity he relates to his Guests, the Loves of* Phœbus *and* Psamathe, *and the Story of* Chorœbus. *He enquires, and is made acquainted with, their Descent and Quality; The Sacrifice is renew'd, and the Book concludes with a Hymn to* Apollo.

The Translator hopes he needs not apologize for his Choice of this Piece, which was made almost in his Childhood. But finding the Version better than he expected, he gave it some Correction a few Years afterwards.

---

6 Etheocles. Jupiter] Etheocles: *The Murmurs of the People on this occasion are describ'd in an excellent Speech.* Jupiter *1712–14.*

21 Chorœbus.] Coræbus. *1712–14*; Choræbus. *1717–36b.*

25-7 But finding . . . afterwards.] But finding the Version better, upon Review, than he expected from those Years, he was easily prevail'd upon to give it some Correction, the rather, because no Part of this Author (at least that he knows of) has been tolerably turn'd into our Language. *1712–14. 1717 omits entirely this last paragraph of The Argument.*

FIRST BOOK

OF

STATIUS his Thebais.

Fraternal Rage, the guilty *Thebes* Alarms,
    Th'Alternate Reign destroy'd by Impious Arms,
    Demand our Song; a sacred Fury fires
My ravish'd Breast, and All the Muse inspires.
O Goddess, say, shall I deduce my Rhimes   5
From the dire Nation in its early Times,
Europa's Rape, *Agenor*'s stern Decree,
And *Cadmus* searching round the spacious Sea?
How with the Serpent's Teeth he sow'd the Soil,
And reap'd an Iron Harvest of his Toil;   10
Or how from joyning Stones the City sprung,
While to his Harp Divine *Amphion* sung?
Or shall I *Juno*'s Hate to *Thebes* resound,

---

1 *Thebes*] *Thebe's 1712–14.*

---

2. *Th'Alternate Reign*] See the "Argument".

5. *deduce*] To trace the course of, treat, deal with (OED).

6. *dire*] A Latinism: ill-omened, unfortunate.

7. *Agenor's stern Decree*] Agenor, king of Phoenicia, sent his son Cadmus to search for Europa, forbidding him to return should he fail.

8. Cadmus's search proved vain. In obedience to the oracle of Delphi he went into Boeotia, where his followers were killed by a dragon. Cadmus slew the dragon and sowed its teeth in the earth, whence sprang up armed warriors whom Cadmus caused to fight amongst themselves till only five remained. With their help he founded the city of Thebes and fulfilled the oracle.

10. *Iron Harvest*] Cf. *Aen.*, xii 662–4, and Dryden's tr., xii 964: "An Iron Harvest mounts . . ."

11. *from joyning Stones*] Another legend attributed the foundation of Thebes to Amphion and Zethus, twin sons of Jupiter and Antiope.

13. *Juno's Hate*] Juno's jealous hatred of Europa extended to all her family and descendants, the house of Thebes.

Whose fatal Rage th'unhappy Monarch found;
The Sire against the Son his Arrows drew,   15
O'er the wide Fields the furious Mother flew,
And while her Arms her Second Hope contain,
Sprung from the Rocks, and plung'd into the Main.
    But wave whate'er to *Cadmus* may belong,
And fix, O Muse! the Barrier of thy Song,   20
At *Oedipus*—from his Disasters trace
The long Confusions of his guilty Race.
Nor yet attempt to stretch thy bolder Wing,
And mighty *Cæsar*'s conqu'ring Eagles sing;
How twice he tam'd proud *Ister*'s rapid Flood,   25
While *Dacian* Mountains stream'd with barb'rous Blood;
Twice taught the *Rhine* beneath his Laws to roll,

17 her Second] a second *1741–51*.
25–7 How twice the Mountains ran with *Dacian* Blood,
      And trembling *Ister* check'd his rapid Flood;
      How twice he vanquish'd where the *Rhine* does roll,

                                                1712–14.

---

14. *unhappy Monarch*] Athamas, who was married to Nephele, but fell in love with Ino, daughter of Cadmus, by whom he had two sons. At Juno's instigation the fury Tisiphone caused Athamas and Ino to go mad. Athamas slew one of his sons, and Ino, with the other son, Melicertes, in her arms, flung herself into the sea. Ino and Melicertes were changed into sea deities, under the names of Leucothea and Palaemon. Cf. ll. 167–8, below.

17. *Second Hope*] See preceding note. Cf. Dryden, *Æn.*, XII 254: "The second Hope of *Rome*'s Immortal Race".

19. *wave*] Waive.

20. *Barrier*] Either the boundary line (Statius, 16, has "limes"), or perhaps an allusion to the "carcer", or starting-place, in the ancient race-course. Dryden, *Æn.*, XII 1300–1, has: ". . . the common Bound / Of Neighb'ring Fields; and Barrier of the Ground".

22. *long Confusions*] The troubled histories of Polynices, Eteocles, Antigone.

24. *mighty Cæsar*] Domitian, emperor of Rome, A.D. 81–96.

25. *proud Ister*] The Danube. Far from "taming" Dacia, the Romans, owing to Domitian's defeat by the Marcomanni, were obliged to make peace with the Dacian general, Decebalus, and pay tribute for the first time in Roman history.

27. Domitian annexed the Taunus district between the Rhine and the Main.

And stretch'd his Empire to the frozen Pole;
Or long before, with early Valour strove
In youthful Arms t'assert the Cause of *Jove*.   30
And Thou, great Heir of all thy Father's Fame,
Encrease of Glory to the *Latian* Name;
Oh bless thy *Rome* with an Eternal Reign,
Nor let desiring Worlds intreat in vain!
What tho' the Stars contract their Heav'nly Space,   35
And crowd their shining Ranks to yield thee place;
Tho' all the Skies, ambitious of thy Sway,
Conspire to court thee from our World away;
Tho' *Phœbus* longs to mix his Rays with thine,
And in thy Glories more serenely shine;   40
Tho' *Jove* himself no less content wou'd be,
To part his Throne and share his Heav'n with thee;
Yet stay, great *Cæsar*! and vouchsafe to reign
O'er the wide Earth, and o'er the watry Main,
Resign to *Jove* his Empire of the Skies,   45
And People Heav'n with *Roman* Deities.
   The Time will come, when a diviner Flame
Shall warm my Breast to sing of *Cæsar*'s Fame:
Mean while permit that my preluding Muse
In *Theban* Wars an humbler Theme may chuse: 50

---

28. *frozen Pole*] Statius, 18, has simply: "nec Arctoos ausim spirare trium-
phos . . ."

29–30. Perhaps an attempt to glorify the occasion when Domitian, eighteen
years old, was forced to hide in the temple of the capitol in order to escape from
his father's enemies.

31. *thy Father*] Vespasian, emperor A.D. 69–79.

35 *ff.* Members of the imperial family were deified, and as divinities were
placed among the constellations. See l. 46 below.

39–40. The suggestion is that Phoebus would like to mix the rays from his
nimbus with those from the nimbus Domitian will acquire when he is divinized.
In ancient art emperors and consuls are occasionally represented with a nimbus.

47. EC compare Stephens (*An Essay Upon Statius: Or, The Five First Books Of
. . . his Thebais*, 1648), 39: "The time may come, when a diviner rage . . ." See
Intro., p. 349.

Of furious Hate surviving Death, she sings,
A fatal Throne to two contending Kings,
And Fun'ral Flames, that parting wide in Air,
Express the Discord of the Souls they bear:
Of Towns dispeopled, and the wandring Ghosts   55
Of Kings unbury'd, on the wasted Coasts;
When *Dirce*'s Fountain blush'd with *Grecian* Blood,
And *Thetis*, near *Ismenos*' swelling Flood,
With Dread beheld the rolling Surges sweep
In Heaps his slaughter'd Sons into the Deep.   60
      What Hero, *Clio*! wilt thou first relate?
The Rage of *Tydeus*, or the Prophet's Fate?
Or how with Hills of slain on ev'ry side,

56 on] in *1736b–51.*
62 The Rage of *Tydeus*,] The raging *Tydeus, 1712–17.*

51–4. The smoke from the bodies of Eteocles and Polynices, who were placed on the same funeral pyre, did not mingle.

53–4. EC note that Pope is closer to Stephens, 47–8,
                    funerall flames
        Divided, like the soules they carry,
than to the original, 35–6: "flammasque rebelles / seditione rogi . . ."

57–8. *Dirce . . . Ismenos*] The two streams which gave Thebes its name of διπόταμος.

57. *Grecian Blood*] EC cite Stephens, 51: "When *Dirce* blush'd, being stain'd with *Grecian* Blood."

58. *Thetis*] Daughter of Nereus, and chief of the fifty Nereids.

60. *his slaughter'd Sons*] The Thebans, descendants of Cadmus; or perhaps here considered as descendants of the river Ismenos. There is no authority for Pope's phrase in the Latin text.

61. *What Hero*] Which one, that is, of the famous seven who fought against Thebes. They were Polynices, Adrastus (king of Argos), Tydeus, Amphiaraus, Hippomedon, Parthenopaeus, and Capaneus.

62. *The Rage of Tydeus*] An allusion to the horrible episode related later in the *Thebais*, VIII 751–62, in which the dying Tydeus gnaws the head of his dead adversary Melanippus in a frenzy of hatred.

the Prophet's Fate] Amphiaraus, who prophesied the destruction of all the leaders except Adrastus. Jupiter saved him from the spear of the Theban Periclymenus by causing the earth to swallow him with his chariot and horses.

Hippomedon repell'd the hostile Tyde?
Or how the Youth with ev'ry Grace adorn'd,   65
Untimely fell, to be for ever mourn'd?
Then to fierce *Capaneus* thy Verse extend,
And sing, with Horror, his prodigious End.
   Now wretched *Oedipus*, depriv'd of Sight,
Led a long Death in everlasting Night;   70
But while he dwells where not a chearful Ray
Can pierce the Darkness, and abhors the Day;
The clear, reflecting Mind, presents his Sin
In frightful Views, and makes it Day within;
Returning Thoughts in endless Circles roll,   75
And thousand Furies haunt his guilty Soul.
The Wretch then lifted to th'unpitying Skies
Those empty Orbs, from whence he tore his Eyes,
Whose Wounds yet fresh, with bloody Hands he strook,
While from his Breast these dreadful Accents broke.   80
   Ye Gods that o'er the gloomy Regions reign
Where guilty Spirits feel Eternal Pain;
Thou, sable *Styx!* whose livid Streams are roll'd
Thro' dreary Coasts which I, tho' Blind, behold:
Tisiphone! that oft hast heard my Pray'r,   85
Assist, if *Oedipus* deserve thy Care!
If you receiv'd me from *Jocasta*'s Womb,
And nurst the Hope of Mischiefs yet to come:
If leaving *Polybus*, I took my Way

---

   64. *Hippomedon*] The bodies of the enemy slain by Hippomedon dammed the Ismenos.

   65. *Parthenopæus.* [P. *1712–51*.]. He was the son of Atalanta of Calydon.

   67. *Capaneus*] He defied Jupiter, who slew him with a thunderbolt as he was scaling the walls of Thebes.

   79. *Whose Wounds*] The original, ll. 54–5, is somewhat ambiguous: "manibus-que cruentis / pulsat inane solum . . ." The lines could mean that Oedipus struck the ground, normal practice in summoning infernal deities.

   85. *Tisiphone*] One of the three Furies, the avenger of murder. Cf. l. 14*n*.

   89. *Polybus*] King of Corinth, who raised Oedipus as his son.

To *Cyrrha*'s Temple on that fatal Day,   90
When by the Son the trembling Father dy'd,
Where the three Roads the *Phocian* Fields divide:
If I the *Sphynxe*'s Riddles durst explain,
Taught by thy self to win the promis'd Reign:
If wretched I, by baleful Furies led,   95
With monstrous Mixture stain'd my Mother's Bed,
For Hell and Thee begot an impious Brood,
And with full Lust those horrid Joys renew'd:
Then self-condemn'd to Shades of endless Night,
Forc'd from these Orbs the bleeding Balls of Sight.   100
Oh hear, and aid the Vengeance I require;
If worthy Thee, and what Thou might'st inspire!
My Sons their old, unhappy Sire despise,
Spoil'd of his Kingdom, and depriv'd of Eyes;
Guideless I wander, unreguarded mourn,   105
While These exalt their Scepters o'er my Urn;
These Sons, ye Gods! who with flagitious Pride
Insult my Darkness, and my Groans deride.
Art thou a Father, unregarding *Jove!*
And sleeps thy Thunder in the Realms above?   110
Thou *Fury*, then, some lasting Curse entail,
Which o'er their Childrens Children shall prevail:
Place on their Heads that Crown distain'd with Gore,

100 Forc'd] Tore *1712–14.*
112 Which shall o'er long Posterity prevail: *1712–14.*

---

90. *Cyrrha's Temple*] The spring at Delphi, beneath the peaks of Parnassus, where Oedipus went to consult the oracle.

96. Stephens, 89: ". . . stain'd my Mothers bed".

106. *o'er my Urn*] There is nothing to justify this in the Latin. Cf. Stephens, 99: "Grown proud, they raise their Scepters from my urne."

111. Cf. Stephens, 104: "Entaile a Curse . . ."

112. EC compare Dryden, *Æn.*, III 132: "And Children's Children shall the Crown sustain."

113–14. EC cite Stephens, 105–6:
> Put on that Diadem besmear'd with gore,
> Which from my fathers head these fingers tore.

Which these dire Hands from my slain Father tore;
Go, and a Parent's heavy Curses bear;   115
Break all the Bonds of Nature, and prepare
Their kindred Souls to mutual Hate and War.
Give them to dare, what I might wish to see,
Blind as I am, some glorious Villany!
Soon shalt thou find, if thou but arm their Hands,   120
Their ready Guilt preventing thy Commands:
Cou'dst thou some great, proportion'd Mischief frame,
They'd prove the Father from whose Loins they came.
    The Fury heard, while on *Cocytus*' Brink
Her Snakes, unty'd, Sulphureous Waters drink;   125
But at the Summons, roll'd her Eyes around,
And snatch'd the starting Serpents from the Ground.
Not half so swiftly shoots along in Air
The gliding Lightning, or descending Star.
Thro' Crouds of Airy Shades she wing'd her Flight,   130
And dark Dominions of the silent Night;
Swift as she past, the flitting Ghosts withdrew,
And the pale Spectres trembled at her View:
To th'Iron Gates of *Tænarus* she flies,
There spreads her dusky Pinions to the Skies.   135
The Day beheld, and sick'ning at the Sight,
Veil'd her fair Glories in the Shades of Night.
Affrighted *Atlas*, on the distant Shore,
Trembl'd, and shook the Heav'ns and Gods he bore.
Now from beneath *Malea*'s airy Height   140
Aloft she sprung, and steer'd to *Thebes* her Flight;

139 bore.] bore, *1712–17*.
141–3 She mounts aloft, and steers to *Thebes* her Flight,
        Does with glad Speed the well-known Journey go,
        Nor here regrets the Hell she left below. *1712–14*.

   134. *Tænarus*] The southernmost promontory of the Peloponnesus, considered
to be one of the gates of Hades.
   140. *Malea*] Promontory at the south-eastern point of the Peloponnesus.

With eager Speed the well-known Journey took,
Nor here regrets the Hell she late forsook.
A hundred Snakes her gloomy Visage shade,
A hundred Serpents guard her horrid Head,   145
In her sunk Eye-balls dreadful Meteors glow,
Such Rays from *Phœbe*'s bloody Circle flow,
When lab'ring with strong Charms, she shoots from high
A fiery Gleam, and reddens all the Sky.
Blood stain'd her Cheeks, and from her Mouth there came
Blue steaming Poisons, and a Length of Flame;   151
From ev'ry Blast of her contagious Breath,
Famine and Drought proceed, and Plagues, and Death:
A Robe obscene was o'er her Shoulders thrown,
A Dress by Fates and Furies worn alone: 155
She tost her meagre Arms; her better Hand
In waving Circles whirl'd a Fun'ral Brand;
A Serpent from her left was seen to rear
His flaming Crest, and lash the yielding Air.
      But when the Fury took her Stand on high,   160
Where vast *Cythæron*'s Top salutes the Sky,

---

147 Such Light does *Phœbe*'s bloody Orb bestow, *1712–14.*
158 A curling Serpent from her left did rear *1712–14.*
159 lash] lash'd *1712–14.*

---

142. *well-known Journey*] Tisiphone had had occasion to visit Thebes before.
Cf. l. 14*n.*

146. Cf. Garth, *Dispensary*, VI 120: "In her parch'd Eye-balls fiery *Meteors*
reign".

148. Cf. *Par. Lost*, I 665–6: ". . . while the labouring Moon / Eclipses at thir
charms."

156. *better Hand*] Not in Statius. EC cite Dryden, *Æn.*, x 582: "And from
Strimonius hew'd his better Hand."

159. Statius, 113, says only: "haec vivo manus aera verberat hydro." Possibly Pope was influenced by Dryden, who constantly attributes crests to snakes
in his translations of Virgil (e.g., *Æn.*, II 515, 643; *Georgics* III 641, 648), where
nothing indicates this in the original, and thus gives to snakes the characteristics
of the cerastes or fabulous dragon (cf. Ovid, *Met.*, IV 598*ff.*).

161. *Cythæron's Top*] The mountain range between Athens and Thebes, from
which the Fury looked down on her goal.

A Hiss from all the Snaky Tire went round; ⎫
The dreadful Signal all the Rocks rebound, ⎬
And thro' th' *Achaian* Cities send the Sound. ⎭
Oete, with high *Parnassus*, heard the Voice;   165
Eurota's Banks remurmur'd to the Noise;
Again *Leucothoë* shook at these Alarms,
And press'd *Palæmon* closer in her Arms.
Headlong from thence the glowing Fury springs,
And o'er the *Theban* Palace spreads her Wings,   170
Once more invades the guilty Dome, and shrouds
Its bright Pavilions in a Veil of Clouds.
Strait with the Rage of all their Race possest, ⎫
Stung to the Soul, the Brothers start from Rest, ⎬
And all the Furies wake within their Breast. ⎭   175
Their tortur'd Minds repining Envy tears,
And Hate, engender'd by suspicious Fears;
And sacred Thirst of Sway; and all the Ties

169–70 Headlong from thence the Fury urg'd her Flight,
        And at the *Theban* Palace did alight, *1712–14*.
175 the Furies] their Furies *1736b–51*.

165. *Oete*] A mountain south of Thessaly, a land famous for spells and witches.

165*ff.* Pope here intentionally softened the original, which, in a letter to Cromwell (*Corr.*, 1 64), he describes as "most extravagantly hyperbolical". See Intro., p. 351.

166. *Eurota*] The Eurotas, a river in Sparta. Cf. Dryden, *Æn.*, VI 964: "The Rivers and the Rocks remurmur to the sound."

167–8. See l. 14*n*.

171–2. Statius, 123–4, has:
      Atque ea Cadmeo praeceps ubi culmine primum
      constitit adsuetaque infecit nube penates . . .
"Dome" means here a mansion; "Pavilions" calls to mind the tents represented in the illustrations to Ogilby's Homer, which Pope pored over as a child.

173. Gentilisque animos subit furor, *seems* ⟨*seems to me 1717–41*⟩ *a better reading than* Gentilesque. [P. *1717–51*.]

178. *sacred Thirst*] *Sacred* here means *accursed* (Latin *sacer*), and alludes to Virgil's famous phrase, *Aen.*, III 56–7: "auri sacra fames". Pope told Cromwell (*Corr.*, 1 36), when he first sent him his MS, that he had omitted translating the

Of Nature broke; and Royal Perjuries;
And impotent Desire to Reign alone,   180
That scorns the dull Reversion of a Throne;
Each wou'd the sweets of Sovereign Rule devour,
While Discord waits upon divided Pow'r.

　　As stubborn Steers by brawny Plowmen broke,
And join'd reluctant to the galling Yoke,   185
Alike disdain with servile Necks to bear
Th'unwonted Weight, or drag the crooked Share,
But rend the Reins, and bound a diff'rent way,
And all the Furrows in Confusion lay:
Such was the Discord of the Royal Pair,   190
Whom Fury drove precipitate to War.
In vain the Chiefs contriv'd a specious way,
To govern *Thebes* by their Alternate Sway;
Unjust Decree! while This enjoys the State,
That mourns in Exile his unequal Fate;   195
And the short Monarch of a hasty Year
Foresees with Anguish his returning Heir.
Thus did the League their impious Arms restrain,
But scarce subsisted to the Second Reign.

　　Yet then no proud aspiring Piles were rais'd,   200
No fretted Roofs with polish'd Metals blaz'd,
No labour'd Columns in long Order plac'd,
No *Grecian* Stone the pompous Arches grac'd;

198 the] this *1712–17*.   201 No] Whose *1712–17*.
203 No] Nor *1712–14*.

---

passage from l. 178 to l. 199 (Statius, 128–43). These lines were translated at a
later date. Cf. *Ess. on Crit.*, 521–2.
　181. *Reversion*] "The right of succession to an office or place of emolument,
after the death or retirement of the holder" (OED).
　188. Bowles points out that *Reins* and *bound* suggest that Pope was thinking of
horses, not bullocks. Bullocks may be harnessed like horses, however, as they
still are in parts of France and Germany. But in that case they are not "joined
. . . to the . . . Yoke".
　201. *fretted Roofs*] Cf. *Temple of Fame*, 138 (vol. II, p. 253).

No nightly Bands in glitt'ring Armour wait
Before the sleepless Tyrant's guarded Gate;   205
No Chargers then were wrought in burnish'd Gold,
Nor Silver Vases took the forming Mold,
Nor Gems on Bowls emboss'd were seen to shine,
Blaze on the Brims, and sparkle in the Wine—
Say, wretched Rivals! what provokes your Rage?   210
Say to what End your impious Arms engage?
Not All bright *Phœbus* views in early Morn,
Or when his Evening Beams the West adorn,
When the South glows with his Meridian Ray,
And the cold North receives a fainter Day;   215
For Crimes like these, not all those Realms suffice,
Were all those Realms the guilty Victor's Prize!
   But Fortune now (the Lots of Empire thrown)
Decrees to proud *Etheocles* the Crown:
What Joys, oh Tyrant! swell'd thy Soul that Day,   220
When all were Slaves thou cou'dst around survey,
Pleas'd to behold unbounded Pow'r thy own,
And singly fill a fear'd and envy'd Throne!
   But the vile Vulgar, ever discontent,

204 No] Nor *1717*.   Armour wait] Arms did wait *1712–14*.
205 sleepless] wakeful *1712–14*.
216 Not all those Realms cou'd for such Crimes suffice, *1712–14*.

204. Cf. *Par. Lost*, IV 684–5: ". . . oft in bands / While they keep watch, or nightly rounding walk . . ."
221. EC compare Stephens, 206–8:
                              How wast thou lost
            In thine own joyes, proud Tyrant then? when all
            About thee, were thy slaves?
Of the Latin original Pope wrote to Cromwell (*Corr.*, 1 64): "Nor did I ever read a greater piece of Tautology than
                         —*Vacua cum* solus *in Aula*
            Respiceres jus omne tuum, cunctosque Minores,
            Et nusquam par *stare* caput."
224 *ff.* From here to l. 443 (ll. 168–311 in Statius) was omitted by Pope in his first attempt, according to a letter to Cromwell (*Corr.*, 1 36–7). Pope states his reasons thus: ". . . between these two Last places *Statius* has a Noble Description

Their growing Fears in secret Murmurs vent,   225
Still prone to change, tho' still the Slaves of State,
And sure the Monarch whom they have, to hate;
New Lords they madly make, then tamely bear,
And softly curse the Tyrants whom they fear.
And one of those who groan beneath the Sway   230
Of Kings impos'd, and grudgingly obey,
(Whom Envy to the Great, and vulgar Spight
With Scandal arm'd, th'Ignoble Mind's Delight,)
Exclaim'd—O *Thebes*! for thee what Fates remain,
What Woes attend this inauspicious Reign?   235
Must we, alas! our doubtful Necks prepare,
Each haughty Master's Yoke by turns to bear,
And still to change whom chang'd we still must fear?
These now controul a wretched People's Fate,
These can divide, and these reverse the State;   240
Ev'n Fortune rules no more:—Oh servile Land,
Where exil'd Tyrants still by turns command!
Thou Sire of Gods and Men, Imperial *Jove!*
Is this th'Eternal Doom decreed above?
On thy own Offspring hast thou fix'd this Fate,   245
From the first Birth of our unhappy State;
When banish'd *Cadmus* wandring o'er the Main,
For lost *Europa* search'd the World in vain,
And fated in *Bœotian* Fields to found

228 New . . . make,] Madly they make new Lords, *1712–17*.
231 obey,] obey; *1712–17*.

---

of the *Council* of the *Gods*, & a *Speech* of *Jupiter*; which Contain a peculiar beauty
& Majesty; & were Left out for no Other reason but because the Consequence
of this Machine appears not till the 2d Book. . ." The word *Machine* designated
the supernatural personages introduced into a poem. See Intro., p. 347.
    226. Cf. Dryden, *Æn.*, VII 62: "Still unresolv'd, and still a Slave to Fate?"
    228–9. This couplet was interpolated by Pope, and seems to have been sug-
gested by his hostility to the revolution of 1688 [EC].
    236. *doubtful Necks*] Statius, 175, has "dubitantia . . . colla". Pope uses *doubtful*
in its older meaning, "full of fear or apprehension".

A rising Empire on a foreign Ground,   250
First rais'd our Walls on that ill-omen'd Plain
Where Earth-born Brothers were by Brothers slain?
What lofty Looks th'unrival'd Monarch bears!
How all the Tyrant in his Face appears!
What sullen Fury clowds his scornful Brow!   255
Gods! how his Eyes with threatning Ardour glow!
Can this Imperious Lord forget to Reign,
Quit all his State, descend, and serve again?
Yet who, before, more popularly bow'd,
Who more propitious to the suppliant Crowd,   260
Patient of Right, familiar in the Throne?
What Wonder then? he was not then Alone.
Oh wretched we, a vile submissive Train,
Fortune's tame Fools, and Slaves in ev'ry Reign!
    As when two Winds with Rival Force contend,   265
This way and that, the wav'ring Sails they bend,
While freezing *Boreas* and black *Eurus* blow,
Now here, now there, the reeling Vessel throw:
Thus on each side, alas! our tott'ring State
Feels all the Fury of resistless Fate,   270
And doubtful still, and still distracted stands,
While that Prince Threatens, and while this Commands.
    And now th'Almighty Father of the Gods
Convenes a Council in the blest Abodes:
Far in the bright Recesses of the Skies,   275
High o'er the rowling Heav'ns, a Mansion lyes,
Whence, far below, the Gods at once survey ⎫
The Realms of rising and declining Day,   ⎬
And all th'extended Space of Earth, and Air, and Sea. ⎭

---

252. Cf. l. 8*n*.
265. Cf. Dryden, *Æn.*, x 496: "As wint'ry Winds contending in the Sky".
267. *Eurus*] The east wind.
271. Cf. Stephens, 241–2: ". . . such fate / Hangs o're this doubtfull, this distracted State."
279. An Alexandrine. One should perhaps recall Cowley, *Davideis*, 1 354,

Full in the midst, and on a Starry Throne,   280
The Majesty of Heav'n superior shone;
Serene he look'd, and gave an awful Nod,
And all the trembling Spheres confess'd the God.
At *Jove*'s Assent, the Deities around
In solemn State the Consistory crown'd: 285
Next a long Order of Inferior Pow'rs
Ascend from Hills, and Plains, and shady Bow'rs;
Those from whose Urns the rowling Rivers flow,
And those that give the wandring Winds to blow,
Here all their Rage, and ev'n their Murmurs cease, 290
And sacred Silence reigns, and universal Peace.
A shining Synod of Majestick Gods
Gilds with new Lustre the divine Abodes,
Heav'n seems improv'd with a superior Ray,
And the bright Arch reflects a double Day.   295
The Monarch then his solemn Silence broke,
The still Creation listen'd while he spoke,
Each sacred Accent bears eternal Weight,
And each irrevocable Word is Fate.

How long shall Man the Wrath of Heav'n defy,   300
And force unwilling Vengeance from the Sky?
Oh Race confed'rate into Crimes, that prove
Triumphant o'er th'eluded Rage of *Jove!*

"Nor can the glory contain it self in th' endless space", and Cowley's note 25:
"I am sorry that is necessary to admonish the most part of *Readers*, that it is not
by *negligence* that this verse is so loose, long, and as it were, *Vast*; it is to paint in
the number the nature of the thing which it describes . . ."

282. Placido quatiens tamen omnia Vultu, *is the common reading; I believe it
should be* Nutu, *with reference to the word* quatiens. [P. *1717–51.*]

Vultu is the accepted reading; the universe trembles at the expression of
Jupiter's face as easily as it does at his nod.

284–5. Cf. *Il.*, x 231–2 (of the Greek kings):
          The Trenches past, th'assembl'd Kings around
          In silent State the Consistory crown'd.

291. Cf. Dryden, *Æn.*, xi 370–1:
          When *Venulus* began, the murmuring Sound
          Was hush'd, and sacred Silence reign'd around.

This weary'd Arm can scarce the Bolt sustain,
And unregarded Thunder rolls in vain: 305
Th' o'erlabour'd *Cyclop* from his Task retires;
Th' *Æolian* Forge exhausted of its Fires.
For this, I suffer'd *Phœbus'* Steeds to stray,
And the mad Ruler to misguide the Day,
When the wide Earth to Heaps of Ashes turn'd, 310
And Heav'n it self the wandring Chariot burn'd.
For this, my Brother of the watry Reign ⎫
Releas'd th'impetuous Sluices of the Main,— ⎬
But Flames consum'd, and Billows rag'd in vain. ⎭
Two Races now, ally'd to *Jove*, offend; 315
To punish these, see *Jove* himself descend!
The *Theban* Kings their Line from *Cadmus* trace,
From God-like *Perseus* those of *Argive* Race.
Unhappy *Cadmus'* Fate who does not know?
And the long Series of succeeding Woe: 320
How oft the Furies from the deeps of Night
Arose, and mix'd with Men in Mortal Fight:
Th'exulting Mother stain'd with Filial Blood;
The Savage Hunter, and the haunted Wood;
The direful Banquet why shou'd I proclaim, 325
And Crimes that grieve the trembling Gods to name?

---

304. *This weary'd Arm*] In Statius, 217–18, the Cyclopes are tired, not Jupiter. Pope follows Stephens, 270: "This arme is tir'd with thundering".

307. *Th' Æolian Forge*] Vulcan's forge, where he worked with the Cyclopes, was supposed to be on Hiera, one of the Æolian islands, off Sicily. EC suggest that Statius introduced this remark because in his days "the eruptions had ceased in Hiera".

309. *mad Ruler*] Phaethon.

312–14. An allusion to the deluge. Cf. Ovid, *Met.*, 1 283 *ff.*

323. *Th'exulting Mother*] Agave, daughter of Cadmus, who, blinded by bacchic fury, tore to pieces her own son, Pentheus.

324. *The Savage Hunter*] Athamas. Cf. l. 14*n.*

325. *direful Banquet*] This allusion to the story of Tantalus, the king of Argos who served up his own son as meat for the gods, occurs in Statius at the end of the paragraph. See Pope's l. 347, below.

E'er I recount the Sins of these Profane, ⎫
The Sun wou'd sink into the Western Main, ⎬
And rising gild the radiant East again.   ⎭

Have we not seen (the Blood of *Laius* shed)   330
The murd'ring Son ascend his Parent's Bed,
Thro' violated Nature force his way,
And stain the sacred Womb where once he lay?
Yet now in Darkness and Despair he groans,
And for the Crimes of guilty Fate attones;   335
His Sons with Scorn their Eyeless Father view,
Insult his Wounds, and make them bleed anew.
Thy Curse, oh *Oedipus*, just Heav'n alarms,
And sets th'avenging Thunderer in Arms.
I from the Root thy guilty Race will tear,   340
And give the Nations to the Waste of War.
Adrastus soon, with Gods averse, shall join
In dire Alliance with the *Theban* Line;
Hence Strife shall rise, and mortal War succeed;
The guilty Realms of *Tantalus* shall bleed;   345
Fix'd is their Doom; this all-remembring Breast
Yet Harbours Vengeance for the Tyrant's Feast.
    He said; and thus the Queen of Heav'n return'd;
(With sudden Grief her lab'ring Bosom burn'd)
Must I whose Cares *Phoroneus*' Tow'rs defend,   350
Must I, oh *Jove!* in bloody Wars contend?
Thou know'st those Regions my Protection claim,
Glorious in Arms, in Riches, and in Fame:

---

337. *Insult his Wounds*] Statius, 238-9, has:
                            at nati—facinus sine more!—cadentes
                    calcavere oculos.
Cf. Stephens, 299: "Triumphing o're his Blindnesse".
    338-9. Cf. Addison, *An Account of the Greatest English Poets* (1694), 62-3:
                    Shakes heav'ns eternal throne with dire alarms,
                    And sets th' Almighty Thunderer in arms.
345-7. Cf. l. 325*n*.
350. *Phoroneus' Tow'rs*] Argos, of which Phoroneus was reputed founder.

Tho' there the fair *Ægyptian* Heifer fed,
And there deluded *Argus* slept and bled; 355
Tho' there the Brazen Tow'r was storm'd of old,
When *Jove* descended in Almighty Gold.
Yet I can pardon those obscurer Rapes,
Those bashful Crimes disguis'd in borrow'd Shapes;
But *Thebes*, where shining in Cœlestial Charms 360
Thou cam'st Triumphant to a Mortal's Arms,
When all my Glories o'er her Limbs were spread,
And blazing Lightnings danc'd around her Bed;
Curs'd *Thebes* the Vengeance it deserves, may prove,—
Ah why shou'd *Argos* feel the Rage of *Jove*? 365
Yet since thou wilt thy Sister-Queen controul,
Since still the Lust of Discord fires thy Soul,
Go, rase my *Samos*, let *Mycenè* fall,
And level with the Dust the *Spartan* Wall:
No more let Mortals *Juno*'s Pow'r invoke, ⎫ 370
Her Fanes no more with Eastern Incense smoke, ⎬
Nor Victims sink beneath the Sacred Stroke; ⎭
But to your *Isis* all my Rites transfer,
Let Altars blaze and Temples smoke for her;
For her, thro' *Ægypt*'s fruitful Clime renown'd, 375
Let weeping *Nilus* hear the Timbrel sound.
But if thou must reform the stubborn Times,
Avenging on the Sons the Father's Crimes,
And from the long Records of distant Age
Derive Incitements to renew thy Rage; 380
Say, from what Period then has *Jove* design'd
To date his Vengeance; to what Bounds confin'd?

---

354. *Ægyptian Heifer*] Io.

361. *a Mortal's Arms*] Semele's.

368–9. Mycenae and Sparta were Juno's favourite cities.

373. *Isis*] Io, with whom Isis, worshipped by the Egyptians, was sometimes identified.

378. *Father's*] So in all editions. Ward suggests that this is a misprint, for the Latin has "auctorum crimina". Pope, overlooking the original, may allude to Oedipus alone. See Note on the Text.

P

Begin from thence, where first *Alphëus* hides
His wandring Stream, and thro' the briny Tydes,
Unmix'd, to his *Sicilian* River glides.   385
Thy own *Arcadians* there the Thunder claim,
Whose impious Rites disgrace thy mighty Name,
Who raise thy Temples where the Chariot stood
Of fierce *Oenomäus*, defil'd with Blood;
Where once his Steeds their savage Banquet found,   390
And Human Bones yet whiten all the Ground.
Say, can those Honours please? and canst thou love
Presumptuous *Crete*, that boasts the Tomb of *Jove?*
And shall not *Tantalus* his Kingdoms share
Thy Wife and Sister's Tutelary Care?   395
Reverse, O *Jove*, thy too severe Decree,
Nor doom to War a Race deriv'd from thee;
On Impious Realms, and barb'rous Kings, impose
Thy Plagues, and curse 'em with such Sons as those.

    Thus, in Reproach and Pray'r, the Queen exprest   400
The Rage and Grief contending in her Breast;
Unmov'd remain'd the Ruler of the Sky,
And from his Throne return'd this stern Reply.

389 *Oenomäus*,] *Oenömaus, 1712–17.*
394 *Tantalus* his] Tantalus's *1751.*

383–5. EC compare Dryden, *Ecl.* x 6–7:
        So may thy Silver Streams beneath the Tide,
        Unmix'd with briny Seas, securely glide.
    387. *impious Rites*] EC suggest that this is a reference to "the worship of Jupiter with human sacrifices". The original, 273–7, seems to refer merely to the establishment of temples to Jupiter on the ground defiled by Oenomaus (cf. 389*n*).
    389. *fierce Oenomäus*] King of Pisa. Warned that he would die by the hand of his son-in-law, he challenged all suitors for his daughter Hippodamia to a chariot race against his own horses. The defeated suitors were fed to these man-eating horses.
    393. The Cretan Zeus, born on Mount Ida, was thought to die and to be re-born at certain periods.
    394. Cf. l. 325*n*.
    399. *Etheocles* ⟨*Tydeus 1712–17*⟩ and *Polynices.* [P. *1712–51.*]

'Twas thus I deem'd thy haughty Soul wou'd bear ⎫
The dire, tho' just, Revenge which I prepare   ⎬ 405
Against a Nation thy peculiar Care: ⎭
No less *Dione* might for *Thebes* contend,
Nor *Bacchus* less his Native Town defend,
Yet these in Silence see the Fates fulfil
Their Work, and rev'rence our Superior Will.   410
For by the black infernal *Styx* I swear,
(That dreadful Oath which binds the Thunderer)
'Tis fix'd; th'irrevocable Doom of *Jove*;
No Force can bend me, no Persuasion move.
Haste then, *Cyllenius*, thro' the liquid Air,   415
Go mount the Winds, and to the Shades repair;
Bid Hell's black Monarch my Commands obey,
And give up *Laius* to the Realms of Day,
Whose Ghost yet shiv'ring on *Cocytus*' Sand
Expects its Passage to the farther Strand: 420
Let the pale Sire revisit *Thebes*, and bear
These pleasing Orders to the Tyrant's Ear;
That, from his exil'd Brother, swell'd with Pride
Of foreign Forces, and his *Argive* Bride,
Almighty *Jove* commands him to detain   425
The promis'd Empire, and Alternate Reign:
Be this the Cause of more than mortal Hate;
The rest, succeeding Times shall ripen into Fate.

407. *Dione*] Venus was occasionally referred to by the name of her mother, Dione.

408. Bacchus was the son of Semele, a daughter of Cadmus, founder of Thebes.

415. *Cyllenius*] Mercury, born on Mount Cyllene.

419. *yet shiv'ring*] Because he had been killed by his own son.

428. Pope (*Corr.*, 1 63) owned to Cromwell that the latter's objections to this line "may well be grounded, in relation to its not being the exact sense of the words—*Cætera reliquo* [sic] *ordine ducam*" (Statius, 302). "But", he added, "the duration of the Action of *Statius*'s poem may as well be excepted against, as many things besides in him. . . For instead of confining his narration to *one year*, it is manifestly exceeded in the very first two books. . ."

The God obeys, and to his Feet applies
Those golden Wings that cut the yielding Skies;   430
His ample Hat his beamy Locks o'erspread,
And veil'd the Starry Glories of his Head:
He seiz'd the Wand that causes Sleep to fly,
Or in soft Slumbers seals the wakeful Eye;
That drives the Dead to dark *Tartarean* Coasts,   435
Or back to Life compells the wondring Ghosts.
Thus, thro' the parting Clouds the Son of *May*
Wings on the whistling Winds his rapid way,
Now smoothly steers through Air his equal Flight,
Now springs aloft, and tow'rs th'Ethereal Height,   440
Then wheeling down the Steep of Heav'n he flies,
And draws a radiant Circle o'er the Skies.
    Mean time the banish'd *Polynices* roves
(His *Thebes* abandon'd) thro' th'*Aonian* Groves,
While future Realms his wandring Thoughts delight,
His daily Vision, and his Dream by Night;   446
Forbidden *Thebes* appears before his Eye,
From whence he sees his absent Brother fly,
With Transport views the airy Rule his own,
And swells on an imaginary Throne.   450

433 the] his *1712–17*.   436 wondring] wand'ring *1741–51*.
449 Enjoys an airy Empire, all his own, *1712–14*.

430. Cf. Dryden, *Æn.*, I 412 (of Cyllenius): "And cleaves with all his Wings the yielding Skies."

432. *Starry Glories*] Statius, 305, says that Mercury put on a hat to temper the heat of the stars: "et temperat astra galero". Stephens, 379, has "starry head".

434. Cf. Dryden, *Æn.*, IV 358 (of Hermes): "With this he seals in Sleep, the wakeful sight".

437. Mercury was the son of Jupiter and Maia, daughter of Atlas.

438. *whistling Winds*] Cf. Dryden, *Æn.*, IX 927 (of trees): "Dance to the whistling Winds". Cf. also XII 404.

441. Cf. *Par. Lost*, III 741: "Throws his steep flight in many an Aery wheel..." Dryden, *Æn.*, I 413, has: "Down from the Steep of Heav'n *Cyllenius* flies".

446. Cf. *Sapho to Phaon*, 143–4 (p. 399, above).

449. *airy*] "Unsubstantial, vain, empty; unreal, imaginary" (OED).

Fain wou'd he cast a tedious Age away,
And live out all in one triumphant Day.
He chides the lazy Progress of the Sun,
And bids the Year with swifter Motion run.
With anxious Hopes his craving Mind is tost,   455
And all his Joys in length of Wishes lost.
   The Hero then resolves his Course to bend ⎫
Where ancient *Danaus'* fruitful Fields extend, ⎬
And fam'd *Mycene*'s lofty Tow'rs ascend, ⎭
(Where late the Sun did *Atreus'* Crimes detest   460
And disappear'd, in Horrour of the Feast.)
And now by Chance, by Fate, or Furies led,
From *Bacchus'* consecrated Caves he fled,
Where the shrill Cries of frantick Matrons sound,
And *Pentheus'* Blood enrich'd the rising Ground,   465
Then sees *Cythæron* towring o'er the Plain,
And thence declining gently to the Main.
Next to the Bounds of *Nisus'* Realm repairs,
Where treach'rous *Scylla* cut the Purple Hairs:
The hanging Cliffs of *Scyron*'s Rock explores,   470

470 Rock] Rocks *1712–14.*

458. Danaus was a former king of Argos.

459–61. Pope remarked to Cromwell (*Corr.*, I 64) upon this passage (l. 325 in Statius): ". . . *Caligantes abrupto sole Mycænas*, is not consistent with what he tells us, in Lib. 4. lin. 305: 'that those of *Mycænæ* came not to the war at this time, because they were then in confusion by the divisions of the Brothers, *Atreus* and *Thyestes*:' Now from the raising the *Greek* army against *Thebes*, back to the time of this journey of *Polynices*, is (according to *Statius*'s own account) three years."

460–1. The sky was darkened when Atreus, son of Pelops, served up the sons of his brother Thyestes as a meal for their father.

463–5. Cf. l. 323*n.*

468–9. Scylla, daughter of Nisus, king of Megara, fell in love with Minos when he besieged Megara, and pulled out the purple hair on which her father's life depended.

470*ff.* Pope altered the order of the original. Statius says that Mercury flew over Sciron and Corinth, and that from the middle of the isthmus he could hear the waves beat on both shores. This, says Pope in a letter to Cromwell (*Corr.*,

And hears the Murmurs of the diff'rent Shores:
Passes the Strait that parts the foaming Seas,
And stately *Corinth*'s pleasing Site surveys.
 'Twas now the Time when *Phœbus* yields to Night,
And rising *Cynthia* sheds her silver Light,   475
Wide o'er the World in solemn Pomp she drew
Her airy Chariot, hung with Pearly Dew;
All Birds and Beasts lye hush'd; Sleep steals away
The wild Desires of Men, and Toils of Day,
And brings, descending thro' the silent Air,   480
A sweet Forgetfulness of Human Care.
Yet no red Clouds, with golden Borders gay,
Promise the Skies the bright Return of Day;
No faint Reflections of the distant Light
Streak with long Gleams the scatt'ring Shades of Night;
From the damp Earth impervious Vapours rise,   486
Encrease the Darkness and involve the Skies.
At once the rushing Winds with roaring Sound
Burst from th'*Æolian* Caves, and rend the Ground,
With equal Rage their airy Quarrel try,   490
And win by turns the Kingdom of the Sky:
But with a thicker Night black *Auster* shrouds
The Heav'ns, and drives on heaps the rowling Clouds,

---

1 64), "could hardly be; for the *Isthmus* of *Corinth* is full five miles over". EC
correct him and say it is but three miles and a half. Pope may have been hyper-
critical, but his remark shows how carefully he considered every detail in the
text he translated.

477–81. See Intro., p. 350.

480–1. Pope remembered this couplet in his *Il.*, IX 841–2.

482–3. Statius, 342–3, has:

    sed nec puniceo rediturum nubila caelo
    promisere iubar . . .

Pope's lines recall the common saying: Red sky at night, shepherd's delight.

490–1. EC compare Dryden, *Æn.*, II 567–8:

    Thus, when the Rival Winds their Quarrel try,
    Contending for the Kingdom of the Skie;

and also IV 638: "As when the Winds their airy Quarrel try".

492. *Auster*] The south wind.

From whose dark Womb a ratling Tempest pours,
Which the cold North congeals to haily Show'rs.   495
From Pole to Pole the Thunder roars aloud,
And broken Lightnings flash from ev'ry Cloud.
Now Smoaks with Show'rs the misty Mountain-Ground,
And floated Fields lye undistinguish'd round:
Th'*Inachian* Streams with headlong Fury run,   500
And *Erasinus* rowls a Deluge on:
The foaming *Lerna* swells above its Bounds,
And spreads its ancient Poysons o'er the Grounds:
Where late was Dust, now rapid Torrents play,
Rush thro' the Mounds, and bear the Dams away: 505
Old Limbs of Trees from crackling Forests torn,
Are whirl'd in Air, and on the Winds are born;
The Storm the dark *Lycean* Groves display'd,
And first to Light expos'd the Sacred Shade.
Th'intrepid *Theban* hears the bursting Sky,   510
Sees yawning Rocks in massy Fragments fly,
And views astonish'd from the Hills afar
The Floods descending and the watry War,

494 From whose dark Womb] Then down on Earth *1712–14*.
498 Mountain-Ground,] Mountain-Ground. *1712–14*; mountain-
    ground *1741–51*.
509 Sacred] Venerable *1712–14*.
510–11 The Prince with Wonder did the Waste behold,
      While from torn Rocks the massy Fragments roll'd;
                          1712–14.
512 views] heard *1712–14*.

500–1. Inachus and Erasinus were rivers in Argos.
503. *ancient Poysons*] Those of the Hydra killed by Hercules in the marshes of
Lerna.
508. *dark Lycean Groves*] The groves on Mount Lycaeus, which the sun did not
penetrate, were sacred to Jupiter.
512–13. EC cite Dryden, *Æn.*, II 415–16:
      The Shepherd climbs the Cliff, and sees from far,
      The wasteful Ravage of the wat'ry War.

That driv'n by Storms, and pouring o'er the Plain,
Swept Herds, and Hinds, and Houses to the Main.   515
Thro' the brown Horrors of the Night he fled,
Nor knows, amaz'd, what doubtful Path to tread,
His Brother's Image to his Mind appears,
Inflames his Heart with Rage, and wings his Feet with Fears.

   So fares a Sailor on the stormy Main,   520
When Clouds conceal *Boötes'* golden Wain,
When not a Star its friendly Lustre keeps,
Nor trembling *Cynthia* glimmers on the Deeps;
He dreads the Rocks, and Shoals, and Seas, and Skies,
While Thunder roars, and Lightning round him flies.   525

   Thus strove the Chief on ev'ry side distress'd,
Thus still his Courage, with his Toils, encreas'd;
With his broad Shield oppos'd, he forc'd his way
Thro' thickest Woods, and rouz'd the Beasts of Prey.
Till he beheld, where from *Larissa*'s Height   530
The shelving Walls reflect a glancing Light;
Thither with haste the *Theban* Hero flies;
On this side *Lerna*'s pois'nous Water lies,
On that, *Prosymna*'s Grove and Temple rise:
He pass'd the Gates which then unguarded lay,   535
And to the Regal Palace bent his way;
On the cold Marble spent with Toil he lies,

---

515. EC compare Dryden, *Georgics* I 652: "Bore Houses, Herds, and lab'ring Hinds away."

516. Cf. Dryden, *Æn.*, VII 40–1: ". . . a Wood, / Which thick with Shades, and a brown Horror, stood". Cf. *El. to Abel.*, 170 (vol. II, p. 312 and *n*).

524. Pope perhaps recalled *Par. Lost*, II 947–50:
                     So eagerly the fiend
      O'er bog or steep, through strait, rough, dense, or rare,
      With head, hands, wings, or feet pursues his way,
      And swims or sinks, or wades, or creeps, or flies.

530. *Larissa*] The citadel of Argos.

534. *Prosymna's Grove*] Part of the temple of Juno (Heraeum) was situated near Prosymna.

And waits 'till pleasing Slumbers seal his Eyes.
　Adrastus here his happy People sways,
Blest with calm Peace in his declining Days,　　540
By both his Parents of Descent divine,
Great *Jove* and *Phœbus* grac'd his noble Line;
Heav'n had not crown'd his Wishes with a Son,
But two fair Daughters heir'd his State and Throne.
To him *Apollo* (wondrous to relate!　　545
But who can pierce into the Depths of Fate?)
Had sung—"Expect thy Sons on *Argos*' Shore,
"A Yellow Lyon and a bristly Boar."
This, long revolv'd in his Paternal Breast,
Sate heavy on his Heart, and broke his Rest;　　550
This, great *Amphiaraus*, lay hid from thee,
Tho' skill'd in Fate and dark Futurity.
The Father's Care and Prophet's Art were vain,
For thus did the Predicting God ordain.
　Lo hapless *Tydeus*, whose ill-fated Hand　　555
Had slain his Brother, leaves his Native Land,
And seiz'd with Horror, in the Shades of Night,
Thro' the thick Desarts headlong urg'd his Flight:
Now by the Fury of the Tempest driv'n,
He seeks a Shelter from th'inclement Heav'n,　　560
Till led by Fate, the *Theban*'s Steps he treads,

548 Boar."] Boar. *1712–41.*　　557 in] 'midst *1712–14.*
559 Tempest] tempests *1717–36a.*

542. *Phœbus*] Statius does not mention Phoebus as an ancestor of Adrastus.
Pope may have observed Stephens's note, l. 486, that Adrastus was "Son to
Talaus the grandchild of *Jupiter*, and *Eurynome* daughter to *Apollo*."
　544. *heir'd*] EC compare Dryden, *Æn.*, VII 79: "One only Daughter heir'd the
Royal State", and also VII 367.
　549. Cf. Dryden, *Æn.*, VI 454: "Revolving anxious Thoughts within his
Breast."
　551. *Amphiaraus*] Cf. l. 62*n.*
　555. *Tydeus*] Son of Oeneus, king of Calydon. He is called Oenides at l. 572.

And to fair *Argos'* open Court succeeds.

When thus the Chiefs from diff'rent Lands resort
T'*Adrastus'* Realms and Hospitable Court,
The King surveys his Guests with curious Eyes,   565
And views their Arms and Habit with Surprize.
A Lyon's yellow Skin the *Theban* wears,
Horrid his Mane, and rough with curling Hairs;
Such once employ'd *Alcides'* youthful Toils,
E're yet adorn'd with *Nemea*'s dreadful Spoils.   570
A Boar's stiff Hyde, of *Calydonian* Breed,
Oenides' manly Shoulders overspread,
Oblique his Tusks, erect his Bristles stood,
Alive, the Pride and Terror of the Wood.

Struck with the Sight, and fix'd in deep Amaze,   575
The King th'accomplish'd Oracle surveys,
Reveres *Apollo*'s vocal Caves, and owns
The guiding Godhead, and his future Sons.
O'er all his Bosom secret Transports reign,
And a glad Horror shoots through ev'ry Vein: 580
To Heav'n he lifts his Hands, erects his Sight,
And thus invokes the silent *Queen* of *Night*.

Goddess of Shades, beneath whose gloomy Reign
Yon spangled Arch glows with the starry Train,
You who the Cares of Heav'n and Earth allay, ⎫   585
Till Nature quicken'd by th'Inspiring Ray,   ⎬
Wakes to new Vigor with the rising Day.   ⎭
Oh thou who freest me from my doubtful State,
Long lost and wilder'd in the Maze of Fate!

562 *Argos'*] *Argos 1712–14*.   579 secret] sacred *1712–14*.
585 You who] Who dost *1712–14*.

562. Here Pope left out a long passage in the Latin text (ll. 408–81) which
describes a fight between Tydeus and Polynices. In Statius the fight takes place
at the entrance to the palace; Adrastus awakes and stops it, and they enter the
palace. See Intro., p. 351.

563–4. This couplet is introduced by Pope to bridge the portion of the Latin
text he omitted.

Be present still, oh Goddess! in our Aid;   590
Proceed, and firm those Omens thou hast made!
We to thy Name our Annual Rites will pay,
And on thy Altars Sacrifices lay;
The Sable Flock shall fall beneath the Stroke,
And fill thy Temples with a grateful Smoke: 595
Hail faithful *Tripos!* Hail ye dark Abodes
Of awful *Phœbus*: I confess the Gods!
    Thus, seiz'd with Sacred Fear, the Monarch pray'd;
Then to his Inner Court the Guests convey'd;
Where yet thin Fumes from dying Sparks arise, ⎫   600
And Dust yet white upon each Altar lies,   ⎬
The Relicks of a former Sacrifice.   ⎭
The King once more the solemn Rites requires,
And bids renew the Feasts, and wake the Fires.
His Train obey; while all the Courts around   605
With noisie Care and various Tumult sound.
Embroider'd Purple cloaths the Golden Beds;
This Slave the Floor, and That the Table spreads;

601 lies,] lies; *1712–17.*
604 the Fires.] the sleeping Fires. *1712–14.*

---

591. *firm*] A Latinism, for *confirm.* Statius, 504, has: "tuaque omina firmes".
EC compare Dryden, *Æn.*, VIII 107–8:
        But, oh! be present to thy Peoples Aid;
        And firm the gracious promise thou hast made.
596. *faithful Tripos*] The tripod on which the Pythoness seated herself when
prophesying.
596–7. Cf. Stephens, 625–6:
        Haile faithfull *Tripos*, and ye close aboads
        Of the dark Oracle. I've found the gods.
The phrase "dark abodes" is common in Dryden. See *Æn.*, IV 874.
601–2. Cf. Stephens, 628–30:
                Where th' Altars still look'd white
        With their late fires; In th' ashes yet there fumed
        Some sparkes alive . . .
604 var. EC compare Dryden, *Æn.*, VIII 725: "And on his Altars wak'd the
sleeping Fires."

A Third dispels the Darkness of the Night,
And fills depending Lamps with Beams of Light;   610
Here Loaves in Canisters are pil'd on high,
And there, in Flames the slaughter'd Victims fry.
Sublime in Regal State, *Adrastus* shone,
Stretch'd on rich Carpets, on his Iv'ry Throne;
A lofty Couch receives each Princely Guest;   615
Around, at awful Distance, wait the rest.
    And now the King, his Royal Feast to grace,
Acestis calls, the Guardian of his Race,
Who first their Youth in Arts of Virtue train'd,
And their ripe Years in modest Grace maintain'd.   620
Then softly whisper'd in her faithful Ear,
And bad his Daughters at the Rites appear.
When from the close Apartments of the Night,
The Royal Nymphs approach divinely bright,
Such was *Diana*'s, such *Minerva*'s Face;   625
Nor shine their Beauties with superior Grace,
But that in these a milder Charm indears,
And less of Terror in their Looks appears.
As on the Heroes first they cast their Eyes,
O'er their fair Cheeks the glowing Blushes rise,   630
Their down cast looks a decent Shame confest,
Then, on their Father's rev'rend Features rest.
    The Banquet done, the Monarch gives the Sign
To fill the Goblet high with sparkling Wine,
Which *Danaus* us'd in sacred Rites of old,   635
With Sculpture grac'd, and rough with rising Gold.

612 fry.] fly. *1736b–51.*
618 Guardian] Tutress *1712–14.*
622 at the Rites appear.] to the Rites repair. *1712–14.*
624 approach] approach'd *1712–17.*

618. *the Guardian*] The nurse of his two daughters.
636. Cf. Dryden, *Æn.*, v 704: "Accept this Goblet rough with figur'd Gold".
Cf. *Spring*, 37 (p. 64, above).

Here to the Clouds victorious *Perseus* flies; ⎫
Medusa seems to move her languid Eyes, ⎬
And, ev'n in Gold, turns paler as she dies. ⎭
There from the Chace *Jove*'s tow'ring Eagle bears   640
On golden Wings, the *Phrygian* to the Stars;
Still as he rises in th'Æthereal Height,
His native Mountains lessen to his Sight;
While all his sad Companions upward gaze,
Fix'd on the Glorious Scene in wild Amaze,   645
And the swift Hounds, affrighted as he flies,
Run to the Shade, and bark against the Skies.
    This Golden Bowl with gen'rous Juice was crown'd,
The first Libations sprinkled on the Ground;
By turns on each Celestial Pow'r they call;   650
With *Phœbus*' Name resounds the vaulted Hall.
The Courtly Train, the Strangers, and the rest,
Crown'd with chast Laurel, and with Garlands drest,
(While with rich Gums the fuming Altars blaze)
Salute the God in num'rous Hymns of Praise.   655
    Then thus the King: Perhaps, my Noble Guests,
These honour'd Altars, and these annual Feasts,

644 upward] upwards *1712–14.*   651 *Phœbus*'] *Phœbus 1712–14.*
654 *No parentheses 1736a–51.*

---

    641. *the Phrygian*] Ganymede, carried off to be the cup-bearer of the gods.
    648. Cf. Dryden, *Æn.*, I 1013: "The Golden Bowls with sparkling Wine are crown'd".
    649. Cf.Dryden, *Æn.*, I 1031: "Sprinkling the first Libations on the Ground..."
    655. *num'rous*] Measured, rhythmic, harmonious. Cf. *Par. Lost*, v 150: "... in Prose or numerous Verse".
    656. Cf. Stephens, 675: "Then saies the King: Perhaps my noble guests ..."
For the entire passage, cf. Dryden, *Æn.*, VIII 246–51:

> These Rites, these Altars, and this Feast, O King,
> From no vain Fears, or Superstition spring:
> Or blind Devotion, or from blinder Chance;
> Or heady Zeal, or brutal Ignorance:
> But, sav'd from Danger, with a grateful Sense,
> The Labours of a God we recompence.

To bright *Apollo*'s awful Name design'd,
Unknown, with Wonder may perplex your Mind.
Great was the Cause; our old Solemnities   660
From no blind Zeal or fond Tradition rise;
But sav'd from Death, our *Argives* yearly pay
These grateful Honours to the God of Day.
    When by a thousand Darts the *Python* slain
With Orbs unroll'd lay covering all the Plain,   665
(Transfix'd as o'er *Castalia*'s Streams he hung,
And suck'd new Poisons with his triple Tongue)
To *Argos*' Realms the Victor God resorts,
And enters old *Crotopus*' humble Courts.
This rural Prince one only Daughter blest,   670
That all the Charms of blooming Youth possest;
Fair was her Face, and spotless was her Mind,
Where Filial Love with Virgin Sweetness join'd.
Happy! and happy still She might have prov'd,
Were she less beautiful, or less belov'd!   675
But *Phœbus* lov'd, and on the Flow'ry Side
Of *Nemea*'s Stream the yielding Fair enjoy'd:
Now, e'er ten Moons their Orb with Light adorn,
Th'illustrious Off-spring of the God was born.
The Nymph, her Father's Anger to evade,   680

665 covering] stretch'd o'er *1712–14*.
668–9 The Victor God did to these Realms resort,
    And enter'd old *Crotopus*' humble Court. *1712–14*.
670 rural] *Argive 1712–14*.   674 prov'd,] prov'd; *1712–17*.
678 Now,] And *1712–17*.

664*ff.* Python was the dragon who guarded the oracle of Delphi. He was killed by Apollo, who then took possession of the oracle. Warton reproaches Pope with omitting "some forcible expressions of the original: Septem—atris—terentem—nigro—centum per jugera. All of them picturesque epithets." Pope's phrase, "a thousand Darts", apparently comes from Ovid's description of the same incident, *Met.*, I 443–4.
667. "The water was not itself poisonous, but it turned to venom in the serpent" [EC].
669. *Crotopus*] Former king of Argos.

Retires from *Argos* to the Sylvan Shade,
To Woods and Wilds the pleasing Burden bears,
And trusts her Infant to a Shepherd's Cares.
    How mean a Fate, unhappy Child! is thine?
Ah how unworthy those of Race divine?   685
On flow'ry Herbs in some green Covert laid,
His Bed the Ground, his Canopy the Shade,
He mixes with the bleating Lambs his Cries, ⎫
While the rude Swain his rural Musick tries, ⎬
To call soft Slumbers on his infant Eyes.   ⎭ 690
Yet ev'n in those obscure Abodes to live,
Was more, alas! than cruel Fate wou'd give!
For on the grassie Verdure as he lay,
And breath'd the Freshness of the early Day,
Devouring Dogs the helpless Infant tore,   695
Fed on his trembling Limbs, and lapt the Gore.
Th'astonish'd Mother when the Rumour came,
Forgets her Father, and neglects her Fame,
With loud Complaints she fills the yielding Air,
And beats her Breast, and rends her flowing Hair; 700
Then wild with Anguish, to her Sire she flies;
Demands the Sentence, and contented dies.
    But touch'd with Sorrow for the Dead, too late,
The raging God prepares t'avenge her Fate.
He sends a Monster, horrible and fell,   705
Begot by Furies in the Depths of Hell;
The Pest a Virgin's Face and Bosom bears; ⎫
High on her Crown a rising Snake appears,   ⎬
Guards her black Front, and hisses in her Hairs:⎭

681 Retires from] Now flies from *1712–17*.
688 Cries,] Cries; *1712–17*.   694 early] rising *1712–17*.
708 her] a *1741–51*.

682. Cf. *Fable of Dryope*, 19n (p. 386, above).
706. EC compare Sandys, *Met.*, vi 663: "And cites the Furies from the depth of hell."

About the Realm she walks her dreadful Round,   710
When Night with sable Wings o'erspreads the Ground,
Devours young Babes before their Parents' Eyes,
And feeds and thrives on Publick Miseries.
    But gen'rous Rage the bold *Chorœbus* warms,
Chorœbus, fam'd for Virtue as for Arms;   715
Some few like him, inspir'd with Martial flame,
Thought a short Life well lost for endless Fame.
These, where two Ways in equal Parts divide, ⎫
The direful Monster from afar descry'd;   ⎬
Two bleeding Babes depending at her Side;   ⎭   720
Whose panting Vitals, warm with Life, she draws,
And in their Hearts embrues her cruel Claws.
The Youth surround her with extended Spears;
But brave *Chorœbus* in the Front appears,
Deep in her Breast he plung'd his shining Sword,   725
And Hell's dire Monster back to Hell restor'd.
Th'*Inachians* view the Slain with vast Surprize,
Her twisting Volumes, and her rowling Eyes,
Her spotted Breast, and gaping Womb imbru'd
With livid Poyson and our Children's Blood.   730
The Crowd in stupid Wonder fix'd appear,
Pale ev'n in Joy, nor yet forget to fear.
Some with vast Beams the squallid Corps engage,

712 Parents'] Parent's *1712–17*; parents *1736a–51*.
714 *Chorœbus*] *Chorœbus 1712–17*.
715 *Chorœbus*,] *Chorœbus, 1712–17*.   723 Youth] youths *1751*.
724 *Chorœbus*] *Chorœbus 1712–17*.   727 view] view'd *1712–17*.
730 Children's] Infant's *1712–17*; childrens *1736a–51*.

712–13. EC compare Stephens, 728–30:
                        devouring some
    With rav'nous jaws, before their Parents eyes,
    And fats herself with publike miseries.
  727. *Th'Inachians*] Descendants of Inachus, founder of Argos.
  728. *Volumes*] Coils. Describing the Python, Statius (l. 562) had said: "caeru-
lei sinuosa volumina monstri". Cf. *Windsor-Forest*, 143.

And weary all the wild Efforts of Rage.
The Birds obscene, that nightly flock'd to Tast,   735
With hollow Screeches fled the dire Repast;
And ravenous Dogs, allur'd by scented Blood,
And starving Wolves, ran howling to the Wood.
   But fir'd with Rage, from cleft *Parnassus'* Brow ⎫
Avenging *Phœbus* bent his deadly Bow,   ⎬ 740
And hissing flew the feather'd Fates below;   ⎭
A Night of sultry Clouds involv'd around
The Tow'rs, the Fields, and the devoted Ground:
And now a thousand Lives together fled,   ⎫
Death with his Scythe cut off the fatal Thread, ⎬ 745
And a whole Province in his Triumph led.   ⎭
   But *Phœbus*, ask'd why noxious Fires appear,
And raging *Sirius* blasts the sickly Year,
Demands their Lives by whom his Monster fell,
And dooms a dreadful Sacrifice to Hell.   750
   Blest be thy Dust, and let Eternal Fame
Attend thy *Manes*, and preserve thy Name;
Undaunted Hero! who, divinely brave,
In such a Cause disdain'd thy Life to save;
But view'd the Shrine with a superior Look,   755

---

736 hollow] hallow *1736b–41. An evident misprint.*
738 And] With *1712–14.*

---

741. *feather'd Fates*] Statius, 630, has "pestifera arma". Cf. Dryden, *Iliad*, I
73–4 (of Apollo):
> Then with full Force his deadly Bowe he bent,
> And Feather'd Fates among the Mules and Sumpters sent.

743. *devoted*] Consigned to evil or destruction, doomed (OED).

745. *Scythe*] Statius, 633, has "ense metit". Pope perhaps preferred the medieval image of Death armed with a scythe.

746. Cf. Stephens, 762: ". . . and captive townes in triumph led."

749–50. Cf. Stephens, 765–6:
> The same Power bids, their lives should pay to hell
> A sacrifice, by whom his monster fell.

752. *Manes*] Here probably the soul or spirit of Choroebus.

753. *Undaunted Hero*] Choroebus.

And its upbraided Godhead thus bespoke.
  With Piety, the Soul's securest Guard,
And conscious Virtue, still its own Reward,
Willing I come; unknowing how to fear;
Nor shalt thou, *Phœbus*, find a Suppliant here: 760
Thy Monster's Death to me was ow'd alone,
And 'tis a Deed too glorious to disown.
Behold him here, for whom, so many Days,
Impervious Clouds conceal'd thy sullen Rays;
For whom, as Man no longer claim'd thy Care,   765
Such Numbers fell by Pestilential Air!
But if th'abandon'd Race of Human-kind
From Gods above no more Compassion find;
If such Inclemency in Heav'n can dwell; ⎫
Yet why must un-offending *Argos* feel   ⎬ 770
The Vengeance due to this unlucky Steel? ⎭
On me, on me, let all thy Fury fall,
Nor err from me, since I deserve it all:
Unless our Desart Cities please thy Sight,
Our Fun'ral Flames reflect a grateful Light.   775
Discharge thy Shafts, this ready Bosom rend,
And to the Shades a Ghost Triumphant send;
But for my Country let my Fate attone,
Be mine the Vengeance, as the Crime my own.
  Merit distress'd impartial Heav'n relieves;   780
Unwelcome Life relenting *Phœbus* gives;
For not the vengeful Pow'r, that glow'd with Rage,
With such amazing Virtue durst engage.

775 Our] And *1712–17*; Or *1751*.

---

772. Cf. *Par. Lost*, III 236–7:
    Behold mee then, mee for him, life for life
    I offer, on mee let thine anger fall.
Cf. also x 852–3. Dryden, *Æn.*, IX 571–2, has:
    Me, me, he cry'd, turn all your Swords alone
    On me; the Fact confess'd, the Fault my own.

The Clouds dispers'd, *Apollo*'s Wrath expir'd,
And from the wondring God th'unwilling Youth retir'd. 785
Thence we these Altars in his Temple raise,
And offer Annual Honours, Feasts, and Praise;
These solemn Feasts propitious *Phœbus* please,
These Honours, still renew'd, his antient Wrath appease.
    But say, Illustrious Guest (adjoin'd the King)   790
What Name you bear, from what high Race you spring?
The noble *Tydeus* stands confess'd, and known
Our Neighbour Prince, and Heir of *Calydon*:
Relate your Fortunes, while the friendly Night
And silent Hours to various Talk invite.   795
    The *Theban* bends on Earth his gloomy Eyes,
Confus'd, and sadly thus at length replies:
Before these Altars how shall I proclaim
(Oh gen'rous Prince) my Nation or my name,
Or thro' what Veins our ancient Blood has roll'd?   800
Let the sad Tale for ever rest untold!
Yet if propitious to a Wretch unknown,
You seek to share in Sorrows not your own;
Know then, from *Cadmus* I derive my Race,
Jocasta's Son, and *Thebes* my Native Place.   805
To whom the King, (who felt his gen'rous Breast
Touch'd with Concern for his unhappy Guest)
Replies—Ah why forbears the Son to Name
His wretched Father, known too well by Fame?
Fame, that delights around the World to stray,   810
Scorns not to take our *Argos* in her Way.
Ev'n those who dwell where Suns at distance roll,
In *Northern* Wilds, and freeze beneath the Pole;
And those who tread the burning *Lybian* Lands,
The faithless *Syrtes* and the moving Sands;   815
Who view the *Western* Sea's extreamest Bounds,
Or drink of *Ganges* in their *Eastern* Grounds;

---

815. *Syrtes*] Quicksands off the northern coast of Africa.

All these the Woes of *Oedipus* have known,
Your Fates, your Furies, and your haunted Town.
If on the Sons the Parents' Crimes descend,   820
What Prince from those his Lineage can defend?
Be this thy Comfort, that 'tis thine t'efface ⎫
With Virtuous Acts thy Ancestor's Disgrace, ⎬
And be thy self the Honour of thy Race. ⎭
But see! the Stars begin to steal away,   825
And shine more faintly at approaching Day;
Now pour the Wine; and in your tuneful Lays,
Once more resound the Great *Apollo*'s Praise.
 Oh Father *Phœbus!* whether *Lycia*'s Coast
And snowy Mountains thy bright Presence boast;   830
Whether to sweet *Castalia* thou repair,
And bathe in silver Dews thy yellow Hair;
Or pleas'd to find fair *Delos* float no more,
Delight in *Cynthus* and the Shady Shore;
Or chuse thy Seat in *Ilion*'s proud Abodes,   835
The shining Structures rais'd by lab'ring Gods!
By thee the Bow and mortal Shafts are born,
Eternal Charms thy blooming Youth adorn:
Skill'd in the Laws of Secret Fate above,
And the dark Counsels of Almighty *Jove*,   840
'Tis thine the Seeds of future War to know,
The Change of Scepters, and impending Woe;

819 Fates,] Fates; *1712–14.*   820 Parents'] Parents *1712–51.*
823 Ancestor's] Ancestors *1712–14.*
832 bathe] bath *1712–14.*
841 Thou dost the Seeds of future War foreknow, *1712–14.*

829. *Lycia*] A state in Asia Minor where the worship of Apollo was active.
833. *float no more*] Delos supposedly drifted through the Aegean until Jupiter moored it as a refuge for Latona. There she gave birth to Apollo and Diana.
834. *Shady Shore*] The shadow cast by Mount Cynthus, the mountain in Delos, on the Aegean shore.
836. *lab'ring Gods*] According to legend, the walls of Troy were built by Apollo and Neptune.

When direful Meteors spread thro' glowing Air
Long Trails of Light, and shake their blazing Hair.
Thy Rage the *Phrygian* felt, who durst aspire   845
T'excel the Musick of thy Heav'nly Lyre;
Thy Shafts aveng'd lewd *Tityus*' guilty Flame,
Th'Immortal Victim of thy Mother's Fame;
Thy Hand slew *Python*; and the Dame who lost
Her num'rous Off-spring for a fatal Boast.   850
In *Phlegias*' Doom thy just Revenge appears,
Condemn'd to Furies and Eternal Fears;
He views his Food, but dreads, with lifted Eye,
The mouldring Rock that trembles from on high.

    Propitious hear our Pray'r, O Pow'r Divine!   855
And on thy Hospitable *Argos* shine.
Whether the Style of *Titan* please thee more,

853–4 He views his Food, wou'd taste, yet dares not try;
       But dreads the mouldring Rock that trembles from on high.
                          1712–14.

843–4. Cf. *Par. Lost*, ii 708–11:
                  . . . and like a Comet burn'd
      That fires the length of *Ophiucus* huge
      In th' Arctic Sky, and from his horrid hair
      Shakes Pestilence and War.

845. *the Phrygian*] Marsyas, a river god who competed with his flute against Apollo and his lyre. He was defeated and flayed alive by the god.

847. *Tityus' guilty Flame*] Tityus, a giant, attempted to violate Latona. He was killed by Apollo and Diana and hurled by them into Tartarus, where two vultures fed perpetually on his liver.

849. *the Dame*] Niobe.

851–4. Phlegyas set fire to Apollo's temple at Delphi because the god had seduced his daughter Coronis. Statius, 713, speaks of the rocks which threaten him as being hollow ("subter cava saxa iacentem"), and makes it clear that Phlegyas did not eat his food because it had been made repulsive ("sed mixta famem fastidia vincunt"). As EC suggest, Pope was probably influenced by Dryden's description of the punishment of Pirithous and Ixion, *Æn.*, vi 817–8:
      High o're their Heads a mould'ring Rock is plac'd,
      That promises a fall, and shakes at ev'ry Blast.
Cf. also Stephens, 862–3: ". . . hungry *Phlegias*, who does fear / The ever-falling Stone."

Whose Purple Rays th'*Achæmenes* adore;
Or great *Osyris*, who first taught the Swain
In *Pharian* Fields to sow the Golden Grain;   860
Or *Mitra*, to whose Beams the *Persian* bows,
And pays in hollow Rocks his awful Vows,
Mitra, whose Head the Blaze of Light adorns,
Who grasps the strugling Heifer's Lunar Horns.

865 *The End of the first Book. 1712–14.*

858. *Achæmenes*] The people of Achaemenes, the legendary ancestor of the
Persian kings.
860. *Pharian*] Egyptian.
861. *Mitra*] Mithras, the Persian god of light. He was identified by the Greeks
with Apollo and introduced later into Roman mythology. Statius alludes to the
famous relief representing Mithras slaying a bull. Pope expands the two lines in
Statius, adds the "hollow Rocks" which recall the artificial grottoes of Mithraic
temples in Rome, and in the last couplet underlines the interpretation, generally accepted in his day, of Mithras as representing the sun, and the bull (or
heifer) with its horns, the moon.

THE
EPISODE
OF
SARPEDON,

Translated from the
Twelfth and *Sixteenth* BOOKS

OF
HOMER's *ILIADS*.

NOTE ON THE TEXT

The Episode of Sarpedon first appeared, along with *January and May*
and the *Pastorals*, in *Poetical Miscellanies : The Sixth Part*, on May 2,
1709. This was Pope's first appearance in print. A second edition
of the Miscellany was published in 1716 with the title, *The Sixth
Part of Miscellany Poems*. The texts of the two editions are practically
identical : there is an obvious misprint at l. 334 in the first edition,
and the variant at l. 33 may also be a misprint. In 1717 vol. III of
Pope's *Iliad* appeared, and a portion of the *Episode* was worked into
its proper place in Book XII. In 1718 vol. IV of the *Iliad* was published, and the remaining portion of the *Episode* appeared in Book XVI.

The changes Pope made when he fitted *The Episode of Sarpedon*
into the *Iliad* are noted in the textual apparatus, but form no part
of the text, that of the first edition, printed here.

KEY TO THE CRITICAL APPARATUS

1709 = Poetical Miscellanies, The Sixth Part, octavo, Griffith 1.
1716 = The Sixth Part of Miscellany Poems, duodecimo, Griffith
        61.
1717 = The Iliad of Homer, vol. III, quarto, Griffith 75.
1718 = The Iliad of Homer, vol. IV, quarto, Griffith 93.

THE

EPISODE

OF

SARPEDON,

Translated from the
Twelfth and *Sixteenth* Books

OF

HOMER's *ILIADS*.

The ARGUMENT.

Sarpedon, *the Son of* Jupiter, *commanded the* Lycians *who came to the Aid of* Troy. *In the first Battel when* Diomed *had put the* Trojans *to flight, he incourag'd* Hector *to rally, and signaliz'd himself by the Death of* Tlepolemus. *Afterwards when the* Greeks *had rais'd a Fortification to cover their Fleet, which the* Trojans *endeavour'd to overthrow, this Prince was the Occasion of effecting it. He incites* Glaucus *to second him in this Action by an admirable Speech, which has been render'd in English by Sir* John Denham; *after whom the Translator had not the Vanity to attempt it for any other reason, than that the Episode must have been very imperfect without so Noble a part of it.*

THUS *Hector*, great in Arms, contends in vain
To fix the Fortune of the fatal Plain,
Nor *Troy* cou'd conquer, nor the *Greeks* wou'd yield,
'Till bold *Sarpedon* rush'd into the Field;
For Mighty *Jove* inspir'd with Martial Flame   5
His God-like Son, and urg'd him on to Fame.
In Arms he shines, conspicuous from afar,
And bears aloft his ample Shield in Air,

1–2   Thus God-like *Hector* and his Troops contend
      To force the Ramparts, and the Gates to rend; *1717.*
4 bold . . . into] great *Sarpedon* tow'r'd amid *1717.*
6 God-like] matchless *1717.*

449

Within whose Orb the thick Bull-hides were roll'd,
Pondrous with Brass, and bound with ductile Gold;   10
And while two pointed Jav'lins arm his Hands,
Majestick moves along, and leads his *Lycian* Bands.
    So prest with Hunger, from the Mountain's Brow,
Descends a Lion on the Flocks below;
So stalks the Lordly Savage o'er the Plain,   15
In sullen Majesty, and stern Disdain:
In vain loud Mastives bay him from afar,
And Shepherds gaul him with an Iron War;
Regardless, furious, he pursues his way;
He foams, he roars, he rends the panting Prey.   20
    Resolv'd alike, Divine *Sarpedon* glows
With gen'rous Rage, that drives him on the Foes.
He views the Tow'rs, and meditates their Fall;
To sure Destruction dooms the *Grecian* Wall;
Then casting on his Friend an ardent Look,   25
Fir'd with the Thirst of Glory, thus he spoke.
    Why boast we, *Glaucus*, our extended Reign,
Where *Xanthus*' Streams enrich the *Lycian* Plain?
Our num'rous Herds that range each fruitful Field,
And Hills where Vines their Purple Harvest yield?   30
Our foaming Bowls with gen'rous *Nectar* crown'd,
Our Feasts enhanc'd with Musick's sprightly Sound?
Why on those Shores are we with Joy survey'd,

24 the *Grecian*] th'aspiring *1717*.   29 each] the *1717*.
31 gen'rous] purer *1717*.   33 those] these *1716*.

12. Cf. Dryden, *Æn.*, I 225: "Majestick moves along, and awful Peace maintains."
    15. *Lordly Savage*] Cf. *Windsor-Forest*, 57n.
    23. *meditates*] Cf. *Windsor-Forest*, 102n.
    27 ff. For a discussion of Denham's tr. of these lines, see Intro., p. 357, above. Cf. also *Rape of the Lock*, v 9–34 (vol. II, pp. 195–7).
    33–4. Cf. Denham, *Sarpedon's Speech to Glaucus*, 10–11:
                Why as we pass, do those on *Xanthus* shore
                As Gods behold us, and as Gods adore?
See Intro., p. 357, above.

Admir'd as Heroes, and as Gods obey'd?
Unless great Acts superior Merit prove,   35
And Vindicate the bounteous Pow'rs above:
'Tis ours, the Dignity They give, to grace;
The first in Valour, as the first in Place:
That while with wondring Eyes our Martial Bands
Behold our Deeds transcending our Commands,   40
Such, they may cry, deserve the Sov'reign State,
Whom those that Envy dare not Imitate!
Cou'd all our Care elude the greedy Grave,
Which claims no less the Fearful than the Brave,
For Lust of Fame I shou'd not vainly dare   45
In fighting Fields, nor urge thy Soul to War.
But since, alas, ignoble Age must come,
Disease, and Death's inexorable Doom;
The Life which others pay, let Us bestow,
And give to Fame what we to Nature owe;   50
Brave, tho' we fall; and honour'd, if we live;
Or let us Glory gain, or Glory give!
      He said, his Words the list'ning Chief inspire
With equal Warmth, and rouze the Warrior's Fire;
The Troops pursue their Leaders with Delight,   55
Rush to the Foe, and claim the promis'd Fight.
Menestheus from on high the Storm beheld,
Threat'ning the Fort, and black'ning in the Field;
Around the Walls he gaz'd, to view from far
What Aid appear'd t'avert th'approaching War,   60
And saw where *Teucer* with th'*Ajaces* stood,

39 while] when *1717*.   43 greedy] gloomy *1717*.

45–6. Cf. Dryden, *Æn.*, vɪɪɪ 685: "In fighting Fields from you shall learn to dare".

52. Hobbes, *The Iliads and Odysses of Homer* (1677), has: "And either honour gain or honour give."

58. Cf. Dryden, *Æn.*, ɪx 40: "Blackning the Fields, and thickning thro' the Skies."

60. *War*] Soldiers in fighting array (OED). Cf. l. 134, below.

Insatiate of the Fight, and prodigal of Blood.
In vain he calls, the Din of Helms and Shields
Rings to the Skies, and ecchoes thro' the Fields,
The Gates resound, the Brazen Hinges fly,   65
While each is bent to conquer or to die.
Then thus to *Thoos*;—Hence with speed (he said)
And urge the bold *Ajaces* to our Aid;
Their Strength united best may help to bear
The bloody Labours of the doubtful War: 70
Hither the *Lycian* Princes bend their Course,
The best and bravest of the *Trojan* Force.
But if too fiercely, there, the Foes contend,
Let *Telamon* at least our Tow'rs defend,
And *Teucer* haste, with his unerring Bow,   75
To share the Danger, and repel the Foe.
  Swift as the Word, the Herald speeds along
The lofty Ramparts, through the Warlike Throng,
And finds the Heroes, bath'd in Sweat and Gore,
Oppos'd in Combate on the dusty Shore.   80

62 Of Fight insatiate, prodigal of Blood. *1717*.
65–6 The brazen Hinges fly, the Walls resound,
      Heav'n trembles, roar the Mountains, thunders all the
          Ground. *1717*.
72 *Trojan*] hostile *1717*.   78 Warlike] martial *1717*.
80 *Add. 1717:*
            Ye valiant Leaders of our warlike Bands!
            Your Aid (said *Thoos*) *Peteus'* Son demands,
            Your Strength, united, best may help to bear
            The bloody Labours of the doubtful War:
            Thither the *Lycian* Princes bend their Course,
            The best and bravest of the hostile Force.
            But if too fiercely, here, the Foes contend,
            At least, let *Telamon* those Tow'rs defend,
            And *Teucer* haste, with his unerring Bow,
            To share the Danger, and repell the Foe.

70. Cf. Dryden, *Æn.*, x 1090: "And dauntless undertook the doubtful War."

Strait to the Fort great *Ajax* turn'd his Care,
And thus bespoke his Brothers of the War:
Now valiant *Lycomede*, exert your Might,
And brave *Oïleus*, prove your Force in Fight:
To you I trust the Fortune of the Field,   85
'Till by this Arm the Foe shall be repell'd;
That done, expect me to compleat the Day:
Then, with his Sev'nfold Shield, he strode away.
With equal Steps bold *Teucer* prest the Shore,
Whose fatal Bow the strong *Pandion* bore.   90
High on the Walls appear'd the *Lycian* Pow'rs,
Like some black Tempest gath'ring round the Tow'rs:
The *Greeks* oppress'd, their utmost Force unite,
Prepar'd to labour in th'unequal Fight;
The War begins; mix'd Shouts and Groans arise;   95
Tumultuous Clamour mounts, and thickens in the Skies.
Fierce *Ajax* first th'advancing Host invades,
And sends the brave *Epicles* to the Shades,
Sarpedon's Friend; Across the Warrior's Way,
Rent from the Walls, a Rocky Fragment lay;   100
In modern Ages not the strongest Swain
Cou'd heave th'unwieldy Burthen from the Plain:
He poiz'd, and swung it round; then tost on high,
It flew with Force, and labour'd up the Sky;
Full on the *Lycian*'s Helmet thundring down,   105
The pondrous Ruin crush'd his batter'd Crown.
As skilful Divers from some Airy Steep
Headlong descend, and shoot into the Deep,
So falls *Epicles*; then in Groans expires,
And murm'ring from the Corps th'unwilling Soul retires.
    While to the Ramparts daring *Glaucus* drew,   111
From *Teucer*'s Hand a winged Arrow flew,

95 begins;] renews, *1717*.
110 And murm'ring to the Shades the Soul retires. *1717*.

96. Cf. l. 58*n*, above.

The bearded Shaft the destin'd Passage found,
And on his naked Arm inflicts a Wound.
The Chief who fear'd some Foe's insulting Boast   115
Might stop the Progress of his warlike Host,
Conceal'd the Wound, and leaping from his Height,
Retir'd reluctant from th'unfinish'd Fight.
Divine *Sarpedon* with Regret beheld
Disabl'd *Glaucus* slowly quit the Field;   120
His beating Breast with gen'rous Ardour glows,
He springs to Fight, and flies upon the Foes.
Alcmaon first was doom'd his Force to feel,
Deep in his Breast he plung'd the pointed Steel,
Then from the yawning Wound with Fury tore   125
The Spear, pursu'd by gushing Streams of Gore;
Down sinks the Warrior, with a thundring Sound,
His Brazen Armour rings against the Ground.
    Swift to the Battlement the Victor flies,
Tugs with full Force, and ev'ry Nerve applies;   130
It shakes; the pondrous Stones disjoynted yield;
The rowling Ruins smoak along the Field.
A mighty Breach appears, the Walls lye bare,
And like a Deluge rushes in the War.
At once bold *Teucer* draws the twanging Bow,   135
And *Ajax* sends his Jav'lin at the Foe;
Fix'd in his Belt the feather'd Weapon stood,
And thro' his Buckler drove the trembling Wood;
But *Jove* was present in the dire Debate,
To shield his Off-spring, and avert his Fate.   140
The Prince gave back; not meditating Flight,
But urging Vengeance and severer Fight;
Then rais'd with Hope, and fir'd with Glory's Charms,
His fainting Squadrons to new Fury warms.

143 Hope,] Hopes, *1717*.

119–20. See Intro., pp. 354–5, above.
143–4. See Intro., p. 355, above.

O where, ye *Lycians*, is the Strength you boast,   145
Your former Fame, and ancient Virtue lost?
The Breach lyes open, but your Chief in vain
Attempts alone the guarded Pass to gain:
Unite, and soon that Hostile Fleet shall fall,
The Force of pow'rful Union conquers All.   150
   This just Rebuke inflam'd the *Lycian* Crew,
They join, they thicken, and th'Assault renew;
Unmov'd, th'embody'd *Greeks* their Fury dare,
And fix'd support the Weight of all the War:
Nor cou'd the *Greeks* repell the *Lycian* Pow'rs,   155
Nor the bold *Lycians* force the *Grecian* Tow'rs.
As on the Confines of adjoyning Grounds,
Two stubborn Swains with Blows dispute their Bounds;
They tugg, they sweat; but neither gain, nor yield,
One Foot, one Inch, of the contended Field: 160
Thus obstinate to Death, they fight, they fall;
Nor these can keep, nor those can win the Wall:
Their Manly Breasts are pierc'd with many a Wound,
Loud Strokes are heard, and ratling Arms resound,
The copious Slaughter covers all the Shore,   165
And the high Ramparts drop with Human Gore.
   As when two Scales are charg'd with doubtful Loads,
From side to side the trembling Balance nods,
'Till poiz'd aloft, the resting Beam suspends
Each equal Weight, nor this, nor that descends.   170
So Conquest loth for either to declare,
Levels her Wings, and hov'ring hangs in Air.

168 *Add. 1717:*
     (While some laborious Matron, just and poor,
     With nice Exactness weighs her woolly Store)
171–4 So stood the War, till *Hector*'s matchless Might
     With Fates prevailing, turn'd the Scale of Fight. *1717.*

153. *embody'd Greeks*] Cf. *Par. Lost*, I 574: "imbodied force".
157. Cf. Hobbes's tr., "As two men on the Confines of their ground".

'Till *Hector* came, to whose Superior Might
Jove ow'd the Glory of the destin'd Fight.
Fierce as a Whirlwind, up the Walls he flies,   175
And fires his Host with loud repeated Cries:
Advance ye *Trojans*, lend your valiant Hands,
Haste to the Fleet, and toss the blazing Brands!
They hear, they run, and gath'ring at his Call,
Raise scaling Engines, and ascend the Wall: 180
Around the Works a Wood of glitt'ring Spears
Shoots up, and All the rising Host appears.
A pondrous Stone bold *Hector* heav'd to throw,
Pointed above, and rough and gross below:
Not two strong Men th'enormous Weight cou'd raise,   185
Such Men as live in these degen'rate Days.
Yet this, as easie as a Swain wou'd bear
The snowy Fleece; he tost, and shook in Air:
For *Jove* upheld, and lighten'd of its Load
Th'unwieldy Rock, the Labour of a God.   190
Thus arm'd, before the folded Gates he came,
Of massy Substance and stupendous Frame,
With Iron Bars and brazen Hinges strong,
On lofty Beams of solid Timber hung.
Then thundring thro' the Planks, with forceful Sway, 195
Drives the sharp Rock; the solid Beams give way,
The Folds are shatter'd, from the crackling Door
Leap the resounding Bars, the flying Hinges roar.
Now rushing in the furious Chief appears,
Gloomy as Night, and shakes two shining Spears;   200
A dreadful Gleam from his bright Armour came,
And from his Eye-balls flash'd the living Flame:

187 wou'd] could *1717*.

---

181. Cf. *Par. Lost*, I 547: "A Forrest huge of Spears . . ."
    198. An Alexandrine, in which the sound is perhaps an echo to the sense.
    200. Cf. *Par. Lost*, II 670–2 (of Death): ". . . black it stood as Night. . . And
shook a dreadful Dart."

He moves a God, resistless in his Course,
And seems a Match for more than Mortal Force.
Then pouring after, thro' the gaping Space   205
A Tide of *Trojans* flows, and fills the Place;
The *Greeks* behold, they tremble, and they fly,
The Shore is heap'd with Death, and Tumult rends the Sky.

Connection of the foregoing
with the following Part.

The Wall being forc'd by Hector, *an obstinate Battel was fought before
the Ships, one of which was set on fire by the* Trojans. *Patroclus thereupon obtaining of* Achilles *to lead out the* Myrmidons *to the Assistance
of the* Greeks, *made a great Slaughter of the Enemy, 'till he was oppos'd
by* Sarpedon. *The Combate betwixt these Two, and the Death of the
latter, with the Grief of* Jupiter *for his Son, are describ'd in the ensuing
Translation, from the Sixteenth Book of the* Iliads.

WHEN now the Chief his valiant Friends beheld
Grov'ling in Dust, and gasping on the Field,   210
With this Reproach his flying Host he warms,
Oh Stain to Honour! oh Disgrace of Arms!
Forsake, inglorious, the contended Plain;
This Hand unaided shall the War sustain:
The Task be mine the Hero's Strength to try,   215
Who mows whole Troops, and makes whole Armies fly.
    He said, and leap'd from off his lofty Car;
Patroclus lights, and sternly waits the War.

209 the . . . valiant] *Sarpedon* his brave *1718.*
212 of] to *1718.*   215 the] this *1718.*
216 whole Armies] an Army *1718.*
217 He spake; and speaking, leaps from off the Car; *1718.*

214. Cf. Dryden, *Æn.,* XII 27: "This Arm unaided shall assert your Right".

Q

As when two Vulturs on the Mountain's Height
Stoop with their sounding Pinions to the Fight;   220
They cuff, they tear, they raise a screaming Cry;
The Desart ecchoes, and the Rocks reply:
The Warriors thus oppos'd in Arms engage,
With equal Valour, and with equal Rage.
    Jove view'd the Combate, whose Event foreseen,   225
He thus bespoke his Sister and his Queen.
The Hour draws on; the Destinies ordain,
My God-like Son shall press the *Phrygian* Plain:
Already on the Verge of Death he stands,
His Life is ow'd to fierce *Patroclus*' Hands.   230
What Passions in a Parent's Breast debate!
Say, shall I snatch him from Impending Fate;
And send him safe to *Lycia*, distant far
From all the Dangers and the Toils of War;
Or to his Doom my bravest Off-spring yield,   235
And fatten, with Celestial Blood, the Field?
    Then thus the Goddess with the radiant Eyes:
What Words are these, O Sov'reign of the Skies?
Short is the Date prescrib'd to Mortal Man;
Shall *Jove*, for one, extend the narrow Span,   240
Whose Bounds were fix'd before his Race began?
How many Sons of Gods, foredoom'd to Death,
Before proud *Ilion* must resign their Breath!

220 their sounding] re-sounding *1718*.
224 Valour,] Clamours, *1718*.

---

  220. *Stoop*] "Of a hawk or other bird of prey: To descend swiftly on its prey, to swoop . . ." (OED). Cf. Garth, *Dispensary*, VI 28: "Stoops on his sounding Pinions from above".
  239 *ff.* Cf. Dryden, *Æn.*, x 657–61:
        Short bounds of Life are set to Mortal Man,
        'Tis Vertues work alone to stretch the narrow Span.
        So many Sons of Gods in bloody Flight,
        Around the Walls of *Troy*, have lost the Light:
        My own *Sarpedon* fell beneath his Foe . . .
Cf. *Ess. on Crit.*, 476n.

Were thine exempt, Debate wou'd rise above,
And murm'ring Pow'rs condemn their partial *Jove*.   245
Give the bold Chief a glorious Fate in Fight;
And when th'ascending Soul has wing'd her Flight,
Let *Sleep* and *Death* convey, by thy Command,
The breathless Body to his Native Land.
His Friends and People, to his future Praise,   250
A Marble Tomb and Pyramid shall raise,
And lasting Honours to his Ashes give;
His Fame ('tis all the Dead can have!) shall live.
    She said; the Cloud-Compeller overcome,
Assents to Fate, and ratifies the Doom.   255
Then, touch'd with Grief, the weeping Heav'ns distill'd
A Show'r of Blood o'er all the fatal Field.
The God, his Eyes averting from the Plain, ⎫
Laments his Son, predestin'd to be slain, ⎬
Far from the *Lycian* Shores, his happy Native Reign. ⎭ 260
    Now met in Arms the Combatants appear,
Each heav'd the Shield, and pois'd the lifted Spear:
From strong *Patroclus*' Hand the Jav'lin fled,
And pass'd the Groin of valiant *Thrasymed*,
The Nerves unbrac'd no more his Bulk sustain,   265
He falls, and falling, bites the bloody Plain.
Two sounding Darts the *Lycian* Leader threw,
The first aloof with erring Fury flew,
The next more fatal pierc'd *Achilles*' Steed,
The gen'rous *Pedasus*, of *Theban* Breed;   270
Fix'd in the Shoulder's Joint, he reel'd around;
Rowl'd in the bloody Dust, and paw'd the slipp'ry Ground.
His sudden Fall the entangled Harness broke;
Each Axle groan'd; the bounding Chariot shook;

269 The next transpierc'd *Achilles*' mortal Steed, *1718*.
274 Each Axle crackled, and the Chariot shook: *1718*.

253. Cf. Dryden, *Æn.*, VII 6: "Thy Name ('tis all a Ghost can have) remains."

When bold *Automedon*, to disengage						275
The starting Coursers, and restrain their Rage,
Divides the Traces with his Sword, and freed
Th'incumber'd Chariot from the dying Steed:
The rest move on, obedient to the Rein;
The Car rowls slowly o'er the dusty Plain.						280
    The towring Chiefs to fiercer Fight advance,
And first *Sarpedon* tost his weighty Lance,
Which o'er the Warrior's Shoulder took its Course,
And spent, in empty Air, its dying Force.
Not so *Patroclus* never-erring Dart;			&#125;			285
Aim'd at his Breast, it pierc'd the mortal Part
Where the strong Fibres bind the solid Heart.
Then as the stately Pine, or Poplar tall,
Hewn for the Mast of some great Admiral,
Nods, groans, and reels, 'till with a crackling Sound				290
It sinks, and spreads its Honours on the Ground;
Thus fell the King; and laid on Earth Supine,
Before his Chariot stretch'd his Form divine:
He grasp'd the Dust, distain'd with streaming Gore,
And, pale in Death, lay groaning on the Shore.						295
So lyes a Bull beneath the Lion's Paws,
While the grim Savage grinds with foamy Jaws
The trembling Limbs, and sucks the smoking Blood;
Deep Groans and hollow Roars rebellow thro' the Wood.
    Then to the Leader of the *Lycian* Band,						300
The dying Chief address'd his last Command.
Glaucus, be bold, Thy Task be first to dare

282 tost] whirl'd *1718*.
288–90 Then, as the Mountain Oak, or Poplar tall,
        Or Pine (fit Mast for some great Admiral)
        Nods to the Axe, till with a groaning Sound *1718*.

287. Cf. Chapman's tr., ". . . where life's strings close about the solid heart."
289. Cf. *Par. Lost*, i 293–4: "to be the Mast / Of som great Ammiral . . ."
291. *Honours*] The foliage of the tree.

The glorious Dangers of destructive War,
To lead my Troops, to combate at their Head,
Incite the Living, and supply the Dead. 305
Tell 'em, I charg'd them with my latest Breath,
Not unreveng'd to bear *Sarpedon*'s Death.
What Grief, what Shame must *Glaucus* undergo,
If these spoil'd Arms adorn a *Grecian* Foe?
Then as a Friend, and as a Warrior, fight; 310
Defend my Corps, and conquer in my Right;
That taught by great Examples, All may try
Like thee to vanquish, or like me to die.
  He ceas'd; the Fates supprest his lab'ring Breath,
And his Eyes darken'd with the Shades of Death: 315
Th'insulting Victor with Disdain bestrode
The prostrate Prince, and on his Bosom trod;
Then drew the Weapon from his panting Heart,
The reeking Fibres clinging to the Dart;
From the wide Wound gush'd out a Stream of Blood, 320
And the Soul issu'd in the Purple Flood.
  Then thus to *Phœbus*, in the Realms above,
Spoke from his Throne the Cloud-compelling *Jove*:
Descend my *Phœbus*, on the *Phrygian* Plain,
And from the Fight convey *Sarpedon* slain; 325
Then bathe his Body in the crystal Flood,
With Dust dishonour'd, and deform'd with Blood:
O'er all his Limbs *Ambrosial* Odours shed,
And with Celestial Robes adorn the mighty Dead.
Those Honours paid, his sacred Corps bequeath 330
To the soft Arms of silent *Sleep* and *Death*;
They to his Friends the mournful Charge shall bear;
His Friends a Tomb and Pyramid shall rear;

321 *1718 adds 184 lines here.*   329 mighty] *Om. 1718.*
330 Those Honours paid,] Those Rites discharg'd, *1718.*

305. Cf. Dryden, *Æn.*, IX 1052: "To save the living, and revenge the dead".

These unavailing Rites he may receive,
These, after Death, are All a God can give!   335
   Apollo bows, and from Mount *Ida*'s Height
Swift to the Field precipitates his Flight;
Thence, from the War, the breathless Hero bore,
Veil'd in a Cloud, to silver *Simois* Shore:
There bath'd his honourable Wounds, and drest   340
His Manly Members in th'Immortal Vest,
And with Perfumes of sweet *Ambrosial* Dews,
Restores his Freshness, and his Form renews.
Then *Sleep* and *Death*, two Twins of winged Race,
Of matchless Swiftness, but of silent Pace,   345
Receiv'd *Sarpedon*, at the God's Command,
And in a Moment reach'd the *Lycian* Land;
The Corps amidst his weeping Friends they laid,
Where endless Honours wait the Sacred Shade.

334 unavailing] unvailing *1709*.
334–5 What Honours Mortals after Death receive,
      Those unavailing Honours we may give! *1718*.

   337. Cf. Dryden, *Æn.*, VIII 565 (of Vulcan): "Through the brown Air precipitates his Flight."

THE
ARRIVAL
OF
ULYSSES
IN
ITHACA.

Being Part of the XIIIth Book of *HOMER*'s
ODYSSES.

NOTE ON THE TEXT

The Arrival of Ulysses in Ithaca was first published in *Poetical Miscellanies, Consisting of Original Poems and Translations. By the best Hands... Publish'd by Mr. Steele*. The volume appeared on December 29, 1713, but the title page bears a misprinted date of MDDCXIV. A second issue of the volume, designated *variant b* by Griffith, appeared some time later with the date on the title page corrected to MDCCXIV. Pope next printed the piece in the 1717 *Works*, and in 1725 it appeared as part of Book XIII of *The Odyssey*.

Pope altered a number of passages in 1717, and a few more in 1725. The text printed here follows the spelling, punctuation, and typography of the first edition but observes the corrections of *1717*. In order that the reader may follow the history of the text until its inclusion in *The Odyssey*, the changes introduced in 1725 are recorded in the textual notes.

KEY TO THE CRITICAL APPARATUS

1714a = Poetical Miscellanies, octavo, Griffith 24.
1714b = Poetical Miscellanies, octavo, Griffith 25.
1717　 = Works, quarto, Griffith 79.
1725　 = The Odyssey, vol. III, quarto, Griffith 159.

Part of the
THIRTEENTH BOOK
OF
HOMER's ODYSSES.

The Beginning of this Book describes the Parting of Ulysses *from* Phæacia; *with the Gifts of* Alcinous *to his Guest; and his taking Ship for his Native Country* Ithaca.

THE Sun descending, the *Phæacian* Train
Spread their broad Sails, and launch into the Main:
At once they bend, and strike their equal Oars,
And leave the sinking Hills, and less'ning Shores.
While on the Deck the Chief in Silence lies,   5
And pleasing Slumbers steal upon his Eyes.
As fiery Coursers in the rapid Race,
Urg'd by fierce Drivers thro' the dusty Space,
Toss their high Heads, and scour along the Plain;
So mounts the bounding Vessel o'er the Main: 10
Back to the Stern the parted Billows flow,
And the black Ocean foams and roars below.
    Thus with spread Sails the winged Gally flies;

Title] 1714ab have: THE/ARRIVAL/OF/*ULYSSES*/IN/*ITHACA.*/ Being Part of the XIIIth Book of *HOMER's*/*ODYSSES.*/—/By Mr. *POPE.*
1 The Sun descending,] Now plac'd in order, *1725.*
2 Spread their broad Sails,] Their cables loose, *1725.*

---

   1. Pope translated Homer's ll. 78 to 125, and 187 to 360.
   2. *Spread their broad Sails*] Not in Homer. The use of sails here and in l. 13 is not compatible with l. 3. Note the revision of *1725.*
   4. Added by Pope, who possibly remembered *Aen.*, III 72: "terraeque urbesque recedunt".
   11–12. Cf. Chapman's tr., 133–4:
      About whom [the ship] rusht the billowes, blacke, and vast;
      In which the Sea-roares burst.

Less swift, an Eagle cuts the liquid Skies:
Divine *Ulysses* was her Sacred Load,   15
A Man, in Wisdom equal to a God.
Much Danger long, and mighty Toils he bore,
In Storms by Sea, and Combats on the Shore:
All which soft Sleep now banish'd from his Breast;
Wrapt in a pleasing, deep, and death-like Rest.   20
    But when the morning Star with early Ray
Flam'd in the Front of Heav'n, and promis'd Day,
Like distant Clouds the Mariner descries
Fair *Ithaca*'s emerging Hills arise.
Far from the Town, a spacious Port appears,   25
Sacred to *Phorcys*' Pow'r, whose Name it bears;
Two craggy Rocks, projecting to the Main,
The roaring Winds tempestuous Rage restrain;
Within, the Waves in softer Murmurs glide,
And Ships secure without their Haulsers ride.   30
High at the Head a branching Olive grows,
And crowns the pointed Cliffs with shady Boughs.
Beneath, a gloomy *Grotto*'s cool Recess
Delights the *Nereids* of the neighb'ring Seas;

21–4   But when the rising Star did Heav'n adorn,
        Whose radiant Fires foretell the blushing Morn,
        Like distant Clouds the Mariners survey
        Th'emerging Hills and Rocks of *Ithaca*. *1714ab*.

---

14. Cf. *Windsor-Forest*, 185–7 (p. 167, above). Chapman and Ogilby use *falcon*, and Homer has *hawk*.

16. Hobbes's tr. has "Bearing a man for wisdom like a God."

23–4. Not in Homer. Spence (*An Essay on Pope's Odyssey*, 1726, p. 67) thought the lines showed Pope's "excellent Hand" in "drawing poetical Prospects", especially "in the appearance of Land off at Sea." Cf. Dryden, *Æn.*, III 684–5:
        When we from far, like bluish Mists, descry
        The Hills, and then the Plains, of *Italy*.

34. *Nereids*] Homer and Chapman use *Naiads*. Pope may have remembered Dryden's use of *Nereids* in a similar context, *Æn.*, I 228*ff*.

Where Bowls and Urns were form'd of living Stone, 35
And massie Beams in native Marble shone,
On which the Labours of the Nymphs were roll'd,
Their Webs Divine of Purple mix'd with Gold.
Within the Cave, the clustring Bees attend
Their Waxen Works, or from the Roof depend. 40
Perpetual Waters o'er the Pavement glide;
Two Marble Doors unfold on either side;
Sacred the South, by which the Gods descend,
But Mortals enter at the Northern End.
　　Thither they bent, and haul'd their Ship to Land, 45
(The crooked Keel divides the yellow Sand)
Ulysses sleeping, on his Couch they bore,
And gently plac'd him on the Rocky Shore:
His Treasures next, *Alcinous*' Gifts, they laid
In the wild Olive's unfrequented Shade; 50
Secure from Theft: Then launch'd the Bark again,
And tugg'd their Oars, and measur'd back the Main.
　　Mean while *Ulysses* in his Country lay,
Releas'd from Sleep; and round him might survey
The solitary Shore, and rowling Sea. 55
Yet had his Mind, thro' tedious Absence, lost
The dear Remembrance of his Native Coast;

50 Olive's] Olives *1714ab*.
52 And tugg'd] Resum'd *1725. 1725 here adds 76 lines.*

---

35. *living Stone*] "In its native condition and site" (OED, *living*). Cf. Dryden, *Æn.*, I 78: "Where in a spacious Cave of living Stone . . ."

36. *Beams*] The wooden rollers or cylinders in a loom, on which the warp is wound before weaving (OED).

38. There is no question of gold in the original. Possibly Pope remembered *Georgics* IV 342, where two sea-nymphs are wearing gold girdles: "ambae auro . . . incinctae".

46. Repeated in Pope's *Il.*, I 631.

52. Cf. Dryden, *Æn.*, X 931–2: ". . . the Vessel plows the Sea, / And measures back with speed her former Way."

Here Pope added 76 lines in the final version, relating the return of the Phaeacians and the revenge of Neptune.

Besides *Minerva* to secure her Care,
Diffus'd around a Veil of thicken'd Air:
For so the Gods ordain'd, to keep unseen   60
His Royal Person from his Friends and Queen,
Till the proud Suitors, for their Crimes, afford
An ample Vengeance to her injur'd Lord.
    Now all the Land another Prospect bore,
Another Port appear'd, another Shore,   65
And long-continu'd Ways, and winding Floods,
And unknown Mountains, crown'd with unknown Woods.
Pensive and slow, with sudden Grief opprest,
The King arose, and beat his careful Breast,
Cast a long Look o'er all the Coast and Main,   70
And sought around his Native Realm in vain;
Then with erected Eyes stood fix'd in Woe,
And, as he spoke, the Tears began to flow.
    Ye Gods (he cry'd) upon what barren Coast,
In what new Region is *Ulysses* tost?   75
Possest by wild Barbarians fierce in Arms?
Or Men, whose Bosom tender Pity warms?
Where shall this Treasure now in Safety lie?
And whither, whither its sad Owner flie?
Ah why did I *Alcinous*' Grace implore?   80
Ah why forsake *Phæacia*'s happy Shore?
Some juster Prince perhaps had entertain'd,
And safe restor'd me to my Native Land.
Is this the promis'd, long expected Coast;
And this the Faith *Phæacia*'s Rulers boast?   85
Oh righteous Gods! of all the Great, how few
Are just to Heav'n, and to their Promise true!

63 her] their *1725*.   85 Rulers] Princes *1714ab*.

67. *unknown*] Cf. *Windsor-Forest*, 87*n* (p. 158, above).
    69. In the original, and in Chapman, Ulysses beats his thighs. See Intro.,
p. 359, above.
    86–7. Not in Homer. See Intro., p. 359.

But He the Pow'r, to whose All-seeing Eyes
The Deeds of Men appear without Disguise,
'Tis his alone, t'avenge the Wrongs I bear;   90
For still th'Opprest are his peculiar Care:
To count these *Presents*, and from thence to prove
Their Faith, is mine; the rest belongs to *Jove*.
     Then on the Sands he rang'd his wealthy Store,
The Gold, the Vests, the Tripods number'd o'er;   95
All these he found, but still, in Error lost,
Disconsolate he wanders on the Coast:
Sighs for his Country; and laments again
To the deaf Rocks, and hoarse-resounding Main.
When lo! the Guardian Goddess of the Wise,   100
Celestial *Pallas*, stood before his Eyes;
In show a youthful Swain, of Form divine,
Who seem'd descended from some Princely Line:
A graceful Robe her slender Body drest,
Around her Shoulders flew the waving Vest.   105
Her decent Hand a shining Jav'lin bore,
And painted Sandals on her Feet she wore:
To whom the King: Whoe'er of Human Race
Thou art, that wander'st in this desart Place,
With Joy to thee, as to some God, I bend,   110
To thee my Treasures and my self commend.
O tell a Wretch, in Exile doom'd to stray,
What Air I breath, what Country I survey?
The fruitful Continent's extreamest Bound,
Or some fair Isle which *Neptune*'s Arms surround?   115
     From what far Clime (said she) remote from Fame,
Arriv'st thou here, a Stranger to our Name?
Thou seest an Island, not to those unknown,
Whose Hills are brighten'd by the rising Sun.

110 bend,] bend *1714ab*.

93. *the rest belongs to Jove*] Cf. *Ep. to Arb.*, 419 (vol. IV, p. 127).
99. Dryden, *Iliad*, I 54, has "hoarse-resounding Shore".

Nor those, that plac'd beneath his utmost Reign,   120
Behold him sinking in the Western Main.
The rugged Soil allows no level Space
For flying Chariots, or the rapid Race;
Yet not ungrateful to the Peasant's Pain,
Suffices Fulness to the swelling Grain;   125
The loaded Trees their various Fruits produce,
And clustring Grapes afford a gen'rous Juice;
Woods crown our Mountains, and in ev'ry Grove
The bounding Goats and frisking Heyfers rove;
Soft Rains and kindly Dews refresh the Field,   130
And rising Springs Eternal Verdure yield.
Ev'n to those Shores is *Ithaca* renown'd,
Where *Troy*'s Majestic Ruins strow the Ground.
      At this, the Chief with Transport was possest,
His panting Heart exulted in his Breast: 135
Yet well dissembling his untimely Joys,
And veiling Truth in plausible Disguise;
Thus, with an Air sincere, in Fiction bold,
His ready Tale th'inventive Hero told.
      Oft have I heard, in *Crete*, this Island's Name,   140
For 'twas from *Crete*, my Native Soil, I came;
Self-banish'd thence, I sail'd before the Wind,
And left my Children and my Friends behind.
From fierce *Idomeneus*' Revenge I flew,
Whose Son, the swift *Orsilochus*, I slew,   145
(With Brutal Force he seiz'd my *Trojan* Prey,
Due to the Toils of many a bloody Day.)
Unseen I scap'd; and favour'd by the Night,
In a *Phænician* Vessel took my Flight;
For *Pyle* or *Elis* bound; but Tempests tost,   150
And raging Billows drove us on your Coast:
In dead of Night an unknown Port we gain'd,

148. Here Pope omits the few lines in which Ulysses relates how he killed
Orsilochus.

Spent with Fatigue, and slept secure on Land;
But ere the Rosie Morn renew'd the Day,
While in th'Embrace of pleasing Sleep I lay,   155
Sudden, invited by auspicious Gales,
They land my Goods, and hoist their flying Sails.
Abandon'd here, my Fortune I deplore,
A hapless Exile on a Foreign Shore.

   Thus while he spoke, the blue-ey'd Maid began   160
With pleasing Smiles to view the God-like Man;
Then chang'd her Form, and now divinely bright
Jove's heav'nly Daughter stood confess'd to Sight,
Like a fair Virgin in her Beauty's Bloom,
Skill'd in th'illustrious Labours of the Loom.   165

   O still the same *Ulysses!* she rejoin'd,
In useful Craft successfully refin'd;
Artful in Speech, in Action, and in Mind!
Suffic'd it not, that thy long Labours past
Secure thou seest thy Native Shore at last?   170
But this to me? who, like thy self, excel
In Arts of Counsel, and Dissembling well:
To me, whose Wit exceeds the Pow'rs Divine,
No less, than Mortals are surpass'd by thine:
Know'st thou not me, who made thy Life my Care,   175
Thro' ten Years Wand'ring, and thro' ten Years War;
Who taught thee Arts, *Alcinous* to persuade,
To raise his Wonder, and ingage his Aid?
And now appear, thy Treasures to protect,
Conceal thy Person, thy Designs direct,   180
And tell what more thou must from Fate expect;
Domestick Woes, far heavier to be born,
The Pride of Fools, and Slaves insulting Scorn.
But thou be Silent, nor reveal thy State,
Yield to the Force of unresisted Fate,   185

159 A] An *1714ab.*

185. Cf. *Rape of the Lock*, III 178 (vol. II, p. 179).

And bear unmov'd the Wrongs of base Mankind,
The last and hardest Conquest of the Mind.
   Goddess of Wisdom! (*Ithacus* replies) ⎫
He who discerns thee must be truly wise,   ⎬
So seldom view'd, and ever in Disguise. ⎭   190
When the bold *Argives* led their warring Pow'rs
Against proud *Ilion*'s well-defended Tow'rs,
Ulysses was thy Care, Celestial Maid,
Grac'd with thy Sight, and favour'd with thy Aid:
But when the *Trojan* Piles in Ashes lay,   195
And, bound for *Greece*, we plow'd the Watry way;
Our Fleet dispers'd, and driv'n from Coast to Coast;
Thy sacred Presence from that Hour I lost;
Till I beheld thy radiant Form once more,
And heard thy Counsels on *Phæacia*'s Shore.   200
But by th'Almighty Author of thy Race,
Tell me, oh tell, is this my Native Place?
For much I fear, long Tracts of Land and Sea
Divide this Coast from distant *Ithaca*.
The sweet Delusion kindly you impose,   205
To sooth my Hopes and mitigate my Woes.
   Thus he: The blue-ey'd Goddess thus replies:
How prone to Doubt, how cautious are the Wise?
Who vers'd in Fortune, fear the flatt'ring Show,
And taste not half the Bliss the Gods bestow.   210
The more shall *Pallas* aid thy just Desires,
And guard the Wisdom which her self inspires.
Others, long absent from their Native Place,   ⎫
Strait seek their Home, and fly with eager Pace, ⎬
To their Wives Arms, and Childrens dear Embrace. ⎭

191–2 When the bold *Argives* did their Arms imploy
     Before the Walls of well-defended *Troy*, *1714ab*.
195 the *Trojan* Piles] proud *Ilion*'s Tow'rs *1714ab*.

186–7. See Intro., p. 359, above.
195. Cf. Dryden, *Æn.*, III 4: "And *Ilium*'s lofty Tow'rs in Ashes lay".

Not thus *Ulysses*; he decrees to prove 216
His Subjects Faith, and Queen's suspected Love,
Who mourn'd her Lord twice ten revolving Years,
And wastes the Days in Grief, the Nights in Tears.
But *Pallas* knew (thy Friends and Navy lost) 220
Once more 'twas giv'n thee to behold thy Coast:
Yet how cou'd I with adverse Fate engage,
And Mighty *Neptune*'s unrelenting Rage?—
Now lift thy longing Eyes, while I restore
The pleasing Prospect of thy Native Shore! 225
Behold the Port of *Phorcys* fenc'd around
With Rocky Mountains, and with Olives crown'd!
Behold the gloomy *Grot*, whose cool Recess
Delights the *Nereids* of the neighb'ring Seas;
Whose now neglected Altars, in thy Reign 230
Blush'd with the Blood of Sheep and Oxen slain.
Behold where *Neritus* the Clouds divides,
And shakes the waving Forests on his Sides!
    So spake the Goddess, and the Prospect clear'd,
The Mists dispers'd, and all the Coast appear'd: 235
The King with Joy confess'd his Place of Birth,
And, on his Knees, salutes his Mother Earth;
Then, with his suppliant Hands upheld in Air,
Thus to the Sea-green Sisters sends his Pray'r.
    All hail! Ye Virgin Daughters of the Main; 240
Ye Streams, beyond my Hopes beheld again!
To you once more your own *Ulysses* bows,
Attend his Transports, and receive his Vows.
If *Jove* prolong my Days, and *Pallas* crown

232–3. Cf. Chapman's tr., 526–7: "Here, Mount Nerytus shakes his curled Tresse / Of shady woods." Spence remarks (*An Essay on Pope's Odyssey*, p. 38): "Mr. *Pope questions* [in a note to l. 510 of *Odyssey*, bk XIV] *whether the nodding of a Mountain be a natural Image;* shou'd not You be apt to think too, that *a Mountain shaking the Forests on his sides*, is fitter for an Earthquake, than a *Metaphor*?"

244. Pope omits, probably for reasons of decorum, the epithet Homer uses, l. 359, to designate Athena as "she that drives off the spoil".

The growing Virtues of my youthful Son,   245
To you shall Rites Divine be ever paid,
And grateful Off'rings on your Altars laid

APPENDIXES

APPENDIX A

WALSH'S CRITICISM OF
LINES FROM THE *PASTORALS*

AT an early stage in the composition of his *Pastorals*, Pope submitted to his friend William Walsh a number of passages for criticism. The record of this interchange, consisting of four pages, quarto, is reproduced below by kind permission of Mr Arthur A. Houghton, Jr. As far as possible, the actual appearance of the manuscript is imitated. The lines which separate passages are to be found in the original. To distinguish the hands of the two men, Pope's words are printed in roman type, Walsh's in italic. A photographic reproduction of the manuscript has previously been published in *A Catalogue of the First Editions of the Works of Alexander Pope*, The Grolier Club, New York, 1911.

[page one]

Alterations to the Pastoralls:
(The Solutions of the Queries are written by Mr. Walsh.)

Past. 1. lin. 1.　　First in these Fields I sing the Sylvan Strains,
　　　　　　　　Nor blush to sport on Windsor's peaceful Plains;
　　　　　　　　Fair Thames flow gently from thy sacred Spring,
　　　　　　　　While on thy Banks Sicilian Muses sing.

　Objection.　That the Letter is hunted too much—Sing the Sylvan—Peaceful Plains—and that the word Sing is us'd two lines after, Sicilian Muses sing.

　Alteration.　　First in these Fields I try the Sylvan Strains,
　　　　　　　　Nor blush to sport on Windsor's happy Plains. &c.

　Quere.　If Try be not properer in relation to First; as, we first attempt a thing; and more modest? and if Happy be not more than Peaceful?

*Try is better than sing—Happy does not sound right, y*ᵉ *first Syllabl being short, perhaps you may finde a better word than Peaceful as Flowry.*

477

Past. 1. lin. 23.   I'll stake my Lamb that near the Fountain plays,
                     And his own Image from the Brink surveys.
            Or,   And from the Brink his dancing Shade surveys.
     Quere. Which of these 2 lines is better?   *The second*

Past. 1. lin. 43.   Me lovely Chloris beckons from the Plain,
                     Then hides in Shades from her deluded Swain;
                     But feigns a Laugh to see me search around,
                     And by that Laugh the willing Fair is found.
     Objection.   That hides without the Accusative herself is not
        good English, and that from her deluded Swain is needless.
     Alteration.   Me wanton Chloris beckons from the Plain,
                     Then hid in Shades, eludes her eager Swain; &c.
     Quere.   If wanton be more significant than lovely: If Eludes be
        properer in this case than deluded: If eager be an expressive
        Epithet to the Swain who searches for his Mistress?
        Wanton apply'd to a woman is equivocal & therefore not
        proper— Eludes is properer than deluded.   Eager is very well

                                                              Past.

[page two]
Past. 1. lin. 57.   If Sylvia smile, she brightens all the Shore,
                     The Sun's outshin'd, and Nature charms no more.
                                     be
                 Whether to say the Sun is outshin'd, is too   *For Pastoral*
     Quere.   bold & Hyperbolical? If it shou'd be soften'd   *it is*
                 with seems,   Do you approve any of these Alterations)
                     If Sylvia smile, she brightens all the Shore,
     Quere which (All Nature seems outshind, and charms no more.
     of these   { Or, Light seems outshind, and Nature charms no more.
     three?   (Or, And vanquishd Nature seems to shine no more.
                     The last of these I like best

Past. 1. lin. 81.　　Nay tell me first what Region canst thou find,
　　　　　　　　　　In which by Thistles Lillies are outshin'd?
　Or,　Nay tell me first in what *more happy Fields　　* This Epithet re-
　　　　The Thistle springs to which the Lilly yields?　fers to something
　　　　　　　　　　　　　　　　　　　　　　　　　　going before.

　Quere.　Which of these Couplets are better express'd and better
　　Numbers? and whether it's better here to use Thistle or
　　Thistles, Lilly or Lillies, Singular or Plural? (Alluding to
　　ye Arms of Scotland & France)
　　　The second Couplet is best; & singular, I think better than Plural

---

Past. 2. lin. 1.　　A Shepherds Boy (he seeks no better Name)
　　　　　　　　　　Led forth his Flocks along the silver Thame.
　　Objection.　against the Parenthesis (he seeks no better name)
　　Quere.　Wou'd it be any thing better to say
　　　　　　　　　　A Shepherds Boy, (who sung for Love, not Fame)
　　　　　Or,　A Shepherds Boy, who fed an Am'rous Flame,
　　　　　　　　　　Led forth his Flocks along the silver Thame.
　　Quere　which of all these is best, or are none of them good?
　　　The first is Spensers way, & I think better than the others.

Past. 2. lin. 7.　　Relenting Naïads wept in ev'ry Bow'r,
　　　　　　　　　　And Jove consented in a silent Show'r.
　　Objection.　That the Naïads weeping in Bowers is not so proper being
　　　Water Nymphs. and that the word consented is doubted by some
　　　to whom I have shown these Verses.

　　　　　　　　　　　　　　　　　　　　　　　　　　Alteration

[page three]
　　Alteration.　　The Naïads wept in ev'ry watry Bow'r,
　　　　　　　　　　And Jove relented in a silent Show'r.
　　Quere.　which of these Couplets you like best?— ~~The First~~ Upon y^e
　　　second thought, I think the second is best

Past. 2. lin. 35.   Of slender Reeds a tuneful Flute I have,
                       The tuneful Flute which dying Colin gave.
   Objection.   That the first line is too much transposd from the
                 natural Order of ye words: and that the Rhyme is unharmonious.
   Alteration.   That Flute is mine which Colin's tuneful Breath
                    Inspir'd when living, and bequeath'd in Death.
   Quere.   Which of these is best?   *The second*

Past. 2. lin. 41. Some pitying God permit me to be made
                  The Bird that sings beneath thy Mirtle Shade:
                  Then might my Voice thy listning Ears employ,
                  & I those Kisses he receives, enjoy.
        Or,   Oh, were I made by some transforming Pow'r
              The Captive Bird that sings within thy Bow'r! Then might—&c.
   The Epithet Captive seems necessary to explain the Thought, on account
   of those Kisses in ye last line. Quere. If these be better than the
   other?   *The second are best, for tis not enough to permitt*
                          you to bee made, but to make you

Past. 2. lin. 67. Oh deign to grace our happy rural Seats,
                  Our mossy Fountains, and our Green Retreats:
                  While you y^r Presence to the Groves deny,
                  Our flow'rs are faded, and our Brooks are dry;
                  Tho' withring Herbs lay dying on the Plain,
                  At y^r Return they shall be green again.

        Or,   Oh deign to grace our happy Rural Seats,
              Our mossy Fountains, & our green Retreats:
              *Winds, where you walk, shall gently fann the Glade,   *Or,
              Trees, where you sit, shall crowd into a Shade,   Where'er you
              *Flow'rs, where you tread, in painted Pride shall   walk, fresh
                  rise,   Gales shall
                                                                  fann ye Glade,
              And all things flourish where you turn your Eyes!   *or
   Quere.   Which of these you like better?   Where'er you
              The second, with the alterations on ye side   tread, the purple
                                                                    flow'rs shall
                                                                        rise,

[page four]

Past. 4. lin. 5.   Now in warm folds the tender Flock remains,
                    The Cattle slumber on the silent Plains,
                    While sleeping Birds forget their tuneful lays,
                                            Daphne's
                    Let us, dear Thyrsis, sing in   Delias   Praise.

Objection to the word remains:

I do not know whether these following be better or no, & desire
yʳ opinion.

                    Now while the Groves in Cynthia's Beams are drest,
                    And folded Flocks on their soft Fleeces rest;
                    While sleeping Birds——

Or,

                    While Cynthia tips with silver all the Groveˢ
                    And scarce the Winds the topmost Branches move;
                        not a Breeze   quivring   moves

Or,

                    While the bright Moon wᵗʰ silver tips yᵉ gro
                    &c.

                            *I think yᵉ last best but might not even yᵗ bee
                            mended*

Past. 4. lin. 29.   Tis done, and Nature's chang'd since you are gone,
                    Behold the Clouds have put their Mourning on.
         Or,   Tis done, and Nature's various Charms decay,
                    See sable Clouds eclypse the chearful Day.

Quere, which of these is the better?   *Clouds put on mourning is too
                                            conceited for Pastoral. The second is
                                            better & the thick [?] or the dark I
                                            like better than Sable*

Past. 4. lin. 39.   No rich Perfumes refresh the fruitful Field,
                    Which, but for you, did all its Incense yield.
                            for yʳ sake

Quere, Will the second line be better'd by being altred thus?
                    No rich Perfumes refresh the fruitful field,
                    Nor fragrant Herbs their native Incense yield.
                            The second is better

Pas. 3. lin. 91.   Thus sung the Swains, while Day yet strove with Night,
     And Heav'n yet *languish'd with departing light; *Quere,
                     if lan-
     When falling Dews with Spangles deck'd the guish be a
       Glade,   proper word?
                     Not very proper
     And the low Sun had lengthend ev'ry Shade.

Objection. That to mention the Sunsett after Twilight (Day yet strove
   wth Night) is improper, Is the following Alteration any thing
   better?
      Thus sung the Swains while Day yet strove wth Night,
      The Sky still blushing wth departing light;
      When falling Dews with Spangles deck'd the Glade,
      And the brown Evening lengthen'd evry Shade.

 *Tis not ye Evening but ye Sun being low y^t lengthens ye Shades. otherwise
ye second please [?] mee best.*

APPENDIX B

MANUSCRIPT MEMORANDA
RELATING TO
AN ESSAY ON CRITICISM

POPE's manuscript version of the *Essay on Criticism* in the Bodleian Library
(MS Eng. Poet. C. 1) is accompanied by a page of manuscript memoranda
(fol. 15). On this page the poet jotted down attempts to improve lines in the
Essay which had been criticized by John Dennis and perhaps also by his own
friends. Some of the corrections were perhaps inspired by his own second-
thoughts, but in the main they seem to show his willingness to "make use of
ev'ry *Friend*—and ev'ry *Foe*". The record also shows his decision to disregard
some of the criticisms his poem had received.

This page of memoranda is reproduced here as an interesting example of
Pope's procedures in revision. Most of the notations were scored through by the
poet, but no attempt has been made to reproduce these strokes of the pen. The
page numbers which follow Dennis's name refer to that critic's *Reflections Critical
and Satyrical, Upon a Late Rhapsody, Call'd, An Essay upon Criticism* (1711). All other
page numbers conform to the manuscript pages of the *Essay* itself (or to the preliminary page count for the printer found on the manuscript[1]), not to the pages
of printed texts of the poem. It is impossible to reproduce in print the appearance of these manuscript jottings, but so far as possible the order in which they
occur is preserved. The manuscript is reproduced by kind permission of the
Bodleian Library.

---

1. See Intro., p. 203, above.

P   Be silent always w^n y^u doubt y^r sense, —Dennis p. 21.
    Speak w^n youre sure, yet speak wth diffidence. alter y^e
                Inconsi[stenc]y

P.   A Work t'outlast immortal Rome— alter ye seeming Incōsistēcy.

    W^n first his voice ye youthful Maro tryd
    Eer Phebus touchd his ear & checkd his pride

      Perhaps—&—but—nature—each line
     His boundless Soul perhaps disdaind—

    Arms and ye Man then rung ye World around,
    & Rome commencd Īmortal at ye Sound
     †Learn hence for ancient rules—To—
     †Some beauties yet—

    W^n first great Maro sung of Kings & Wars,
    Eer warning Phœbus touchd his trembling Ears,
    Perhaps—

P. 23. Nay fly to Altars—

P. 8. Triumphant Pæans—and again—3 lines off—Bards Triumphant.

P. 9. lin. 9. read it thus—But more advancd behold wth strange surprise.
    on acc^t of survey being usd after.

P. 24.   Wit & Faith nihili

          (ye 2 lines left out
   Where wanted scornd—of Wit—to be alterd—See Dennis. p. 20.

not to be   Horace judgd wth Coolness—& Longin wth Fire.
alterd)   Supreme alike in Judgm^t—He boldly censurd & he boldly writ
      He judgd wth Spirit as he sung

    bare threescore, w^h if it were, & threescore years is all—

P. 4.—one Science— So vast is art— not only— But oft in
                                                                those,   stet sic

   Such as Chaucer is, may Dryden be.

   Those may be Stratagems—

   And   less often than
   Nor Homer nods so often as we dream

   *Fool, let it not be usd so often.

   *Licence represt, and sacred Laws maintaind—quere of
                                                                this.

   *Much was believd, but little understood.

   *Schismatics ye plain believers quitt

                                       & speak   yet speak
   *w^n you doubt y^r Sense,   Tho sure, wth seeming diffidence—

   *At the last Couplett, which alone is fraught—

APPENDIX C

THE DON QUIXOTE EPISODE IN
AN ESSAY ON CRITICISM

THE comical episode of Don Quixote in the *Essay on Criticism*, ll. 267–84, was
inspired by a chapter in a sequel to the history of Don Quixote written, as Pope
says in *The Critical Specimen*, by a "false Cervantes".[1] This "false Cervantes"
published his "Continuation" under the name of Alonzo Fernandez de Avellaneda, and his work was translated into English in 1705. The passage used by
Pope was quoted in part by Warton in his edition of the poet's *Works*, and it is
quoted in full here in order that Pope's skilful abbreviation of the episode may
be the better appreciated. The English translation of the Spanish source was
entitled: A Continuation Of the Comical History Of the most Ingenious Knight,
Don Quixote De la Mancha. By the Licentiate Alonzo Fernandez de Avella-

---

1. See *Prose Works*, I 5.

neda. . . Translated by Captain John Stevens . . . London . . . 1705. The passage quoted occurs in Book III, pp. 164–6, and is a portion of Chapter x, entitled *"How* Don Quixote *met two Schollars, and what Discourse they had."*

[One of the scholars says to Don Quixote:]

". . . but since I have not any thing to read to you Sir Knight; shall I advise with you about the Plot of a Play I have in my Head? You will oblige me, re-ply'd *D. Quixote,* but pray tell me, whether in your Plays, you stick close to *Aristotle's* Rules? No, truly, said the Batchelor, I do not. So much the worse, answer'd *Don Quixote,* for *Aristotle* is an infallible Oracle in that point. Not to follow his Rules, is to swerve from Nature and Reason; and that is the cause why Strangers do not approve of our Performances, which in all other respects are Excellent. I own, quoth the Batchelor, that most of our Dramatick Poets, seem to make little account of *Aristotles Rules.* For my own part, I like them very well; I never depart from them out of meer lightness, but ever follow them when they will suit with my Plot; but to deal ingeniously, I do not pay so much de-ference to them, as to lose any surprising turn for their sake, which cannot sub-sist with them. That Turn must be cast away, quoth *Don Quixote,* Interrupting him; all must be sacrific'd to the severe Rules of that wise Master. But let us come to your Plot. This is it, reply'd the Batchelor. An Earl of *Barcelona* takes a Voyage into *England,* where he falls in Love with the King's Daughter, and is Belov'd again; but the King for Politick Ends, Marries the Princess to the King of *Bohemia.* The Earl of *Barcelona* in Despair, Embarks and returns to his own Dominions. The King and Queen of *Bohemia* live very happily together, tho' that Princess always preserves a tender Affection for the Earl of *Barcelona:* But soon after, a Favourite of the King of *Bohemia,* falls passionately in Love with the Queen, and has the boldness to let her know it. She reproves him, and threatens to acquaint the King her Husband with his Baseness. The Favourite changing his Love into Rage, prepossesses that weak Prince, and accuses the Queen of being in Love with an Officer of his Guard. The King, who only sees with his Favourite's Eyes, causes the Officer to be put to Death, and would do the same by the Queen; but she Demands, that according to the Custom of those Times, she may have leave to find Knights to defend her Honour against her Accuser. The King not knowing how to refuse the Combat the Queen demands, appoints a day, which is proclaim'd in *Bohemia* and *England.* When the day comes, the Favourite appears in the Lists to make good his Accusation, but no Body comes against him till it is late, and the Queen is like to suffer; then a Knight Arm'd at all Points, enters the Lists, fights her Battel, and Kills the Favourite. This Knight proves to be the very Earl of *Barcelo~a,* brought thither by the fame of the Queen's Accusation, of whose Innocence he is satisfy'd. This Sir, is the whole Plot of my Play. It is a very good one, answer'd the Knight, but I know not whether you can make a regular Play of it. It is true, said the Batche-lor, our Authors who follow *Aristotle* the closest, would make the first Act in *England;* the Second in *Barcelona,* and the Third in *Bohemia:* But I am bringing this Play to answer all the Rules; and I do not despair of Success. I am satisfy'd you'll compass it, said the other Scholar, provided you omit the Combat in the Lists. Let him have a care of that, said *Don Quixote*, Interrupting him, that is the best part of the Plot. But Sir, quoth the Batchelor if you would have me adhere to *Aristotle*'s Rules, I must pass by the Combat. *Aristotle*, reply'd the Knight, I grant was a Man of Parts; but his Capacity was not Unbounded; and in short, his Authority does not extend over Combats in the Lists, which are above his Rules. Would you suffer the Queen of *Bohemia* to Perish? Or how can you clear her Innocence? Believe me, Combat is the most Honourable way; and besides, it will add such Grace to your Play, that all the Rules in the World must not stand in Competition with it. Well Sir Knight, reply'd the Batchellor, for your sake and for the Honour of Chivalry I will not leave out the Combat; and that it may appear the more Glorious, all the Court of *Bohemia* shall be present at it from the Princes of the Blood, to the very Footmen. But still one difficulty occurs, which is that our common Theaters are not large enough for it. There must be one built a purpose, answer'd *Don Quixote*; and in a word, rather than leave out the Combat, the Play had better be acted in a Field, or Plain.''

INDEX

Italic numerals indicate that a reference is to the text of a poem

R

R*